JEREMY
THORPE

JEREMY
THORPE

Michael Bloch

Little, Brown

LITTLE, BROWN

First published in Great Britain in 2014 by Little, Brown

3 5 7 9 10 8 6 4

PICTURE CREDITS

1–10, 12, 16: private collections; 11, 21, 40, 44: Popperfoto;
26: Camera Press; 35, 43: Jane Bown/Camera Press; 36: Nick
Garland/*Daily Telegraph*/Centre for the Study of Cartoons,
University of Kent at Canterbury; 37: Warren Harrison/Times
Newspapers; 39: *Punch*; 42 Bryan Wharton/Times
Newspapers; 45: Press Association; 47: Simon
Kreitem/Popperfoto/Reuters

*Every attempt has been made to trace copyright-holders in
uncredited photographs. Please contact the publisher
if copyright had been inadvertently infringed.*

A CIP catalogue record for this book
is available from the British Library.

ISBN 978-0-316-85685-0

Typeset in Berkeley by M Rules
Printed and bound in Great Britain
by Clays Ltd, St Ives plc

Papers used by Little, Brown are from well-managed forests
and other responsible sources.

MIX
Paper from
responsible sources
FSC
www.fsc.org FSC® C104740

Little, Brown
An imprint of
Little, Brown Book Group
100 Victoria Embankment
London EC4Y 0DY

An Hachette UK Company
www.hachette.co.uk

www.littlebrown.co.uk

to four friends I made
writing this book

Celia Thomas
Leo Abse
Stephen Carroll
and
Jonathan Fryer

CONTENTS

PREFACE AND
ACKNOWLEDGEMENTS

SOMETHING MUST BE said about the circumstances in which this book was conceived and written. Ever since boyhood, I have been fascinated by Jeremy Thorpe, Leader of the Liberal Party from 1967 to 1976, and imagined it would be an intriguing task to try to unravel the intricacies of his career and personality. In 1990, I proposed a biography of him to the excellent Ursula Mackenzie, then Publishing Director at Bantam Press, who duly commissioned me to write it. Other projects prevented me from getting down to work immediately, but by the end of 1992 I had familiarised myself with most of the published literature on Jeremy Thorpe's life: this included a huge mass of press cuttings (which I perused thanks to the *Daily Telegraph* and its librarian, Alexandra Erskine); the reminiscences of his former colleagues, notably Peter Bessell and David Steel; works on the history of the Liberal Party; and books relating to his trial at the Old Bailey in 1979 on charges of conspiracy and incitement to murder. (The only work in the nature of a biography then existing, *Jeremy Thorpe: A Secret Life* by the *Sunday Times* journalists Lewis Chester, Magnus Linklater and David May, came out soon after the trial and was intended to explain its background: it is a model work of its kind. Later, in 1996, there appeared *Rinkagate: The Rise and Fall of Jeremy Thorpe* by Simon Freeman and Roger Penrose, which concentrates on the story of the intended victim of the alleged murder plot, Norman Scott, and is a work of lesser historical and literary merit.)

My preliminary research had made me aware that Jeremy Thorpe had led a life far more mysterious and complex than I had originally supposed, that he was as gregarious as he was secretive, and that the most interesting material for his biography was likely to be found in the spoken rather than the written word. I therefore devoted 1993 and 1994 to meeting hundreds of people who had known him in various ways, accumulating thousands of pages of notes. My informants included his school and university contemporaries, fellow barristers and broadcasters, politicians and political workers of every complexion, journalists and civil servants, friends and enemies, relations and lovers. Some provided me with a few details, others with masses of material, communicated over many months, which in several cases might have formed the basis of books in themselves. Indeed, there were moments when I felt that a volume entitled *The Quest for Jeremy Thorpe*, in the tradition of A. J. A. Symons and Hugh Trevor-Roper, would be at least as interesting as this one.

Those two years were an adventure; but as they progressed, the puzzle of Jeremy Thorpe seemed to get no nearer a solution, and indeed to grow ever more labyrinthine. As one of the first parliamentarians I visited, the venerable and formidable Baroness Seear, prophesied: 'You'll never get to the bottom of him.' I smiled at the time; I often had cause to recall her words. Indeed, that there was more to Jeremy Thorpe than met the eye was virtually the only thing about him that everyone could agree on. To some he was the Lost Leader, potentially the outstanding statesman of the age, misunderstood by millions and thwarted by envious pygmies; to others he was the most devious and amoral person who ever existed; yet others saw him either as a man of great gifts whose life was tragically ruined by fatal flaws, or a shallow and unattractive character partly redeemed by some charming qualities. Many regarded him as an actor on life's stage; but was he Hamlet or Macbeth, Richard II or Richard III, Othello or Iago?

Meanwhile, a few days before his sixty-fourth birthday in April 1993, I had met Jeremy Thorpe with his wife Marion at their house in Orme Square, Bayswater, the first of some twenty such meetings. He was a sick man, but his mind was still active and his will to live manifest; she was protective towards him. They always received me courteously; and if the direct help they offered was somewhat limited in scope, the opportunity to meet him face-to-face gave me an insight which I could not otherwise have gained. When I showed him my chapter on his under-graduate years at Oxford, he wrote to me that it had filled him with nostalgia and he thought it 'a fair cop'. I like to think that this would have been his verdict on the book as a whole (though when I showed him the draft manuscript in 2001 – I am not sure he actually read much of it – his reaction was confined to an urgent insistence that it should not appear in his lifetime).

By the spring of 1995 my basic research was almost complete. Yet further years passed before I could bring myself to write the book. I knew a vast amount about the man, in some respects more than he knew about himself; I had known him personally for two years; yet what did I really know of him? There were times when I felt that nothing was what it seemed, that behind every façade lay another façade. But when I finally took the plunge, the biography seemed to write itself. At last it was fin-ished and delivered to Ursula Mackenzie (now CEO of Little, Brown & Co., but able to take the book with her, to my joy and relief). I cannot deny that my feelings about Jeremy Thorpe changed somewhat in the course of the decade during which

I worked on his life; but I hope I have managed to be reasonably dispassionate. It somehow seemed right to call him 'Jeremy' throughout rather than 'Thorpe', but this should not be taken to imply that I felt an intimacy with him greater than that of a zoologist who studies the doings of a fascinating specimen over a period of several years.

Brief biographical notes on most of those figures mentioned more than once in the text, including all those Liberals who sat in Parliament with Jeremy Thorpe or were nominated by him for life peerages, will be found at the end of the book.

The list of acknowledgements which follows is necessarily long, but some particular debts must first be mentioned. Celia Thomas (now Baroness Thomas of Winchester), a sometime personal secretary of Jeremy and for long years Secretary to the Liberal Democrat Peers, was of enormous help in persuading often reluctant Liberal Democrats to meet and talk to me. Jonathan Fryer was also full of useful suggestions as to whom I ought to see, and cast fascinating light on Liberal politics and personalities down the decades. Jeremy's sister Lavinia Bradley provided me with a wealth of detail on his early life and family background. That most delightful of mentors, Dr R. B. McDowell, was always ready with useful advice. For access to unpublished written material, I am grateful to Lord Beaumont and Stuart Mole, who showed me their diaries; to Susan Crosland and Magnus Linklater, who generously allowed me to use the interview and other notes of their own previous researches into Jeremy Thorpe; to Gerald Hagan, who gave me the original transcripts of David Holmes' interviews with the *News of the World* in 1981 (only a small proportion of which was published at the time); to Sybille Bedford and Auberon Waugh, who showed me their manuscript notes on the Thorpe trial; to Dominic Carman, who let me see his father's notes on Jeremy's defence; and to Tony Maycock, custodian of the papers of Henry Upton. Many others showed me letters they had received from Jeremy Thorpe, and

Jeremy himself showed me some papers relating to his early life. I am grateful to the staff at the National Archives (formerly Public Record Office), where I consulted the papers relating to Jeremy's 1974 coalition talks with Ted Heath after they were declassified in 2005, and at the London School of Economics, which holds the papers of the Liberal Party Organisation, of the Society for Homosexual Law Reform, and of David Steel. Edith Stokes and her staff at Mount Pleasant provided me with a delectable haven whenever I needed it. My friends at the Savile Club were a constant source of encouragement. I was fortunate in having Andrew Best, Peter Robinson, Andrew Hewson and Ed Wilson as my agents during the long saga, and Broo Doherty, Andrew Gordon, Tim Whiting and Vivien Redman as my editors. And Ursula Mackenzie showed an angelic patience towards an often moody author who must at times have seemed as if he was never going to produce his book.

In expressing my thanks to the following, I have indicated where persons were formerly known by other names which have been used in the text, but I have not graced the deceased with 'the late', as in most cases I simply do not know whether those I spoke to in the last century are still alive or not.

Leo Abse; John Addey; Ian Aitken; Anthony Alffrey; Rupert Allason; Elkan Allen; Patrick Allen; Richard Allen; Bruce Anderson; Lady Anson (Elizabeth Clarke); Mike Arlen; Vivienne Arnell (Viv Franklin); Stephen Atack; Lord Avebury (Eric Lubbock); Kina, Lady Avebury; Peter Avery; Guy Avis; Lord Aylmer; Tim Baistow; Judge John Baker; Carol ('Pixie') Balfour-Paul; Lord Banks (Desmond Banks); Simon Barrington-Ward; Lord Beaumont of Whitley; Sybille Bedford; Alan Beith MP; Tony Benn MP; Humphry Berkeley; Julian Berkeley; Lady Berkeley; Diane Bessell; Paul Bessell; John Bigelow; Viv Bingham; Lord Blaker; Anthony Blond; Sir Richard Body; Stephen Bonarjee; Lord Bonham-Carter; Christopher Booker; Stanley Booth-Clibborn;

Christopher Bourke; Roderic Bowen; Lord Boyd-Carpenter; Simon Bradish-Ellames; Lavinia Bradley (Thorpe); Stanley Brodie QC; Natalie Brooke; Percy Browne; George Bull; Peter Burton; Johanna Butt (Norton-Griffiths); Julian Byng; Richard Came; Myra Campbell; Robin Carey Evans; Dominic Carman; George Carman QC; Edward Carpenter; Dr Christian Carritt; Stephen Carroll; Michael Cartwright-Sharp; Baroness Castle; Rupert Cavendish; 'Scottie' Cheshire; Lewis Chester; Susan Chitty; John Christie-Miller; Stanley Clement Davies; Nigel Cockburn QC; Michael Cockerell; Judge Arthur Cohen; Christopher Coker; Susan Crosland (Barnes); Hugh Cudlipp; Tom Dale; Tam Dalyell MP; Sir Francis Dashwood, Bt; Arthur Davidson QC; James Davidson; Ann Dawson; Michael De-la-Noy; Judge Thomas Dewar; Patric Dickinson; Nadir Dinshaw; Piers Dixon; Judge George Dobry QC; Sir John Drinkwater QC; Andrew Duff; Anne Dummett (Chesney); Michael Edwardes; Bob Edwards; Nick Elan; Tim and Sue Elliott; Tim Ellis; Sir Peter Emery MP; Giles Eyre; Dan Farson; Neil Feiling; Thomas Field-Fisher QC; Mark Fisher MP; Robert Fisher; Neil Flanagan; Antony Fletcher; Robin Fletcher; Sir Charles Fletcher-Cooke QC; Lord Foot (John Foot); Michael Foot; Sir Denis Forman; James Fox; Nigel Foxell; Arnold and Frances Francis; Sir Clement Freud; Jonathan Fryer; John Gaze; Dr William George; Sir Eustace Gibbs; John Goldsmith; Stephen Govier; Michael Gow; James Graham; Martin Graham; Bernard Greaves; Chris Green; John and Sheila Gregory; Antony Grey (Edgar Wright); John Grigg; Inga Haag; Gerald Hagan; Peter Hain MP; David Hall; John Hall QC; Nick Hamel-Smith; Dr Marcus Harbord; Illtyd Harrington; Gladys Harris; Dominic Harrod; Robin Hart; Nick Harvey MP; Patricia Hastings; Lady Selina Hastings; Richard Hawkins; Jerry Hayes; Clifford Henderson; Peter Hennessy; Sir Denis Henry; Ruth Heywood (Araujo); Bevis Hillier; Christopher Hitchens; Henry Hobhouse; Hermione Hobhouse; Neil Hobhouse; Paul Hobhouse; Mary Hodgkinson; Charles Hodgson; Lord Holme; Charles Holmes;

David Hooper; Lord Hooson; Mrs Hopkins (archivist of Trinity College, Oxford); Richard Hough; Tom Houston; Anthony Howard; David Howie; Christopher Hurst; Derek Ingram; Dion Irish; Ronald Irving; Sir Anthony Jacobs; Lord Jenkins of Hillhead (Roy Jenkins); Grenville Jones; Sir Hugh Jones; Gerald Kaufman; Brigadier Robin Keigwin; Fred Kendal; Sir Ludovic Kennedy; Oleg Kerensky; Richard Kershaw; Francis King; Lord Kingsdown (Robin Leigh-Pemberton); Uwe Kitzinger; George Knapp; Colin Knowles; Keith Kyle; Enid Lakeman; Richard Lamb; Trevor Langford; Jan Latham-Koenig; Michael Launder; Dominic le Foe; Sir Andrew Leggatt; Anthony Lejeune; John Lewes; Jason Lindsey; Prince Rupert Loewenstein; Helen Long; the Countess of Longford; Mary Lutyens; Margaret Lyle; Dame Moura Lympany; Patrick Lyndon; the Rev. Douglas Macdonald; Edward Mace; Lord Mackie of Benshie; Michael Maclagan; Bryan Magee; Terry Maher; the Rev. Victor Malan; Philip Mansel; Anthony Marecco; Lord Marlesford (Mark Schreiber); Patrick Marlowe; John Marshall; the Rev. Christopher Martin; David May; the Rev. Anthony Maycock; Lord Mayhew of Wimbledon (Christopher Mayhew); Lord Mayhew of Twysden (Patrick Mayhew); R. B. McDowell; Robin McNaghten; Ian McPhail; Michael Meadowcroft; Colin Merton; Nelson Mews; Sir Anthony Meyer; Keith Middlemas; Judge Arthur Mildon QC; Tina Miller; Sir Patrick Moberly; Stuart Mole; Lord Montagu of Beaulieu; Pierre Montocchio; Richard Moore; Anne Morgan (Norton-Griffiths); Richard Morgan; John Morrell; Alastair Morrison, George Moser; Lady Mosley; James Moxon; Chris Mullin MP; Christopher Murray; Venetia Newall; Derek Nimmo; Francis Noel Baker; Florence O'Donoghue; Michael Ogle; Mereil Oliver; David Owen-Jones QC; Bruce Page; Nigel Palmer; John Pardoe; Sir Hugh Park; Matthew Parris; Margaret Parsons; Indar Pasricha; Lord Peyton of Yeovil; Hubert Picarda QC; Sir Michael Pickard; Roger Pincham; Tom Pocock; Robert Ponsonby; Suna Portman; Stephen Potel; Julian Potter; Heather Prescott; Michael Prest;

Stuart Preston; Paul Quarrie; Lord Reay; Lord Rees-Mogg; Sir Robert Rhodes James; Tony Richards; Andrew Roberts; Denys Robinson; Baroness Robson; Dodl Romayn; Kenneth Rose; Lady Henrietta Rous; Mary Rous; Frances Rubens; Earl Russell; Lord Russell-Johnston; Michael Ryle; Robin Salinger; Bill Schultz; Ruth Sebag-Montefiore; Baroness Seear; John Shakespeare; Sir William Shakespeare; William Shawcross; Moira Shearer; Judge George Shindler QC; John Shirley; Howard Shuman; Elizabeth Sidney; Alan Sked; Adrian Slade; Godfrey Smith; Graham Snell; Lord Snowdon; John Spiller; Tom Stacey; Michael Steed; Lord Steel of Aikwood (David Steel); Mike Steele; George Steiner; Ian Stewart; Mervyn Stockwood; Aidan Sullivan; Lord Taverne; Brian Taylor; Viscount Tenby; Celia Thomas; Sir Swinton Thomas; Richard and Annette Threlfall; Rebecca Tinsley; Viscount Tonypandy; Lord Tope; Lord Tordoff; Raleigh Trevelyan; Patrick Trevor-Roper; Baroness Trumpington; Michael Turner-Bridger; Paul Tyler; James Vallance-White; Graham Viney; Sir Henry de Waal QC; Richard Wainwright; David Walter; Allan Warren; Robin Warrender; Gerald Watkin; Philip Watkins; George Watson; Moray Watson; Judge Victor Watts; Auberon Waugh; Philip Wearne; Ted Wheeler; Francis Wheen; Christina White (Morgan); Nicholas Wickham-Irving; Lord Wigoder; Margaret Wilks (Lady Henderson-Stewart); John Wilkinson; Wynyard Wilkinson; Desmond Willcox; Baroness Williams of Crosby; Marcelle Williams; Victoria Williams (Ellinger); Stephen Willinck; Margaret Wingfield; Dr Timothy Wood; Lord Woolf; Nesta Wyn-Ellis; Philip Ziegler.

I thank them all, together with any helpers or owners of rights whom I may inadvertently have left out.

JEREMY
THORPE

1

ANCESTRY

THORPE OR THORP, still included in the dictionary but now classed as archaic, is an Old English noun of Scandinavian origin meaning 'village, hamlet or small town', and is a common English family name. In 1929, the year Jeremy Thorpe was born, the births of 358 Thorpes were registered in England and Wales, along with 56 Thorps. Historically it is associated with the areas of Danish settlement in eastern England: there are a host of Thorpe place-names all along the east coast from Northumberland to Essex (including Thorpeness in Suffolk, where Jeremy's second wife Marion had a house by the sea). *The Dictionary of National Biography* mentions sixteen Thorpes: these include Sir Robert de Thorpe of Norfolk, Lord Chancellor in 1372, and Thomas Thorpe of Northamptonshire, Speaker of the House of Commons under the Lancastrians in 1452 and lynched by a Yorkist mob in 1461. Jeremy Thorpe, himself a barrister and parliamentarian, always claimed descent from both these men, though they came from different parts of the country and do not appear to have been obviously connected.

If we turn to Volume XII of *The Complete Peerage*, we read of

a barony of Thorpe, which was granted in 1309 to John de
Thorpe, a great landowner of Norfolk and Suffolk, and fell into
abeyance when the 5th Baron, Edmund, was killed in France in
1418, leaving only daughters. There is nothing to suggest that
Jeremy Thorpe is descended from this family, whose estates eventually passed to Edmund's great-great-grandson, the 2nd Lord
Berners.* However, it was common a century ago for middle-
class families to claim association with noble families of the same
name; and Jeremy's grandfather, the Venerable John Henry
Thorpe, seems to have used the arms of John de Thorpe without
having established his right to do so.† These arms include a
handsome crest of a Stag on a Cap of Maintenance which Jeremy
himself used on every possible occasion, engraving it on his personal jewellery, his silver and glass, his invitation cards and his
stationery. He went further: on his twenty-first birthday in 1950,
he astonished his guests by announcing that he was thinking of
calling the Thorpe barony out of abeyance in his favour;[1] and he
spoke of this again thirty years later after losing his seat in the
House of Commons. These claims were pure fantasy since, even
in the improbable event of his being able to prove a title, it has
been legally impossible since the 1920s to revive peerages which
have been in abeyance for centuries; but they are of interest in
that they illustrate the element of romanticism which was central to his personality.

Jeremy Thorpe's identifiable ancestors were Protestant
Irishmen. According to family tradition, the Irish Thorpes

---

* Ancestor of the painter and composer Gerald Tyrwhitt, 14th Lord Berners, who
   died without male heirs in 1950 – the year Jeremy first seems to have mentioned his 'claim'.
† In a notebook shown to the author by his grandson Dr Colin Knowles, J. H.
   Thorpe claimed that these arms were 'supplied' to his father by Ulster King of
   Arms, who was responsible for heraldry in Ireland. Ulster's office may have
   provided a copy of their design, but there is nothing in his records to suggest
   the right to use them was ever granted or confirmed. (Information from Patric
   Dickinson, sometime Ulster King of Arms.)

descend from two English brothers who fought in Cromwell's bloody campaign in Ireland in 1649–50, and were afterwards rewarded with confiscated land there – the elder (Jeremy's ancestor) in County Wexford, the younger in County Carlow.[2] The two branches enjoyed different fortunes. The Carlow Thorps (they eventually dropped the 'e') prospered in the business and professional life of Dublin, where one of them was High Sheriff in 1789 and another Lord Mayor in 1800. Meanwhile the Wexford Thorpes lost their land and were reduced to tenant farmers and tradesmen. They remained fervent, however, in their loyalty to the Crown: they fought as yeomen against the Wexford Uprising of 1798, and when the Irish Constabulary was subsequently set up to deal with agrarian unrest, several of them enlisted in it. Jeremy's great-great-grandfather William Thorpe (1805–79) was born in County Wexford but moved to Queen's County in the Irish Midlands, where he served as a constable at Abbeyleix, seat of the county magnate Viscount de Vesci. He was remembered by his grandson as a proud, boastful man of military bearing, fond of story-telling. The third of his five sons, Jeremy's great-grandfather, another William, was born at Abbeyleix in 1830 and enlisted as a constable in the Dublin Metropolitan Police in 1856, giving his previous occupation as labourer.[3]

The Dublin Metropolitan Police (DMP), like its London counterpart, had been founded in the 1830s to cope with the rising crime and disorder of that city. Less smart than the military-style Irish Constabulary, it was notorious for its low pay and harsh discipline, and its officers were not known for their intelligence: the oafish Dublin policeman is a stock figure in the Irish literature of the period.[4] William Thorpe seems, however, to have been a man of some talent. As a sergeant in 1873, he was the star witness before a Commission of Enquiry into the DMP: as a result of his evidence (which included the observation that his brother, holding the same rank in the London Metropolitan Police, was better paid for less arduous work) there was an increase in the

Dublin force's pay.[5] He was promoted to Inspector in 1874 and in 1883, after a mutiny in the DMP during which he had kept a cool head, he became a Superintendent in charge of one of Dublin's six police divisions, with his headquarters in the prosperous district of Rathmines. He retired in 1890 on a tidy pension of £250 per annum, and died in 1898. In 1854 he had married Maria Byrne: she died in 1904, leaving an estate valued at £213.[6]

William and Maria Thorpe had no fewer than nineteen children. It must have been a struggle to raise them; and ten of them died in infancy, mostly of tuberculosis, a hereditary curse from which Jeremy himself was to suffer. A fierce devotion to the Church of Ireland sustained the family; and the eldest son, Jeremy's grandfather John Henry Thorpe – born on 12 July 1855, the anniversary of the Battle of the Boyne which had secured Protestant rule in Ireland – set his sights on ordination in that Church, a not inconsiderable ambition for the child of a police officer. He was a gifted youth, for despite an incomplete secondary education,[7] he managed to enter Trinity College, Dublin at the age of twenty, complete the four-year degree course in three,[8] and get ordained without having obtained the usual Testimonium in Divinity, becoming a curate in Cork. The Church of Ireland, to which fewer than 750,000 of Ireland's 5 million belonged, had been disestablished by Gladstone in 1869, but remained the religion of the ruling elite in Ireland: having to operate in an overwhelmingly Catholic country, it was more staunchly Protestant than its English counterpart. John Thorpe attracted attention as a vigorous preacher, his main theme being that all truth was to be found in the scriptures.[9] He was an ambitious man, and did no harm to his prospects by his marriage in 1884 to Martha Aylmer (Amy) Hall, a lady six years younger than himself. Her father, Alderman Robert Constable Hall, was one of the leading merchants of Cork. And her mother was an Aylmer.

The Aylmers are one of the oldest Anglo-Irish families, who came over with the Norman invasions of the twelfth century. The branch from which Jeremy is descended were landowners in County Kildare and acquired one of the first Irish baronetcies. Like many such families, they clung to their Catholic faith: Jeremy's ancestor Sir Gerald Aylmer went to prison rather than acknowledge Elizabeth I as Supreme Governor of the Church. Only in the eighteenth century did they embrace Anglicanism. Through the Aylmers, Jeremy descended from an aristocratic clan which was prepared to fight and suffer for its beliefs, and had more than its fair share of swashbucklers, martinets, libertines and other eccentrics. General Sir Fenton Aylmer VC, 13th Baronet (1862–1935), a hero of the Burma Wars who led the unsuccessful British relief expedition to Mesopotamia in 1915, was his grandmother's first cousin. Another cousin, whose Aylmer grandmother was a sister of Jeremy's great-grandmother, was Sir Edward Spears (1886–1974), the soldier, politician and man of letters who was Winston Churchill's intimate and brought General de Gaulle to London in 1940: Jeremy knew him well, reading the address at his memorial service.[10]

Soon after his marriage, John Thorpe was appointed vicar of St Peter's, Cork. There was but one drawback to life in that fine city: he felt patronised and slighted by his rich and prominent in-laws. He had a pronounced chip on his shoulder as the son of that figure of fun, a Dublin policeman: it was around this time that he claimed to be descended from the Barons de Thorpe, hoping to show his wife's relations that he was as good as they. Eventually he could stand it no longer and decided to move with his growing family to England.[11] It so happened that, around this time, a group of wealthy Low Church industrialists in the burgeoning northern town of Stockport – notably Wakefield Christie-Miller, owner of Christy & Co., the world-famous hat manufacturers – were dismayed that their rector had become an Anglo-Catholic, and obtained permission to found a new parish.

No expense was spared: they built a neo-Gothic church of cathedral-like proportions, with a palatial vicarage attached. It remained to find an incumbent with suitable credentials; and the patrons of the new living were impressed by John Thorpe's remarkable preaching talents and impeccable doctrinal beliefs.[12] He was appointed to St George's, Stockport in 1896 and remained there until his death in 1932, becoming Rural Dean of Stockport in 1912, an Honorary Canon of Chester Cathedral in 1917 and Archdeacon of Macclesfield in 1922. In 1908, his pretty eldest daughter Olive married Geoffry (later Colonel Sir Geoffry) Christie-Miller, son of his patron Wakefield: this alliance with one of the richest families in Cheshire was to bring many advantages to the Thorpes, the Christie-Millers paying for the education of Jeremy's father and later Jeremy himself.

Although he failed to become a bishop, Archdeacon Thorpe achieved national renown as a preacher and theologian. He was a leading campaigner for the Low Church Evangelical wing of Anglicanism (with its emphasis on the scriptures, simplicity of worship and personal salvation) in its struggle with the High Church Anglo-Catholic wing (with its emphasis on the Sacraments, elaborate ritual and the universality of the Church). It was repugnant to him that the 'Roman' practices he had learned to despise in Ireland should be imitated by so many of his co-religionists. Through his friend in the Government, Sir Thomas Inskip, he organised the successful parliamentary resistance in 1927–28 to the revised Prayer Book, which to his mind reeked of 'Romanism'. A stream of pamphlets poured from his pen, warning Anglicans against Catholic doctrines and practices and the tendency to treat worship as a sensual experience of art and music. Above all, he loathed the cult of the Virgin Mary, which he denounced as a form of sexual perversion.[13]

Interviewed by Susan Barnes in 1973, Jeremy Thorpe (who was but two when his grandfather died) described the Archdeacon as 'a bullying and bigoted man, a really monstrous man'. This is not entirely fair: other grandchildren remember him for his sense of humour, generosity and kindness. He was, however, what would nowadays be regarded as a fanatic of rigid and intolerant views; and he was a caricature of a fierce, argumentative Irishman. Jeremy, who bore some physical resemblance to him, inherited his campaigning spirit and determination, as well as his quick wit and ability to inspire. At the same time, Jeremy's lifelong antipathy to Ulster Unionism suggests a reaction against all his grandfather stood for. The Archdeacon was a particularly harsh parent; as if by way of compensation, Jeremy's father and Jeremy himself were both indulgent parents.[14]

The Archdeacon had nine children (three of whom died of tuberculosis) by his wife Amy, a gentle and vague woman who was forever wondering how her kinsfolk who had departed this world were faring in the next. We are only concerned here with Jeremy's father, called John Henry after his father but known to the world as Thorpey, who was born in Cork on 3 August 1887. A handsome but delicate boy, he attended St John's School, Leatherhead and proceeded to Trinity College, Oxford, Alma Mater of the Christie-Millers. Trinity was the leading Oxford rowing college and Thorpey hoped to win his oar, but the sport proved too much for his health. After taking a fourth in history, he read for the Bar, being called by the Inner Temple in 1911 and practising on the Northern Circuit. When war broke out in 1914, he was commissioned into the Manchester Regiment and sent to Egypt; but just as his battalion was about to sail for Gallipoli, his health again collapsed, and he spent the rest of the war doing censorship and court-martial work, for which he was awarded an OBE. He became friendly with his commanding officer, Gerald Hurst, another Northern Circuit barrister who became Coalition Unionist MP for Manchester Moss Side at the 'coupon' election of December 1918. When, soon afterwards, a by-election was declared in the nearby seat of Rusholme, Hurst secured the

Unionist candidature for Thorpey, who was duly elected to Parliament in October 1919 at the age of thirty-two.[15]

Captain Thorpe (as he was known after the custom of the day) sat in the House of Commons for four years, during which he spoke in only a dozen debates. He appears to have been a lazy and unambitious politician, who concentrated his energies on earning a living at the Bar. When he did speak, he was liberal in his views, courteous towards opponents, and generally had something interesting to say. He championed the welfare of ex-servicemen, and the equality of women in the civil service. He called for an end to discrimination against illegitimate children, criticising the Church for hypocrisy on this subject;[16] and he tried to introduce an amendment giving soldiers facing court-martial the right to be defended by an officer with legal training.[17] His most interesting contribution was to apply for leave to introduce a Bill in April 1923 to enable ministers to speak in either House of Parliament: had this been carried (it was defeated by 244 votes to 100), it might have resulted in Lord Curzon becoming Prime Minister five weeks later instead of Stanley Baldwin, one of the objections to Curzon being his inability to speak in the Commons.[18]

Thorpey seems to have been liked by all. He was not intel-lectually outstanding, but invariably courteous, charming and kind. He had 'the gift of the gab' and was a superb raconteur and mimic, possessing the quality (which he passed on to his son) of being able to lighten any atmosphere and entertain any company. Like many sensitive men who suffer from precarious health, he was in his element at funerals and memorial services. It is pos-sible that he possessed homosexual inclinations (as was later believed by his son Jeremy): he was to become closely attached during the 1930s to Christopher Hobhouse, a beautiful, brilliant and bisexual young barrister who died on active service during the Battle of Britain. His interest in women, as he confided in Hurst, was largely guided by the desire to marry an heiress.[19] He had not made much progress in this direction when, in January 1922, he was asked to represent his father at the wedding in Westminster Abbey of the Princess Royal and Viscount Lascelles.* Thorpey was thirty-four, and in the next stall sat a striking girl of eighteen, Ursula Norton-Griffiths. She too was representing her father, a famous (and reputedly rich) MP popularly known as Empire Jack; and it is to this man, Jeremy Thorpe's other grandfather, that we must now turn.

At first sight, it is difficult to think of two men more different than Archdeacon Thorpe and Sir John Norton-Griffiths; but they had two things in common which mark them out as typical products of the late Victorian age. They were both men of restless, violent energy who fought passionately for the things in which they believed. And they were both ambitious men who advanced from relatively humble origins to the upper levels of society, becoming slightly ashamed of their backgrounds and marrying women socially much grander than themselves. Towards the end of her long life, Gwladys Norton-Griffiths wrote a book of memoirs in which she confessed that she found her husband's relations so vulgar that she married him on the condition that he never see them again.[20] In fact Sir John's paternal ancestors, rugged Welsh from the mountainous county of Breconshire, appear to have been modest but proud farming folk much like the Wexford Thorpes. His father John Griffiths (1825–91), like the Archdeacon's father, seems to have done rather better than the rest of the family: he set up as a building contractor in Brecon and eventually moved his business to London, but did not prosper there and left an estate valued at £153. He married as his second wife Juliet Avery; and their only son, John Norton Griffiths, known as Jack, was born in Williton in Somerset on 13 July 1871.

---

* Whose elder son married Marion Stein, who would later marry Jeremy Thorpe.

He had a stormy upbringing in Hammersmith: his father had a violent temper, his mother drank, and Jack himself was a wild and rebellious boy. He later claimed to have attended St Paul's School; but there is no record of him there, and whatever education he had was interrupted when at sixteen he ran off to enlist as a trooper in the Horse Guards, giving his age as eighteen. He looked the part, but did not take to military discipline and was 'bought out' ('I never quite understood why', writes Gwladys) by Sir Henry Kimber, a rich businessman and MP. The colonies seemed appropriate for this hardy and tempestuous youth; and Kimber sent him to South Africa to work as a sheep farmer. His farm failed, and he turned to prospecting and shaft-drilling in the Transvaal goldfields, in which he picked up a rudimentary knowledge of engineering. It was a rough life in a lawless world: in later years, he boasted that, one night in the goldfields, he had strangled a man with his bare hands. (In the 1970s, some of his descendants remarked that, if he had received the attentions of a blackmailer, he would have known what to do about it, and would have carried out the job himself.) What young Jack needed was conflict; and in 1896–97, he won his spurs as a scout in the war of Cecil Rhodes' British South Africa Company against the Matabele. In the wake of this, he was awarded some mining concessions in the new territory of Rhodesia; and in 1899 he sailed for London to find backers to enable him to exploit these. It was during a stop at Zanzibar that he met and fell instantly in love with a formidable Englishwoman two years younger than himself, Gwladys Wood.

Gwladys, the only grandparent Jeremy was to know, came from the upper middle class which dominated the business and professional life of Victorian London. Her mother's grandfather, 'Mud' Mills, said to have been a natural son of King George IV, was the engineer who invented the dredge. Her great-uncle by marriage, a Jew named John Coleman, founded the modern profession of accountancy in England. Other well-known uncles included a surgeon, an artist and an archaeologist, while an aunt was a popular songwriter. Her paternal grandfather, the timber merchant Thomas Wood, had married Elizabeth Browning, daughter of a prominent distilling family; and Gwladys' father, another Thomas Wood (1821–85), owned the distillery of Browning, Wood & Fox in Worship Street. He was an unwilling businessman, whose main interests seem to have been literary: he was a member of the Garrick, where his friends included both Dickens and Thackeray. At the age of forty-eight he married Emma-Jane Mills, a woman of strong personality twenty years his junior who had quarrelled with her family. Gwladys, the youngest of four children, was born on 2 January 1873 and brought up in a large house in Marylebone teeming with servants. But when she was only twelve her father died at the age of sixty-four, apparently of worry after a series of business disasters which left the family almost destitute.

The widowed Emma-Jane and her children moved out of their house into cheap lodgings and became poor relations, dependent on the charity of rich Browning uncles. This turn in family fortunes during her childhood had a marked effect on Gwladys' personality. She became resourceful, cheerfully adapting to changing circumstances and able to make the best of any situation. She also developed a degree of snobbery remarkable even for that period, for the impoverished Woods consoled themselves with a sense of being 'gentry' who maintained superior values in spite of hard times. In the late 1880s, the family left London for the continent, where life was cheaper. Gwladys studied music in Germany: she seems to have had talent, as those who praised her singing or piano-playing included (as she tells us) Brahms, Clara Schumann, Joseph Joachim and Jules Massenet. Back in London in the 1890s she tried to make a career as a singer, and received a favourable notice from George Bernard Shaw; but her progress was handicapped by stage fright. Meanwhile her eldest brother, Ralph – Jeremy's 'Great-Uncle

Mumpy', an amiable eccentric who was to become a friend of
Max Beerbohm and marry the suffragette Violet Ruffer – had
been appointed the Johannesburg agent of an Anglo-French trading company; and in 1898, Gwladys and her mother went out to
visit him. It was at Zanzibar on the return journey that she met
Jack Griffiths ('the handsomest man I ever saw') and returned his
love, while aware that here was a rough character she would
have to take firmly in hand.[21]

Chaperoned by Emma-Jane, the couple proceeded together to
London; but before they could marry, the Boer War broke out.
Griffiths rushed back to South Africa and was commissioned
into a company of scouts known as Lord Roberts' Bodyguard, in
which he greatly distinguished himself, being mentioned in dis-
patches three times. He returned to London in 1900, married
Gwladys the following year, and then embarked on a career as a
contractor which carried him from obscurity to fame within the
span of King Edward's short reign. He owed his success to a combination of imagination, ruthlessness and charm: his wife
provided the brains. In short, Griffiths believed, and persuaded
others to believe, that he could carry out engineering projects
in distant parts of the world which were thought to be near-
impossible. He made his name with the construction of the
Benguela railway in Portuguese Angola (1905–8), a contract no
one else wanted to touch, and followed this with spectacular railways in inaccessible parts of South America, and an aqueduct
across the Caucasus supplying the Russian oil industry in Baku.
These were remarkable achievements for a man of no formal
education who spoke no foreign language; they were realised by
slave-driving huge armies of workers who laboured under terrible conditions and many of whom died. In the years before 1914,
Griffiths also constructed the first skyscrapers of Vancouver and
the modern sewerage systems of South London and
Manchester. With his mesmeric personality, he had no difficulty
in finding powerful backers: he was financed from 1908 to 1914

by a consortium consisting entirely of rich peers, led by Lord Howard de Walden who owned most of Marylebone.

His biographer, Keith Middlemas, gives the following portrait of him in 1908:

> At thirty-seven he could pass for thirty; tall, unusually handsome, tanned and sporting the moustache of the born imperialist; powerful as a prize-fighter, impetuous and passionate, rarely restrained yet, schooled by domestic satisfaction, no longer foreign to the drawing-rooms of London; idolised by women, sought after by men; no brilliant talker, but so full of gaiety and fun, enthusiasm and absurdity, he drew everyone to him; while preserving cloaked, except in moments of rare emergency, a nature ruthless in its crude force, entirely elemental; he was the expression of all that characterised the empire-builders of the Edwardian era.[22]

It was natural that this rugged character should support the aggressive imperialism of Joseph Chamberlain. The peers who backed his business provided him with political contacts; and in 1909 he was adopted as Conservative candidate for the traditionally Liberal seat of Wednesbury near Birmingham. At the General Election of January 1910, he threw himself into the unlikely task of capturing this seat with the same determination he brought to his railways. He fascinated voters with the eloquence and fire with which he expressed his imperialist creed, and was not afraid to visit the roughest districts and engage in physical combat with his opponents. To the surprise of all, he won the seat by a majority of some 600. (Fifty years later, his grandson would win a Tory seat for the Liberals by some 300: both victories were due to a combination of hard work, showmanship and an ability to persuade voters of concern for their lot.) Upon his election, John Norton Griffiths began using his middle name as part of his surname; but during the campaign, the press had dubbed him Empire Jack, the sobriquet by which he would be known for the rest of his life.

He remained in the House of Commons for fifteen years, never losing an election. Like his grandson, he was both an outstanding constituency member and a talented self-publicist, forever thinking up wheezes likely to make a splash in the press.[23] As a parliamentarian, however, he was a notorious windbag, returning every year to a pet proposal for an 'Imperial Senate' in London through which the Dominions might bind themselves more closely to the mother country.[24] Sir Maurice Hankey, Secretary of the Committee of Imperial Defence (and later a friend of the Thorpe family), described Empire Jack in 1917 as 'a clever man in the technical sense, but stupid, unpractical and visionary in his ideas', who led a small, obscure group of 'insufferable bores' in 'woolly' discussions about Imperial Federation.[25]

True to his imperialist image, he combined a capacity for feats of endurance in rough places with an enjoyment of all the luxuries life had to offer. He was a lavish host and entertainer, regarded by many as fast and flashy: he kept a fleet of the latest motor cars. He had strong sensual appetites and was a notorious philanderer. His wife, however, was the only person who really mattered to him, and he had reason to be grateful to her. She tamed his nature, shared his hardships, guided him in his decisions, taught him how to behave in society. As she wrote in her memoirs: 'All his affection he poured out into me . . . and everything outside was purely a means to an end. He was always charming to people, even after he had finished with them, but none of his casual friends really meant anything at all in his life.'

If Empire Jack's career reads like an adventure story, this was never more so than during the First World War. He raised a private army from old soldiers who had fought in Southern Africa, and had this recognised as an official regiment of the British Army, the 2nd King Edward's Horse. In an exploit for which he was awarded the DSO, he brought over to France his labourers who had been building the Manchester sewers, and set them tunnelling under enemy lines. He became a legend for his amorous escapades: he was the model for the final scene of Evelyn Waugh's *Vile Bodies*, in which a general drives around a battlefield in a Rolls-Royce loaded with pretty girls and champagne. In the autumn of 1916, he was sent on a mission well suited to his talents: the Germans had invaded Romania, and it was essential for the Allies to destroy the Ploesti oilfields, the richest in Europe, before they fell into enemy hands. After an adventurous journey, Empire Jack arrived at Ploesti just ahead of the Germans; brushing aside local opposition with the help of Queen Marie of Romania (with whom he had an affair), he personally sabotaged the oil wells, setting on fire an area of 200 square miles. For this service, Tsar Nicholas II, whom he visited in St Petersburg just before the February Revolution, invested him with the Order of St Vladimir and presented him with the Order's magnificent decorated sword, destined to become the proudest possession of his grandson Jeremy.[26]

During the first years of peace, Empire Jack was riding high. Construction was booming in the aftermath of war, and the Norton-Griffiths firm was deluged with contracts: among its achievements during this period were a harbour in Portugal, a railway in East Africa, the rebuilding of the Romanian oil industry after its recent destruction and the South London section of the Northern Line. In 1914, he had announced he would not stand again at Wednesbury; but in 1918 he accepted the candidature at Wandsworth, where he was elected as one of the few Conservative MPs opposing the Lloyd George coalition. Although unable to spare much time for Parliament during these years, he was close to many leading politicians: all three men who were to become Conservative premiers between the wars – Bonar Law, Baldwin and Neville Chamberlain – were his friends at this time. Empire Jack and Gwladys became fashionable political hosts, dispensing lavish hospitality at Wonham Manor, a huge pile in Surrey built by Wyatt in 1810, which they had bought towards the end of the war and which cost a fortune to run.

Like most socially ambitious people of the time, the Norton-Griffithses were keenly interested in titles. In 1917, following his Romanian exploits, Empire Jack had been created a KCB, whereupon he hyphenated his surname. In 1922, on Austen Chamberlain's recommendation, he was promoted to the rank of baronet. A few years later, having left Parliament, he tried in vain to get Baldwin to nominate him for a peerage, explaining that his firm was 'always fighting Yanks, Italians, Germans etc. .... for the benefit of British trade' and hinting that the increased business resulting from his elevation would enable him to make handsome donations to the Conservative Party.[27] Half a century later, his grandson Jeremy was also to be greatly interested in questions of honours and patronage.

The years 1923–24 saw a turn in Empire Jack's fortunes. The defeat of the Conservatives at the 1923 election finally dashed his dreams of imperial unity, and he bowed out of Parliament the following year. Meanwhile, a life of relentless activity had taken its toll, and in 1924 he was weakened by a long attack of typhoid. His business also began to go badly. The post-war construction boom had fizzled out; and Empire Jack, whose high-handed behaviour had won him enemies in both business and official circles, found it hard to get orders in a more competitive world. He experienced a series of disasters due to a mixture of bad luck and poor judgement. He embarked on massive public works in Brazil, only to find that the Government there was unable to meet its obligations. He won important concessions from the new Kingdom of Iraq, but found no one to underwrite them. In 1926, Wonham had to be sold. He showed increasing signs of mental instability, and became desperate for one spectacular contract to restore his fortunes. In the summer of 1929, the Egyptian Government invited tenders for the heightening of the Aswan Dam: so intent was Empire Jack on obtaining this commission that his winning tender, at £1,960,000, turned out to be nearly half a million pounds lower than that of his nearest competitor. As the work progressed, it became evident that he had seriously underestimated his costs. He needed to raise loans to continue, but this proved impossible in the climate of the world stock market crash. He faced ruin – if not also prison, for in his desperation he had resorted to some dubious ploys. At dawn on 29 September 1930, in his sixtieth year, Sir John left the seaside hotel at which he was staying near Alexandria, paddled out into the Mediterranean in a small pleasure craft, and shot himself. His last communication had been to telegraph his wife in London, assuring her of his undying love.

Though Jeremy Thorpe was but a year old at the time of Empire Jack's suicide, he had much in common with this remarkable ancestor. Both were visionary men of ruthless ambition who believed nothing was impossible; both operated through a mixture of charm and bullying; both pushed themselves to the limits of their endurance; both were risk-takers who disregarded the normal rules. Both had a gift for making friends, but did not hesitate to take advantage of or discard those friends when it suited them. Both came to grief in money matters owing to a combination of unscrupulousness and over-optimism. As politicians, both were outstanding campaigners and constituency MPs who possessed a flair for publicity and enjoyed the glamour of public life. Both were given to dramatic mood swings, and sought relief from life's stresses in risky and promiscuous sex lives. Both were exhibitionists who struck dramatic poses and longed for the applause of the multitude. Both suffered from bursts of violent temper. In the view of many of their contemporaries, both had a touch of brilliance but were more than a trifle mad.

But there were also important differences. Jeremy was a polished performer, Empire Jack a rugged force. Whereas Jeremy was always sensitive to the mood of the moment, Norton-Griffiths clung to an out-of-date vision of Empire. Indeed, Empire Jack's philosophy was based on a conviction of the superiority of the British race to both European and coloured peoples, while Jeremy championed the causes of European unity and racial equality. Yet his grandfather's devotion to Empire found an echo in Jeremy's devotion to a multi-racial Commonwealth: both rejected insularity, and saw themselves as statesmen on a global stage.

The Norton-Griffithses' eldest son and the heir to the baronetcy, Jeremy's Uncle Peter (1904–83), was a gifted man who took a brilliant degree at Oxford and was a fine linguist and pianist, but is remembered by most of those who knew him as an odious and selfish bully. He married an American heiress, Kay Schrafft, whom he enjoyed humiliating in public. Outside his marriage, he pursued homosexual interests. (Jeremy could do a devastating impersonation of his outrageous mannerisms.) After a chequered wartime secret service career, he went on to become a leading executive of Shell, but missed getting to the top of that corporation owing to his scandalous private life. In 1979, he attended Jeremy's trial at the Old Bailey and seemed to derive pleasure from the thought that his nephew might be convicted and sent to prison.

The eldest child of Empire Jack and Gwladys, Jeremy's mother Ursula, was born on 27 February 1903. She was adored by her father, whom in turn she adulated: even as a small girl, she imitated his noisy and determined manner. After a patchy education, she proceeded in 1919 to a finishing school near Paris, where she met and formed a close friendship with Lloyd George's daughter Megan, another girl of forthright personality who suffered from a father-fixation. (Megan was in France with her father, then at the height of his premiership and attending the Paris Peace Conference.[28]) As the best friend of the Prime Minister's favourite daughter, and with her own parents at the height of their career as political hosts, Ursula became accustomed, while still in her teens, to moving in ruling circles. She attracted attention through some exotic affectations such as the sporting of a monocle. In 1921, she fell in love with the young heir to a Scottish earldom; but his family forbade their marriage, to Ursula's woe. A few weeks later, meeting the handsome figure of Jack Thorpe in Westminster Abbey, she at once decided to marry him, partly on the rebound from her recent unhappy infatuation, perhaps partly because she saw this eloquent parliamentarian, who was twice her age and possessed much charm and a handsome appearance, as something of a reflection of her father. Thorpey for his part was captivated by her striking looks and vigorous personality.

Both families were horrified by the proposed match. Archdeacon Thorpe considered Empire Jack, with his chequered past and flashy style of living, as an agent of the devil, while Gwladys was that abominable thing, an Anglo-Catholic. As for the Norton-Griffithses, they had planned a brilliant marriage for their daughter: the impecunious son of a North Country clergyman, who had failed to make much of a mark as a barrister, soldier or MP, was not what they had in mind at all. Gwladys examined the Thorpe pedigree with her sharp social eye and found it wanting. Empire Jack was about to leave on business for South America and took Ursula with him, hoping to distract her from such foolishness. But Ursula was her father's daughter and not one to give up: back in London, she retired to bed and announced she would stay there until her parents allowed her to be reunited with Thorpey. Eventually they relented: they had been won over by Thorpey's charm and evident devotion to Ursula.

Before the wedding could be arranged, there was an important change in politics: meeting at the Carlton Club on 19 October 1922, Conservative MPs voted to end the coalition which kept Lloyd George in power.[29] A General Election was called for

15 November and resulted in victory for the Conservatives under
Bonar Law, both Empire Jack and Thorpey retaining their seats.
This represented a dramatic moment for Empire Jack, who
hoped his imperial dreams might at last be realised under Bonar
Law, a Canadian and tariff reformer. It was also an exciting
moment for Ursula, who helped Thorpey campaign in
Manchester and was thrilled at the prospect of becoming a politi-
cian's wife.

The marriage took place at St Margaret's, Westminster on
19 December 1922. It was a glittering occasion. The guests
included the new Prime Minister, the Lord Chancellor (Viscount
Cave), the Secretary of State for War (the Earl of Derby), the
President of the Board of Trade (Sir Philip Lloyd-Greame), the
Attorney-General (Sir Douglas Hogg) and the Postmaster
General (Neville Chamberlain), along with other peers and MPs
and a host of ambassadors, judges and industrialists. Friends
of the Archdeacon, on the other hand, were conspicuous by their
absence from the ceremony, which was conducted by an Anglo-
Catholic priest. Megan Lloyd George was the principal
bridesmaid; and Ursula caused a sensation by wearing her monocle. *The Times* published a photograph of the happy couple over
the caption 'MP Weds MP's Daughter': both look handsome and
confident, but whereas Thorpey wears an easy-going look,
single-mindedness is already written on the features of Ursula.

Thorpey and Ursula were in love, but their marriage was
based on false hopes. He imagined her to have great financial
expectations; she imagined him to be at the outset of a brilliant
political career. But within twelve months, Thorpey was out of
Parliament, defeated in his Manchester seat by the Liberal free
trader C. F. G. Masterman at the 'tariff reform' election of
December 1923; and it was not long afterwards that the Norton-
Griffiths business empire began to reveal itself as hollow. Under
the circumstances, Thorpey felt it his duty to devote himself to
earning an income at the Bar which would enable his wife to

keep up something of the manner to which she had become accustomed. He thus abandoned both his political career and his practice on the Northern Circuit to concentrate on the Parliamentary Bar – that small body of counsel acting for the promoters of private Acts of Parliament, particularly involving local authority construction projects. It was unexciting but lucrative work, and by the time he took silk in 1935, Thorpey had become one of its most successful practitioners.

Ursula, meanwhile, developed from a bossy and petulant girl into a formidable and intimidating woman, exhibiting the traits associated with Lady Bracknell, Bertie Wooster's Aunt Agatha, and the terrifying matrons in Saki. She had her father's temper, she was always determined to get her way, and she was capable, if thwarted, of making a scene which would leave her victims quivering. If anything displeased her, such as the dress or behaviour of the person she was with, or the half-delivered sermon of some hapless vicar, she would express her disapproval audibly. Her monocle resembled a searchlight, seeking out faults on which to unleash her wrath. She had inherited the snobbery of her mother as much as the bullying of her father, and could be ruthless in putting in their places those she considered her inferiors. There were some who admired her spirit or found it amusing; but she herself notably lacked a sense of humour. Children and servants adored Thorpey; they were terrified of Ursula.

Like Gwladys, Ursula loved society and entertaining. She was a good housekeeper and hostess, and could be charming, particularly if her guests were distinguished or might be useful in some way. She was determined to keep up with many rich friends. By the late 1920s, the Thorpes resided in some style in South Kensington, where Ursula ran a large household and gave nightly dinner parties. This was tedious for Thorpey, whose health was never robust and who would have preferred a quiet life with a few chosen friends: as it was, he had to work long hours to pay for his wife's social life, and was then expected to participate in it. It was his fate to endure first an oppressive father, then a demanding wife. While devoted to her, and anxious to do his best to satisfy her wishes, he often found her behaviour and opinions hard to bear.

This was notably the case when she came into contact with his family, whom she regarded with a scorn she did not trouble to conceal. Her relations were particularly bad with that other opinionated and hot-tempered personality, the Archdeacon: their rare meetings usually ended in rows, in which the nimble-witted clergyman tended to get the better of his daughter-in-law. Four times a year, Thorpey went up to the north-west to sit as Recorder of Blackburn, staying with his sister Olive and her husband Geoffry Christie-Miller on their hunting estate at Nantwich in Cheshire. At first Ursula came too – as rich gentry, the Christie-Millers were spared her disapproval of her husband's relations – but she soon got bored with country life and left him to go alone, to the relief of her former hosts who had found her a most troublesome guest.

At the outset of their married life, Ursula was intensely ambitious for her husband: he was more active in Parliament during the first months of his marriage than during the whole of his previous three years as an MP. It was a severe disappointment to her when he lost his seat and failed to resume his political career. But though denied the chance to play much of a role as the daughter or wife of a politician, she might still become the mother of one: she longed for a son. Her first two children, however, were daughters: Lavinia, born in 1923, and Camilla, born in 1925. Lavinia was a quiet, reflective girl who took after her father; Camilla was pretty and mischievous with something of her mother's spirit. Brought up by nannies, they received affection from their father but suffered cruelty and neglect from their mother. Finally, on 29 April 1929, a son was born, to his parents' joy. They called him John Jeremy: John after his two grandfathers, Jeremy because they thought it sounded well with John.

2

CHILDHOOD
1929–43

JEREMY THORPE WAS born into what appeared to be a secure and prosperous world.[1] His parents lived at 3, Onslow Gardens, a large, fashionable terrace house in South Kensington: in 1933, when he was four, they moved to 2, Egerton Gardens, a similar house in still more fashionable Knightsbridge. These residences were stylishly furnished and decorated, and staffed by a cook, a chauffeur, four maidservants and two nannies. The Thorpes belonged to the professional upper middle classes; but their son might be forgiven for assuming that they were connected to the aristocracy. His maternal grandmother was a formidable titled dowager; his mother had the airs of a duchess; while his father romantically sported on his signet ring the crest of the medieval Barons de Thorpe. As he grew up in the decade before the war, Jeremy can have been but little aware that his parents were short of capital and lived to the full extent of their income; or that, of his two illustrious grandfathers, both of whom died before he was three, one was the son of a policeman, the other the son of a builder.

Thorpey and Ursula had prayed for a son and were overjoyed

at his arrival; but like most parents of their time and class, they barely concerned themselves with the early upbringing of their children. The Thorpes' head nanny was Nanny Wynne, a strict practitioner of the old school whom even Ursula, with her sergeant-major attitude towards servants, treated with respect: she brooked no outside interference, and insisted on her employers making an annual visit to the South of France in order to safeguard her leading social position among the Kensington nannies. The under-nanny was Nellie Hoskins, a sweet-natured Sussex girl who remained in touch with many of her charges (including Jeremy) up to her death in 1991. Under the care of these contrasting matrons, Jeremy endured the usual English nursery regime of unappetising meals, perambulations in the Park, rewards and punishments. He had a teddy bear and a gollywog, and his favourite toys were a wind-up train set and a sentry box in which he could stand to attention in a miniature guardsman's uniform, complete with bearskin.

Jeremy developed into an angelic but rather sickly boy. He was prone to chills, contracted the whole gamut of childhood diseases, and (like his sister Camilla) suffered from the *petit mal* form of epilepsy. (It may be noted here that Freud, in his famous essay on Dostoevsky, advances the theory that *petit mal* tends to be associated with two other conditions – homosexuality, and a love of gambling and risk-taking.[2]) In the winter of 1935, shortly before he was six, he underwent a serious health crisis: after acting as a page at a society wedding, he was convulsed with pains and found to have developed tubercular glands in his stomach. (Tuberculosis was the curse of the Thorpes, which had carried off three siblings of his father and ten of his grandfather.) For two weeks, he hovered between life and death at Great Ormond Street Hospital, his parents beside themselves with anxiety. That February, Thorpey was due to be sworn in as a King's Counsel: before the ceremony, he went to see his son in hospital, wearing his silk gown and full-bottomed wig. In his delirium,

Jeremy imagined this strangely attired figure to be the devil come to fetch him: he screamed and screamed.

He pulled through, but faced a long and hazardous recuperation. In the pre-penicillin age, the cure for tuberculosis was a regime of immobilisation; and as the London smogs were thought to be fatal to his condition, he endured six months of this treatment at a seaside villa at Rustington in Sussex, spending his days lying on a veranda in a spinal carriage, being looked after by Nanny Hoskins and a maid called Daisy, his parents visiting him when they could. When he was finally cured, he had to learn to walk again, which he did in the company of George, a smooth-haired fox terrier presented to him by his godfather, Sir Ernest Hiley.* These early experiences lent an element of stoicism to his character: they also left him with a tendency to backache, and an awkward, shuffling gait.

Back in the family home in London in the autumn of 1935, Jeremy attended a nearby day school called Wagner's[3] and began to see more of his parents. Thorpey had a natural affinity with children and a great capacity for entertaining them: he was a gifted story-teller and could produce much laughter with his imitations, especially in the Irish and North Country dialects of his own childhood. Jeremy's wit, his talents as a raconteur and mimic, may be traced to the early influence of his father. The result of his mother's influence, on the other hand, was to fill him with precocity and a sense of his own importance: for Ursula (who did not like children as such, and treated her daughters severely) was fiercely ambitious for her son and determined that he should make his mark upon the world. The normal parental roles were therefore reversed, as Thorpey

---

* Sir Ernest Varvill Hiley (1868–1949), a solicitor specialising in parliamentary business who gave Thorpey most of his work at the Bar. Jeremy's other godparents were Colonel Andrew Kingsmill of the Grenadier Guards and Sibyl Howard, an Australian heiress and London County Councillor.

represented the relaxed, artistic side of life, while Ursula pushed her son forward, her eyes fixed firmly on the future. Another early influence was that of his grandmother, Gwladys, Lady Norton-Griffiths, a tough old dragon living nearby in Evelyn Gardens, surrounded by the relics of a glorious past and struggling to maintain her social position: she helped instil in Jeremy a love of music and an acute class-consciousness.

His parents and grandmother were all gregarious people endowed with abundant outward self-confidence, and Jeremy was brought up in an atmosphere which imbued him with an unashamedly forward nature. His mother (like her mother before her) was an assiduous lion-hunter; his father had eminent friends through politics and the law; and from infancy, Jeremy was introduced to prominent personages and encouraged to shine in their company. Visitors to Egerton Gardens included illustrious soldiers such as Field Marshal Sir Claud Jacob; members of the aristocracy such as Lord and Lady Sackville; rich industrialists such as the Langs of Black & White whisky; and numerous lawyers and politicians. In the autumn of 1935, when he was six and a half, his father took him to the service at Westminster Abbey marking the start of the legal year, where he was photographed by the press chatting to a high court judge.[4] Ursula later recalled:

> It never occurred to him that anybody might not be glad to see him. Once when he was a little boy and we were at a concert, he said: 'I want to talk to Sir Thomas Beecham.' I replied: 'You can't, Jeremy, we don't know him.' He was quite determined and went backstage ... 'What do you want?' asked Sir Thomas. 'I just wanted to talk to you,' said this little boy. After that – we always sat in the front stalls – when Beecham made his bow he would turn and give this boy an enormous wink.[5]

It is ironic that Ursula should mention this episode, for if Jeremy had a tendency to seek out the great and assume their goodwill, he inherited it from his mother: during her long widowhood, she was to be notorious for inviting herself to stay with anyone of importance she knew wherever she happened to be, at home or abroad.

As might be expected of a child who enjoyed such precocious relations with adults, Jeremy was not universally popular with his contemporaries. Owing to his delicate health, he was discouraged from playing with boys of his own age; and those he did get to know were invariably alarmed by his mother, who was in the habit of glaring at them through her monocle and criticising their appearance and behaviour. He was also considered to be a terrible show-off. On one occasion, Jeremy turned up at a children's party better dressed than any of the other children, and proceeded to draw attention to himself: when the time came to go home, his smart clothes were in rags. Sir William Shakespeare, son of the Thorpes' close friends the Geoffrey Shakespeares, later remembered him as 'a mother's boy'; while Baroness Trumpington (then Jean Campbell-Harris), who met him during pre-war summer holidays in Wales, recalled that she and her brothers considered him 'a spoilt brat'.[6]

On the other hand, Jeremy was doted on by his sisters, Lavinia being six years and Camilla four years older than himself. They were a contrasting pair: Lavinia quiet, studious and romantic; Camilla (the prettier of the two) noisy, mischievous and temperamental. They longed to fuss over 'Jayjay' (as they called him) but were given little chance to do so, since Ursula (and her proxy Nanny Wynne) guarded him with a jealous possessiveness. Jeremy was the apple of his mother's eye and could do no wrong, whereas Ursula was forever scolding her daughters, both of whom would always have difficult relations with her and come to regard her as a selfish, unfeeling woman.

Encouraged by the daredevil Camilla, Jeremy soon developed a taste for being naughty and getting away with things. Once, visiting the nursery of a schoolfellow from Wagner's, he discovered a collection of Dinky toys which he purloined by stuffing them into his Wellington boots. (He returned them a few days later, explaining it was just a jape.[7]) In Ursula's drawing room there was a table draped with a large damask cloth under which two small boys could disappear and not be seen: Jeremy called this his 'secret house' and would sometimes lure a friend there, where they would engage in such intimacies as small boys are capable of. On at least one occasion this happened while a fashionable and unsuspecting tea party hosted by his mother was taking place in the room beyond.[8] Thus from earliest childhood Jeremy experienced the thrill of forbidden pleasure in reckless proximity to a conventional world, with the risk of exposure and disgrace adding to the excitement.

Religion played a part in Jeremy's upbringing. Thorpey, reacting against his father, was not much of a churchgoer, but Ursula was a regular Sunday worshipper with her children at St Peter's, Cranley Gardens, where the vicar was firmly under her control. As an adult, Jeremy would show a broad-minded interest in spiritual matters: he enjoyed the sensual theatre of Anglo-Catholicism, found solace in the stark individualism of the Evangelicals, explored other faiths (including the occult) and detested all religious bigotry. The Archdeacon's legacy was not wasted on him, however: traditionally there was a preaching tone in Liberal speechmaking, and Jeremy would find this came to him naturally.

Ursula encouraged Jeremy's early interest in two aesthetic pursuits – playing the violin and collecting Chinese ceramics. Neither of these ran in the family and both seem to have been inspired by the Thorpes' friendship with prominent Greeks living in London, Alexandre Fachiri and George Eumorfopoulos. Fachiri was an international lawyer practising at the Inner Temple whose wife Adila (née d'Aranyi) was a violinist and great-niece of Joseph Joachim.[9] It was a pupil of Adila, Ruth Araujo, who undertook to teach the six-year-old Jeremy the instrument: from the start, he was one of those musicians who make up in flair what they lack in application.[10] Eumorfopoulos, a rich merchant, was a famous collector of Chinese porcelain; having no children of his own, he became attached to Jeremy, to whom he presented some fine small specimens from his collection, along with a copy of its printed catalogue which appeared in 1938. He even spoke of making Jeremy his heir: unfortunately he died a ruined man, but his gifts formed the nucleus of an interesting collection built up over the years by Jeremy, who at one moment thought of making a career as a professional expert in the subject. (Jeremy was always to be an ardent supporter of the Greeks, a fact which would later become evident in his attitude as a politician towards the Cyprus question.)

But the most remarkable talent which Jeremy exhibited as a boy was that of mimicry: almost as soon as he could talk he was doing brilliant impersonations, imitating not just the voices but the expressions and mannerisms of his subjects. He was encouraged in the exercise of this irreverent ability by his unusual opportunities to study the speech and behaviour of distinguished grown-ups, and presented with ideal practice material in the form of his own relations. There can have been few more welcome gifts to a boy who delighted in the art of parody than Uncle Peter, the louche baronet, with his pompous voice and camp gesticulations; Uncle Geoffry, the crusty colonel, with his limping gait and habit of repeating his expressions; or that fiery little eccentric, Great-Uncle Mumpy.

On the whole, Jeremy's childhood, though marred by illness and subject to some unusual influences, was a happy one. But the Thorpe household, for all its outward jollity and normality, was haunted by ancestral secrets which were spoken of in whispers. The spectres of homosexuality, alcoholism, violence and mental instability hovered in the background. Whistling in the wind at night were echoes of the shot with which Empire Jack had taken his life, and of the Archdeacon's fiery denunciations of sin. The brazen self-confidence which appeared to characterise the family owed something to a sense of inferiority deriving from a consciousness of its recent humble origins. These 'dysfunctional' aspects of the world in which Jeremy grew up would affect him in various ways.

Although his father's parliamentary career was long over, Jeremy was brought up in a household which continued to have strong connections with Conservative politics. At the time of his birth in April 1929 the Prime Minister was Stanley Baldwin, a sometime associate of Empire Jack who had sent the Thorpes a silver tea service for their wedding: various leading members of his administration were friends either of Jeremy's father or one or other of his grandfathers.* When Jeremy was a month old, Baldwin's ministry was replaced by a Labour Government whose members were outside the Thorpe circle; but friends of Thorpey again held office in the Conservative-dominated National Government of 1931–40. These included Lord Swinton (Colonial Secretary 1931–35, Air Minister 1935–38), on whose Yorkshire estate Thorpey often went shooting; Sir Donald Somervell (Solicitor-General 1933–36, Attorney-General 1936–45), a fellow Northern Circuit barrister and friend of the Christie-Millers; and the Liberal National MP Geoffrey Shakespeare, who had been Thorpey's closest friend in the House of Commons. Such men and their wives were frequently entertained at Egerton Gardens: their proximity helped instil in Jeremy an early awareness of the glamour and excitement of public life.

---

* In particular, the Lord Chancellor (Lord Hailsham) and the War Secretary (Sir Laming Worthington-Evans) were friends of Empire Jack; the Home Secretary (Sir William Joynson-Hicks) and Attorney-General (Sir Thomas Inskip), both fervent Evangelicals, were friends of the Archdeacon; while the President of the Board of Trade (Sir Philip Cunliffe-Lister) and the Solicitor-General (Sir Boyd Merriman) were friends of Thorpey.

The people who contributed most to Jeremy's early interest in politics were not, however, Conservatives. For his parents were on close terms with the Lloyd George family. This might seem odd, for not only were the Lloyd Georges Liberals, but Empire Jack had been Lloyd George's sworn enemy, while Thorpey had helped vote him out of office in October 1922. Ursula, however, had kept up the close friendship she had formed in 1919 with Lloyd George's daughter Megan; while Thorpey, after his marriage, similarly befriended Megan's brother Gwilym, a gentle and humorous man like himself who served with him in the Parliament of 1922–23. (There was, however, a strong mutual antagonism between Ursula and Gwilym's pretty wife Edna.) Every September from the mid-1920s onwards Thorpey and Ursula went to stay with Gwilym and Megan at Brynawelon, the Lloyd George family home at Criccieth in North Wales. This was presided over by the matriarchal figure of Dame Margaret Lloyd George, as 'LG' spent most of his time in Surrey with his secretary-mistress Frances Stevenson; and Dame Margaret seems to have fallen mildly in love with Thorpey, whose delightful company helped her forget her husband's adultery and neglect. But the Thorpes also seem to have been popular with Lloyd George himself, who entertained them both at his London house in Addison Road, Kensington, and Bron-y-de, his country house at Churt with its famous orchard.

Though Lloyd George had fallen from power in 1922, he remained an immense figure on the national scene, venerated by millions both as the social reformer who had introduced National Insurance and 'the man who won the war'. He continued to take a vigorous part in politics: as late as 1940, he was widely expected to return to office in some form. His personality was such that he could never be ignored; indeed, he was feared by many of the politicians in power. He was too much of an individualist to be held down by party allegiances: in 1910, he had been the most radical member of the Liberal Government;

in 1920, he tried to persuade his followers to merge with the Conservatives. He split the Liberals in 1916; he led an ostensibly reunited party from 1925 to 1931, while refusing to hand over to it the large political funds he had amassed; in 1931 he effectively split from it again, henceforth leading a tiny family parliamentary group made up of Gwilym and Megan (both returned for Welsh constituencies in 1929), and Goronwy Owen, who was married to Gwilym's sister-in-law.

The Thorpe children were brought up to consider themselves honorary members of the Lloyd George family. Lloyd George and Dame Margaret were 'Tada' and 'Nain' (grandfather and grandmother); Megan (who was Lavinia's godmother*) was 'Aunty Megs', Gwilym 'Uncle Gil'. Gwilym's two sons, and the four children of Megan's elder sister Olwen Carey Evans, stood in a cousinly relationship (though they did not always appreciate Jeremy: Gwilym's son William, a normally placid boy, almost drowned him at Criccieth after some intolerable provocation).[11] Jeremy liked afterwards to recall his first sighting of the great man. It was September 1935: as a treat after his long recovery from tuberculosis, Jeremy was allowed to take part for the first time in his parents' annual visit to Criccieth, where Lloyd George was about to make one of his periodic descents. A figure in the news was Haile Selassie, Emperor of Ethiopia, whose country was threatened with imminent invasion by the Italians; as a lark, Gwilym and Thorpey decided to greet Lloyd George at Brynawelon dressed up as the Emperor and Empress. Lloyd George's private secretary, A. J. Sylvester, recorded in his diary the memorable scene:

> Gwilym wore a black beard and whiskers, which he had pulled
> out of his mother's hearth rug and stuck on his chin and
> cheeks ... Thorpey wore one of Dame Margaret's best dresses,

---

* Not Jeremy's, contrary to what he often asserted.

with a cushion underneath to form a more than adequate bust . . .
Olwen, Megan, Mrs Thorpe and the children, carrying a huge flag
of the Welsh dragon, stood behind. As LG alighted from the car,
the Emperor welcomed him in broken English to Addis Ababa,
while the Empress, with a delightful charm and attractive shyness, made two graceful bobs . . . LG was thrilled.[12]

Jeremy glimpsed Lloyd George at perhaps a dozen pre-war
encounters – at Criccieth, during the great man's occasional visits
to Egerton Gardens, or when the Thorpes went down to have tea
at Churt. Like so many of all ages, he was strongly affected by
LG's magnetic personality, his zest for life, his infectious sense of
fun. Sometimes he would sit silently in a corner while 'the Welsh
wizard' performed to a luncheon table or drawing room. He
would then notice LG's power to captivate an audience for hours
on end, his ability to tune in mentally to each of his listeners, his
beautiful speaking voice, his poetical language with its sparkling
wit and powerful imagery. He would listen to the easy flow of LG's
conversation – a seductive mixture of gossip and reminiscence,
spiced with sharp observations (including mimicry) on the personalities of the current scene. He would catch the atmosphere of
intrigue which Lloyd George carried about with him, the raffish
and roguish air. Slightly though Jeremy knew him, Lloyd George
became his boyhood hero, and a role model for the rest of his life:
one of his favourite books was a volume of the great man's
speeches, from which he frequently quoted as a child.

Although they had disliked each other, Lloyd George had
much in common with Empire Jack. Both were unclassifiable
individualists, *enfants terribles*, radicals impatient with the existing order; men of energy and imagination for whom nothing was
impossible; seducer types who got their way through a mixture
of charm and bullying; larger-than-life characters who led
colourful private lives. In Jeremy's imagination, his honorary
grandfather Lloyd George and his own late grandfather Empire

Jack seem to have merged into a kind of composite being which he set out to imitate.* He came to regard himself as Lloyd George's spiritual heir, and was encouraged in such feelings by Megan, who adored her father and saw much of the Thorpe children. She was particularly fond of Jeremy, and seems to have helped foster within him the dream that he might be destined to complete the leadership tasks LG had begun. A schoolfriend of Camilla recalls Jeremy walking with Megan in 1938, proclaiming: 'One day, I shall be Prime Minister ...'[13] It became a kind of childhood refrain, and not one which endeared him to his contemporaries.

In January 1938, shortly before he was nine, Jeremy was sent to Cothill, a fashionable school in Oxfordshire owned and run by a Major Pike which prepared boys for Eton. He disliked the spartan regime, missing home comforts and his mother's protective influence. The other boys thought him precious with his violin, his Chinese pots, and his assertions that he was descended from a Lord Chancellor and destined to become Prime Minister. He cannot have been entirely lacking in social and leadership qualities, however, for despite a lack of aptitude for sports and games, he became captain of the school wolf cub pack, run by the headmaster's daughter.[14] But his unhappiness was palpable, and when he came home for the school holidays in the summer of 1939, his parents decided not to send him back. Thirty-four years later, asked in a BBC interview how he proposed to educate his own son Rupert (then aged four), Jeremy replied that he would quite like him to go to Eton if he proved suitable, and perhaps to his old Oxford college, but under no circumstances would he think of sending him to 'a toffee-nosed prep school'.[15]

---

* I once asked Jeremy whether he knew of any meetings between his two grandfathers: he automatically assumed I was referring to Empire Jack and Lloyd George.

The prospect of war now loomed. The Thorpes were particularly conscious of the threat posed by Hitler owing to their friendship with Richard Weininger, a flamboyant Jewish businessman who had been born in Vienna, taken Czech nationality, lived on an estate near Augsburg and spent much time in London. In September 1935, when the Nuremberg Laws were proclaimed, the Thorpes had been staying with the Weiningers in Germany and were shocked to witness the indignities suffered by their hosts at that time. By the spring of 1939, Weininger was living in London, a refugee from Nazism but still able to carry on part of his business. Warned by him that war could not be far away and would make city life uncomfortable, the Thorpes decided to give up Egerton Gardens and move to the picturesque and fashionable village of Limpsfield on the Surrey-Kent border, where the North Downs meet the Weald.* They had spent summers there in the past and had friends in the neighbourhood, notably the wealthy Prest family. The new residence into which they moved in June 1939 was Little Heath House, a substantial gabled villa set in a walled garden. Limpsfield was to be Ursula's home for the remaining half-century of her life, and she quickly set about establishing herself as a leading influence in the village.

Around the time of the Thorpes' move, some of their English servants left to work in munitions factories, being replaced by two middle-aged Jewish sisters from Prague whom Richard Weininger had helped emigrate to England. One of these, Mrs Fischer, had been Prague's leading *patissière* and became the Thorpes' cook, to the delight of Ursula who found herself able,

---

* Since Edwardian times, Limpsfield had been a favourite haunt of writers such as Ford Madox Ford and E. V. Lucas, and musicians such as Frederick Delius and Thomas Beecham. It also had associations with radical politics through such residents as the humanitarian campaigner Octavia Hill and the Fabian statesman Sydney Olivier. Winston Churchill lived just four miles away at Chartwell, where Jeremy's sister Lavinia was sometimes asked to tennis parties by the youngest Churchill daughter Mary.

in the months before rationing, to serve meals of sensational quality; Mrs Fischer's sibling Josée toiled as a housemaid. The presence of these refugees (who had left behind husbands they would never see again), and the visits of the Weiningers with their grim reports of continental developments, left their mark on Jeremy: he was always to abhor racial and religious persecution, and would devote much of his political career to helping refugees and political prisoners.

The family had barely settled down at Limpsfield when war broke out in September 1939. The Parliamentary Bar which had provided Thorpey with a livelihood ceased to operate owing to the suspension of civilian construction work by local authorities. However, both Thorpey and Ursula were intensely patriotic and soon found themselves occupied with useful jobs. Thorpey became personal assistant to his friend Geoffrey Shakespeare MP, then serving as a junior minister under Winston Churchill at the Admiralty. ('His gay and charming personality,' recalled Shakespeare in his memoirs, 'cheered many a heavy day.'[16]) Ursula became billeting officer for the Limpsfield district – a job in which she was highly effective, since it was a brave household which, faced with Ursula in all her monocled formidability, dared question what she considered to be its proper quota of evacuees. Indeed, Ursula's rage could be terrible if she ever suspected that anyone was failing to 'do their bit' or evading wartime regulations.

Jeremy was meanwhile sent to a local school, Hazelwood, as a weekly boarder. He seems to have been quite happy there. His school runs took him past home where he would be joined by his beloved dog George. He also saw much of his sister Lavinia, then sixteen, who was living at home studying for her Oxford responsions. Jeremy was allowed to bring schoolfriends to stay when he returned to Little Heath House for weekends; and it soon became evident that he had learned at least one lesson from his unhappy spell at Cothill. On his first weekend, he brought with him a particularly surly and oafish boy. When his mother asked him why he had befriended such a person, he replied: 'Oh, he's the biggest bully in the school!'

Around the time of Dunkirk, when Britain seemed likely to be invaded, many parents sought to send their children to safety on the (still quite numerous) ocean-going passenger ships. Most of those who could afford to do so organised this privately; but at the Admiralty, Thorpey was responsible for setting up the Children's Overseas Reception Board, designed to organise the evacuation of British schoolchildren at public expense to the Dominions and United States. The pressure for places was enormous – only about 3,000 out of 200,000 child applicants (some of them lost when their vessels were sunk) had been shipped by the time the scheme was abandoned in September 1940[17] – but thanks to Thorpey's influence, passages were found for Jeremy and Camilla on the *Duchess of Richmond* sailing for Canada in June 1940. They were destined to join their rich American aunt Kay Norton-Griffiths, who had returned to her native Boston with her own children after her husband Peter had been posted to the British Embassy in Madrid. There was a tearful parting at Euston Station, parents and children not knowing if or when they would ever see each other again. Lavinia was worried to think of the eleven-year-old Jeremy being at the mercy of the fourteen-year-old Camilla, whose behaviour was increasingly wild: at Benenden, where she had spent the past two years, she had become notorious for her St Trinian's-style escapades and for turning girls against each other by spreading tales.

Jeremy was seasick during the Atlantic crossing,[18] but when they arrived in America it must have seemed a paradise compared to wartime Britain. The Schrafft dynasty to which Kay belonged lived at West Newton, the smartest suburb of Boston, in princely style. The family fortunes had been founded by her grandfather, a Catholic German immigrant of 1849 who had purveyed confectionery to the Union Army during the American

Civil War. His son had gone on to found the largest chocolate factory in the world along with a chain of popular restaurants; at an advanced age he had married a young Irish nurse, produced several daughters (of whom Kay was the eldest), and died. His brother took charge of the business, while his widow, Bertha Schrafft, continued to display the exuberance and extravagance of the chorus girl who marries the millionaire in a musical comedy, her daughters being muted versions of herself. The household which received Jeremy in America was therefore a colourful one which encouraged him in a theatrical view of life.

Jeremy and Camilla did not remain long in Boston, for after the Fourth of July celebrations the entire Schrafft household moved to Lochland, their country estate on Squam Lake in New Hampshire, where their huge clapboard mansion (now part of Dartmouth College) could accommodate up to fifty guests. It must have been an odd experience for the young Thorpes to be dwelling in this lotus land at a time when their own country was fighting for its life, especially in view of the ambiguous attitude of the Schraffts towards Hitler and the war. They were fiercely conservative Republicans, who opposed President Roosevelt and his desire to give Britain 'all aid short of war'; they were also highly conscious of their German origins. One of their visitors at Lochland that summer was the German Consul in Boston: during his visit, Jeremy provocatively hoisted a Union Jack.[19] Certainly some of the things he heard and saw that summer seem to have filled him with a lasting distaste for right-wing politics and caused him to question certain elements in his own background.

In the autumn of 1940, Jeremy was admitted to the Rectory School at Pomfret, Connecticut, where he would spend the next three years, his school holidays generally being spent at Lochland (where he kept an outboard motor) or Dartmouth College Summer Camp. Founded in 1928, the Rectory was an Episcopalian establishment which attempted to model itself on an English public school: it laid particular emphasis on smartness of dress, the boys being required to change their clothes several times a day. In other respects the regime was a comfortable one, every boy having his own room; the headmaster, the 'Boston Brahmin' John Bigelow, was a warm, inspiring character who imbued the school with a family atmosphere. Jeremy (as he later recalled) was very happy there, his homesickness assuaged by the presence of other English evacuees.[20] He began to cultivate the art of making friends and influencing people. He won particular admiration for his gifts as a mimic: it was not long before he could reproduce the characteristic accents and expressions of almost every part of the United States.

Two events stood out during Jeremy's American schooldays. The first was the Presidential Election of November 1940, which returned Roosevelt for an unprecedented third term. This was the first great political event of which Jeremy was conscious and he followed it with fascination: braving the disapproval of his schoolmates, who mostly came from Republican backgrounds, he declared himself enthusiastically for 'FDR', whom he saw as an American Lloyd George. (Years later, he was delighted to discover that Roosevelt had indeed been an admirer of Lloyd George and had studied his writings and speeches.) The second event was America's entry into the war following the attack on Pearl Harbor in December 1941. After the call-up of the school's ancillary staff, the boys were organised to run their own facilities: Jeremy's job, which he enjoyed, was to look after the piggery on the school's home farm. He was fiercely patriotic: collecting garbage to feed his pigs from neighbouring properties, he delivered stern warnings to anyone who appeared to be exceeding permitted rations.[21]

Twenty years later, when Jeremy liked to think of himself as a potential British 'JFK', he would say that his childhood sojourn in the United States had had the salutary effect of making him thoroughly egalitarian and free of snobbery. However, neither the

Schrafft milieu nor the Rectory School was particularly lacking in elitism, and if Jeremy experienced a surge of democratic feeling, it can only have been by way of reaction. But his personality certainly seems to have been affected by the greater uninhibitedness of Americans, their receptiveness to new ideas, their love of showmanship. One may also wonder whether he had any adolescent homosexual experiences while in America: certainly his sister Camilla returned from that country having been confirmed in a distinct and flamboyant preference for her own sex.

3

ETON
1943–48

BY JULY 1943, the Allies were winning the war, and it was time for Jeremy Thorpe and his sister Camilla, now fourteen and eighteen, to return from America, he to take up his place at Eton, she to 'do her bit'. Passages were hard to come by, but thanks to Thorpey's Admiralty connections they were able to cross the Atlantic in a Royal Navy cruiser. The country to which they returned was much changed from the one they had left three years earlier. Large areas of London and its surroundings had been devastated by bombing. Air raids, shortages and queueing were the commonplaces of civilian life. A great American military establishment was building itself up for the coming invasion of Europe: Lavinia worked for it, having obtained her job through a USAF colonel she would later marry. In addition to his duties at the Admiralty and BBC, Thorpey had become Deputy Chairman of Middlesex Sessions (the criminal court next to the Houses of Parliament), Chairman of the Central Price Regulation Committee, and a Bencher of the (much-bombed) Inner Temple.* Ursula did a variety of strange jobs,

---

* During Jeremy's absence, Thorpey had also been trying to help Richard Weininger, who was imprisoned and deported after being implicated, with

including cutting up dead horses for dog-food on her kitchen
table. Gwladys, still vigorous at seventy, ran a forces canteen at
Victoria Station. All of them lived at Little Heath House, where the
staff had been reduced to a gardener and one maid-of-all-work. It
was a far cry from America where the war was a distant happening and there was plenty of everything, but Jeremy was happy to
be home and reunited with his family.

On 15 September 1943, Jeremy entered Eton.[1] He was the first
member of the Thorpe family to go there, though he had been preceded by his Norton-Griffiths uncles and Christie-Miller cousins.
There was, however, an older family connection. Oscar Browning
(1837–1923), a first cousin of Gwladys' father, had been one of the
outstanding Eton housemasters of the Victorian period, renowned
for the manner in which he both inspired his boys and charmed
their parents. In 1875 he was forced to leave, ostensibly on account
of a minor irregularity in the management of his house, in reality
because he was thought to have become too intimate with some of
his charges – notably George Curzon, the future Viceroy and
Foreign Secretary. Browning went on to become a well-known
Cambridge don and writer of popular historical works; he kept in
touch with his old Eton boys to the end of his long life, as well as
maintaining a huge correspondence with young soldiers and sailors
who wrote to him from all over the Empire, expressing gratitude
for past kindnesses and usually requesting further assistance.[2]

Jeremy's own housemaster was another eccentric bachelor,
though not one possessing the reputation of harbouring romantic
feelings towards boys in his care. Julian Lambart, known as 'Leggy'
(from his middle name of Legge), was fifty in 1943 and had been
running his house for almost twenty years. He was an old-maidish
character, absorbed in the classics and a lifelong study of cathedral

---

Robert Boothby MP, in the so-called Czech Assets Affair. More than twenty
years later, Jeremy would succeed in clearing Weininger's name and enabling
him to return to the United Kingdom.

architecture, endlessly fussing about rules but easily deceived (and thus a gift to an accomplished prankster such as Jeremy). The true centre of power in his house, however, resided in the House Dame, Nora Byron, a legendary figure 'of gigantic girth, stupendous energy, and boundless kindness'.[3] She was a keen musician, who pressed all her boys to learn an instrument and organised them into a house orchestra, often an unusual combination for which she would arrange the music herself. Jeremy tried her sorely with his mischief, but came to have an affectionate relationship with her.

During the 1960s, Nora Byron wrote, in the third person, a book of memoirs of her years at Eton, and though she does not mention any boy by name, some have claimed to recognise aspects of Jeremy in the following (possibly composite) portrait:

> Every now and then a boy would turn up who was really a first-class mimic, and M'Dame had an experience she found hard to bear with one boy. She was ringing up a master who was easy game for a mimic, and ... the mimic had entered the room unbeknown to M'Dame ... She was then aware that not only was the master himself answering the telephone, but another identical voice from inside the room at exactly the same moment said, 'Speaking.' M'Dame ... vowed never again to ring up anybody when a boy was within hearing.
>
> And then there grew an almost professional aesthete ... If a boy came into the room carrying a football, he would close his eyes and ... make a strange gesture of feeling ill, and the number of times he tried to get round M'Dame to let him off exercise on the flimsiest of excuses were unending ... He was an amusing conversationalist, and in many ways laughed at himself, and having found himself accepted for what he was trying to be, he rather cleverly managed to keep himself on the right side of authority, but he was not *persona grata* with the members of the Library [the house prefects], before whom he played his most exaggerated personality.

To give him his due, he learnt a musical instrument and gave plenty of time to practise ... However, he provided the House with a good deal of entertainment, as there was no end to the ingenuity with which he could produce excuses for avoiding exercise. Even London dentists ... were brought into play more often than would have been possible with any other boy ...[4]

Certainly some key elements of Jeremy's Eton personality are here: his exhibitionism; his skill in getting out of arduous physical activity; his propensity for shocking 'authority' while managing to stay out of trouble; his musicianship; his gift for mimicry.

Jeremy did not possess those qualities which make for automatic popularity at public school. He had no aptitude for games; he was not academically distinguished; and he was a self-conscious boy who loved to show off. His propensity for sucking up to masters while making fun of them behind their backs won him the unflattering nickname 'Oily Thorpe'. Schoolboys tend to be obsessed with conformity, but Jeremy, while generally keeping out of trouble, was keen to establish his credentials as a rebel. During his first weeks, he showed a disinclination to wear the regulation top hat: when told off about this, he went to the opposite extreme and wore it more often than any other boy, removing it with bows and flourishes. He trumpeted the superiority of all things American and suggested that 'The Battle Hymn of the Republic' be added to the Eton chapel repertoire. Everything he did seemed designed to attract attention and set himself apart from other boys.

It is traditional at Eton for junior boys to confine their friendships to their own house. Jeremy, however, had only one friend at Lambart's – Patrick Marlowe, a boy he had known since early childhood whose parents were friends of the Thorpes.*

---

* Son of Anthony Marlowe KC, Conservative MP for Hove 1941–65, and Patricia, daughter of the celebrated Sir Patrick Hastings KC (1880–1952).

Otherwise he had no inhibitions about making friends in other houses, as well as among the Scholars living in College, generally frowned on by 'Oppidans' living in houses and known as 'tugs'. Friends made in his first year at Eton included Christopher Hurst,* nephew of Thorpey's former commanding officer and fellow MP Sir Gerald Hurst; Piers Dixon, a diplomat's son (and 'tug');† and Simon Barrington-Ward, son of the Editor of *The Times*.‡ Jeremy also befriended the only American boy at wartime Eton, the genial and bespectacled Richard Morgan, who had been brought up in a French château and whose mother was then a prisoner of the Germans. (Morgan would later marry Jeremy's cousin, Sir Peter Norton-Griffiths's daughter Anne.) All these boys shared something of Jeremy's unconventional outlook, and (apart from Barrington-Ward, who managed to keep a foot in both camps) none of them can be said to have belonged to the Eton 'establishment'.

Among his circle, Jeremy was known for aesthetic posing. He set out to be a dandy, only seemed interested in books about art, and decorated his room with his Chinese pots. He loved dressing up and acting out parts: during one vacation, he got friends to join him in donning velvet jackets and skull caps and going out to smoke clay pipes in cafés and pubs. The school society patronised by Jeremy and his friends was the Archaeological Society, in reality the aesthetes' society, which had adopted its misleading name to appease the notoriously 'robust' Head Master, Claude Elliott: they read each other papers on literary and artistic subjects, and recited Firbank and Proust. Jeremy's conversation, however, was light-hearted and jocular. Apart from

---

* Later a publisher, and author of an interesting autobiography, *The View from King Street* (London: Thalia, 1997). Of Jeremy, he writes on page 100: 'I treasure the memory of his un-Etonian ebullience and wit, agreeably mixed with a touch of rascality ...'
† Conservative MP for Truro, 1970–74.
‡ Bishop of Coventry, 1985–97.

his imitations of masters and other boys, he gave hilarious renderings of a series of goon-like characters he had invented, such as the elderly squire Sir George and his wife Mildred.* He was also given to practical jokes, and such whimsy as conducting conversations with a wooden parrot.

He also drew attention to himself by showing unusual kindness to other boys. It was normally considered 'bad form' to visit a sick friend in the school infirmary, but Jeremy made a point of doing so whenever any friend of his was laid up, bearing gifts of food and books. He tried to protect some vulnerable boys from bullying, including David 'Loopy' Lutyens, a misshapen, hypersensitive boy who responded to Jeremy's protective attentions by developing a crush on him.† An episode which casts light on his personality took place at the end of his second half in the winter of 1944. For some weeks, a gang of boys (not including Jeremy) had been climbing out of their houses at night and conducting a campaign of practical jokes: this strayed into the realms of vandalism when they planted trees on a football ground and sabotaged the organ in Lower Chapel. One of the culprits was eventually identified as Michael Lindsay Watson. During the twenty-four hours before his premature departure from Eton, Lindsay Watson was shunned by the entire school – except for Jeremy, who made a public show of friendliness towards him and invited him to join him for a walk in Windsor Great Park.

---

* He carried on developing these characters in adult life: during dark moments for the Liberal Party, fellow workers might be cheered by some absurd new reflection from Sir George.

† David Lutyens (1929–90) was on his father's side a grandson of the architect Sir Edwin Lutyens and great-grandson of the Viceroy Lord Lytton; on his mother's, a great-nephew of the Zionist leader Chaim Weizmann. Having shown some early promise as a playwright, he later descended into a life of louche homosexuality and died in a mental home. When Jeremy was awaiting trial in the late 1970s, his mother was alarmed, going through his old books at Limpsfield, to discover a volume Lutyens had presented to him at Eton, containing what to her mind was a highly compromising inscription.

Academically, his progress at Eton was adequate but undistinguished. Patrick Marlowe felt that 'he never wanted to go deeply into anything, but always aimed to know just enough to get by' – an assessment which might apply to the whole of his life. He was perhaps unfortunate in his housemaster, as Lambart only gave much encouragement to boys who, unlike Jeremy, showed promise as classicists. Later, he claimed to have been inspired by two famous teachers at Eton, the English master George Lyttelton and the historian G. B. ('Gibbers') Smith: but his contact with these legendary figures was in fact rather limited, and he may have been more intrigued by their (highly imitable) personalities than influenced by them in his intellectual development. Nor was he much of a reader, usually preferring to ask a friend what was in a book than look at it himself. Yet Jeremy was a clever boy who could achieve most of what he wanted if he put his mind to it: arriving at the school two years late, he soon caught up with his contemporaries, obtaining his School Certificate in the summer of 1946.

On the other hand, outside the formal curriculum, he made outstanding progress in the field of music, which flourished at Eton at that period under two remarkable musicians who successively held the post of Precentor – Henry Ley and Sidney Watson. With encouragement from Nora Byron and the school string tutor Mr Yonge, he worked hard at his violin and became one of the leading Eton violinists of his generation, along with Simon Streatfeild (later a distinguished professional performer) and Eustace Gibbs (a future diplomat): all three won the school violin prize, the Boyle Cup. At Eton concerts, Jeremy's violin provided him with an opportunity to make a theatrical impression on the entire school: beautifully dressed, with a red handkerchief flowing from his breast pocket, his dark looks lending him a mephistophelean air, he played with panache, sometimes performing the works of little-known composers such as Nardini. Like many performers who rely on a strong sense of style, he was a poor sight reader but had an excellent ear and memory as well as a talent for improvisation: when a string snapped in mid-recital, he swore vigorously and simply carried on.

Another factor which set Jeremy apart at Eton was that his mother was more in evidence there than any other parent (apart from those employed at the school). With her monocle and fierce personality, Ursula created something of a sensation during her frequent visits: few of the boys had met anyone like her. Jeremy was always anxious to impress her and win her approval. Whenever his friends asked whether he was wise to go ahead with some proposed exhibitionist prank, he would reply: 'I'm doing it for Ursula – it would *amuse* her so much!' When he was training for the Boyle Cup, she was determined that he should win it, especially as his main rival Eustace Gibbs was the son of Lord Wraxall, whom Ursula had once hoped to marry but who had not responded to her overtures: she would turn up at Jeremy's house several times a week to check on his practising, often bringing with her his old violin teacher, Ruth Araujo.

In spite of posing as an aesthete, Jeremy was not particularly known at Eton for homosexual escapades. (Most of those who do acquire such a reputation there go on to lead heterosexual adult lives.) He did, however, develop the usual crushes on schoolfellows, and gave his friends to understand that some of these went beyond the purely platonic. And there was one 'incident', notorious among those who got to hear of it, when he tried to force his attentions on a younger boy in the house lavatories, the ensuing scuffle and the escape of his victim being witnessed by at least one other boy.* Though this does not seem to have led to serious trouble, he caused astonishment by subsequently approaching every boy in the house (most of whom as yet knew nothing of the episode) with the words: 'I know what they're

---

* The victim was Michael Haslam, elder brother of the future designer and socialite Nicky; the witness was the future night-club tycoon Mark Birley.

saying about me – and it's *not true!*' It was a technique of stout denial which he would employ throughout life.

Jeremy was fifteen and had been at Eton little more than a year when there occurred, on 31 October 1944, an event which affected him profoundly: the death of his father at the age of fifty-seven. A few months earlier, Thorpey had been thrown across St James's Street by a bomb blast while emerging from the Carlton Club; and shortly afterwards he had suffered a stroke. During his school holidays, it had been painful for Jeremy to witness his father, formerly so witty and lively, in a state of dumb distress: he hitch-hiked all the way to the West Country to find a faith healer of whom he had heard and fetch him to his father's bedside, but to no avail. The night before the funeral, there was a terrific thunderstorm: at Little Heath House, Jeremy and his sisters huddled together and wondered if their father was 'coming back'.

By his will dated 1929, Thorpey left his entire estate to Ursula. However, there was not much to leave: his property was valued at £2,243 16s 3d. His large pre-war earnings had been used up, mostly on Ursula's *train de vie*, partly on pensions paid to impoverished relatives. Ursula had some money of her own, and received a substantial sum from Thorpey's life insurance, but it was clear that she would have to adjust to sharply reduced circumstances. This she did uncomplainingly, one friend remarking that she had 'come down in the world better than anyone I know'. At the end of the war, she left Little Heath House and bought a smaller property in Limpsfield, a castellated Edwardian building with an acre of garden and a fine rolling view: the upper of its two storeys was converted into a separate flat which could be let. Solidly built by a local stonemason, it was named Stonewalls: Ursula would live there for the rest of her life, and it was there that certain events allegedly took place in November 1961 of which the whole country would eventually read in the newspapers.

One problem was how to provide for Jeremy's education. Happily his rich uncle Colonel Geoffry Christie-Miller came to the rescue, setting up a trust to see him through school, university and reading for the Bar. Nor was he likely to have any trouble following his father to Trinity College, Oxford, to which Uncle Geoffry had made a large benefaction in memory of a son killed in North Africa. Jeremy visited his uncle in Cheshire and asked how he might repay his kindness. The Colonel, who owned Christy's hat manufactory in Stockport, suggested that Jeremy should always wear a hat. Jeremy promised to do so, and indeed became a walking advertisement for the declining hat industry throughout his adult life, favouring first a brown bowler and later a trilby or homburg. He also lectured his friends on the health-promoting properties of hat-wearing, which he claimed prevented loss of heat through the head.[5]

Another relation who showed kindness to Jeremy at this time was his great-uncle Ralph Wood (1871–1945), Gwladys's brother, known in the family as 'Mumpy', who was Thorpey's executor and to whom Jeremy bore some physical resemblance. A cultivated but splenetic little man, he was regarded as a great eccentric, as was his wife, the former suffragette Violet Ruffer. They lived at Flint Cottage, Box Hill, a charming Regency folly with an Elizabethan knot garden which had once belonged to the novelist George Meredith: they were joined there in August 1944 by the great satirist and 1890s survivor Sir Max Beerbohm and his American wife Florence, who had been bombed out of their own house nearby. Jeremy (who was told by Mumpy that he would one day inherit the property, though in the end it passed to Violet's brother) was a frequent visitor, and made a hit with Max, with whom he shared a keen sense of the ridiculous. That Max became another of his boyhood heroes is evident from Jeremy's contribution to a 1972 radio programme devoted to recollections of that delightful character:

My great-uncle was himself a great eccentric and collector of superb things – he used to eat off Ming plates with James II silver and Charles I glass – so it was a perfect backdrop for Max. I stayed there as a child I suppose nine or ten times while Max was there. I remember him coming down to breakfast in a perfectly cut tweed suit with a double-breasted waistcoat and a pearl pin and then after breakfast getting out an ivory cigarette holder. It was a bad period of the war and on one occasion Max put down his newspaper with a look of anguish and his wife said, 'What is the matter, dear?' and he replied, 'Florence, my dear, the toast is cold.'* I was just old enough to ask such questions as whether he had known Meredith, and he said he had come down there to see him just before he died ... And then one would ask what Lytton Strachey looked like and so he offered to do a wash drawing ... and there in three minutes was a devastating cartoon. He did one or two more for me – Sir William Harcourt and Whistler and others ...[6]

It is possible to discern Max's influence in several of the qualities Jeremy developed: a taste for wearing beautiful clothes of a type long out of fashion; a love of elaborate practical jokes; a talent for writing short witty letters garnished with humorous little drawings. Even Jeremy's handwriting – flowing, crystalline, minuscule, exotic – bears a passing resemblance to Max's. Max also helped him perfect his mimicry: he was an acknowledged master of this art, his specialities being turn-of-the-century royalty and stuffy old colonels holding forth in London clubs.

Ursula's brother Peter had meanwhile returned to England after his chequered wartime career, and told the Thorpe children that he would try to take their father's place, an announcement which they greeted with mixed feelings coming as it did from that dubious character. True to his promise, he visited Jeremy at school (Jeremy

---

* In quoting these words, Jeremy reproduced perfectly Florence's American accent and Max's precise enunciation.

afterwards entertaining his friends with impersonations of the louche baronet); and Jeremy spent his Christmases at Kempsford Manor, the house in Gloucestershire taken by the Norton-Griffithses when Kay and her children returned from America. It is difficult to say what contribution was made to Jeremy's education by his uncle, who was sexually interested in adolescents.

Another person of whom Ursula and Jeremy saw much after their bereavement was Megan, who suffered the loss of her own father at Criccieth on 26 March 1945. It was an emotionally complex time for her, since Lloyd George, during the last two years of his life, had distressed her first by marrying his mistress Frances Stevenson, then by accepting an earldom. Ursula and Megan comforted each other and resumed something of the intimate friendship they had enjoyed after the First World War. With the end of the Second World War in sight, party politics were resuming; and Megan, who remained MP for Anglesey, often discussed politics with Jeremy and urged him to join the Liberal Party. He began to develop romantic feelings for her: it will be remembered that something in the nature of a platonic romance had existed between Jeremy's father and Megan's mother, Dame Margaret, who had died in 1941.

Following Thorpey's death, Jeremy thus received kindness and support from several quarters. But there was no one to take his father's place, to give him wise and sympathetic guidance in the formative years ahead, to restrain his more extravagant enthusiasms. At this critical stage of his emotional development, he fell entirely under the powerful influence of his mother, who drummed into him that he was the most important person in the world, that he could do no wrong, that he should exploit every opportunity to advance his career and that he must succeed at all costs. In years to come, he would often rebel against her possessiveness; but the egotism, ambition and ruthlessness she had implanted would never be far away.

*

When Eton reassembled in September 1945, it was a time of political excitement. The past few months had witnessed not only the end of the war, but the first General Election for a decade and the coming to power of a Labour Government. One of the new boys in Jeremy's house was Mark Schreiber (later Lord Marlesford), who recalled:

> I entered his room and there he was sitting cross-legged on a leather pouf smoking an ivory pipe. His room was quite unlike the rooms of other boys. Instead of being a mess with football boots etc. lying about it was immaculate – lots of leather-bound books and a desk with a magnificent blotter and green blotting paper. 'Come in, Schreiber,' he said, 'I want you to shake hands with the future Prime Minister of England.' I offered him a grubby paw, and asked him: 'Which party, Thorpe?' 'Oh, I favour the old Liberal Party,' he replied.[7]

At the age of sixteen, Jeremy had nailed his colours to the Liberal mast. This reflected both his developing personal convictions and the influence of the Lloyd George family; but his decision, made at a time when the Party had been returned to Parliament with a mere dozen seats and was widely regarded as defunct, also fitted in with a general policy of stylish nonconformity. Along with the outlandish arrangement of his room, a dandified mode of dress, the self-conscious panache of his violin-playing and his indulgence in the forbidden pleasures of smoking, it seemed designed to set him apart from other boys and show he did not intend to follow the normal path. Such tendencies attracted admiration from other individualists, but disapproval from the Eton establishment. His smoking eventually earned him a beating from his house captain – an episode he jocularly recalled in later years, saying that it represented a good case for corporal punishment since it had cured him of the habit. Another action which set him apart was his resignation from the school

'Corps' when it technically ceased to be obligatory in the autumn of 1945: only a handful of boys dared draw attention to themselves in this way, including his friend Piers Dixon.

He was already much given to elaborate flights of fantasy. Not only did he talk of becoming Prime Minister, but he would give a moving rendering of the balcony speech which, clad in a silk-lined cloak, he would one day deliver on his retirement from the premiership, before waving farewell to a tearful audience and driving off in a state coach. Another fantasy to which he sometimes gave voice, which sat rather oddly with his political ambitions, was that he meant one day to marry Princess Margaret, who was sixteen at the time Jeremy left Eton and second in line to the throne. But perhaps his most extravagant fantasy was his declared belief that he would end his schooldays as a member of the Eton Society or 'Pop', the privileged, self-electing club of senior boys, clad in brocade waistcoats, who act as school prefects. Only boys possessing qualities endearing them to the Eton establishment have any realistic possibility of attaining that sought-after honour,* and Jeremy, who failed even to become a house prefect, never stood a chance. When his friends expressed amazement that he should harbour such an ambition, he would say: 'But I must do it for Ursula: it would *please* her so much!' And when they asked him how he proposed to achieve his aim, he would tell them that he was compiling dossiers of compromising information on the current Pop members with a view to putting pressure on them to give him their vote.

While still at Eton, Jeremy became known for his love of flaunting his acquaintance with the great and famous. Whenever anyone visited him in his room, a letter from Max Beerbohm or some other celebrity would be prominently displayed; and he was eager to show off such eminent visitors as Megan to his

---

* Curzon famously said that becoming Foreign Secretary was as nothing compared with being elected to Pop.

friends. His circle of distinguished acquaintances was an ever-expanding one, for he knew how to be engaging in his dealings with the adult world. The eccentric old philanthropist Lord Courtauld-Thompson thought him 'one of the most remarkable young men in England' and begged him to visit Dorneywood, his country house near Eton, whenever he chose. With his talent to amuse, Jeremy was popular with the parents (especially the mothers) of those friends with whom he stayed during school holidays, and formed a lasting tie with such families as the Barrington-Wards. After the war, his accomplishments as a guest enabled him to travel on the continent to an extent that would not otherwise have been possible for him: he made the first of many visits to the Château d'Oursières, Richard Morgan's family home in Lower Normandy, stayed in Mallorca with a schoolfriend named Hillgarth (whose father ran MI6 in Spain), and visited the Beerbohms at Rapallo. Of course, though he always gave good value for his board and lodging, he could be merciless afterwards in parodying his hosts.

Although he inevitably failed to get into Pop, Jeremy distinguished himself in several ways during his last weeks at school in the freezing winter of 1947. He succeeded in winning the school violin prize for the second time. He had his great moment at the Archaeological Society, when he delivered a paper on the Tang Dynasty, illustrated with items from his collection of Chinese pots.* He also dazzled a meeting of the school debating society (of which he was not a member, but to which he was

---

* Though unremarkable from a literary point of view, Jeremy's paper is not without interest for his biographer. He expressed the view that the flourishing of art under the Tang owed much to the dynasty's 'religious toleration and open-mindedness' and its wide contacts with foreign countries. He described the poet-artist Wang-Wei as 'the Max Beerbohm of his age'. He showed a particular interest in the Empress Wu-Hou, 'whose history is more than fascinating and packed with corruption and intrigue'. And he carefully noted at the bottom of each page how long it would take to read.

taken as a guest) with a fluent and witty speech from the floor on a subject he knew nothing about, based entirely on what he had managed to pick up from previous speeches – a foretaste of a talent he would make his own.

Jeremy left Eton in March 1947, a few weeks short of his eighteenth birthday: characteristically, his 'leaving' photograph shows him wearing not traditional Eton garb, but bright checks like a bookie. He spent Easter in Paris with Richard Morgan and the latter's friend Francis Dashwood. One night, after the three of them had dined in Montmartre, Morgan and Dashwood suggested that Jeremy lose his virginity with one of the local girls: Jeremy responded with good-humoured eagerness, and was conducted by his hosts to a well-known bordello. When he returned to England, Jeremy entertained his friends with a colourful and detailed account of his adventures in the bordello. This, however, was yet another example of his romanticism: the truth – as ascertained by his companions when they next visited the establishment – was that the visit had not been a success.[8]

Jeremy's next ambition was one which he had already confided to several friends – to get out of National Service as soon as possible. By mid-1947, eighteen months (soon to be extended to twenty-one) of compulsory military service had come to be seen by many of those who were liable to do it as a tedious and unnecessary chore. Jeremy felt (as he told friends) that he had little to offer the army, and that he might steal a march on his contemporaries by making his time in it as short as possible. His plan was simple: having suffered as a boy from mild epileptic 'absences', he intended to stage a dramatic blackout during his training leading to a discharge on medical grounds. He spent some time poring over medical books, lent to him by a friend whose father was a doctor, studing the symptoms he aimed to reproduce, and boasted to this friend and others that he expected to be 'out by Christmas'.

Jeremy began his stint in August 1947 with six weeks' basic

training with a local regiment in Surrey. Having survived this, he proceeded to Palace Barracks at Holywood, Northern Ireland for a Warrant Officers' Training Course with the 28th Training Regiment, after which he was due to become an officer cadet in the Rifle Brigade. There he befriended three fellow members of his company from a public-school background – Douglas Spankie (later in MI6), Tom Houston (a cousin of Jeremy's Eton friend Patrick Marlowe, later an academic) and David Sheppard (later to be famous as England's cricket captain and Bishop of Liverpool). They would go out together on free evenings, Jeremy entertaining the others with the speech he proposed to make on coming to power as the first Liberal Prime Minister since Lloyd George. About a month after they had arrived, the company was put through an assault course which involved crossing a wire bridge suspended between a post and a tree. Jeremy intimated to his friends that he proposed to 'black out' in the course of this exercise. He was as good as his word, managing to fall off the bridge no less than three times while giving a convincing impression of some kind of seizure. As he had predicted, he obtained his discharge in time to attend the annual Eton Concert that December.[9]

What is one to make of this episode? In one sense it represented the culmination of his schoolboy talent for getting off games. It was also characteristic of much of his future behaviour in that, among friends, Jeremy made little secret of his wheeze: on the contrary, he positively revelled in his ingenuity. Some of those who knew of it were shocked and held it as a permanent black mark against him; others reacted with envious admiration. His fellow trainees were demoralised by the circumstances under which he had left them; 'but one couldn't help liking him', recalled Houston, 'for all his faults'. (It may be noted that Jeremy's inglorious military career did not affect his lifelong fascination with uniforms, or stop him brandishing his grandfather's sword to cut the victory cake after various electoral triumphs.)

Jeremy was unable to take up his place at Oxford until the

following autumn, and in January 1948 enlisted for a couple of terms as an assistant master at a preparatory school, Southey House at Great Bookham near Leatherhead. (The local public school was St John's, Leatherhead where his father had been a pupil and later a governor.) It occupied a fine but run-down Georgian house set in an estate which had once belonged to Lord Howard of Effingham, who had commanded the fleet that defeated the Spanish Armada. Morning prayers took place in the former ballroom under a painted ceiling of cupids and nymphs. The school's headmaster and owner was Denys Fussell, who had inherited it from his father and whose career would end a few years later after allegations of misconduct with boys in his care.

Jeremy took over the job – teaching 'general studies' to younger boys – of another lively young man, Douglas Macdonald, who had been promoted to be the school's Latin master and was also due to go up to Oxford later that year. Macdonald recalled:

> In the early stages he used to come to me to discuss what to do, and I found him eager to learn the ropes so that he could do this, his first job, as well as possible. I think the boys liked and respected him, for he never seemed to have disciplinary problems. He had a generally light-hearted approach to his work, which made him a pleasant colleague . . .
>
> To begin with we were rather overawed by him. He was the first Old Etonian we had seen. He knew an awful lot of people in High Society about whom we could only read in the newspapers. He was better dressed than we were (for whom clothes rationing was a very limiting reality), with a fresh tie nearly every day. His conversation was entertaining, and occasionally he would skilfully mimic some eminent politician he had heard from the gallery of the House of Commons. He clearly had ambitions not only to be on the floor of the House himself but to be the next Liberal Prime Minister, as he once actually said. Gradually we came to take his utterances with ever-increasing pinches of salt,

for the man (or rather youth) did not seem to have his feet firmly planted on the floor. We thought he was living in a fantasy world far removed from the realities of life as experienced by mere mortals such as ourselves. And when he dressed himself up in his finery to go to a royal garden party at Buckingham Palace, most of us just laughed . . .[10]

Jeremy lived at the school, but continued to see much of his mother at Limpsfield, only a few miles distant. Though their relationship remained close, he was starting to be troubled by her possessiveness. Wishing to escape from their formidable parent, both of his sisters had gone to live abroad, Lavinia to the Philippines to join her American lover Colonel Bradley, Camilla to Geneva to do secretarial work for an international organisation. Alone at home with his mother, Jeremy found the atmosphere claustrophobic. Tension was further increased by the fact that Ursula, a fierce Tory, strongly disapproved of Jeremy's interest in the Liberal Party, telling everyone that she hoped he would soon come to his senses and become a Conservative (though she gradually relented and eventually came to support him in his chosen path).

Jeremy's Liberalism was encouraged as always by Megan, whom he visited both at Criccieth (where she had inherited Brynawelon) and London (where she remained an MP). Through her he met the nine other Liberal MPs,* including the Party Leader, the orotund Welsh barrister Clement Davies, and the Chief Whip, the brusque and energetic Colonel Frank Byers. At this period, the Liberals, though seriously short of money, were still in reasonably good heart, having persuaded themselves that their disastrous result of 1945 was a fluke and that they

---

* In 1945, twelve MPs had been elected as Independent Liberals (as opposed to the Liberal Nationals allied to the Conservatives), but since then, one of these (Lloyd George's son Gwilym) had effectively become a Conservative, while another (the former Chief Whip T. L. Horabin) had defected to Labour.

would do better next time. Among other Liberals Jeremy got to know at this time, two were to loom large in his future. The barrister Dingle Foot had been Liberal MP for Dundee from 1931 to 1945 and was a longstanding admirer of Megan. He was one of four remarkable sons of the leading Devon Liberal Isaac Foot, the others (all of whom Jeremy would come to know well) being the Plymouth solicitor John (later Lord Foot), the Labour MP Michael (later Leader of his Party) and the colonial civil servant Hugh (later Lord Caradon). Dingle, who had been President both of the Liberal Club and Union at Oxford and gone on to become a barrister and (while still in his twenties) an MP, became something of a role model for Jeremy, who was also influenced by his sympathy with the nationalist aspirations of the peoples of the British Empire. Jeremy did a fine imitation of him, with his mild Devon accent and precise lawyer's enunciation. He also befriended (and splendidly imitated) Lady Violet Bonham Carter, Asquith's daughter, who was still active in politics (she was President of the Liberal Party from 1945 to 1947) and had become a radio celebrity with her strident personality and acid wit.* Her intelligence was shared by her son Mark, who had contested the Barnstaple Division of Devon at the 1945 election, and her daughter Laura, married to the dashing young Scottish Liberal Jo Grimond. Violet had a feuding relationship with Megan, a hangover of the bitter antagonism between their fathers, and it is a tribute to Jeremy's social skills that he managed to retain the friendship of both.

During the summer of 1948, shortly before going up to

---

* In her diary around this time, she described him as 'intelligent & rather nice looking', though 'pushing & *exhibitioniste*' and '*terribly* anxious to show one that he knows Max Beerbohm etc.'. But she was impressed by his Liberal zeal, later writing that 'if faith can move mountains he should be able to . . . make the Himalayas skip like mountain goats'. (Mark Pottle [ed.], *Daring to Hope: The Diaries and Letters of Violet Bonham Carter, 1946–69* [London: Weidenfeld & Nicolson, 2000], p. 396.)

Oxford, Jeremy met and befriended at a party in London a larger-than-life character who was to have an important influence on his development. The Honourable Henry Eric Patrick Mountjoy Spalding Upton was the only son and heir of the 5th Viscount Templetown, an Irish peer residing in Scotland. He was then thirty-one, twelve years older than Jeremy, tall and strongly built with a mop of blond hair, and would have been handsome but for a dent in his forehead resulting from a motorcycle accident. High-speed motorcycling was one of his twin passions: the other was a compulsive, sadistic homosexuality. He had no inhibitions and believed in taking his pleasure where he found it: in 1942, as an officer in the Indian Army, he had been cashiered and imprisoned on forty charges of gross indecency, after a court-martial at which he had unrepentantly boasted that his men had thoroughly enjoyed the experiences to which he had subjected them. This setback had done nothing to tame his wild nature, and after the war his respectable family had been anxious to keep him out of the United Kingdom. For a while he lived in Canada, where his escapades got him into the usual trouble, from which he extricated himself by marrying the daughter of a Canadian Army chaplain. As soon as he was in the clear, he dumped his new wife and set out for India: it was while he was in England awaiting his onward passage that he met Jeremy.

Henry was a forceful personality – noisy, dashing, reckless, sinister. His talk was racy and violent: he enjoyed describing how he had allegedly 'removed' various people who had been foolish enough to get in the path of his motorcycles, or cross him in other ways. Possibly he reminded Jeremy of that other forceful, devil-may-care character, his grandfather Empire Jack. In any event, Jeremy, an impressionable nineteen at the time, fascinated by the exotic and aristocratic, already fancying himself something of a rebel to whom the normal rules did not apply, seems to have been swept off his feet by the older man during the time they spent together that summer.

Henry went on to join two young English friends in Calcutta (both of whom would later become friends of Jeremy) – Tony Maycock, a schoolmaster, and John Wilkins, a journalist. To them he spoke rapturously of his new friend Jeremy Thorpe, an attractive and ambitious Etonian who was determined to become President of the Oxford Union, husband of Princess Margaret and eventually Prime Minister. He believed he had persuaded Jeremy that life was for living and that laws regarding personal morality were not made to be observed by the great ones of this world. Though separated for the present, they were, he felt sure, destined to be useful to each other in the future. They were not to meet again for three years; but Henry's part in Jeremy's life was far from over.[11]

4

OXFORD
1948–52

FOLLOWING IN THE footsteps of his father – and 'rich Uncle Geoffry' who footed the bills – Jeremy Thorpe was admitted to Trinity College, Oxford to read jurisprudence on 8 October 1948.[1] At nineteen, he was young in a college much of whose student membership had seen active service in the war. Trinity, founded in 1554, was a small, intimate college: it had some 300 under-graduates in 1948, but numbers had been swelled by the influx of ex-servicemen and would fall to around 200 by 1952. It was known for its traditionalism, its elegant buildings and gardens, its atmosphere of dim gentility. Its admissions policy tended to pay more attention to social background and sporting prowess than academic talent: Trinity excelled at rowing and games but produced few notable scholars. The majority of its members came from well-known public schools, with a high proportion of Old Etonians. There was a traditional rivalry with neighbouring Balliol, a far more earnest and intellectual college whose members came from a wide range of backgrounds at home and abroad.

Fourteen fellows sat at the college high table – all destined to

be mercilessly imitated by Jeremy, from the President, the shy
medievalist J. R. H. Weaver, down to the flamboyant young economics tutor (and future Labour Cabinet Minister) Anthony
Crosland. But none lent himself more to caricature than Jeremy's
own tutor, Philip Landon, who was sixty in 1948 and had been
college bursar as well as law tutor for some thirty years. A lazy,
snobbish, piano-playing bachelor, he was notorious throughout
Oxford for his favouritism and wire-pulling. He also had something of a homosexual reputation: stories abounded about his
penchant for muscular sportsmen (he refused to have his own
bathroom in college, preferring to join the undergraduates in
their communal showers) and his dislike of women (whom he
chased out of his university lectures on criminal law by dwelling
on details of cases involving sexual cruelty). Fortunately for
Jeremy, he was an easy taskmaster and did not expect his law students to do much work if they could show they had other
interesting things to do, particularly if they were Etonians, whom
he regarded as a privileged species.

In the formal group photograph of the Trinity freshmen who
came up in the Michaelmas term of 1948, Jeremy is seated in the
dead centre of the front row; the other men are all cross-legged
as they squeeze into the picture, but Jeremy sits majestically with
his legs apart, his hands on his knees, his upper body thrust forward, his face set with a singleminded expression. Clearly, from
the moment he arrived at Oxford, he was determined to stand
out and be noticed. In college, this ambition was quickly
achieved: dining in hall with his fellow undergraduates, he was
soon famous for his witty remarks and imitations, delivered in a
penetrating voice to guffaws of laughter from his neighbours. He
also attracted attention through some high-spirited japes. In his
first year he was fined £1 by the Dean for allowing his rooms to
be used for 'throwing water at Balliol College'. One night in hall,
he won a wager by drinking a sconce of ale in a single draught.

It was indeed impossible to ignore him because of his

tremendous theatricality. In that drab period when clothes were still rationed, he sported a wardrobe of beautifully cut Edwardian suits, frock coats and brocade waistcoats, along with such colourful accessories as silver-topped canes, jewelled tie-pins and a curly-brimmed brown bowler hat. (For the most part, the clothes had been inherited from his father, while the hats were presents from his uncle's factory in Stockport: he thus managed to contrive an impression of opulence without incurring much expense.) His rooms in college, carefully adorned with his Chinese porcelain collection and silver-framed photographs of the celebrities he was cultivating, exuded an exotic atmosphere. From time to time, he would hold spiritualist séances there with a ouija board. On other occasions, he would entertain his guests with his flamboyant violin-playing. His pallid complexion, dark hair and eyes, and angular features gave him a diabolonian air. There was a whiff about him of the music hall stage.

At Eton, Jeremy's outlandish appearance and behaviour had won him a coterie of admirers but the disapproval of the conventional majority, and some of this feeling followed him to Trinity, where his reputation was not enhanced by rumours of his inglorious National Service career. He was not taken very seriously at first and tended to be regarded, even by those who enjoyed his company and jokes, as a rather clownish figure. But as he rose to fame in the wider world of university politics, where few Trinity men made their mark at the time, his college came to treat him with a new respect, and laugh with him rather than at him. By the end of his second year, Jeremy had become something of a college hero, admired not just as an entertainer who relieved the drabness of post-war Oxford but as a shrewd and skilful operator destined to make a mark in the wider world.

Jeremy was on terms of jovial friendship with many of his Trinity contemporaries, who included Nigel Davenport,* Robin

---

* British film actor and sometime President of Equity.

Leigh-Pemberton,* Patrick Moberly† and Angus Ogilvy.‡ His
closest friend was Michael Ogle, a man in many ways different
from himself – a hearty Carthusian who played rugby and cricket
for the college as well as being gifted academically, having won
a scholarship to Trinity. (He came up to read history, but changed
to law to keep Jeremy company.) They seemed inseparable, and
when seen together were jocularly known as 'Oglethorpe' – the
name of the bishop who had crowned Elizabeth I. Some saw
Ogle as 'Jeremy's Rasputin', the mastermind hovering in the
wings and guiding the brilliant but erratic performer in his
Oxford career; but Ogle always insisted he did little more than
act as a sounding board for Jeremy's speeches and try to restrain
some of his more extravagant enthusiasms. Ogle was one of several male friends to whom Jeremy became closely attached in the
days of his youth, but there was nothing overtly homosexual
about such relationships – in those days of single-sex education,
they were considered perfectly normal. There is no doubt that
Jeremy had a gift for friendship, and for inspiring lasting devotion: a quarter of a century after they had left Oxford and drifted
apart, Ogle would stand by Jeremy and support him in the greatest crisis of his life.

Jeremy felt a strong attachment to Trinity: little in life would give
him greater satisfaction than the honorary fellowship to which
he was elected there in 1972. But his main interests lay outside
the college walls. For he arrived at Oxford with a burning ambition to succeed in the byzantine world of university politics and
carry off its greatest prize, the Presidency of the Union. His Eton
career had ended with his ludicrous failure to get into Pop, but

---

* Governor of the Bank of England, 1983–93; created Lord Kingsdown, 1993.
† Ambassador to Israel (1981–84) and South Africa (1984–87); knighted 1986.
‡ Younger son of 12th Earl of Airlie; married HRH Princess Alexandra of Kent,
  1963; knighted for charitable work, 1989.

he would not allow himself to fail again. Indeed, he still dreamed of becoming Prime Minister, seeing the Oxford Union (as many had done before him) as the first step. As ever, he was influenced by a longing to impress the formidable figure of his mother, who visited him frequently at Oxford as she had done at Eton and always made it clear that she expected great things of him. He laid his plans with care. Wisely, he decided that, before attempting to storm the Union citadel, he would win his spurs in a less daunting field. His starting-point was obvious: on his first day at Oxford, Jeremy, already a declared supporter of the Liberal Party for at least three years, signed up as a member of the Oxford University Liberal Club (OULC).

The OULC had been founded in 1913 and claimed to be the first English university political club.* It had declined after the First World War owing to the splits in the Liberal Party, but experienced a spectacular revival during the 1930s under two energetic young Liberals – Frank Byers (now Liberal Chief Whip in the Commons and tipped to be next Party Leader) and Harold Wilson (who went on to become a Labour MP and join the Cabinet in 1947 aged thirty-one). After 1945 it continued to flourish and was indeed the most active and fastest-growing of the Oxford political clubs – ironically in view of the virtual collapse of Liberalism as a national political force. As the Club's historian has written, there were times when it seemed 'the only living element in a moribund party', one of its attractions being that success in its ranks automatically made one an important figure in the Party at large. When Jeremy joined, it had more than 800 members (out of a total student population of less than 8,000), including such notable undergraduates as Robin Day and Godfrey Smith who were already regarded (as Jeremy soon

---

* In the sense of being an active affiliate of a national political organisation: until then, undergraduates interested in politics had only been able to join political dining clubs and debating societies.

hoped to be) as serious candidates for office at the Oxford
Union. The Club held three meetings a week during term,
including talks by distinguished speakers, political debates and
discussions, and divers social events. It had its own premises,
over a shoe shop in the Turl, and even its own fortnightly newspaper, the *Oxford Guardian*, which at times reflected a high
standard of student journalism.[2]

It did not take his fellow members long to recognise Jeremy's
political gifts. Here was a brilliant and original performer, filled
with infectious energy and enthusiasm, a natural campaigner and
fundraiser, able to inspire and win over both individuals and
large audiences. He was given an opportunity to demonstrate
these talents soon after joining the OULC when he volunteered
to help with recruitment at Oriel, where the Club had no college
representative: as he knocked on the doors of the Oriel undergraduates, men with no obvious interest in politics were
sufficiently dazzled by him to ask him in, and soon persuaded to
part with half a crown as their first term's subscription.

He loved the game of politics, and did so with a roguish
delight. From the first, he was jockeying for position among the
young hopefuls who sought to achieve office in the Club's termly
elections, revelling in the plots and intrigues which are the stuff
of student politics, out to win support among the membership
at large. Some mistrusted him, finding him over-ambitious; but
on the whole he was highly popular. Few doubted that the
sparkling manner which so enlivened meetings was combined
with a serious belief in the Liberal Party and its principles. Nor
did he shirk the drudgery that falls to the aspiring lower ranks
in university clubs, such as addressing envelopes. His popularity was also assisted by his impressive personal connections,
which both lent him glamour and were likely to be extremely
useful to the OULC. When his mother came to see him, she was
often accompanied by his beloved Megan Lloyd George; Dingle
Foot (a former OULC President) was another frequent visitor;

and he was never shy in introducing such famous friends to his fellow Oxford Liberals.

Jeremy's main handicap as an undergraduate politician (as throughout his career) was that he was an intellectual lightweight who lacked a serious grasp of the issues of the day. On the other hand, such was his quickness of mind and effectiveness as a speaker that he was usually able, if he had someone to brief him, to give the impression that he knew and understood far more than he did. (This was one of many attributes which he shared with his late hero Lloyd George.) A friend and contemporary in the OULC was Ann Chesney, an attractive young woman with a keen intellect; and Jeremy often picked her brains if he was called upon to discuss policy. He once burst into her room with the words: 'Chesers, I've got to make a speech tonight and can you tell me all about economic development in five minutes?'

At the end of his first term, Jeremy had no trouble getting elected to the OULC Committee, and the question was not whether he would become President but when. At the end of his second term, Keith Kyle, an intellectually gifted undergraduate with a distinguished war record, was elected President: not being interested in the social side of the presidency, he offered to leave this to Jeremy, who had a splendid time organising dinners and other functions, notably the annual May Morning punt party on the Cherwell, at which members were serenaded by a floating string orchestra and he appeared resplendent in Regency dress. Jeremy could have stood for President at the end of his third term with every prospect of success; but he chivalrously stood aside to allow Ann Chesney to be elected, playing much the same role under her presidency as he had under Kyle's.

An important function of the OULC was to send undergraduates to campaign in various parts of the country on behalf of Liberal parliamentary candidates, many of whom were former OULC members. This was useful training for the aspiring politicians and appreciated by the candidates, who received little support from the impoverished central party organisation in their efforts to make a respectable showing and save their deposits. Jeremy eagerly participated in such activities, injecting a note of merriment into the heroic cause of keeping the Liberal flame alive until such time as the Party's fortunes revived. In April 1949, just before his twentieth birthday, he addressed his first public meeting in support of a by-election candidate at Uckfield, attracting an audience of 102 and raising the impressive sum of £108. During the summer vacation of 1949, due to be the last before the General Election, he campaigned throughout southern England, developing a hustings manner which would become celebrated. Wearing such dandified outfits as a bold striped suit with spats, twirling a cane and invariably sporting his brown bowler hat, he would launch self-confidently into a speech both rousing and full of jokes, making ribald use of the local dialect and putting down hecklers with witty repartee. This exotic spectacle, more redolent of the music hall stage than the political platform, drew large and appreciative audiences even in remote villages and apathetic suburbs. The response was particularly warm in the West Country, where Jeremy campaigned that summer for Dingle Foot's brother, John:* thus began his association with the region which he would represent for twenty years and love for the rest of his life.

These early campaigning experiences made him aware both of the enormous difficulties faced by the Liberals in winning seats and his own power to sway the public and galvanise local party organisations. He believed that by means of the latter he could transform the former, reinforcing his conviction that he would one day be Liberal Prime Minister. Visiting London with Ann Chesney to find speakers for the OULC, he remarked as they passed Downing Street: 'I'm going to get there, Chesers – you'll see!'

In November 1949, little more than a year after coming up to

---

* Prospective Liberal candidate at Bodmin, Cornwall (where his father Isaac had been MP from 1929 to 1935).

Oxford, Jeremy was elected President of the OULC for the coming (Hilary) term, an event unusually announced in both *The Times* and the *Daily Telegraph*. He spent the vacation recruiting an impressive list of speakers, including the Party Leader, Clement Davies. The Annual Dinner was due to take place in February, and as guests of honour Jeremy, who dearly loved a lord, invited two members of the higher nobility who still supported the Liberal Party, the Duke of Montrose and the Marquess of Reading. He was also determined to increase the OULC membership to the magic figure of 1,000: after a vigorous recruiting drive, it reached 995, and Jeremy made up the balance by creating ten new honorary members. As the Oxford Conservatives had some 950 and the Labour Club fewer than 700 members at this time, the Liberals now ran the biggest as well as the most active of Oxford's political clubs.

It was a different picture in the country; for the Party, though optimistically fielding 475 candidates, was woefully unprepared for the General Election due to take place within a few months. Jeremy announced that, during the Easter vacation, the OULC would undertake 'an election tour of all major towns and cities in England and Wales in twenty caravans'.[3] Mr Attlee was unwilling to wait so long, however, and announced the election for 23 February. In the event, the Club had to concentrate its efforts on Oxford itself and neighbouring constituencies, where the local party organisation had all but collapsed. Jeremy himself campaigned in North Oxfordshire for the Liberal candidate Lawrence Robson, a rich accountant: Robson and his formidable Swedish wife Stina had frequently entertained him at Kiddington Hall, their beautiful early Georgian house near Woodstock, and contributed handsomely to the OULC's coffers.* He also went down to North Dorset to work for the Liberal Chief Whip and great

---

* Jeremy was not one to forget such kindness: as Liberal Leader in 1974, he would nominate Stina for a life peerage.

future hope Frank Byers, a former OULC President. In the run-up to the election, the parties held rallies at Oxford Town Hall which were addressed by the leaders of the political clubs: Jeremy gave a fine performance (including his Churchill imitation) which everyone agreed to be the best. He was in equally fine fettle at the final meeting at Woodstock, dealing wittily with Tory hecklers and urging the Duke of Marlborough to join the Liberal Party.

Alas, the election was a disaster for the Liberals worse than anything they had imagined. They lost most of their deposits, picked up only 9 per cent of the national vote and held on to a mere nine seats. Thanks to the efforts of Jeremy and his friends, Robson did respectably in North Oxfordshire, saving his deposit; but in North Dorset, Frank Byers lost his seat by a few dozen votes. The Party could no longer dismiss the (rather better) 1945 result as an aberration, and now had to fight for its very survival.

Jeremy did not lose heart: as soon as he came of age two months later, he applied to have his name added to the Liberals' candidates list. Had he switched to one of the two main parties,* he would probably have had little trouble finding a safe seat and, once his party was in power, rapidly ascending the ladder to Cabinet rank. But even fellow Liberals who disliked him had to admit that he was a Liberal through and through, in love with the Party's historical traditions and steeped in its principles of freedom and tolerance. The Conservatives he viewed as reactionary and Labour as doctrinaire. Asked what he would do if the Liberals folded, he replied that he would become a professional actor rather than continue his political career elsewhere.

---

* A number of men who began their careers in the OULC later achieved prominence in other parties. Harold Wilson, OULC Treasurer in 1935, became Labour Prime Minister; and Peter (later Lord) Blaker, Treasurer the term after Jeremy was President, became a Foreign Office minister under Margaret Thatcher.

But he never doubted that he would have a brilliant future as a Liberal: he was convinced that the Party would survive and (with his assistance) eventually revive as a national force. Meanwhile, there was much to be said for being a big fish in a small pond. He foresaw that his charisma would carry him into Parliament within a decade and that a lack of competition would then enable him to rise quickly to the Party Leadership. For Jeremy, thanks to his impact at the OULC and his developing reputation as a speaker and campaigner, was already a considerable personality in the Liberal Party, well known to all its leading figures and viewed as one of its rising stars: he might hope to lead it while still a relatively young man as none of his contemporaries could hope to lead the Labour or Conservative Party.

As his term as OULC President drew to an end, Jeremy began to devote himself to achieving the Union Presidency. Before winning that coveted prize, however, he picked up two other distinguished Presidencies on the way, lending further lustre to his name as he struggled to the top.

First there was the Oxford University Law Society: Michael Ogle was its President during the Trinity term of 1950 and thought it would be fun to have Jeremy succeed him in that office. It must be said that there were others who aspired to preside over the Law Society who had a more worthy claim than Jeremy, an undistinguished law student who only just scraped by on a minimum of work. The main activity of the Law Society was to organise moots, hypothetical law cases argued by undergraduates and adjudicated by visiting judges; and Jeremy's one contribution to a moot, in May 1949, had been a fiasco. ('No idea how to open the case,' he candidly noted at the time, '& equally ignorant how to close it.') His only qualification was that he knew many distinguished lawyers and judges who had been friends of his father and would thus find it easy to set up an interesting programme.

According to contemporary witnesses, Ogle and Jeremy used every device to influence the outcome of the election. They got their friends (many of them non-lawyers) to join the OULS with the sole object of voting for him, and persuaded Oxford-educated lawyers who had long since left the university, but technically remained life members of the Society, to come up to vote. As there was a (much ignored) anti-canvassing rule, they even got some of their friends to canvass for Jeremy's opponents with a view to disqualifying them should they win. When Jeremy won, the unscrupulous methods he had used or condoned damaged his reputation among some onlookers – though on the whole he seems to have been a popular choice. Distinguished visitors to the Society during Jeremy's term (Michaelmas 1950) had a distinctly Liberal tinge, including as they did Lord Simon, the wartime Lord Chancellor and relic of the Asquith Government; Sir John Morris (later Lord Morris of Borth-y-Gest), a brilliant Welsh judge who was close to the Lloyd George family; and Sir Alfred (later Lord) Denning, who as Master of the Rolls would become famous for his championship of individual freedom.

In May 1950, Jeremy revived a dormant Liberal dining club which had flourished in pre-1914 Oxford, the Russell & Palmerston. He was inspired to do so by two ancient dons who had presided over the 'R & P' in Edwardian times and revealed to him that a bank still held a collection of old silver in its name – Gilbert Murray, doyen of Oxford Liberal historians, and Nathaniel Micklem, principal of an Oxford theological college. He appointed himself President and Michael Ogle Secretary and invited a dozen of their friends to join, provoking comparisons with Christ and the Apostles. In the manner of the societies at Eton, the members, attired in white tie, would meet in Jeremy's rooms after dinner, drink port, and discuss a paper read by one of their number on some topical subject. The 'R & P' flourished for many years, its membership (limited to eighteen) much sought after by Liberal undergraduates and its meetings often attended by its re-founding President.[4]

The Liberal Club, the Law Society, the 'R & P' – these were but steps on the ascending path to the Union. In his determination to preside for a term over that historic institution, Jeremy displayed in abundance his usual energy and flair; but he also won a reputation as a trickster and almost came to grief.

Founded in 1825, the Oxford Union Society performed two distinct roles. On the one hand it was a gentleman's club,* in whose well-appointed premises members could eat and drink, play indoor games, read newspapers and use the facilities of a splendid library. It was also the most famous debating society in the world, which modelled its procedure on the House of Commons and was regarded as the classic preparation for a national political career. Its weekly debates were often attended by well-known speakers and reported in the national press. Undergraduates who made reputations there were not only university celebrities but considered to be destined for brilliant futures in the world outside. Former Union lions were prominent in every profession, especially that of politics; they often returned as speakers, and as the new generation rubbed shoulders with them, they felt themselves to be embryo members of the ruling class. To be elected President for a term was an achievement which remained with one for the rest of one's life; and even to have served in one of the junior offices of Secretary, Treasurer or Librarian, or on the Union's governing body, the Standing Committee, meant something as one embarked on a career. There was intense rivalry between the gifted young men who aimed at office, many of whom, like Jeremy, dreamed of

---

* Women were not admitted as members until 1963.

becoming Prime Minister, following in the footsteps of ex-
Presidents Gladstone and Asquith.*

Jeremy made the Union his social headquarters at Oxford,
where his flamboyant presence quickly made itself felt.[5] He
soon got to know both the established lions and those gifted
novices who were likely to be his own future rivals for office.
The first category included his fellow Liberals Robin Day,
Keith Kyle and Godfrey Smith, as well as his fellow Trinity
undergraduate Peter Kirk, who as President during Jeremy's
second term helped launch him on his Union career.
Prominent among those who started and competed with
Jeremy were two clever men who had come up together to
Balliol from Charterhouse, the owlish William Rees-Mogg, a
Conservative, and the handsome Dutchman Dick Taverne, a
Socialist. Jeremy's closest friend at the Union was another
Labour Party supporter, John Gilbert, who shared something
of his flamboyant manner: they also slightly resembled each
other (though Gilbert was better-looking) and when seen
together were dubbed 'the heavenly twins'. Contemporaries
remember them whispering and giggling together, as if forever
engaged in some lark or plot.

His prospects in Union politics, however, depended not so
much on his social popularity as his impact as a debater. There
was still at that time a characteristic style of Oxford Union debating, of which the main elements were cleverness, quickness and
lightness of touch. Jeremy came to be widely regarded as one of
the finest exponents of this style during his period, perhaps bet-
tered only by the older and weightier Robin Day. Like most
aspiring Union men, he spent much time preparing his speeches
and trying them out on friends; but his real talent was the

---

* Heath was the first ex-President to become Conservative Prime Minister –
  though it is said that Harold Macmillan would have been elected but for the outbreak of the First World War. The great Lord Salisbury had served as Secretary.

instinctive one of being able to hold an audience. He knew how to sense their mood and play on their emotions. He had an actor's sense of timing, and knew the right moment to deliver some well-polished epigram or imitation. He also knew how to give the impression that he had a good grasp of his subject, even when this was not really the case. His critics would say that his speeches were mere brilliant displays behind which lay little substance: but he was more effective at getting listeners on his side than more sober and reasoned debaters.

Some idea of his style can be gleaned from the Union reports in the Oxford student magazine *Isis*. He is first mentioned in his second term,* when he made 'a promising speech' against a humorous motion deploring the Fall of the House of Stuart, delivering a stream of witticisms. 'He was interested in legitimacy and fascinated by illegitimacy. He dwelt on Oxford in Stuart times, when disaffected Tories threw chamber pots. It was a time of sentiment and infidelity, of witty hairdressers and enterprising mountebanks.'[6]† When we next read of him the following term, he is supporting the motion that the Partition of Ireland was a Grievous Blot on English History. 'A good case well argued by a speaker who took care that the House wanted to hear what was coming,' was the verdict.[7] In his fourth term he spoke in favour of creating a Third Force in International Affairs to hold the balance

---

* It is unusual for an undergraduate to be invited to be a paper speaker (that is, one of the official speakers of the evening, mentioned on the order paper) so early in his career. Jeremy owed this honour to the favour of the President, his fellow Trinity man Peter Kirk.

† An allusion to Trollope's scornful criticism of Disraeli's novels: 'The wit has been the wit of hairdressers, and the enterprise has been the enterprise of mountebanks. An audacious conjurer has generally been the hero – some youth who, by wonderful cleverness, can obtain success by every intrigue that comes to hand. Through it all there is a feeling of stage properties, a smell of hair-oil, an aspect of buhl, a remembrance of tailors ...' (Anthony Trollope, *An Autobiography*, Chapter XIII.) These words might be considered by some to apply to Jeremy Thorpe's life.

between the Americans and Russians, expressing 'somewhat gloomy' opinions 'in his usual lively, cheerful and interesting manner'.[8]

By the end of his fourth term, he had made sufficient impact to secure election to the Standing Committee. Then, in January 1950, he had his first real triumph, proposing the motion that South Africa was unworthy of membership of the Commonwealth. It was a subject about which he felt deeply, and he delivered a passionate speech in the Gladstone manner, thundering against the iniquity of the Malan Government which had come to power eighteen months earlier with its policy of 'apartheid', denounced by Jeremy as contrary to the Commonwealth tradition. Journalists were rather sniffy about the speech, finding it contrived and exaggerated.[9] There could be no doubt, however, of his effect on his audience, and the motion was carried by a resounding 298 votes to 131.

Jeremy had now arrived as a serious contender for Union office. He could have stood that term for one of the junior offices with good prospects of success,* but instead decided to try for the presidency itself. This was bold, for he stood little chance against the front-runner Robin Day, a forceful and larger-than-life ex-serviceman six years older than himself. Day completely eclipsed Jeremy in the Presidential Debate (the termly debate held on the eve of the presidential election, with the candidates as speakers): the motion concerned the workings of the international currency system, a subject about which even Jeremy found it difficult to speak confidently. Jeremy came third in the election with 89 votes to Day's 283, but retained his seat on the Standing Committee.

Day, the future grand inquisitor of the small screen, had begun by admiring Jeremy for his wit and debating skills, but now

---

* The previous term he had stood for the office of Librarian, but come third with a bare hundred votes.

regarded him with strong dislike, a feeling intensified by two episodes which occurred during his presidential term. Day proposed a rule change whereby men whose university careers had been interrupted by military service would be eligible to stand for President: this would have enabled Keith Kyle to be a future candidate. On the Standing Committee, Jeremy supported the proposal; but suddenly there was opposition to it from some quarters, and both Day and Kyle had reason to believe that Jeremy, hoping to eliminate Kyle as a future rival to himself, had covertly inspired this. The second episode was ludicrous. By a Union tradition which would soon be abolished, a humorous debate was held annually in Eights Week* at which the President and Officers wore Hunting Pink. However, just before the debate in May 1950, Day's 'pink' outfit vanished. As he had taken the precaution of hiring two sets, he was spared the embarrassment of appearing wrongly dressed; but he took a serious view of the prank and went so far as to call in the Oxford police. It was generally believed that Jeremy and his friend John Gilbert were responsible for the removal of the clothes (which were soon returned).[10]

That spring, Jeremy gave another memorable debating performance, proposing ('as the grandson of a venerable archdeacon') the disestablishment of the Church of England and evoking the spectacle of the Socialist radical Aneurin Bevan becoming premier and appointing bishops. Wisely, however, he decided to bide his time and stood only for the Treasurership in the termly elections, scoring an easy victory. Keith Kyle was elected Secretary and William Rees-Mogg Librarian. The favourite for President was Dick Taverne, who had successively held all three junior offices during 1949–50; but to the general surprise, he made a poor showing in the Presidential Debate and was

---

* The week of the annual inter-collegiate rowing tournament, known for its social activities.

defeated by the charming but lightweight Godfrey Smith. All thoughts were now concentrated on the *next* presidential election, due in November 1950, at which the candidates would be Taverne, Rees-Mogg and Jeremy. This would be a veritable battle of the titans. All three men were unusually gifted and ambitious; between them, they represented all three political parties; and their contest evoked the traditional rivalry between Balliol (the college of both Jeremy's opponents) and Trinity.*

By tradition, the Opening Debate of each term is on a motion attacking the government of the day; the speakers are generally that term's presidential candidates,† and they are allowed to decide among themselves the order in which they speak. Before the vacation, it was agreed that, come October, the motion should be proposed by Jeremy and opposed by Taverne, while Rees-Mogg would speak third, supporting the motion. However, during the summer, Jeremy started behaving like a prima donna. First he wrote to Smith that he would rather speak third than first: but Rees-Mogg, who as Librarian took precedence over Jeremy as Treasurer, would not agree to this. Then Jeremy announced that, as a Liberal, he did not feel able to attack the Labour Government with its record of social reform, and wished to be first speaker against rather than for the motion. Smith told him that he could change sides if he wished, but that Taverne had already been chosen as the main opposing speaker and Jeremy would have to speak fourth rather than second. Jeremy seems to have felt that, as a fellow Liberal, Smith should have helped him get his way: he vented his pique by speaking disparagingly about him that September

---

* Two decades later, when Jeremy was Liberal Leader, Rees-Mogg Editor of *The Times* and Taverne had left the Labour Party to sit as an independent MP, these former rivals were to become friends and allies. See Chapter 15.

† These men speak again in the Presidential Debate, the sixth debate of term, thus giving the Union electorate two chances to hear them, with a month or so in between, before casting their vote.

at the Liberal Assembly at Scarborough. As a result, when the President turned up at the Assembly in the hope of finding speakers for the coming term, he found the atmosphere poisoned against him.

Smith was furious at being crossed by Jeremy in this way. Encouraged by Robin Day and others who disapproved of Jeremy, he set up a committee at the Union to enquire into his conduct:* its remit included not only the latest matter but also 'the affair of the Hunting Pink'. But Jeremy had covered his tracks well – after conducting extensive interviews, the committee concluded that, while it was clear that he had misbehaved and that his explanations had lacked frankness, there was no evidence against him which would stand up in a court of law. In the end, after Jeremy had apologised for the fact that 'in a moment of extreme anger' he may have made 'statements likely to detract from the prestige of the Society', the Standing Committee decided to take no action against him – though Smith used his presidential privilege to exclude him altogether from the Opening Debate.[11]

Passions ran high over the episode. Robin Day said that no one who had known Jeremy at Oxford would ever trust him again, while another ex-President feared that Jeremy's 'acquittal' would encourage him to believe that he could get away with anything in future. Others predicted (as they would recall three decades later) that his lack of scruple would one day bring his career to a sticky end. On the whole, however, the view among Union members was that he was one of their brightest stars and it would be absurd to prejudice his chances of becoming President merely on account of a few indiscretions. In retrospect, it does seem rather childish of Jeremy's peers to have made such a fuss about his conduct, especially as many of those who aspired

---

* It consisted of Uwe Kitzinger, an ex-President; Max Beloff, an ex-Librarian; and the current Secretary, Keith Kyle, as record-taker.

to Union office engaged in some form of illicit activity, if only by ignoring the anti-canvassing rule.

Yet it must be said that, even by the lax standards of student politics, Jeremy was notorious for his plotting and his bending of the rules. One of his Union contemporaries remembers him as 'an artful dodger, always up to tricks', while another has described him as having the outlook and morals 'of a bookie'. His unscrupulousness partly sprang from his ruthless ambition: he believed (as he had been taught to do by his mother) that almost anything was permissible if it helped him get on. But there can be no doubt that he also had a natural love of devious behaviour, of being naughty, of getting away with things. These tendencies were closely linked to the theatrical side of his personality: he was a kind of fantasy gangster, revelling in little acts of skulduggery, most of which did little real harm. He was also influenced by a desire to emulate that other great trickster and intriguer, his hero Lloyd George.

Jeremy also earned a reputation at Oxford for being unreliable in financial matters. He was not considered blatantly dishonest, but (again like Lloyd George) he wanted to get control of whatever funds were going and use them in ways calculated to enhance his own authority and prestige. His idea of hiring twenty caravans for an OULC campaigning tour presaged his later controversial expenditure of Liberal Party election funds on helicopters and hovercrafts. As Union Treasurer, he was criticised for spending too much money furnishing the Society's new bar. Philip Watkins, Treasurer of the Russell & Palmerston Club (and later of the Liberal Party), once tried to stop Jeremy using some of the Club's limited funds to add to its silver collection. 'But he talked me into it,' Watkins later recalled, 'as he always did.'[12]

Jeremy's trouble at the Union at the outset of the Michaelmas Term seemed to do him little long-term harm. His exclusion from the Opening Debate was forgotten after a brilliant performance in a subsequent debate on European policy in China, a subject he knew something about: while criticising his speech for its indifferent construction, *Isis* marvelled at 'his self-confident parliamentary manner, his command of gesture, his way with interrupters, his ability to play with the hand – and the signet ring – of a master on the emotions of his audience'.[13] Two weeks later, in the Presidential Debate, Jeremy had his great moment, when he proposed the motion that the Philosophy of Conservatism was Irrelevant to the Present Age. His speech, said *Isis*, succeeded 'by the relentless force of its delivery ... a succession of short, biting sentences forced through a jet'. The Tories, said Jeremy, were in favour of every reform except the next one. They believed in £2,000 a year for everyone who had got more than £2,000. He imitated Churchill and quoted Disraeli 'before working up to his final onslaught on a party that was held together by no greater bond than self-preservation'.[14] The motion was carried by 338 votes to 290; and the following day, in the presidential election, Jeremy polled a decisive 352 votes to Taverne's 295 and Rees-Mogg's 155.

At the age of twenty-one, he had achieved the first of his great ambitions. In accordance with tradition, *Isis* celebrated his election with a profile in their 'Idol' column, giving a vivid picture of his life and achievements to date and describing him as 'a personality whose vivacity, wit and easy manner stand in sparkling relief to the drab stage of Oxford life'. But it ended on a warning note: 'His likes and dislikes are often too violently felt and expressed, and some feel that as a future politician, he would be wiser to be more discreet. An interesting and stimulating career lies ahead of him, provided he does not let his enthusiasm overreach his wisdom.'[15]

A President is remembered at the Union for the quality of the debates he organises during his term and of the speakers he persuades to take part in them; and Jeremy's term (Hilary 1951) was a vintage one in this respect. He persuaded the Tory Viscount

Hailsham to speak in favour of the foreign policy of the Labour
Government and the Socialist Viscount Stansgate to oppose it,
while Stansgate's sons, Anthony and David Wedgwood Benn,
also spoke and took opposing sides in the debate.* A motion
sending up lawyers was proposed by the great humorist Stephen
Potter and opposed by the famous judge Norman Birkett. The
Prime Minister of Southern Rhodesia spoke – the first time a
serving premier had been heard at the Union. In the (traditionally humorous) Farewell Debate, on the motion that This House
Prefers the Devil to the Deep Blue Sea, Lord Chatfield, an elderly
admiral, defended the navy against Nathaniel Micklem, an elderly cleric, who brought the house down with his opening
remark that he was infernally pleased to be there.

Jeremy also had to decide which undergraduates to invite to
speak – always a delicate task for a president as there are limited
'slots' each term for paper speakers, many of which are filled as
of right by current committee members and election candidates.
He took care to give suitable opportunities to such rising stars
(all destined to be future presidents) as Peter Blaker, Patrick
Mayhew† and Bryan Magee.‡ But he also invited some less well-
known names to speak, such as David Lutyens, the highly strung
youth who had been infatuated with him at Eton, who discussed
the 'dark erotic tendencies' of the age and its 'arid formalism in
art and literature', and George Carman, a clever Balliol lawyer,

---

* Hailsham, formerly Quintin Hogg, had been MP for Oxford before inheriting
his peerage six months earlier. Stansgate, who had begun his career as a
Liberal, had been Attlee's Secretary of State for Air in 1945–46. Anthony
Wedgwood Benn (as he was then known) was a former Union President who
had recently become a Labour MP, while David, a contemporary of Jeremy,
would be elected Secretary of the Union for the following term.

† President, Michaelmas 1952; Conservative MP for Tunbridge Wells, 1964–97;
Attorney-General, 1987–92; Secretary of State for Northern Ireland, 1992–97;
life peer, 1997.

‡ President, Hilary 1953; philosophy don, writer and broadcaster; MP (Labour,
later Social Democrat) for Leyton, 1974–83.

whom *Isis* praised for 'the careful construction of his speech ...
and an immaculate delivery'.* Twenty-eight years later, Carman
would be chosen again – this time to be Jeremy's defence counsel
at the Old Bailey.

Jeremy got on well with his Secretary, the American Howard
Shuman, and had satisfactory relations with his Treasurer, the
eccentric and literary Ivan Yates,† and Librarian, the handsome
but dim Geoffrey Dalzell-Payne. He now presided over the
Standing Committee, but it is clear from the minutes that he
contributed little to its proceedings. Throughout his career, he
was bored by the detail of committee work and administration,
preferring to leave this to others while he operated behind the
scenes. Paradoxically, it was his antagonist Robin Day, still
attending the Committee as a former President, who took the
most active part on it and formulated most of its proposals.
Jeremy only seemed to show a keen interest when they discussed
exchange visits with other societies; and the only significant
innovation for which he was responsible was the introduction of
a permanent reciprocal arrangement with the Cambridge Union,
which continues to this day.

When Jeremy, much praised for a memorable term, retired
from the presidency in March 1951,‡ to be succeeded by William
Rees-Mogg, he felt he had something to look forward to. Every

---

* According to his son, Carman 'wrote a few of Jeremy's more demanding law
  essays' in return for Jeremy's help in launching his Union career. (Dominic
  Carmen, *No Ordinary Man* [2002], Chapter 2.)
† Said to be the author of Jeremy's anonymous *Isis* 'Idol' profile quoted above.
  He became a political journalist and died in a road accident in middle life.
‡ Among the Presidents during Jeremy's four years at Oxford, he alone would go
  on to become a household name in British politics. Taking the decade 1945–55
  as a whole, with its thirty Presidents, the only others destined to make an
  impression on the political scene were Tony Benn, Edward Boyle, Tony
  Crosland, Michael Heseltine and Patrick Mayhew. With Britain's decline, politics no longer had the same allure for Union men, many of whom went on to
  seek careers in journalism, television, business and academia.

other year (in rotation with their Cambridge counterparts), two representatives of the Oxford Union embarked on a debating tour of American universities sponsored by the English Speaking Union: such a tour was due to take place in the autumn of 1951, and it was generally expected that Oxford would be represented by Jeremy and Taverne. Jeremy (already familiar with the United States) was considered the most brilliant speaker of his generation, while Taverne was thought to deserve selection after twice failing to secure the presidency. However, the selection committee (consisting of those Union ex-officers still in residence at the university) chose Rees-Mogg, a popular and gifted man but an indifferent speaker, to accompany Taverne. Jeremy was dismayed: he had even given up his Oxford rooms in the confident expectation of being chosen. It was said at the time that the memory of his past escapades still rankled with some of the ex-officers, who no doubt felt it would do him good to be thwarted at least once in his Oxford career.

With his rollicking style and celebrity in university politics, Jeremy cut a brilliant figure on the Oxford undergraduate scene. Everyone knew him, and many sought to be included in his burgeoning circle. He always welcomed an audience, and loved parties of every description. At the end of his second year, he moved out of college to share digs with Michael Ogle at Number 69, High Street, where their spacious first-floor sitting room, its grand piano covered with Jeremy's silver-framed photographs and its mantelpiece littered with a profusion of invitation cards, was the scene of many jolly gatherings – so much so that Ogle eventually moved out, unable to work while Jeremy was holding court to their endless visitors.

There was rarely a dull moment in his company. He had a lightning verbal repartee. With his elaborate sense of fantasy, he could make a hilarious joke out of the most mundane situation: if he saw two strangers together, he would indulge in some fanciful speculation as to their background; and if he entered a room for the first time, he would make up some ribald story about the furniture. His gift for mimicry was remarkable, and not just confined to the famous. He once joined a dinner table of fellow undergraduates none of whom he knew well: within an hour he was not only impeccably reproducing their voices and mannerisms but had got inside their minds, knew the sort of things they would say. One of his tricks was to slip into the personality of a person he was with: when he walked down the High with Dingle Foot, both were heard to talk in Foot's characteristic, over-precise, mild Devonian tones. Of course, some were irritated to hear themselves parodied by Jeremy, while some of his imitations were thought to be in questionable taste: an accurate rendition of King George VI with his tortured speech aroused few laughs. He was also given to lavatorial jokes, often funny if not to everyone's taste.

While delighting in his company, many found him insincere and superficial. It was often hard to tell whether the things he said or did really meant something or were just for show. His conversation consisted mostly of social gossip, political intrigue and jocularity of one sort or another; he was rarely heard to discuss abstract ideas, or go very deeply into any subject unless it concerned his career. And there was a price to be paid for all the hectic activity and manic high spirits: like his hero Winston Churchill, he experienced periodic bouts of 'Black Dog' during which he would shut himself away in a darkened room. (He would ascribe these depressive reactions to his Irish paternal ancestry – though they were probably more closely linked to his Welsh maternal side, to the rages and suicidal despair of Empire Jack.) He was a man of paradoxes: it was often suggested that his brilliance was counterbalanced by a dangerous streak of mental instability; that the confident exterior concealed an insecure nature; that, as with the proverbial clown, tragedy lurked behind the comic mask.

Although Jeremy had numerous friends at Oxford, he always seems (then and afterwards) to have needed a close crony, an inseparable soul-mate upon whom to rely and with whom to conspire. For the first two and a half years of his Oxford career, this role was fulfilled at different times by Michael Ogle and John Gilbert. In the middle of his third year, when Gilbert had left Oxford and Ogle was busy reading for exams, their place was taken by Christopher Bourke, a jovial law undergraduate at Oriel from an old Roman Catholic family: meeting for the first time at a Union party in January 1951, they immediately (to quote Bourke) struck up 'a firm and faithful friendship' based on 'a shared sense of fun'. Like Jeremy, Bourke was a flamboyant dandy (he once dyed all his clothes green); and the well-known sight of them walking about Oxford together with their springy gait, Jeremy pale and angular in appearance, Bourke rather florid and rotund, had a touch about it of a music-hall double act.

While close and romantic, none of these friendships could be described as homosexual. Indeed, Gilbert got married while at Oxford, while Bourke failed to distinguish himself academically owing to a distracting weakness for women. At Oxford, few seem to have imagined that Jeremy himself might be homosexual: he was regarded (in so far as such matters were then thought about) as a basically asexual character, wrapped up in politics and his career. He once told Bourke that politics provided him with all the excitement he needed, rendering sex unnecessary, and he does not yet seem to have devoted much time or thought to the latter, though his tastes must by this time have been set. He did not frequent either of the two 'queer sets' at the university – one theatrical, based on the Oxford University Dramatic Society; the other aristocratic, revolving around the rich young Lord Montagu of Beaulieu. And although he made some long-term friends at Oxford, such as David Holmes and Philip Watkins, who would go on to lead homosexual double lives, it is unlikely that they made each other aware of their shared interests at this stage. Years later, some contemporaries saw possible significance in the fact that he had attended the all-male midnight parties of Stanley Parker, a raffish Australian artist who kept rooms in the Broad, but not much seems to have happened at these beyond some drunken embracing. Before he left Oxford, Jeremy was also visited by Henry Upton, whose disreputable acquaintance he had made just before coming up to the university, but he managed to pass off such friends as merely eccentric.

As for Oxford women (a rare commodity in those days, making up less than one-sixth of the student population), Jeremy was full of gallant gestures towards them; but they, while often amused by his company, found his efforts to play the stage lover absurd. In so far as he exhibited any serious romantic feelings, it was towards older women such as Megan Lloyd George rather than his contemporaries. If he ever seemed to be getting close to a female undergraduate, as he did to Ann Chesney when they were both involved in the OULC, the relationship was likely to arouse the destructive attention of the one who was long to remain the principal woman in his life – his mother.

For during her frequent visits to her son at Oxford, Ursula followed his doings with passionate interest and revelled in his successes as if they were her own. It was unusual for an undergraduate's mother to be so much in evidence, and her formidable, monocled presence lent yet another exotic touch to Jeremy's Oxford life. Before every Union debate, the President held a dinner for the Society's officers and the speakers of the evening, each of whom was entitled to bring one guest; most men brought girlfriends, but Jeremy usually his mother. Among his friends, she provoked mixed reactions: some disliked her or regarded her as a joke; others admired her for her strident personality, her devotion to her son and her familiarity with the pre-war ruling class world. Jeremy himself now enjoyed something of a love–hate relationship with her: he relied on her for many things and longed for her to be there at his great moments, but resented her possessiveness and interference in his life. They had fierce rows, often provoked by politics, for Ursula, who was now Vice-Chairman of her local Conservative Association and had been elected to Surrey County Council in 1949 in the Tory interest, found it as hard as ever to reconcile herself to Jeremy's Liberalism. Yet she remained his greatest ally, devoted to his future and spurring him on to success. And some felt his dead father, of whom he spoke often, was as much an influence as his highly alive mother – a legend to be glamorised, whose successes he could emulate and failures avenge.

Absorbed by his political and debating activities and varied social life, Jeremy had little time or inclination at Oxford for academic work. When it came to essay-writing and other tests, he just managed to get by with the help of Michael Ogle and other more studious friends. He was fortunate that his tutor, Philip Landon, expected little work from his students if they were distinguishing themselves and their college in other ways. The other members of Jeremy's tutorial class included a leading cricketer and a famous oarsman; in the autumn of 1950, after the cricketer had been selected for the university team, the oars-man had become stroke of the college eight, and Jeremy had been elected President of the Union, they were summoned by Landon to be told that they would all be very busy and he did not expect to see them again until the end of the following term.

Like most undergraduates who devote their third year to sporting achievements or Union office, Jeremy secured a fourth year to prepare for his finals. During that year, however, he gave little thought to his studies. He was one of the lions of Oxford and basked in his celebrity. He regularly gave and attended parties, and continued to put in a periodic appearance *ex officio* on the committees of the OULC and Union. Much time was spent in idle enjoyment with Christopher Bourke: rationing was coming to an end, and they spent long hours at tailors and restaurants, revelling in the luxury of previously forbidden indulgences. Most days they lunched with their friends at the Shamrock, a small hostelry where they kept their own table: this was next to a low window facing the street through which Jeremy, perfecting his technique in communicating with the electorate, would engage in ribald conversation with the passers-by.

He was already looking to the future beyond Oxford, and much of his time and interest were now absorbed by national politics. In October 1951, just after he had come up for his fourth year, Attlee with his dwindling majority called another General Election – to the dismay of the Liberals, who had not yet recovered from their disaster of February 1950 and were able to contest fewer than one-fifth of the seats. Again, Jeremy campaigned energetically in various parts of the country. The result was an even worse catastrophe for the Liberals, who only succeeded in holding on to six of their nine seats, the casualties including Jeremy's greatest friend in the House of Commons, Megan Lloyd George in Anglesey. The Party's very existence seemed in danger when the victorious Winston Churchill tried to tempt its leader, Clement Davies, to join the new Conservative Government.* Although Davies refused, having been urged to do so by Jeremy and other Oxford Liberals,† the Party was in danger of splitting into pro-Labour and pro-Tory factions: Jeremy attended the post-election meeting of the Liberal Council in London at which Violet Bonham Carter, an admirer of Churchill, had a famous public row with Megan, now flirting with Socialism.

---

* Davies was offered the Cabinet post of Education Secretary. Churchill also offered the Ministry of Food to Lloyd George's son Gwilym, and the Lord Chancellorship to Asquith's son Cyril, a judge: Gwilym accepted, effectively becoming a Conservative, but Cyril refused.

† A number of prominent Liberals, including the Oxford historian Gilbert Murray, had urged him to accept the offer and merge the Liberals with the Conservatives, but the OULC sent him a telegram urging him to stand firm, which Davies claimed to have been a leading factor in his decision to refuse.

None of this discouraged Jeremy, however: if anything, the Party's wretched fortunes favoured his cause by deterring other young Liberals from seeking an active political career.* In April 1952, while still at Oxford, he was invited to seek adoption as a prospective parliamentary candidate by the North Devon Liberals (as will be described in the next chapter).

Jeremy also spent much time in London during his final Oxford year, where he had started eating his dinners at the Inner Temple and had been elected (proposed by Dingle Foot) to the National Liberal Club.† During these visits to the capital, he strove in his usual robust way to extend his contacts and impress his personality on influential people. While waiting to see MPs in the Central Lobby at Westminster, he would introduce himself heartily to any well-known politician or journalist who happened to pass through: many were surprised, but few forgot him. Once, dining at the Inner Temple, he marched up to the high table and started chatting to the Benchers,‡ adopting a tone of easy familiarity and congratulating them on their recent performances in the courts. 'Who the devil was that?' asked one

---

* Of the other Liberals active at the Oxford Union in Jeremy's time – Robin Day, Godfrey Smith, Keith Kyle and Peter Blaker – the only one to make a career in national politics was Blaker. None of the others even stood as a Liberal candidate, with the exception of Day's one-off effort at Hereford in 1959, shortly before he left the Party.

† The Club, with which Jeremy would be closely associated for the rest of the century, was founded in the 1880s during the Gladstonian heyday and occupied one-third of a huge neo-Gothic palace on the Westminster Embankment. As well as serving as a gentleman's club, its vast tiled rooms, filled with statues and portraits of Liberal heroes, were used for party meetings. It still occupies the lower part of its original premises, now handsomely restored, while the upper floors containing its library and bedrooms were sold off during the 1970s to the hotel next door.

‡ The Masters of the Bench or 'Benchers', generally drawn from distinguished judges or practising barristers, form the self-elected governing bodies of the Inns of Court, and sit at the high table when lunching or dining in the hall of their Inn. Jeremy's father had been a Bencher of the Inner Temple from 1941 until his death in 1944.

astounded Bencher after he had gone. 'That's Thorpey's boy,' came the reply, 'and you haven't heard the last of him!'[16]

Soon after Easter 1952, Jeremy gloomily confided to Christopher Bourke that he had decided to leave Oxford without taking a degree. He had done no work, and did not want to sit his law finals as he was likely to fail them. Bourke had himself sat and passed them the year before, and had kept his excellent set of revision notes: he suggested they both obtain a month's leave from the university and retreat to his parents' country house in Worcestershire, where he would put Jeremy through his paces and help him cram four years' work into four weeks. This they did: Jeremy spent his mornings memorising Bourke's notes, and his afternoons being tested on them as they wandered through the countryside in glorious spring weather. The result was that Jeremy managed to scrape a third-class degree, while Bourke, who had inadequately prepared himself for the postgraduate BCL examination, had the misfortune to fail. Yet he had no regrets at having sacrificed himself for his friend, a striking example of the devotion Jeremy could inspire.[17]

5

CAREER
1952–59

WHEN, SOON AFTER his twenty-first birthday in April 1950, Jeremy Thorpe, then in his second year at Oxford, was interviewed by the Liberal Party's Candidates Committee in London, so impressed were they by his energy and flair, his political gifts and the reputation he had built up, that they thought of recommending him as the future candidate in the Welsh constituency of Montgomeryshire, the nearest thing then existing to a 'safe' Liberal seat,* when the sitting MP, the Party Leader Clement Davies, eventually chose to retire.[1] Though this seemed a distant prospect, as Davies was an energetic sixty-six and showed no signs of stepping down from the leadership, let alone Parliament, Jeremy went so far as to take some Welsh lessons from Megan Lloyd George, impressing his friends with his beautiful pronounciation of the phrase *cofwyeh eich egwriddorion!*† By the

---

* Davies enjoyed a majority of almost 10,000, but only in a straight fight with Labour: after his death in 1962, the seat began to be contested by the Conservatives, who eventually captured it in 1979.
† 'Remember your principles!'

spring of 1951, however, he had another plan: he told friends that he now intended to seek adoption for a seat in Devon or Cornwall, where the Liberals possessed a long tradition but no MP since the war, with a view to winning on the second attempt.[2] He knew he could count on the support there of the influential Foot family, just as in Wales he would have benefited from his association with the Lloyd Georges. Soon after the 1951 election, with its disastrous outcome for the Liberals, he duly received invitations from the party associations in the adjacent seats of North Devon, Torrington and North Cornwall. Of these, it was in North Cornwall that the Liberals had come closest to victory; but Jeremy chose North Devon. In April 1952, during his last university vacation, he travelled down to meet the North Devon Liberals, making a scintillating impression; and the following November he was enthusiastically adopted as their prospective parliamentary candidate at a packed meeting addressed by Clement Davies and Dingle Foot.

The North Devon constituency had been created by the parliamentary boundary redistributions of the late 1940s and succeeded to the old Barnstaple Divison of Devon, its only sizeable town (of some 15,000) being that historic borough situated at the mouth of the Taw estuary. It covered over a thousand square miles of agriculturally rather poor land, mostly given over to dairy pasture and much of it owned by the Tory magnate Lord Fortescue. It was thinly populated, most of its inhabitants being farming folk living in and around small villages. Its thirty-odd miles of coastline included stretches of picturesque cliffs, punctuated by Ilfracombe and other small seaside towns in which summer tourism had overtaken fishing as the main source of livelihood. Though its borders lay within a few dozen miles of the great centres of Bristol and Exeter, it was geographically isolated, cut off by Exmoor to the east, Dartmoor to the south, the Taw and Torridge to the west, the Bristol Channel to the north and north-west. Its main communications with the rest of the country were the narrow secondary roads and slow branch railways which joined Barnstaple to Taunton and Exeter. It was a remote backwater in which public services were poorly developed and national trends slow to penetrate. In so far as it impinged on the national consciousness, it was as a summer tourist destination, the home of the Jack Russell terrier, and the setting of Henry Williamson's best-selling rustic novel *Tarka the Otter*.*

Like so much else in North Devon, politics were highly traditional. Elections were great local events at which public meetings attracted large audiences. Both Conservatives and Liberals had long traditions, which to some extent still followed the historic divisions between church and chapel, squire and tenant, drinking and temperance; but the personalities of candidates tended to count for as much as their party labels. The Barnstaple seat had been Liberal up to the 1920s and then Conservative until 1935, when it was regained for the Liberals (one of only two gains that year) by the eccentric young radical Sir Richard Acland. But during the war, Acland left the Liberals to found the short-lived Common Wealth Party; and in the 1945 election, Brigadier Peto, son of the Tory MP who had preceded Acland, comfortably defeated Asquith's grandson Mark Bonham Carter. Peto won again in 1950 and 1951: in the latter year, the Liberals, handicapped by a chronic shortage of members and cash, experienced the unprecedented humiliation of being beaten into third place by the Labour candidate, receiving less than one-fifth of the vote.

---

* Both the Barnstaple Museum and the Barnstaple–Exeter railway have now been renamed in honour of Tarka, though Williamson himself, having published the novel in 1927, was drummed out of the locality in the 1930s on account of his fascist sympathies. North Devon can boast of few other figures of national stature: the medieval lawyer Bracton, the eighteenth-century composer John Gay and the Victorian writer Charles Kingsley were all brought up there but made their mark elsewhere.

Jeremy therefore had a mountain to climb. Yet he had chosen well by investing his political future in North Devon. Perhaps more than any other constituency within two hundred miles of London, it was a self-contained world in which a charismatic candidate might capture the imagination of voters and build up a personal following. Its people, largely descended from seafaring folk, enjoyed a touch of exhibitionism and were not averse to colourful outsiders. Sir Ernest Soares, a flamboyant solicitor of Portuguese–Jewish origin, was still remembered as the popular Liberal MP of Edwardian times; while Bonham Carter, despite being the nephew of an important local landowner, made a luke-warm impression owing to his cold and superior manner. Jeremy, with his Edwardian dress and extrovert style, his rousing oratory combining fervour and jocularity, his keenness to befriend the North Devonians and learn of their concerns, his impish habit of addressing them in a perfect imitation of their own dialect, made an instant hit.

Of course, it was one thing to win hearts and another to win votes. As a newcomer based in London, he would need time to familiarise himself with the sprawling constituency and its inhabitants and traditions. It would take years of hard work to build up the neglected local party organisation, and persuade voters that Liberalism was not a lost cause. But he was confident that, within a decade, he would not only have captured the seat but fashioned it into a powerful base for his wider ambitions. 'After I am elected,' he would declare during his seven years as a prospective candidate, 'no-one will have to ask who is the Member for North Devon.'

It was an odd thing to be a Liberal in 1952, the year Jeremy came down from Oxford and was adopted for North Devon. The Party's days of power and glory were still a recent memory. Only forty years earlier, Asquith had been Prime Minister, presiding over an outstanding Liberal Cabinet which had included the present Prime Minister, Winston Churchill. Thirty years earlier, Lloyd George had been in power, widely considered the greatest statesman of his age. Twenty years earlier, the Liberals had still been partners in a governing coalition, with the leaders of its two wings serving as Home Secretary and Foreign Secretary. Less than ten years earlier, the Liberals had been participants in the wartime government, the Party Leader Sir Archibald Sinclair occupying the key post of Air Minister.

Since 1945, however, the Party had experienced an electoral catastrophe so overwhelming that its very survival now hung in the balance. At the 1951 election, not only had it been reduced to a mere six seats, but five of these were held by courtesy of the now governing Conservatives. The three Welsh MPs – Roderic Bowen in Cardigan, Clement Davies in Montgomeryshire, Rhys Hopkin Morris in Carmarthen – had won in straight fights with Labour; while the two North Country MPs – Arthur Holt in Bolton and Donald Wade in Huddersfield – owed their success to local pacts with the Conservatives.* Only in Orkney and Shetland had the dynamic Jo Grimond managed to survive as a Liberal in a three-cornered fight. Moreover, Hopkin Morris no longer counted as a party politician as he had accepted the Deputy Speakership of the House of Commons; while three of the remaining five devoted much of their time to careers outside Parliament. The Liberal MPs behaved more like independents than a parliamentary party, turning up when they could, meeting irregularly, and generally voting according to their individual consciences.

In grotesque contrast to the parliamentary party was the elaborate structure of the party in the country, known as the Liberal Party Organisation or LPO, which had hardly changed in eighty years and was more suited to a party with 750,000 members than one commanding that number of national votes. Under a complex

---

* These were two-seat towns, in which Conservatives and Liberals agreed to contest one seat each and support each other to exclude Labour.

constitution, based on federal principles and voting by PR, local branches sent delegates to constituency associations, which in turn sent representatives to regional federations, which elected members of the Party Executive (which met monthly to discuss strategy) and the Party Council (which met quarterly to discuss policy). These bodies engaged in endless futile debates, rarely agreed on anything and had become largely divorced from reality.* Jeremy sat on both Executive and Council in the 1950s: this entitled him to sit on the platform at the annual Liberal Assembly, but he rarely turned up to meetings[3] and soon realised that, if the Party was to revive nationally, a new machinery would have to be found.

There was little contact between the LPO and the Liberal MPs, who drew the funds (such as they were) for their parliamentary activities from a separate body known as the Liberal Central Association. The MPs were *ex officio* members of the Executive and Council but hardly ever bothered to attend. In theory, they were supposed to put forward 'party policy' in Parliament, as laid down by the Council and Assembly, but they rarely gave much thought to this. This gulf between the parliamentary and national parties hardly mattered much in the dire circumstances of 1952, but would produce serious trouble fifteen years later under Jeremy's leadership.

A great party which has existed for generations and recently participated in government does not crumble overnight. There were still many distinguished and talented people in the Liberal Party, some of whom belonged to the National Liberal Club, whose splendid Victorian palace on the Embankment with its portraits and statues was a living reminder of a glorious past.

---

* The Executive and Council were in effect fantasy bodies, in which men and women who had virtually no chance of being elected to public office were able to imagine themselves sitting at the Cabinet table or debating in the House of Commons. As such they served the purpose of sustaining the morale of party workers at a dismal time. Later on, they were easily infiltrated by the radical extremists of the Young Liberals.

Two of the most influential economic and social thinkers of recent years, Keynes and Beveridge, had been Liberals; and Liberalism (as demonstrated by the flourishing OULC over which Jeremy had recently presided) was still a force at the universities. A sizeable if increasingly demoralised body of volunteer workers still toiled in the constituencies. But none of this counted for much electorally because of a chronic shortage of funds. Unlike the Conservatives, supported by big business, and Labour, financed by the unions, the Liberals had no source of income other than donations from individual members. Party Headquarters in Victoria Street were just kept going by the generosity of a few wealthy supporters; there was little left over to hire professional officers, fight proper campaigns or buy national publicity. Under these circumstances, some feared the Party could not long survive: contingency plans existed to wind it up in six weeks, with special funds set aside to pay off the staff. One result of the Party's poverty was that it was easy for plausible rogues to become officers or candidates, and thus acquire respectability, if they made significant donations or offered to pay their own deposits. Another was that Liberals with a natural talent for fundraising, such as Jeremy, were likely to be cherished by the Party and rise high in its counsels.

Another problem was that it was no longer at all clear what the Liberals stood for politically. Their traditional rallying cry had been that of Free Trade, but this hardly made sense at a time when, in Britain as elsewhere, domestic industry and agriculture were protected by tariffs and state subsidies. Some Liberals believed in the *laissez-faire* economics of Gladstone, others in the interventionist philosophy of Lloyd George. There was a risk that what remained of the Party might split between right and left, or even defect *en masse* to the two main parties: the famous row after the 1951 election between the daughters of the last two Liberal premiers, Violet and Megan, in which the former expressed support for the new Conservative Government and the latter for the outgoing Labour one, seemed an ominous portent. Jeremy belonged to a growing body of opinion, particularly prevalent at the universities and among Young Liberals, that they should establish themselves as a 'radical' party, vigorously opposing the Conservative Government while offering a clear alternative to the socialist policies of Labour.

He made his feelings known in characteristic fashion in April 1953 at the annual Party Assembly at Ilfracombe, situated in the North Devon constituency where he had been adopted just five months earlier. When the Chairman of the Party Executive proposed a resolution calling for the gradual phasing-out of state subsidies, Jeremy seized the microphone and declared that he and his fellow candidates in Devon and Cornwall would refuse to fight an election on such a programme. While this piece of bravado went down badly with the audience, and Jeremy was forced to apologise, his stand inspired like-minded Liberals to found the Radical Reform Group to counter right-wing tendencies in the Party. Its leading members, the schoolmaster E. F. Allison and the pensions expert Desmond Banks, published a book in 1954 entitled *Radical Aims*, advocating 'social reform without socialism'. Jeremy was their agriculture spokesman and hosted meetings of the Group's Agriculture Committee at his law chambers, which Banks recalled as 'hilarious ... Jeremy talking about everything except agriculture'.[4] He was not much of a political philosopher, but felt that Liberalism had no future unless it could offer something progressive, imaginative and distinct: at this time, he described himself as the Prospective *Radical* Liberal Candidate for North Devon.

One policy on which all Liberals could agree was that of electoral reform, and Jeremy was a vigorous campaigner for a 'proportional' voting system which would more accurately reflect the popular will and enable the Liberals to increase their parliamentary representation. He wrote a number of popular newspaper articles on the subject, and was co-author of a report advocating the Single

Transferable Vote system which appeared in January 1953 under the title *To All Who Are Interested in Democracy*. In February 1955, he took part in an all-party delegation to the Home Secretary to lobby for PR:* the minister was none other than his father's old friend Gwilym Lloyd George, now a Conservative, who received the delegates courteously but could hardly have had much to offer them with an election looming which, under the existing system, the Government was likely to win.

Having already attracted notice during his Oxford years, Jeremy had now made a personal impact on the Liberal Party as well as a contribution to its thinking and direction. The great question was whether it would survive the next few years. If it did, he might aspire to lead it if he could show two things: that he could help raise the money it so desperately required, and that he could win and hold his seat.

Although Jeremy's mind was focused on politics during his post-Oxford period, he was also preparing for a career at the Bar.[5] This had been the profession of his father, whose reputation and connections were likely to come in useful; and it was traditionally regarded as a natural base from which to pursue a political career.†

---

* The delegation's leader was the Thorpe family friend and former National Liberal MP Sir Geoffrey Shakespeare, and it also included Lady Violet Bonham Carter, the Labour MP Anthony Greenwood and an Ulster Unionist MP.

† The links between the Bar and Westminster politics were then still very strong. The titular head of the profession, the Attorney-General, was a member of the Government; the Lord Chancellor was always a distinguished former silk; and until quite recently, some judges (all drawn from the Bar) had been political appointees. Junior barristers who sat in the House of Commons could become QCs on request (a practice discontinued in the 1960s, just before Jeremy tried to take advantage of it). Barristers were thought to make ideal MPs, being steeped in the arts of debating and lawmaking and belonging to a gentlemanly profession from which they could take time off when they chose. The legal profession was well represented in the Liberal Party: of the six Liberal MPs, three (Davies, Bowen and Morris) were QCs, one (Grimond) a junior barrister and one (Wade) a solicitor.

Jeremy had not distinguished himself as a university law student, and cannot be said to have possessed either a legal mind or a learned interest in the law. But he had a quick and inventive brain; he was an accomplished debater; and he loved the theatrical side of the profession – dressing up in wig and gown, acting out the rituals of the courtroom, addressing juries, performing before public and press. The legal world was also crowded with colourful and eccentric characters, providing ample scope for his mimetic talents.

The steps needed to become a barrister were similar then to now: one had to join one of the four Inns of Court and 'keep terms' by dining there with fellow students; pass professional examinations (from parts of which one was exempted by a university law degree); and serve a year's apprenticeship with a junior barrister, known as pupillage. Jeremy joined his father's Inn, the Inner Temple, whose Benchers included such family friends as Lord Merriman, President of the Probate, Divorce and Admiralty Division of the High Court, and Sir John Morris, the eminent Welsh judge who was close to the Lloyd George family. He next had to prepare himself for exams: it was then customary to 'read' for these with a barrister offering private tuition, and in September 1952, he enrolled in the chambers of Gerald Hart, a one-armed South African considered one of the top tutors at the Bar. Hart had many Commonwealth students, who at that time included the famous West Indian Test cricketer (and future Trinidadian High Commissioner) Learie Constantine; Tissa Wijeyeratne, son of Ceylon's High Commissioner in London; and several members of the future governments of Cyprus and Malaysia: Jeremy got on particularly well with these students, whose friendship would later prove invaluable when he became politically interested in Commonwealth affairs. Academically, he seems to have made less use of his time with Hart: it was not until February 1954 that he finally managed to secure a third-class pass in the Bar Finals.

Meanwhile, in the spring of 1953, he moved from Hart's chambers in Farrer's Building to 10, King's Bench Walk to start a pupillage* with Rodger Winn, an outstanding junior who would go on to become a leading judge. Winn was an austere intellectual lawyer who did not suffer fools (or third-class law students) gladly, and had only offered a place to Jeremy after being implored to do so by Ursula, who had been told by Lord Merriman that he was the most sought-after pupil master at the Temple. But Ursula in her over-enthusiasm had done her son a disservice: Winn, who demanded total dedication from his pupils and a firm grasp of legal principles, was an unsuitable mentor for Jeremy, who rarely satisfied his high standards and sorely tried his patience. He also disapproved of Jeremy's flamboyance, which may have reminded him of his brother, the exuberant homosexual journalist Godfrey Winn, whom he disliked. Nor, as a hunchback with a notoriously short temper, is he likely to have appreciated the impersonation of himself with which Jeremy entertained his fellow pupils.

Winn took three or four pupils at a time, and Jeremy was always popular with the others† for the amusement he brought into their often dull days. It struck them that he was extremely democratic in some ways and absurdly snobbish in others. He went out of his way to be friendly to overseas students and those from modest social backgrounds, and was always charming to clerks and other lesser mortals. On the other hand, he never missed a chance to impress himself on the great. Winn once gave a party at his house to which he invited Lord

---

* Unlike now, it was then permissible to embark on a pupillage before passing final exams and being called to the Bar.
† Those overlapping with Jeremy included Elizabeth Clarke (later Lady Anson), Andrew (later Sir Andrew) Leggatt (subsequently a Lord Justice of Appeal), George Shindler (subsequently Presiding Judge of the Inner London Crown Court), and Henry (later Sir Henry) de Waal (subsequently First Parliamentary Counsel).

Goddard, the Lord Chief Justice. As soon as the great man entered, Jeremy sprang forward to the astonishment of all and declared in a loud voice: 'My dear Lord Chief Justice, I believe you knew my father!'

On 9 February 1954, having finally passed his exams, Jeremy was called to the Bar in the traditional after-dinner ceremony in the hall of his Inn, his proposers being Merriman and Morris. After the proceedings, a crowd of Benchers who remembered his father came down from their high table to offer him their personal congratulations, while less well-connected callees looked enviously on. Soon afterwards, to the relief of the long-suffering Winn, his pupillage came to an end, and he was able to commence practice as a barrister. He joined a new set of chambers on the ground floor of Lamb Building, where the clerk was an old clerk of Thorpey's.* These were Western Circuit chambers,† which suited Jeremy as it enabled him to practise in the Devon courts and so keep in touch with his constituency.

At that time, newly called barristers who had yet to prove themselves tended to be notoriously short of work; and Jeremy was no exception. During his first year of practice, he would often be found leaning out of an open window at the Temple, chatting idly to passers-by. He had better luck in Devon, where Liberal solicitors were willing to instruct him in run-of-the-mill criminal cases. His first brief, and much of the work which came his way during the next six years, he owed to John Foot, the Plymouth solicitor (brother of Dingle, Michael and Hugh) for whom he had campaigned in Bodmin in the summer of 1949. Jeremy did not forget this kindness, which he sought to

---

* The head of chambers was George King-Anningson, a dour character with a large common law practice, and the clerk was the much-loved Bill Gough. There were some ten tenants, none of them silks.

† That is, its members, while doing much of their work in London, were entitled to practise in the courts of the West of England and dine in the Bar Messes there and built up close professional relationships with West Country solicitors.

repay on becoming Liberal Leader in 1967 by nominating Foot for a life peerage.*

As a barrister, Jeremy was courteous, self-confident, quick to learn and never at a loss for a reply, but suffered from an irresistible desire to show off and a haphazard knowledge of the law. In one of his early cases before Plymouth Quarter Sessions, he opened with an impassioned speech to the jury, though this was contrary to the rules of procedure as he had no evidence to call other than that of the client he was defending: behind him, John Foot tugged frantically at his gown to get him to shut up. He was an indifferent cross-examiner, being too theatrical, but good at making a plea in mitigation of sentence, which gave scope to his histrionic gifts. His proudest achievement was his successful defence of a Romford newspaper editor who, at the time of Suez, had been hauled before the House of Commons Privileges Committee for publishing an attack on the petrol allowances of MPs.[6] Most contemporaries felt that he was not terribly serious about the Bar and saw it as something to keep himself going until he got into Parliament. Had he dedicated himself to the profession, it was thought that he might ultimately have built up quite a successful practice in one of those areas – crime or defamation – where there is a jury to impress and showmanship plays a part.

Whatever his shortcomings as a practitioner, Jeremy (like his father before him) was considered by his fellow barristers to be a delightful colleague who cheered up many a dreary hour. In the robing room after a long session in court, he would lighten the atmosphere with gossip, anecdotes and imitations of the day's cases. His table rocked with laughter whenever he lunched in Inner Temple Hall or dined in the Bar Mess of the Devon Sessions at the Clarence Hotel at Exeter. It was felt that, if he did not love the law, he loved the Bar; and there was much rooting

---

* Or as Jeremy characteristically put it to the author: 'He gave me my first brief; I made him a life peer.'

for him there in 1979 during what might be described as his most famous case.

On 3 April 1955, Winston Churchill retired from the premiership at the age of eighty. With his buccaneering spirit and rousing oratory, he had long been a hero of Jeremy, who did a famous imitation of him, and as a fellow MP would relish the occasional chance to sit with him and ask about his days in the Asquith Cabinet – 'the best team ever', as Churchill admitted. He was succeeded by Anthony Eden, who called a snap General Election for 26 May. Jeremy, who had just appeared in the Liberals' annual party political broadcast,* rushed down to North Devon and threw himself into the campaign.

Since his adoption three years earlier, he had spent much of his spare time in the constituency, where he had worked his magic and become a well-known figure. Not only did he know hundreds of voters by name, but he could usually remember some personal fact about them – to do with their family or their pets, their house or their work – which made them feel he cared for them as individuals. He hoped to do well, but knew he could not yet win. The local party was short of both money and members and its organisation left much to be desired; the Liberal agent, the amiable but ineffectual Major Ralph de Pomerai, did little more than put up posters. As with other candidates in traditionally Liberal areas, Jeremy suffered from the fact that many voters, while sympathetic to the cause, believed their vote would be wasted on a party with such meagre prospects: it was necessary to motivate them by setting up a network of thriving branch associations, and this it had not yet been possible to achieve.

---

* At that time, party political broadcasts were live and went out simultaneously on radio and television. The Liberal broadcast of April 1955, a transcript of which was published in the Listener, consisted of Lord Rea, Liberal Leader in the Lords, talking with a somewhat unconvincing show of informality to Jeremy and two other Young Liberals, who explained what Liberalism meant to them.

He was undaunted by these handicaps. In three weeks, he visited every village in the constituency and addressed sixty indoor and twenty-five outdoor meetings. Swallowing her Tory principles, his mother, still sporting her monocle, came down and acted as his chauffeur. He also received support from eminent Liberals he had helped in their own past election battles, such as Frank Byers and Isaac Foot. His Conservative opponent, the Honourable James Lindsay, brother of the 28th Earl of Crawford, was a Bertie Woosterish character and natural target for Jeremy's satire: while he delivered the same dreary speech every time, Jeremy constantly adapted his remarks to suit his audience, and was not afraid to hold forth on such large issues as the Cold War and the future of the British Empire – remote from the immediate concerns of his rustic listeners, but giving them a sense of drama and excitement.

The election results (with 1951 figures in brackets) were as follows:

Lindsay, the Hon. J. L. (Conservative):   16,784   (19,780)
Thorpe, John Jeremy (Liberal):   11,558   (7,326)
Heslop, Harold (Labour):   7,272   (10,632)

The Liberals' share of the vote had risen from one-fifth to one-third, and they had driven Labour back into third place. It was a fine result for Jeremy, for in the country the Party did no better in 1955 than in 1951, picking up fewer than 750,000 votes nationally* and just hanging on to their six existing seats. As North Devon recorded the greatest increase in the Liberal vote of

---

* The total Liberal vote actually fell from 743,512 in 1951 to 722,402 in 1955, although the Party was contesting one more seat. But the turnout in 1955 was lower, so that the average share of the vote polled by Liberal candidates rose from 14.7 per cent to 15.1 per cent, enabling the Party to claim a marginal improvement in their fortunes.

any of the 110 contested seats, Jeremy could claim to be one of the heroes of an otherwise dismal election.

He was determined to win next time, but realised that he could not do so without a good agent. Lilian Prowse, a local party worker in her thirties, married to an insurance agent who was honorary secretary to the local association, had impressed him by her pleasant personality and dedicated work, and replaced the incompetent de Pomerai in 1956. She and Jeremy proved a perfect team, her organising abilities complementing his inspirational talents. She knew the constituency intimately, and arranged busy schedules for his weekend visits to build up support where it was most needed. She came to understand him well and assume something of a mothering role, offering him sensible advice and ensuring that he always showed himself at his best in the constituency. Inevitably, she tended to clash with Ursula whenever that formidable matron descended upon North Devon; but Lilian was also formidable in her way, and Jeremy made it clear that, while he welcomed his mother's visits, Lilian was in charge.

With her support, he aimed to build up the local party to the point where every village had a branch association which was the centre of both political and social life. To this end, he set out to persuade the voters not only that he was a winner who could improve their lives, but that being a Liberal was fun. Apart from addressing political meetings, he was in his element presiding over such occasions as ox-roasts, beauty competitions, quiz nights and the annual Liberal Fair in Barnstaple's Pannier Market. He also caused excitement in those remote parts where national celebrities were rarely seen by asking down such personalities as Lady Violet Bonham Carter and Ludovic Kennedy to appear in 'Any Questions' evenings and present certificates to local Liberals who had recruited twenty new members. Such razzmatazz provided scope for his talents and relief from the dullness of rural life.

He was never one to miss a chance to celebrate; and in the

summer of 1957 he marked the fifth anniversary of his adoption
with a rally addressed by Jo Grimond, a dinner with toasts and
speeches, and a booklet emblazoned with the Thorpe crest and
stuffed with tributes to him solicited from Liberals all over the
country. It was an odd jamboree for an as-yet-unelected candidate, but Jeremy had some cause for self-congratulation. In the
two years since his encouraging 1955 result, Liberal membership
in North Devon had grown from hundreds to thousands, while
the number of local branches had increased from six to thirty.
Victory seemed within his grasp.

A problem which dogged Jeremy from the outset of his career was
lack of money. Until his forties he possessed no significant capital of his own; and though occasional windfalls came his way, his
instinct was not to save these but to spend them on living it up.
Since his father's death he had been supported by his rich Uncle
Geoffry's educational trust; but this had come to an end by the
mid-1950s, and like most young barristers of the time, he found
it hard to live off his fees. He economised by living at home with
his mother and wearing his father's clothes; and when he went
down to North Devon, local Liberals contributed to his travelling
expenses and keep.* But it was clear that, until he had managed
to build up a practice, he would have to find some way of sup-
plementing his legal earnings: there were moments during those
early days when he was reduced to supplying 'tips' to the gossip
columns to bring in a few extra pounds.†

---

* They did not always do so willingly: at one point, Jeremy threatened to resign
as a candidate unless his expenses were met.

† Some details of Jeremy's circumstances may be gleaned from letters written to
his friend Tony Maycock (see Chapter 6). In May 1954 he writes that 'at the
moment cash is frightfully difficult as the Bar has not yet yielded a livelihood'.
A year later he is having trouble meeting 'basic expenses of £750 a year'. And
in August 1956, he writes that his finances are 'desperate' as he is £300 over-
drawn with no immediate prospect of clearing this off. (Papers of the late
Major Maycock in possession of Stephen Carroll.)

Tutoring and journalism are the two traditional standbys for the struggling young barrister. Jeremy had no aptitude for either, but was ideally suited to a new area of part-time employment which also promised to be highly useful experience for his political career – television. Soon after leaving Oxford, he had made his TV début on *Teleclub*, a programme for teenagers presented by the legendary Gilbert Harding.* He had all the qualities to be a successful presenter himself – a polished appearance, a lively manner and (important at that period when almost all TV was live) a talent to improvise. But since its reintroduction in 1946, television had been the preserve of the BBC, which generally employed full-time professionals. However, the commercial network ITV was due to start broadcasting in the autumn of 1955, and the new independent companies were recruiting outside talent on limited contracts. One of them, Associated Rediffusion, advertised that summer for a chairman to present a projected series entitled *The Scientist Replies*: Jeremy, fresh from his election campaign in North Devon, and able to point to an effective recent appearance in a party political broadcast, applied for and got the job.[7]

The Scientist Replies was the brainchild of Norman Macqueen, a film-maker with a scientific background, and produced by the young and talented Brian Taylor, who had worked with the great documentary directors Grierson and Rota. It was a 'Brains Trust' type of programme, in which a panel of experts answered questions submitted by the public; but it proved a refreshing contrast to similar science programmes put out by the BBC in which experts talked down to viewers and no controversial subjects were ever mentioned. The series started on 26 September 1955, going out live from Wembley Studios every Monday evening

---

* Gilbert Harding (1907–60), the first British television star, famous for his sparkling wit and often belligerent manner. In private life, he was notorious for his rudeness, drunkenness and homosexuality.

following the ten o'clock news, and was an instant success with both public and press. This was due in equal measure to the daring questions chosen,* the personalities taking part and Jeremy's talent as chairman. Though he was but twenty-six and knew no more about science than most of the listening public, he was not in the least intimidated by such distinguished regular contributors as the Astronomer Royal, and got everyone going with an easy flow of banter.

The critics were unanimous in their praise. 'Why hasn't the BBC got a programme like *The Scientist Replies*?', asked the *Listener*. The *Daily Mail* praised the series for its 'brisk, straightforward approach'; the *Manchester Guardian* found it 'an admirable blend of serious information and speculation'; the *Observer* thought it 'the most exciting half-hour of popular science in the history of TV'. As chairman, Jeremy was considered 'lively' and 'efficient', one critic finding him so smooth that he looked as if he had stepped out of the electric razor advertisements in the intervals. 'He has an extraordinary but not in the least irritating self-assurance,' wrote the *Evening News*, 'and is wisely content to signpost the discussion with his questions and then leave the experts to get on with it without interruption.' He was particularly congratulated when, on 21 November, he deftly chaired a panel of four Fellows of the Royal Society as they spent half an hour attempting to answer the question: What is Life?

Then, in February 1956, after the programme had been running for five months, to ever-increasing audiences and more enthusiastic notices, it was suddenly announced that it would be axed. This was purely to do with the politics of the television companies: Rediffusion had entered into a close business

---

* The questions touched upon such controversial subjects as sex and reproduction or nuclear physics, which had never before been dealt with so frankly on TV. Each week, Macqueen, Taylor and Jeremy would meet some hours in advance of the broadcast to choose the questions, or if necessary make them up.

relationship with Lew Grade's Birmingham-based ABC Company, which wanted no competition with its own science programme *Meet the Professor*, drawing its 'experts' from Birmingham University. The production team of *The Scientist Replies* were stunned, as were the critics. The *Daily Mail* referred to the 'indignation' which the decision had aroused throughout broadcasting circles and thought it represented 'a sinister trend in ITV'. *The Scientist Replies* had been 'remarkably good of its kind' while the ABC alternative was 'sickeningly dull'.

It was bad luck for Jeremy, deprived of the chance to become a national celebrity at a moment when millions were tuning in to ITV. But he had established himself as a minor television personality, and another opportunity soon beckoned. In March 1956, a month after the end of *The Scientist Replies*, Rediffusion launched *This Week*, one of the great British television programmes which would run for more than thirty years. Brian Taylor became its assistant producer, and recruited Jeremy as a regular interviewer and occasional presenter. This did not give him the same prestige as presenting his own show; nor did it represent as much financial security, since Rediffusion would only sign him up to work on four programmes at a time. On the other hand, *This Week* was produced not in distant Wembley but at the company headquarters, St Catherine's House in the Aldwych, convenient for Jeremy's chambers in the Temple nearby.

Jeremy made regular contributions to *This Week* for the next eight years, relying on them for a large part of his income and becoming well-known to the viewing public. In March 1957, he was sent to cover the independence ceremonies of Ghana, the first British African colony to achieve self-rule;[8] and he soon established himself as the programme's expert on independence movements in colonial territories, often interviewing their leaders (many of whom he befriended) either in London or their own lands. He also contributed to various other programmes, including *Kingsway Corner*, an afternoon show based on live interviews with the public on the pavement outside St Catherine's House. As his law practice increased, it required careful planning to juggle the two careers: sometimes he arrived at a studio from a courtroom or railway station with only minutes to spare. From time to time, he was offered attractive full-time contracts by Rediffusion or other companies – but this would have meant giving up his active political career, which he refused to do.[9] Perhaps had he failed to win his seat he would have changed his mind and gone on to become a leading television personality, as did two other disillusioned Liberals who lost in 1959, Ludovic Kennedy and Robin Day (both of whom worked for ITN at this time but later achieved fame at the BBC).

As an interviewer, Jeremy was polished and slick, adept at establishing a rapport with his subject and switching to a lighter or more serious mood as the moment required. He rarely probed very deeply into anything and tended to give his interviewees an easy ride (though the whole approach was infinitely more respectful in those days than it would subsequently become). Some felt he played up too much to his huge invisible audience, so that he failed to achieve the intimate effect of 'a friend in the room': this was noticeable in his political broadcasts, highly professional but lacking the 'fireside' touch mastered by both Macmillan and Wilson. But when as a broadcaster he faced a real audience, Jeremy was at his superb best. In the late 1950s, he began to appear regularly on BBC Radio's *Any Questions*, then chaired by Freddy Grisewood and based in the West Country; and it is for his sparkling contributions to that programme over twenty-five years that he is probably still best remembered by millions.

After each of its General Election disasters, the Liberal Party ritually established a high-powered committee with the aim of reorganising and revitalising itself for the next election; and following his creditable result in 1955, Jeremy was appointed to the new committee, chaired by Sir Andrew McFadyean. This discussed various reforms and strategies, but felt that little more could be achieved under the leadership of Clement Davies: though a man of courage and integrity who had held the Party together during the dark years, he was now in his seventies, suffered from a drink problem and had become something of a joke on account of his long-winded speeches (imitated by Jeremy in a perfect Welsh accent). Jeremy was involved in the delicate manoeuvres which resulted in Davies reluctantly standing down in September 1956 at the Liberal Assembly at Folkestone. Of the five remaining Liberal MPs, Bowen had no ambitions for the leadership and Hopkin Morris was disqualified from it by holding the Deputy Speakership, while Holt and Wade were handicapped by the fact that they held their seats thanks to pacts with the Conservatives: this left just the Chief Whip Jo Grimond, MP for Orkney and Shetland since 1950 and the only sitting Liberal to have won against both a Labour and a Tory opponent, who was duly confirmed as Davies' successor.

He was in any case the obvious choice – a youthful forty-three, splendidly handsome with a patrician manner, a fine speaker who relished the cut-and-thrust of intellectual debate. As a product of Eton and Balliol, and Asquith's grandson-in-law (his wife Laura was the daughter of Lady Violet), he belonged to Liberalism's social elite. But his political instincts were radical: he sought to establish the Liberals as 'the radical alternative to socialism', and was a man after the hearts of the Radical Reform Group set up by Jeremy and others in 1953 (which effectively dissolved itself now that the Party was led by an advocate of its views). The arrival of this inspiring new leader boosted both the morale of the Party and its standing in the country. The donnish Grimond was especially popular at the universities, recovering for the Liberals something of their reputation as 'the party of the intellectuals' which they had lost to Labour in 1945. With his youthful energy and receptiveness to new ideas, he appealed to students as well as dons: it was during his leadership, and partly due to his encouragement, that the Young Liberals emerged as an aggressively radical movement.

Like many of the younger generation, Jeremy looked up to Grimond with hero-worshipping admiration. Grimond for his part saw Jeremy as an asset to the Party, but never warmed to him personally – 'not a man whose company I enjoy', he told his godson Magnus Linklater twenty years later.[10] Despite their common educational background, they were opposites in many ways: Jeremy representing style, Grimond substance; Jeremy a product of Trinity, Grimond of Balliol; Jeremy the Lloyd Georgian, Grimond the Asquithian; Jeremy the gregarious show-man, Grimond the lofty patrician. In reality, there was a touch of the poseur about Grimond, whose intellectualism was rather shallow; but while the two men worked closely together over the next decade, and Grimond appeared to treat Jeremy as his heir presumptive, there always remained an imperfect sympathy between them. ('He's the life and soul of the Party,' Grimond would exclaim sarcastically when Jeremy was showing off. 'What would we do without him?'[11]) On the other hand, Jeremy got on splendidly with Grimond's wife and mother-in-law and could rely on their support: Lady Violet was now a kind of Dowager Empress to the Liberal Party, and Jeremy took his place as her court entertainer.

Grimond's appointment as leader coincided with the disas-trous Suez venture of the Eden Government. Although Liberals were at first divided in their reactions to this, the invasion of the Canal Zone at the beginning of November 1956 was roundly condemned by Grimond, and his parliamentary colleagues fell into line. In the country, this produced a modest wave of defec-tions to the Liberals by disillusioned Conservatives. Jeremy, with his gut dislike of blimpish Toryism and sympathy with nation-alist movements in former imperial territories, was particularly vociferous in his denunciation of Eden, even at the risk of alienating some patriotic Liberals in his constituency. Suez was also the occasion for what many considered his finest performance at the Oxford Union, where he was invited to debate against his old Conservative rival William Rees-Mogg.* Beginning quietly and humorously, he gradually built up a blistering attack on the Government: at a key moment of his speech, he caused a sensation by breaking the dramatic news that Sir Edward Boyle, another ex-President, had just resigned from the Government over their handling of the crisis.

Jeremy's desire to win the approval of his new leader may have owed something to the fact that his two closest friends in the Liberal Party, Megan Lloyd George and Dingle Foot, who had been like political parents to him, had both recently deserted to Labour – a step prompted mainly by their desire to get back into Parliament, though Megan could not bear to be in the same party as Violet, while Dingle could not bear *not* to be in the same party as Megan. In 1957, both were returned as Labour MPs at by-elections, Megan at Carmarthen in March, Dingle at Ipswich in October. Jeremy, who felt 'shattered and bitter'† about their defections, campaigned against them with a heavy heart. Carmarthen was particularly galling, as the vacancy had arisen through the death of the much-respected Liberal MP Sir Rhys Hopkin Morris; the lacklustre Liberal candidate took a pro-Suez line in an effort to win the votes of local Conservatives (who were not fielding a candidate), causing embarrassment to those Liberals who came to support him. In his discursive memoirs,

---

* Then chief leader-writer for the *Financial Times*. Jeremy was supported by the young socialist Bryan Magee, and Rees-Mogg by Peter Tapsell, a former socialist who had become a Conservative: all four had been Presidents of the Oxford Union within the past few years. It was said to be the most important debate at the Union since 'King and Country' in 1933.

† His words to the author in 1994. But it was not in Jeremy's nature to allow politics to influence personal relationships, and even before he had joined them in the House of Commons, he had resumed his close friendship with both 'renegades'.

Grimond hardly mentions Jeremy, except to pay tribute to his support during that grim winter campaign when 'his good humour made the whole experience more tolerable'.[12] The Liberals' loss of the seat reduced their parliamentary party to five, giving rise to the joke that they could all share a London taxi or squeeze into a telephone box.

Despite Carmarthen, the period 1955–59 was quite successful for the Liberals in terms of by-elections, in the sense that, unusually for them, they tended on each occasion to do distinctly better than at the last General Election at which they had contested the seat. Though victory remained elusive, it was nevertheless an exciting time for the Party, which experienced (admittedly from a miserably low point) the first significant revival in its fortunes since the 1920s. In the canon of Liberal history, the names and dates of these by-elections read like a roll of battle honours. For instance, at Torquay in December 1955, just six months after the General Election, the flamboyant local businessman Peter Bessell increased the Liberal vote by 10 per cent. At Hereford in February 1956, the journalist Frank Owen, who had been Liberal MP there from 1929 to 1931, came within 2,000 votes of recapturing the seat. At North Dorset in June 1957, Frank Byers' old seat, the Conservative majority was halved. At Rochdale in February 1958, the television presenter Ludovic Kennedy won 36 per cent of the vote and beat the Conservatives who had previously held the seat into third place.

In such spare time as he had, Jeremy took an eager part in these campaigns and threw himself into the fray. In the four contests mentioned above, he won the gratitude and friendship of the candidates, who were both cheered by his participation and convinced that it had contributed to their good results. At Torquay, he formed a close personal and political friendship with Bessell, who shared his sense of showmanship and fantasy: it was a relationship destined to last twenty years and have dramatic consequences. At Rochdale, Kennedy feared Jeremy might be lynched when he addressed a working-class audience wearing one of his most extravagant outfits, complete with brown bowler and yellow gloves: in fact, they were enchanted.[13] Christopher Booker, who came from a prominent Liberal family in North Dorset and was nineteen in 1957, has recalled what it was like campaigning there with Jeremy in that summer's by-election:

> For me, that was Jeremy's golden age, before he got into Parliament and lost his youthful edge. He gave total enthusiasm to whatever he was doing and treated a by-election as if it was the most important event in the world. He had an extraordinary ability both to cheer up his followers and send up his opponents. On the eve of poll, he addressed two open-air rallies from a farm cart, at Blandford and Wimborne: thousands came to hear, and Jeremy was superb and baited the Conservatives as they emerged from their indoor meetings. At Wimborne, he reduced a heckler to silence by saying: 'Sir, what you say reminds me of what I heard in Canada when I met Mr Diefenbaker . . .' He admitted to me later that he had never met Diefenbaker – a typical example of his *chutzpah*.
>
> On polling day, I accompanied him as he toured the constituency with a loud-hailer: he hailed almost everyone he saw and would have something personal to say to each of them, such as: 'You up there on the ladder, as the son and grandson of Tory MPs let me tell you why you should vote Liberal . . .' He got so carried away that it was a while before we noticed that people were not responding and we had accidentally strayed into Somerset. He was not worried and suggested we call for tea on the local Liberal magnate, Sir Arthur Hobhouse. When we reached his seat, Hadspen House, Jeremy blared through his megaphone: 'Come out, Sir Arthur, we've come for tea!' Such fun it was . . .[14]

From Jeremy's point of view, the most significant of these by-elections took place in March 1958 in Torrington, a constituency bordering on North Devon and sharing its traditions. The vacancy had arisen when the sitting MP, George Lambert, succeeded to the peerage of his father who had been MP before him. The Lamberts had 'ruled' the division since 1891: originally they were Liberals, but since 1931 they had adhered to the National Liberal Party* which had become virtually indistinguishable from the Conservatives. The 'real' Liberals had therefore long ceased to have a base there; they had not contested the seat in 1951 or 1955; and although in 1956, largely through Jeremy's influence, they had adopted a prospective candidate in the form of Ambrose Fulford, a prosperous local farmer, he stood down when faced with the national publicity of a by-election.† To fight it, the Liberals chose Mark Bonham Carter, son of Lady Violet, who had been the unsuccessful Liberal candidate in Barnstaple in 1945: though superior in manner and unimpressive in appearance, he had a sharp intellect, a brilliant war record, good local connections‡ and the glamour of being Grimond's brother-in-law and Asquith's grandson.

---

* The National Liberals (or Liberal Nationals as they had been known until 1948) were the old 'Simonite' wing of the Party which had split from the main 'Samuelite' wing in 1931 over the issue of protection. From 1932, the Samuelites were in opposition while the Simonites continued to participate in the Conservative-dominated National Government. Under the Woolton–Teviot Agreement of 1947, Conservatives and National Liberals agreed to field joint candidates in former Liberal seats under the ticket 'Liberal and Conservative', to the fury of traditional Liberals (including Jeremy, who wrote heated letters to the press on the subject) who saw this as a trick to mislead their supporters into voting Conservative.

† Both Jeremy and Fulford's daughter Gladys have assured the author that Fulford stood down voluntarily on health grounds; but others (including Bonham Carter) believed that he was reluctantly persuaded to do so by Jeremy to make way for a more high-profile candidate.

‡ His aunt-by-marriage, Betty Asquith, owned the beautiful Clovelly estate near Bideford.

There was little love lost between Jeremy and 'my brother of Torrington' (as he addressed him at his adoption meeting): they were incompatible personalities, and whereas Jeremy saw himself as Lloyd George's spiritual heir, Bonham Carter was in every sense an Asquithian.* But it was clear that Bonham Carter could achieve nothing without the support of Jeremy and the political machine he had built up in the neighbouring seat; and Jeremy threw all his weight behind him, planning a military-style campaign and raising money for the fray. Laura Grimond later told Susan Crosland that Jeremy had 'flogged his guts out to get Mark [her brother] in'.[15] No doubt an element of self-interest played a part: he relished the chance to try out his new organisation and conduct a dress rehearsal for his own coming fight. It was a historic contest, one of the first by-elections to be televised and in which opinion polls played a part. It was also marked by the strident participation of Lady Violet, who was said to lose the Liberals votes every time she referred in public to 'my boy': on that account at least, Jeremy could warmly sympathise with the candidate.[16]

When the poll was declared on the night of 21 March, Bonham Carter had won by 219 votes – the first Liberal by-election gain since 1929. It was ironic that Asquith's grandson should have made good the damage done to the Liberal Parliamentary Party a year earlier by Lloyd George's daughter; and Jeremy, though he may have seen in the victor a possible future rival for the leadership, sensed in the victory a precursor of his own.

Something must be said about Jeremy's domestic life and family relationships at this period. Throughout the 1950s, he was precluded by lack of money from setting up an establishment of his

---

* 'What do you consider my greatest electoral asset?' Bonham Carter once asked Jeremy. 'That your arrogance passes for shyness,' came the frank reply.

own. He continued to live with his mother at Limpsfield, Surrey, from where he commuted by rail to his chambers at the Temple.* If he wished to spend a night in London, he could stay either at the National Liberal Club or with his doting and still formidable octogenerian grandmother, Gwladys Norton-Griffiths, at her mansion flat in Cadogan Gardens, Chelsea. In North Devon, he resided at Broomhills, a Victorian villa set in wooded grounds outside Barnstaple, as a paying guest of the owner Mrs Chappel, a Liberal widow who adored Jeremy and provided yet another mother figure in his life.

Jeremy and his mother continued to have much the same double-edged relationship as before, involving intense closeness and stormy rows. As always, Ursula was devoted to her son's career. She was constantly inviting to dinner people she thought it would be useful for him to know, such as the rising Tory politician Ted Heath. For his sake, she gradually abandoned her own involvement in Conservative politics, helped him campaign in North Devon, and stood as an Independent when she offered herself for re-election to Surrey County Council in 1958. Jeremy for his part was his mother's ally in her rivalries with other leading women of the locality: he saw to it that she took the credit when he persuaded their neighbour, the pianist Eileen Joyce, to come out of retirement and give a concert at the Albert Hall in aid of local charities. In the eyes of friends and relations, mother and son seemed almost unnaturally attached; but he increasingly resented her possessiveness and interference in his life, and their quarrels were frequent and bitter.

Both of his sisters, to whom he had been close in childhood, had ended up living abroad with their much older husbands, father figures who offered escape from the mother who had treated them with such cruelty and neglect. After their long affair

---

*Jeremy, who had passed his driving test while at school, also kept a Baby Austin motor car at Limpsfield.

in London and the Philippines, Lavinia married Colonel Eric Bradley in the United States as soon as he was able to get a divorce. Camilla, who had worked in advertising and become known in London lesbian circles, caused surprise in 1955, aged thirty, by marrying Enrique Ellinger, a German–Jewish mining engineer in his fifties who had made a fortune in South America; he had fallen in love with her after meeting her at a party to which she had gone dressed as a man; neither Ursula nor Jeremy was invited to the wedding in London, following which the couple departed for Buenos Aires. Both marriages were happy and blessed with children, and by the 1960s both sisters had returned to live in England with their families: Bradley was posted as a defence attaché to the United States Embassy in London, while the Ellingers settled prosperously in Sussex following Enrique's retirement from business. Though there were periodic family reunions, and Ursula took a close interest in her five grandchildren, the sisters remained wary of their mother; and Jeremy's closeness to Ursula and absorption in his own career left little room for a resumption of the old fraternal intimacy (though he made frequent and futile efforts to persuade Ellinger to donate some of his fortune to the Liberal Party).

Despite his professional and political commitments, Jeremy continued to lead a hectic social life. He had the reputation of making a party go. He was much in demand as an after-dinner speaker, godfather and best man, his participation generally guaranteeing merriment. He often entertained his friends with wonderful performances as a mimic. One of his best 'turns' was a skit of the Tory Cabinet in which he imitated not just voices but such physical peculiarities as Macmillan's stoop, Macleod's limp and Butler's withered arm. When Dr Bodkin Adams was tried at the Old Bailey in 1957 for having allegedly hastened the deaths of female patients who had mentioned him in their wills, Jeremy attended the hearings and later gave superb renderings of the highlights of the case, imitating everyone. Similarly, anyone going with him to the theatre might afterwards be treated to a take-off of the entire cast. He could have had an outstanding career as a professional entertainer – as Nicholas Parsons, who befriended him during this period, later wrote in his memoirs.[17]

Foreign travel played a part in his life. He often went to stay with that swaggering baronet, his uncle Peter Norton-Griffiths, who became chief executive of Shell first in Lisbon and then in Brussels and lived with his rich wife in great style in both capitals. His work as a television interviewer involved frequent trips abroad, sometimes to distant parts of the Commonwealth; and he always brought a spirit of enjoyment to these short professional journeys and made new friends. On a less exalted level, cheap package holidays were coming into vogue and Jeremy was an eager subscriber to these, visiting such destinations as the South of France, the Balearics and Corsica; not only did they suit his modest purse, but he enjoyed meeting the people from varied backgrounds to be encountered on such excursions; he often went with friends, who would be entertained by imitations of their fellow travellers and humorous fantasies arising out of small incidents.[18]

Although Jeremy had a gift for making friends and was liked by most of those who knew him, he was not universally popular. Some saw him as a snob, a poseur and a vulgar exhibitionist; some found him sinister and devious; some were put off by what they regarded as his extreme ambition and egocentricity. Many of his admirers would undoubtedly have been horrified had they known that he was leading a secret homosexual life (as will be examined in the next chapter); but this was suspected by remarkably few of his acquaintances, even among those who shared his tastes in this regard.

Jeremy was thirty in April 1959, and already something of a national celebrity. Every month, millions saw him on *This Week* or heard him on *Any Questions*. His doings were often mentioned (not always flatteringly) in gossip columns such as the *Sunday Express*'s 'Crossbencher'. His name had recently become associated with a number of high-profile causes. He was an ardent platform campaigner against the apartheid regime in South Africa, and a ceaseless critic of Sir Roy Welensky's Central African Federation which stood in the path of native aspirations to self-government. At home, he launched colourful attacks, in the press and sometimes in the courts, on the Potato and Egg Marketing Boards, which he saw as sinister monopolies designed to force out small producers: he called them 'packers' rackets' and 'the fiddle on the griddle'.

In North Devon, his and Lilian Prowse's efforts to build up a political organisation had been crowned with success. The Liberal Association, which in 1955 had consisted of six branches with thirty-five officers, now had thirty-eight branches with some seven hundred officers and over four thousand members, one-tenth of the entire electorate. The victory at Torrington had boosted their morale and demonstrated that Liberalism was not a hopeless cause. Jeremy had built up good relations with the local newspaper, the *North Devon Journal Herald*, which gave wide coverage to his activities and speeches. He also benefited from the assistance of Dominic le Foe, a gifted young man involved in the theatrical world who lent his talents to Liberal candidates in their campaigns. Meanwhile there seemed little to fear from James Lindsay, or 'Mr Utter Complacency' as Jeremy dubbed him, who had proved a lacklustre and ineffective MP.

When the General Election was called for 8 October 1959, the machine was ready to roll. As before, Jeremy toured the constituency addressing dozens of indoor and outdoor meetings: but this time, his audiences consisted more of cheering supporters than bemused strangers. Again, his mother came down to support him, having finally been persuaded to exchange her monocle for a pair of spectacles. (He afterwards wrote to a friend that 'Mama was SUPERB throughout'.[19]) Among the others who

campaigned for him was Keith Kyle, who intended to join the
Labour Party after the election but first wished to help Jeremy
and other old friends from the Oxford University Liberal Club.
During the final days, wearing his brown bowler at a rakish angle
and a rosette in each lapel, Jeremy drove through Barnstaple and
the other main towns with a loud-hailer, using a technique he
had perfected in recent by-elections. 'Good morning, Mrs Smith.
Let's see the victory torches blazing in the streets! Hello, removal
men. Let's see some more removals on Thursday!'

Tom Pocock, a young *Evening Standard* journalist, was sent to
cover the campaigns of Jeremy in North Devon, Mark Bonham
Carter in Torrington and Peter Bessell in Torquay. He later
recalled his first meeting with Jeremy:

> He sat at a desk at the end of a long room and I recall this strange,
> rather hypnotic face looking up: round, chimpanzee eyes, great
> arched eyebrows, high cheekbones, humorous mouth; a face that
> was part Mephistopheles, part clown. He was direct and amusing
> and (as I soon saw) had completely bewitched his future con-
> stituents. This was the period when St James's dandies were
> dressing in Edwardian clothes, as indeed were Teddy Boys;
> Thorpe's wardrobe was even more eccentric but it was accepted
> by most of the blunt Devonians without raising an eyebrow. He
> was a 'mother's boy' but that did not bother the robust Devonians
> either. He seemed something fresh, original and enormously
> attractive. He did seem a metropolitan man but then so did
> Bonham Carter and Bessell. Yet Bonham Carter was rather dry,
> humourless and donnish and Bessell, who was usually dressed in
> a very clean, belted trench coat, seemed a bit 'fly'. Thorpe was just
> highly original . . .[20]

Jeremy told Pocock that he expected to win by 'a close margin'.
To Kyle, the old friend who had witnessed his first steps in politics, he confided that, balancing all the factors, including the

membership of the thirty-eight branches of the local party, the promises received during the campaign, the likely effect of his personality on wavering and uncommitted voters, and the natural advantage his Tory opponent would have as the sitting MP, he expected to win by about 350 votes.[21]

In fact, when the votes were counted at the Queen's Hall in Barnstaple, he turned out to have a majority over Lindsay of 362. The result (with 1955 figures in brackets) was:

Thorpe, John Jeremy (Liberal):   15,831   (11,558)
Lindsay, the Hon. J. L. (Conservative): 15,469   (16,784)
Pitt, G. W. (Labour):   5,567   (7,272)

Having increased the Liberal vote by some 4,200 in 1955, Jeremy had now increased it again by roughly the same number, stealing some 3,000 further votes from the other two parties and persuading some 1,300 people to vote for him who had not turned out last time. It was an impressive achievement, for it in no way reflected a national trend. Despite Grimond's national popularity, their performance in the country was bitterly disappointing to the Liberals, whose average vote in the seats they contested rose only from 15.1 per cent to 16.9 per cent.* Of the six Liberal MPs sitting at the dissolution, only five were returned, the loser being Jeremy's recently elected neighbour, Mark Bonham Carter in Torrington, who after holding the seat for just eighteen months was comfortably defeated by the charismatic Tory racing personality Percy Browne.

As befitted Jeremy's great moment, the night of the count was one of high drama in Barnstaple. The result was clearly going to be close, the crowd was large, and the tension and excitement were intense. When the figures were read out just before

----

* On the other hand, almost twice as many seats were being contested (216 as opposed to 110 in 1955), while the number of lost deposits fell from 60 to 52.

midnight from the small balcony, Jeremy's supporters went wild
with joy and cheered for a full half-hour. He was carried
shoulder-high to the Liberal Club in Cross Street where, his
mother at his side, he made an emotional speech of thanks. 'This
is not my victory but our victory. I think you know how much
I love North Devon and the people who live within its borders.'
The following evening saw the magnificent spectacle of a torchlight victory procession, the River Taw resplendent in the
reflected light: 6,000 took part, led by Jeremy carrying a banner
which had been made to commemorate the last Liberal victory
there in 1935.*

---

* These victory processions became known as 'Jeremy's Nurembergs', but had in
  fact originated with his Edwardian predecessor Sir Ernest Soares. The figure
  of 6,000 included Torrington Liberals who, following Bonham Carter's defeat,
  had come over to celebrate Jeremy's success.

6

TENDENCIES

DURING THE 1950s, while Jeremy Thorpe was involving himself in politics, broadcasting and the law, he was also engaging in a secret homosexual life. This does not seem to have played much part at Oxford, where he concentrated on short-term ambitions and lived in a close-knit world. But on coming down from the university and entering the great anonymous world of London, he drifted into the shadowy homosexual subculture of the period. This partly involved casual affairs with men met in bars and other public places. It also involved close and conspiratorial friendships (sometimes overtly sexual, often not) with men who shared his tastes and whom he felt he could trust.

Homosexual behaviour was still highly illegal and regarded as shockingly immoral at this time. Those who engaged in it were liable to blackmail and, if exposed, risked social ostracism, vicious criminal penalties and the ruin of their careers. There was a traditional tolerance in certain aristocratic and 'artistic' circles, but not among the respectable professional classes from which Jeremy hailed. In the early 1950s, the defection of the raffishly homosexual double agent Guy Burgess to Moscow led to something of a witch hunt in Britain: some prominent men were prosecuted, including Lord Montagu of Beaulieu whom Jeremy had known at Eton and Oxford, sent to prison with two friends in 1954 on dubious evidence following a sensational trial. However, partly as a result of the controversy surrounding that case, the Government set up the Wolfenden Committee to examine the law relating to homosexuality, which reported in 1957.

On the other hand, for at least some of its aficionados at the time, homosexuality also represented an exciting and conspiratorial world. The idea of operating clandestinely outside the normal scheme of things lent a bohemian spice to life, and there was an element of thrill inherent in the risks involved, 'like feasting with panthers'. Homosexual circles, obsessed as they were by secrecy, loyalty and code language, had something of a masonic air. Homosexuality could also overcome barriers between classes: gentlemen traditionally sought pleasure with working-class youths such as guardsmen, often to the benefit of both parties.

There has been much discussion as to whether homosexuals are born or made, whether their inclinations result mainly from their genes or environment. What can one tell in Jeremy's case? On the genetic front, his sister Camilla was known in London lesbian circles; his father may have been bisexual; his mother's brother, Sir Peter Norton-Griffiths, led a louche homosexual life; and the three brothers of his maternal grandmother (one of whom committed suicide) all appear to have had homosexual leanings. On the environmental front, he had a gentle, rather feminine father and a formidable, rather masculine mother. His father died when he was fifteen, leaving his mother the dominant influence in his life – a classic 'Oedipal' situation. From his earliest years, he displayed a love of fantasy and intrigue, dissimulation and exhibitionism, play-acting and risk-taking – all characteristics associated with a homosexual double life.* He also sought to emulate his hero Lloyd George, who had thrived and kept up his political adrenalin on a risky and promiscuous (though in his case heterosexual) sex life.

When it came to sexual relations with men, Jeremy generally took the dominant role. Like many of his generation, he was conditioned by early experiences to act quickly to avoid getting caught. He did, however, enjoy the preliminaries, the pick-up, the art of seduction. He had a strong sex drive and threw himself lustfully into the act. He would arrive for an amorous assignation in his formal clothes, lay aside his furled umbrella and copy of *The Times*, carefully undress – and then behave with animal passion. He seems to have been excited by the idea of fitting rapid amorous escapades into the mainstream of a busy conventional life. His choice of partners seems to have embraced all classes, from heirs to peerages to rough proletarian youths. On visits to Africa, he developed a taste for 'beautiful black bodies'. If he had a general preference, it seems to have been for men who were young, handsome, slightly effeminate and easily dominated.

There is no doubt that Jeremy derived much pleasure from homosexuality – both the physical pleasures of sex and the cerebral pleasures of belonging to a secret society. At the same time, he suffered intense feelings of guilt. The thrills he experienced were those of a man who knows he is breaking the rules and will be crucified if caught. As a result, with one exception, he would never be able to admit publicly to his homosexuality or talk about it openly – even forty years later, when attitudes had changed and everyone knew about his past. The sole exception was the admission made on his behalf by his defence counsel at his trial that as a young man he had possessed

---

* As a boy, he also suffered from *petit mal* epilepsy, said by Freud to be a condition associated with both homosexuality and a 'gambling' personality: see Note 2 to Chapter 2.

'homosexual tendencies' – an admission made with reluctance to prevent the prosecution calling witnesses to his past sex life. (It must, however, be noted that Jeremy was always sympathetic to the campaign to change the law on homosexuality in which, as will be seen, he became active after his election to Parliament.)

Some people claimed to deduce the fact that Jeremy was homosexual from his exhibitionist manner, his relationship with his mother and the fact that he was frequently to be seen in the company of handsome youths. When a dinner party of Liberal MPs asked Jo Grimond in 1976 when he had first become aware of it, he replied: 'I suspected it from the moment I met him and when I met his mother, I had no further doubts.'[1] On the whole, however, remarkably few who knew Jeremy seem to have had much inkling of his proclivities. He was protected by the fierce cult of secrecy which pervaded the homosexual world, and the fact that it simply never occurred to most people then to think of anyone as homosexual unless they were advertising their preferences or involved in scandal. Indeed, even fellow homosexuals among his acquaintance were often slow to realise that he shared their interests: although Lord Montagu knew him at Eton, Oxford and later in Parliament, they never discussed their common tastes, though Montagu gradually got to know of them through rumour and seeing him in certain company.

In pursuing his homosexual adventures, Jeremy was generally discreet. He made his sexual arrangements with care and accomplished them with speed. He tended to be 'cellular' in his relationships, most of his partners being unaware of each other. Yet as time passed he became less cautious in his behaviour and began to take unnecessary risks. He made little attempt to disguise his intentions from those he was trying to seduce, and seemed to get a kick out of flaunting his acquaintance with rough working-class youths before conventional middle-class

friends, presenting them as young people he was trying to help.*
He also developed a taste for sending mildly compromising
romantic letters which were liable to cause embarrassment if a
recipient turned nasty or they fell into the wrong hands: as an
MP, he often tempted providence by writing such letters on
House of Commons stationery. It was as though he were playing
a game with himself, seeing how close he could sail to the wind,
how far his mental agility and social talents could see him
through hazardous situations. Possibly he suffered from a subconscious longing to be caught and punished, for however often
he 'got away with it', he was bound to face a degree of exposure
and retribution sooner or later: even before his election to
Parliament, there were episodes which might have proved disastrous but for a mixture of deft handling and good luck.

A conspicuous and colourful figure in Jeremy's early homosexual life was Henry Upton, the gigantic and scandalous heir to
Viscount Templetown, twelve years older than Jeremy, who had
met him in London during the summer of 1948 and fascinated
him with his outrageous hedonism.[2] When Jeremy went up to
Oxford, Henry had gone out to Calcutta to join two English
friends, both of whom were to play a part in Jeremy's story –
Tony Maycock and John Wilkins. Major Anthony Maycock
(1921–95), a gallant survivor of the Burma Campaign, had been
Henry's closest wartime friend in India, and had gone up to
Oxford in 1945 where his admirers included the historian A. L.
Rowse. Wilkins (1930–94) was the handsome but delinquent
son of a wealthy family who had run away from his public school

---

*For example, Jeremy once surprised Lloyd George's daughter Lady Olwen
Carey Evans by visiting her in Wales with a handsome working-class youth
whom he introduced as his chauffeur. (Information from Robin Carey Evans.)
And later on, he had no compunction about introducing Norman Josiffe to
various respectable people, many of whom were frankly puzzled as to why he
should know such a person.

after trying to set fire to it, and at the age of sixteen had become the lover of both Upton and Maycock: it was largely to protect him from police inquiries that Maycock had taken him out to India, where Maycock obtained a job as a schoolmaster and helped Wilkins embark on a career as a journalist.

In 1951, after Henry had got himself and his friends into trouble in India by abusing the position Maycock had obtained for him as a PT instructor at his school, the three of them returned to England and visited Oxford to see Jeremy, who seemed delighted to meet them all. Henry had two requests to make of him. John Wilkins was about to be prosecuted for his past misdeeds, and Henry wondered if Jeremy, with his legal connections, might be able to help him. And Henry himself, who was in financial straits and no longer on speaking terms with his parents, asked if Jeremy might intercede with them on his behalf. Jeremy's Oxford friend Christopher Bourke begged him not to get involved with 'this chilling character': but the double invitation to help a young man of angelic beauty and mediate between the members of a noble family was a challenge he could not resist. He was able to do little for Wilkins, who went to prison for six months. But he did succeed in helping Henry: he visited the dour Lord and Lady Templetown at Kirkudbright in Scotland and persuaded them to give their son some money to meet current expenses, a windfall which Henry immediately spent on new clothes and other non-essentials.

After further discussions through Jeremy, the Templetowns agreed to give Henry £1,500 to go out to Western Australia, holding out the prospect of further sums from a family trust once he had settled down there. Henry set out at the end of 1952, having charged Jeremy with negotiating the release of the trust money. Jeremy was making progress when the news arrived that Henry had been arrested in Perth and sent to prison for molesting adolescent boys. Jeremy nevertheless managed to reassure the Templetowns that Henry, if he got his money, would change his ways. In July 1954, on the eve of Henry's release, Jeremy wrote to Maycock that after much bargaining he had achieved 'a very good settlement' amounting to some £16,000 for Henry (worth about £500,000 today). He hoped Henry would now settle in a country such as Sweden, which possessed liberal laws.

Henry in fact made for India again, where he took a house in Poona and sent Jeremy a first-class air ticket to join him there that autumn for a celebratory reunion. Jeremy duly spent a fortnight in Poona celebrating with Henry. On the eve of his return to England, he ran into his Oxford friend Michael Ogle at the Taj Mahal Hotel at Bombay, where he was sharing the bridal suite with Henry. After Jeremy's departure, Ogle accepted out of curiosity an invitation from Henry to return with him to Poona, where he found his host living with a harem of Anglo-Indian boys, cavorting around on massive motorcycles and sporting a large collection of whips. Henry explained that he had been admitted to the murderous Thugee cult, but Ogle felt he was just an outrageous poseur.

By the end of 1954, Henry was back in England, where Jeremy invited him to stay with his mother at Stonewalls for Christmas and the New Year. This was not a success: Ursula was alarmed by Henry's violent remarks,* got to hear of his shady past and eventually threw him out of her house. In April 1955, Henry, who had purchased an Aston Martin sports car with what remained of his money, offered to act as Jeremy's chauffeur in North Devon during the General Election campaign – an offer which Jeremy accepted, though Henry was an inconvenient helper as he told all and sundry that he believed 'the common people' ought not

---

* When Jeremy's sister Lavinia and her husband Colonel Bradley turned up late for Christmas lunch, explaining they had been held up by traffic, Henry burst out: 'If anyone got in my road in India, I'd crush them like a chicken!' During Jeremy's trial, Ursula told various people that he was not truly homosexual but had been 'led astray' by this nobly born reprobate. (Information from Lavinia Bradley.)

to have the vote, and he unceremoniously fled as soon as he heard that Ursula was coming down to help her son. Even now, Jeremy continued to associate with Henry and help him out of scrapes. He acted for him in a lawsuit arising out of a road accident; and when the *Sunday Pictorial* threatened to expose the murky past of Henry, then teaching at a preparatory school, Jeremy tried in vain to intercede with the editor.

Bombarded at his law chambers with irate letters from Henry's trustees and creditors, Jeremy had now had enough. He belatedly understood what friends such as Christopher Bourke and Michael Ogle had tried to tell him – that here was a man who would be a drain on his goodwill and cause him endless embarrassment. In just two years, Henry had run through the inheritance Jeremy had worked to obtain for him. In August 1956, Jeremy wrote to Maycock asking him to tell Henry he could do no more for him.

Some months later, Henry was back in trouble. Having sold the Aston Martin and spent the money, he was again in debt; following his exposure in the press, he had lost his teaching job and the police were once more on his trail. With the shadows closing in, he drew up a will couched in flamboyant language, declaring that he was disinheriting Jeremy Thorpe, 'whose friendship has proved limited', in favour of Maycock, to whom he sent his signet ring and other valuables. Using money borrowed from a widow, he then chartered a fifteen-ton motor cruiser on the Sussex coast. In February 1957, the vessel ran aground near Chichester: there was no sign of Henry and (so far as is known) he was never seen again. The press ran headlines about the mystery of the 'peer's missing heir'. There were no other heirs to the Templetown viscountcy, which was deemed extinct when Henry's father died in 1981.

Jeremy did not escape notice in the police investigations that followed Henry's disappearance. Among the articles found in the cabin of the deserted boat was Henry's passport, naming J. J.

Thorpe Esq. of Lamb Building, Temple, as the person to be contacted in an emergency. Jeremy accordingly received a visit from the police at his chambers, but regretted that he could cast no light on the mystery, having seen nothing of Henry for months. Jeremy meanwhile remained close to Henry's two long-suffering friends Maycock and Wilkins, now living together on Brixton Hill. Maycock became a confidant of Jeremy, who proposed him for membership of the National Liberal Club; and Jeremy began a long, intermittent affair with the handsome but unstable Wilkins, which came to an end in June 1966 in circumstances which will be described in Chapter 10.

Jeremy's association with Henry Upton illuminates various aspects of his personality: his willingness to help an outcast; his fascination with devil-may-care aristocrats, and with louche and outrageous characters; his ability to switch between the respectable (winning the confidence of Henry's parents) and the shady (hobnobbing with Henry himself). Henry undoubtedly influenced Jeremy, encouraging him to regard sex as an act of crude domination, and instilling a play-acting interest in violent fantasies: as Maycock put it to the author, 'the whole Norman Scott business was pure Henry'.

There was one man acquainted with both Jeremy and Henry Upton who was convinced that the former was responsible for the disappearance of the latter. He believed that Jeremy, while in control of Henry's affairs during 1952–4, had helped himself to more of Henry's money than he was entitled to; that Henry had belatedly become aware of this fact, and was threatening to use it against Jeremy; and that Jeremy had consequently arranged for a couple of alluring toughs to join Henry on his boat and dispose of him at sea. While it would be hard to find any evidence for this story after fifty years, it is lent some credence by the fact that the man who later related it to various friends and relations, the art expert David Carritt (1927–82), began an affair with Jeremy

around the time of Henry's disappearance, and was undoubtedly
in his confidence for a period.

Carritt was an Oxford contemporary of Tony Maycock,
through whom he befriended both Jeremy and Henry. During
the 1950s he worked as an independent art dealer and contributed regular art history articles to the *Burlington Magazine*.
While still in his twenties he made a great reputation in the art
world through his spectacular discoveries of lost or unrecog-
nised masterpieces, starting with Caravaggio's *Concert* in 1952.
He was known as something of a flirt and heartbreaker: the
editor of the *Burlington*, Benedict Nicolson, was one of several
unhappy men who were unrequitedly in love with him at
various times.

Carritt and Jeremy had much in common. Both were small,
charismatic men with quick minds and sparkling wit; and
though Carritt possessed a more solid intellect than Jeremy, both
owed much of their success to remarkable memories. Like
Jeremy, Carritt was renowned as a mimic and gossip; and both
possessed a viperish streak. Each had a burning passion – Jeremy
for politics, Carritt for art. Jeremy admired Carritt's artistic talents (he later recalled his excitement when Carritt identified a
ceiling at the Egyptian Embassy as as a Tiepolo), while Carritt
was rather less interested in Jeremy's political career. At some
point in the late 1950s, they began an affair, mostly conducted
at Carritt's bachelor flat in Davies Street, Mayfair. They also twice
went on holday to Tangier. They were sexually compatible, Carritt
being a passive homosexual; but friends believed the relationship
was doomed as both men were tremendous egoists each of whom
wished to be the centre of attention.

With time, Jeremy became increasingly infatuated with Carritt,
while Carritt's ardour for Jeremy cooled. He began to resent that
Jeremy was using his flat as 'a convenient bar where he could come
and drink and tell anyone who would listen about his dreary speeches'.
One night in 1960, Jeremy called on Carritt, who refused to let him

in. Jeremy made a tearful scene beneath Carritt's windows, begging to be admitted and even threatening suicide, but Carritt would not relent and threatened to call the police unless Jeremy went away. Finally Jeremy resigned himself to the situation and ceased trying to see his former lover.

Interviewed in February 1979 by Magnus Linklater, Carritt expressed the view that Jeremy (then awaiting trial)

> doesn't add up to anything likeable. One of the most self-centred people I've ever met. *Mildly* entertaining, slightly sinister. Said to be witty, but his wit consists entirely of impersonations and if one doesn't care for impersonations, he's really a bit of a bore. He had a form of ambition so extraordinary it was hard to believe in, because it was ambition *in the abstract*, an ambition for vulgarities – to be rich, powerful, famous. He took these ambitions so seriously that one really considered him a bit dotty. Cultured? Not by my standards. Can play the violin a bit, that's all. He was all dressed up like a ham actor ... a character out of Disraeli rather than Thackeray ...

David Carritt died of cancer in 1982 aged fifty-five. He had become celebrated as an art detective and popular socially; but his firm of art dealers had not been successful and he had published no works, his expertise dying with him. His memorial service at St James's, Piccadilly was crowded with famous names but these did not include Jeremy Thorpe.

The associations mentioned above did not end well, but there were others which do seem to have been happy and given pleasure and satisfaction to both parties. Some were just fleeting encounters, others more durable affairs which ripened into lasting friendship. Some of his lovers were men of his own class such as fellow barristers. Others were men from modest social backgrounds towards whom he could play a protective role: like many homosexuals of the period (their longings described in the novels of Robin Maugham), he dreamed of meeting some attractive but rootless youth who was alone in the world, who might look up to him as a friend and mentor and whom he could effectively adopt and call his own.

In London, Jeremy's homosexual life was to some extent centred on the two gentleman's clubs to which he belonged, the National Liberal Club in Whitehall Place and the Reform Club (to which he was elected upon his becoming an MP) in Pall Mall. Though both these august establishments were eminently respectable and most of their members thoroughly conventional, at that time they both possessed clandestine homosexual coteries which flourished under the aegis of like-minded club secretaries. At the National Liberal Club, some of the male staff were available 'after hours' for assignations with members on the *Hispaniola*, a ship moored on the Embankment which then operated as a bar and nightclub. At the Reform Club, a distinguished homosexual circle which included QCs, museum curators, civil servants, dons, writers and an eminent eye surgeon met regularly for a quiet gossip in the upstairs room known as the Committee Room, and Jeremy quickly became absorbed into their fraternity. One fellow member of the Reform later recalled periodically dining there with Jeremy and then going off with him to visit either the Standard at Piccadilly Circus, a pub known for soldier prostitutes, or the Salisbury on St Martin's Lane, a theatrical hang-out: on such occasions, Jeremy, who would often be going on to the House of Commons to vote, would pull his homburg low over his eyes in a furtive, play-acting way.

Jeremy's sexual preferences were (to quote a secret report of April 1960) 'fairly common knowledge' in North Devon, where they tended to be regarded merely as another of his many eccentricities. As in all isolated rural areas, there was much rampant if furtive sexual activity, and he conducted a number of affairs with local farmers and others. He was also in the habit of taking

London friends down there to act as political helpers: thus Henry Upton made a brief appearance during the 1955 election, and Jeremy would (ill-advisedly) introduce Norman Josiffe to the locality in 1962. Occasionally he got into trouble by flaunting such friendships in what was still a traditional part of the world: at the annual Liberal Garden Party at Lanhydrock in Cornwall in June 1960, where he stood in for the local candidate, Peter Bessell, who was then abroad, Bessell's wife Pauline took exception to his turning up with a handsome youth who had no apparent interest in politics. ('Your relationship with that young man is obvious: please send him away!'[3]) On the whole, however, his private life caused him few serious difficulties in the West Country until the General Election of 1966.

Jeremy also tended to let him himself go when he went abroad (though there were men, friends from Oxford and the Bar, who accompanied him on foreign holidays during the 1950s without being aware of his proclivities at that time). When he visited distant parts of the Commonwealth to report for *This Week*, he was known to make indiscreet advances towards such persons as hotel barmen, not always troubling to conceal his behaviour from colleagues who soon became used to his ways. After his election to Parliament, political travel also provided a pretext for occasional sexual adventures. After his tour of America (sponsored by the State Department) in the spring of 1961, he wrote to Maycock and Wilkins (on the inevitable House of Commons stationery) expressing his delight at the 'gay' (he already uses the word) life of San Francisco, in which he had joyously indulged and from which he had found it hard to tear himself away.[4]

Jeremy's sexual nature seems to have been brought to the attention of the authorities for the first time not on account of any particular indiscretion on his part, but as an indirect result of Princess Margaret's marriage in 1960. As we have seen, ever since Eton days it had been his fantasy ambition to marry the Princess, who was a year younger than himself. During the late 1950s, he had begun to see something of her through their mutual friend Anthony Armstrong-Jones (later Earl of Snowdon), the fashionable photographer, who had been at Eton with Jeremy and whose father had been a colleague of Thorpey at the Bar. Armstrong-Jones and Jeremy seem to have known each other quite well at this time: they discussed making a television series together on 'The Islands Around Britain', and in the November 1959 issue of *Queen*, Jeremy's photograph by Armstrong-Jones appeared next to Princess Margaret's in an article on London's 'top talkers'.

In March 1960, the Princess announced her engagement to Armstrong-Jones. This seems to have come to Jeremy as a complete and unwelcome surprise. Two friends who saw him immediately after the announcement later recalled his reactions. David Carritt remembered: 'He was "dead serious" about marrying Margaret. But I doubt if the lady herself knew anything about these grisly plans for her future. He hadn't yet got round to asking her or even talking to her. He was caught completely unawares by the Snowdon announcement, and was furious ...' The other witness, a business associate of Jeremy's at the time, recalled:

> In March 1960, Thorpe dined with me one evening at the Dorchester. He arrived late and appeared to be upset. It was the evening of the announcement of the news of Princess Margaret's engagement. I asked what was the matter and he utterly dumbfounded me by saying he was furious at 'Maggie pulling the wool over his eyes and getting herself engaged'. He went on to say that he had been after her for a long time and considered himself in with a top chance. I thought he was joking but very soon saw he was in earnest. It made me think a lot.[5]

Jeremy himself was to leave one extraordinary trace of his feelings at the time. He sent a House of Commons postcard to his

1. Theatre party at the time of Jeremy's parents' engagement, 1922. Ursula and Thorpey in the background; unknown couple in the foreground; 'Empire Jack' on the right, clutching two of his daughter's friends.

2. Jeremy's christening at the Temple Church, 1929. L to R: Lady Worthington-Evans (godmother); Colonel Andrew Kingsmill (godfather); Ursula with Lavinia and Camilla; Thorpey; the Archdeacon; Nanny Wynne, holding Jeremy; Lady Hiley; Sibyl Howard (godmother); Sir Ernest Hiley (godfather); Emma-Jane Wood (great-grandmother); Empire Jack; Gwladys.

3. Ursula looking her most formidable.

4. Jeremy aged six, at the opening of the legal year, with his father (left) and the judge Sir Alfred Tobin (right). The monocled figure of Ursula hovers as ever in the background.

5. Posing as a guardsman.

6. Jeremy aged about ten, showing an early penchant for three-piece suits.

7. Eton, 1943.

8 & 9. Two of Jeremy's boyhood role models. Megan Lloyd George, pictured with Jeremy in North Wales, and Max Beerbohm, photographed by Jeremy at Rapallo.

10. Henry Upton, the nobly born and sinister motorcyclist who so fascinated Jeremy in the summer of 1948.

11. Jeremy, President of the Oxford Union, in evening dress, receives a visit from the President of the Cambridge Union, the future Labour MP Jack Ashley, in lounge suit, March 1951.

12. The young barrister dozes on a train.

13. On the BBC Overseas Service (1958), Jeremy discusses with a general and a professor the question, 'What nationality are fish?'

14 & 15. Jeremy with his sister Camilla, and with the new Party Leader Jo Grimond, at a Liberal dinner in 1957.

16. The prospective candidate for North Devon helps wash up.

equestrian friend Norman van de Vater bearing the jocular words: 'What a pity about HRH. I rather hoped to marry the one and seduce the other.' This indiscreet missive would later fall into the hands of the police and would have been produced at Jeremy's trial but for the determination of the judge to keep the names of the Snowdons (who had just been divorced) out of the proceedings.

Towards the end of March 1960, the inventor Jeremy Fry suddenly withdrew as Armstrong-Jones' best man, ostensibly on health grounds but in reality because it had become known that, in 1952, he had pleaded guilty to a charge of gross indecency and been fined £2. Jeremy Thorpe's name was then mooted, whereupon MI5 asked the Chief Constable of Devon, Colonel Ranulph 'Streaky' Bacon, if he could provide some information on Jeremy's private life as 'Fry, Thorpe and Armstrong-Jones were apparently mates together . . .'* Having made discreet enquiries, Bacon reported that the friendship between Jeremy and Armstrong-Jones seemed to amount to 'nothing more than two Old Etonians catching up with each other', but that it was 'fairly common knowledge in Devon' that Jeremy himself was homosexual. In the event, Jeremy was not even invited to the wedding in Westminster Abbey: on 9 April 1960, it was announced by Buckingham Palace that the best man would now be Dr Roger Gilliat.

These events had little effect on Jeremy's relations with the Snowdons, who continued to enjoy his company and entertain him at Kensington Palace.† But the authorities had been made

---

* The author has been assured by them both that Thorpe and Fry hardly knew each other, a misunderstanding possibly having been created by the fact that they shared the same Christian name.

† It has been alleged that when the Snowdons decided to divorce in 1976, they agreed to a suggestion of Harold Wilson that they make their announcement on a date when it was likely to help Jeremy by drawing press attention from his then troubles: see Chapter 20.

aware that he was leading a private life which might make him a security risk if he ever achieved more than backbench status.

In his posthumously published memoirs *Ruling Passions*, the outrageously homosexual Labour MP Tom Driberg* wrote: 'If anything, I became more promiscuous after my election to Parliament, relying on my new status to get me out of tight corners.'[6] He might have added that the atmosphere of politics, by increasing the production of adrenalin, often produces a powerful aphrodisiac effect both on politicians themselves and those they seek to seduce. Like Driberg (whom he was to befriend), Jeremy became no less active as a homosexual once he had become an MP. However, he also became active in the parliamentary campaign to change the law relating to homosexuality, in which he had already been interested for some years. When, in 1954, the Home Secretary, at the prompting of Sir Robert Boothby MP, had appointed a committee to examine the subject, Jeremy wrote excitedly to Tony Maycock of his hopes for reform.[7]

'Bob' Boothby, Conservative MP for Buchan from 1924 to 1958 and then a life peer, was a family friend of the Thorpes, the original link between them having been the German businessman Richard Weininger, whom both Boothby and Thorpey had known in the 1930s. He was a man after Jeremy's heart, a brilliant rogue with liberal political instincts who combined a long-standing affair with the wife of the Prime Minister Harold Macmillan with hair-raising homosexual adventures with

---

* Famous before the war as the William Hickey columnist in the *Daily Express*, and noted for his left-wing and High Church views, Driberg sat as MP for Maldon 1942–55 and Barking 1959–74. As Chairman of Labour's National Executive, he exchanged 'fraternal' visits with Chairman Khrushchev. The excellent biography of him by Francis Wheen (London: Chatto & Windus, 1990) shows his life to have been a rollercoaster of homosexual scrapes. He was elevated to the peerage as Lord Bradwell shortly before his death in 1976.

characters from the criminal underworld. His ministerial career had ended during the war owing to his unlucky involvement (with Weininger) in the so-called Czech Assets Affair; but during the 1950s he made a new career as a media celebrity, being instantly recognisable on television with his gruff voice, handsome, beetle-browed appearance and forthright opinions. He and Jeremy often appeared together on BBC Radio's *Any Questions*. In 1964, he was to be involved in sensation when the *Sunday Mirror* published the (true) story that he was on close terms with the notorious East End gangsters, the Kray brothers: with the help of powerful friends (and the solicitor Arnold Goodman), Boothby forced the newspaper to retract the allegation and pay him in compensation the huge sum of £40,000.* (Some years later, Jeremy significantly remarked to Susan Crosland that, although it was true that Boothby knew the Krays, he had been justified in reacting as he did, as the action of the *Mirror* in publishing the story had been 'monstrous: they had no right . . .'[8])

It was Boothby who, as an MP in 1954, initiated the adjournment debate in the Commons which led to the setting-up of the Wolfenden Committee. Wolfenden reported in 1957 in favour of decriminalising homosexual acts in private between consenting adults. However, the Conservative Government refused to introduce or support the necessary legislation and there began a ten-year lobbying campaign for its enactment: in contrast to later 'gay rights' campaigns, this was led by distinguished liberals who were mostly not homosexual. During 1958, a letter in *The Times* supporting Wolfenden signed by many eminent people was followed by the formation of the Homosexual Law Reform Society

---

*When confronted with embarrassing allegations, Boothby's policy, like Jeremy's, was one of stout denial: his assertion that he hardly knew the Krays (whom he had in fact met quite regularly) was similar to Jeremy's that he had hardly known Norman Josiffe.

(commonly known as 'the Society'), its first committee including such well-known figures as the human-rights campaigner Canon Collins, the publisher Victor Gollancz, the archaeologist Jaquetta Hawkes and the poet Stephen Spender, all of whom had been signatories to the *Times* letter. The Society had an office on Shaftesbury Avenue and a full-time secretary; it published reports, lobbied ministers and collected data on the harassment of homosexuals. In May 1960 it held its first public meeting; and a month later its committee member, the Labour MP and future health minister Kenneth Robinson, introduced a private member's motion in the Commons to implement the Wolfenden recommendations, defeated by 213 votes to 99. Jeremy naturally supported this, as did three of the other five Liberal MPs.*

On 23 November 1960, Jeremy wrote to Maycock that he had joined the committee of the Society. That month, Spender and Gollancz stood down and were replaced by two recently elected young MPs, Jeremy and the Conservative former Olympic runner Christopher Chataway: they attended their first meeting in January 1961. The minutes show that Jeremy, though irregular in his attendance, took an active part at meetings, recommending new members (such as the ballerina Moira Shearer), offering his free services to the Society as a barrister and broadcaster,† and suggesting names (including Boothby) who might contribute to a book. He became more active in 1963, after the homosexual civil servant Edgar Wright,‡ a friend with whom he felt able to discuss his own private life, had become secretary: from 1963 to 1966, the committee held most of its meetings at Jeremy's parliamentary office in Bridge Street, and he

---

* Grimond, Holt and Wade supported it; the two Welsh MPs, Clement Davies and the bachelor Roderic Bowen, opposed it.
† Having made this generous offer, Jeremy does not actually seem to have either appeared in court or broadcast on behalf of the Society: it would certainly have been rashly brave of him to do either.
‡ Later known by the pseudonym of Antony Grey.

took a close interest in the various attempts to introduce reforming legislation (though he was not in the forefront of these attempts, which were promoted by the Conservative MP Humphry Berkeley, the Labour MP Leo Abse and, in the House of Lords, the Earl of Arran).

Edgar Wright recalls: 'Jeremy was a useful member of the committee. He did not do much but did it very well, and was always helpful with suggestions or contacts. Unlike many other homosexuals, he was not afraid to stand up and call for reform. Of course, the Society was quite respectable in those days, before it was taken over by the gay radicals and opposition had been organised by Mary Whitehouse and others.' It must have taken courage for Jeremy, naturally so secretive about himself and fearful of exposure, to involve himself publicly in the campaign to change the law. Or perhaps, in his mind, it was another case of sailing close to the wind.

Another colourful friend of Jeremy's was Norman van de Vater, a man of his own age who combined a hot temper with much raffish charm. He was a well-known figure in the equestrian world and ran Kingham Stables near Brize Norton in Oxfordshire, where he trained horses for three-day events in which (rather unusually) he also rode himself. He hinted at mysterious aristocratic origins, though journalists in the 1970s discovered that he was the son of a Welsh miner, born Norman Vivian Vater.[9] Jeremy seems to have met him around the time of his election to Parliament, and wrote him a number of intimate letters on parliamentary stationery, including the postcard on Princess Margaret's engagement mentioned above. (Jeremy was to be best man at Vater's marriage to Miss Helen Tomkinson in 1961 and subsequently godfather to his son: the couple separated in 1968 and Vater went to live in Ireland, where he became a leading figure in the dressage world and a distinguished international competition judge.)

During one of Jeremy's visits to Kingham in the summer of 1960, Vater mentioned that he had a young groom whom Jeremy might be interested to meet. Jeremy went to find the lad – another Norman, Norman Josiffe – and discovered him leaning against a stable door and (as he allegedly later told Peter Bessell) 'looking simply heaven'.[10] Josiffe was wild-eyed, tousle-haired, looked younger than his twenty years and had an arresting, rather androgynous appearance. They talked for a few minutes, Jeremy showing interest in Josiffe and suggesting that he get in touch at the House of Commons should he ever need help or be in London.

Jeremy was to hear no more of Josiffe for more than a year. But meanwhile, early in 1961, Josiffe left Vater's employment, having first stolen the 'Dear Norman' letters Jeremy had written Vater, which he would proceed to show various people, claiming they had in fact been addressed to himself. Indeed, he would sometimes claim, on the basis of their one fleeting conversation, that Jeremy was his most intimate friend. In June 1961, he was admitted to a psychiatric clinic at Oxford, where he would spend much time during the coming months. After being released from there in November 1961, following a short spell of compulsory detention, Josiffe set out for London to look up Jeremy at the House of Commons. It would prove a fateful encounter.

7

PARLIAMENT
1959–64

JEREMY THORPE'S NARROW victory in North Devon was one of the great surprises of the 1959 election, and caused a mild sensation. It was one of a handful of seats lost that year by the triumphant Tories, and the Liberals' first General Election gain since 1951. Only thirty, but already well known to the public through television, he had the air of a magician who had pulled off an apparent miracle. He was much fêted socially in the weeks following his election, while the press hailed him as the most stylish and eloquent of the new MPs, who would 'liven things up no end'.[1] When he next spoke at the Oxford Union, he brought the house down with imitations of Tory squires and matrons spluttering with bewildered outrage at the capture of one of their strongholds by an enemy thought to be extinct. Those were heady days for him; but how would he get on once the novelty of his election had worn off?

An MP may be said to play four distinct roles. First, he is a House of Commons man, a privileged member of an exclusive club, steeping himself in the traditions and procedures of his ancient chamber and making his mark with fellow MPs of all parties. Secondly, he is a member of a parliamentary party, supporting his party's policies, jockeying for position with party colleagues, usually hoping for office when his party comes to power. Thirdly, he is an individual with his own personal views and convictions, which he is able (within the constraints of party discipline) to air in parliamentary debates and translate into parliamentary votes. And fourthly he is a constituency MP, dedicated to upholding the interests of the people he represents, both collectively, by pressing upon the Government the particular needs of his division, and individually, by using his position to try to help the many constituents who approach him with their problems.

Jeremy quickly built up a reputation in all four roles. He became recognised as a good parliamentarian and accomplished debater; he established himself as the most prominent Liberal next to Jo Grimond; he did much to advance his personal views on human-rights issues at home and abroad; and he showed himself to be an outstanding constituency member. Each of these four areas needs to be examined in turn.

Jeremy was not one of those who regard the House of Commons as a mere route to status and power. He loved it with a passion which never wavered during the twenty years he was in it. He loved its long history, its imposing buildings, its intricate procedures, its club-like atmosphere. This love had been nurtured in him from the cradle: it owed much to his political family background, his childhood contacts with the Lloyd Georges, the early ambitions fostered by his mother. Although the parliamentary careers of his father and grandfather had ended before he was born, he had always felt the House to be a natural home. Tea there with Megan, followed by a visit to the gallery, had been a common treat in childhood, since when he had often frequented its lobbies and refreshment rooms, recruiting speakers or visiting friends. When he took his seat, Jeremy (as other newly elected MPs noticed with a touch of envy) suffered from none of the ignorance of the 'new boy': he was already familiar both with the precincts and procedures of Parliament. He was also well acquainted with dozens of his fellow MPs from all parties, including his old Liberal mentors Megan and Dingle (both now sitting on the Labour benches), family friends such as Nigel Fisher, Eton contemporaries such as Robin Balniel and Tam Dalyell, colleagues from the Bar such as Geoffrey Rippon, and fellow human-rights campaigners such as Philip Noel-Baker and Kenneth Robinson.

Above all, he felt at home at Westminster thanks to the Oxford Union, that traditional preparation for the House of Commons. Not only had he mastered the elements of parliamentary proce- dure and the art of parliamentary debate there, but he now found himself surrounded by MPs (including the Prime Minister, Harold Macmillan) who had also started their political careers there, many of whom Jeremy had already got to know as visitors to the Union and among whom there was an almost masonic sense of fraternity. Indeed, in 1959 Jeremy was just one of five young MPs who had been President of the Oxford Union since 1945, along with Edward Boyle, Tony Crosland, Peter Kirk and Anthony Wedgwood Benn; and during the next fifteen years he would be joined in the House by many other Union contempo- raries, including Peter Blaker, John Gilbert, Michael Heseltine, Gerald Kaufman, Bryan Magee, Patrick Mayhew, Norman St John-Stevas* and Dick Taverne.

---

* The only man to have held office at both the Cambridge Union (of which he was President) and Oxford Union (of which he became Secretary in Jeremy's fourth year), St John-Stevas, who was Conservative MP for Chelmsford, 1964–87, subsequently being raised to the peerage as Lord St John of Fawsley, shared Jeremy's flamboyance and homosexual tastes (about which he was as open as it was then possible to be); unlike Jeremy, he was also a considerable intellectual and possessed a substantial inherited fortune. Though they served together on the committee of the Homosexual Law Reform Society, they never particularly got on.

Jeremy has often been described as an Oxford Union politician who never grew up. In 1971, Tony Benn wrote of him as 'very nice, agreeable and kind but . . . no weight . . . just thinks of the House of Commons as the Oxford Union . . .'[2] Certainly he never lost the light touch and element of showmanship which are the hallmarks of a Union debater. But it would be wrong to represent him as a frivolous parliamentarian: a study of *Hansard* reveals that the majority of his contributions, though delivered with panache and seasoned with quips, were well argued and informed. His reputation as a jester rested mainly on his questions to ministers, when a certain levity is traditionally allowed, and on what he said to journalists and fellow MPs outside the chamber. It is noteworthy that neither of his best-known *bons mots*, the one about Harold Macmillan 'laying down his friends for his life' or the other about the House of Lords being 'proof of life after death', was uttered inside the House.

The circumstances of his maiden speech on 10 November 1959 illustrate this combination of seriousness in debate and frivolity on the fringe. By tradition, maiden speeches are low-key affairs; but some hoped Jeremy would try to take the House by storm, as had been attempted in their day by Disraeli (disastrously) and F. E. Smith (successfully). Recalling how he had won his Presidential Debate at the Union with a speech imitating Churchill, the *Spectator* offered him a hundred guineas if he would 'make his maiden speech in imitation of the Prime Minister'.[3] Jeremy was certainly out to attract notice and, before the debate in which he was due to speak, caught the amused attention of fellow MPs and the Press Gallery by holding up a filthy antimacassar he had discovered on his rail journey from the West Country that morning, demanding an explanation from the Transport Minister, Ernest Marples. But there was nothing ribald about the speech he proceeded to make (though one journalist thought it 'slickly competent, as though Mr Thorpe had been addressing the House for the past ten years and had got

rather tired of the exercise'[4]). Speaking in the debate on the Local
Employment Bill, he described the problem of bringing jobs to
his constituency, much of which suffered from poor communications and a lack of such basic amenities as water, electricity
and proper drainage. 'Is it any wonder that people are leaving the
land?' His effort won a respectful reply from the Minister of
Labour, Edward Heath, and a flurry of congratulatory notes, of
which the one he most cherished was from Megan.[5]

As an MP with a wide range of interests, and one of only six
Liberal members (two of whom rarely turned up), Jeremy spoke
unusually often for a recently elected MP, contributing to almost
a hundred debates during the five years of his first term in
Parliament. Although he never quite succeeded in holding the
attention of the House as he had done the Union,[6] he quickly
developed a reputation as a fine parliamentary orator with an
original style. He capitalised on the fact that, as a Liberal, he was
in a position to attack both sides of the House. When he spoke in
a debate on share ownership in June 1960, the *Guardian* commented that 'his combination of wit and sense further expectation
that he will develop into an outstanding speaker. He is devastat-
ingly impartial and never tries to curry favour. No sooner did he
have the Conservatives nodding their agreement at some of the
wise things he said than he turned on them with scorn ...'[7] And
when, at the time of the United Kingdom's application to join the
Common Market in 1961, he attacked both Government and
Opposition for their former complacency on the subject, *Punch*
congratulated him on 'his best innings yet ... Belonging to neither of the main parties, he could hit out uninhibitedly all round
the wicket. His victims protested but there was a squeak of
masochistic delight in their protests and they enjoyed the vigour.'[8]

It need hardly be said that, in the corridors and bars of
Westminster, Jeremy tremendously entertained his fellow MPs
with his imitations: he was generally regarded as the best mimic
among them since the war. Tory ministers and pompous

backbench MPs were favourite targets, though some of his best imitations were of colleagues for whom he had affection, such as Grimond and Dingle Foot. He thought up comic nicknames for his victims: Frederic Bennett, the blimpish Conservative MP for Torquay, was 'Jowly Swine', while the junior minister John Boyd-Carpenter, a small man with a bouncy gait, was 'Spring-Heel Jack'. He was also given to practical jokes based on impersonations – as when he telephoned his friend Nigel Fisher, just appointed to a junior post in the Government, pretending to be the Prime Minister. His besetting sin was that he did not know when to stop: more than once, a politician with a limited sense of humour stumbled upon a devastating rendering of himself being delivered by Jeremy to an appreciative audience, and took offence.

From the moment he took his seat, Jeremy campaigned both inside and outside the House for better working conditions for MPs. He constantly needled Lord John Hope, the Minister of Works, about the inadequate facilities of the Palace of Westminster. ('Last night the temperature in the Members' Dining Room soared above eighty degrees. How much longer are MPs going to be cooped up for hours on end in a building with the stifling conditions of a Turkish Bath and precluded from removing the necessary minimum of clothing to make such conditions tolerable?'[9]) In a newspaper article published in 1962, he wrote that it was all very well for MPs to have red loops on their coatpegs to hang their swords; but the ordinary member had no telephone, desk or room of his own.

> He must dictate to his secretary in a draughty corridor, keep all his papers in a schoolboy's locker, and transact his business from a telephone box. If a deputation wishes to see him he may be able to book a committee room. Otherwise the nearest corridor must do. Who else would be expected to look after 50,000 people in such outrageous conditions?[10]

He also spoke out against the unsocially late hours MPs were expected to sit and their inadequate pay, fixed in 1957 at £1,750 per annum. In November 1962, he was one of three 'pay nego-tiators' appointed by backbenchers of the three parties to lobby for an increase, later giving a witty account of how Macmillan had received them 'like a deputation of parlourmaids'. But their efforts were successful: the Lawrence Committee was set up, which in 1964 awarded a rise to £3,250.

As with all institutions with which he was associated, it had not taken Jeremy long to impress his personality on the House of Commons. He was heartily disliked by some right-wing Tories (particularly from the West Country) who saw him as a rene-gade, and by some who disapproved of or suffered from his showmanship, but on the whole he was popular with his fellow MPs. They saw him as a companionable and entertaining col-league, a fine debater, a natural parliamentarian dedicated to upholding their traditions and improving their conditions. As for his political impact, that would depend on the fortunes of the Liberal Party and himself within it.

Jeremy was the toast of the Liberals after his dramatic victory in North Devon. There had been few new MPs for them to welcome in the past thirty years; and the circumstances of his win, as a non-local man defeating a sitting Conservative member, had been inspiring. He was now by far the youngest of the six Liberal MPs, the only one in the south of England, and the first to rep-resent the Liberal heartland of Devon and Cornwall since 1942. For almost a decade he had been a well-known figure in the Party, and great things were expected of him.

Of his five colleagues, the lofty and glamorous figure of Grimond, now forty-six, towered over the rest: to many people (including himself) he *was* the Liberal Party. Jeremy continued to regard him with near-adulation. As before, Grimond did not reciprocate this admiration, but recognised Jeremy as one of the

Party's greatest assets; and Laura Grimond and her mother Lady Violet remained firm supporters of Jeremy, whose company they enjoyed and whom they regarded as 'one of us' on account of his social background and political ancestry. The other four MPs were all compromised politically by the fact that they had held their seats in straight fights with Labour, without having to face Conservative opponents. The former leader Clement Davies, seventy-five, still sat for Montgomeryshire, which he had represented since 1929; but he had been broken by a series of family tragedies and become a sad figure. The two North Country MPs, Donald Wade, fifty-five, and Arthur Holt, forty-five, were respected party idealists; but both were lacklustre men, scarcely known to the public. Roderic Bowen, forty-six, was the longest-serving MP next to Davies, being the only other survivor of the twelve Liberals elected in 1945; but though genial, he was lazy and unambitious, appearing irregularly at Westminster in the intervals of his career as a Welsh barrister.

Technically, the second position in the parliamentary party belonged to the Liberal Chief Whip,* a post held by Wade until 1962 and then by Holt. However, almost as soon as he took his seat, there was a general feeling, both inside and outside the Party, that Jeremy, despite his youth and inexperience, had in effect become Grimond's heir presumptive. Apart from Grimond, he alone had won his seat in a three-cornered contest, possessed leadership qualities and charisma, was recognised as a fine speaker and was well known outside the House. Grimond never seems to have said anything in recognition of this fact, either to Jeremy or anyone else, and doubtless hoped that, before he stood down as Leader, another gifted Liberal more to his taste (such as his brother-in-law,

---

* There were no other whips at this time, but the title remained as a reminder of better days and so that the incumbent could continue to enjoy parliamentary privileges comparable to the Chief Whips of the two main parties.

Mark Bonham Carter) would enter (or re-enter) the House and succeed him; but meanwhile he tacitly admitted Jeremy's primacy in various ways. For example, in May 1960 he invited Jeremy to appear with him in the Liberals' first party political broadcast of the new Parliament, in which they argued that the Party with its 'radical alternative' would make a better Official Opposition than Labour.

In 1959, the Liberal MPs were a parody of a parliamentary party. In theory, each had a range of 'portfolios' (Jeremy's main one was initially agriculture), they held meetings to discuss tactics, and they aimed to present party policy as laid down by the Liberal Council and Assembly. The reality was different. Grimond was an inspiring speaker but a poor organiser who did little to co-ordinate the work of the MPs. He spent much of his time in his remote constituency or campaigning around the country; and his five colleagues (none of whom held a seat within 100 miles of London) were also often absent in their constituencies or pursuing other careers. Owing to lack of funds, the MPs had little support by way of assistants or researchers,* making it difficult for them to speak on any subject with which they were not already familiar. In consequence, their contributions in the House tended to be made not with a view to presenting a party programme but merely according to whether they happened to be present and personally interested in the subject under debate and able to get called. This meant that Jeremy, as the most lucid and vigorous of Grimond's colleagues, was to some extent able to stamp his imprint on parliamentary Liberalism. It is interesting that the subjects on which he spoke most often during his early years in Parliament – Commonwealth relations (particularly regarding

---

* This situation changed in the late 1960s thanks to the Rowntree Trust, which provided funds to the Parliamentary Liberal Party to enable it to hire support staff, popularly known as 'chocolate soldiers'.

Africa), Britain's future in Europe, human rights, constitutional reform, immigration, broadcasting – have ever since remained high on the parliamentary agenda of the Liberal Party and its successor.

As after previous depressing election performances, the Liberals were quick to set up a committee to overhaul the Party with a view to their doing better next time. This came into existence in December 1959 and was known as the Standing Committee. It was to have wide powers for two years and was originally confined to six members. The Chairman and Deputy Chairman were the Liberal ex-MPs Frank Byers and Mark Bonham Carter; and it included two sitting MPs, Arthur Holt and Jeremy. Jeremy's special responsibilities included fundraising and by-elections, and his efforts in these areas took up much of his time and energy during his first year in Parliament.[11] He hosted a series of fundraising lunches and dinners at the House of Commons, and secured one really important donor – Tim Beaumont, an upper-class eccentric who had been a 'hearty' contemporary of Jeremy at Oxford, subsequently taken Anglican orders, and recently come into a large fortune. In by-elections, Jeremy continued to campaign vigorously as he had done throughout recent years; and he persuaded the committee that in future they should aspire to fight every by-election. This decision had an unforeseen and unfortunate result, for 1960 saw a by-election in Bolton North-East, in contesting which the Liberals put an end to their local pact with the Conservatives which had enabled Holt to hold the neighbouring seat of Bolton South-West. With Byers as their candidate, the Liberals only managed to pick up a quarter of the vote in Bolton North-East, coming third, though on the same day they achieved a heartening result in the Devon seat of Tiverton, where their candidate James Collier, much supported by Jeremy, cut the Conservative majority from 11,000 to 2,000.

Jeremy was never much of a committee man, and felt that his

talents could be put to better use running his own show and working on the ground. Early in 1961, he resigned from the Standing Committee to devote himself to a new organisation he had created, known as Winnable Seats. His aim was to help Liberals elsewhere in the country repeat his own achievement in North Devon – the transformation of a constituency Liberal association into an election-winning machine. To achieve maximum effect, he decided to concentrate long-term effort and limited resources on a short-list of those former Liberal seats in which the Party stood the best chance of success.* To help him, he chose two charismatic assistants: Dominic le Foe, the young music-hall entertainer who had managed his campaign in North Devon, and Ted Wheeler, a devoted professional officer of the Party who had recently been appointed to the post of its Chief Agent. Together, they drew up a list of what they regarded as the most winnable seats, and then they toured Britain, visiting Liberals in these constituencies and assessing their potential and requirements.[12]

In terms of morale, the results were immediate. Once proud but now languishing Liberal associations which for years had received virtually no support from the creaking Liberal Party Organisation (LPO) were amazed to meet the sparkling trio, full of advice and encouragement and asking them to list their needs. Jeremy showed ingenuity both in raising funds for his new organisation and using them. Dazzling them with seductive talk of the brilliant future to which they would be contributing, he obtained large sums from the Liberals' new millionaire patron Tim Beaumont (who gave some £50,000 to the Party between 1959 and 1964), and the rich widows of some former Liberal MPs. He offered money to the chosen associations on two conditions: that they met targets for

---

* Thus Jeremy may be said to have invented the concept of 'targeting', used to such devastating effect by the Liberal Democrats in the General Election of 1997.

improving their organisation and raising their membership, and that they laid out the specific purposes for which they needed cash. (This in turn helped fundraising, for it was always easier to approach donors if they could be told where their money was going – such as to buy a car for the agent in a particular constituency.) It remained to be seen how many of the Winnable Seats would actually be won at the next election; but in almost all of them, the Liberals were soon in better shape than for some time. Only occasionally did Jeremy's irresistible desire to show off produce a setback – as at Huddersfield West, where he so antagonised local Liberals by making a colourful scene at a hotel that the MP Donald Wade had to ask him to refrain from revisiting the seat.[13]

Winnable Seats enabled Jeremy to concentrate on the sort of activity at which he was superbly good. It also amounted to a bid for the future leadership of the Party. He had in effect created a rival organisation to the LPO with its cumbersome machinery of committees: if he succeeded where they had failed, and enabled the Liberals to increase their parliamentary representation, he could hope to become master of the Party in the country. Meanwhile, he had constructed a power base for himself, for Winnable Seats was his own private operation: he was not responsible to anyone for the way he ran it, and the money he raised for it remained effectively under his personal control.* Indeed, it was reminiscent of the controversial 'Lloyd George Fund' which Jeremy's hero had used to give selective help to Liberal candidates and thus maintain his influence over the Party between the wars: in true Lloyd George style, Winnable Seats was also a semi-secret organisation, Jeremy arguing that to give any publicity to its existence or activities

---

*Accounts of the organisation were, however, kept by Dominic le Foe as Treasurer, and found to be in order when examined by the police in the late 1970s.

would alert the other parties to where the Liberals were making their strongest efforts.

Apart from his parliamentary activities and Winnable Seats, Jeremy made an impact on the Party through brilliant set-piece speeches to the annual Liberal Assemblies. A notable moment occurred at the Eastbourne Assembly in September 1960, when his eloquence secured the defeat of a unilateral nuclear disarmament motion put forward by the popular Treasurer, Colonel Lort-Phillips: this was particularly striking as the Labour Leader, Hugh Gaitskell, humiliatingly failed to have a similar motion defeated at his own party conference later that month. At the Edinburgh Assembly of 1961, Jeremy spoke in favour of Britain's current negotiations to join the European Economic Community, accusing both the Conservatives and Labour of dithering over this historic step. At Llandudno in 1962, he spoke on foreign affairs; and at Brighton in 1963, he advocated constitutional reform and improved conditions for MPs.

While building up Winnable Seats, Jeremy continued to be active on the by-election circuit. During 1961, as the Macmillan Government became unpopular, the Liberals did well, picking up votes from the Conservatives and coming a good second in several seats where they had been third in 1959. But nothing prepared them for their phenomenal win at Orpington on 14 March 1962, where the youthful Eric Lubbock transformed a Conservative majority of 14,760 into a Liberal one of 7,855, a swing not seen since the war. This result was no fluke, for at the same time the Liberals came within a thousand votes of capturing Blackpool North from the Conservatives, while forcing them into third place in Middlesborough East. Jeremy could claim much of the credit for Orpington: Lubbock, a handsome Old Harrovian and Oxford Boxing Blue who had strong local connections and was heir to a Victorian peerage, was not much of a public speaker, and Jeremy had done most of the speaking in his campaign. When Lubbock (who was a few months older than

Jeremy) came to Westminster, Jeremy took him under his wing rather in the manner of a school prefect patronising a 'new boy'; and they became friends.

The sudden and seemingly miraculous Liberal upsurge at the expense of the Conservatives certainly owed something to Grimond's personal popularity, though it was in fact rather embarrassing for Grimond, who since becoming Leader had based his strategy on the hope that the Liberals would take votes from Labour and eventually replace them as the main opposition to the Conservatives. Meanwhile, Grimond's predecessor Clement Davies lived just long enough to witness the revival of the party he had kept alive during its darkest days: he died the week following Orpington aged seventy-eight, precipitating a by-election in Montgomeryshire. In normal times this would have been worrying for the Liberals, as the local party organisation had run down, Davies having relied on his personal vote, and the Conservatives were now contesting the seat for the first time. Jeremy worked hard in support of the Liberal candidate, the 37-year-old Welsh barrister Emlyn Hooson, who was duly elected in May 1962 with a majority of over 7,000. But with Hooson, a sober Celt who mistrusted Jeremy's showmanship and was conscious of coming from a different educational background, Jeremy was to develop none of the friendship he came to have with Lubbock.

The Liberals now had more than half a dozen MPs for the first time since 1951, and were riding high. They did well in local elections that spring, and some opinion polls even put them fractionally ahead of the other two parties. Their resurgence was one of the factors which caused Macmillan to lose his nerve and sack one-third of his Cabinet that July, enabling Jeremy to secure a future place in *The Oxford Dictionary of Quotations* with the quip that 'greater love hath no man than this, that he should lay down his friends for his life'.[14] If, over the next two years, they maintained even part of their increased support, and Jeremy's work for

Winnable Seats bore fruit, he might soon find himself the second figure in a parliamentary party which numbered itself in dozens.

Jeremy regarded himself not merely as an MP involved in domestic politics, but as a player on a wider stage. As a Liberal, in touch with the Party's traditional strains of internationalism and humanitarianism, and perhaps also as the grandson of Empire Jack, who had carried out great engineering works in every continent and dreamed of a British Empire encompassing the world, he had something of a global outlook. The late 1950s and early 1960s were a time of excitement and hope for liberals everywhere, who were encouraged in the belief that countries were drawing closer together and that tyranny and oppression were on the decline. There were few open military conflicts between states; Communism seemed less threatening under Khrushchev than Stalin; nations all over the globe were being 'liberated' from 'colonialism' as new independent states; and international organisations appeared to be flourishing. Jeremy was no starry-eyed utopian: he understood the realities of the Cold War, and the need for Britain to maintain her defences and close relationship with the USA as a member of the NATO alliance. But at the same time he believed in the great liberal concepts of international unity and human rights, and throughout his political career would work to promote their advancement. His attitude was inspired as much by egoism as altruism: at Westminster he might be no more than the MP of a small opposition party, but in the counsels of international liberalism he could aspire to be an influential, even a heroic, figure.

Africa had been the scene of Empire Jack's first triumphs; and Jeremy was always fascinated by that continent and warmly sympathetic towards the nationalist movements seeking independence from British rule. As early as 1953 he had been a prominent campaigner against the setting-up of the Central African Federation, which united the colonies of Southern

Rhodesia, Northern Rhodesia and Nyasaland under a constitution which ensured indefinite dominance by a small white
minority.* During the following years, two circumstances helped
him pursue his interest in Africa: his friendship with Dingle
Foot, who had a large colonial practice at the Bar and
represented many of the nationalist leaders, and his television
work for *This Week*, which sent him to colonial Africa to interview representatives of both the rulers and the ruled. In
Parliament, he upheld the right of Africans to self-determination:
in this respect, he had little quarrel with the Conservative
Government, which following Macmillan's 'wind of change'
speech of February 1960 took a similarly 'enlightened' view.† By
the mid-1960s Britain had withdrawn from virtually all her
African possessions; and Jeremy found himself on terms of personal friendship with many of the leaders of the newly
independent states – notably Banda of Malawi, Kaunda of
Zambia, Kenyatta of Kenya, Khama of Botswana, Nyerere of
Tanzania and Obote of Uganda – whom he had got to know on
his visits and who were grateful for his longstanding and
unwavering support for their cause.‡

---

* In August 1953, Jeremy devoted his first public speech in North Devon to
attacking the Federation (which had come into existence that month), pointing out that nine federal MPs would represent 6 million Africans while
twenty-six MPs represented 170,000 whites, 'a flagrant breach of the trust
which the Africans have placed in the British Government'. He was accompanied by Learie Constantine, his fellow Bar student and a noted campaigner
for racial equality who may have inspired the speech.

† Jeremy's only serious clash with the Government on colonial issues occurred
during 1961–62, when the Colonial Office, under pressure from the elder
statesman Lord Salisbury, gave consideration to a proposed new constitution
for Northern Rhodesia which would have prolonged white rule there. Jeremy,
who had become a close friend of the local nationalist leader Kenneth Kaunda,
warned that this might produce 'an Algerian situation' with 'five, ten or fifteen
years of bloodshed'.

‡ On the other hand, in 1961, both in the House of Commons and on *This Week*,
Jeremy denounced the leader of the first African colony to become independent, Kwame Nkrumah of Ghana, as a tyrant and megalomaniac. This may

The rapid pace of decolonisation left South Africa as an incongruous example of uncompromising white rule on the continent; and Jeremy, like all liberals, was a fierce and unremitting critic of the local policy of apartheid which had the effect of humiliating the black majority and keeping them in a position of permanent inferiority. In 1950, during the early days of apartheid, he had delivered an impassioned speech at the Oxford Union arguing that South Africa ought to be expelled from the Commonwealth; and in May 1961, after the Sharpeville massacre, he spoke there again with equal passion on the same theme. (The South Africans only avoided explulsion by voluntarily leaving the Commonwealth that month.) He was prominent in public protests against apartheid, including vigils outside Lancaster House (then the venue of the annual Commonwealth Prime Ministers' Conference) and rallies in front of the South African Embassy in Trafalgar Square. He also gave practical support to the cause by helping raise money for various exile groups and chairing an organisation which published a 'liberationist' newspaper in London for underground circulation in South Africa. When Nelson Mandela and his co-defendants were sentenced to death at the 'Rivonia trial' in June 1964, Jeremy organised an international petition which helped secure their reprieve – a service for which Mandela, by then President of South Africa, was finally able to thank him when they met in London for the first time in 1996.[15]

Jeremy took a special humanitarian interest in the fate of political prisoners under authoritarian regimes. South Africa was a case in point, as was Franco's Spain, and for some years he was effectively banned from both countries on account of

---

have owed something to the fact that he had recently been given an unfriendly official reception there and been attacked in the local press as 'an imperialist twerp': in later years, he was slow to criticise those African leaders who were his friends when their regimes became odious.

his outspoken criticisms. In June 1961, he helped launch a new organisation called Appeal for Amnesty, later known as Amnesty International, which aimed at publicising the plight of political prisoners throughout the world and securing their release or better treatment: at the inaugural press conference, he declared that their campaign had no frontiers and would 'pierce as many prisons as possible with a shaft of light'.[16] For the rest of his political career, he would take a close interest in Amnesty's work and try to help in many individual cases. Amnesty represented Jeremy's most lasting contribution to the defence of human rights; but down the years he also supported many other humanitarian causes, in Britain and overseas. His involvement in the campaign to decriminalise homosexuality has already been noted; he was adamantly against all forms of racial and religious discrimination; he fervently opposed the Immigrants Act of 1962, which restricted the right of Commonwealth citizens to settle in Britain; and he was not afraid to say where he stood on such issues, even in North Devon, where voters tended to be old-fashioned in their attitudes.

He was always an enthusiast for bodies which aimed at strengthening international co-operation, such as the United Nations, the Commonwealth and the European Economic Community. Liberals tended to be prominent in these organisations; and he cultivated the friendship of such figures as the UN Secretary-General U Thant, the Commonwealth Secretary-General Arnold Smith, and Jean Monnet, the 'Father of Europe'. His statements in praise of these bodies sound naively idealistic today but were sincerely meant at the time: in 1961, he described the Commonwealth as representing 'a microcosm of the sort of world society we want to see created', in which respect for the rule of law would mingle with the concept of 'racial partnership'.[17] When the Macmillan Government launched their unsuccessful bid to join the EEC in 1961, Jeremy, while criticising them for not having applied earlier, declared himself

strongly in favour of British membership, which he supported
not just on economic grounds but as a prelude to 'the political
unification of Europe'[18] – another example of his courage in
expressing views which were not likely to be popular in his constituency. He was also keenly interested in Anglo-American
relations, especially after the inauguration in January 1961 of
President John F. Kennedy, with whom Jeremy strongly identified
as a 'liberal', a ruthless political operator, and a glamorous young
leader with a gift for oratory.* During the spring of 1961, he
undertook a whirlwind tour of the USA as a guest of the State
Department, where he greatly enjoyed himself and made many
friends and useful contacts – though, to his regret, his contact
with the President was limited to his attendance at a White
House press conference.†

   There was always an element of fantasy surrounding Jeremy's
overseas political activities: even at this early stage, he liked to
see himself as a kind of world statesman, flitting around the
globe on important missions, participating in splendid international occasions, rubbing shoulders with the great. But behind
the fantasy lay a reality of sincerely held ideals, useful high-level
contacts and a sense of how the world might be changed for the
better. There could be no doubt that he did much good according to his lights; nor was he insensible to the fact that his doings

---

* In an article published in the *Sunday Times* following his election as Liberal
Leader in January 1967, Jeremy wrote that he aspired to establish the Liberals
as a 'non-socialist, Kennedy-type new democratic party of the left'. This
prompted a reader to write to the editor that 'if Mr Thorpe really wants what
Kennedy actually led, he will get a conservative, almost reactionary, undemocratic party of the industrial–military right'.
† Interviewed on his return to England, Jeremy's main memories of the six-
week tour were of his meetings with Eleanor Roosevelt and the Duke of
Windsor, his visit to the United Nations in New York, his receiving the
Freedom of the City of San Francisco, his reunions with friends from Oxford
and his American schooldays, and his reception by state legislatures whose
members seemed to enjoy facilities vastly superior to those of the House of
Commons.

abroad could only enhance his standing at home, both in Parliament and the Liberal Party.

Even Jeremy's opponents had to admit that he proved himself a model local MP in North Devon.[19] During the election, he had promised to improve the lives of his future constituents; and once elected, he set out to achieve dramatic things for them and secure a permanent place in their affections. There was much to be done in so backward an area, particularly regarding public services. Assisted by his agent Lilian Prowse, with her local knowledge and organising talents, Jeremy immersed himself in the constituency, discussing roads and railways, water and electricity, employment and housing, health and education with the relevant public authorities, always ensuring that his efforts were well reported in the local press. Quite soon, in most departments, improvements became noticeable; he knew how to exercise influence and get things done.

The main problem in North Devon, as in all isolated rural communities, was the steady drain on the population as people left for the cities. In his maiden speech, Jeremy pleaded for greater government investment in both the public services and economies of constituencies like his own in order to stem the flow. More than four years later he returned to this theme when, in February 1964, he tabled a private member's motion calling for the south-west and certain other rural areas of Britain to be given special help to improve amenities and attract jobs.[20] He sent a copy of his speech to each of his constituents. It was not long afterwards that North Devon was granted 'assisted area status', a development which owed much to his campaigning efforts: he was said to have 'put North Devon on the map' by constantly mentioning its special character and needs in his parliamentary speeches.

He helped the North Devonians in other ways. He was responsible for initiating two important long-term projects requiring central government finance, a large modern general hospital and a link road joining Barnstaple to the Exeter–Taunton motorway at Tiverton. (Ironically, both were to be completed just after Jeremy lost his seat in 1979.) At the time of the 'Beeching Axe' in 1963, he fought to prevent the closure of the railway lines joining Barnstaple to Taunton, Ilfracombe and Exeter: he failed to save the first two, but the third survives to this day. When local industries were threatened, he was prominent in organising consortia to rescue them: he thus helped save the S & P Cabinet Works, Barnstaple's biggest employer, in the 1960s, and the Appledore Shipyards in the 1970s. He devoted much time to constituency surgeries and casework at a period when many MPs did not yet bother much about this side of things. And he performed many acts of personal kindness, particularly where these promised to attract useful publicity – as when he took over the running of a village post office for a week to enable the postmaster and his wife to take a much-needed holiday.*

Despite being a solitary Liberal among Conservatives, he also did much to galvanise his fellow Devon MPs (there then being ten in all). In his devotion to the welfare of his constituents, he set a standard which they were obliged to follow; and they went along with various ideas he put forward to improve public services throughout the county. In 1962, several of them followed his example and defied the Government whip to vote against a price review which threatened the interests of local small farmers. Some right-wingers such as Frederic Bennett (Torquay) and Robert Maxwell-Hyslop (Tiverton) disliked him on both

---

* This colourful episode took place in October 1966, the beneficiaries of Jeremy's gesture being Squadron Leader and Mrs Leslie Farrell who ran the post office and general stores at Landkey near Barnstaple. It produced a tongue-in-cheek rebuke from the Postmaster-General, Jeremy's old friend Tony Benn, who pointed out that it was technically illegal for an MP to work for the GPO, as this amounted to 'an office of profit under the Crown' under the terms of the Act of Settlement of 1701.

personal and political grounds; but he got on splendidly with his immediate neighbour Percy Browne, the youthful and charismatic Old Etonian who had defeated Mark Bonham Carter in Torrington. A man of moderate and humane views, Browne co-operated with Jeremy on many issues both local and national; he also shared Jeremy's ribald sense of humour, and they developed something of a comic double act during their frequent joint appearances at public dinners or on *Any Questions*.

Even before his election, Jeremy had enjoyed a large personal following in North Devon: one political journalist reckoned that as much as one-third of his vote was 'personal', bestowed upon him by people who were uninterested in his politics but had been captivated by his vivid personality and extraordinary ability to remember their names and concerns.[21] As the benefits of having him as their MP became apparent, this following swelled in numbers, while their feelings towards him became more those of adulation than admiration. They called him 'the King of North Devon' and treated him like royalty, rushing out to hail him as he travelled around the constituency. Stories about him became the staple gossip of the region, while the local paper, the *North Devon Journal Herald*, became largely devoted to reporting his sayings and doings. During his weekend visits to Barnstaple, he would deliver speeches on the issues of domestic or international politics currently engaging his interest, which were attended by large audiences and reported in the *Herald* as if they were the weighty utterances of some great statesman.

It need hardly be said that Jeremy adored being the local hero and played up to the role. He was a compulsive organiser of celebrations; and in April 1962 he held a tremendous rally to celebrate the tenth anniversary of his adoption, complete with fanfares of trumpets and drums and closed-circuit TV to enable those at the back of the hall to see what was happening at the front. Over 3,000 came, making it the largest political gathering in the West Country for years. The numerous guests included

Lubbock, fresh from his victory at Orpington, and Jeremy's grandmother Lady Norton-Griffiths, almost ninety, who was cheered when she announced that she had last been there forty years earlier to support the Conservative candidate. By chance, the event coincided with the high point of the Party's political revival: in a rousing speech, Jeremy spoke of 'a furnace of Liberalism ablaze in the land'. To those who were present that day and witnessed the adulation of his constituents, it seemed that he was truly 'King' in North Devon, that he could soon look forward to a much increased majority, that the seat would be his for life.

Like most MPs, Jeremy was unable to live on his parliamentary salary. As noted, this amounted to £1,750* in 1959, rising to £3,250 in 1964 thanks to the efforts of Jeremy and his fellow pay negotiators. At that time, MPs received travel allowances and such perks as free postage, but most other expenses arising from their parliamentary duties, including the cost of secretarial assistance and London accommodation, had to come out of their salary, which was in any case hardly adequate to maintain a lifestyle appropriate for an MP. Jeremy received some help from prosperous well-wishers;† his constituency association contributed towards his local living expenses; and he could draw on the funds of Winnable Seats when he went on the stump. But like most of his backbench colleagues, he was obliged to supplement his income through professional activities outside Parliament. Indeed, so limited were his means that, for more than two years after his election, he still had no private residence

---

* According to the Retail Prices Index, £1,750 in 1959 was the equivalent of about £35,000 in 2011.

† These included his grandmother, left moderately well-off by a Canadian trust set up by Empire Jack before his suicide: after Jeremy's election, she bought him two motor cars, a Rover for London and a Sunbeam Rapier for the West Country.

of his own, continuing to live with his mother at Limpsfield and
Mrs Chappel at Barnstaple: only in 1962 did he feel sufficiently
secure to rent a one-bedroom service flat in Marsham Court, a
pre-war block in Westminster.

Before his election, Jeremy had earned his living in two main
ways – as a barrister and broadcaster. After six months in
Parliament, he decided to give up the Bar: such occasional practice as he might have had as an MP was not worth the expense
of maintaining a tenancy in chambers. He still occasionally
appeared in court without fee in cases involving human rights:
in June 1961, for example, he represented twelve anti-apartheid
demonstrators who had been charged with causing an affray outside South Africa House. And in 1966, he briefly toyed with the
idea of becoming a QC with a view to doing 'just two or three big
cases a year'.* But his legal career, which had never been much
more to him than a stop-gap until he got into Parliament, was
effectively at an end.

On the other hand, his broadcasting career continued to flourish, particularly his television interviewing for *This Week*. Apart
from boosting his income, this kept him before the public eye
and enabled him to make interesting overseas journeys to meet
important personages, many of whom became useful friends. As
noted, he was the programme's expert on African affairs and
often went out to see both the colonial rulers and nationalist
leaders, his great 'scoop' being his exclusive interview with Dr
Hastings Banda in London immediately after his release from
prison in Nyasaland in April 1960. He also conducted some
notable interviews with Middle Eastern rulers, including Nasser
of Egypt, the Shah of Iran, King Hussein of Jordan and Makarios

---

* Previously, MPs who were barristers had been able to apply to be made QCs
as of right, being known as 'the artificial silks'. But this practice was discontinued by the Labour Lord Chancellor Gardiner, who informed Jeremy that,
if he wished to take silk, he would have to return to regular practice as a junior
barrister for at least a couple of years. (Diary of Kenneth Rose, 1 March 1966.)

of Cyprus. Meanwhile, he continued to be a regular and popular panellist on BBC Radio's *Any Questions*, where he was famous for dropping into local dialect and giving authentic imitations of his fellow panellists: there was even a plan to record a programme consisting of Jeremy *solo* impersonating an entire panel of well-known figures, unfortunately scotched by strait-laced controllers at the BBC.

Though no one could accuse him of possessing much literary talent, Jeremy dabbled in popular journalism and wrote occasional political articles for the left-wing *Daily Herald* and its (then fairly respectable) successor the *Sun*. Meanwhile, the upmarket *Sunday Telegraph*, founded in 1961, paid him an annual retainer of £500 to supply parliamentary gossip to its 'Albany' columnist Kenneth Rose. This was the idea of Lady Pamela Berry, wife of the proprietor and a brilliant hostess and networker, who believed Jeremy and Rose would be useful to each other and introduced them at her dinner table. The two men became friends, sharing as they did a common interest in political history and anecdote, and their friendship survived the end of Jeremy's professional connection with the newspaper in 1965.[22]

In September 1963 Jeremy was appointed Negotiating Secretary of the National Association of Fire Officers, succeeding a Conservative MP. This brought in £1,500 a year (the cost of maintaining his London flat) and gave him useful experience of trade union matters. Meanwhile, he had acquired a superficial knowledge of business by accepting a number of company directorships. Though he enjoyed dabbling in the world of commerce, Jeremy did not show much business sense and was fatally drawn to rather dubious promoters. In 1960 he was persuaded by a fellow West Country Liberal (who was later forced to resign as a parliamentary candidate when unmasked as an undischarged bankrupt) to join the board of the television company Univision: within a year, Jeremy's involvement with both the man and the firm had ended in a welter of mutual recrimination. Another West Country Liberal, Peter Bessell, the candidate at Bodmin and a flamboyant fantasist with whom Jeremy then enjoyed a close friendship, made him a director of two small Cornish businesses he had set up under American franchises, manufacturing drink-vending machines and felt-tip pens: while these were modestly successful, Bessell went on to get into serious trouble with more ambitious schemes. Jeremy was of course invited on to these boards mainly on account of his kudos and connections as an MP: as a businessman, he enjoyed discussing grandiose plans but lacked the ability to master detail.[23]

He was also employed as a consultant by External Development Services (EDS), a firm set up in the late 1950s by the Welsh Liberal Grenville Jones to provide research and advice to new foreign governments. For this he was paid an annual retainer of £750 plus extra fees for any specific work he undertook. Jeremy accompanied Jones and his partner George Knapp on missions to Nigeria and Tunisia in 1960, Uganda and Zanzibar in 1962, and Dubai in 1963 and 1964: though he did not always have much to contribute to practical discussions, he was a useful intermediary who knew how to make the most of his contacts and create a relaxed atmosphere for talks. Through his friendships with Makarios and Banda, he was also able to obtain business for EDS from the new governments of Cyprus and Malawi. There is, however, little to suggest that Jeremy improperly used his parliamentary position to advance the interests of the governments represented by EDS: indeed, his politics were often highly embarrassing to EDS. For example, the fact that the principal client of EDS was an Arab ruler, the Emir of Dubai, never affected Jeremy's Zionist sympathies: he once astonished Jones by asking if he might stop off to see friends in Israel on his way to visit the Emir, who was paying for the trip. And his attacks on the regime in Ghana threatened EDS business with the South African exile ANC organisation, which counted Nkrumah among its backers.[24]

Given the variety and scale of his political work, it seems amazing that Jeremy should have had much time or energy left over for other professional activities. As it was, his contributions to television, radio and the press, his trade union secretaryship, his company directorships and his EDS consultancy, together with his parliamentary salary, brought in (so Jeremy told Grenville Jones) a combined annual income of around £7,500 towards the end of the 1959–64 Parliament, no great fortune but enough to enable him to live in reasonable comfort and style. But financial anxiety was never far away, and would resurface in the autumn of 1965 when his election as Liberal Party Treasurer obliged him to give up much of this outside work.

During the early 1960s, Jeremy was involved in a number of colourful parliamentary episodes which, though outside the mainstream of politics, caused him to hit the headlines and illustrate his love of controversy and his quixotic and impulsive nature. The first of these occurred in the autumn of 1960, when the News Chronicle, the last national daily newspaper supporting the Liberal Party, suddenly ceased publication after its proprietor, the chocolate millionaire Laurence Cadbury, sold it to the rival and Conservative-supporting Daily Mail which closed it down. It had been in financial difficulties for some time, but its closure caused consternation among its staff, which included many journalists with radical political sympathies who had (perhaps understandably) not been consulted by their capitalist employer about his decision. Jeremy had many friends among the aggrieved staff* and keenly felt the loss of this traditional mouthpiece of

---

* Notably the whiggish young leader writer Richard Moore, who had been Liberal candidate at Tavistock in 1955 and 1959. He also knew the veteran foreign correspondent James Cameron and the cartoonist Vicky. The Barnstaple-born A. J. Cummings, political editor until his death in 1957, had also been a friend of Jeremy and had commissioned him to write occasional articles.

Liberalism. In a magnificent thundering performance in the House of Commons, he launched a vitriolic personal attack on Cadbury, 'the butcher of Bouverie Street', accusing him of 'murdering' the paper and betraying the principles of his philanthropic Liberal and Quaker family. Cadbury's reputation never recovered from the onslaught; and while nothing could bring the *News Chronicle* back to life, Jeremy's colourful invective ensured that it died in a blaze of publicity which was useful both to the Liberal Party and himself.[25]

On 17 November 1960, while the fuss over the *News Chronicle* was in progress, the death occurred of the Labour statesman Viscount Stansgate. As the law then stood, his eldest surviving son Anthony Wedgwood Benn automatically succeeded to the viscountcy with its seat in the House of Lords, and thus forfeited the seat in the House of Commons which he had held for the past ten years as Labour MP for Bristol South-East – an outcome which Benn regarded as scandalous and was determined to reverse. Jeremy knew and admired Benn from the Oxford Union;* and when Benn announced his intention of refusing to take up his peerage and fighting to retain his membership of the Lower House, Jeremy offered his full support. On 27 November, Jeremy issued a joint statement with the Conservative MP Gerald Nabarro and the Labour MP Barbara Castle, contending that it was 'unjust to expel an elected MP from the House of Commons by reason of an inherited disqualification over which he has no control' and 'undemocratic to deny a constituency the right to choose anyone ... it wants to represent it in Parliament'.[26]

---

* Benn, who was four years older than Jeremy, had been President shortly before Jeremy came up to Oxford and was still in residence during Jeremy's first term. During the 1950s, Jeremy sometimes went to hear Benn at the House of Commons, and would afterwards congratulate him 'rather in the manner of an elder statesman bestowing approval on some youngster'. (Tony Benn to the author, April 1994.)

When it came to questions of inherited rank and privilege, Jeremy was torn between two positions. As a young radical, he purported to regard the hereditary peerage as 'a medieval farce';[27] but he adored the romance of titles, and cherished the fantasy that he himself was the rightful claimant to the ancient and splendid barony of Thorpe. Writing to Benn on the eve of his historic struggle to disclaim his viscountcy, he could not resist mentioning that 'only a lack of funds ... prevents me from claiming a Barony!!!!'[28] Nevertheless, Jeremy was Benn's stalwart ally in his complex legal battle, lasting almost three years, to divest himself of his unwanted peerage and return to the House of Commons. When, in May 1961, Benn defiantly insisted on standing in the by-election at Bristol South-East caused by his own disqualification from the Commons, Jeremy saw to it that he faced no Liberal opponent. And it was in reply to a parliamentary question from Jeremy in November 1961 that the Government finally agreed to set up a Joint Select Committee to consider reform of the law regarding peerages. He also contributed to the fund set up to help Benn meet his legal costs, regretting he could not give more as 'it is almost as expensive being in the House of Commons as it is being forcibly ejected from it!'[29]

Jeremy was not invited to sit on the Joint Select Committee, on which the more senior Donald Wade represented the Liberal MPs. But when, in the spring of 1963, the Government acted on the committee's report and introduced the Peerages Bill, enabling peers to stand for the Commons after disclaiming their titles, Jeremy made his mark in the debate. He (unsuccessfully) proposed an amendment which would have made disclaimed peerages redundant for all time and not just a single generation, inevitably mentioning his own imaginary claim to 'a discreditable Norman barony'.[30] Finally, on 29 July, the Bill received the Royal Assent, and Jeremy attended the victory party thrown by Benn, who was at last able to rid himself of his *damnosa hereditas* and return as MP for Bristol South-East at another by-election the following month.*

On 5 June 1963, while the Peerages Bill was making its progress through Parliament, the Government was rocked by the resignation of the War Minister John Profumo, who admitted having lied to the House of Commons in denying a relationship with Christine Keeler, a prostitute whose other patrons included a member of the Soviet Embassy. Jeremy was always fascinated by scandals concerning other people; and a few weeks later, speaking in his constituency on 21 July, he caused a sensation by declaring that 'two further ministers will soon have to resign for personal reasons'. Though he mentioned no names or details, he seems to have been alluding to fairly widespread gossip in parliamentary circles concerning the Transport Minister Ernest Marples and the junior minister Denzil Freeth: though neither was actually involved in the events surrounding Profumo, the first was rumoured to have fetishistic interests and the second a homosexual past. Jeremy's remarks were picked up by the national press and caused an outcry among Conservative MPs, who demanded that he either explain what he meant by them or retract them.

He was summoned to appear before the official enquiry investigating Profumo, chaired by Lord Denning, the Master of the Rolls.† This had two contradictory consequences. First, Jeremy

---

* After all he had done for his friend, Jeremy was dismayed in June 1963 to learn that Benn was to address the North Devon Labour Association that month. In an injured letter, he complained that, as a matter both of tradition and good manners, Benn should at least have let him know of his intention to speak in his constituency. When he spoke, however, Benn warmly praised Jeremy for his 'wonderful and sustained support throughout my long battle'.

† Fortunately for Jeremy, Denning seems to have been personally well-disposed towards him: he had Liberal sympathies, and had once been engaged to Jeremy's Aunt Pheobe, Ursula's younger sister. In 1979, he was to give Jeremy a favourable judgement in his efforts to ban the election address of his adversary Auberon Waugh.

explained to Denning the gossip which had prompted his remarks, which led to secret investigations as a result of which Freeth was quietly sacked from the Government some months later. Secondly, as Denning's official report concluded that no other public figures were implicated in the Profumo affair itself, Jeremy was forced to apologise for his offending remarks when the Commons debated the report in December 1963.* Skilful parliamentarian that he was, he seems to have turned this humiliation to his advantage: the New Statesman reported that 'the normally ebullient Thorpe never looked more diffident than he did as he sat twisting his handkerchief in lonely isolation on the Liberal bench, but in the end he won over even the Tory benches by his modesty ...'[31]

Considering that Jeremy was himself leading a dissolute and illegal sex life at this period, which involved immense risks for his career and had already brought him to the notice of the police both in Britain and America, this episode does not present him in an attractive light. Quite apart from the element of hypocrisy, it shows up some of his worst qualities – his irresistible tendency to show off, his reckless disregard of consequences, the streaks of mischief and prurience in his nature which inclined him to cast stones. But for all his faults, he had by this time built up a unique position for himself as a parliamentary performer, a party politician, an international humanitarian and a constituency MP. There was no one quite like him; and with an election looming which promised to change the political map of Britain, an interesting future seemed to lie ahead.

---

* In paragraph 338 of his report, Denning wrote: 'There were other rumours arising indirectly out of the Profumo affair ... I investigated them and have to report there is not a shred of evidence in support of them.' However, in a secret letter which he sent Macmillan at the same time, Denning wrote that he had investigated the rumours concerning Freeth 'and regret to inform you that [he] did three years ago go to a party of a homosexual character and there participated in homosexual conduct'.

8

NORMAN
1961–64

JEREMY THORPE'S FIRST TERM in Parliament, during which he distinguished himself in various ways, also witnessed the unfolding of the secret drama which would eventually result in the destruction of his career. As we have seen, he conducted many clandestine homosexual affairs during this period, often with rather insecure men, younger than himself and from earthier social backgrounds, who looked up to him and towards whom he could play a protective role. In the homosexual world of those days, such relationships could bring satisfaction to both parties; but they could also be dangerous, as there was always a risk that the younger party might turn nasty and resort to some form of blackmail. Jeremy enjoyed the danger, and on the whole handled such episodes with skill. But he had the misfortune to encounter one situation which was beyond his power to control, when he formed an attachment with a neurotic parasite who would not let go, made constant demands, persuaded himself that he had been the victim of serious mistreatment and became obsessed with thoughts of revenge. This was Norman Josiffe, later to call himself Norman Scott, whom Jeremy had fleetingly met while visiting Norman Vater in

Oxfordshire in the summer of 1960, and who re-established contact with him in November of the following year.

From that moment, they saw each other regularly over a period of fourteen months, then intermittently during a further two years. The story is complicated by a conflict of evidence between them as to the nature of their relationship. In numerous outbursts and statements down the years, the details of which varied, Josiffe portrayed Jeremy as a callous sexual vampire whose interest in him had been based not on altruism or affection but merely a constant desire for crude self-gratification. Jeremy, for his part, although he eventually confessed that his relationship with Josiffe had been 'close, even affectionate', always insisted that it never involved a sexual element, and was essentially a case of his trying to help a soul in distress. Neither version can be accepted at face value: Josiffe was a compulsive liar and fantasist, while Jeremy was caught out in repeated evasions as the scandal unfolded, and finally admitted at his trial to having had 'homosexual tendencies' at the time, of which Josiffe had tried to take advantage. But two things are clear. First, whether or not Jeremy's relations with Josiffe were sexual, he certainly for a time showed tender feelings towards him and a genuine concern for his welfare. And secondly, it must be judged reckless folly for someone in Jeremy's position to have formed any sort of relationship with a person of Josiffe's character and background – though, to be fair, Josiffe was a persuasive teller of hard-luck stories and skilled at taking people in.[1]

Born on 12 February 1940, Norman Josiffe was the wayward son of a broken marriage in suburban Kent. His father, Albert Josiffe, was an accountant; his mother, Ena, née Lynch, had had several children by a previous marriage to a shipping clerk who had died before the war. Norman saw virtually nothing of his father as he grew up. Nor did he see as much as he would have liked of his mother, who worked long hours in an airline office to keep her large family and tended to spend her evenings at the

Bexleyheath Conservative Club. (From 1950, the local Tory MP was Ted Heath, who would one day offer a place in his Government to Jeremy Thorpe, then persecuted to distraction by the son of Ena Josiffe.) The strongest influence on his childhood was his grandmother Lynch, a formidable Irishwoman who saw to it that her grandchildren received a Catholic upbringing.

At his secondary modern school, Norman did not shine either at work or games and became shy and withdrawn. He preferred animals to people, lavishing his affections on a beloved pony. When he was fifteen, a juvenile court convicted him of stealing a saddle and some animal feed and put him on probation. By this time, two dangerous elements of his personality had become established. He was a dreamer, forever 'looking for some Shangri-la' (as his mother put it) and fantasising about romantic backgrounds far from the suburban dullness of Bexleyheath: in particular, he began to daydream that the father he did not know might have been someone rather more glamorous than Albert Josiffe. And he had begun to see himself in the role of victim: he felt he had been driven to crime by his mother's neglect and the fact that no one would help him provide for the pony. Soon it would become second nature to him to exaggerate his misfortunes and blame them on others.

During his probation, Josiffe attended riding school and proved to have talent as a horseman. At seventeen, he was working as a riding instructor in Cheshire. The equestrian world is one in which people of modest origins rub shoulders with those from a higher social sphere, and Norman started putting on airs, changing his surname to Lianche-Josiffe ('Lianche' being the supposed original Norman French form of his mother's maiden name of Lynch) and hinting that, though alone in the world, he hailed from some mysterious aristocratic background. At nineteen, he moved to Kingham in Oxfordshire to become a groom to Norman Vater, hoping to learn dressage and compete in the Badminton Trials. Vater was another man of mysterious origins who claimed aristocratic antecedents, but he was also a distinguished figure in the eventing world and an energetic, hot-tempered personality. Josiffe seems at first to have fallen under his spell but later became terrified of him and, around the time of his twenty-first birthday in the winter of 1961, ran away from the job. In June of that year he suffered a nervous breakdown, attempted suicide, and was admitted as a voluntary patient to an Oxford psychiatric hospital, the Ashurst Clinic.

By this time, Josiffe had met Jeremy precisely once, at Kingham in 1960, on which occasion they had had a few minutes' conversation, enough (as he later claimed) to be made aware of Jeremy's homosexual interest in him. Jeremy (according to Josiffe's account) had told him that Vater was a curious character and that if he had any trouble he should come to see him at the House of Commons. Josiffe also claimed to have received a subsequent letter from Jeremy, which he was never able to produce. What Josiffe did know, however, was that Vater possessed a genuine cache of letters from Jeremy; and when he fled from Kingham early in 1961, Josiffe (as he later admitted) stole these letters and made off with them. They included the ribald postcard in which Jeremy lamented Princess Margaret's marriage to Lord Snowdon, having hoped to 'marry the one and seduce the other', and other letters of an intimate nature on House of Commons writing paper. As most of them began 'Dear Norman', this being Vater's first name as well as Josiffe's, Josiffe was able to pass them off to people he subsequently met as having been written to himself, which he did (as he confessed at the Old Bailey) to several fellow patients at the Ashurst.

At twenty-one, Josiffe was a striking youth. 'Tall and slim, with strong features, he would have been formally handsome but for the troubled expression about his eyes and the pouting set of his mouth which suggested sensuality and petulance in equal measure.'[2] He had developed skill at engaging the sympathy of people he met for the first time. He was sexually attractive to both men and women: several patients at the Ashurst developed crushes on him, and on leaving the clinic he briefly set up house in Oxford with two of them, a woman and a homosexual man. He was widely considered to be homosexual himself, and while denying this vehemently, he was clearly uncertain about his orientation. Following the break-up of his *ménage à trois*, he formed a close friendship with a man who lived in the Oxfordshire village of Church Enstone: when this friend eventually took up with a girlfriend, Josiffe again tried to commit suicide, which led to his briefly returning to the Ashurst under a compulsory detention order. Josiffe was now telling everyone – including the village GP and constable at Church Enstone, and the doctors treating him at the Ashurst – that he had a powerful and intimate friend in London, to whom he referred mysteriously as 'JT', who he believed would help him sort out his problems. As soon as he was released from the Ashurst on Wednesday 8 November 1961, Josiffe, accompanied by his Jack Russell terrier Mrs Tish, duly made his way to London to take up the offer which Jeremy had made to him so casually so many months before.

Having deposited his dog at the Westminster branch of the Anti-Vivisection League, Josiffe went to the Central Lobby of the House of Commons and filled out a green card asking to see Jeremy Thorpe MP. He had no appointment and it was fortuitous that Jeremy, who was due to go overseas next day, happened to be in the House. As it was, Jeremy remembered him and saw him willingly. Josiffe was by now a skilled teller of hard-luck stories. He spoke of how he had been mistreated by Vater, claiming (among much else) that the latter had stolen his National Insurance card. He said that he had no family, no work and nowhere to go.* As Peter Bessell later wrote, Jeremy ought

---

* According to one of his later accounts, he also handed Jeremy some (not all) of the letters he had stolen from Vater, explaining that he feared they might be used for blackmail purposes.

at once to have done two things – contacted his friend Vater to hear his side of the story, and advised Josiffe to approach his own (Oxfordshire) MP. Instead, he offered to take Josiffe and his dog to spend the night at Stonewalls, his mother's house in Limpsfield, where Jeremy was himself still living at this time, not yet having acquired his own London flat.

They drove down to Surrey in Jeremy's Rover, stopping on the way at a South London address to see a man named Tony, to whom Jeremy introduced Josiffe as a friend down on his luck.* The following day, Jeremy was due to fly to Jamaica† with a television crew, to make a programme for *This Week*; and as they approached Limpsfield, he suggested to Josiffe that he introduce him to his mother as one of the cameramen, 'Peter from Colchester'. Josiffe went along with this and signed Ursula Thorpe's visitors' book with the name he had been given. After they had dined, Josiffe said he was exhausted and asked to go to bed. It is possible that Ursula was not unused to Jeremy bringing strange young men to spend the night. The ground-floor flat in which she lived (she let the upper floor of her house) consisted of a large central area which served as entrance hall, drawing room and dining room, off which ran two corridors in opposite directions, one leading to Jeremy's bedroom, a room which served both as Jeremy's study and the spare bedroom, and a bathroom, the other to Ursula's sitting room, bedroom and bathroom. (Owing to the layout and thickness of the walls, whatever happened at one end of the dwelling was inaudible at the other.) Jeremy saw Josiffe to the spare room, and provided him with water for the pills he had to take and some books to

---

* Who was 'Tony'? Jeremy had two friends of that name in South London – Lord Snowdon, who had a house in Dulwich, and Tony Maycock, who had a flat in Brixton. At Jeremy's trial, the judge refused to allow any discussion of 'Tony' – presumably to prevent the name of Lord Snowdon, who had recently been divorced by Princess Margaret, being dragged into the proceedings.

† Not Malta, as Josiffe later alleged in his trial evidence.

read: these, according to Josiffe, included James Baldwin's novel
Giovanni's Room (1957), an account, then considered daring, of
a homosexual affair in Paris between an American expatriate and
an Italian barman.

According to Josiffe, some time later Jeremy returned to his
room, embraced him, and told him banteringly that he looked
like 'a frightened rabbit'. (Such was the origin of the nickname
'Bunnies', used by Jeremy in his subsequently famous letter to
Josiffe.) What happened next varies according to Josiffe's several
accounts. In a statement he gave the police a year later, he
claimed that Jeremy proceeded to have sexual relations with him,
but that these did not include an act of penetration. In the
famous evidence at the Old Bailey in 1979, he claimed that
Jeremy produced a towel and jar of vaseline and effectively proceeded to rape him, while Josiffe bit the pillow to prevent himself
crying out in pain: he was then left alone for the rest of the night
with only his dog for company. However, at the Committal
Proceedings at Minehead a few months earlier, Josiffe had
claimed that Jeremy had returned several times during the night
to repeat the performance. In other accounts, Josiffe claimed that
Jeremy had already tried to seduce him during the car journey to
Limpsfield. One feature common to all these accounts is that
Josiffe insists that he found the alleged experience novel and
traumatic and was forced unwillingly to engage in acts which,
with his Catholic upbringing, he regarded as sinful. Seeing that,
only a few months earlier, he had been boasting to his fellow psychiatric patients that he was already engaging in a homosexual
affair with Jeremy, whom he had then met once for a few minutes, and that since then he had been cohabiting in romantic
circumstances with at least two men, these claims do not entirely
convince.

The next morning, Jeremy put his head round Josiffe's door
and asked him how he liked his eggs done. (It was on hearing
this detail, which 'rang true of Jeremy's usual concerns and

courtesies', that David Steel, years afterwards, decided that 'there must be something' in Josiffe's story.)³ They returned to London together. Before proceeding to Heathrow to catch his plane, Jeremy gave Josiffe some money and advised the youth (who does not seem to have lived in London before) to rent one of the inexpensive furnished flats advertised in the windows of newsagents in the King's Road. Josiffe duly became a tenant at 21, Draycott Place, and awaited Jeremy's return from abroad.

Jeremy returned from Jamaica on 15 November, and for the next few weeks seems to have spent much time in Josiffe's company. He paid the rent of Josiffe's flat; he gave him pocket money; he entertained him at the House of Commons, the Reform Club and Chelsea restaurants; he gave him presents and letters authorising him to order clothes at his tailor and shirt-maker. (This must have represented a fair sum to a man with heavy expenses whose annual pre-tax earnings cannot then have exceeded £6,000.) Whether or not Jeremy engaged in nightly acts of buggery at Josiffe's flat, as alleged by Josiffe, or the friend-ship was merely 'close and affectionate', as claimed by Jeremy, it certainly seems to have contained a powerful romantic element at this stage. Jeremy evidently enjoyed the sensation of intro-ducing a responsive youth to a new and enchanted world, knowing that Josiffe was looking up to him as a protector and worldly sophisticate. But there are dangers in introducing an impressionable young person to a dazzling and unfamiliar environment, from which he may later find it hard to come down to earth and resume normal life and work.

It has been noted that Josiffe had become skilful at engaging the sympathy of strangers, and two elements in his story seem to have touched Jeremy particularly. First, he gave Jeremy to under-stand that he was entirely alone in the world, effectively an orphan. The truth was that both his separated parents were lead-ing respectable and prosaic lives in Kent, and Josiffe remained in touch with his mother; but the tale he spun for Jeremy (which he had already put about in Oxfordshire during the past year) was that his father was a famous architect who had been killed in a plane crash in the Amazon jungle while designing a new Brazilian city,* while his mother had long ago disappeared with another man. He also claimed to have been cheated out of an inheritance from his deceased father's estate; and Jeremy asked a solicitor friend, James Walters, to make enquiries about this. Jeremy was also apparently affected by Josiffe's assertion that he had been denied a proper chance in life and only needed some help to get on his feet. As a first step, Jeremy got Josiffe a job assisting Len Smith, a professional officer at Liberal Headquarters in Smith Square who was then organising an appeal for the relief of the victims of a hurricane which had struck British Honduras at the end of October. Smith was a kindly man who tried to show understanding towards the obviously disturbed youth; but on one occasion, Josiffe walked off with his briefcase and Smith had to ask for Jeremy's help in getting it back – not the first time Josiffe had been tempted to purloin papers which did not belong to him.

During these weeks, Jeremy continued to be active in the many political and professional roles outlined in the last chapter, though the fact that he made no parliamentary speeches that November and December might be taken to signify that he was unusually absorbed in his private life. Josiffe too seems to have had other fish to fry: he later claimed that, while conducting his affair with Jeremy in London, he was also sleeping with two women who had been his fellow psychiatric patients at the Ashurst.

Jeremy was due to spend Christmas 1961 with his mother at Broomhills, Mrs Chappel's house outside Barnstaple which he

---

* It may seem surprising that Jeremy should have given any credence to this improbable-sounding story; but it must be remembered that he too lived in something of a fantasy world.

used as his constituency base. He arranged for Josiffe to stay at Tiverton, some twenty miles away, on the farm of the local Liberal candidate James Collier and his wife Mary, helping with their horses and political canvassing. Collier, who had two small daughters, was not happy at the prospect of playing host to an evidently neurotic youth, but was indebted to Jeremy for his support in the previous year's Tiverton by-election, which he had come within 2,000 votes of winning. Early in the New Year, the Colliers visited Jeremy at Broomhills and brought Josiffe with them: Josiffe later alleged that Jeremy had made love to him in a bathroom while Ursula Thorpe and the Colliers were walking in the garden. The Colliers later confirmed that Jeremy had urged them to go for a walk while he stayed behind with Josiffe for some twenty minutes, explaining that he wanted the young man to try on some shirts.

Josiffe stayed on with the Colliers for most of January 1962, while Jeremy returned to London to attend Parliament after the recess. The book *Rinkagate* quotes from a letter which was allegedly sent from Jeremy to Josiffe at this time. On House of Commons paper, it appears to be little more than a scribbled note, and carries no date; but it begins with a description of Jeremy's move into a new office which, as a backbench MP, he had been allotted that month, across the road from the House of Commons at No.1, Bridge Street.* It ends with a declaration of love, and an expression of Jeremy's impatience to see Josiffe again.[4]

The Colliers were the first of a string of kindly rural employers who started off feeling sorry for Josiffe but after a few weeks had had enough of him and asked him to leave. He was a

---

* Only a handful of offices were then available for backbench MPs, and whenever one became vacant, it would be re-allocated through a draw. As one of some five hundred office-less MPs, Jeremy was lucky to get one after just two years in the House, even outside the precincts of Parliament.

disturbed and disturbing presence, had little discipline for work and was inclined to say strange things. (Josiffe later claimed to have told them about his 'relationship' with Jeremy.) Jeremy took steps to find him another job. He placed an advertisement in *Country Life* in the following romanticised terms: 'Ex-public schoolboy, 21, wishes to live with family and work on farm. Skilled horses. Former Badminton competitor. Willing to undertake any work. Pocket money only expected.' But Jeremy did not encourage Josiffe to follow up the replies received, most of which hinted at homosexual interest. Meanwhile, Jeremy read in the newspapers that the groom of a Major Hambro, a farmer at Dulverton in Somerset, had been killed in a riding accident: he telephoned the Hambros (whom he did not know) to ask if he would accept Josiffe as a replacement and they agreed to give him a try.

Between the Colliers and the Hambros, Josiffe returned to London for a couple of weeks, staying at Draycott Place. Two substantiated incidents took place around this time. Jeremy took Josiffe to Limpsfield again to visit his mother (who had already been reintroduced to him at Broomhills), and this time the false name he had originally entered in Ursula's visitors' book was erased and he substituted *Norman Lianche Josiffe.** And Ann Gray, a former girlfriend of Josiffe – stung, according to Josiffe, by the knowledge, which he had decided to share with her, of his affair with Jeremy – went to the police alleging that Josiffe had stolen her suede coat. When the police asked to see Josiffe about this, Jeremy arranged for the interview to take place under his auspices at his new parliamentary office in Bridge Street. In his record of the interview, Detective Constable Raymond Whitmore-Smith noted that Jeremy claimed to be 'more or less a guardian to Norman Josiffe, who had lost both parents', and added:

---

* A police handwriting expert at Jeremy's trial confirmed that the entry had been altered in this way.

During the interview in the presence of Thorpe, it was patently obvious that Josiffe was a rather weak personality, apparently labouring under considerable mental strain, and completely dominated by Thorpe who was acting in an advisory capacity to Josiffe. During the period when Josiffe was writing his statement, Mr Thorpe left his office to attend a Division and during his absence Josiffe was noticeably relaxed and more talkative.

Josiffe later alleged that one of the reasons for his nervousness was that Jeremy had been fondling him at the moment the police arrived.

It was five days later, after Josiffe had started work for the Hambros, that Jeremy wrote him the letter which would subsequently become famous and cost him his career:

House of Commons
13 February 1961*

My dear Norman,

Since my letters normally go to the House, yours arrived all by itself at my breakfast table at the Reform, and gave me tremendous pleasure.

I cannot tell you just how happy *I* feel that you are settling down, and feeling that life has something to offer.

This is really wonderful and you can always feel that whatever happens Jimmy and Mary [Collier] and I are right behind you. The next thing is to solve your financial problems and this James Walters and I are on to. The really important thing is that you are now a member of a *family* doing a useful job of work – with

---

* This is clearly a mistake for 13 February 1962 – an unfortunate error which would later give rise to the misapprehension that Jeremy had become close to Josiffe while the latter was still a minor.

Tish – which you enjoy. Hooray!! Faced with all that no more bloody clinics.

I think you can now take the Ann Gray incident [regarding the alleged theft of her coat] as over and done with.

Enclosed another letter!!* I suggest you keep them all – just in case – but will you send back the photo? Thank the guy but say you are fixed up.

Bunnies *can* (and *will*) go to France.†

In haste.

Yours affectionately

Jeremy

I miss you.

In itself, this letter reads innocently, even touchingly; but when it was published in May 1976, it made a mockery of Jeremy's then assertion that he had scarcely known Norman Josiffe, and led within days to his resignation as Leader of the Liberal Party. It unmistakably suggests that, three months after getting involved with him, Jeremy was still fond of 'Bunnies' and concerned for his welfare.

These feelings, however, were soon to cool. During the next few weeks, three events must have made him realise that, in befriending and patronising Josiffe, he had made a serious mistake. First, James Walters, the solicitor he had asked to investigate the matter of the estate of the deceased architect Josiffe claimed to be his father, wrote to Jeremy that he doubted whether any such person existed. He suggested they tread softly since, if Josiffe's fantasy world were exposed, there was no telling how he might react. Jeremy agreed they must be careful not 'to open a Pandora's box'. Walters' doubts were soon justified. Josiffe's father was alive and well and living in Orpington. Moreover, his mother,

---

* In reply to the *Country Life* advertisement.
† A reference to Josiffe's ambition to study dressage in that country.

who according to Josiffe had long since disappeared to distant parts and whom he had not seen for years, turned out to be not only living in Bexleyheath but closely in touch with her son and informed by him about his relationship with Jeremy. 'She is vicious about you,' wrote Walters to Jeremy, 'as being largely responsible for the rift between her son and herself.'

Secondly, by Josiffe's admission, he had 'a dreadful row' with Jeremy while they were driving one afternoon in Devon, during which he threatened to expose Jeremy's homosexuality. Jeremy seems to have laughed off the incident, telling Josiffe that he would find it hard to harm him as he had powerful friends; but it was a foretaste of things to come. Thirdly, the hope that Josiffe would make a success of his job with the Hambros proved wishful thinking: like the Colliers, they asked him to leave after a month, finding his work unsatisfactory and behaviour alarming. (According to Josiffe, Olga Hambro was yet another person to whom he confided his relationship with Jeremy.) The only lasting result of his time there was that it provided Josiffe with material for a new fantasy paternity, now he could no longer use the architect father who had perished in Amazonia: in future, he would claim to be the illegitimate son of John Scott, 4th Earl of Eldon, a neighbour of the Hambros at Rackenford Manor.

The spring of 1962 represented a busy and exciting moment in Jeremy's life, marked by the victorious by-elections at Orpington and Montgomeryshire and his rally in Barnstaple. He must by now have regarded Josiffe as a terrible nuisance, but he still (as he told his friend Tony Maycock) felt some residual responsibility for him and a desire to see him settled. For a short time, until he could find other work, he personally employed him (though Josiffe knew nothing about politics) as a Liberal canvasser in the seaside resorts of Lynton and Lynmouth in his constituency – an unfortunate decision, as it later enabled Josiffe to claim that Jeremy had responsibilities towards him as an ex-employer. Eventually, Josiffe was offered a job at a riding school in Minehead, but required a National Insurance card, which he asked Jeremy to obtain for him. Jeremy went to some trouble to do so, and a new card was posted to Josiffe by the Ministry of Pensions; but Josiffe claimed never to have received it. Had he received it, it is likely that he would have contrived to lose it, for in Josiffe's fantasy world it was essential *not* to have a valid card: this enabled him to rationalise his lack of self-identity and to 'blame' his lack of a proper job on former employers such as Vater and Jeremy. (It may be recalled that, when Josiffe saw Jeremy at the House of Commons in November 1961, one of his main accusations against Vater was that he had stolen his National Insurance card; and this was an accusation which, in years to come, he was constantly to level against Jeremy himself.)

In May or June 1962, Josiffe found a new patron: a GP he consulted about his problems, Dr Lister, took pity on him and invited him to stay with his family on their farm at Porlock Weir, Somerset. He stayed the entire summer, though letters sent by Lister to Jeremy, whom Josiffe had described as his 'guardian', received short replies to the effect that the doctor ought to address himself to Josiffe's mother. He left there in September after his dog Mrs Tish had been put down for killing Dr Lister's ducks. When he wrote to Jeremy about this episode, and asking if he might return a photo of the dog, the reply he received was kindly but evasive, indicating a distinct change in the relationship since the letter sent in February:

House of Commons
30 September 1962

My dear Norman,

This is indeed terribly sad news about poor little Mrs Tish, and I know what a blow this must have been to you. You have all my sympathy.

I am afraid I shall not be home for a little while and cannot
therefore send you the photo (at the moment I'm in North
Devon). I have a horrible feeling that I may have pasted it into an
album which will make it difficult for me to dislodge.
However . . .

I hope otherwise things go well.

Yours

Jeremy

Josiffe spent most of the autumn of 1962 staying in Kent with
his disapproving mother; but during visits to London he stayed
with Jeremy at his recently acquired service flat at Marsham
Court. According to Josiffe, he was only allowed to stay in return
for services rendered: once Jeremy had gratified himself, he
would retire alone to the single bedroom of the small flat, while
Josiffe would have to make do with an uncomfortable camp-bed
in the sitting room. Yet elsewhere in his litany of accusations,
Josiffe complained that Jeremy now cared for him so little that he
preferred to have sex with sailors and other casual pick-ups
rather than resume anything of their alleged former relationship.
Possibly Jeremy hoped, by showing kindness, to assuage Josiffe's
resentments: if so, it was a forlorn hope. Indeed, the knowledge
that Jeremy no longer loved him, had lost his heart to newer
friends, seems to have driven Josiffe mad with jealousy. He also
claimed to have been devastated when a priest at Westminster
Cathedral, to whom he had confessed his 'sins' with Jeremy,
refused him absolution.

A crisis occurred on 19 December 1962, when Josiffe went to
see Caroline Barrington-Ward, sister of Jeremy's old Eton schoolfriend Simon Barrington-Ward, whom he had met while staying
with the Colliers. Years earlier, the hypersensitive Caroline had
developed a crush on Jeremy when he visited her family home
during school holidays, and this infatuation, while evoking no
response in Jeremy, had persisted down the years. Possibly

supposing that she would understand his feelings of rejection, Josiffe poured out the story of his 'relationship' with Jeremy, adding that he was at the end of his tether and proposed to go to the House of Commons with a gun to kill both Jeremy and himself. Horrified, Caroline suggested that Josiffe go to the Easton Hotel in Victoria, which was co-owned by Mary Collier's sister and where Mrs Collier herself then happened to be acting as receptionist; she then telephoned the police and asked them to go to the hotel.

When the police arrived, Josiffe announced that he wished to make a statement about his homosexual affair with Jeremy, as evidence of which he gave them the two letters of February and September 1962 quoted above as well as several items of the 'Vater' correspondence, including the 'Snowdon' postcard. (The documents handed over are also said to have included a third, rather more compromising letter from Jeremy to Josiffe, written on blue paper rather than the usual House of Commons stationery, which unlike the other two never re-emerged from police custody.) He accompanied them to Chelsea police station, where a doctor examined him and confirmed he was a passive homosexual. He then made a lengthy statement to Detective Inspector Bob Huntley. This began: 'I have come to the police to tell you about my homosexual relationship with Jeremy Thorpe, who is a Liberal MP, because these relations have caused me so much purgatory that I am afraid it might happen to someone else.' There followed a lubricious account of various sexual acts, beginning with the alleged incident at Limpsfield on the night of 8 November 1961. It was a vindictive document, designed to cause maximum embarrassment to Jeremy: Josiffe did nothing to correct the false impression (created by Jeremy's letter of February 1962 mistakenly dated 1961) that he had been a minor at the outset of the alleged affair, and named another man who, he claimed, had supplanted him as Jeremy's lover, the handsome Cambridge undergraduate son of a North Devon doctor. (It should be borne in mind that all homosexual acts were illegal at this time but that offences with minors, then construed as persons under the age of twenty-one, were regarded as especially serious.)

Huntley considered Josiffe a dangerous hysteric, and the documents he handed over, while certainly suggesting that 'the association was more than just friendly', could hardly be said to have corroborated his tale of rampant sodomy. As it amounted to the word of an unknown and unstable individual against that of a respected public figure, he had no intention of taking action on the basis of Josiffe's allegations or of troubling Jeremy Thorpe. Nevertheless, he could not entirely ignore the matter: it was only two months since the homosexual Admiralty clerk W. John Vassall had been convicted of spying for the Soviets. He therefore felt obliged to pass the file up to his superiors. (It ended up along with other sensitive files on the private lives of public figures in the Assistant Commissioner's safe.) He also made further inquiries: he requested the report quoted above from DC Whitmore-Smith who had taken evidence from Josiffe at Jeremy's office the previous February, and interviewed the Cambridge undergraduate Josiffe claimed to be Jeremy's current lover, who indignantly denied the imputation. Perhaps most seriously for Jeremy, he also sent a copy of the file to Devon and Cornwall CID, suggesting that they discreetly check out various aspects of the story.

At the time, Jeremy knew nothing of this episode, so potentially compromising to his career: indeed, he does not seem to have found out about it until more than two years later. Josiffe also claimed that, having given his 'evidence', he actually returned to stay with Jeremy at Marsham Court, hoping to be present when the police came to arrest him. But nothing happened. When the New Year arrived and Jeremy was still at liberty, Josiffe left to take up a job he had seen advertised as a riding instructor in Northern Ireland. Jeremy must have been relieved to see him go, but cannot have been pleased to receive a string of bills Josiffe had run up on his account at various London shops: these he refused to settle, insisting that the purchases had been made without his authority. 'I do not know his current whereabouts,' he wrote to a Savile Row firm which had supplied Josiffe with silk pyjamas, 'but believe he has gone abroad.'

The next two years of Josiffe's life may be briefly described. He spent most of 1963 in Northern Ireland, but was unable to regularise his employment there as he could not produce a National Insurance card: he absurdly claimed that this had been 'stolen' by Jeremy Thorpe who was his longstanding 'employer' but had been too mean to keep the card up to date by paying contributions. As in the West Country in 1962, he found a succession of kindly farmers with horses who took pity on him and gave him work, accommodation and pocket money, but after a short time asked him to move on. He also had a homosexual relationship with a man in Belfast. As well as speaking abusively of Jeremy, he told anyone who would listen that he was the illegitimate son of Lord Eldon, and also invented a wife who had been killed in a car crash. In the autumn of 1963, he moved to Wolverhampton, where for a few months he held down a job with a stables which trained show-jumpers. Although he inevitably fell out with his employer, he had meanwhile acquired a sympathetic friend in the shape of one of his riding students, a married woman of means, and he spent another few months staying at her house and enjoying something of a champagne lifestyle until he was finally thrown out by her husband. Josiffe then made another of his periodic suicide attempts, ending up at St George's Hospital in London.

Throughout this time, Josiffe kept in touch with Jeremy, who continued to put him up on his visits to London. Josiffe later claimed that Jeremy's motive in doing so was purely selfish – 'so he could screw me', as he told the judge at the Old Bailey; but it may well be that Jeremy, who still knew nothing of the police incident, felt he ought to humour him out of fearfulness as to what he might otherwise say or do. Then, after Jeremy's success in holding his seat with an increased majority at the October 1964 General Election, Josiffe, who had just recovered from another breakdown, went to see him at Marsham Court and demanded his help. In the latest issue of *Horse and Hound*, a Dr François Choquard of Porrentruy near Basle, Switzerland was advertising for a groom to look after his horses, and Jeremy persuaded Josiffe that this was the answer to his problems. Jeremy fixed up the job by an exchange of telegrams, helped Josiffe with his passport application, paid his outward fare and gave him a little sterling and Swiss money to take care of immediate expenses. Josiffe departed for Switzerland in December.

To Jeremy's horror, within a week he was back at Marsham Court, explaining that he had not liked either his new employer or the accommodation he had been offered and had found the Swiss winter climate intolerable. Moreover, he had had to borrow money for his return journey from Choquard, who had impounded his luggage as security – luggage which included intimate letters Josiffe had received from Jeremy.* Jeremy was furious: he undertook to recover the luggage, but made it clear that he never wished to see Josiffe again. And indeed, they were not to see each other again for fourteen years, and then only across a courtroom. But Jeremy's long ordeal of persecution by Josiffe was only beginning; and as prosecuting counsel at the Old Bailey would later put it, the higher he climbed on the political ladder, the greater the threat Josiffe represented to his ambition.

---

* Excluding, of course, the items which had been given to the police in December 1962, an episode of which Jeremy was presumably still ignorant.

9

MANOEUVRING
1964–66

THE LIBERAL REVIVAL of 1962 proved short-lived. For all the efforts of Jeremy Thorpe and others, the Liberals lacked the money and organisation which might have enabled them to sustain the burst of success which had delivered them Orpington. Events conspired against them, for during 1963 both Labour and the Conservatives managed to improve their electoral appeal by changing their leaders. Following Gaitskell's death in February, Labour chose Harold Wilson, a wily political manager with a comfortable Yorkshire image who reconciled his party's squabbling factions and offered to 'modernise' Britain after years of 'Tory misrule'. Like Jeremy, he had started his political career in the Oxford University Liberal Club:* he now made Labour look attractive in the eyes of disillusioned Conservatives who might otherwise have voted Liberal. In October, Macmillan, whose government had been plunged into new depths of unpopularity by Profumo, suddenly resigned from the premiership on health

---

* During his premiership, a Liberal once asked him why he had changed colours. He replied: 'But look where it has got me!'

grounds, being succeeded by the Foreign Secretary Lord Home, who thanks to the Peerages Act was able to disclaim his title and return to the House of Commons as Sir Alec Douglas-Home.* That a fourteenth earl should become premier in an egalitarian age was a gift for satirists (not least Jeremy); but some voters found Douglas-Home an honest and rather endearing figure, and Conservative fortunes began slowly to improve, again at Liberal expense.

The Liberal vote was therefore squeezed: less than two years after Orpington, some by-elections were producing even poorer results than had been recorded in 1959. Under the circumstances, Grimond became depressed: though only fifty, and still popular both in the Party and the country, he seemed to be losing his enthusiasm for the leadership. Jeremy, on the other hand, remained confident that, thanks to Winnable Seats, the Liberals would register an advance at the coming General Election. Shortly before polling was announced for 15 October 1964, Tim Beaumont (who remained the main financial backer of Winnable Seats) noted in his diary that 'Jeremy is very cock-a-hoop . . . and confident of winning 14 seats. It sounds too good to be true but he should know.'[1] A sign of Liberal optimism and improved organisation was that 365 seats were contested in 1964 as opposed to 216 in 1959.

Jeremy threw himself into the campaign with his usual energy and verve, devoting a week to touring the West Country with Mark Bonham Carter before concentrating on his own constituency. The Liberal slogan in North Devon (thought up by Dominic le Foe, who was again managing his campaign) was the simple one of 'Keep Jeremy Thorpe at Westminster', a powerful appeal since even his political opponents had to admit that he

---

* Jeremy was rather liked by the showman Macmillan but disapproved of by Sir Alec, while Grimond got on badly with Macmillan but well with the ex-Earl. They were all Old Etonians.

had proved an outstanding constituency MP. Whereas in 1959 Jeremy's Conservative rival had been the sitting MP, his current challenger, Michael Peto, was the son and grandson of former Tory Members for the Division, enabling Jeremy to dismiss him with the quip that, having had the Father and the Son, they were now being invited to vote for the Holy Ghost.

The result (with 1959 figures in brackets) was as follows:

Thorpe, John Jeremy (Liberal):	19,031	(15,831)
Peto, M. H. B. (Conservative):	13,895	(15,469)
Paton, A. F. (Labour):	4,603	(5,567)

Jeremy had scored a dramatic victory, increasing his majority from 362 to 5,136. Tom Pocock, reporting for the *Evening Standard*, later recalled 'an electioneering scene drawn by Rowlandson: roistering, apple-cheeked Devon farmers, full of cider, shouting "We want Jeremy"; then Thorpe, with his mother, coming out on to the balcony and flinging his arms above his head in triumph to a roar of cheering.'[2]

In the rest of the country, it was a different tale. Despite almost doubling their national vote to more than 3 million and coming second in fifty-five seats,* the Liberals only managed to increase their parliamentary representation from seven to nine. Their greatest success was in Scotland, where they captured three seats, all of which had received support from Jeremy's organisation: Caithness and Sutherland,† won by the robust Scottish Liberal Chairman, George Mackie; Ross and Cromarty, won by the Gaelic-speaking farmer Alisdair Mackenzie; and Inverness, won

---

* The key statistic was that, in seats contested both in 1959 and 1964, the Liberals increased their average share of the vote from 16.9 per cent to 20.6 per cent.

† Formerly the seat of Sir Archibald Sinclair (Viscount Thurso), Leader of the Liberal Party from 1935 to 1945, who, though much reduced in health, still lived in the constituency and owned much of it.

(and held for the next thirty-three years) by the young party officer Russell Johnston. In England, thanks to the ending of local pacts with the Conservatives, Wade and Holt lost their seats in Huddersfield and Bolton, while the Liberals made the solitary gain of Bodmin in Cornwall,* won by Jeremy's friend Peter Bessell with a majority of more than 3,000. Under the circumstances, it was a cause for satisfaction that Lubbock had managed to hold Orpington, while Wade had come within 1,500 votes of retaining Huddersfield West and Mark Bonham Carter within 2,000 of recapturing Torrington, all results owing something to Winnable Seats.

Jeremy's efforts had not been in vain: his tactic of targeting money and resources had resulted in improvements in almost all the targeted seats, and although only four of them had fallen to the Liberals in 1964, a dozen more would follow during the next decade.† Nevertheless, it was a depressingly meagre result; and his mood of frustration may explain his behaviour with regard to North Cornwall. This had been considered the most winnable seat in England, but the Liberal candidate Meddon Bruton, a retired naval commander of reputed homosexual tastes, had failed to win it by a few hundred votes. Jeremy rounded upon him with bitter recriminations, which caused surprise as it was Jeremy himself who had persuaded both Bruton to stand and the local association to adopt him.[3] The North Cornwall Liberals now had to find a new candidate, and the two main applicants, both charismatic men in their thirties, were Dominic le Foe and John Pardoe. Le Foe, who for seven years had greatly helped

---

* Last held for the Liberals from 1929 to 1935 by the recently deceased Rt Hon. Isaac Foot.

† These were Roxburgh in 1965; South Aberdeenshire, Colne Valley, Cheadle and North Cornwall in 1966; Birmingham Ladywood in 1969; Rochdale in 1972; Berwick and Isle of Ely in 1973; Hazel Grove, Isle of Wight and Truro in 1974. Many of the seats won by the Liberal Democrats in their *annus mirabilis* of 1997 had first been cultivated by Jeremy during the early 1960s.

Jeremy both in North Devon and with Winnable Seats, expected
to receive his personal support; but Jeremy instead persuaded his
Oxford friend Michael Ogle to stand as a third candidate, as a
result of which Le Foe lost the nomination to Pardoe by a single
vote and, feeling betrayed, decided to quit politics.[4]* (Pardoe in
fact proved an excellent candidate and was a fervent admirer of
Jeremy at this time, though they would later have a sparring
relationship.)

On a happier note, in March 1965 the Liberals scored a welcome gain, and Jeremy a new protégé, in one of the first
by-elections of the new Parliament, when the young David
Steel, Assistant Secretary of the Scottish Liberal Party, having
failed to capture the winnable seat of Roxburgh, Selkirk and
Peebles at the General Election by some 1,700 votes, now won
it by more than 4,500 votes. As Steel acknowledges in his memoirs, Jeremy, who had 'scented victory' from the first, was 'a
tower of strength' in the campaign, speaking 'all over the countryside' with the Liberal team and boosting their morale with his
'high humour and effervescence'.[5] At twenty-six (but looking
younger), 'the boy David' became the youngest MP at
Westminster, where he swelled the Liberal numbers to ten:
Jeremy took him under his wing and they became friends,
though Steel knew nothing of Jeremy's unorthodox private life
until six years later.

The 1964 General Election and the departure of Wade and
Holt had the effect of confirming Jeremy's position as the second
most prominent Liberal in Parliament. Only Grimond and
Bowen had been there longer – but Bowen, the last Liberal survivor from 1945, had long been tiring of politics and was now

---

* Jeremy thus lost a friend whose support he was to miss in future: after his poor
  result in 1966, he visited Le Foe and offered him various inducements to
  return, but Le Foe was not to be moved and soon afterwards resigned from the
  Liberals to join the Conservatives.

the least conspicuous of the ten MPs. Next to Grimond, Jeremy remained the best speaker in the parliamentary party and the best-known Liberal MP. Though the deputy leadership techni- cally belonged to Lubbock as Chief Whip, and the newly elected Mackie exercised clout as the leading Scottish Liberal (in a Parliament where five out of ten Liberals were Scots), it was Jeremy who assumed the mantle of Grimond's lieutenant in the realm of parliamentary politics. And the seventeen months of the 1964–66 Parliament presented the Liberals with a difficult problem.

Wilson had won the election with an overall majority of four, which soon fell to two with the loss of the Leyton by-election in January 1965. Given that the survival of Labour's precarious administration might soon depend on the votes of the ten Liberal MPs, to what extent ought they to support the Government? On the one hand, as a radical party, the Liberals could only welcome the end of the long period of Conservative rule and its replacement by a regime which gave the appearance of being reforming and progressive – and there was the prospect of their securing important advantages in return for maintain- ing Labour in office. On the other hand, until quite recently, Grimond's declared aim had been for the Liberals to replace Labour as the main opposition to the Conservatives; and there were painful memories of 1924 and 1929, when the Liberals suffered at the polls after supporting minority Labour adminis- trations. The official Liberal policy, agreed by the parliamentary party after the election, was to consider each vote on its merits: thus they opposed Labour's steel nationalisation plans as too left-wing and immigration policy as too right-wing, while sup- porting such 'liberal' measures as the Redundancy Payments Bill, the Race Relations Bill and the reform of the Rent Acts. But how far would they sustain Labour when it came to the general management of the economy? And how would they vote in the event of a confidence motion?

The view taken by both Grimond and Jeremy was that the Liberals ought to be prepared in principle to support the Wilson Government. During much of 1965, the Conservatives were ahead in the polls, and it seemed likely that Wilson, rather than face another election, would try to struggle on despite his vanishing majority. By selling their favours, the Liberals might acquire their first serious influence in public affairs since 1945. Grimond and Jeremy both personally liked Wilson and felt they could do business with him: he had been a Liberal originally, and though he pandered to the left for tactical reasons, there was some reason to suppose that his basic instincts remained liberal rather than socialist. For his part, Wilson, though he made no promises to the Liberals and discussed no deals except over specific votes, wooed and flattered them, which was a novel experience for them after being shunned by Conservative governments. For example, since introducing life peerages in 1958, the Conservatives had refused to give any to the Liberals, but before 1964 was out Wilson had allowed them three – bestowed on Lady Violet Bonham Carter* and the ex-MPs Byers and Wade. For the first time since the war, the Liberals were at least engaging in political talks with the Government, the main channels of communication being between Grimond and Wilson, Lubbock and the Government Chief Whip Ted Short, and Jeremy and his old friend Dingle Foot, now Solicitor-General.[6]

There were, however, two insuperable difficulties in the way of a Lib–Lab pact. First, the Liberals disposed of a mere ten parliamentary votes, which would hardly do much to shore up a tottering Labour Government facing the threat of rebellion from its own left-wing backbenchers. Secondly, there were many in

---

* She took the title of Baroness Asquith of Yarnbury, but continued to be generally known by her old name. Soon afterwards, her son Mark left politics to accept the new post of Chairman of the Race Relations Board, offered to him by his friend Roy Jenkins, now Home Secretary.

both parties who, for either ideological or tactical reasons, were opposed to the very idea of a pact.* Indeed, Grimond could not even be sure of delivering his ten votes, since three of them belonged to right-wingers – Bessell, Hooson and Mackenzie – who disagreed with the Government on most issues. The moment of truth came in June 1965, soon after Wilson had announced that there would be no election that year, when Grimond declared in a *Guardian* interview that he was prepared to 'come to terms' with Labour in return for 'a serious agreement on long-term policies': this aroused such a storm of protest from party workers that Grimond was obliged to retract his remarks. A few weeks later, just before the summer recess, the Liberals had to decide how to vote in a confidence motion put down by the Conservatives: Grimond and Jeremy wanted to support the Government but Bessell and Hooson refused to agree to this, so that in the end they all abstained.[7]

Despite these difficulties, Grimond and Jeremy continued to be mesmerised by the prospect that their tiny parliamentary army might soon hold the balance and be in the position of power-brokers. This was illustrated in September 1965 after the sudden death of the Speaker of the House of Commons, the Conservative Sir Harry Hylton-Foster. There had never been a Speaker from the Labour Party, but to appoint one now threatened to wipe out the Government's majority: Wilson and Short therefore let it be known that they were prepared to support the candidature of Roderic Bowen, the longest-serving Liberal MP. There was no good reason why Bowen should not become Speaker: he had been in Parliament for twenty years, was well liked by fellow MPs and possessed judicial qualities which might

---

*Wilson thought sufficiently seriously about a pact to ask his aide Gerald Kaufman to take soundings about it among Labour MPs. Kaufman reported that for every three MPs against it, two were in favour and one uncommitted. (Philip Ziegler, *Wilson* [London: Weidenfeld & Nicolson, 1993], p. 207.)

have suited him to the job. Grimond and Jeremy, however, were opposed to his nomination on the ostensible grounds that it would have reduced the effective Liberal parliamentary force from ten to nine.* As a result of their objections, the Speakership went instead to the Labour MP Horace King, but they could not stop Bowen accepting the Deputy Speakership, so they lost his vote anyway.

During the febrile period of the 1964–66 Parliament, Jeremy was more concerned with political tactics than political issues; but one issue which permanently engaged his interest was that of Rhodesia. After the election, he had been appointed his party's official spokesman on Commonwealth Affairs, giving him a pretext to visit those newly independent countries whose rulers he had befriended, as well as to be present on the fringes of such gatherings as the Commonwealth Prime Ministers' Conference in London in June 1965. It has been seen that he had been a vociferous campaigner against the Central African Federation, which had fallen apart in the early 1960s; in 1964, two of its three former components, Nyasaland and Northern Rhodesia, had become independent as Malawi and Zambia, and Jeremy was regarded by their new rulers Banda and Kaunda as a good friend who had helped them attain independence. It was a different story with the third unit of the old Federation, Southern Rhodesia (known simply as Rhodesia after the name-change of its northern counterpart), which had both a large white minority of over 200,000 and an unusual constitution which allowed it virtually complete internal self-government under an electoral system ensuring white dominance. Here Ian Smith's Rhodesia Front had come to power committed to perpetuating white rule on the South African model and threatening, if London did not

---

* It has been suggested that personal considerations may also have played a part, as Grimond is said to have wanted the Speakership for himself some time in the future.

grant them independence on their own terms, to take it for themselves.

In July 1965 Jeremy embarked on an African tour, in the course of which he visited both Rhodesia and Zambia. On his return, he saw Wilson and told him that he believed the Rhodesians would make a Unilateral Declaration of Independence (UDI) before the end of the year unless deterred by a threat of coercion by the British Government. He suggested that, if 1,500 British troops* were sent to Zambia on 'extended manoeuvres', they would provide the necessary deterrent and be welcomed by Kaunda (who had made a similar proposal to Wilson during the Prime Ministers' Conference). However, Wilson refused to countenance the use of force against the Rhodesian whites, which he believed would be unacceptable to British public opinion. As the autumn progressed, the prospect of UDI loomed ever larger. Twentieth-anniversary celebrations of the United Nations were due to take place at the beginning of November, and Jeremy took part in these, declaring at a rally in Trafalgar Square that the UN might have to step in to 'prevent massacre' in the event of UDI, and visiting the UN Headquarters in New York, where he discussed the situation with the Secretary-General U Thant and the British Permanent Representative Lord Caradon (who, as one of the Foot brothers, was something of a friend of Jeremy).

On 11 November 1965, the Rhodesians announced UDI. This presented a difficult problem for Wilson, who had to perform a tightrope act by doing enough on the one hand to satisfy outraged international opinion, while nothing on the other which risked prejudicing a bi-partisan approach with the Conservatives and turning the crisis into a divisive domestic political issue. He therefore ruled out the use of force and introduced a phased

---

* At this time, the regular Rhodesian armed forces numbered only 3,400, including some 1,000 Africans under the command of European officers.

programme of economic sanctions, holding out the prospect of negotiations with the Rhodesians provided they returned to the path of legality. This policy was bitterly criticised by African states and also by Jeremy, who in repeated public statements and parliamentary interventions accused the Government of irresolution and the Opposition of being lukewarm in support of sanctions. He was particularly critical of the fact that Wilson did not impose oil sanctions until more than a month after UDI and that, just before doing so, he failed to prevent an oil tanker (belonging to British Petroleum, in which the Government had a controlling stake) from delivering a cargo to Rhodesia. Without being specific, Jeremy suggested that force should be contemplated if sanctions failed. 'From the military point of view,' he declared on 25 November, 'it would be a fantastic position if this country, with its tremendous imperial past and its present Commonwealth tradition, were incapable of putting down a rebellion of a population the size of that of Portsmouth.' Sanctions were not, however, effective, owing to the economic support the Rhodesians received from the South Africans and Portuguese; and the crisis dragged on.

Another issue with which Jeremy was concerned at this time was that of Commonwealth immigration. While in opposition, Labour had opposed the Immigrants Act of 1962; but now they were in power and having to face reality, they not only continued the Conservative policy of controlling Commonwealth immigration but began to introduce still more restrictive measures. Jeremy endorsed the official Liberal view that any attempt to restrict the right of Commonwealth citizens to enter Britain was both socially unnecessary and morally wrong. This was the theme of his speech at the Liberal Assembly at Scarborough in September 1965. The aim of the 1962 Act, he said, had been to 'keep Britain white', and Labour were going along with this in their 'aptly named White Paper'. He believed, 'as one proud to be the son of a Southern Irish father', that Commonwealth citizens ought to have the same free right of entry as those from Eire.

Jeremy's bold pronouncements in favour of using force against Rhodesia and allowing free immigration were typical of his approach to policy. As an MP of a small party which was unlikely to hold office in the near future, he did not need to worry about the practical consequences of his proposals. He was therefore able to give free rein to his personal convictions and achieve a satisfying splash in the press. By taking an uncompromising stand on these emotive issues, he also gained further prestige in Commonwealth and international liberal circles.

By the autumn of 1965, Jeremy wished to give himself a higher profile in the Party, especially as Grimond was intimating that he might retire before long. For five years now he had been running a private empire in the form of Winnable Seats, showing skill both in raising money and targeting expenditure; and he wanted to practise his talents and exercise influence on a wider scale. During that time, the Party Treasurer, responsible for the funds of the LPO, had been Sir Andrew Murray, a former Lord Provost of Edinburgh: but the Party now faced a financial crisis, and in the party elections of October 1965 Jeremy challenged him for the office and defeated him by some 400 votes to 250. Jeremy made it clear that he intended to devote himself to the Treasurership, giving up most of his professional work outside Parliament such as television interviewing. With a typical flourish, he also nominated four Deputy Treasurers (a post unknown to the party constitution): these were Len (later Sir Leonard) Smith, a long-standing professional officer of the LPO; Hugo Brunner, Liberal candidate at Torquay and son of the Party's leading benefactor, the chemicals tycoon Sir Felix Brunner; Stanley Brodie, a barrister who had been at Oxford with Jeremy and was a nephew of the Chief Rabbi; and the Manchester-based merchant banker David Holmes, a fellow homosexual befriended by Jeremy at Oxford who was little-known in the Liberal Party. Of these, only Smith was seriously involved on the administrative side: the others were widely perceived as glorified fundraisers, who also satisfied Jeremy's need to be surrounded by admiring cronies.

There have been mixed views about Jeremy's fifteen months as Party Treasurer. He brought a new zeal to the office: Len Smith (who was to succeed him as Treasurer) remembered him as 'a tremendous worker with an enormous range of contacts, able to inject great enthusiasm in fellow workers, willing to have a crack at anything'.[8] He cut through bureaucracy: the Treasurer traditionally reported to the Party Council, but Jeremy only appeared once before that dismal body, merely to say that they would be seeing little more of him as he proposed to devote himself to raising money up and down the country.[9] The level of donations certainly shot up during his term: he had a natural flair for persuading people to part with their cash, and was not overly scrupulous about where it came from or what inducements (such as the prospect of future honours) might be offered to secure it. His critics, however, would allege that he manipulated the figures to make them look better than they really were: promised donations would appear in the accounts before they had been received, and as Jeremy independently controlled Winnable Seats, he could juggle funds between that body and the LPO to create a desired impression. And although Jeremy was a great inspirer of the faithful, at Party Headquarters in Smith Square he acquired a reputation for bullying arrogance: he expected the staff to work long hours and obey his orders unquestioningly, and if they failed to come up to scratch, he could round upon them bad-temperedly.

Still, Jeremy must rank as a successful Treasurer; the Party's overdraft was soon substantially reduced; and it was bad luck for him that, within six months of his taking office, the Liberals experienced the financial disaster of having to fight another General Election less than eighteen months after the last. For the prosaic new Conservative Leader Edward ('Ted') Heath, who had replaced Douglas-Home in July 1965, was proving unpopular;

the Government was experiencing a sudden surge in the polls; and Wilson, aware that this situation was unlikely to last with an economic crisis on the horizon, decided to go the country on 31 March 1966. The Liberals were caught unprepared and only able to field 311 candidates as compared to 365 in 1964. Despite Labour's poll lead, Jeremy hoped for another narrow result which might pave the way for a Lib–Lab pact: he even telephoned Wilson during the campaign to say that the Liberals might be prepared to support him after the election in return for the dropping of Labour's steel nationalisation programme and the introduction of PR for the following election. Wilson replied that this seemed a high price to pay, to which Jeremy replied: 'If necessary, I think you will pay it.'[10]

In North Devon, despite campaigning as energetically as ever, Jeremy experienced an unexpected reverse. The result (with 1964 figures in brackets) was as follows:

Thorpe, John Jeremy (Liberal):   16,797   (19,031)
Keigwin, T. C. (Conservative):   15,631   (13,895)
Rayner, J. H. (Labour):   6,127   (4,603)

His majority had declined from over 5,000 to barely 1,000. ('Is that all?' he remarked with dismay to the Returning Officer.) There appear to have been four reasons for this. First, he had been less active in his constituency (where his personal vote required constant nurturing) since his comfortable result there in 1964. Secondly, in North Devon as elsewhere, the Liberal vote was squeezed: the main election issue was the record of Harold Wilson's Government and people tended to vote Labour or Conservative according to whether they approved or disapproved of this. Thirdly, the Conservative candidate, the landowner and former Irish Guards officer Tim Keigwin, appealed to some voters with his right-wing views on such issues as the EEC, immigration and Rhodesia. Fourthly, as will be seen in the next chapter,

Jeremy suffered as a result of a local whispering campaign about his homosexuality. 'The Tories fought a pretty filthy campaign,' he wrote afterwards to a friend, 'but we will put that right next time.'[11]

In the country, the result was a curious one for the Liberals. Compared with 1964, their total vote declined dramatically from 3,101,103 to 2,327,533 and their national percentage from 11.2 per cent to 8.5 per cent. This could not be explained simply by the smaller field of candidates, for the Liberals came second in only 29 seats as opposed to 55, while their lost deposits doubled from 52 to 104. Yet they found themselves with more seats in Parliament than at any time since 1945. As in 1964, two seats were lost and four gained, bringing the total to twelve. The gains were all 'winnable seats' targeted by Jeremy: North Cornwall, won at last by the dynamic John Pardoe; Colne Valley, gained from Labour (their only loss in 1966) by the much-respected Yorkshire Methodist Richard Wainwright; the north-western town of Cheadle, captured by the television doctor Michael Winstanley; and West Aberdeenshire, won by the young farmer James Davidson. The seats lost were by the narrowest of margins, Roderic Bowen failing to hold Cardigan by 523 votes and George Mackie Caithness and Sutherland by a mere 64. Just as the winners recognised that their victories owed much to Jeremy and Winnable Seats, so the two losers (perhaps unfairly) rather blamed their failure on his lack of support: Bowen felt that Jeremy bore him a grudge for having accepted the Deputy Speakership, Mackie that Jeremy welcomed his removal as a future rival for the leadership.*

The 1966 General Election represented a setback for the

---

* On one occasion in 1965, Jeremy had seized Mackie by the lapels with the words: 'They say you're after the leadership when Jo goes. If you support me, I'll make you deputy leader, but if you stand, I'll finish you!' Mackie just laughed: he did not in fact have leadership ambitions for himself, but hoped to promote Emlyn Hooson as a candidate. (Information from Lord Mackie of Benshie.)

Liberals not only in that it produced the first serious drop in their vote since 1951, but also because it returned Labour to power with a landslide majority of ninety-six. Gone was the brief period in which the Government made up to the Liberals in the hope of securing their few parliamentary votes. Gone too was Grimond's dream that the Liberals would prevail as 'the radical alternative to socialism'. Wilson, however, continued to be most friendly to the Liberals, partly out of sentiment but also because he calculated that a flourishing Liberal Party would help keep down the Conservative vote. He also calculated that, by treating the Liberals with almost the same degree of consideration as the Official Opposition, he would cause much annoyance to Heath, for whom Wilson nurtured an intense personal dislike.

As may be deduced from the fact that he was able to ring up the Prime Minister during the election campaign, Jeremy himself had established close personal relations with Wilson by this time. There was a natural sympathy between them on account of their common liberal faith and gut dislike of the Conservatives. Both Oxford men, they also shared a penchant for showmanship, intrigue and springing surprises. Wilson enjoyed Jeremy's wit, and was pruriently fascinated by his private life troubles.* Jeremy took care to cultivate Wilson's influential political secretary Marcia Williams, who was susceptible to his charm and proved a useful ally. Two events in the spring of 1966 illustrate Jeremy's easy relationship with the premier. First, he asked if some public recognition might be given to his beloved Megan Lloyd George, who was dying of cancer (though returned at the General Election as Labour MP for Carmarthen). The PM willingly agreed, and Megan was made a Companion of Honour a few days

---

*Jeremy would have been horrified to think that Wilson knew of these; but that he should have done so was hardly surprising (as will be seen in the next chapter) since Bessell had been approaching various members of the Government on his behalf to help him out of scrapes.

before her death (which left Jeremy disconsolate) on 14 May at the age of sixty-four. Secondly, Wilson, knowing of Jeremy's closeness to African leaders, consulted him over the continuing Rhodesia crisis, even though Jeremy was an outspoken public critic of Wilson's policy of seeking a negotiated compromise with the Smith regime. On 6 May, Jeremy lunched at 10 Downing Street to discuss the current situation in Rhodesia, which he had just visited: Wilson and his Commonwealth Secretary Arthur Bottomley were eager to have his impressions in view of the imminent arrival of a Rhodesian delegation in England for 'exploratory talks' – though once those talks were under way, Jeremy, speaking at a rally in Trafalgar Square on 26 June, denounced them as 'a farce' whose 'explorations' could only be 'archaeological'.

Rhodesia was the subject of Jeremy's big speech to the Liberal Assembly at Brighton on 23 September 1966. It came at a tense moment, for a Commonwealth meeting had just taken place in London at which Wilson had been bitterly attacked by most of his fellow premiers for not taking more decisive action to end the rebellion and for his willingness to deal with Smith. 'For the British people,' declared Jeremy, 'the choice is stark. Do they want to preserve the Commonwealth or perpetuate the Smith regime? They cannot have both.' He called on the Government to rule out any deal which granted independence to Rhodesia before the establishment of majority rule, and to implement 'stronger measures to bring down the regime'. One measure in particular he had in mind. 'The main supply of oil [to Rhodesia] now travels by the rail line which crosses the [Mozambique] border at Malvernia. If that supply were to continue, it might be necessary to consider whether, with the backing of a UN resolution, it might be feasible for that line of communication to be nipped on Rhodesian soil by the use of high flying planes . . .'*

---

* This plan had originally been suggested to Jeremy by Archie Levine, a wealthy South African exile moving in London liberal circles.

Objectively considered, there was nothing shocking about these remarks. Ever since UDI, Jeremy had expressed the view that force might eventually have to be used if sanctions failed; and his plan to 'nip' the railway was still presented as a last resort in the event of sanctions continuing to be ineffective. As he was to stress during the next few days, the line in question passed through virtually uninhabited territory, so there was little risk of bloodshed as a result of 'aerial intervention' (he guarded himself from using the word 'bomb' or its derivatives in his speech). Moreover, the threat of armed force was already being used to disrupt Rhodesian trade communications: following a UN resolution in April, a British naval patrol lay off the Mozambiquan port of Beira ready to intercept any ship believed to be carrying oil for Rhodesia. And Jeremy may have been right in thinking that his plan would deal a decisive blow to the Rhodesians: for during the 1980s, the railway in question *was* bombed by South African-backed Renamo terrorists, as a result of which the local economy almost collapsed.

However, it is hard to believe that an experienced politician such as Jeremy could have failed to anticipate the furore his remarks would cause.* The white Rhodesians were 'kith and kin'; they were led by a former Battle of Britain pilot; the very notion of British bombs raining down on their country, however bloodlessly, was bound to alarm public opinion and cause an outcry in the press. The next day, the front pages were full of lurid headlines about Jeremy's call to 'bomb Rhodesia', and a torrent of criticism descended on his head. Wilson declared that his proposals would amount to an act of war, and even Grimond disowned them, saying that he did not quite understand what

---

* It is interesting to compare Jeremy's controversial remarks at the time of Profumo (see Chapter 7). On that occasion he had also played the innocent, claiming to have been surprised at the fuss his remarks had caused. One suspects that in both cases he knew what he was doing and was secretly delighted to have made a stir.

Jeremy had meant but that he had certainly not been expressing party policy. The right of the Conservative Party, which had always regarded Jeremy as something of a renegade, were confirmed in their antipathy towards him: for the rest of his parliamentary career they would call him 'Bomber Thorpe' and bait him with a low chorus of 'bomber' whenever he entered the Commons chamber.

Although the Rhodesia speech tended to confirm the public view of Jeremy as a maverick, it was not without positive consequences both for the Party and himself. It further enhanced his prestige in black African and international liberal circles.* It was the first time for years that a Liberal Assembly had made front-page news. And one of the features of the Brighton Assembly was that it marked the emergence of the Young Liberals as a force on the extreme left of the Party. After two years in office, the Labour Government showed no sign of bringing about radical change; and students with radical instincts, inspired by Grimond's rhetoric, were flooding into the Young Liberal ranks. At their own conference at Colwyn Bay a few months earlier, the YLs had already called for British withdrawal from NATO and workers' control of nationalised industries, and expressed approval of the Cultural Revolution then convulsing China, describing themselves as Britain's 'Red Guards'. Using Trotskyite methods, they sought to infiltrate the main organs of the Party; and at Brighton, where they proposed a series of resolutions alarming to traditional Liberals, they made their presence aggressively felt for the first time. The idea of 'bombing' Rhodesia was just what they wanted to hear; and they cheered Jeremy to the echo.

If his Rhodesia speech won the hearts of the Young Liberals, Jeremy's speech as Party Treasurer confirmed his popularity with

---

* It did Jeremy little harm in these circles that, not long afterwards, he was banned from entering Rhodesia and depicted in official propaganda there as a public enemy who had called for the mass bombing of civilians.

the rank and file. He claimed that, in the year since his taking office, twice as much revenue had been raised as in the previous year, while the Party's overdraft, despite the financial strain of the General Election, had been reduced from £70,000 to £20,000. In fact, the figures had been juggled somewhat and the truth was not quite as spectacular as this;* but it was nevertheless evident that he was proving an effective Treasurer, and his speech inspired the Assembly with a keen sense of future possibilities.

At Brighton that September, many Liberals felt they were hearing Grimond speak as Leader for the last time. He was visibly tiring of the leadership, which he had taken on at the 1956 Assembly with the words that he would give himself ten years to 'get on or get out'. There was a general expectation that Jeremy would soon take over: he was by far the best-known of the other Liberal MPs, and had proved himself through his campaigning talents, his parliamentary skills, his fundraising abilities, his inspiring speeches. His popularity in the Party was far from universal: many found him shallow or regarded him as a trickster. Nevertheless, had a vote on the succession been taken at Brighton, Jeremy would undoubtedly have received a comfortable mandate.

One thing alone stood in the way of his smooth ascent to the leadership. His secret homosexual life was catching up with him. During recent years, a number of skeletons had threatened to emerge from his closet, often with a noisy rattle. The most serious of these concerned Jeremy's past association with Norman Josiffe – and it is to the further developments of that affair that we must now turn.

---

*Beaumont had intended to raise during the Assembly the matter of alleged irregularities in the accounts, but was intimidated by Jeremy into remaining silent.

10

EDGE
1964–66

IN THE COURSE of cross-examination at the Old Bailey on 22 May 1979, Norman Scott (formerly Josiffe) burst out: 'Jeremy Thorpe lives on a knife-edge of danger!' Certainly the greatest danger Jeremy ran in the course of a career not lacking in risk and adventure arose out of his folly and misfortune in befriending the vindictive character that was Josiffe himself.[1] Although they had met for the last time shortly before Christmas 1964, after Josiffe's precipitate return from Switzerland where he had failed to take up the job Jeremy had obtained for him, Jeremy's hope that he would hear no more of him proved short-lived. To be sure, early in 1965, Josiffe moved to Ireland, where he would continue to be based for the next two and a half years. In March, however, Jeremy received a letter from a Mrs Quirke who ran a stud farm in County Wicklow, where Josiffe had arrived three weeks earlier to work and train: 'I am writing to you as he told us you were his Guardian and we feel there is something wrong with the boy.' Josiffe had claimed to be the illegitimate son of a prominent English peer; his behaviour had been neurotic and quarrelsome, and it had been impossible to teach him anything as he claimed to know everything. 'It's such a pity as he can be such a charming boy and just as quickly he can be very nasty.' Josiffe had now returned to Dublin, having borrowed money from the Quirkes. Jeremy replied that he was not Josiffe's guardian 'but merely tried to help him on occasions which have at times proved hair-raising' and regretted he could take no responsibility for his actions.

Worse was to come. Stung by Jeremy's refusal to acknowledge himself as his guardian (which he had virtually claimed to be some three years earlier), Josiffe decided to write to Jeremy's mother. The letter, sent in late March and seventeen pages long, began: 'For the last five years, as you probably know, Jeremy and I have had a "homosexual" relationship.' This, Josiffe went on, had begun in November 1961 under Ursula's own roof – 'through my meeting with Jeremy that day I gave birth to this vice that lies latent in every man'. He went on to describe how he had been 'kept' by Jeremy in Chelsea; his stay with the Colliers; and his nights at Marsham Court. 'When he had satisfied himself he put me to sleep on a little camp-bed. This was when I realised that he didn't care for me as a friend.' Josiffe (who had in fact been boasting about it to almost everyone he had met and had given a long statement about it to the police) claimed that, up to then, he had told no one about the affair, as he was 'too loyal – a quality your son fails at miserably'. The ostensible purpose of the letter was to enlist Ursula's help in getting Jeremy to recover Josiffe's abandoned luggage in Switzerland, as he had promised to do but not yet done. It concluded: 'You are probably shattered by all this . . . I'm so sorry. Please believe me, I'm desperate for help.'

One may wonder to what extent these revelations would have come as a shock to Ursula. She was nobody's fool and cannot have been ignorant of the facts of life: her husband and three of her uncles are said to have had homosexual leanings, and her bisexual brother Peter had been involved in various escapades. One may presume that Josiffe was not the first young man of unknown background Jeremy had brought home: it is probable that she turned a blind eye to her son's peccadillos or even, like many possessive mothers, encouraged them with a view to remaining the leading influence in his life. Some years later, a friend of Ursula, the widow of a baronet, told her that her daughter was divorcing her husband whom she had discovered to be homosexual: to the lady's astonishment, Ursula replied that she had little sympathy with the daughter, as many men had inclinations of this sort and it was the duty of their womenfolk to support and protect them. But however much Ursula may have understood such matters, women of her generation never liked being confronted with the details; and Jeremy, whose filial relations were already complex and strained, must have been appalled when his mother passed him the letter, having doubtless digested its contents.* At all events, such was his anxiety that he made the fateful decision to find a sympathetic and resourceful confidant who might help him sort out the trouble caused by Josiffe. His choice fell on Peter Bessell, who had been his friend for ten years and at the 1964 election had become MP for Bodmin in Cornwall and thus his solitary Liberal parliamentary colleague from the West Country, as well as being one of the few fellow politicians with whom he had discussed the secret of his homosexuality.

Bessell, who hailed from a West Country family of Liberal and Nonconformist small businessmen, was eight years older than Jeremy. Although destined to be the principal prosecution witness at Jeremy's trial in the 1970s, there can be no doubt that,

---

* When the scandal broke in the late 1970s, Ursula denied having received the letter; but she also denied having received Josiffe at her house, which we know she had done at least twice. It is possible that Jeremy, who was no longer living at Stonewalls in 1965 but still going there often, recognised the handwriting and intercepted the letter before Ursula received it, though he told Bessell (according to the latter's memoirs) that she had in fact read it, though not believed it.

throughout the 1960s, a strong friendship had existed between them based on much similarity of character. Like Jeremy, Bessell was a showman and extrovert, witty and imaginative, an elegant charmer with a theatrical touch who enjoyed intrigue and danger. He indulged in a promiscuous heterosexuality hardly less dangerous in terms of career and reputation (particularly among the God-fearing Cornish) than Jeremy's homosexuality: he kept a wife and family in Cornwall and mistress in London, and was a compulsive and accomplished seducer of women. He was a fantasist and in this respect went further than Jeremy: he developed a habit of telling everyone what they most wanted to hear, causing many to regard him as a liar, hypocrite and mischief-maker. As a lay preacher who practised little of what he preached but had a power to hold audiences, he was also seen, by those who knew the truth about him, as a crook of the Elmer Gantry variety. His sense of fantasy was particularly marked when it came to his business career: he was not without talent, and set up a number of successful small enterprises (including the felt-tip pen and vending-machine companies of which Jeremy became a director), but he overreached himself by launching a series of wildly ambitious transatlantic schemes which he hoped would make him rich but merely landed him in debt. The fact that he managed to hold off his creditors for so long was a tribute to his persuasive powers. (He looked to his political career to help rescue him from his business troubles, writing to a creditor that 'the letters MP are worth more than stocks and shares ...')

Jeremy first met Bessell at the Torquay by-election of December 1955, and struck up a rapid rapport with this exuberant campaigner who shared his own gift for making a joke out of every situation. It was largely thanks to Jeremy that Bessell was adopted in 1957 as prospective candidate for Bodmin, the former seat of the legendary (and then still living) West Country Liberal, Isaac Foot. With his colourful style, Bessell built up a devoted personal following there much like Jeremy's in North

Devon. (Bessell's style was rather different from Jeremy's: while the latter presented an Edwardian image and gave an impression of genteel poverty, the former wore the latest Italian suits, radiated an air of opulence and drove about in the biggest and flashiest motor cars. But both were metropolitan men whose success was largely based on an ability to dazzle countryfolk.) He also won the confidence of the local Liberal grandee, the elderly and heirless Viscount Clifden, and the heart of his spinster sister, the Honourable Everilda Agar-Robartes: one of his many fantasies was that he was destined to inherit their fortune and fine seventeenth-century house, Lanhydrock, both of which were in fact left to the National Trust.[2] At the 1959 General Election, Bessell cut the Conservative majority by more than half; and in 1964, following a campaign full of razzmatazz in which he had travelled around the constituency in an enormous motorcade, making speeches through a megaphone in his rich, sonorous voice, he was elected by a majority of over 3,000.

As fellow MPs, Jeremy and Bessell, despite political differences (Bessell being far to the right of Jeremy on most issues), continued their friendship, entertaining each other on the Liberal bench with jokes about their fellow members. They had not yet discussed their private lives, but Bessell, who had long suspected Jeremy's homosexuality, felt the time for such confidences had come. One day, when they were alone in the Members' Dining Room, he casually mentioned that he had enjoyed homosexual adventures in his youth. This lowered Jeremy's defences and they were soon exchanging secrets, Bessell telling Jeremy about his current mistresses and Jeremy pointing out which of the young journalists in the press gallery he most fancied. It was therefore natural that, when Josiffe wrote to Ursula some weeks later, Jeremy should have sought Bessell's help. He asked him to lunch at the Ritz, showed him the letter and told him the story of his relations with Josiffe. ('It was the first and indeed the last time,' recalled Bessell in his memoirs, 'that I heard Jeremy speak with gentleness or affection of any of the men in his life. I was immediately aware that, whatever he had felt later, Jeremy had genuinely cared for Josiffe.') Bessell urged Jeremy to do nothing rash which might further provoke the neurotic Josiffe, and offered to go to Dublin to assess the situation for himself. Jeremy (writes Bessell with Freudian innuendo) breathed a grateful sigh of relief and wolfed down a spicy Steak Tartare.

Bessell duly made an overnight trip to Dublin in April 1965. He first visited Josiffe's current mentor, the Jesuit Michael Sweetman. (Josiffe seems always to have managed to find someone to take a sympathetic interest in his 'case' and look after him.) Father Sweetman agreed Josiffe had been wrong to write as he had done to Ursula, but was not convinced that the story the letter told was essentially untrue. He thought Jeremy had something to answer for, if only because he had introduced Josiffe to a glamorous world after which it was difficult for him to settle down to ordinary life and work. However, he agreed to do his best to get Josiffe to forget Jeremy, and meanwhile urged Bessell to see him for himself. Bessell telephoned Josiffe and asked him to join him the following morning for breakfast at his hotel. Looking nervous and dishevelled, Josiffe only turned up when Bessell had finished his breakfast and was about to take a taxi to the airport, a journey on which Josiffe joined him. Bessell was stern with Josiffe, saying that if he wrote any more letters he would be extradited to Britain to face trial for blackmail. At this, Josiffe broke down and became a pathetic spectacle of contrition.* He promised to give no more trouble; and Bessell in return promised to try to recover his

---

* At this point, Josiffe's account differs from Bessell's in two respects. Josiffe says that Bessell claimed to have an extradition warrant in his briefcase, signed by the Home Secretary; he also says that he called Bessell's bluff by saying that he would be pleased to return to England to face charges which would enable him to air his relationship with Jeremy in court. However, a letter sent by Josiffe to Bessell in 1967 tends to confirm Bessell's story that Josiffe did not wish to return to England in 1965 and was fearful of the prospect of extradition.

luggage and send it to him in Ireland. At the airport, Bessell gave Josiffe £5 and invited him to get in touch at any time.

Bessell felt he had done his job well, particularly when he received a pathetic letter from Josiffe in which the latter expressed his regret for any trouble he had caused and his determination to make a clean start. He told Jeremy that he believed he had neutralised Josiffe as a threat for the foreseeable future. However, a few weeks later, Bessell received a bill which Josiffe had run up at a Dublin hotel with instructions to forward it to the MP. As Bessell wrote to Father Sweetman: 'Further trouble over this wretched boy: as you will see from the enclosed, he is now trying to make *me* responsible for his debts! This coincides hideously with Mr Thorpe's experience, and I suppose it is only a matter of time before you or somebody else is placed in a similar position.'

Meanwhile, Jeremy had been working to recover Josiffe's luggage, which had got lost on the continent, and had even invoked the help of British consular authorities. Eventually it was located, and he arranged for it to be delivered to Bessell for onward transmission to Josiffe in Dublin. As Bessell was away when it arrived in June 1965, it was collected by his secretary, Diana Stainton, who took it to her flat. As she later recalled, Jeremy invited himself over to see her one evening, ostensibly on amorous grounds ('Diana darling, are you wearing a gorgeous *négligée*?') but in reality so he could recover the letters he had written Josiffe. Josiffe later complained that, when he finally received the suitcase, Jeremy's letters were missing and much besides. However, although he continued to speak to all and sundry of his 'betrayal' by Jeremy, he was to cause no further serious trouble for another two years. (During that time, in the intervals of the usual nervous breakdowns and suicide attempts, he succeeded to a remarkable degree in his ambition to rub shoulders with the Irish gentry, becoming for a time the kept lover of an Irishman prominent in political and social life, and getting to stay with such people as the Desmond Guinnesses at Leixlip Castle.)

However, even if Josiffe were to do no more damage in the future, he had already compromised Jeremy in the past. This was brought home to Jeremy when he belatedly learned, early in 1965, of the statement Josiffe had made to the police in December 1962. A copy of this, and of the letters from Jeremy which Josiffe had given the police, had been sent at the time to Devon and Cornwall CID, and it was from that quarter that he had now been tipped off about the existence of this damaging material. Jeremy was anxious to know two things: whether a file on the matter was still being kept at Scotland Yard; and what, if anything, his friends the Colliers, who had accommodated Josiffe in January 1962 and must also have known about the 'incident' of December 1962 (which had partly taken place at the Easton Hotel where Mary Collier had been acting as receptionist), had told the Devon police. Feeling unable to undertake these enquiries himself, he again appealed to Bessell.

Jeremy's plan to sound out the Colliers was a mistake: it reminded them of something they had been anxious to forget. Over tea at the Clarence Hotel at Exeter, Bessell informed them that Josiffe had sent Ursula Thorpe a letter accusing Jeremy of being homosexual, and invited their views. The Colliers recalled that Josiffe had been a terrible nuisance and they had at first been at a loss to understand why Jeremy had wished to help such a person. However, they thought that Josiffe, though not always truthful, was probably telling the truth in the letter. At all events, they were alarmed at being approached in this way; and it was not long afterwards that Collier resigned both his prospective candidature at Tiverton and his Liberal Party membership, stating openly in a letter to the *Western Morning News* that his reason for doing so was a lack of confidence in the Party's West Country MPs, Bessell and Thorpe.

With the question of the police file, Bessell seemed to have more success. He approached a junior minister at the Home Office, the Welsh MP George Thomas (later to be famous as

Speaker of the House of Commons), whom he knew personally.
Like Bessell, Thomas was a lay preacher and member of the
interdenominational Brotherhood Movement; and like Jeremy,
he was a bachelor with homosexual inclinations (though he was
obsessively discreet about these and Bessell may not have been
aware of them). Thomas showed himself cautiously sympathetic
to Jeremy's problems and offered to arrange an interview
between Bessell and the Home Secretary, Sir Frank Soskice. This
took place during May 1965, both parties subsequently agreeing on the outlines of what occurred.[3] Like Thomas, Soskice was
sympathetic to Jeremy's troubles, but as an elderly MP who soon
intended to retire from public life, he did not (unlike Thomas)
have to worry about career considerations. He told Bessell that,
as Josiffe was presumably unable to prove his allegations, he did
not believe they would lead to further trouble; he also made it
clear that he personally considered it outrageous that homosexuals should have to suffer penalties on account of consensual
acts. He added, however, that it was 'a pity about those letters',
and urged Bessell to prevent any further contact between Jeremy
and 'the Creature' (as he called Josiffe) which might allow the
latter to establish a hold over the former. The minister concluded with the words: 'It's good of you to spend time on
Jeremy's problems ... I'm very fond of Jeremy: he's an asset to
the House.'

(It is worth recalling here that, while coping with Josiffe and
trying to cover up his own past indiscretions, Jeremy continued
to be active on the committee of the Homosexual Law Reform
Society, which from 1963 to 1966 held most of its meetings at his
parliamentary office. Indeed, in April 1965, the month before the
Bessell–Soskice meeting, Jeremy and Norman St John Stevas, the
Society's Conservative MP, had met the Attorney-General, Sir
Elwyn Jones, to discuss the bill which Lord Arran proposed to
introduce in the House of Lords to give effect to the Wolfenden
proposals, a meeting at which Jones made it clear that Arran's

initiative, though its prospects did not seem good at that stage, had the Home Secretary's personal support.)

During the interview, Soskice kept patting a buff file on the desk in front of him, which Bessell assumed contained Josiffe's police statement and 'letters'; and at one point Bessell mentioned how anxious Jeremy was that the documents in question should not remain on record. Soskice had made no reply at the time; but when Bessell next ran into George Thomas, the latter said that he had spoken to Soskice who had told him that Jeremy had 'nothing more to worry about'. Bessell interpreted this as meaning that the file had been destroyed, and reported this to a delighted Jeremy – though all Soskice seems to have meant was that, on the existing evidence, there was no prospect of any further official action being taken. Meanwhile the file remained in existence, and the letters it contained remained the property of Josiffe, to do with as he wished.

Even if he had somewhat exaggerated his achievements, Bessell had done much to help his friend. He had been to see Josiffe, arranged for him to get his luggage, and intimidated him into ceasing (for the moment) his harassment of Jeremy; and he had conducted friendly discussions which had the effect of confirming the sympathy towards Jeremy which existed in current government circles and ensuring that he would be given the benefit of the doubt in relation to any compromising evidence possessed by the police. As a token of his gratitude, Jeremy presented him with a gold cigarette lighter. Bessell, however, required help of a more practical kind. As a result of his fantasy business schemes of recent years, he had got into serious financial trouble and urgently needed £20,000 (worth some £500,000 today) just to keep afloat. During the summer recess of 1965, Jeremy responded to his plea for assistance: he approached the two richest benefactors of the Liberals, the millionaire clergyman Tim Beaumont and the chemicals tycoon Sir Felix Brunner, convinced them that it would be a calamity for the Party if Bessell went bankrupt and had to resign the seat he had laboured so hard to win, and persuaded each of them to lend £10,000 to Bessell, who expressed confidence that he would be able to repay them within a short time. Now it was Bessell's turn to be grateful, and he presented Jeremy with a pair of gold cufflinks adorned with the Thorpe crest. (This, according to Bessell, was a significant gift; for Jeremy had apparently confided to Bessell that he had given Josiffe, early in their relationship, a similar pair of cufflinks inherited from his father, an act of generosity which led to embarrassment as his mother kept asking him why he no longer wore them.)

At the time, Brunner was cruising in his yacht in the Mediterranean; and Jeremy, who had planned a holiday in Greece, took Bessell with him so that they could meet the tycoon and get him to part with his cheque at Corfu. Bessell was still present when Jeremy was reunited in Athens with the Oxford contemporary with whom he was sharing his holiday, the Manchester-based merchant banker David Holmes. Bessell was impressed by Holmes' distinguished appearance, lively conversation, sophisticated sense of humour and quiet good manners. He assumed they were lovers and thought Holmes, unlike Josiffe, a most suitable paramour for Jeremy to have. (The truth was rather more complex: Holmes, who travelled much on business, led a multiple life, conducting a discreet and stable 'marriage' in Salford with Gerald Hagan, a drama producer for Granada Television, while leading a promiscuous homosexual life in London and also having relationships with women. He certainly had a close and confidential friendship with Jeremy, but if they had been lovers, it was probably only for a short time. He remained, however, an infatuated admirer of Jeremy, taking a romantic delight in making himself useful to his eminent friend and through him rubbing shoulders with a glamorous world.)

Having shared each other's secrets and helped each other out of serious problems, Jeremy and Bessell seemed bound together by unshakable bonds. They were regarded in the West Country as twin Liberal heroes, joined after the 1966 election by the new MP for North Cornwall, the charismatic John Pardoe. Two things, however, stood in the way of their friendship. First, Bessell's political views were often far to the right of Jeremy's: in particular, he took the opposite position on two matters which were close to Jeremy's heart, being pro-Rhodesia and anti-EEC. It was therefore inevitable that some friction should have developed between them, particularly when rumours began to circulate that Bessell had mentioned to the whips of both the main parties that he might be prepared to consider changing his political colours.

Secondly, Bessell, though undoubtedly close to Jeremy at this time, proved incapable of keeping a secret, particularly when he was in bed with a woman. It later transpired that he had told several of his secretaries how he had helped his sexually unconventional colleague out of scrapes. He also felt the urge to share the burden of Jeremy's secret with at least one other fellow Liberal MP. He told George Mackie, Chairman of the Scottish Liberals, about the Josiffe affair when he visited him in his constituency in north-eastern Scotland in August 1965; and when Mackie lost his seat at the 1966 election, he went on to confide in one of the new Liberal MPs, the Methodist Richard Wainwright. He was also approached by Alisdair Mackenzie, the elderly and upright Liberal MP for Ross and Cromarty, who had been shocked to hear of Josiffe's allegations from a constituent who had visited Ireland: at least Bessell realised how inappropriate it would be for a man of Mackenzie's temperament to know the truth, and tried to reassure him by telling him that Jeremy was in fact conducting an affair with his own wife.*

Also, although Bessell had on the whole done Jeremy good by discussing Josiffe with government ministers, in doing so he

---

* It will be seen that, during the Liberal Leadership contest which followed, both Mackenzie and Wainwright voted against Jeremy, while Mackie, though out of Parliament, campaigned strongly for one of his opponents.

inevitably risked giving greater currency to the affair in ruling circles. George Thomas and Frank Soskice were both sympathetic to Jeremy, but the matter also got to the ears of another Home Office minister, Alice Bacon, who was less sympathetic and made her disapproval known to other colleagues. By the time of the 1966 General Election, the matter was known to the new Home Secretary, Roy Jenkins; to his junior minister, Jeremy's old Oxford Union sparring partner Dick Taverne;* and to Harold Wilson himself. (Fortunately for Jeremy, all these men, like Thomas and Soskice, were sympathetic to him and concerned to spare him embarrassment.) For good measure, the affair probably lingered in the memory of the Conservative Henry Brooke, who had been Home Secretary at the time of Josiffe's allegations to the police in 1962, while his predecessor R. A. Butler had been informed of the investigation regarding Jeremy's suitability to be best man at Princess Margaret's wedding in 1960. (By 1966, both Brooke and Butler were sitting in the House of Lords.)

However, during the mid-1960s, Josiffe was not the only skeleton from Jeremy's private life which threatened to emerge from the cupboard to haunt him. At this period, a number of other potential scandals arose relating to his homosexual past: any one of these might have caused him serious trouble, and collectively they ensured that far more people, including prominent individuals in political and government circles, got to hear of his tendencies and indiscretions.

The first 'scandal' arose out of his trip to America in the spring of 1961, during which he had visited San Francisco where (as we have seen) he had enjoyed himself in the thriving homosexual subculture of that city. He had in particular got to know a young man there called Bruno, to whom, over the next couple of years, he had sent a stream of romantic letters on House of Commons

---

* Taverne already knew about Jeremy's homosexuality from their Oxford Union contemporary, the ballet critic Oleg Kerensky.

writing paper, addressing him by the affectionate nickname of 'Brewin'. As fate would have it, Bruno came under investigation by the FBI, who censored his mail and thus became aware of his homosexual association with a British MP. Ever since the Burgess affair a decade earlier, the American authorities had been paranoid about the 'security risks' presented by British homosexuals in official or public positions; and at some point during 1963, the United States Ambassador in London approached the Foreign Secretary, Lord Home (shortly to become Prime Minister) to suggest that it would be prudent if Jeremy Thorpe refrained from visiting America in the near future. The only action Home took was to share this information with his fellow Etonian Jo Grimond. It seems unlikely that Grimond, who had a natural distaste for confronting people with such matters, went on to share it with Jeremy; but he dissuaded Jeremy from accompanying him to President Kennedy's funeral in November 1963, and around the time of the 1964 General Election confided the story to two of his closest friends – Mark Bonham Carter and Frank Byers. As a result of this episode, of which Jeremy himself probably knew nothing at the time, some of the most senior people in the Liberal Party were made aware of his indiscreet behaviour.[4]

A whole series of potential scandals arose from the fact that Jeremy, with his love of risk-taking, was often unable to resist making passes at attractive young men in potentially hazardous situations. At various times he claimed (perhaps 'boasted' would be more appropriate) to likeminded friends that he had succeeded in seducing cameramen filming his television interviews, footmen at Buckingham Palace receptions,* even policemen on duty at the House of Commons. Such was the deftness of his approach that those who declined his invitations generally did so without rancour and kept the matter to

---

* See below, pp. 289–90.

themselves; but there was always the danger of a hostile reaction. Such a case occurred on a visit, during the summer recess of 1965, to Tangier, where he stayed with his fellow Reform Club member Patrick Thursfield, being popular in the British expatriate community which was then led by such colourful aristocratic homosexuals as David Herbert and Robin Maugham. On this occasion, he attempted to seduce a young English male tourist who reacted angrily and later contacted both the Liberal and Conservative Associations in North Devon to denounce his behaviour. Faced with this embarrassment, Jeremy sought the advice of Leo Abse, the brilliant and charismatic Welsh Labour MP who had become prominent in the campaign for homosexual law reform, who advised him to stick to stout denial. This Jeremy did, but he suffered the consequence that, during the General Election campaign of March 1966, his meetings were disrupted by anti-homosexual abuse from young Conservative farmers – one of several factors which appear to have contributed to the slashing of his majority. This episode, like the 'Brewin' one, meant that more Liberals got to hear of his dangerous secret life.

Yet another scandal involved John Wilkins, the handsome runaway public schoolboy whom Jeremy had first met with Henry Upton during the early 1950s and who had subsequently worked as a journalist, living with Tony Maycock on Brixton Hill. Since Henry's mysterious disappearance in 1957, Jeremy had been conducting an intermittent affair with Wilkins, whom he also employed as a parliamentary researcher; but by the mid-1960s they were seeing less of each other and Wilkins, who had started drinking heavily, somewhat resented the fact that Jeremy so rarely asked him to dine at the House of Commons as of old. On the evening of 23 June 1966, Wilkins was due to meet Jeremy at the House – for dinner, as he supposed – but on his arrival he received a note from Jeremy to say that he had been called away, though he had arranged for Richard Wainwright to sign him in to watch the debate from the public gallery. Wilkins somehow found his way to a bar in the precincts, and got drunk; he then created a disturbance in the gallery, shouting that he was Jeremy Thorpe's jilted lover. Wainwright was called and saw him out into the street; but Wilkins succeeded in returning to the Central Lobby, where he made a second scene, following which Wainwright took him home in a taxi. Jeremy, anxious to behave discreetly since his trouble at the General Election four months earlier, was appalled to learn of the incident. Next morning, Wilkins was filled with remorse and wrote apologetic letters to Wainwright and Jeremy, but the latter was not to be appeased. Wainwright already knew about Josiffe from Bessell: this episode made him feel that Jeremy (whom he had previously admired) might not be suitable to succeed Grimond, and he confided his doubts to his fellow North Country Liberal MP, Michael Winstanley, who shared his view.[5]

By the autumn of 1966, therefore, with Grimond's resignation in the offing, Jeremy's private troubles had become known to many important people: to the former Prime Minister Douglas-Home and the current Prime Minister Harold Wilson; to government ministers on both sides of the House who had served at the Home Office since Josiffe had made his police statement four years earlier; to Grimond himself; to Jeremy's fellow Liberal MPs Bessell, Mackenzie, Wainwright and Winstanley; to the leading Liberal ex-MPs Byers, Bonham Carter and Mackie; and to others besides. With so much known to so many, could he still hope to lead the Party?

11

SUCCESSION
1966–67

JEREMY THORPE SOMETIMES told intimate friends of his anxiety lest Grimond, who was both his party leader and personal hero, should hear about his private life. He need not have worried. Grimond and his family circle belonged to a sophisticated world which had few illusions as to Jeremy's nature but took a relaxed view of homosexuality as an alternative preference. Down the years, Grimond had heard rumours about Jeremy's escapades, and been informed of such episodes as the 'Brewin' affair; but he took the liberal view that it did not matter what Jeremy did in private so long as public scandal was avoided, and he protected Jeremy by reassuring those Liberals (such as Richard Wainwright) who came to see him to report such rumours that it was 'just talk' and no cause for concern.[1]

Yet, as we have seen, it cannot be said that Grimond particularly liked Jeremy. He recognised Jeremy's talents and by the 1964 election had more or less adopted him as his deputy in political matters; but, much to Jeremy's discomfiture, he declined ever to discuss with him the question of his eventual successor, though Jeremy was widely perceived in the Party as the heir apparent, and Grimond's wife Laura and mother-in-law Lady Violet (the latter still formidable in her eightieth year and now sitting in the House of Lords) enjoyed Jeremy's company and wanted him to succeed as Leader.*

It has been seen that, by the time of the Brighton Assembly in September 1966, Grimond was widely expected to retire from the leadership in the near future. Indeed, those close to him were aware that he had been bored with the job ever since the collapse of the 'Orpington revival' in 1963. During the election campaigns of 1964 and 1966 he seemed to have lost much of his old sparkle; and though he got on well with Harold Wilson, he had never recovered from the shattering of his 1950s dream that Liberalism would prevail as 'the radical alternative to socialism'. In December 1965, after he had been criticised in some party circles for being too supportive of the Labour Government, there was speculation that he was about to step down, only ended when he issued a statement that he intended to lead the Party into the next General Election. (In fact, he *had* considered giving up at that time, but was persuaded to carry on by Jeremy and others, who warned that Emlyn Hooson seemed to be the current favourite to succeed him. Grimond and his Asquithian in-laws disliked Hooson's right-wing views and did not want to see another Welsh lawyer leading the Liberal Party. But had a leadership election then occurred, Hooson would have had the support of Mackie and Bowen, both of whom lost their seats in 1966, and Mackie would have sought to bring his fellow Scots MPs into line behind Hooson.[2])

There was a further flurry of speculation after the 1966

---

* In her diary, Lady Violet wrote that, although there was 'no one even approaching' the stature of her son-in-law, and Jeremy lacked judgement and 'was not a thinker in depth', he was nevertheless her choice on account of his 'vitality & colour & passionate zest' – as well as her somewhat optimistic belief that, as Leader, he would 'always seek and take the advice' of Grimond. (Pottle, *Daring to Hope*, entries for 17–18 January 1967.)

election (during which Grimond experienced the personal tragedy of his son's suicide); but it was not until December 1966 that Grimond finally made up his mind to go in the New Year. Subsequent events are interestingly described in the unpublished diary of Tim Beaumont,[3] the Oxford contemporary of Jeremy who after an intemperate youth had taken holy orders and inherited a fortune which he used to become a leading benefactor of the Liberal Party, recently serving as Head of the LPO. The diary reveals that, by mid-1966, Grimond had lost interest in the leadership and effectively delegated his authority to a 'gang of four': the warhorse Byers (aged fifty-one), now Party Chairman and back in Parliament as a life peer; Pratap Chitnis (aged thirty), the professional party officer who had recently succeeded Beaumont as Head of the LPO; Richard Holme (aged thirty), the ex-Gurkha officer who was Vice-Chairman of the Party Executive (deputising for the Chairman, Gruffydd Evans, who lived on Merseyside); and Beaumont himself (aged thirty-eight). Having reached his decision to resign, Grimond confided it to Byers, who in turn confided in the other three: no one else (least of all his fellow MPs) was supposed to know.[4] Between mid-December and mid-January, the four met on several occasions to discuss the succession. Having tried and failed to persuade Grimond to change his mind, they decided that his resignation should be announced on Tuesday 17 January 1967, his successor being elected by the twelve MPs from among their number within two days (leaving no time for the development of a divisive national debate within the Party). And they were unanimous that that successor should be Richard Wainwright.

The genial and rather saintly Leeds accountant and Member for Colne Valley was then forty-eight. Though only elected to Parliament the previous March, he had long been a popular figure in the Party's counsels, regarded by many as the embodiment of traditional Liberalism. He was a devout Methodist, and a wealthy supporter of good causes; though a product of Shrewsbury and Cambridge, he had never (being like Harold Wilson in this respect) lost his homely Yorkshire accent. Beaumont and his colleagues agreed that Grimond was irreplaceable, but that Wainwright was best fitted to follow him among the current MPs; and they hoped to 'fix' his election by getting friendly journalists (such as Robert Carvel of the *Evening Standard*) to write articles in his praise to coincide with Grimond's resignation announcement.[5]

Chitnis and Holme were 'adamant against Jeremy' and talked of 'launching a Keep Jeremy Out campaign'; but as they played the parlour game of speculating who would vote for whom, the quartet concluded that, although both Jeremy and Hooson would probably stand, neither was likely to survive the first round of voting. If there was a serious potential challenger to Wainwright, it was Lubbock. Jeremy, they believed, could at best get just four first-round votes: his own; Pardoe's (unless he voted for Lubbock); Bessell's (unless he voted for Hooson); and Lubbock's (if he decided not to stand himself). They assumed Grimond would loftily abstain.[6] However, during the weekend prior to the announcement, these calculations were thrown to the winds. As Chief Whip, Lubbock was the first MP to be informed of Grimond's decision, and decided not to be a candidate. Moreover, the letter he received from Grimond spoke of Jeremy having 'a certain claim'.[7] Then Beaumont saw Wainwright to 'offer' him the leadership; but to Beaumont's consternation, this prize was 'flatly refused' by Wainwright, who did not wish politics to interfere with his family life.* Wainwright did, however, hope that Lubbock would change his mind and stand, as he considered Hooson's politics to be unacceptable while 'Jeremy's

---

* To the author in 1993, Wainwright gave two further reasons for his decision: he feared he might lose his marginal seat at the next election (as proved to be the case), and felt the Party might be hampered by his strongly pacifist views.

security standing is a most unfortunate one ... [which] might stop him getting a Privy Counsellorship'.[8] (Beaumont knew what Wainwright meant, having heard rumours of a homosexual blackmail situation 'and there is a file on this in the possession of the Home Office ... a serious matter ... at least two Ministers on each side of the House are known to have seen it ... it probably made all the difference to Wainwright not supporting Thorpe'.[9] In addition, Byers confidentially told Beaumont, Holme and Chitnis about the 'Brewin' affair around this time.[10])

Up to this moment, Jeremy had remained unaware both of Grimond's decision and the botched attempt to fix the succession: he received no more notice of the resignation than the other MPs, a few hours in advance of the public announcement on 17 January. The news electrified him and threw him into a frenzy of calculation. Of his eleven fellow MPs, he believed he could count on the support of four – Bessell, Lubbock, Pardoe and Steel. Lubbock and Steel remained indebted to him for his contribution to their by-election victories, and looked up to him as a political mentor. Bessell and Pardoe were his fellow West Country MPs: Bessell had been a close friend for more than a decade, and Pardoe (though later to be an adversary) was at this stage a warm admirer of Jeremy's inspirational style. True, Bessell's political views were far to the right of Jeremy's, and just a few weeks earlier there had been some unpleasantness between them over Rhodesia.* But during the previous two years, they had confided in each other and helped each other out of their respective private difficulties: it hardly occurred to Jeremy that Bessell might fail to support him.

---

* In November 1966, following the failure of the talks between Wilson and Ian Smith aboard HMS *Tiger*, Bessell was involved in an attempt by some right-wing backbench MPs (including the maverick Labour member Reginald Paget) to avert the imminent imposition of mandatory UN sanctions against Rhodesia by getting Smith to agree to receive a Royal Commission: his efforts were disowned by the other Liberal MPs, in Jeremy's case with some anger.

With the ballot fixed for the afternoon of the following day (Wednesday the 18th), events unfolded swiftly.[11] Steel immediately declared himself for Jeremy and offered to act as his campaign manager, canvassing the other MPs. Pardoe also rallied to Jeremy's side. ('Why bother to ask?' he replied when approached by Steel.) Bessell, however, acted in a characteristically devious fashion. Motivated, it would seem, by a certain resentment against Jeremy, who had used and patronised him, as well as by strong political differences and a first-hand knowledge of the skeletons which might make Jeremy's leadership disastrous, he first approached Hooson, to whom he promised his support; but then he began to have second thoughts. It occurred to him that his failure to back Jeremy would be greeted with anger and incomprehension in the West Country. He then went to see Jeremy, who assumed as a matter of course that Bessell would be supporting him and was pacing excitedly around his office in a manic mood. In his memoirs, Bessell depicts the vivid scene:

> Jeremy's brain was already at work on how he would use the leadership: the reorganisation of Party Headquarters; the appeal he would make for funds; the campaign to be fought at the next election; the speaking tours he would undertake; the seats we would win. His enthusiasm was contagious. As he paced the room he epitomised the quality so essential for political leadership: charisma. Like all his audiences, I was captivated. The longer he talked, the more certain I became that, whatever the risks, Jeremy was the only MP who could lead the party. Suddenly he grasped my shoulders and literally shook me, as was his habit in moments of exhilaration ... 'We'll shake up this old party ... I'll lead it as ruthlessly as Lloyd George. Harold and Ted won't know what's hit them. Now it's a crusade!'[12]

Thus Bessell joined Jeremy's bandwagon, without bothering to tell either Jeremy that he had already promised to support

Hooson, or Hooson that he had changed his mind. According to his own account, Bessell went on to canvass Alisdair Mackenzie and Michael Winstanley on behalf of Jeremy, but without success: Mackenzie thought Jeremy too pro-EEC, while Winstanley remarked that the Party needed 'a leader and not an impersonation of a leader'. (As Bessell had reason to know, both had also heard something about Jeremy's secret life.)

Two dramatic developments now occurred. First, Lubbock declared he *would* be a candidate after all: he had been reluctantly persuaded to do so by Wainwright and Winstanley who, though unwilling to stand themselves, considered Hooson unacceptable owing to his right-wing views and Jeremy because of his homosexuality. Jeremy took Lubbock's candidature in a sporting spirit and they agreed that whichever of them lost would serve as Chief Whip under the other. (There was no such mutual regard between Jeremy and Hooson, nor did Jeremy readily forgive Wainwright and Winstanley for getting Lubbock to stand against him.) Secondly, Grimond finally made it known that he would be supporting Jeremy, which filled Jeremy with relief. Subsequently, Grimond told various intimates that he had regarded the prospect of handing over the Party to Jeremy without enthusiasm, but nevertheless considered him to be the most able and acceptable of the eleven potential candidates. Grimond was also under pressure from his wife and mother-in-law to support Jeremy; and although, like Wainwright, he knew about Jeremy's homosexuality, this (as in the past) was not something which worried him provided it remained discreet.

Within a few hours of the announcement, therefore, Jeremy had emerged as the favourite for the leadership in a three-cornered fight. He could count on at least five votes out of twelve. He had the endorsement of the retiring leader, who was still held in huge affection and respect. It was also becoming clear that he had the overwhelming support both of English Liberals in the constituencies and of the Young Liberals, who bombarded the MPs and Party Headquarters with telegrams declaring Jeremy to be their choice. Although they would have preferred the less colourful but more virtuous Wainwright, most senior party figures, including Beaumont, Byers and Evans, were willing to accept Jeremy as leader, hoping he would mend his ways. A few, including Chitnis and Holme and a group of Liberals in the north-west of England,* were appalled at the prospect, fearing that his homosexuality would mire the Party in scandal and considering him arrogant, devious and lacking in intellectual substance; but there was little they could do. There were calls for the election to be postponed so that the membership could be consulted; but there could be no doubt in any case that Jeremy was the members' choice.

If there was a threat to his chances, it came from Scotland. The Scottish Liberal Chairman, the ex-MP George Mackie, was not one of Jeremy's admirers and hoped to get the Scottish Liberal MPs to back Hooson. He failed with Steel and Grimond, but succeeded with Russell Johnston and Alisdair Mackenzie. There remained James Davidson, the popular and easy-going farmer who had been elected for West Aberdeenshire in 1966: as soon as he arrived in London from his constituency, Mackie and Steel began grappling for his soul. Eventually, late on Tuesday night, Davidson was taken by Steel to see Jeremy at Marsham Court, where 'after much talk and whisky' he finally agreed to give Jeremy his vote.[13] Jeremy could now be sure of six votes out of twelve – his own, Grimond's, Steel's, Pardoe's, Bessell's and Davidson's.

The leadership ballot took place at half-past two on the afternoon of Wednesday 18 January 1967 in the Liberal Whips' Office

---

* These included the solicitor Roger Cuss (President of the North-Western Liberal Federation), the future MP Michael Meadowcroft and the future Liberal peer Geoffrey Tordoff. They rang around the Liberal associations of the region to see if they could whip up a campaign against Jeremy, only to find that he was widely popular.

at the House of Commons, the ex-MP Lord Wade acting as returning officer and a champagne cooler serving as ballot box. Jeremy's office being outside the parliamentary precincts, his old friend Tony Benn, now Minister of Technology, had lent him his room further down the corridor as a headquarters for the afternoon. Once the MPs had cast their votes, it was half an hour before they were summoned to hear the result. This was because the election was being conducted under the Single Transferable Vote system of proportional representation, as a result of which the outcome was one of total deadlock. As expected, Jeremy received six first preference votes and his opponents three each; as all who voted for Hooson gave Lubbock as their second preference, and vice versa, it was impossible to proceed to a conclusion.[14] It was a grotesque outcome to what had been intended as an advertisement for the voting system which the Liberals wished to see used nationally.

In a state of intense nervousness, Jeremy retired to Benn's room accompanied by Steel and Bessell. They were discussing whether, in the event of a re-run, it might be possible to prise Russell Johnston from the Hooson camp, when Wainwright appeared and asked to have a private word with Bessell in the corridor. Wainwright referred to what Bessell had told him some months earlier about the Josiffe affair, and asked if there was 'any risk of that matter – or anything else – becoming public'. With a confidence he did not feel, Bessell replied: 'If I thought there was, I wouldn't have supported Jeremy.' 'That's good enough for me,' said Wainwright, who went off to confer with Hooson and Lubbock.[15] At 3.35 PM, the MPs again congregated in the Whips' Office. A smiling Lubbock announced that both he and Hooson had now decided to withdraw and hoped their supporters would unanimously accept Jeremy as leader. Obviously unhappy, but doing his best to appear gracious, Hooson added that he was sure Jeremy would do a great job for the Party. The other MPs all shouted, 'Hear! Hear!' Jeremy was declared elected, and made a short speech of thanks. 'I have no recollection of what he said,' Bessell later wrote, 'only that he looked and sounded more nervous than I had ever known him to be.'

It was the greatest moment of his life, the fulfilment of a childhood dream. At thirty-seven, he was the youngest leader of a British parliamentary party since mass politics had begun a century earlier, even since Pitt the Younger. The party of which he took charge was very different from that which Grimond had inherited a decade earlier – a party with a rising membership and improving organisation which gathered more seats at each election, a magnet for radical youth, its leader treated by the press as a national figure and by the current Prime Minister as a near-equal to the Leader of the Opposition. And who could tell what greatness lay ahead? If he could solve the Party's funding problems and capture the imagination of the voters, if future elections resulted in further gains for the Liberals and their support was eventually sought by a minority government, if they could thus secure a change in the voting system ... was it not conceivable that Jeremy might one day hold public office, and even realise his ultimate dream, planted in his young mind by Megan (how he missed her in his hour of glory![16]), of becoming the first Liberal Prime Minister since Lloyd George?

But all he had achieved or dreamed of achieving was a hostage to fortune: all might be ruined in a moment were it to become generally known that his private life was of a character which, in the eyes of the law and most of his fellow citizens, was beyond the pale. Even were he now to lead an entirely respectable life, any one of a score or more of scandalous incidents in the past might still rise up to haunt and ultimately destroy him. His secret was already known to most of the leading figures in the Party and at least half his fellow Liberal MPs.

An hour after his election as leader, Jeremy was alone with Bessell, who explained that Wainwright had voted against him on account of his knowledge of the Josiffe affair, and had only changed his attitude when Bessell had reassured him that there was no risk of 'that or anything else' becoming public.* Bessell now said to Jeremy: 'If you do anything that puts the party at risk, you'll have betrayed everything we've fought for. If anything in the past ever became public, you'd have to resign immediately.' Jeremy replied with apparent seriousness: 'Peter, I give you my word that, should anything become public, I shall blow my brains out.'† To which Bessell replied: 'I hate to say it, but you'd have no alternative.'[17]

---

* In his memoirs, Bessell admits that he deceived Jeremy by concealing from him the fact that it was he himself who had originally told Wainwright of Josiffe and of Jeremy's homosexuality.

† Jeremy may have been thinking of the fates of two pre-war Liberal statesmen who had been exposed as homosexuals, the 1st Viscount Harcourt (1863–1922) and the 7th Earl Beauchamp (1872–1938). Harcourt committed suicide by taking an overdose of sleeping draught; Beauchamp resigned his offices and fled abroad, giving rise to King George V's remark: 'I thought men like that shot themselves.'

12

LEADERSHIP
1967

JEREMY THORPE'S FIRST days as Liberal Leader passed in a whirl of celebration. He was photographed for the press beaming broadly and surrounded by congratulatory telegrams. He visited Party Headquarters, where he kissed every woman and shook hands with every man. He made his first public appearance at an agricultural show at Shrewsbury, eclipsing the Agriculture Secretary Fred Peart. He was showered with garlands when he next crossed into his constituency. A series of parties took place in his honour, such as Cynthia Gladwyn's* champagne reception to which flocked 'a huge crowd' including half the Cabinet and such celebrities as Yehudi Menuhin and David Frost.[1] He seemed determined to prolong the celebratory atmosphere: some felt that he continued to behave throughout his leadership as if it had never come to an end.

His election received wide coverage in the press. Jeremy was popular with journalists, having always given them good copy;

---

* Wife of Gladwyn Jebb, 1st Baron Gladwyn, Liberal Foreign Affairs spokesman in the House of Lords.

and with the rise in the Party's fortunes over the past decade, to be Liberal Leader meant something again. His showmanship was remarked on, one commentator describing him as 'above all a *performer* politician – one is reminded of a professional conjurer'.[2] But the *Guardian* complimented the Liberals on choosing 'a good radical leader' who would 'continue to make the Liberals matter ... by questioning questionable things ... and by shouting aloud for the rights of individuals'.[3] The *Daily Telegraph* devoted an editorial to his election, depicting him as

> a character, the most vivid available personality ... Mr Thorpe has most of the gifts that make a man a success as a professional politician – those of the statesman in high office are unlikely to be required of him. He has the youth; the debonair self-confidence cultivated at Eton; the logical capacity of one trained in the law; the fluent speech and ready wit of a President of the Oxford Union ... What lies behind the glossy façade will become more apparent as his leadership develops.[4]

In interviews, he spoke soberly of the need for 'a radical alternative' to the 'caution and conservatism' of the Labour Government,[5] but he was also full of quips, remarking that he regretted he could not now deliver his gallant loser's speech.[6] His mother was also interviewed. 'I suppose I've always known he would lead the Party some day,' declared this recent convert to Liberalism, 'but I didn't think it would be this soon.' She had done her best to support her son's political career – 'it's always nice to have someone in the background you can rely on, isn't it?' – but saw little of him these days as he was so busy. 'He doesn't even have much time for girlfriends ... Any wife will have to understand that his career comes first.'[7]

Of all the congratulations he received, none can have pleased him more than the warm words of welcome delivered by Harold Wilson to a cheering House of Commons when Jeremy made his debut there as Leader.[8] Wilson had a soft spot for the Liberals, having been one himself; he personally liked Jeremy, sharing his sense of intrigue and showmanship and appreciating his humanitarianism and wit; and he hoped, by building up Jeremy's stature, to irritate Edward Heath and keep down the Conservative vote. Thanks to Wilson, Jeremy was appointed a Privy Counsellor only six weeks after becoming Liberal Leader, an honour for which Grimond had had to wait five years: this gave him kudos as well as access to official secrets, enabling him to be briefed on such matters as Rhodesia and Northern Ireland. (In offering him this status laden with security implications, Wilson was evidently undeterred by Jeremy's private life, concerning which, unbeknown to Jeremy, he was well-informed and indeed intrigued.) The genial premier also favoured him in other ways. He invited him to nominate three new Liberal life peers, and allowed the Liberals parliamentary time to introduce occasional bills. He ensured that the Liberal Leader was always prominently included in public events, including visits by foreign statesmen. (Within a month of becoming Leader, Jeremy was meeting the Soviet Prime Minister Alexei Kosygin at a Buckingham Palace banquet and informing him that his grandfather had been the last foreigner to be decorated by the Tsar.) Jeremy was much entertained at 10, Downing Street, where his wit and mimicry were particularly enjoyed by Wilson's influential political secretary Marcia Williams: he was a regular fixture at the PM's 'celebrity parties', attended by such personalities as the Beatles, Bobby Charlton and Morecambe and Wise.

Jeremy enjoyed no such friendly relations with Heath, who cannot have appreciated either this prime ministerial favouritism or the fact that, with his plebeian vowels and gauche manners, he was a prime target for Jeremy's mimicry. In personal terms, the exuberant and slapdash Jeremy had little in common with the introverted and plodding Heath, apart from a shared love of music, nor was the fact that they were both bachelors at this time calculated to draw them together. A week after Jeremy became Leader, Heath had still failed to offer his congratulations; and the press interpreted other small incidents down the years as slights to Jeremy on Heath's part.* But the Conservative Leader was naturally awkward in his behaviour; and if there was little fellow feeling between them, there does not seem to have been any strong mutual animosity either. They were both pragmatic, centrist politicians who passionately believed (as Wilson never did) that Britain's future lay with the European Economic Community: when the great moment arrived at which the Liberals came close to holding the balance, it would significantly be Heath and not Wilson who would try (albeit half-heartedly) to tempt Jeremy into a coalition.

Following his election,[9] Jeremy left his office in Bridge Street and moved into the room reserved for the Liberal Leader in the corridor behind the Speaker's Chair, which he redecorated by ordering new carpets and curtains and covering the walls with photographs of himself meeting eminent personages and newspaper cartoons in which he featured. He then appointed a small personal staff. He secured the services of two trusted assistants, both old friends a couple of years younger than himself. Richard Moore, a journalist of patrician background and whiggish outlook, who had become President of the Cambridge University Liberal Club soon after Jeremy had occupied the equivalent position at Oxford, became his political secretary, writing his speeches and advising him on policy. Tom Dale, an LSE graduate with Elvis-type good looks whom Jeremy had befriended one Sunday afternoon in 1960 when they had found themselves alone together in the library of the National Liberal Club, became his personal assistant, organising his diary and acting as his 'eyes and ears' in the Liberal Party. In addition, he had two

---

* For example, early in 1968 Heath accidentally damaged Jeremy's car while parking his own at Westminster, and failed to offer apologies.

excellent personal secretaries, one of whom, the devoted Judy
Young, would remain in his service for the rest of his life. He also
inherited a press officer from Grimond in the form of Mike
Steele, a young Australian journalist of republican sympathies
with whom his relations were often difficult: Steele found Jeremy
'vain and bullying', while Jeremy considered him inefficient and
disrespectful and regarded him as a spy for his enemy Pratap
Chitnis, still Head of the LPO; but Steele knew his job and got
on with the Lobby, and despite periodic attempts by Jeremy to
get rid of him, he remained in his post until 1972.

Apart from this regular staff, Jeremy also relied on several
unofficial advisers, notably his Oxford friend David Holmes and
the flamboyant German-born banker Robin Salinger. Both had
originally helped him with fundraising, but he came to confide
in them and seek their advice about many things. They had
scarcely been heard of in the Party before Jeremy became Leader
and were regarded with suspicion by many Liberals, though
Holmes continued to use the dubious title of Deputy Party
Treasurer which Jeremy had purported to confer on him as
Treasurer, while Salinger married Miss Iona Jones, Secretary to
the Liberal Peers. Both exuded a raffish air: Salinger (a philandering heterosexual) wore scent and had a habit of putting his
arm around his interlocutor, while Holmes (a promiscuous
homosexual) displayed a fastidiousness which some found
unnerving. They satisfied Jeremy's need for admiring cronies outside his official circle with whom he could discuss his problems
without inhibition and on whose loyalty he could absolutely
depend.

From the first, money was an obsession for Jeremy as Leader:
throughout his decade in office, he devoted more time to raising
and spending it than to any other activity. Although he claimed
virtually to have solved the Liberals' financial problems as Party
Treasurer, the truth was that those problems were continuing
and chronic, and threatened to cripple the Party's organisation

and electoral prospects. He displayed his usual skill at securing donations from potential benefactors, and expressed confidence that he would one day find a fabulously rich donor who would permanently relieve the Party of its fiscal embarrassments and open up a new world of political possibilities: he frequently exasperated colleagues by going off into flights of fancy on this theme when they wished to discuss practical matters of tactics and policy. Apart from the question of party finance, an immediate problem for him was that he had no salary as Leader, nor were there any party funds specifically available for the running of his office. To meet his expenses and pay his staff, he relied on the largesse of a few wealthy private supporters – notably the Welsh patent lawyer and industrialist Gerran Lloyd, rewarded in Lloyd George fashion with a life peerage in 1969.

Jeremy took an essentially theatrical view of party leadership. He loved the trappings of his position – the invitations to the Palace and elsewhere, the participation in the annual wreath-laying ceremony at the Cenotaph and other national occasions. He loved being interviewed on television, having his picture in the newspapers, giving his views on *The World at One* and *Any Questions* on the issues of the day. He loved such publicity stunts as posing for photographers next to his waxwork statue at Madame Tussaud's. He loved being one of 'the great and the good': he was probably the most 'social' party leader since the age of Balfour and Asquith, his wide circle including Princess Margaret, the Archbishop of Canterbury, and many leading figures in the arts. This flamboyant outlook was to be harshly criticised by many in his own party, yet it benefited the Liberals in two important ways. Through the drama and style that attended his public doings, he conveyed the impression that the Liberals possessed a far greater political significance than was suggested by their 2.5 million votes and twelve MPs. And he believed that, given time, he could establish himself as a familiar and reassuring national figure, to whom voters would gratefully turn at a time of crisis. This belief – which may be said to have been the basis of his political strategy throughout his leadership – struck many as grotesquely narcissistic: but seven years after he had become leader, it would very nearly translate itself into reality.

Besides, it was no disadvantage to be an actor in British political life in 1967. Thanks to television and the introduction of advertising techniques into politics, party leaders were increasingly becoming identified in the public mind with the parties they led and having to project suitable images. This was no hardship for Wilson, who possessed the common touch, but the prosaic Heath presented a problem for the image-makers, and the media turned with relief to Jeremy's showmanship. The late 1950s and early '60s had been the age of Macmillan and Gaitskell, with Grimond included as something of an extra; but the period from the mid-'60s to the mid-'70s was to be the age of Wilson, Heath and Thorpe. They were an ideal trio for cartoonists and impersonators: Wilson with his round face, homely manner and nasal Yorkshire accent; Heath with his square face, awkward deportment and grating vowels; Jeremy with his expressive, angular features, flamboyant mannerisms and rich theatrical voice.

A feature of Jeremy's leadership, particularly marked during its early stages, was the opposition he faced from within his own party. This was not a feature unique to the Liberal Party; for the 1960s marked the heyday of 'consensus politics', the leading figures of all three parties basically agreeing (in accordance with the known wishes of the electorate) on such fundamental policies as a 'mixed' economy of private and state enterprise, the maintenance of the welfare state, and Britain's role in NATO. This agenda, however, was too right-wing for many in the Labour Party, too left-wing for many Conservatives, and too lacking in 'radicalism' for many Liberals. All three leaders therefore faced trouble from both party activists and backbench (occasionally frontbench) MPs. In Jeremy's case the trouble was worse than that faced by Wilson or Heath, first because he led a party unlikely in the near future to enjoy the consolations of office and patronage, secondly because he irritated many Liberals through his leadership style.

Even among most of the other Liberal MPs he never enjoyed more than lukewarm support. Of his eleven colleagues, only five had voted for him in January 1967, and no fewer than three of these – Davidson, Pardoe and Grimond himself – would admit, little more than a year later, that they regretted having done so.[10] He continued to have an ambivalent relationship with Bessell, who remained his leading confidant in personal matters but whose loyalty and discretion were never wholly to be trusted and who pursued as before his own political agenda, pro-Rhodesia and anti-EEC. Hooson, Mackenzie, Wainwright and Winstanley never made much secret of their doubts concerning Jeremy's fitness to lead: he viewed them as enemies. Russell Johnston was loyal, but carried little weight. The only MPs he could truly regard as friends and allies were David Steel and Eric Lubbock. Having managed his leadership campaign, Steel became his loyal Parliamentary Private Secretary; having stood against him in a friendly spirit, Lubbock was henceforth his devoted deputy as Chief Whip. On these two alone could he certainly rely. Although a sense of self-preservation made it unlikely that the others would actually turn on him, he could never be sure how much support he would get from them when the going got rough.

He felt more at home among the Liberal peers. Some thirty-five hereditary peers still took the Liberal whip, and Jeremy, who dearly loved a lord, counted many of them as friends. Of the three Liberal life peers created in 1964, Violet Bonham Carter was his vociferous supporter, while the ex-MPs Frank Byers and Donald Wade, though frequently exasperated by him, remained loyal. One of the few constitutional reforms he accomplished as Leader was to include the Liberal peers in the weekly meetings of the Parliamentary Party, which led to a welcome increase in both the numbers and political expertise of that gathering. In March 1967, Lord Rea stood down as Liberal Leader in the House of Lords, a position he had held since 1955. In the ensuing ballot (in which thirty-nine peers were eligible to vote and twenty-one actually did so), Byers was elected as the new Leader, with Lord Gladwyn (a distinguished diplomat ennobled on his retirement who had joined the Liberals in 1965 as their foreign affairs spokesman in the Lords) as his deputy: both were to be an asset at PLP meetings, and personally supportive of Jeremy. In June 1967, Wilson invited Jeremy to nominate three new Liberal life peers. The allocation of these peerages, announced in November, was typical of Jeremy: one went to the millionaire benefactor, Tim Beaumont; one to a public celebrity, the former Scottish rugby international John Bannerman; and one to John Foot, the Plymouth solicitor who had given Jeremy his first brief at the Bar.* Jeremy never ceased to be fascinated by the possibilities of patronage presented by the Upper House: he was to dangle the prospect of future peerages before many people he wished to flatter, particularly with a view to securing important donations, and was always on the lookout for stray hereditaries who might be persuaded to take the Liberal whip. He was deeply interested in the multi-party attempt to reform the House of Lords which began towards the end of 1967.

During Grimond's last year, the Party had effectively been run by the 'cabal' of Beaumont, Byers, Chitnis, Evans and Holme. None of these had particularly welcomed Jeremy as Leader, and

---

* The peerage which Foot reluctantly accepted had already been refused by three others to whom Jeremy had offered it – Ludovic Kennedy (who was about to defect to the Scottish National Party), and the ex-MPs Arthur Holt and Mark Bonham Carter. (Diary of Lord Beaumont, November 1967.)

Chitnis and Holme, as we have seen, were frankly hostile to him. Although they had lost their controlling position with Grimond's resignation, they all still held senior offices in the Party: Chitnis remained Head of the LPO; Byers was now Leader in the Lords, Beaumont (who joined Byers in the Lords that autumn) replacing him as Party Chairman; Evans remained Chairman of the Party Executive, with Holme as his Vice-Chairman. They still met regularly, and regarded themselves as the Party's guardians: they were prepared to wait to see how Jeremy would get on, but if in their eyes he proved unsatisfactory as Leader, they were capable of mounting formidable opposition to him.

Throughout his Leadership, Jeremy enjoyed the support of most ordinary party members in the constituencies. But trouble loomed from that notoriously fractious and ineffective representative body, the Party Executive. Like the Labour Party Executive, this took a more radical view of policy than the Parliamentary Party; and it resented the fact that it was virtually ignored by the MPs in general and the Leader in particular, who rarely bothered to attend its meetings. The Executive had no constitutional means of controlling the MPs or the Leader, but could embarrass them by passing votes of censure. That its opposition would not be long in manifesting itself was virtually guaranteed by two aspects of the Executive – that it was under the influence of its Vice-Chairman, Richard Holme, and that it had been infiltrated by the Young Liberals.

In recent years, the Young Liberals – along with their sister body, the Union of Liberal Students – had mushroomed both in numbers and influence. Using Trotskyite methods, they had infiltrated constituency associations, and through them the Party Council and Executive,* and they aspired to dominate the

---

* A couple of seats on both bodies were reserved for the YLs and ULS, but through their control of run-down constituency associations, they managed to fill many more.

annual Party Assembly. Jeremy's attitude towards them was ambivalent. On the one hand, his 1966 Rhodesia speech had made him a hero among them; he had been their choice for Party Leader; and there could be no doubting their energy and success in recruiting new members. On the other hand, their militant views and methods were intensely alarming both to moderate Liberals and much of the electorate. Jeremy's tactic was to flatter them – in early speeches, he praised their 'red blood' – while trying to minimise their influence. At their Assembly in April 1967, the YLs elected a radical Chairman and Secretary, George Kiloh and the gay campaigner Bernard Greaves, while the ULS chose two even more militant characters, Terry Lacey and Philip Kelly. When these officers went to see Jeremy to propose a programme of radical tactics and policies, he was welcoming, assuring them that he thoroughly agreed with their aims and ideas and would merely need a little time to decide how to put them into effect. By the time of the Party Assembly in September, however, it was obvious to the YLs that Jeremy had no serious intention of going along with their programme: they felt betrayed by him and ready to do battle with him.[11]

With mounting opposition from the Party Executive and Young Liberals, limited support from his fellow MPs and growing scepticism about his leadership from senior party figures, Jeremy's position was precarious. His assets were his own toughness and ingenuity; the support of the grass roots; an excellent intelligence service run by Tom Dale, which gave early warning of any developing threats to his leadership; the absence of any constitutional machinery for the removal or re-election of the Leader; and the fact that, ultimately, most responsible Liberals shrank from public rows which threatened to inflict serious damage on their party. On the other hand, dissatisfaction with him was certain to grow unless the Liberals registered some political advance; and he did not make things easy for himself, in a party which had more than its fair share of nonconformists, intellectuals and militant radicals, with his exhibitionism and ribaldry, his lack of interest in ideas, his evident delight in being a 'member of the establishment'.

The first months of Jeremy's leadership were hectic and strenuous. An opposition leader wears a multitude of hats. He is leader of a mass membership spread across the country, responsible for rallying them to the cause; leader of a national political organisation, responsible for reconciling conflicts between its various components; leader of a parliamentary party, responsible for planning its tactics, acting as its spokesman, managing its relations with the Government. He presides over some species of shadow administration. He is his party's chief public relations officer, its main fundraiser, its ambassador in contacts with similar parties abroad. The leaders of the Labour and Conservative parties, with their hundreds of MPs and extensive financial resources, had large staffs organised in various departments to which they were able to delegate most of these multifarious functions. But the Leader of the impoverished Liberals had only a handful of (doubtfully loyal) colleagues, a few paid assistants, an understaffed Party Headquarters which found itself virtually overwhelmed by everyday organisational tasks, and such volunteers as were willing to come to his aid.

Under the circumstances, Jeremy had to choose, during the early months of his leadership, whether to make an impact in Parliament or (through public meetings attracting media publicity) in the country: he simply did not have the resources to do both. Given the need to bolster both the electoral appeal of his party and his standing within it, he chose the latter: during his first six months as leader, he addressed about 150 meetings up and down the land. In an effort to inspire audiences, he spoke with exaggerated optimism both of the present condition of the Party and its prospects under his leadership. He claimed for it a current membership of 300,000, which he hoped soon to double; he claimed to have reduced the party overdraft as Treasurer from £50,000 to £5,000, and was hopeful of raising a further £100,000 in the short term and £1 million in the long term to put its finances firmly in the black. The political message he put forward was one which had been worked out since the General Election by a party 'think tank' run by Richard Holme and his friend in the advertising world, Adrian Slade. In essence, it was that Labour and the Conservatives represented the same tired, failed, outmoded politics, while the Liberals stood for something fresh and exciting. The slogans used were 'The Liberal Crusade', 'The Radical Alternative', 'Down With Politicians!' and 'Power to the People!'. The problem was that it was far from clear exactly *what* alternative the Liberals were proposing; and it was difficult to lay down any definite programme which would satisfy both the traditionalists and radicals in the Party, beyond some vague proposals for constitutional reform and greater popular participation in government. When, soon after Jeremy became Leader, a thirty-page pamphlet appeared under his name entitled *The Liberal Crusade: People Count*, it was filled with the woolliest generalities.

On 1 March, Jeremy attempted to 'relaunch' the 'repackaged' Liberal Party under his leadership at a much-heralded rally at the Albert Hall, relayed by closed-circuit television to audiences in Bristol and Newcastle – the first time such a thing had been attempted at a British political meeting. (It was typical of Jeremy to be the first to try out such a gimmick: later that year, he also became the first British politician to give a televised party political broadcast in colour.) Inevitably, it contained more style than substance – but the style was spectacular, reminiscent of the mass presentation techniques used by Billy Graham and John F. Kennedy. A warmed-up audience burst into thunderous applause as Jeremy, wearing television make-up, strode down the aisle and then appeared on stage as if through some trap door, to a magnificent show of lights. His speech was full of rhetorical flourishes, calling for 'a Liberal crusade' to 'quicken the heartbeat of the British people' and 'kindle the hope of millions':

> Power was wrenched from our hands or let fall by our own inadequacy. So the Century of the Common Man became the Century of the Concentration Camp. As Liberalism faltered the world was defiled. So we owe it not only to this nation but to civilisation to resume our advance. This is the Great Crusade.

The audience was stirred, and the press took note (though their reports were satirical in tone) – but what had been conceived as a fundraising exercise proved a financial disaster, the enormous cost of the occasion far surpassing the contributions from those attending. It had, however, given a boost to Jeremy's personal prestige, followed as it was a couple of days later by the announcement of his Privy Counsellorship.

Liberals waited anxiously to see whether the change of leader and Jeremy's barnstorming efforts were having any effect on their electoral fortunes in the country. The first half of 1967 was a fairly stable time in domestic politics – a lull before the storm which would break in the autumn. A wage freeze imposed by the Wilson Government in the second half of 1966 had been unpopular, but had led to some strengthening of the economy. On the whole, opinion polls showed (as was natural at that stage of a Parliament) the Opposition slowly gaining in popularity at the expense of the Government, while the Liberals remained roughly static, their national tally fluctuating between 7 per cent and 10 per cent. They made a fractional advance at a round of by-elections on 9 March, but lost their deposit at Brierley Hill on 13 April (after a campaign in which Young Liberals had been caught tearing down Conservative posters), and won no seats in the elections to the Greater London Council that month. At the local elections in May, they did respectably, losing thirty-five seats and gaining sixty-two; but opinion polls over the summer showed their vote declining. The simple fact, which no number of dazzling performances by Jeremy could alter, was that the Liberals generally only did well under an unpopular Conservative Government: an unpopular Labour Government caused uncommitted voters to drift towards the Conservatives, including many 'temporary' Liberals who had voted Conservative in the past.

Jeremy's decision to give priority to public and party meetings meant that he did not make much impression in Parliament during those early months. He was able to spend little time there, only appearing in important debates or those of special interest to him, and tending to make rather brief statements, usually written for him by Richard Moore. Even on these occasions he often surprised fellow MPs by his failure to shine: having taken to heart the advice of colleagues that he should try to acquire *gravitas*, he seemed to lose much of his sparkle and come over as rather pompous. His most impressive contributions were on the two great foreign affairs issues which dominated the news in the spring of 1967 – Britain's reapplication to join the EEC, and the war crisis in the Middle East. Otherwise, his only parliamentary performance to attract much attention was his unsuccessful introduction in April, following the Aberfan disaster, of a private member's motion providing that all monies paid to disaster appeals should go into a national fund if not distributed after two years.

A role Jeremy especially enjoyed as Liberal Leader was that of pundit, airing his views on the great issues of the day at home and abroad. On subjects he knew and cared about, he spoke with originality and verve (though he measured his words more carefully now – there were to be no more 'bomb Rhodesia' speeches). In theory, he was supposed to express 'party policy' as agreed with fellow MPs or laid down by the Party Council and Assembly; but such restrictions never much bothered Jeremy, who in any case, on matters which were important to him, generally got his way both with the Parliamentary Liberal Party and Assembly. As well as expressing his opinions in Parliament, public meetings, and media interviews, he reached an audience of millions through BBC Radio's *Any Questions*, to which he continued to be a regular and popular contributor, his appearances always being followed by a huge and mostly admiring postbag.

He was especially interested in foreign affairs: he had a natural understanding of these and often went abroad to visit people and places in the news, seeing himself as an ambassador of international liberalism. His first such trip as Leader was to Canada that spring, to attend 'Expo 67' and meet the Liberal premier Lester Pearson. As noted, two great international issues arose at that period about which he had much to say both inside and outside the House – the Wilson Government's application to join the EEC, and the Middle Eastern crisis arising out of the pressure put on Israel by her Arab neighbours. Jeremy's views on both issues were clear: it was vital for Britain to join the EEC (though her application was flawed by Cabinet divisions on the subject), and equally vital to stand by Israel while she was threatened with destruction (though Palestinian rights and the role of the UN had to be respected). Both issues were soon resolved, when De Gaulle vetoed Britain's application and Israel inflicted a crushing defeat on the Arabs in the Six-Day War. During the following months, he made a Middle Eastern tour, meeting leading figures in both camps, and visited European Liberals to discuss Britain's future relations with the EEC: he became well informed in both these areas, on which he always spoke with assurance and was listened to with respect.

There were two other international issues that spring on which he had rather less to say, being involved to some extent in conflicts of interest. When Biafra began its long and bloody attempt to secede from Nigeria, he was torn between the Commonwealth position of strict neutrality and the fact that, a few years earlier, he had advised the Biafran (then Eastern Nigerian) Government through his work for the EDS consultancy, which was said to have encouraged the secessionists. And when the Greek Colonels seized power, Jeremy's natural desire to condemn their regime was tempered by the fact that it was condoned by his friend Francis Noel-Baker,* an eccentric right-wing Labour MP with extensive property interests in Greece whom he hoped to persuade to cross the floor and join the Liberals: Jeremy was in fact staying with Noel-Baker on his Greek estate in August 1967 when two of the Colonels came to lunch, though he avoided meeting them by pleading a diplomatic illness. (Later, Jeremy, always a fan of royalty, became a friend of the exiled King Constantine, to whom he offered advice on how he might regain his throne.)

He was fascinated by the international politics of the Cold War. The YLs and other party radicals were becoming increasingly anti-American owing to Vietnam, but Jeremy always insisted that Britain must continue to stand by the United States and play a leading role in NATO. (He did, however, acquiesce in a Party Council resolution of December 1967 calling on the Government to offer asylum to American draft-dodgers: having himself contrived to get out of National Service, he could hardly object to this.) He remained a staunch supporter of the Commonwealth, visiting the African leaders who were his friends, and showing interest in the relations between Britain and India.† He continued to lambast the illegal regime in Rhodesia, warning that its continuance might lead to a break-up of the Commonwealth or even a future world war between the white

---

* Francis's father, the internationalist statesman Philip (Lord) Noel-Baker, had for decades conducted a famous love affair with Jeremy's late heroine Megan Lloyd George. Surprisingly, Francis knew nothing of this until informed of it by Jeremy. (Information from Francis Noel-Baker.)
† Cyril Smith, elected in 1972 as Liberal MP for Rochdale in Lancashire, which had a large Pakistani population, thought Jeremy disturbingly pro-Indian.

and coloured races. He denounced Britain's precipitate withdrawal from Aden in the autumn of 1967 without having made arrangements for its future: 'It is surely without precedent for this country to grant independence to a territory when, within days of leaving, there is no Government and the country is in a virtual state of Civil War.'[12]

Jeremy was less effective when he spoke on domestic affairs. He had a poor grasp of economics; and owing to his friendship with Wilson and admiration of such 'liberal' ministers as the Home Secretary Roy Jenkins, his instinct was to give the Government an easy ride. There were, however, four issues in 1967–68 on which he expressed strong views: Northern Ireland, regional devolution, immigration and the reform of the House of Lords. (It is interesting that all these issues were to be high on the Liberal Democrat agenda when they made their parliamentary breakthrough thirty years later in 1997.)

Northern Ireland was not yet much in the news in 1967: its troubles would only hit the headlines the following year. Jeremy, however, was unusually interested in the province, partly on account of his own Irish Unionist family background, against which he had strongly reacted, but also because, as a Liberal, he considered that the position of the Catholic minority constituted the leading 'civil rights' issue in the United Kingdom, comparable to the position of blacks in America's Deep South. One of his first acts as Leader was to visit Belfast. Speaking at Queen's University, then represented by a Liberal in the local Stormont parliament, he spoke out against alleged injustices suffered by Catholics in votes, jobs and housing, predicting serious disorder unless these were removed. Addressing the annual conference of the local Liberals the following October, he described the province as 'a reactionary backwater ... the dark corner of the British Isles'. Some would say that his words were prophetic, others that they helped provoke the explosion which would not be long in coming.

The question of Scottish devolution came to the fore after the

Hamilton by-election in November 1967, in which the Scottish National Party secured its first and most spectacular victory, driving the Liberals into fourth place. The Liberals had long urged self-government for Scotland and Wales, and there was much debate within their ranks as to whether they should now seek an electoral pact with the SNP to fight for a Scottish Parliament: the idea was fiercely opposed by the Scottish Liberal Chairman, George Mackie, but supported by Jeremy's friend Ludovic Kennedy, who eventually resigned from the Liberals to join the SNP. Jeremy kept out of the row, but during the early months of 1968 made devolution one of his main themes, advocating not only parliaments for Scotland and Wales but also the establishment of twelve provincial English assemblies and a reduction in the number of Westminster MPs from around 600 to 400: in February 1968, he obtained leave to introduce a parliamentary bill providing for such reforms, though it did not get far. 'Time and again in our constitutional history,' he declared in the House, 'we have conceded in bitterness what should and could have been granted in logic ...'[13]

Immigration was a subject upon which his views were well known: he believed in a free right of entry for Commonwealth citizens, and campaigned inside and outside Parliament against the various legislative measures from 1961 onwards to restrict this right, culminating in the Immigrants Bill introduced by the Labour Government early in 1968. He joined in the outcry against Enoch Powell's 'rivers of blood' speech in April 1968. He was presented with a problem, however, in that Wallace Lawler, the leading Midlands Liberal who had been elected to Birmingham City Council at the time of Orpington as the first Liberal there since the war, showed some sympathy with Powell's views. To the scorn of the Young Liberals and other radicals, Jeremy declined to criticise Lawler, whose populist stance resulted in his re-election as a city councillor in May 1968 and his sensational victory in a parliamentary by-election the following year.

It has been noted that Jeremy was deeply interested in the House of Lords and proposals for its reform. His views, as revealed by his participation in the events leading to the Peerages Act of 1963, were contradictory. He claimed to be eager to 'modernise' that anachronistic institution, yet he revelled in its ancient traditions, in his own fantasy belief that he himself had a claim to a medieval peerage, and above all in the possibilities of patronage: nothing gave him greater pleasure, during his first year in office, than having three life peerages to hand out to his chosen candidates. At the start of the new parliamentary session in November 1967, a cross-party Joint Committee was set up to discuss House of Lords reform, on which the Liberals were represented by Jeremy and Byers: the favoured proposal was that the hereditary peers should lose their voting rights* and be replaced by new life peers nominated by the three party leaders. The prospect of having further peerages to hand out delighted Jeremy. It remained to be seen what final form the reform proposals would take, and whether they would succeed; but meanwhile he dropped broad hints of future peerages to allies he wished to encourage, adversaries he wished to disarm, and above all (following the Lloyd George tradition) rich businessmen whom he hoped to persuade to donate some of their fortunes to the Liberal Party.†

In the autumn of 1967, his political honeymoon over, Jeremy experienced the first serious tests of his leadership. The Party

---

* It was, however, proposed that existing hereditaries should be allowed to carry on sitting in the House and enjoying its facilities for the rest of their lives.
† In the course of his leadership, Jeremy nominated nine life peers and two peeresses, of whom six – Beaumont, Lloyd, Tanlaw, Mackie, Wigoder and Baroness Robson – had made substantial contributions to party funds. Lord Tanlaw (Simon Mackay, elevated in 1971) was little known in party circles, and ennobled after offering money to the Party which he would otherwise have applied to a business career. (Diary of Lord Beaumont, April 1969.) Jeremy also spoke of getting a peerage for his benefactor Jack Hayward, who was not even a member of the Liberal Party.

Assembly at Blackpool in September promised to be stormy: the Young Liberals had put down motions calling for withdrawal from NATO and workers' control of nationalised industries, and many moderate Liberals were threatening to resign if these were carried. Jeremy, however, had been quietly working behind the scenes to ensure that the YLs did not have an automatic majority, and their motions were ultimately defeated. His two speeches were lively and statesmanlike, their main theme being that the difference between Labour and Conservative was 'like the difference between a crocodile and an alligator': Wilson, Jeremy declared, was a better Conservative Prime Minister than Heath, but the country wanted a 'radical alternative'. He tried to appease the YLs with flattery, calling them the Party's 'intellectual sparking plugs'. The press congratulated him on a fine performance, but compared him unfavourably to the magisterial figure of Grimond, and claimed to be mystified as to the meaning of his so-called 'radical alternative'.

In fact, the Party faced a difficult time which was not of Jeremy's making. The gap between its traditional and radical wings was widening, and any programme which aspired to satisfy both – such as that put forward by Jeremy at Blackpool – was bound to consist largely of hot air. Moreover, as the Labour Government became increasingly unpopular, the electorate was turning not to the Liberals' much-vaunted (but little explained) 'radical alternative', but to the traditional alternative presented by the Conservatives. This became clear from the Liberals' performance at four by-elections that autumn, in all of which Jeremy campaigned personally. At Cambridge and Manchester Gorton – their candidate in the latter being the fiery Terry Lacey of the Federation of Liberal Students – they lost their deposits. At Walthamstow and South Derbyshire, where they had made great efforts with excellent candidates and expected to do well, they achieved little advance. Their opinion-poll ratings continued to stand well below 10 per cent. The Party was also heading for another severe financial crisis, though this would not become fully apparent until the following year: Jeremy was partly to blame here, for his extravagant leadership style (epitomised by the Albert Hall rally) had resulted in the expenditure of much more money than had been raised. Meanwhile the tempers of the Young Liberals, who had been checked at Blackpool, and the Party Executive, who felt increasingly ignored by the Leader and MPs, were becoming frayed. These tempers were not improved when, on Remembrance Sunday, Jeremy appeared at the Cenotaph dressed, in contrast to Wilson and Heath in their ordinary suits, in full morning dress and a silk top hat.

November 1967, the Government's worst month, also proved hazardous for Jeremy. After weeks of crisis, the pound was devalued on the 18th – a humiliation for Wilson, whose policy since the election had been to keep the currency strong by means of drastic and painful financial controls. James Callaghan resigned as Chancellor, and there was speculation that Wilson too would resign. Speaking in the House of Commons on the 21st, however, Jeremy congratulated the Government on its decision, which he described as 'a necessary step ... for which we must be profoundly grateful' and which would 'make it easier for this country to join Europe' – even if its timing had been 'unfortunate' and the economic measures accompanying it 'inadequate'.[14] These were hardly the words of a heavyweight parliamentarian rounding on a discredited ministry, and Jeremy was harshly criticised for them at an angry joint meeting of the PLP and Party Executive to discuss the national crisis. He mollified his critics by announcing that he was about to make an important statement, both in a speech in North Devon and a party political broadcast, which would capture the national imagination. His listeners assumed that this would attack the Government; but when they saw an advance copy of his speech, it transpired that the mystery 'statement' consisted of a proposal for a coalition government under Wilson which would include prominent industrialists brought into Parliament with life peerages.*

The Executive were furious. They held an impromptu meeting at Birmingham on 25 November at which Richard Holme proposed a resolution effectively censuring Jeremy. There was some debate about the wording of this, Tim Beaumont (just ennobled on Jeremy's recommendation) arguing that it should not read too obviously as an attack on the Leader.[15] The final version deplored 'the failure of the Liberal Party to make an impact on the electorate as an alternative to the two discredited main parties' and called on the Party to 'campaign militantly against the system of which the Wilson Government is the sorry symptom': this was adopted unanimously and immediately issued to the press. It was greeted with consternation by Jeremy and his allies, who had been given no warning of it, but with delight by the press, which published huge articles about how the Liberals were tearing themselves apart. 'Can the Liberals survive?', asked the *Sunday Telegraph*, while the *Daily Express* ran the double-page headline, 'WHO IS LEADING THE LIBERALS?'. When, in the wake of the resolution, Holme and Lubbock proceeded to launch vituperative personal attacks on each other, this too was eagerly reported in the newspapers.

Even the Executive realised that such disastrous publicity served the interests of no one in the Party; and when Jeremy met them on 10 December, he won their grudging support after admitting 'mistakes' and agreeing to drop the coalition proposal from his coming broadcast. (He had already mentioned it in his North Devon speech, which had been widely reported in the context of

---

* The Joint Committee on the Reform of the House of Lords (see above) had just begun its proceedings, and was likely to recommend the creation, through the patronage of the party leaders, of new life peers to replace disenfranchised hereditary peers, Jeremy having it in mind to nominate businessmen who might help relieve the Liberal Party of its financial problems.

the general furore.) But having tasted blood, the Executive soon returned to the attack. In the New Year, they threw out a proposal put forward by Jeremy for the reform of the party constitution, whereby the (notoriously useless) Party Council would have been replaced by a new policy-making body dominated by MPs and parliamentary candidates. Always at his best when presented with a challenge, Jeremy prepared to do battle, aware that 1968 would make or break him in his relations with his Party.

On the day of Jeremy's election as Leader, Bessell had made him promise to be more circumspect in his private life. It was all right, Bessell had told him, to conduct discreet relationships with such friends as David Holmes; but there must be no more Norman Josiffes.[16] But however discreetly Jeremy behaved in future, he still had to contend with his past; and it was not long before he again had need of Bessell as the manager of problems arising from his history of homosexual escapades.

That he had continued to lead a dissolute and risky life right up to the time of his election became clear to Bessell when Jeremy showed him a letter he had received dated 5 April 1967.[17] The writer, one Bill Shannon, referred to having met Jeremy the previous November and spent two 'very pleasant nights' with him at Marsham Court. After offering congratulations on his election and assurances that he had told no one of 'our secret', he asked for a 'loan' of £150 – 'in cash and, if possible, by the end of the week'. Jeremy admitted to Bessell that the writer was a rent boy he had picked up in the King's Road, and begged for his help in getting him out of what looked like a blackmail situation. Bessell offered to write to Shannon, explaining that he was handling Jeremy's financial affairs and asking him to a meeting at his office. 'I don't know where I'd be without you, Beseli,'* replied Jeremy.

---

* Jeremy's pet name for Bessell, based on a whimsy that the latter was an Italian count.

Interviewed in 1979, Shannon gave some details of his contacts with Jeremy. They had met while Shannon had been looking at the window of an antique shop in the King's Road, Jeremy approaching him with the words: 'Looking for anything in particular?' After a romp at Marsham Court, Shannon – like Josiffe – had been invited to spend the night there on the camp-bed, and in the morning been asked how he liked his eggs done. He had then been given a 'present' of £3. Jeremy had picked him up again a few nights later but at first failed to recognise him from their previous encounter. On this second occasion, Jeremy had said to him: 'Do you know who I am?' Shannon had replied: 'A very nice gentleman.' Whereupon Jeremy had explained that he was an MP with eminent friends and showed him the framed photographs on his mantelpiece.[18]

When the youth (who gave his age as twenty-seven) saw Bessell at his office in Pall Mall, the MP handled him with skill. He began by giving the impression that his proposition was being seriously considered and asked how Shannon proposed to repay the requested 'loan', getting the answer that he might manage to do so at the rate of £20 a week. When Bessell suggested that £150 was a lot of money, Shannon lowered the sum dramatically, saying £30 would be enough for the time being. Although Bessell had formed the view that he was not dealing with a serious blackmailer, he abruptly changed tactics. Waving Shannon's letter in his face, he declared to the horrified youth that it constituted a criminal threat of blackmail. No action would be taken if Shannon gave no more trouble; but if he so much as mentioned Jeremy's name to anyone, 'your letter goes straight to the police'. Shannon stammered that he would tell no one, and rushed off: he was to keep the matter to himself until contacted twelve years later by journalists and (under somewhat different circumstances from those outlined by Bessell) the police, who would have produced him as a prosecution witness at Jeremy's trial had not the latter authorised his lawyers to make an admission as to his past homosexuality.

Shannon had proved easier to deal with than Norman Josiffe. Nothing had been heard from the latter since the summer of 1965; but only a few days after Shannon's visit, Bessell received a letter from him dated 20 April 1967, addressed from 13, Kildare Street, Dublin. Josiffe wrote that he had been 'doing very well' in Ireland as a male model, and that in connection with his change of career he had changed his name to Norman Scott.* He was hoping to go to the United States in July, where he had been offered a job, but he had destroyed his passport 'when I was upset over Jeremy'. He asked for Bessell's help in formally changing his name by deed poll and obtaining a passport under the new name. When Jeremy saw the letter, with its news that Scott (as one must henceforth call him) was happy in life and going abroad, he was delighted. 'Marvellous!' he exclaimed to Bessell, making a show of putting on his glasses and reading it again. However, while Bessell was abroad during May, Scott telephoned his secretary with the uncomfortable news that he had become both ill and short of money and no longer had a job to go to in America.

Bessell next heard from him by a letter dated 14 July, sent from a village near Maidstone. Scott wrote that he had returned from Ireland and was staying with his brother in Kent and had had another nervous breakdown for which he was being treated by Dr Brian O'Connell of St George's Hospital in London, to whom he had confided the details of his alleged affair with and mistreatment by Jeremy. Indeed, the letter consisted mostly of a

---

* He chose the name Scott as it was the family name of Lord Eldon, whose illegitimate son he had claimed to be since 1964. He told friends that he was giving up the name Josiffe lest people confuse him with the Marks & Spencer tycoon Joe Sieff, feeling it might harm his modelling career if he was thought to be Jewish.

rambling recapitulation of those details. He had spent all his savings and was unable to perform either equestrian or modelling work owing to his state of health. He wrote that he was desperately in need of money, London accommodation, a National Insurance card and a job, and hinted that unless all these were forthcoming, others might also get to hear his 'story'. He did, however, confirm that his long-term aim was still to go to work in America if this could be arranged.

Jeremy was alarmed by this letter, especially by the news that Scott was spreading his tale. He decided to consult Lord Goodman, the clever and fashionable solicitor whose many eminent clients included Harold Wilson, who had elevated him to the peerage on becoming Prime Minister; he had already acted for Jeremy in a 1950s libel case. A bachelor of enormous bulk, he had a reputation as a skilful operator independent of party politics whose talents included that of extricating politicians from embarrassing private life situations: three years earlier, he had obtained an apology and a huge settlement for Lord Boothby after the latter had been (justly) accused by the *Sunday Mirror* of being a friend of the Krays. The consultation took place next day and was also attended by Bessell. Jeremy showed Goodman the letter Scott had sent his mother in 1965, and the recent letter to Bessell: he neither confirmed nor denied the allegations they contained, but asked Goodman whether he might write to Scott threatening him with a blackmail charge unless he ceased to cause trouble (the technique Bessell had employed successfully in the case of Shannon). Goodman strongly advised against this course, on the grounds that if Scott called their bluff they would be in a worse situation, and suggested Bessell see Scott with a view to helping him go to America, as Bessell had already offered to do. The meeting had achieved little, but Jeremy had enjoyed the drama of the occasion, and he left with a jaunty air, confident that he could again leave it to Bessell to extricate him from trouble.[19]

A few days later, Scott called on Bessell at his London office.

He was in a highly strung state, sweating and stammering, and sought Bessell's help with obtaining a National Insurance card in Britain and employment in America. When Bessell suggested he apply for a temporary card at Maidstone, Scott insisted that this would involve explaining his 'affair' with Jeremy to the local social security office, so Bessell offered to take up the matter directly with the Ministry of Health. Bessell was going to America on business and promised to try to find a job there for Scott, whom he meanwhile offered to help by paying him a 'retainer' of £5 a week, an offer accepted with alacrity.[20]

When he made this offer, Bessell believed he could find employment for Scott in America, and saw the payments as a temporary measure to secure his good behaviour in the meantime. However, no job suitable for the virtually unemployable Scott presented itself, and the 'retainers' (eventually raised to £7 and supplemented with occasional larger payments) would continue to be paid for some twenty months, totalling between £600 and £700. They would prove disastrous for Jeremy, for Scott predictably showed the weekly envelopes he received, containing cheques or banknotes along with short covering letters from Bessell or his secretary, to all and sundry by way of giving credence to his story that he had had an affair with the Liberal Leader and was now being paid 'hush money' by the Liberal Party: the letters, which Scott carefully kept, would later bear witness to Bessell's long efforts to handle him on Jeremy's behalf. Jeremy, however, seems at the time to have considered the solution a not unsatisfactory one, believing that the payments might keep Scott quiet indefinitely – and indeed, Scott was to give no particular trouble for more than a year. It is not clear how far Jeremy had authorised Bessell to offer Scott money, but he did eventually repay most of the sums expended by Bessell on his behalf.

By this time, however, Jeremy had come to a decision which he hoped would put an end to rumours of his homosexual past.

He had decided, for the sake of his career and the Party, to find himself a wife. He was not to make his final choice until the winter of 1968; but he began his search in the summer of 1967. Meanwhile, that autumn, one newspaper made an inspired guess. On 18 October 1967, the *Daily Express* wrote of 'speculation' caused by Jeremy's friendship with 'willowy, dark-haired art expert Caroline Allpass', and published a photograph of them together at a charity film première. Jeremy protested that there was 'no significance in my friendship with Miss Allpass' who was 'just a friend', while the lady admitted that she had known him for some months, 'but there's really no romance'.

13

CAROLINE

1967–68

IT USED TO be a truth universally acknowledged that a single man in possession of political ambition must be in want of a wife; and ever since boyhood, when he had conceived the fantastic ambition of marrying Princess Margaret, thoughts of eventual matrimony had occupied Jeremy Thorpe's mind. Three factors, however, resulted in the postponement of this project until his late thirties. First, there was his lack of money: as a young MP in 1959, he could scarcely have contemplated supporting a family on a parliamentary salary of £1,750 a year. Secondly, there was the possessiveness of his mother, who was determined to remain the leading influence in his life: towards even his most innocent friendships with women, she tended to take up an attitude veering between suspicion and downright hostility. Last but not least, there were his homosexual inclinations: though he occasionally entertained friends with alleged philandering exploits, the truth was that the act of making love to a woman did not come naturally to him.

Despite this last obstacle, Jeremy, like many homosexual men, enjoyed the society of women, knew how to be gallant towards them and was regarded by many of them as a delightful companion. At various times, he became particularly attentive towards a female friend, giving rise to speculation as to his intentions. Thus at Oxford, he seemed close to his Liberal Club contemporary Ann Chesney, and as a young barrister, to his fellow pupil Elizabeth Clarke. As he became involved in West Country politics, it looked for a time as if he might make a match with Davina or Suna Portman, daughters of the Dorset Liberal grandee Viscount Portman. There was also gossip about his association with a glamorous divorcée living in Wiltshire. All these women got to know him quite well, and liked him – but they were also all aware of his sexual nature, and none of them relished the prospect of having Ursula as a mother-in-law.

While most of the women Jeremy viewed as potential wives seemed uninterested in having him as a husband, there were others who were captivated by him, and these he kept at arm's length. Caroline Barrington-Ward, sister of his old schoolfriend Simon Barrington-Ward, was one of several young women who developed a crush on him, but he did not respond to such feelings or encourage them. He was sexually attractive to many women, with his smooth manner, air of intrigue, and dark, sensual appearance. In the opinion of one voluptuous virago who met him at the Liberal Assembly at Scarborough in 1965, he 'combined the allure of a Renaissance courtier and a Latin American gigolo' – but while she was struck by his charms, he remained impervious to hers.

Someone Jeremy knew quite intimately and contemplated marrying was a friend of his childhood, Charlotte Prest. Born in 1936 and thus seven years his junior, she was Ursula's goddaughter and the only daughter of Tom and Eliza Prest, a wealthy couple who lived at Limpsfield and had been responsible for the Thorpes moving there in 1939. Charlotte was a rather plain girl, not over-endowed either with brains or robust health.

On the other hand, she was devoted to Jeremy and he felt comfortable with her; and along with her two brothers, she was due to inherit a substantial fortune. Ursula and Eliza, a formidable pair who between them ran the village, both set their hearts on the match and did what they could to promote it. For fifteen years, Charlotte accompanied Jeremy to dances and other events at which he needed a partner; and she came down to help him in his General Election campaigns. But she was a romantic girl, and saw him as a brother rather than a lover: Jeremy proposed to her on several occasions – once by taking her to Downing Street and announcing that 'this is where we're going to live' – but she always turned him down. She was to die in 1972 at the age of thirty-six, of an obscure illness following an unhappy love affair with an Italian of whom her family disapproved.

During the 1960s, Charlotte worked for Sotheby's in London, where she shared a flat in Lexham Gardens, Kensington, with two other young women, one of whom, Caroline Allpass, was a Sotheby's colleague. One summer evening in 1966, Jeremy attended a party given by Charlotte and her flatmates, taking with him his friend David Holmes. At this, their first meeting, Caroline made an impact not on Jeremy but the bisexual Holmes. Jeremy, for his part, seems to have made but a vague initial impression on Caroline; when, watching television with her mother in January 1967, she saw that he had been elected Leader of the Liberal Party, she merely remarked: 'Didn't I meet that man with Charlotte?'

Almost everyone who met Caroline liked her, finding her both physically appealing and possessed of an attractive personality – 'beautiful within and without', as one friend of Jeremy described her. Tall and athletic, with a fresh complexion and radiant smile, considerate, resourceful, unaffected, full of fun, she seemed a splendid example of a virtuous, upper-middle-class English girl.

But there were complexities beneath the surface, and her life had not been altogether easy.

She was born on 29 April 1938, thus sharing a birthday with Jeremy, who was nine years her senior. Her father, Warwick Allpass, was a prosperous businessman who had inherited a chain of furniture shops in South London; her mother had married him when she was only nineteen and found it hard to adjust to his world. There was also a son, Derek, four years older than Caroline. While her father was in the army during the war, her mother fell in love with a Worcestershire farmer, A. B. Williams: as a result her parents were divorced and Caroline's post-war childhood was split between two contrasting households, that of her mother and stepfather, who farmed a beautiful rented estate at Great Coxwell near Faringdon in Oxfordshire, where they lived (often in somewhat precarious circumstances) in a seventeenth-century manor house, and that of her father, who resided in suburban prosperity in Surrey with his formidable married sister, Joan Pickard. 'Caroline was deeply hurt by her parents' divorce,' a friend recalled. 'She seemed carefree on the outside but deep down carried scars and became quite private and secretive.' Others who got to know her became aware of a strain of 'steeliness' behind the easy-going exterior.

She received the best education money could buy, at Roedean and a finishing school at Gstaad. During school holidays, she divided her time between her parents. Staying with her father in Surrey, she became close to her practical and ambitious cousin Michael (later Sir Michael) Pickard, destined for a successful business career; staying with her mother and stepfather in Oxfordshire, she became similarly close to Vivienne ('Viv') Franklin, a high-spirited girl who came to work on the farm and was treated as one of the family. At nineteen, she went to work as assistant to John Rickett, head of the Impressionist Department at Sotheby's, where her cheerful nature made her popular with colleagues. In 1960, she left London to spend an adventurous year travelling with three male friends in wild parts of India and Iran, resuming her job on her return.

Caroline had many suitors and a string of love affairs, one of them quite serious. Like John Betjeman's Olympic Girl, she tended to attract rather masochistic heterosexual men who looked up to her on account of her impressive physique and breezy personality and wanted to be dominated by her. After a while, she began to tire of the doglike attentions of such men, and preferred to spend her time with other men, mostly homosexual and older than herself, who appreciated her for her personal qualities and entertained and amused her. Her boss John Rickett was such a man, as was the Chairman of Sotheby's, Peter Wilson. Other friends included the choreographer Freddie Ashton and Philip Frere, a solicitor with interesting social and literary connections with whom she often stayed in the South of France. She had the normal social ambitions of a girl in her position, and was not averse to the idea of marrying a man in public life.

When Caroline met Jeremy and David Holmes in the summer of 1966, it was with Holmes that she first became intimate: there was a mutual physical attraction between them and she found his conversation stimulating. By the spring of 1967, they were lovers, and when Jeremy next met her it was on a visit to Holmes in Manchester. Jeremy and Holmes had planned to holiday together in the Aegean that August, and it was arranged that Holmes should invite Caroline and Jeremy, Charlotte. The holiday – on the Greek islands of Cos and Rhodes, with an excursion to southern Turkey – was successful, Jeremy keeping the two women constantly entertained. 'If you stay here long enough,' Charlotte joked after an hilarious incident in which he had charmed some locals, 'they are bound to elect you to something.'

Jeremy later put it about that he had fallen in love with Caroline in the Aegean sunshine, and that he and Holmes had agreed as friends to compete for her hand, the loser acting as best man to the winner.* This story seems to have been largely a colourful invention of Jeremy's, for Caroline was still having a physical relationship with Holmes at the time, while Jeremy (who may still have been almost a virgin as far as women were concerned) did not propose to her until six months later. But Caroline had come to appreciate Jeremy's company during the holiday, and accepted an invitation to stay with Holmes in Manchester during September so they might go together to hear Jeremy's speech at the Liberal Assembly at Blackpool. After the Assembly, Caroline, Jeremy and Ursula all spent the weekend with Holmes, a visit made memorable by their attendance at a performance of Verdi's *Requiem* by the Halle Orchestra. On Sunday night, having returned to London, Jeremy rang Holmes to report that his mother had astonished him during the rail journey by remarking: 'Why can't *you* find a nice girl like that one? She would be so suitable . . .'[1]

Soon afterwards, Holmes proposed to Caroline. She turned him down on the grounds that she did not want to live in Manchester, but assured him that she would always consider him a good friend. Meanwhile, during the autumn of 1967, Jeremy – having first delicately asked Holmes' permission – began paying court to Caroline in London, giving rise to the premature article in the *Daily Express* of 18 October referring to 'speculation' over their friendship.

Jeremy had now made up his mind to marry, but he was not yet sure that his choice would be Caroline, even though she had now rejected Holmes' proposal and won Ursula's rare approval. Up to the end of the year, he still had hopes of marrying

* 'A friend of mine and I went on holiday and joined two girls in Greece. One I knew already. I wondered whether I might marry her. I decided I wanted to marry the other. So did my friend. So we said, "Right, Queensberry Rules. Whoever wins, the other is best man." I won. He was best man.' (Jeremy Thorpe quoted by Susan Barnes.)

Charlotte; and there was also a third woman he was courting at the time but eventually decided to be unsuitable. Finally, in February 1968, he proposed to Caroline over dinner at the revolving roof restaurant of the Post Office Tower in Marylebone. According to the memoirs of Peter Bessell, Jeremy confided to him that, in making his proposal, he had been honest and told her that he had not fallen in love with her but needed a wife.[2] Whether or not this is to be believed, it must have been clear to her that he was fond of her and could offer her a most interesting life; and she accepted him.

During the autumn of 1967, Jeremy told his press officer Mike Steele that he was thinking of marrying and asked him how far he thought this would improve Liberal ratings in the opinion polls, then hovering around 7 per cent. Somewhat amazed by the question, Steele suggested perhaps a rise of 2 per cent. 'Come on!' replied Jeremy. 'Surely at least five per cent?'[3]

Certainly, the prospect of making a popular marriage to a beautiful young woman could not have come at a more timely moment for Jeremy; for after a year as Liberal Leader, things were not going well for him. During the early months of 1968, the Liberals (as compared with their General Election performances of 1964 and 1966) continued to languish in the polls and fare badly in by-elections. They also faced a new financial crisis, for Jeremy as Leader had proved more adept at spending money than raising it: since his accession, the party overdraft had more than doubled from around £20,000 to £50,000, and so desperate was the position that Party Headquarters were having to move from their fine premises in Smith Square into shabby temporary accommodation behind the Piccadilly Hotel. It was a far cry from his early months as Leader, when he had launched his 'crusade' intended to bring electoral success and overflowing coffers.

From the start, there had been criticism of his style of

leadership: spurred on by his failure to revive the Party's fortunes, such criticism was becoming acute and widespread. It was increasingly said that he had become addicted to the trappings of leadership, and remote from its practicalities; that he had been seduced by Harold Wilson, and provided no serious opposition to the government of the day; that he was surrounding himself with cronies and losing touch with the rank and file; that it was impossible to discuss serious business with him as he would go off into a fantasy world of daydreams and imitations. What particularly dismayed many Liberals was his lack of interest in political ideas. Nineteen sixty-eight was to be a year notable for radical ferment, marked by the student protests which erupted in Paris and elsewhere. There were few votes in radicalism; but under Grimond, the Liberals had regained something of their pre-war reputation as 'the party of the intellectuals' and come to have the most active political youth movement in Britain. To many in the Party, this was a consolation for lack of power; and there was irritation that Jeremy showed so little interest in the new intellectual currents – and a contrastingly great interest in the traditional British social establishment.

During the second half of 1967, Jeremy had experienced outright opposition from two sections of the Party – the Young Liberals, who had originally supported him but soon felt betrayed by his lack of radicalism, and the Party Executive, which had censured him in November 1967 and gone on to veto his plans for reform of the party constitution. Early in 1968, a new and potentially more dangerous centre of opposition arose in the form of the 'cabal' which had run the party during the last year of Grimond's leadership – Byers, Beaumont, Evans, Holme and Chitnis. These men, who still jointly exercised substantial influence, had waited to see how Jeremy would get on as Leader. They now all tended to agree with Beaumont, who wrote in his diary that there was no real hope for the Liberal Party over the next few years with Jeremy Thorpe as Leader. His inability to listen, his personal style, his lack of ability to think deeply about politics, all contribute to perpetual misunderstandings between him and the rest of the Party. It is not just a question of the Young Liberals. The same thing happens within the Parliamentary Party, with academics, and more and more with certain intelligent party workers. The trouble is that Jeremy does not really know what the politics of the late sixties are about. Nor will he ever learn.[4]

It would not be too much to say that, during the first half of 1968, these men (with the exception of Byers, who was often exasperated by Jeremy but had a soldier's sense of loyalty) conspired to secure his replacement as Leader. Their tactic was to encourage the rising dissatisfaction with him, in the hope that the clamour against him would become so great that he would be forced to stand down. This plan had two weaknesses. First, no constitutional machinery existed for removing a leader, and Jeremy was a tough operator who could be relied on to fight to the last. Secondly, there seemed no acceptable alternative among the twelve MPs: Grimond had no desire to return; Wainwright's reasons for refusing to stand in January 1967 still held; and of Jeremy's two opponents at that time, Lubbock was now his loyal supporter, while Hooson (in the eyes of Jeremy's radical critics) remained unacceptably right-wing. However, the 'cabal' did find a parliamentary ally in John Pardoe, MP for North Cornwall since 1966, who had supported Jeremy for the leadership but had since become disillusioned by his lack of interest in policy. Pardoe was too much of a 'new boy' to challenge Jeremy just yet; but the disaffection of his formidable fellow West Country MP posed the greatest threat so far to Jeremy's leadership.

Apart from fostering general discontent against Jeremy, his opponents were implicated in two specific actions against him during the early months of 1968. First, they were instrumental in setting up a pressure group known as the Radical Action Movement, whose programme included the abandonment of sterling as a reserve currency and a drastic reduction in Britain's defence commitments. It was launched on 25 March, though it had been conceived two months earlier, the delay being due to Grimond's hesitation over whether to join it. (He decided against.) It described itself as a non-party organisation bringing together Liberals and others with 'radical' views, but its founding members were all Liberals, including Holme, Pardoe, the party intellectual Christopher Layton, and Terry Lacey of the Union of Liberal Students. It was widely regarded as an act of public opposition to Jeremy, particularly when its inaugural press conference, of which he had been given no prior notice, took place just before he was due to address a party rally. Secondly, Beaumont and his friends, who had previously regarded the Young Liberals as a nuisance, now began to encourage them in their increasingly shrill attacks on Jeremy. Early in May, the YLs announced that a poll in their ranks showed only 18 per cent support for Jeremy as Leader; and later that month the YL firebrand Louis Eaks described the poor Liberal result in the local elections as 'a vote of censure on Mr Thorpe's incapability to give a lead'.

On 27 May, Jeremy hit back in a speech (written for him by Richard Moore) to Liberal candidates in which he referred to 'the antics of a small minority in our midst who believe, against all the evidence, that the British electorate wants Marxism in a new dress'. These were temperate words, and made a valid point; but just a few days earlier, Jeremy had held a conciliatory meeting with the YL leaders at which it had been mutually agreed to call a halt to public attacks. Feeling that he had broken his side of the bargain, the YLs were furious, and their splenetic reactions were well reported in the press. Their retiring Chairman George Kiloh described him as 'talking out of his silk top hat'; his successor Malcolm McCallum thought him 'hysterical' and called on him to resign; while Terry Lacey called his words 'the greatest load of hogswash since Macmillan told us we had never had it so good'. According to Jeremy's press officer, Mike Steele, he was delighted to have provoked such reactions, which fitted in with his plans. ('Let's bring it all to a head!') For it was at this moment, while he was under attack, that the newspapers carried the surprise announcement, on 31 May, that he was to be married that day.

After proposing to Caroline in February and being accepted by her, Jeremy wished to keep their engagement secret for some months: this accorded with his love of springing theatrical surprises, and he hoped to use the various announcements as carefully timed weapons in his struggle with his political critics. Intrigued by the element of political drama, Caroline went along with this plan, and they took few people into their confidence for some weeks. Someone who had to be told at once, however, was David Holmes, who at first felt hurt that Caroline should have turned him down for a better match; but he soon realised she would be the ideal wife for Jeremy, and they both assured him they would always look to him as their best friend. Holmes was indeed to become almost a third party to the marriage, in his dual role as Caroline's former lover and confidant of Jeremy's homosexual life. On 21 March, in characteristic style, Jeremy called at Downing Street to break the news in person to the Prime Minister, insisting that Holmes as prospective best man accompany him on this Trollopian visit.

Though most of those who knew of the engagement were impressed by Caroline, not all of them looked favourably upon the marriage. Some felt Jeremy was marrying her for the wrong reasons and wondered what sort of husband he would prove to be. Tim Beaumont wrote in his diary that, when summoned as Party Chairman to see Jeremy about a private matter, he had at first feared the worst [presumably some scandal arising from Jeremy's personal life]. However, in the event it is only the worst for poor Caroline Allpass who, it appears, is going to marry Jeremy ... She is a rather splendid girl all round and he is very lucky to have got someone like her. On the other hand I can't help but feel she is extremely unlucky 'to have got him, since what he really wants is a wife for public consumption.[5]

Beaumont's view was shared by Peter Bessell (one of the few occasions they agreed on anything). Some months earlier, when Jeremy had decided in principle to marry, he had asked Bessell's advice about the seduction of women; and Bessell, an expert on the subject, had provided some useful tips which had helped Jeremy familiarise himself, in a series of casual encounters, with heterosexual practices. When Bessell met Caroline, however, he inaccurately assessed her to be 'a shy and innocent girl' and feared she would be in for 'a devastating shock'. He urged Jeremy to live with her for a few months before proposing to her, a suggestion which seemed to outrage Jeremy. Bessell was himself somewhat outraged when, during the engagement, Jeremy boasted to him of a recent escapade with a New York street boy he had picked up in Times Square and taken back to the Waldorf Astoria Hotel: to Bessell, this not only boded ill for the marriage but showed Jeremy had already forgotten his promise, which Bessell had extracted from him just after his leadership election a year earlier, to forswear such risky habits.[6]

The Manhattan encounter was by no means an isolated fling. At the time of his engagement to Caroline, Jeremy was also conducting a relationship with a tall, handsome youth of twenty-two named Guy Hunting, who later described their affair in his memoirs *Adventures of a Gentleman's Gentleman* (2002). They had met in February 1967 at a state banquet at Buckingham Palace, where Hunting was then working as a footman. Soon afterwards, Hunting left royal service to spend a few months with Noël

Coward in Switzerland; but on his return to London that autumn, he resumed contact with Jeremy, who had offered to help him get a job at the BBC. Over a period of several months, Hunting spent many enjoyable evenings at Marsham Court, where their affair was spiced with the exchange of much gossip, Jeremy's of the political world, Hunting's of the royal scene. Hunting was however anxious for Jeremy, who admitted to him 'that late at night he was in the habit of driving down certain streets that were known haunts of rent boys and unscrupulous rough trade... It seemed astonishing that a highly intelligent man who aspired to be prime minister in a Liberal government ... could act so irresponsibly.' Hunting encountered another aspect of Jeremy's risk-taking when they were dining together at the Reform Club, and Emlyn Hooson entered the dining room; Jeremy at once invited his Welsh colleague (who was by no means a friend) to join them, introducing the horrified Hunting as an aspiring Liberal candidate.

Hunting clearly felt affection for Jeremy: indeed, he felt sorry for him, seeing him as a sad and lonely figure for all his brilliant gifts. He made no demands on him and never felt ill-used by him, acquiescing in Jeremy's news that he had decided to marry, and their regular meetings must cease. (He was invited to the wedding reception.) This attitude contrasted starkly with that of Norman Scott, who in April 1968, soon after the announcement of Jeremy's engagement, wrote to Bessell to demand, in addition to the weekly £5 'retainer' which he had been receiving since the previous summer, a capital sum of £250 to help him establish his modelling career: Bessell managed to satisfy him with £75, but was anxious lest Caroline get to hear of Scott and his allegations. In fact he need not have worried, for Caroline, as we have seen, was something of a 'queer's moll': she was well aware of Jeremy's homosexuality and quite unshocked by it, though not perhaps wishing to hear much about it. Jeremy did indeed tell her, in Holmes' presence, that he was being pursued by a vindictive lunatic claiming to be his former lover, to which she replied that this did not especially bother her, nor did she care whether the alleged affair had actually taken place or not.[7]

The engagement was finally made public on 1 April, the general reaction being one of pleasure that he should have found such a suitable mate. A month later, it was announced that the marriage would take place in the Private Chapel at Lambeth Palace by special permission of the Archbishop of Canterbury, Michael Ramsey. Since becoming Archbishop in 1961, the impressive but socially shy Ramsey, who as a 1920s Cambridge undergraduate had befriended Asquith and considered pursuing a career in Liberal politics, had been assiduously cultivated by Jeremy, who was the first person to whom he had granted the unusual privilege of marriage in the chapel.

Jeremy told the press that the wedding would be a small and private affair, to be followed later on by a huge party at Burlington House to which he and Caroline were inviting a thousand people. But when asked about dates, he became evasive, implying that nothing would happen before the summer. In fact, the marriage was fixed for 31 May, and Jeremy's original plan was that it should take place in secret and only be made public during the honeymoon, the wedding guests being sworn to silence and no advance notice being given to the press. The Archbishop's press officer, however, protested that the press were bound to discover the date of the ceremony and try to gatecrash it, making both Jeremy and the Archbishop look ridiculous.[8] Finally it was agreed that the press should be officially informed on the eve of the wedding and invited to come in afterwards to meet the newlyweds and take photographs.

The day arrived, news of the marriage filling the front pages. The ceremony was performed by Wilfred Westall, Bishop of Crediton, whose suffragan area included Barnstaple, assisted by Simon Barrington-Ward; the choir of the Temple Church provided the music, and the couple received a blessing from the

Archbishop. The bride wore a beige double organza wedding dress, Jeremy the morning dress in which his father had been married almost half a century earlier. David Holmes was best man, there being no bridesmaids. The fifty guests, who were entertained to lunch in the Palace Guard Room, were in principle limited to family of the bride and groom, though Jeremy also asked his Oxford friend Michael Ogle, his fellow MP Eric Lubbock, his constituency agent Lilian Prowse and Lloyd George's surviving daughter, Lady Olwen Carey Evans. Before the lunch, Jeremy and Caroline made a point of greeting each of their guests individually, a gesture none of them forgot. Asked by journalists why he had gone to such lengths to ensure privacy, Jeremy replied: 'I think certain things in one's life *are* private. My wedding is one of them.'

The next day, Jeremy and Caroline departed abroad to honeymoon at a secret destination – the island of Elba. Meanwhile, the Young Liberals continued to be indignant at Jeremy's recent criticism of them, especially when, just after his departure, an article appeared under his name in *Liberal News*, in which he further criticised them for 'highly personalised attacks' which precluded 'any constructive dialogue'. The unusual circumstances of the marriage – the attempt at secrecy, the involvement of the Archbishop – also irritated those in the Party who disliked his theatrical style. Dissatisfaction with his leadership intensified when the Liberals were humiliated in the Oldham by-election, coming fourth with a mere 1,700 votes.

Under these circumstances, the quintet of Beaumont, Chitnis, Evans, Holme and Pardoe, who for some months had been plotting to replace him, began to feel that this was the moment to strike, while he was out of the country with his bride. They do not seem to have considered what an appalling impression would be made when their machinations against the honeymooning leader became public. During these days (as Beaumont's diary reveals), they held several conspiratorial meetings; and Holme was particularly active, trying to drum up support for an anti-Jeremy 'coup' to take place at the forthcoming meeting of the Party Executive on 28 June. Their problem, as always, was that there was no point trying to oust him unless another MP commanding general acceptance stood ready to fill his place. Their hope was that Grimond would patriotically agree to return. But Grimond told Beaumont that, while he was 'very critical of Jeremy's leadership' and 'would not have put forward Jeremy for Leader ... if he had known then what he knows now', he was 'not prepared to come back as Leader of the Liberal Party as such ...'[9]

Political journalists soon became aware of the plot to stab Jeremy in the back while he was on his honeymoon, and were only waiting for a pretext to run the story. This was provided when Chitnis leaked to the press the text of a speech Holme was due to make to the Cambridge University Liberal Club, containing a veiled attack on Jeremy. On 11 June, the story was on the front page of the *Daily Mail* and even the BBC news headlines. Pardoe was then interviewed, rashly admitting that 'soundings' were taking place within the Party as to whether Jeremy should continue as Leader. Thus the plotters were compromised by having their plans exposed before they were ready or had any alternative to propose.

Jeremy's allies swiftly counter-attacked. Lubbock, holding the fort as Chief Whip, denounced Holme's speech as 'a trivial statement by a person of no consequence', while the octogenarian Lady Violet, still active in the House of Lords, thundered against 'treachery'.* Messages of support for Jeremy flooded into Party Headquarters from shocked Liberals. His right-wing critics,

---

* In her diary for 12 June 1968, Lady Violet wrote: 'A much publicized "revolt" against Jeremy's leadership is taking place in his absence ... Anything more *lunatic* one cannot imagine ... I am furious at the wanton damage to the party ... I was thankful I went [to the PLP meeting which discussed the affair] – as no one else cld have spoken with so little inhibition! & such genuine *amazement* at their madness – nor such rage!' (Pottle, *Daring to Hope*, pp. 348–9.)

Hooson and Mackie, supported him against this attack from the left of the Party. Finally the 'plotters' themselves were forced to declare their loyalty, Beaumont issuing a statement that Jeremy was 'not only the best leader we have but the best possible leader and the best of any of the party leaders in this country'. When the Young Liberals, at their annual assembly, voted by 60 per cent in favour of Jeremy's removal, this was merely further encouragement to all moderate and traditional elements in the Party to rally to his side.

On 17 June, Jeremy, doubtless inspired by Napoleonic parallels, returned from Elba some days earlier than planned to resume the reins of authority. If it was indeed the case (as claimed by Mike Steele) that he had sought to manipulate his adversaries to declare their hand at the moment of his marriage and so make themselves look treacherous and ridiculous, his plan had succeeded brilliantly. Back in London, he set about consolidating his support; but the battle was already won. Further sympathy was generated when Caroline gave the press her views on recent events: 'What a rotten trick it was. Everybody had their say and Jeremy could do nothing. But I suppose in politics they always wait until you aren't there and can't defend yourself . . .'[10]

Under the circumstances, the Thorpes' delayed wedding party at Burlington House on 27 June took on something of the air of a victory celebration. More than eight hundred came, including Wilson and Heath and half their front benches: standing at the head of William Kent's fine staircase, Jeremy and Caroline received their guests in the style of pre-war aristocratic hosts. Once again, Jeremy showed his genius for timing, for the Party Executive at which his future would be decided was to take place next day: he had taken care to invite Richard Holme and other prominent critics to the party, and the spectacle of them plotting in corners only served further to increase his support.

In the event, the Executive was packed with friends of Jeremy who had rarely been seen there in the past. In a skilful speech, he defended himself fiercely against his critics, while accepting a conciliatory proposal of Byers (which would in practice amount to little) that he would henceforth exercise his leadership in 'consultation' with other leading Party figures.* 'Thorpe has this *presence*,' Mike Steele later told Susan Barnes, explaining how the opposition (with which Steele sympathised) simply melted away. 'He can dominate any Party meeting. You have to be very bold to stand up against him ... That meeting was almost fascistic in the way the loyalists attacked anyone who had criticised the leader.'[11] There was a memorable contribution from Lady Violet, making one of her last appearances at a party gathering:† 'Could anything be more *despicable* than to attack a man while he is on his *honeymoon*? Who is this Mr Holme? Who *is* he?' Finally, a resolution expressing confidence in Jeremy's leadership was carried by forty-eight votes to two (both dissentients being Young Liberals), assuring him of political as well as emotional security within a month of his marriage to Caroline.

---

* The figures in question, under the Byers proposal, were the Party Chairman (now Lord Henley, Beaumont having resigned), the Chairman of the Executive (Evans), Richard Wainwright in a new role as liaison officer between the PLP and LPO, and the Leader in the Lords (Byers himself).

† She died the following February aged eighty-one, Jeremy declaring that the Party had lost 'its greatest orator and most loyal supporter'.

14

MISFORTUNE
1968–70

JEREMY THORPE'S MARRIAGE to Caroline seems to have been very happy on the whole. Many onlookers felt that, having married her for practical reasons, he proceeded to fall genuinely in love with her. There could be no doubt that she brought him a new stability and contentment: he became noticeably more relaxed, and relations with colleagues and subordinates became easier. She seemed to complete him as a human being, and give him an inner self-confidence. Some felt she represented a rescue from the emotional tyranny of his mother, and brightened his essentially dark nature. He for his part was an attentive husband. They seemed to make a good partnership, her practical nature complementing his imaginative qualities. She shared his sense of humour and *joie de vivre*. They developed a private language, and in public could be seen exchanging amorous or witty glances across a room or dinner table. She adored the glamour and drama of his life, and enjoyed accompanying him to official dinners at Downing Street and the Palace and such national events as the Investiture of the Prince of Wales at Carnarvon. She was widely admired by other public figures and their spouses and generally regarded as the perfect politician's wife, charming to everyone, devoted to her husband and able to cope if he unexpectedly turned up for lunch with a dozen guests. She would sit on the platform when he made a speech and afterwards go up to him and kiss him. They seemed intensely proud of each other.

It was not, perhaps, quite the idyll Jeremy later made it out to have been. She suffered the usual agonies of a politician's wife, often not knowing where he was or whether she would be spending the evening with him. Ursula inevitably cast something of a cloud over the marriage as an interfering mother-in-law:* she had spoilt Jeremy, who was a job to look after, and perhaps expected too much of his wife as a housekeeper and hostess. As the glamour wore off, Caroline became more aware of the elements of fantasy and intrigue in his nature, and was occasionally exasperated by his exhibitionism. Contrary to what was sometimes later said, she did not feel either shocked or threatened by his homosexuality. But she disliked some of his friends, notably his (flamboyantly heterosexual) financial adviser Robin Salinger, whom she found sinister. But all this represented a challenge for her in the give-and-take of married life; and David Holmes, who remained close to them both, had few doubts that theirs was a successful union between kindred souls who felt they were right for each other.[1]

Their first task was to find somewhere to live, for the cramped quarters in Marsham Court and Mrs Chappel's comfortable lodgings near Barnstaple were bachelor arrangements. The search for a flat in town and house in the country brought them much shared pleasure. In London, they moved into a spacious flat in Ashley Gardens opposite Westminster Cathedral, suitable for entertaining. In North Devon, after spending a few months at a farmhouse belonging to a local Liberal, they fell in love with

---

* Caroline's father, Warwick Allpass, did not greatly care for Jeremy, and in equally classic fashion fulfilled the role of a disapproving father-in-law.

a substantial seventeenth-century thatched cottage with a couple of acres in Cobbaton, a few miles from Barnstaple, which they bought for £5,000. The task of decorating and furnishing these properties provided a happy occupation for them both, the results reflecting something of a compromise between her cheerful taste and his sense of the theatrical. Caroline had many domestic talents, and made her own curtains. Jeremy cultivated his garden, creating an orchard like his hero Lloyd George. Caroline had family connections in the West Country and soon came to share Jeremy's love for his constituency, whose people took her to their hearts.

To their delight, Caroline became pregnant soon after their honeymoon, and their son Rupert was born on 12 April 1969. He was a strikingly beautiful baby. To fanfares of publicity, he was christened by the Archbishop in the Crypt of the House of Commons, where Jeremy's sister Lavinia, as the daughter and granddaughter of sitting MPs, had received her baptism in 1923: the infant (so the nation read) was clad in a christening robe of Brussels lace which had been used on that occasion and which Jeremy and his mother and grandmother had also worn in their day. David Holmes and Eric Lubbock were godfathers and Joan Ramsey, wife of the Archbishop, godmother: down the years, Jeremy would invite others to become honorary godparents, indicating that this was the greatest honour he felt he could bestow. The birth of Rupert, however, led to further friction with Ursula, who showed the same possessive attentions towards her grandson as she had towards Jeremy: this was naturally resented by Caroline, and Jeremy's own relationship with his mother, always stormy and ambivalent, deteriorated further.

His contentment in his private life was matched by a new air of confidence in his political life. He recovered much of the sparkle he had lost during the early days of his leadership in an effort to appear 'serious'. Following his triumph at the Party Executive of 28 June 1968, his critics appeared to retire from the field. Tim Beaumont resigned as Party Chairman; Richard Holme left to work in America; while the Young Liberals declared themselves a virtually independent organisation dedicated to radical protest. All was not well, however, for the Liberals continued to make dismal electoral progress in the country and to be riven by internal quarrels. At the Liberal Assembly at Edinburgh in September – whose theme was 'participation' – Beaumont and Pardoe came out openly against Jeremy, arguing that under his leadership the Party had 'lost its momentum because it had lost its idealism'. Grimond too did little to conceal his disenchantment with his successor: he snubbed Jeremy and Caroline in public and caused something of a sensation by patronising a rival assembly staged by the Young Liberals. The ex-Leader's ungracious behaviour shocked the party faithful, who gave Jeremy a particularly warm ovation when he delivered his platform speech, in which he expressed sympathy with the 'bitterness and frustration' of the electorate while declaring that their remedy lay not in extra-parliamentary action (as recommended by some party radicals) but voting Liberal in parliamentary elections. Jeremy's hopes that he had won the Party over to a moderate policy received a setback, however, at the party elections that autumn, when his radical critics Beaumont and Pardoe comfortably defeated his friends Stina Robson and Len Smith for the posts of Party President and Treasurer.

Jeremy, meanwhile, continued to make a statesmanlike impression on the public. He spoke out against the Russian invasion of Czechoslovakia in August, and Wilson's unsuccessful attempts to negotiate with Ian Smith aboard HMS *Fearless* in October. He engaged in tri-partisan discussions with Wilson and Heath on Northern Ireland and the proposed reform of the House of Lords (though, much to his disappointment – for it would have brought him a wave of patronage – the latter came to nothing, thanks to the joint hostility of right-wing Conservatives who opposed the disenfranchisement of the hereditary peers and left-wing Labour MPs who did not wish the upper chamber to increase its powers). With his love of anniversaries, he held a dinner in December 1968 to celebrate the centenary of Gladstone's first premiership, his speech mentioning the topical Gladstonian subjects of Ireland and Britain's international humanitarian role. When Richard Nixon made his state visit to Britain in March 1969, Jeremy, formerly an admirer of Nixon's late rival Kennedy, had a private meeting with him and was surprised to register a strong liking for the Republican President, who combined an outstanding political imagination with a somewhat dark, gangsterish personality.[2]

Nineteen sixty-nine proved another dismal year for the Liberals, one of its few bright spots being the unexpected capture by Wallace Lawler of the Labour stronghold of Birmingham Ladywood at a by-election in June, bringing the total of Liberal MPs to thirteen. Lawler, who had been elected to Birmingham City Council soon after Orpington, was a pioneer of what was becoming known as 'community politics', which involved campaigning on specific local issues to which voters could directly relate. His victory was unusual, however, in that it owed much to his opposition to Commonwealth immigration, a cause with which Liberals did not generally identify. It was to be their last good electoral news for some years. Jeremy also persuaded Wilson to allow the Liberals a further life peerage to mark the Investiture of the Prince of Wales on 1 July (an event which had a special appeal for him in that it was directed by the Constable of Carnarvon Castle, a post held formerly by his hero Lloyd George* and currently by his friend Lord Snowdon): this he awarded to Gerran Lloyd (Lord Lloyd of Kilgerran), the rich Welsh inventor and patent lawyer who had been subsidising his private office. Despite the generosity of a few such individuals,

---

* In honour of the occasion, Jeremy also obtained a DBE for Lloyd George's surviving daughter, Lady Olwen Carey Evans.

there was little let-up in the dire financial problems of the Party, whose overdraft, despite drastic economies, increased from around £70,000 to £100,000 between mid-1968 and mid-1969.

The poor state of party morale was demonstrated by the fact that only some 900 delegates turned up to the Liberal Assembly at Brighton in September 1969, compared to the 1,400 who had last attended at Brighton three years earlier. They were asked to approve proposals for a revised party constitution, formulated by a committee chaired by Nancy (later Baroness) Seear. They agreed to slightly changed rules for electing the party leader, still by the MPs alone but only after the Party had been consulted through a 'National Committee': Jeremy had worked hard during the previous months to scotch plans by his radical critics for the annual re-election of the leader by a national ballot. But the Assembly threw out a proposal first advanced by Jeremy two years earlier, whereby the Party Council would be scrapped and replaced as a policy-making body by a Quarterly Assembly dominated by parliamentary candidates. Jeremy made a fighting speech, concentrating on the poor state of public housing (which he declared to be symbolic of the Government's 'decrepitude') and the shortcomings of the Unionist regime in Northern Ireland ('a recipe of incompetence, insensitivity, indifference and ignorance unmatched in the democratic world'). This heartened the faithful, but many would have agreed with the press judgement that the Liberals were facing the coming General Election 'in a worse state of morale, organisation and finance than at any time since 1950'.[3]

More enjoyable was a rally at Barnstaple the following month to celebrate the tenth anniversary of his election to Parliament, at which he was presented with a volume bound in white calf containing the signatures of 14,000 constituents, many of them non-Liberals, who wished to pay tribute to him as their MP. There could be no doubt of the personal popularity in the constituency of both Jeremy and Caroline; but his agent, Lilian

Prowse, was becoming anxious, for the North Devon Liberal Association, assuming that his re-election would be guaranteed by his national celebrity and local stature, had done little canvassing in preparation for the election due within eighteen months. And in North Devon as elsewhere, Jeremy's popularity was matched by the Labour Government's unpopularity which inclined people to vote Conservative.

During the autumn of 1969, the Party's financial crisis became so acute that John Pardoe resigned as Treasurer, admitting failure, along with Pratap Chitnis, the Head of the LPO. Jeremy can have shed few tears over their departures, though his personal relations with Pardoe remained good. Chitnis was replaced by Ted Wheeler, the affable official who had helped Jeremy run Winnable Seats in the early 1960s: his first task was to cut the staff at Party Headquarters from thirty to twenty-two. The new Treasurer was the former National Liberal MP Sir Frank Medlicott, with whom Jeremy at first got on well, though there would later be fearsome rows between them over control of funds. Supervision of party expenditure was entrusted to a new Finance and Administration Board chaired by Philip Watkins, a fellow homosexual Jeremy had known since Oxford days who was strongly under his influence. Meanwhile Jeremy spearheaded a new fundraising drive, and by the end of the year was able to report that he had raised £19,000 with promises of another £10,000.

Hopes that the Liberals might recover support as the election approached seemed to be dashed in January 1970 by disastrous publicity arising from the antics of the Young Liberals. In protest against a South African cricket tour, they began digging up cricket pitches all over the country; and their Chairman, the hot-headed Louis Eaks, made a speech praising the PLO and calling for the destruction of Israel. The latter episode was particularly embarrassing for Jeremy, who was at that moment receiving a fraternal visit from the leading Israeli Liberal Moshe Kol. It was in vain that Jeremy (now supported even by the Party Executive) disowned the Young Liberals, protesting that they were a separate and most un-Liberal organisation over which he had no control: their doings were rarely out of the news. The Liberals were again faring badly in by-elections – their result at Bridgwater in March 1970 would have meant Jeremy's defeat if repeated in nearby North Devon. But he had a card up his sleeve which he hoped would transform both the finances of the Party and its electoral prospects.

Back in the spring of 1969, Jeremy, together with a Conservative and a Labour MP, had mounted a campaign to prevent the development of Lundy Island,* the wildlife sanctuary in the Bristol Channel. He was approached by Jack Hayward, an eccentric British philanthropist living in the Bahamas where he had extensive business interests, offering to buy the island for the National Trust. Jeremy did not know Hayward, but he knew how to handle a generous donor and the purchase of the island was quickly arranged for £150,000 of Hayward's money. That summer, Jeremy organised a thanksgiving service at which the islanders expressed their gratitude to Hayward in their tiny church; Hayward congratulated him on the arrangements with the remark that 'you ought to be Prime Minister if you can do a job like this'. 'It's on the cards,' replied Jeremy, who subsequently sought to enlist Hayward as a benefactor of that other threatened British institution, the Liberal Party. Though a Conservative, Hayward sympathised with the Liberals as the 'underdogs' of British politics; he and his wife Jean had taken a strong liking to Jeremy and Caroline, and he may have been flattered by hints of a life peerage or even ministerial office in a future Liberal Government. After lengthy discussions, partly conducted in the Bahamas through the intermediary of Bessell who had business

---

* Lundy was part of the Torrington constituency at this time, though boundary changes would bring it within North Devon from 1974.

there, Hayward finally agreed to give Jeremy a further £150,000 for the Liberal coffers. Jeremy received the cheque – the largest single donation ever received by the Liberal Party – on 15 May 1970, just three days before Wilson called the General Election: it remained to be seen how and by whom it would be spent and whether it would suffice to rescue the Liberals from the electoral setback which threatened them.

While Jeremy was experiencing the joys of married life and fatherhood, and coping with the internal and external difficulties of the Liberal Party, he continued to be haunted by that spectre from the past, Norman Scott. It will be recalled that, since July 1967, Bessell had been attempting to keep Scott at bay by paying him a weekly 'retainer' of around £5. For more than a year, Scott had given little trouble, apart from the episode during the spring of 1968 when he had asked Bessell for extra cash ostensibly to help further his modelling career. Scott, who retained a certain physical allure in his late twenties, does seem to have made some progress as a fashion model, with his photograph on the books of a Kensington agency. To be a model was a glamorous thing in the 'Swinging London' of the late 1960s, and he fell in with a set of affluent young bohemians. By the summer of 1968, he was living with a girlfriend, Katherine Olivier, at her spacious rented flat in Earl's Court Square. She introduced him to Conway Wilson-Young, a wealthy and fast-living Old Etonian in his twenties who aspired to be an opera producer; and soon Scott was living with Wilson-Young at his house in Chester Square and accompanying him to the Bayreuth Festival. Scott informed Bessell that he was being kept by a rich lover and no longer in need of assistance, news which Bessell reported to a relieved Jeremy. However, during the autumn Wilson-Young tired of Scott, who left Chester Square and returned to Earl's Court Square, where he began an affair with Katherine Olivier's friend Sue Myers. Scott contacted Bessell again to say that his source of

17 & 18. The youngest Liberal MP, sporting Old Etonian tie: above, at the Liberal Assembly at Eastbourne, September 1960; left, returning from Africa, October 1961.

19. A 1970s photograph of Norman Scott (formerly Josiffe) with whom Jeremy had a 'close, even affectionate relationship' in 1961–2.

20. To enable the constituents who ran it to take a holiday – and gain useful publicity – Jeremy took charge of a village post office for a week in the autumn of 1966.

21 & 22. The new Leader of the
Liberal Party, January 1967.

23. Examining his waxwork statue at Madame Tussaud's.

24. At the Cenotaph with Edward Heath and Harold Wilson, November 1968.

25. With Jo Grimond.

26. With Eric Lubbock.

27. With Peter Bessell.

28. Jeremy with Caroline and David Holmes (best man) on his wedding day, 31 May 1968.

29. Campaigning in the 1970 General Election, with Caroline in the background.

30. The bereaved statesman,
July 1970.

31. Discussing Britain's entry
into the European Economic
Community with Churchill's
sons-in-law, Christopher
Soames and Duncan Sandys,
January 1972.

32. With Marion Harewood after the announcement of their engagement, February 1973.

33. The ten Liberal MPs at Kiddington Hall, July 1973. L to R: Graham Tope; Cyril Smith; Jo Grimond; Clement Freud; John Pardoe; Emlyn Hooson; Jeremy; David Austick (partly obscured); David Steel; Russell Johnston.

funds had dried up, that his modelling was no longer going well, and requesting a resumption of the 'retainer', but at a higher level: Bessell agreed to allow him £7 a week.

Bessell said nothing about this to Jeremy until they were alone in Jeremy's Westminster office one evening at the beginning of December 1968, a meeting of which he gave a detailed (though uncorroborated) description at Jeremy's trial and in his memoirs. 'Blast! I thought we'd heard the last of him,' exclaimed Jeremy, hearing of Scott's new exactions. Bessell thought Scott would behave himself so long as he continued to receive regular payments, but Jeremy felt he 'would never cease to be a danger' and 'despaired of ever getting rid of the problem' and asked if Bessell had 'any conception what it was like to live in a state of constant apprehension'. He asked if there were still prospects of getting Scott a job abroad, but Bessell did not think it would be possible to find any situation likely to satisfy him. At this, Jeremy allegedly remarked: 'Then, Peter, we've got to get rid of him.' Bessell asked what he meant. Jeremy made it clear he had murder in mind: 'It's no worse than shooting a sick dog.' Concealing the shock which he later claimed to have felt, Bessell asked Jeremy how he proposed to dispose of the body. After a moment's thought, Jeremy triumphantly exclaimed: 'I've got it: a tin mine!' Finally, Bessell asked who was to do the deed. 'The person to do it is David,' replied Jeremy, referring to David Holmes, who was always eager to do him a good turn. Bessell thought this an odd choice: as he later wrote, Holmes was 'not a man upon whom I would depend in an emergency to take on a task requiring a cool head and sound judgement'. Jeremy, however, proposed to contact Holmes and arrange a meeting between the three of them to discuss the matter further.[4]

Both in the evidence he gave at Jeremy's trial and in his memoirs, Bessell suggests that Jeremy seemed serious about murdering Scott; but Bessell's own account hardly bears this out. Jeremy habitually amused himself and his friends with whimsical speculations; and his 'murder plan' sounds more like the plot of a novel than a practical project. (The wild friend of Jeremy's youth, Henry Upton, had enjoyed talking about murder, though seems to have been a harmless poseur.) Moreover, the conversation seems to have taken place in casual circumstances, as Jeremy and Bessell were hanging about waiting for the division bell. Although Jeremy proposed to organise a follow-up meeting with Holmes within days, this actually took place a month later, in January 1969 after the parliamentary recess.* This time there are two sources for what occurred, Bessell and Holmes: as Holmes (interviewed two years after the trial of himself and Jeremy at which Bessell had been the main prosecution witness) broadly agreed with Bessell's account,† it may be assumed to be substantially correct. Interestingly, one of the few points on which the two accounts disagree is that while Bessell recalled that Jeremy asked him to lock the door, Holmes remembered that it remained unlocked and even open some of the time.

Bessell arrived late for the meeting, and gathered from the astonishment on Holmes' face that Jeremy had already broached the subject of his murder plan. This had now assumed elaborate proportions. Holmes, posing as a journalist, was to meet Scott at a hotel in Plymouth and drive him to a pub near St Austell. (Jeremy's decision to 'stage' Scott's murder in Bessell's constituency lent a further fictional touch, as did his insistence that Holmes and Scott should cross the River Tamar dividing Cornwall from Devon by the traditional ferry rather than the new suspension bridge. How the then London-based Scott was

---

* During the intervening month, Jeremy's energies had been absorbed by moving into the cottage in Cobbaton which he had bought with Caroline.

† 'Now Bessell's description [of the alleged murder conversation in January 1969] is remarkably accurate and he's fortunate in having that kind of recall years afterwards.' (Holmes Transcripts.)

to be lured to these remote parts hardly seems to have been considered.) At the pub, Holmes was to get Scott drunk; he was then to drive him out on to Bodmin Moor and kill him, preferably by strangling him but by shooting him if necessary; after carefully removing anything which might identify the body, he was to drag it to a nearby mineshaft and drop it in. Bessell humoured Jeremy, pointing out that Scott might fight off an attempt to strangle him and a shot might be heard. Jeremy agreed that Holmes might alternatively dispose of Scott by putting poison in his drink. When Holmes, entering into the spirit, asked whether it might not look suspicious if Scott suddenly dropped dead off his bar stool, Jeremy suggested he use a slow-acting poison. On this bizarre note, he brought the meeting to an end, asking Holmes to do research on the subject of poisons and Bessell to find a suitable disused tin mine in the area.[5]

Holmes told Bessell that he had at first been alarmed by Jeremy's talk but now thought it just a fantasy: if they carried on humouring him, nothing would ever come of it. Events seemed to bear this out. Holmes had several telephone conversations with Jeremy in which they discussed the plan and the difficulties in the way of its execution, without reaching any conclusion. When Jeremy next raised the subject with Bessell, it was merely to ask him if it might not be better for Holmes to offer Scott the poisoned drink from a hip flask in the car rather than in the pub. Months passed, and Jeremy seemed in no hurry to take things further, though he arranged another meeting with Holmes and Bessell for the middle of May. When this took place, however, Bessell had dramatic news to report: a few days earlier, on 13 May 1969, Norman Scott had married Sue Myers at Kensington Register Office. Bessell and Holmes were relieved that the 'murder' was presumably off, though Jeremy seemed far from elated: Bessell later remarked to Holmes that Jeremy deprived of his murder fantasy was like 'a child who has lost his toy'.

It has been suggested that, in marrying, Scott may have been seeking to emulate Jeremy.[6] Like Caroline, Sue hailed from an upper-middle-class provincial background; whereas Caroline had worked at Sotheby's, Sue had a job at the Tate Gallery. At the time of the marriage, a month after Caroline had given birth to Rupert, Sue was three months' pregnant with Scott's child. Scott may have hoped for financial support from Sue's parents, but they were appalled by their new son-in-law, and the only help the newlyweds received was from Sue's sister, wife of the film actor Terry-Thomas, who lent them a cottage in Dorset, where they went to live. With Scott's modelling career over, Bessell's 'retainers' suspended, and Sue having to give up her job, they soon found themselves short of money. Scott turned to Bessell, complaining that, because he lacked a National Insurance card, for which he continued to blame Jeremy, his wife was unable to obtain maternity benefits, a matter Bessell offered to take up with the Department of Health.

By the end of August, Scott had not yet heard anything from Bessell and began behaving wildly. He rang Cobbaton and found himself talking to Caroline, to whom he described his alleged past association with and continuing grievances against Jeremy, getting short shrift. (What he told her cannot have come to her as a total surprise, as she had been warned about him on a number of occasions by both Jeremy and Holmes.) He then rang the Department in London, speaking with similar abandon to the private secretary of the Social Security Minister David Ennals. Finally he rang Bessell and threatened to sell his 'story' to the press, hanging up before Bessell could reply. Bessell wrote to assure Scott he was doing everything possible to get him a card. 'It would be a great mistake if you jeopardised this in the way you suggested,' he concluded. 'I have spoken to Jeremy Thorpe and put him in the picture regarding the present position.' This was the only time Bessell mentioned Jeremy in writing to Scott, a lapse which (as Scott proceeded to show the letter to all and sundry) was destined to have unfortunate results: but ironically, he had not informed Jeremy of anything at the time, being reluctant to trouble him with Scott's current behaviour – though presumably Jeremy, learning that Scott had telephoned his house and spoken to Caroline, would have asked Bessell what was going on.

Eventually, thanks to Bessell's efforts, Scott obtained maternity benefits for his wife and a National Insurance card for himself, though the card soon lapsed as Scott was unwilling to pay the contributions to keep it up to date. Then as always, he did not seem to want a valid card, the absence of which enabled him to rationalise both his lack of personal identity and his sense of grievance against Jeremy. Meanwhile, he had described the affair to astonished social security officials in Dorset and London. In November, Sue Scott gave birth to a son, Benjamin. By this time, the Scotts had moved back to the flat in Earl's Court Square; but their marriage was on the rocks, Sue having belatedly realised that her husband was both a hopeless wastrel and (for he had resumed his affair with Wilson-Young) a compulsive homosexual. At the end of 1969, she left him to return to live with her parents in Lincolnshire. Scott managed to relieve his own financial problems by establishing rights in the flat, letting out its rooms to foreign students and eventually getting the landlord to pay him a substantial sum to leave. But it was only a matter of time before he returned to plague Jeremy again.

During the spring of 1970, after three years of often intense unpopularity, Labour finally caught up with the Conservatives in the opinion polls following a period of economic recovery: the local elections at the beginning of May confirmed this trend, and on 18 May Wilson called a General Election for 18 June. Although the Liberals had just experienced their worst local election results for a decade, Jeremy was optimistic about their prospects. The latest projections suggested the two main parties would be roughly equal in the new Parliament: if one of them were a few seats short of an absolute majority, the Liberals might achieve their dream of holding the balance. And he was confident that they would gain ground during the campaign and pick up much of the falling Conservative vote, thanks above all to the £150,000 he had secured from Jack Hayward, which providentially arrived just ahead of the election announcement. While saying nothing about the source of this munificent donation (which remained known to only a few people), he disclosed its effect with the air of a conjuror: at the final meeting of the Liberal MPs and peers, he caused astonishment by announcing that the Party was now solvent,[7] while he declared on television that the Liberals were entering the election 'on a sounder financial basis than ever before'.

Inevitably, the sudden appearance of such a large sum raised questions as to how it should be spent and by whom. Then as always, Jeremy took the view that he himself was the best judge of how to use money he had raised through his personal contacts. Like his hero Lloyd George, he also sought to maintain his grip on the Party through control of the purse strings. This brought him into conflict with the Party Treasurer, Medlicott, who believed that all donations should be handed over to and disbursed by the Liberal Party Organisation with its system of committees and accounted for in the Party's official accounts. With an election under way, Medlicott reluctantly acquiesced in the bulk of the Hayward money (after paying off the LPO's overdraft of almost £70,000) being paid into two bank accounts over which Jeremy exercised effective personal control – those of Winnable Seats and the Liberal Central Association. Spats between Leader and Treasurer about the destination of various sums continued throughout the election, however, and would lead to further rows afterwards.[8] Thanks to Jeremy's use of the Hayward money, the Liberals, who only had 286 candidates in place at the outset of the campaign, were finally able to field 332, more than in 1966 though fewer than in 1964.

The campaign was managed in London by the military figure of Lord Byers, while Jeremy based himself in his marginal constituency, from where he made tours all over the country by helicopter, in itself a sensational touch. In North Devon, he was supported by his wife, his mother, the new head of the LPO Ted Wheeler, and a 'court' of helpers including David Holmes, Robin Salinger, Michael Ogle and Peter Bessell (who was not recontesting his seat). Throughout the campaign, he showed indefatigable energy: he might make four helicopter visits to different parts of the country during the day, and in the evening, accompanied by Caroline, address audiences in half a dozen North Devon villages. Both at public meetings and on the broadcast media, he exhibited his usual blend of statesmanship and sparkle. He lambasted both Wilson and Heath for the ineffectiveness of their policies, and argued that the Liberals, being beholden to neither unions nor bosses, were better placed than the other parties to solve Britain's industrial troubles. He denounced the poor state of public housing, and the anti-immigration views of Enoch Powell. The Labour candidate in North Devon, the 22-year-old journalist Chris Mullin, was amazed at his stamina and flair, and admired his courage in speaking out on such issues as Europe and immigration, on which his views were unlikely to win him much support in the constituency, and were eagerly exploited by his right-wing Conservative opponent, Tim Keigwin.[9]

Behind the wit and optimism, the strain must have been considerable. His political future was at stake, for the Party would not readily forgive him if he failed in this, his first serious electoral test as Leader. His irascible correspondence with Medlicott was indicative of his highly strung state. According to Bessell, a blackmailer calling himself Hetherington turned up in North Devon during the campaign, claiming to possess compromising letters from Jeremy to Scott; Jeremy promised Bessell 'the next Liberal peerage' if he could get rid of him, if necessary by murdering him; Bessell saw the man, found that his letters were forgeries and managed to scare him off.[10] There is nothing to corroborate this story (which was to be raised in a curious fashion at Jeremy's trial): but the risk of Scott raising his head at this time must have weighed heavily on Jeremy.

During the last days of the campaign, it became clear that the Liberals were in trouble. Their organisation on the ground had deteriorated since 1966, owing to poor morale and financial crisis, and the Hayward money had arrived too late to revive it. Even worse was the unexpected news that the Conservatives were overtaking Labour in the polls. A falling Conservative vote provided the Liberals with an opportunity; a falling Labour vote meant they were squeezed. Jeremy was rattled: all his calculations had been based on the assumption that Labour would narrowly win the election. The theme of his final party political broadcast was that the country had decided to return a Labour Government, but had yet to decide what official opposition it wanted: it was too late to rewrite it, and such was Jeremy's state of apprehension that it had to be recorded several times, to the surprise of his entourage who had always found him a flawless broadcaster.

On polling day, 18 June, the pollsters again predicted a narrow Labour majority, but were proved wrong. As the results came in, it became evident that the Conservatives had been comfortably returned to power, while the Liberal vote had declined. Of the first seats to be declared which the Liberals were defending, Ladywood (the only by-election to have been won in the late Parliament) reverted to Labour, while Cheadle and Orpington were lost to the Conservatives. Jeremy could hardly contain his emotion at the news of Orpington, for it was a symbol of Liberal revival, and Lubbock had been his best friend in Parliament. His own result, declared after three recounts, was alarmingly close (1966 figures in brackets):

Thorpe, John Jeremy (Liberal):   18,893   (16,797)
Keigwin, T. C. (Conservative):   18,524   (15,631)
Mullin, C. J. (Labour):   5,268   (6,127)
Morris, B. G. (Democrat):   175

Though he had increased his numerical vote, his majority had dwindled to a mere 369, only 7 more than his first electoral margin in 1959.

At least Jeremy had clung on to his seat, at an election in which seven out of thirteen Liberal MPs had lost theirs. The only other English seat to be held was North Cornwall, where John Pardoe had a majority of 630. David Steel had held Roxburgh by 550. Grimond and Hooson saw their 'safe' majorities dramatically reduced. The 'safest' Liberal seat was now Inverness, where Russell Johnston had fractionally increased his majority to 2,674. The Liberals were back to holding six seats as they had done before Orpington, all of them marginal and on 'the Celtic fringe'. The figures gave little comfort however one looked at them. Although twenty-one more seats were contested than in 1966, the Liberal vote had declined numerically by one-tenth and in percentage terms from 8.5 per cent to 7.5 per cent, while their lost deposits shot up from 104 to 182.

What were the reasons for this setback? The main one was simply that hundreds of thousands of voters who had voted Liberal or Labour in 1964 and 1966 now wished to turn out the Wilson Government and so voted Conservative. (Even where the Liberal vote held up, a swing from Labour to Conservative generally proved fatal to Liberal chances in constituencies where the main contest was between Liberals and Conservatives.) The alienation of middle-class voters by the militancy of the Young Liberals was a contributory factor: Winstanley blamed them for his loss of Cheadle. In Scotland and Wales, the nationalist parties ate into the Liberal vote. Finally, there was the run-down state of party organisation in the constituencies, largely due to

lack of money: had the election been postponed until the
autumn, as urged by many of Wilson's colleagues, Hayward's
donation might have had an effect and the Liberals done better.
Under the circumstances, Jeremy may be judged to have done
well to have secured more than 2 million Liberal votes.

The morning after, with Caroline at his side, he received the
press in his garden at Cobbaton and showed not a shred of disappointment. Heath, he said, was now in danger from his own
right wing, and the six Liberal MPs – who would have been
forty-six under a proportional system – would help save him
from Enoch Powell. They would 'stand out as a beacon of compassion, reason, decency and moderation'. The Liberals, he said,
were still in business and he proposed to carry on leading them
for some time. He and Caroline then toured the seventy branches
of the North Devon Liberal Association to thank them for helping him retain his seat and increase his numerical vote. When he
saw Bessell, however, he asked: 'Why didn't the old magic work?'
Bessell said it had done, otherwise the Liberals would have won
no seats at all. 'That's not what they'll say,' replied Jeremy. But to
another friend, the former Conservative MP Humphry Berkeley,
he declared brightly: 'I've still got my seat, an adorable little boy
and a wife I love.'[11]

The election had been a strenuous experience for Caroline.
For a hectic month, while keeping house and looking after her
child with little help, she had had to perform the social duties of
a political wife, keep the flag flying for her husband while he was
touring in his helicopter, and appear with him on local plat-
forms. The presence of her overbearing mother-in-law, and of
Jeremy's financial adviser Robin Salinger, whom she distrusted,
did not help her relax. She told her mother and her old friend
Viv that she was frequently exhausted and sometimes found it
hard to cope. When Jeremy's Oxford friend Michael Ogle came
down to campaign for him, he found her anxious and wondered
if she might be pregnant: and while this does not appear to have

been the case, she and Jeremy were (as he later put it) 'trying for another baby'. She naturally shared his disappointment at the result of the election.

On Monday 29 June, she seemed tired, having spent the previous evening gardening and been woken by Rupert several times during the night. They were to return to London that day, where Jeremy was to attend the first meeting of the new House of Commons and they were both due at a dinner of the United Nations Association. As there was still some packing to do, it was decided that Jeremy, taking Rupert and his nurse, should set out after breakfast by train, Caroline following later with the luggage in their Ford Anglia estate car. Having deposited Jeremy and his two fellow passengers at Taunton station, Caroline returned to Cobbaton, finished packing, closed the house and drove off around noon.*

Some two and a half hours later, as she was approaching Basingstoke, her car suddenly veered across the middle of the road into the oncoming traffic. It struck first a lorry and then another car, somersaulted into the air and landed on its roof. She was trapped in the wreckage, and her luggage – including a bunch of white carnations she had picked in the garden that morning – strewn across the road. When she was freed, she

---

*In his reminiscences published in the *News of the World* in 1981, David Holmes claimed that just before Caroline set out she telephoned him to say that, after Jeremy's departure, she had been upset to receive a surprise visit from Norman Scott, saying things like 'I should be here and not you'. This story has been vigorously denied by Norman Scott, and indeed seems most unlikely. For why should the then London-based Scott, who for more than five years had dealt with Jeremy only through Bessell, suddenly travel all the way to Devon to confront the Thorpes, without any guarantee that they would still be at their constituency home more than a week after the General Election? It seems probable that Holmes invented the story to put himself in a better light by suggesting that his subsequent actions were partly motivated by the belief that Scott may indirectly have contributed to Caroline's accident.

managed to utter a few words to her rescuers; but by the time she reached hospital, she was dead. The accident might not have been fatal but for the fact that the seat-belt she was wearing ruptured her spleen. There has been some speculation as to her behaviour in the moments before the crash, fuelled by conflicting testimony from witnesses.* On the available evidence, the most plausible explanation seems to be that, exhausted from the strain and sleeplessness of recent weeks, she either suffered a momentary blackout or fell asleep at the wheel. She had a reputation as a careless driver. There is often a suspicion of suicide in cases of unexplained fatal car crashes, but most of those who knew Caroline felt it would have been out of character for her to have taken her own life, even had she been seriously upset for some reason.

Meanwhile, at 3.26 PM, Jeremy, following Heath and Wilson, rose in the House of Commons to congratulate the Speaker, Dr Horace King, on his re-election to office. It was the sort of traditional occasion he loved, and he spoke gracefully and wittily.

> The danger which befell one of my ancestors, Mr Speaker Thorpe, of being beheaded by the mob at Harringay, fortunately is no longer one of the dangers attaching to your task. But it is none the less a very arduous job. I suppose the greatest tedium that any Member of Parliament has to face is to listen to any of the speeches of his colleagues. You have to listen to us all ... You are the guardian of the traditions of this House – not only of the majority, not only of the minority, but, I would add, of the extreme minority and, indeed, of the individual backbench Member ... and therefore this House is grateful to you and, if it is not out of order to say so, grateful to your wife too ...[12]

---

* For example, the driver of the lorry believed that she had been 'looking down at the inside of the car', while a passenger in his cab thought she had been staring ahead in a trance.

When he had finished speaking, the House rose, and he withdrew to his office accompanied by Pardoe and Steel. They were discussing the prospects for their depleted parliamentary party when Jeremy was asked to step outside for a word with the Superintendent of Police. A moment later, he returned looking ashen and collapsed into a chair.[13] In the space of two weeks, he had suffered a serious political setback and a crushing personal misfortune. A period of misery lay ahead.

15

ABYSS
1970–72

FOR EIGHTEEN MONTHS, the keynote of Jeremy Thorpe's life was to be mourning for his dead wife. His grief was intense and genuine, but it was not a quiet, private thing: he played the part of the bereaved husband with characteristic theatricality. Both the flat in London and the cottage in Devon became shrines to her memory, filled with images and mementoes of her. He wanted to talk about her with everyone he met, painting an idealised picture of their marriage. He wallowed in the sympathy of friends, and would read out to visitors from letters of condolence he had received, taking special pleasure in those from such eminent personages as Lord Mountbatten and Harold Wilson. He dabbled in spiritualism with a view to communicating with her. In the aftermath of her death, his attention was concentrated on organising her memorial service, which took place before a packed congregation (including most of the new Government) at St Margaret's, Westminster on 22 July. It was a typically (in the view of some, inappropriately) impressive occasion, including an address by the Archbishop and an elegy performed by Yehudi Menuhin: the hymns were the same as those sung at their wedding two years earlier. He then devoted himself to establishing permanent memorials to her. He was successful in arranging for the children's ward of the new North Devon Hospital to be named after her; unsuccessful in his application to have a Victorian stained-glass window in the fine parish church at Chittlehampton (where she was buried) replaced by one dedicated to her. He began planning a spectacular visible shrine – a 'Taj Mahal', as he put it – on the North Devon summit of Codden Hill which they had often climbed together, an absorbing project involving negotiations with several public and private landowners. Affecting though it was, his obsession with her memory struck many as unnatural. Some saw it as signifying a morbid, almost Etruscan interest in death and its rituals, others as a form of escape from all that was troublesome to him (including having to face up to the recent electoral disaster of the Liberal Party), still others as a reaction to subconscious feelings of guilt at having failed her as a husband or even been responsible for her demise. But there could be no doubt of his genuine and overwhelming sense of loss.

In his misery, two people came to the rescue, both of whom had been close to Caroline and felt her loss almost as keenly as he. David Holmes proved a faithful friend, attending to everything during the first days, when Jeremy was in a state of catatonic shock and unable to cope. It was he who organised the funeral in Devon, a private ceremony in the garden at Cobbaton taking place at the same time as a public service in the parish church in Barnstaple during which the whole town observed silence. Then and always, his solicitude was like that of a brother. And Caroline's childhood friend Vivienne Franklin – the jovial 'Viv' who had worked on the farm of her mother and stepfather – came to live with him, to keep house and look after Rupert.* Though

---

* Jeremy generally described Viv, who was rumoured to be the illegitimate daughter of Caroline's stepfather, as 'my stepsister-in-law'.

nothing in the nature of a romantic attachment developed
between Jeremy and Viv, she was to be an important figure in his
life for the next three years, for he needed a confidante with
whom he could talk about Caroline: often while reminiscing
about her late at night he would break down and sob, repeating
such phrases as 'we were so happy' or 'we never had a quarrel'.
He was accompanied by Holmes and Viv when he went to stay
in Portugal that August with his uncle, Sir Peter Norton-
Griffiths, it being perhaps significant that Ursula was not a
member of the party.

All his affection was now lavished on Rupert, the living result
of the marriage, who even as a baby greatly resembled his
mother: whatever his leadership or parliamentary duties, Jeremy
aspired to return to Ashley Gardens to spend part of each day
with him. Everything Rupert did or said was of absorbing interest to Jeremy, who enjoyed arranging such privileges for him as
the right (by courtesy of his godmother Joan Ramsey) to play in
the gardens of Lambeth Palace. At the same time he was made
anxious by the delicate health of the boy, who turned out to
suffer (as Jeremy had himself done during his early years) from
petit mal epilepsy. His attachment to his son was mirrored by new
feelings of antagonism towards his mother. Caroline had provided him with an escape from Ursula's emotional tyranny; after
her death, Ursula made remarks to the effect that she had 'got
her son back' which he found unforgivable. Ursula wanted to
take charge of Rupert's upbringing; but Jeremy would not hear
of this and entrusted Rupert instead to the care of Viv, towards
whom Ursula was rude and snubbing. There were fearsome rows
between mother and son, sometimes witnessed by other people.
'Do you still love me?' she once asked him accusingly. He replied
that it was monstrous to ask him such a question when he had
lost so much and his emotions were in shreds.

Although Jeremy let the world know that he was devastated by
his wife's death, he had little intention of withdrawing from

public life.* Indeed, his status as a public figure was a consolation to him, and he played to perfection the part of a statesman bearing up in the face of personal tragedy. When the new Conservative Chancellor of the Exchequer, Iain Macleod, who as Colonial Secretary had granted British Africa its independence in the early 1960s, suddenly died of a heart attack in the middle of July, Jeremy, who had not been expected to speak in the Commons for some time, paid tribute to him there, adding that the House's 'readiness to share sorrows is something which is deeply comforting and for which I, myself, have cause to be moved and grateful'. A few days later, just after Caroline's memorial service, he had been due to read an address at a service in Westminster Abbey to mark the unveiling of a plaque in memory of Lloyd George: to general surprise, he insisted on going ahead with this, and not only spoke well but was in good form at the reception afterwards, full of anecdotal reminiscence.[1] The plaque had been designed by Clough Williams-Ellis, and Jeremy took advantage of the occasion to invite the great Welsh architect to design the obelisk in memory of Caroline which he was already planning to erect on Codden Hill.

The period of Jeremy's extended mourning coincided with a miserable period in the history of the Liberal Party. In Parliament, it was reduced to a mere six MPs, as in the dark decade before Orpington. In the opinion polls, its ratings rarely rose above 5 per cent (having swung between 7 per cent and 10 per cent during the Wilson years). Its doings were rarely mentioned by the mass media. Its membership was in a demoralised state, which the continuing battle between traditionalists and

---

* Just after Caroline's death, Jeremy did in fact ask David Steel whether he ought to carry on; but the reply was predictable, and on 1 July, the Parliamentary Liberal Party formally re-elected Jeremy as its Leader, at the same time recording its 'shock and grief' at the tragedy which had befallen him and its understanding that he would not resume his duties until after the recess.

radicals did nothing to relieve. Jeremy performed his duties doggedly, sometimes showing a trace of his old sparkle, often just going through the motions in a trance-like state. He received much support from aides and colleagues – from Richard Moore, who wrote his speeches; from Tom Dale, who undertook many of his party functions; from his secretary Judy Young, who saw to it that he had a full diary; from his fellow MPs Steel and Pardoe; and from Holmes and Viv, always on hand to listen to his problems, whether personal or political.

During this period, Jeremy spent more time in Parliament than before: in his bereavement, he seemed comforted by its camaraderie and rituals. There was much for him to do there, for of the six Liberal MPs, three were effectively part-timers, as Jo Grimond continued to pursue an eccentric personal agenda, Russell Johnston was busy as the new Chairman of the Scottish Liberals, and Emlyn Hooson concentrated on his career at the Bar, becoming Leader of the Wales and Chester Circuit. Only Jeremy, David Steel (Lubbock's successor as Chief Whip) and John Pardoe (the Party's chief spokesman on economic and most other domestic issues) attended regularly, and they were deter-mined that the PLP should not become the joke it had been in the 1950s. They battled to make their presence felt and the Liberal voice heard: anxious to preserve their remaining privi-leges, they made it a rule that at least two of them should always be present on the Liberal bench during debates and put in an appearance at the Liberal table in the dining room.[2]

As Prime Minister, Edward Heath was correct in his dealings with Jeremy, but showed him none of the friendship and favour he had received from Wilson, rarely consulting him about any-thing except Northern Ireland. Jeremy accordingly had no compunction in attacking the Government during its first months in office. He lambasted its decisions to sell arms to South Africa and re-open negotiations with the Rhodesian rebels. He led the parliamentary attack on the Government's industrial policy following the bankruptcy of Rolls-Royce in February 1971, opposed an Immigration Bill which gave preference to applicants whose grandparents had been born in the United Kingdom, and criticised a new census which enquired intrusively into citizens' origins. The one major issue on which he supported the Government was its application to join the EEC: although the last application had been made by Wilson in 1967, most of the Labour Party, including Wilson himself, began to take a sceptical stand on Europe soon after the election, to accusations of hypocrisy from Jeremy. As there was a sizeable group of 'anti-mar-keteers' on the Conservative backbenches, led by Enoch Powell, it was possible that the five Liberal Euro-enthusiasts (Hooson being anti-EEC) might rescue Heath's European policy.

He also supported Heath's decision to reintroduce political honours in November 1970,* hoping there would be some for the Liberals: but there were few. Nor was Heath generous when it came to allocating life peerages to the Liberals, allowing them just two to replace Violet Bonham Carter and John Bannerman, both of whom had died in 1969. Jeremy awarded these to Nancy Seear and Simon Mackay in the New Year Honours of 1971. There was universal applause in the Party for the new Baroness Seear, a vibrant personality and one of the Party's leading thinkers; but the peerage of Mackay, a 36-year-old half-brother of the Conservative Earl of Inchcape who took the territorial title of Lord Tanlaw, caused puzzlement: few Liberals had heard of him, though he was candidate for Galloway in 1959 and 1964, and had recently been elected Treasurer of the Scottish Liberals. Jeremy justified his nomination by the need to replace Bannerman with another Scottish working peer, though it was believed to be not unconnected to contributions totalling £100,000 to Jeremy's Winnable Seats fund. Jeremy would dearly

---

* In October 1966, Jeremy, not yet Leader, had applauded Wilson's decision to abolish such honours.

have loved further peerages to distribute to friends and benefactors, and had some explaining to do to several disappointed people (including Bessell) to whom he had earlier promised 'the next peerage'. One consolation was that Eric Lubbock, his best friend in the Commons until his recent defeat at Orpington, inherited the Victorian barony of Avebury from a cousin in the summer of 1971 and was thus able to rejoin the Liberals in Parliament – though Jeremy had some trouble persuading him not to disclaim his peerage under the Act of 1963, as Lubbock had been assuring his family for years that he intended to do in order to continue his career as an MP.

Though not seen much in public following Caroline's death, Jeremy kept himself in the public eye through appearances on radio and television. He continued to be a popular contributor to *Any Questions*. He gave interviews in which he proclaimed that his bereavement had strengthened his religious faith, as 'unless you believe in the resurrection, the whole of this life is a sick joke'.[3] In March 1971, he gave an impressive performance on the Sunday night BBC radio programme *With Great Pleasure*, reading his personal selection of poetry and prose before an invited audience.[4]* In these broadcasts, he combined humour with a certain tragic nobility: at the age of forty-two, after a dozen years in Parliament and four as party leader, he already had the air of an elder statesman. This seems to have had some effect on public opinion, for although the polls continued to show that only a small percentage were willing to vote Liberal, by the summer of 1971 Jeremy topped the popularity ratings as the nation's favourite party political broadcaster.

---

* He began with Gray's 'Elegy' and Milton's 'On His Blindness'; became political with Dryden's attack on Shaftesbury and some repartee of F. E. Smith; quoted Gladstone on the rights of savages and Burke on the duties of an MP; and continued with Lear's 'The Owl and the Pussycat', Tennyson on the death of King Arthur, Belloc on friendship and laughter, Blake's *Tyger*, Macaulay's 'Jacobite Epitaph', and Lord Chesterfield on the art of pleasing.

Meanwhile, the Party in the country was going through a tortured period of self-examination following the 1970 débâcle. The in-fighting between moderates and radicals (the latter now organised in the Radical Bulletin Group) continued, each faction blaming the other for the sorry state in which the Party found itself. Jeremy distanced himself from this squabbling, his bereavement and the need to spend more time in Parliament providing him with a pretext to stay away from party meetings. Party members saw relatively little of him except at the September assemblies at Eastbourne in 1970 and Scarborough in 1971, dismal and poorly attended occasions at which his speeches lacked their usual sparkle. There were, however, two party matters in which he continued to be much involved: the debate over the future of the Young Liberals, and (as ever) the question of party finance.

There could be no doubt that the shrill radicalism of the YLs had brought the Party some disastrous publicity during the late 1960s, and many traditionalists, including Jeremy, were determined to make them scapegoats for the General Election result and bring them to heel. At the Eastbourne Assembly, he rounded upon those 'who for no discernible reasons call themselves Liberal . . . who did not help the Party in the years between the elections by seeking headlines at the Party's expense'. At the end of 1970, he set up a committee to enquire into the status of the YLs, headed by Stephen Terrell QC. Although this eventually reported with some relatively mild proposals – principally that YLs, in order to qualify as voting party members, should also belong to constituency associations – it led to a furore at the Scarborough Assembly, during which some YLs tried to storm the platform. When the YLs held their annual elections in April 1971, Jeremy supported the moderate Chris Green for Chairman against Peter Hain, the South African radical who had led the campaign against the 1970 South African cricket tour: Hain won the contest, despite a suspiciously large number of applications for postal votes from North Devon, where (as a subsequent investigation revealed) a number of elderly persons and even farm animals had been enrolled as Young Liberals.

In fact, the YLs were moving in a new direction which, if no less alarming to party traditionalists, at least made them a potential electoral asset to the Party. The great days of youth protest, culminating in the student riots of the late 1960s, were over. Peter Hain was no Louis Eaks. Under his leadership, the YLs stayed out of the national headlines and concentrated on 'community politics', a technique recently developed by American radicals. This was based on the idea of winning support among small communities (such as housing estates) by consulting local people about their conditions and helping them fight to improve those conditions. This would have been perfectly comprehensible to Jeremy, who had won and held his own constituency by fighting intensely 'local' campaigns. But to radicals like the YLs, community politics carried a wider agenda of ultimately 'politicising' communities and getting them to take power into their own hands, just as workers were to be encouraged to take over their factories and students their universities. Hain declared that 'the party leadership does not understand what community politics is all about, and if they did they wouldn't like it'.[5] Almost unnoticed, the YLs carried a resolution at Eastbourne that the Party should start campaigning at a community level. In the local elections of May 1971, these new tactics already showed some results, particularly on Merseyside, where the Liberals, led by the rugged radical Trevor Jones, began a spectacular revival.

On the financial front, the Party unprecedentedly found itself solvent following a General Election campaign, thanks to the Hayward donation. On the other hand, an unprecedented £100,000 had been spent on that campaign, largely under Jeremy's direction and all to little avail. Meanwhile, rows continued between Jeremy, who wished to control large undisclosed funds through Winnable Seats and the Liberal

Central Association, and the Party Treasurer Sir Frank Medlicott, who wanted all donations paid over to the LPO, to be disbursed by its committees and disclosed in its published accounts. Several senior figures, including Lord Byers, sided with Jeremy in this dispute, and Medlicott eventually resigned himself to the independent existence of Winnable Seats and the LCA; but the antagonism between Leader and Treasurer continued, culminating in a shouting match at the Eastbourne Assembly.* Relations improved slightly during the following year; but it was not until Medlicott died in January 1972, to be succeeded as Treasurer by Jeremy's stooge Philip Watkins, that Jeremy realised his ambition of achieving effective control of the Party's purse strings. Meanwhile, the Party suffered no serious recurrence in the early 1970s of its financial problems of the late 1960s, largely because it had already slimmed down its organisation and expenditure during the earlier period, but also because of Jeremy's ingenuity in raising money from city businessmen, whom he encouraged with the nebulous prospect of obtaining future honours.

Jeremy was also preoccupied by his personal finances. Caroline had died intestate, and he inherited her estate valued at £38,000 as well as a further sum from her life insurance; but he wished to devote much of this to creating memorials to her and assuring Rupert's future, and his own income remained meagre. He complained about having to 'do a minister's job on a back-bencher's salary': the latter had remained fixed at £3,250 a year since 1964,† and even for his expenses as Party Leader he was obliged to rely on private donations. Then, in 1971, an opportunity arose at which he grasped eagerly. His adviser Robin

---

* This was provoked by two matters. Medlicott was questioned about the Winnable Seats fund, and was humiliated to have to confess that he had never had sight of its accounts. And at a press conference, he identified the Liberals' mystery benefactor as Hayward, infuriating Jeremy, who believed this would prejudice his efforts to obtain Hayward's future financial support.

† It was raised to £3,500 in 1972, with generous increases in allowances.

Salinger knew a man called Gerald Caplan who ran a secondary banking firm, London & Counties Securities, whose outlets included branches in supermarkets. Its capital and profits looked impressive on paper, but its accounting procedures were dubious, as was Caplan's city reputation. Caplan was eager to acquire respectability; and through Salinger (who is said to have pocketed a substantial commission for the introduction), he offered Jeremy a 'non-executive' seat on his board at a salary of £5,000 a year, the perks to include an allocation of shares in the company, a Humber motor car and the full expenses of any journey which included company business. As his duties were virtually confined to making public relations appearances at the bank's supermarket branches, this effectively meant that London & Counties would be paying for much of his travel on behalf of the Liberal Party. It seemed a useful sinecure; he took a liking to the raffish and expansive Caplan (who also contributed handsomely to party funds); and he accepted the offer, to the dismay of friends who considered Caplan a most unsuitable associate for a leading politician.

A few months earlier, Jeremy had also accepted a directorship of Indeco Morrison, a respectable trading firm run by his Oxford friend Michael Ogle. It had extensive interests in Africa, and Ogle felt that Jeremy, through his friendship with African leaders, would provide it with useful contacts. In May 1971, the same month as he accepted Caplan's offer, he visited Zambia on Indeco's business, seeing his old friend President Kaunda. It was on his return from that trip that he confronted a crisis in which his private life caught up with his public life.

In the wake of Caroline's death, seeking escape from his wretchedness, Jeremy resumed with gusto his clandestine homosexual life. On most days Parliament was sitting, he would disappear for an hour or two in the late afternoon, telling colleagues he was returning home for 'Rupert's bedtime' – but he often used part of this interval to keep a sexual appointment. (Viv, who was in charge of Rupert's bedtime, was aware of this ploy and did not disapprove of it, feeling that such distractions helped lessen the pain of Caroline's loss.) Many of his associations at this period were with discreet partners whom he met through a member of his entourage who knew many attractive and willing young men. But this relatively safe arrangement could not satisfy his craving for dangerous adventure, and there were moments of madness when he took appalling risks by hobnobbing with rough youths and appearing in places where he ought not to have been seen. Antony Grey, the former civil servant who was Secretary of the Homosexual Law Reform Society (and had been helped by Jeremy in the campaign to bring about the change in the law which was finally enacted in 1967), heard from various sources during 1971 that Jeremy had been recognised in gay bars and clubs and even cruising the streets: he feared a scandal might result which would set back the cause of reform, and tried to warn him through the intermediary of Michael Launder, a handsome blond youth who had been a lover of Jeremy in both Devon and London during the 1960s* and now worked for the Society.[6] Even Tom Driberg, the outrageously homosexual Labour MP for Barking, was alarmed to hear gossip about Jeremy from rent boys they both patronised: as a mere backbencher soon to retire from politics, Driberg himself had little to lose, but he urged Jeremy to take care.[7]

While Jeremy was taking these new risks with his career, he still had to cope with old danger in the form of Norman Scott (now thirty, though looking rather older). After Caroline's death, Scott allowed Jeremy only a few months' respite before returning to the charge. In the autumn of 1970, his wife began suing

---

* Like Norman Scott, Launder considered himself to have been badly treated by Jeremy.

him for divorce; and he informed Bessell that he intended to defend the case and disclose his past relationship with Jeremy in the course of his evidence. Bessell was no longer Jeremy's fellow MP, nor so close to him as a friend; he was spending most of his time on business in America, and getting into financial trouble so desperate that he had begun to contemplate suicide. He nevertheless continued to concern himself with Scott, and suggested to Jeremy that they provide him with a divorce solicitor who might persuade him to keep Jeremy's name out of the proceedings. Jeremy agreed, but expressed the view (as Bessell later wrote) that the safest solution was to 'eliminate' Scott, preferably abroad: Bessell had arranged to meet Holmes in New York in January 1971, and Jeremy suggested they lure Scott out there by some ruse and murder him. Both Bessell and Holmes humoured Jeremy by pretending to go along with this, but they made no attempt to persuade Scott to join them in America, and when they met in New York, merely had a long talk in which they expressed their worries about Jeremy's mental stability. When Holmes returned to England, he explained that it had not been possible to lure Scott to America, by which news Jeremy seemed curiously relieved.

Meanwhile, Scott was consulting the solicitor Bessell had provided for him, Leonard Ross of Dorset Square, who advised that his past association with Jeremy was irrelevant to his divorce, and if raised during the proceedings risked prejudicing his chances of obtaining access to his son. This advice was unwelcome to Scott, but in the end he did not contest the divorce, which was finally granted in September 1972 on the basis of his being able to see his son once a year. Ross had told Scott that, in the event of his not receiving legal aid, he understood that his costs would be paid by 'those who are interested in your future'; and Ross's bill for £77.55 was eventually settled (after several reminders) by Jeremy.[8]

In February 1971, Scott decided to leave London and move to

a mill house at Talybont in North Wales which he had seen advertised in *The Times* for £12 a week. He got in touch with Bessell, who offered to help him with the rent and sent him £25. As an exotic outsider, Scott received a warm welcome from the Welsh villagers; but after a month he began to feel isolated and tried to commit suicide by subjecting himself to exposure on a freezing hillside. He was rescued by a local garage proprietor, Keith Rose, whom he regaled with his 'story'. Soon afterwards, Scott went to London to see Bessell and ask him for a substantial sum to start a riding school in Wales. A few days later, Bessell told Scott on the telephone that he could let him have £500, the call being overheard on an extension by Rose.* However, on 7 April Bessell wrote to him that he had been unable to raise the money and was leaving on business for America. On 4 May, Rose wrote to Jeremy at the House of Commons on Scott's behalf, saying that Scott's 'financial situation is now critical' and that 'it must surely be in your interest to resolve the situation'.

For six years, all Jeremy's dealings with Scott had taken place through Bessell, and the obvious course for him was to await Bessell's return from America later that month and leave it to him to deal with this letter. Instead, shortly before he himself left on his visit to Zambia, he instructed his aide Tom Dale to send Rose the following reply, which he dictated word for word, and of which the prosecution would make great play at his trial:

> As far as [Mr Thorpe] is aware, he does not know Mr Norman Scott. However, he believes that Mr Van de Brecht de Vater [sic] knew a Mr Norman Josiffe who may be the same person. Mr Thorpe asks me to say that he is under no obligation to this gentleman.

---

* It seems that, during this conversation, Bessell merely mentioned the figure 'five', which Scott told Rose meant £5,000, though this seems improbable.

This was a foolish letter to write: it was economical with the truth (in that Jeremy knew perfectly well who Scott was), it was certain to antagonise Scott further, and whomever Scott showed it to was likely to regard it as an evasive communication giving credence to his 'story'. The fact that Jeremy caused it to be sent suggests that, while in one sense he regarded Scott with loathing, in another, he may actually have enjoyed the danger Scott represented and wished it to continue.

Meanwhile, Scott had befriended a widow in Talybont, Gwen Parry-Jones, a former sub-postmistress who devoted herself to good works and had been active as a Welsh Liberal. His lease on the mill having expired, he went to live with her in May 1971 and, according to his account, they became lovers. Once again, he demonstrated his talent for making friends and winning them to his cause: later on, Mrs Parry-Jones would feel that he was 'in need of medical attention' and living in a 'fantasy world', but at first she listened seriously to his tale. Wishing to help him, she decided to write to Emlyn Hooson, who had known her father and since 1966 had been the only Welsh Liberal MP. Her letter explained vaguely that a young man whose life had been 'ruined by a leading member of your Party' had been 'promised expenses to settle in Wales' and she hoped Hooson might 'influence' those concerned 'to keep their word' in the interests of Liberal honour. Hooson replied that he would first need to know who 'they' were. In a second cryptic letter, she asked him to 'tell Mr Peter Bessell that Mr Norman Scott is in a grave situation and if he has any decency he will fulfil his promise to him immediately'.[9] Hooson assumed that Bessell – whom he had never forgiven for his broken promise to support him against Jeremy for the party leadership in 1967 – was the principal in the affair: as Bessell was no longer an MP, he invited Mrs Parry-Jones and her 'young man' to discuss the matter at the House of Commons on 26 May. However, when the couple arrived at Westminster that day, Hooson's secretary explained that he had been called away to

appear in a murder trial in Swansea and had arranged for them
to be interviewed instead by the Liberal Chief Whip David Steel.
She added that the Liberal Leader Jeremy Thorpe would probably have wanted to see them too, but was abroad, which Scott
said was just as well.[10]

Scott duly poured out his story to Steel, accusing Jeremy of
having wrecked his life through their 'affair' and been responsible for every misfortune which had since befallen him, including
his lack of a National Insurance card and the recent breakdown
of his marriage. He was nervous and perspired profusely, and
Steel at first assumed he was one of the many 'nutcases' who
pester MPs and develop fantasies about them. He was alarmed,
however, when Scott produced the notes from Bessell and his
secretary which had accompanied the weekly retainers sent
between the summer of 1967 and spring of 1969. Although
Jeremy was not named in these communications, he was mentioned in the letter Bessell had subsequently written Scott in
August 1969, and Scott also produced the recent letter from Tom
Dale to Keith Rose, which raised more questions than it
answered.

Steel asked Scott to come back the following day to see
Hooson, and looked pale when he broke the news to his Welsh
colleague that night that 'it's not about Bessell, it's about Jeremy'.
Hooson, who represented the Nonconformist strain of Liberalism, had always regarded Jeremy with a degree of disapproval,
and felt that if there turned out to be any truth in Scott's allegations, he should be made to resign. When Scott returned next
day, Hooson, using his skill as a barrister, subjected him, in
Steel's presence, to a searching cross-examination. Both he and
Steel felt that, while Scott clearly had a neurotic fixation about
Jeremy, and some of his allegations seemed absurd, there was
nevertheless something in his story. However, the documents
produced by Scott, while suspicious, did not constitute evidence
in any legal sense. On the other hand, there was one episode in

the story which ought to have been easy to check: Scott claimed that, some years earlier, he had been arrested at the House of Commons carrying a gun with which he had intended to shoot Jeremy, and had given a statement to the police. (This was not quite true: although, in December 1962, he had talked of going to the House with a gun, Scott had never put this plan into effect, and had merely been interviewed by the police in Chelsea, not arrested by them at Westminster.) Hooson resolved to conduct further investigations by asking both Bessell and the police what they knew about Scott and his relations with Jeremy.

Bessell had now briefly returned from America, and Hooson, still in cross-examining mode, telephoned him and asked him whether he knew a man calling himself Norman Scott and whether it was true that he had paid him money over two years to prevent him talking about a homosexual relationship with Jeremy Thorpe. Bessell replied: 'Yes, it was all a long time ago ... It was bound to come out sooner or later and I'm fed up anyway.' Hooson responded by saying that Jeremy would have to resign as party leader and probably give up his seat as well. Suddenly aware that Hooson might use the affair to put an end to Jeremy's political career, Bessell decided to say no more to the former and to try to warn the latter. He learned that Jeremy was due back from Zambia the following day, and saw him immediately upon his return to break the news that Hooson had seen Scott.

Although Jeremy had not slept for forty-eight hours, Bessell found him in battling mood in the face of the crisis. He had a brief respite, Parliament being in the Whitsun recess. They agreed that they should both stick to the story that Bessell had merely been involved on Jeremy's behalf in trying to help Scott with his National Insurance problems. Jeremy was determined not to be forced out of the leadership, which (writes Bessell) he had come to regard as his by right. He was furious with

Hooson – 'I'm not going to let that bastard destroy me and the Liberal Party!' – but Bessell urged him to keep his cool in talking to the Welshman, and show no more than 'mild indignation coupled by puzzlement that anyone should take such stories seriously'. When Jeremy spoke to Hooson, he adopted a tone of injured innocence. Meanwhile, Bessell spoke to Steel and told him, contrary to what he had already told Hooson, that he knew nothing of any homosexual association between Jeremy and Scott. He then returned to America, removing himself as a further witness.

At subsequent meetings with Hooson and Steel, Jeremy explained that Bessell had tried to help Scott over his National Insurance problems, and suggested that Scott had perhaps tried to blackmail Bessell over aspects of his personal and financial life, but vigorously denied all Scott's other allegations. Hooson barely concealed his hostility towards Jeremy: he said that if Scott's story was true, Jeremy was 'a cross between Horatio Bottomley and Oscar Wilde', and asked him whether he would resign if it was shown to be true, to which Jeremy replied: 'Of course, but it isn't and I won't.' Finally they all agreed that a secret party 'enquiry' should be held into Scott's claims, to be conducted by Hooson, Steel and Frank Byers, Liberal Leader in the Lords. The idea of bringing in the 'neutral' Byers to chair the enquiry was a brainwave of Jeremy's, for Byers, though frequently irritated by Jeremy, was a loyal soldier who saw it as his duty to support and protect his leader: he had staunchly helped Jeremy out of his party troubles in June 1968, and could be expected to do so again. He was also likely to regard Scott as a loathsome creature and give him short shrift.

The enquiry convened at Byers' room in the House of Lords on 9 June, when Norman Scott was invited to tell his story yet again for the benefit of Byers: hearing it for the third time, Steel realised that it was a well-rehearsed tale trotted out to whomever would listen. There was one, rather comic addition:

Scott claimed that he had once been spending the evening at Marsham Court when Byers had turned up to see Jeremy, as a result of which Jeremy had hidden Scott in a cupboard. As Jeremy had anticipated, Byers took a violent dislike to Scott: as he later told Magnus Linklater, 'I got an impression of pure evil.'[11] Byers' questioning of Scott was impatient and hostile. Where were the love letters he claimed to have received from Jeremy? Why was he pursuing a vendetta against Jeremy, whom he had not seen since 1964? What made him think he had a continuing right to be supported by Jeremy? Scott finally broke down and said that he loved Jeremy still and felt rejected and badly treated. This was too much for Byers, who (as Steel recalled) 'exploded and told Scott he was nothing but a dirty little blackmailer, or words to that effect' – whereupon Scott burst into tears and brought the interview to an end by picking up his papers and fleeing from the room ('like a jilted girl', remarked Hooson).

As Bessell was in America and evaded all efforts by Hooson to contact him, there seemed only one further source from which the enquiry could take evidence – the police to whom Scott claimed he had given a statement about the affair in the early 1960s, a statement which (since the alleged relationship would have been illegal at the time) had presumably been investigated. As soon as Jeremy heard that Hooson was getting in touch with Scotland Yard, he contacted the Home Secretary, Reginald Maudling, and asked if he might instruct the police to give out a minimum of information on the subject. Jeremy and Maudling were personal friends, fellow members of the political dining club founded by Winston Churchill known as The Other Club; and Jeremy hinted that Hooson was his political rival who might try to use any information he acquired to discredit him. Maudling seems to have used his influence to oblige Jeremy, for although one of the police officers who had interviewed Scott at Chelsea Police Station in December 1962,

Detective Inspector Edward Smith, went to see the Liberal triumvirate at the House of Lords, accompanied by a watchful senior colleague, he was reticent and would do no more than give brief factual answers to questions. In fact, only two points emerged from his evidence: that Scott's story of having gone to the House of Commons with a gun was untrue, and that the police had concluded that there were no grounds for action arising from what Scott had told and shown them in 1962. Subsequently, Jeremy wrote to Maudling ('Dear Reggie') asking him to confirm these two points in writing, as 'Hooson, whose motives are not entirely selfless, is intent to go on rummaging around, seeing if he can't stir up something': Maudling replied tersely and ambiguously that he had discussed the matter with the Metropolitan Police Commissioner and 'neither of us see any reason to disagree'.

Jeremy had gambled that the enquiry would come up with no evidence against him, and had won. As far as Byers and Steel were concerned, the matter was closed. Hooson, however, having heard Bessell's confession, was convinced that Scott's story was essentially true: he was depressed by what he saw as the 'mafia-like atmosphere ... of lies and intrigues' created by Jeremy and henceforth, while continuing as an MP and Chairman of the Welsh Liberals, he played little further part in national politics.[12] Only one other senior Liberal seems to have known about the enquiry at the time – Richard Wainwright, no longer an MP but now Chairman of the Party Executive, who was informed about it confidentially by Hooson, but who had already known for some years, thanks to Bessell, about Scott and Jeremy's homosexual past.

The episode left Jeremy indebted to three people – Bessell, Byers and Maudling – and it is interesting to note how these debts were discharged. He had already defaulted on his earlier promise to award Bessell 'the next Liberal peerage', but he would take a continuing interest in Bessell's financial problems, with results which will be seen. He recommended Byers for a Privy Counsellorship, a promotion which the Leader in the Lords finally received a year later and which he considered long overdue. As for Maudling, Jeremy repaid his help curiously. A year later, in July 1972, Maudling was in trouble, having been implicated both in the collapse of a Bermuda-based investment company and the activities of the architect John Poulson, who had received lucrative public contracts after making gifts to important figures. In the House of Commons, a motion was tabled criticising Maudling, Jeremy's name heading its list of sponsors: in the face of this pressure, Maudling resigned as Home Secretary. Bessell, who knew of the help Jeremy had received from Maudling, was amazed to hear of this and asked Jeremy why he had acted in so ungrateful a fashion. Jeremy explained that the motion had been drafted by Hooson and he had felt obliged to give prominent support to it so as not to betray the fact that he was under an obligation to Maudling. He was worried that Maudling might bear him a grudge, and relieved that the ex-minister was friendly when they next met.

Meanwhile, what of Scott? Following his humiliation by Byers, he was more determined than ever to publicise his story. He returned to the police and gave them another statement, thirty-three pages long, in which he repeated all his old allegations and added the new story of his dealings with Bessell. He contacted Gordon Winter, a journalist with links to the South African secret service BOSS, and told him his tale, which Winter passed on to the South Africans, the British security services MI5 and MI6, and two London popular newspapers, the *People* and *Sunday Mirror*. Then, in March 1972, Scott's former friend Gwen Parry-Jones died at Talybont from alcohol poisoning; and Scott, giving evidence at the inquest, claimed that she had committed suicide as a result of her inability to obtain redress for the past wrongs which he, Scott, had suffered at the hands of his former lover Jeremy Thorpe, an outburst reported to London newspapers by local journalists. The result of all these efforts was precisely nothing: no police officer or newspaper editor was going to accept the word of the former inmate of a mental home against that of a national figure and Privy Counsellor; and even were Scott's story to be proved essentially true, it was old and stale.*

From this, it is tempting to conclude that Jeremy had no need to involve Bessell in the affairs of Scott, or pay Scott money to keep quiet, or indeed plot his physical 'disappearance'. Had he not done any of these risky things, it is unlikely that Scott could have done him much harm. Jeremy turned the affair into a drama because, consciously or unconsciously, he wanted a drama. It was almost as if he had a psychological need to sustain a threat to his career, which provided him with a challenge and gave him a thrill of fear. This became particularly evident after the autumn of 1972, when Scott went to live with friends in Jeremy's constituency. Over the next three years, Scott would relate his story to anyone who would listen in North Devon. This does not seem to have affected Jeremy's electoral popularity in the constituency, which became greater than ever. But it did inflame Jeremy's persecution mania; and the murder plot, which had probably begun as a fantasy, became an obsession which, in the contention of the prosecution at his trial, he sought to bring about in reality.

On 4 December 1971, seventeen months after her death, the monument to Caroline designed by Clough Williams-Ellis was unveiled on Codden Hill, a North Devon landmark some 600 feet above sea level with fine views of the Taw Valley. It

---

* As Auberon Waugh wrote, when the story reached the satirical magazine *Private Eye* during 1972, 'nobody in the office liked it much – it was sordid without being funny, its unsolicited appearance had a faint smell of blackmail, it was defamatory, unprovable and, above all, it was more than ten years old.' (*The Last Word: An Eyewitness Account of the Thorpe Trial* [London 1980], p. 19.)

consisted of a tall column of Portland stone standing on a saucer-like base and topped with a pineapple-like flourish. Engraved at eye level were the words:

TO CAROLINE
WHO LIVED CLOSE BY AT COBBATON
AND LOVED THIS HILL
THE ADORED WIFE OF THE RIGHT HONOURABLE ·
JEREMY THORPE MP
AND MOTHER OF RUPERT
SHE DIED ON JUNE 29TH 1970 AGED 32

For more than a year, the memorial project had kept him busy and helped him forget his unhappiness. He had obtained the consent of four landowners, two of them government depart-ments. He had approved the design and chosen the stone. Finally he had organised the typically elaborate inaugural ceremonies, which included a piano concert by Moura Lympany and a bless-ing by the Archbishop: Jeremy invited 200 guests and planned the day like a military operation, with a fleet of Land Rovers to carry them up the hill and rugs and umbrellas to protect them from the elements. 'When people see [the column] rising into the sky,' he declared, 'they will think of Caroline Thorpe and the sunshine she brought with her during her tragically short stay in North Devon.' The monument gave rise to mixed views: some thought it resembled an eternal candle, while John Pardoe regarded it as 'a socking great phallic symbol' and thought Jeremy must have been 'certifiably insane' to erect it.[13]

This episode seems to have had a cathartic effect on Jeremy; for although he would never cease (even after remarriage) to be obsessed by Caroline's memory, and all who henceforth visited him in North Devon would be whisked off to see her monument before anything else, he was at least able to get her out of his mind to the extent of concentrating on his leadership duties, having taken to heart a warning delivered some months earlier by Pardoe that, unless he did so, someone else would. The moment was well chosen, for after a year and a half in which the Heath Government had enjoyed an easy ride, politics were again becoming exciting and unpredictable, and the Liberals were experiencing a modest revival of their fortunes.

The issue of the hour was Britain's accession to the Treaty of Rome, following the Conservatives' negotiation of terms of entry to the European Economic Community. Jeremy stressed that the Liberals alone of the three parties had consistently advocated British membership since the EEC's formation in 1957: he offered Heath the enthusiastic support of himself and his four pro-EEC colleagues (Hooson remaining in the anti-EEC camp), and was scathing in his criticism of Wilson, who had tried to secure membership in 1967 but now opposed it on the grounds that the terms obtained were inadequate. On 22 January 1972, together with the ex-Prime Ministers Macmillan and Douglas-Home, he was present when Heath signed the Treaty at the Egmont Palace in Brussels. (Wilson had also been asked, but spent the afternoon instead at a football match.) Jeremy was invited to sign his name alongside Heath's, and though he did so not as a plenipotentiary but a witness, it was typical of his sense of fantasy that he would afterwards talk of how he had 'gone to Brussels to sign the Treaty of Rome': he had even suggested to an astonished Heath that the British signatories should wear Privy Counsellors' uniform for the ceremony, complete with swords.*

Then, on 18 February, he had his great hour when the Government, facing a combination of a united Labour opposition and the rebel Tory 'anti-marketeers' led by Enoch Powell, were saved by the five pro-EEC Liberals on the second reading of the European Communities Bill, surviving by a majority of

---

* Jeremy had recently acquired a second-hand set of this expensive and elaborate uniform, discovered by Viv in a Pimlico junk shop.

eight: had he been defeated, Heath would have resigned. Typically, Jeremy kept everyone guessing up to the last moment as to how the five would vote: he allowed the Labour whips to believe that he would seize the chance to bring down the Government, while indicating to Willie Whitelaw, Leader of the House, that he would be prepared to support Heath provided the vote was not too obviously presented as a confidence motion.* When the figures were read out, there was pandemonium: having given a congratulatory wave to the Government benches, Jeremy received a torrent of abuse from Labour MPs and was physically assaulted by one of the Labour whips, who had to be dragged away by colleagues. It was the first time since 1931 that the survival of a Government had hung on Liberal votes, and Jeremy made the most of the moment. Next day, a beaming photograph of him surrounded by congratulatory telegrams appeared on the front pages. 'We are no longer a spent force or an irrelevant minority,' he declared: everyone would have to take them seriously now. When asked how he felt about saving a Government he affected to despise, he replied: 'Why should we assist Mr Powell to help Mr Wilson bring down Mr Heath?', adding that the Liberals would continue to offer vigorous opposition to the Conservatives on other matters.

Apart from Europe, there were three issues during the first half of 1972 on which Jeremy made the Liberal voice heard. First, Rhodesia, Jeremy attacking the provisional deal Sir Alec Douglas-Home had reached in November 1971 with Ian Smith's rebel regime. Secondly, Northern Ireland, Jeremy criticising the support the Conservatives were giving the Stormont Government, their decision to introduce internment in August 1971 and the troop deployments leading to the 'Bloody Sunday' shootings in Londonderry in January 1972. Thirdly, the fate of the Asian

---

* With this in mind, Jeremy had suggested to Whitelaw a formula with which Heath might (and finally did) end his speech.

community expelled from Uganda by Idi Amin in June 1972, Jeremy deploring the fact that they held British passports yet were denied entry into Britain under the Immigration Acts. As it happened, on all three issues, the Conservative Government eventually (albeit reluctantly) came round to Jeremy's point of view. Douglas-Home's Rhodesia settlement was abandoned after a commission had reported that it did not have the support of the African majority; Stormont was suspended in March 1972, Northern Ireland coming under the direct rule of Westminster; and the Government finally agreed in September 1972 to admit some 30,000 Ugandan Asian refugees to the United Kingdom.

During the spring of 1972, there began to be much talk (which would continue for the rest of the century) of a new 'centre grouping' in British politics which might include the Liberals under Jeremy, the right of the Labour Party under Roy Jenkins and 'liberal' elements in the Conservative Party. The 'Jenkinsites' made no secret of their dismay at the Party's leftward trend and hostility towards the EEC, and it seemed that they might break away from Labour and seek allies. Jeremy was quick to catch this mood, and in a party political broadcast during March called for 'a coalition of the centre' to cope with Britain's economic and industrial problems (a notion he had already put forward under the Labour Government towards the end of 1967). In April, Jenkins resigned as Labour's Deputy Leader and toyed with resigning from the Party altogether, confident that he could take with him at least a dozen MPs: but he finally decided to remain in the Labour ranks, believing that Wilson would lose the next election and he would then be in the running to succeed him. Talk of a 'coalition of the centre' continued, however, its main protagonists being Jeremy, the editor of *The Times*, William Rees-Mogg, and the Labour MP for Lincoln, Dick Taverne. It was an interesting combination, for Taverne and Rees-Mogg had been Jeremy's bitter and unsuccessful rivals for the Oxford Union Presidency in November 1950: now, the three were friends, and would meet periodically to discuss their hopes for political realignment.[14] Jeremy hoped that disaffected Labour politicians would start going over to the Liberals, but few did so at this time, the most prominent being David Ensor, a pro-EEC MP who had lost his seat in 1970. In October 1972, Taverne caused a sensation by resigning the Labour whip and declaring that he would re-contest his seat; but although he asked for Liberal support (which was willingly offered by Jeremy), he did not join the Liberals, preferring to style himself 'Democratic Labour'.

In mid-1972, Jeremy made two much-publicised trips abroad. The first was to South Africa in May, where he had been invited to give the annual Lecture on Academic Freedom at Cape Town University. He launched an open attack on the apartheid regime, saying that freedom in South Africa was 'progressively being reduced' by a ruling establishment following 'a totalitarian principle' which would 'eventually inflame the non-white majority'. This went down well with his mostly liberal and English-speaking audience. Speaking in Johannesburg, he criticised the conditions of African workers, calling on the shareholders of British firms with interests in South Africa to mount a campaign to improve those conditions. Though the fact that he was able to make such public remarks there at all rather belied his thesis of a 'totalitarian' South Africa, it took courage to speak out like this, and Jeremy would henceforth be regarded by the Nationalist Government as one of its most dangerous critics. In July, he accepted an official invitation to Moscow with his fellow MP Russell Johnston, where they were lavishly entertained in the Kremlin and met the Rector of Moscow University (who did not, however, invite Jeremy to lecture there on intellectual liberty). This was a time of 'thaw' in the Cold War: on his return, Jeremy hailed the improvement in Anglo-Russian relations, claimed to have taken up the cause of various persecuted individuals, and somewhat fatuously recommended the creation of 'a standing group of NATO and Warsaw Pact parliamentarians' (there being no free elections or genuine parliaments east of the Iron Curtain). Following this trip, he also hoped to go to China in the wake of Nixon's historic visit there, but was unable to secure an official invitation to Peking.

The death of the Duke of Windsor on 28 May 1972 gave Jeremy the opportunity to pay the sort of tribute at which he was superbly good. As a romantic, he had always had a soft spot for the ex-King over the water, whom he had hoped to get to visit the Oxford Union in 1950* and with whom he had had a memorable meeting in New York in 1961 (thereafter doing an imitation of him with his cockney transatlantic accent). In the House of Commons, he spoke of the Duke's work as a royal ambassador and his 'warmth and simplicity of approach'. His love for the Duchess, he added, had been no transitory love; theirs was 'a sublimely happy marriage lasting thirty-five years'.† The Government had tabled a resolution offering the condolences of the House to the Royal Family, making no mention, however, of the widow who was not officially considered a member of that family; and it was thanks to Jeremy (somewhat incongruously supported by the Reverend Ian Paisley) that this unchivalrous wording was amended to include the Duchess of Windsor.[15]

The Liberal Assembly at Margate in September 1972 took place in an atmosphere of excitement, for the Conservatives were rapidly becoming unpopular and the Liberals, who had done

---

* On 2 July 1950, Jeremy, then Treasurer of the Union, had written to the President, Godfrey Smith: 'Do you think it would be a nice gesture, since he has such happy memories of Oxford, and since he seems to lead such a miserable life cut off from all the memories of his youth, to ask the Duke of Windsor if he would like to attend a debate next term?'

† As a small boy, Jeremy had met the then Mrs Ernest Simpson at the house of an American friend of his parents, Minerva Dodge. His one memory of this occasion was not happy, however: he had been playing at the time with a toy fashioned out of cotton wool, and Mrs Simpson found this unsightly and threw it on the fire.

well in local elections that May, were experiencing a steady rise in the opinion polls. The idea of a 'coalition of the centre', first floated by Jeremy in March, was also gaining ground among both public and press. He had now fully shaken off his lethargy and delivered two rousing speeches, criticising the Government for its mishandling of the Ulster situation and an economic strategy which had resulted in galloping inflation and disastrous indus-trial relations. He argued that the Tories were being taken over by the right and Labour by the left and that the Liberals 'can and must break through'. These speeches had an inspirational effect on those who heard them* and were praised in the media. But the ongoing battle between radicals and traditionalists persisted, Jeremy's candidate for Party President being defeated by the 'community politician' Trevor Jones, architect of the remarkable advance of the Liberals on Liverpool City Council.

At Margate, there was a sense that the coming months would see the start of a serious Liberal revival and that, like the Orpington revival of a decade earlier, it would be heralded by a by-election success. Jeremy pinned his hopes on the coming con-test at Rochdale in Lancashire, scene of another famous campaign in 1958 when the Liberals, represented by Ludovic Kennedy, had come a close second. He had been impressed by the General Election candidate, the gargantuan and charismatic Cyril Smith, a popular former Labour mayor of the town: char-acteristically, he had already approached 'Big Cyril' about the by-election in the autumn of 1971, when the vacancy had not yet occurred but the sitting Labour MP was known to be seriously ill. (There is no reason to suppose that Jeremy knew anything about Smith's career as an abuser of children in care homes, the shocking details of which emerged after Smith's death in 2010.) Smith was reluctant to stand again, but Jeremy persuaded him by

---

* Including the author, then a nineteen-year-old undergraduate watching the Assembly on television.

promising to throw the whole weight of the Party behind him. He duly sent two outstanding young campaigners to Rochdale, John Spiller (formerly Pardoe's agent in North Cornwall) and the Old Etonian landowner Aza Pinney, and joined them himself for two days. Smith would later quarrel bitterly with Jeremy; but in his memoirs, published in 1977, he paid tribute to 'the enormous help' which the Liberal Leader, with his 'electioneering talent amounting to genius', had given him in the battle to win the seat:

> He spoke for me at meetings, he knocked on doors for me as a canvasser, he toured the town in a Land Rover shouting for me over a loud-hailer. He is the sort of man who can stop an old lady in the street, give her an unembarrassed hug, and leave her as a Jeremy Thorpe fan – and committed Liberal voter – to the end of her days. With Jeremy on my side to woo over floating Conservative voters, the campaign became a foregone conclusion.[16]

On 27 October 1972, Cyril Smith achieved a comfortable victory at Rochdale with a majority of 5,000 over Labour, the same as that by which he had lost to them in 1970. As much of a showman as Jeremy himself, he hired a train to take himself and his friends to London, where Jeremy, Steel and Pardoe gave him a hero's welcome at Euston in front of the television cameras. Jeremy declared that it was a remarkable achievement for the Liberals to have taken a seat in mid-term not from the Government but from the Opposition, adding: 'Believe me, we are going to cash in on it!'

Six weeks later, on 7 December 1972, the Liberals achieved the staggering capture of the hitherto solidly Conservative suburban seat of Sutton and Cheam. Though heartening, Rochdale had not been unexpected: the Liberals had a long tradition there, the local Labour Party had become discredited, and Smith was a popular local figure. In Sutton, the Liberals had scarcely been heard of before 1972, and the winner, Graham Tope, was an unknown Young Liberal in his twenties. What amazed was the size of his victory: as the Liberal candidate there at the Greater London Council elections of 1970, he had received 6 per cent of the vote; he now won by 7,600 votes on a swing of 33 per cent, larger than that of Orpington. Whereas Smith had fought a traditional campaign, Sutton was a triumph of 'community politics' – the result of months of hard work by Young Liberals who, inspired by Trevor Jones, had for two years been developing the technique of winning votes by helping the residents of small localities address their grievances.

The 'community politicians' of Sutton were no great admirers of Jeremy, though he took part in their campaign and made his usual dazzling impact. And he took advantage of the news of the victory with typical ingenuity. It happened to be the night of the annual Liberal Ball at the Savoy. When the election results arrived soon after midnight, Jeremy dramatically announced them to the assembled company: he then persuaded them to continue the revels into the early hours, alerted the press, and summoned Tope to join them as soon as possible. The result was a vivid clip for the next day's television news – the victorious candidate greeted by the jubilant leader in opulent surroundings to a riot of cheering.

The scene was set for a Liberal revival even more sensational than that of Orpington, which within a few months would bring the Party to a level of popularity it had not known for half a century and present it with a serious chance of breaking through electorally and holding the balance in the House of Commons. With such prospects ahead, and his self-confidence restored, Jeremy decided to embark on a step which, while incidentally consolidating his popularity and dispelling rumours of his homosexuality, would fill the void in his personal life left by the death of Caroline. This was remarriage, and he believed he had found the ideal candidate – Marion, Countess of Harewood.

16

MARION

1972–73

THE WOMAN DESTINED to become the second Mrs Jeremy Thorpe was two and a half years older than him and hailed from a background very different from that of the first. She was born Maria Donata Nannetta Paulina Gustava Erwina Wilhelmina Stein in Vienna on 18 October 1926, only child of the marriage of the Austrian musicologist Erwin Stein and his German wife Sophie, both of whom were then in their forties. Erwin, son of a Jewish publisher who had converted to Protestantism, had been a pupil of the *avant garde* Viennese composer Arnold Schoenberg and began his career as an opera conductor in Germany. It was while he was conducting at Darmstadt in 1920 that he met his wife, a Lutheran pastor's daughter and the widow of an official at the former princely court of Hesse-Darmstadt. They made a contrasting couple – she was large, formidable and Nordic-looking; he was small and dark, with the air of an absent-minded professor – but they were devoted to each other and to their daughter, known as Marion, upon whom they conferred such a royal string of names.[1]

By the time of Marion's birth, Erwin had become a noted

figure in the musical life of his native Vienna. Ill-health had obliged him to abandon conducting, but he had built up a great scholarly reputation as editor of the periodical *Pult und Talkstock* ('Music Desk and Baton') and artistic adviser to the main Viennese firm of music publishers, Universal Edition. As a friend of his old teacher Schoenberg, and Schoenberg's disciples Webern and Berg, he was responsible for explaining their complex atonal music to the world and arranging the performance and publication of their carefully crafted works. Indeed, he knew and was respected by most of the great composers of the day, and was quick to recognise the talent of the young Benjamin Britten when he visited Vienna in 1937. Marion had a comfortable childhood in a leafy suburb, music being as much a part of the atmosphere as the air she breathed. By the age of eleven, she had become familiar with such music as the symphonies of Mahler, and was an eager opera-goer and piano pupil.

When Hitler annexed Austria in March 1938, the Steins were greatly at risk, not only owing to Erwin's Jewish ancestry but also because the 'new music' he publicised was regarded by the Nazis as 'decadent'. Fortunately, he was able to obtain a job with Universal's London agents, Boosey & Hawkes. While he went ahead to England to set up the new family home, Marion went with her mother to visit relations in Germany – an uncomfortable experience, as their 'Aryan' kinsfolk were not keen to be seen with them, and the Czech crisis blew up, making them wonder whether they would ever see England at all. After war had been averted at Munich, the family were reunited in London. Their possessions, including the family furniture and Erwin's library, had been due to follow them, but never arrived. They also learned that, soon after their departure from Vienna, the Gestapo had come to arrest them, possibly provoked by the fact that Sophie, with reckless courage, had earlier made several angry visits to Gestapo headquarters to protest about the treatment of Jewish friends and neighbours.

Erwin quickly integrated himself into the London music world, in which he became a well-known figure. Sophie adapted less easily, but struggled to keep up standards in unfamiliar circumstances. Meanwhile Marion obtained a scholarship to Kensington High School for Girls, then flourishing under a Miss Charlesworth. She did not speak much English at first and resolved to say little until she had mastered the language, a factor which intensified a natural reserve. But she proved herself a clever and talented girl, also being good at games. She worked hard at the piano and attended concerts whenever she could. Her schoolfellows found her impressive, rather distant, and determined to achieve success in her new country.

The war was not an easy time for the Steins. Along with other German nationals, Erwin was interned as an enemy alien for several months after Dunkirk. They were anxious about the fate of relatives on the continent. (Erwin's brother and sister managed to survive in Vienna despite their Jewish origins, but Sophie's 'Aryan' son by her first marriage was killed serving in the Luftwaffe.) However, providence took a benign turn when Benjamin Britten and his partner Peter Pears returned to England from America (whither they had emigrated before the war) in 1942. Britten, still in his twenties but already recognised as a composer of genius, developed a close professional relationship with Erwin, who was responsible for publishing his works at Boosey & Hawkes. In 1944 the Steins, whose flat in Kensington had been damaged by fire, went to live with Britten and Pears in St John's Wood, and the five of them continued to share various London premises for the next few years, Sophie keeping house for the extended family. Marion formed a lasting attachment to Britten, whose music she loved and who (though thirteen years her senior, and homosexual) was brotherly and protective in his attentions towards her.

After the war, Marion studied piano at the Royal College of Music, her mentors including Professor Kendal Taylor and the concert pianist Clifford Curzon. She developed into a young woman of beauty and poise, and had many admirers, whom she kept at a distance. In June 1948, aged twenty-one, she attended the first Aldeburgh Festival, founded by Britten and Pears who lived nearby at Snape, and there met George Lascelles, 7th Earl of Harewood. Then twenty-five and just down from Cambridge, Harewood was a rich and handsome peer with an adventurous war record whose mother, Princess Mary, was the sister of King George VI. He had a fervent interest in music, especially opera, and had been invited by Britten to become President of the Festival on account of his royal connections. He fell in love with Marion, and was also enchanted by her father, whom he came to regard as his musical guru. He proposed to her in March 1949, after they had gone to hear an opera by Berg, whom she had known as a girl in Vienna. She was (as she confided to Britten) rather daunted by the prospect of marrying into such a high social sphere, but accepted him. Some months of uncertainty followed, as the formal consent of the King (legally necessary under the Royal Marriages Act, as Harewood was in the line of succession to the throne*) was held up by disapproval from Queen Mary: but the old dowager relented and the couple were married on 29 September. All the Royal Family attended and Britten wrote his *Wedding Anthem* in honour of the occasion, which the press celebrated as the culmination of a Cinderella-like romance between the dashing, semi-royal earl and the pretty, talented girl from a refugee background.

Marion suddenly found herself transformed from living with her parents in a modest flat in Kensington to being a countess and mistress of Harewood House near Leeds. She rapidly adapted to her new role, and indeed impressed some observers as being rather more 'regal' than her husband – though the transition involved strain, and while sparkling on the surface, her

---

* Tenth in line at the time he met Marion; eleventh when he married her; eighteenth when he was divorced by her.

personality, always somewhat withdrawn, seemed to become more so. (This may also have owed something to the fact that her mother-in-law, the Princess Royal, whom she regarded as a role model, was a woman of legendary reserve.) Although the demands of her new life caused her to give up her career as a pianist, the Harewoods established themselves as the royalty of the music world. The Earl became a director of Covent Garden and served on the Arts Council, while Marion organised the annual Opera Ball in aid of the English Opera Group. They travelled extensively on the continent, persuading leading conductors and singers to perform in England. They bought a substantial 1830s town house in Orme Square, Bayswater, where their three sons were born: it included a large annexe, originally built as a studio by the artist Lord Leighton, which became a music room and the scene of many recitals. (One of these, in aid of a West Country music festival, was attended by the Prospective Liberal Candidate for North Devon, Jeremy Thorpe.) The Harewoods remained staunch supporters of Britten, who had brought them together: when Elizabeth II came to the throne, it was due to their influence that he was commissioned to write an official opera, *Gloriana*, to celebrate the Coronation and also made a Companion of Honour while still in his thirties.

In 1959, Lord Harewood met the Australian violinist and fashion model Patricia Tuckwell in an airport departure lounge. They began an affair. His marriage to Marion was already under strain: in his memoirs, he gives as a possible reason for this that he had 'always looked for a partner from a background unlike my own' and that Marion had 'adapted so completely' that he 'had subconsciously begun to look for someone else to fill the role I had assigned to her'.[2] However, Marion at first refused to agree to a divorce, believing that her husband's infatuation would prove transitory and fearing the effect on their three young sons and the inevitable scandal. The Harewoods led increasingly separate lives, and in 1965, soon after Patricia had given birth to his child, he left Marion. In January 1967 (also the month that Jeremy Thorpe became Leader of the Liberal Party), it was finally announced that the Harewoods were to divorce: this caused a sensation, as it was the first divorce in the royal succession since George IV's unsuccessful attempt to obtain one in 1820, and only thirty years since Harewood's uncle, Edward VIII, had been obliged to give up the throne because he wished to marry a divorced woman. As soon as the divorce became absolute in July 1967, Harewood married Patricia in New York. The years of uncertainty were painful for all three parties and gave rise to much acrimony. Britten supported Marion in her desire to preserve her marriage, and Harewood was made to resign from the Aldeburgh Festival. He was also out of favour at court after breaking the royal taboo on divorce, whereas the Queen went out of her way to be friendly towards Marion when she opened the new Maltings Concert Hall at Snape in June 1967.

Marion was traumatised by the breakdown of her marriage, but kept herself busy. She spent much time with the Britten–Pears circle in Suffolk, living at Curlews, a pre-war villa on the seafront near Aldeburgh. She remained heavily involved in musical events and activities, notably the annual Leeds International Piano Competition which she had founded with Fanny Waterman in the early 1960s. In London, where she kept the house in Orme Square as part of her divorce settlement, she was close to her three teenage sons, bright and rascally boys who attended Westminster School but were influenced by the rebellious youth culture of the period and more interested in rock than classwork. Following the divorce, her name was sometimes 'linked' with various men, including the unlikely figure of Ted Heath: but although the Conservative Leader and eventual Prime Minister escorted her to concerts, it was never suggested to her by him or anyone else that she should marry him. Then, on 27 January 1972, she met Jeremy Thorpe, five days after he had accompanied Heath to Brussels to sign the Treaty of Rome.

They were brought together by the pianist Moura Lympany, who has described the occasion. Moura – one of several musical celebrities Jeremy had befriended during the 1950s – had been escorted by Jeremy that evening to a recital given by her friend, the violinist Nathan Milstein; and Marion gave a dinner party at Orme Square afterwards for the Milsteins, in which Moura (whom Marion did not know well) and Jeremy (whom she did not know at all) were included at the request of Madame Milstein. Beforehand, Moura (who the previous month had given the concert at Barnstaple to celebrate the dedication of the memorial to Caroline) had told Jeremy that he ought to marry again and that Marion would make him an ideal wife, to which he replied that he could not consider such a thing. However, by the end of dinner, as Jeremy offered to help Marion pour the coffee, Moura felt a certain electricity developing between them, and he later confirmed this to her, saying: 'Moura, I think you're psychic!'

Thus began a year's courtship, culminating in his proposal of marriage at the Ritz on 15 February 1973. Although they often dined or attended concerts together, they remained relative strangers to each other. When he proposed to her, he had not yet met her sons, nor she his mother; he had yet to be introduced to the Suffolk side of her life, and she to his Devon side. One observer noted that it was only after their marriage that she discovered he could not dance, and wondered what else she had not known about him. In years to come, there was speculation as to how far she had been aware of his homosexual past. In view of her close friendship with Britten, whose operas give expression to his complex homosexual personality and who lived in a semi-public relationship with Pears, it is hard to believe that she was either unaware of it or would have been dismayed by it; but she was fastidious in such matters and would probably not have wished to hear much about it. As in the case of Caroline, however, he did tell her in general terms about the trouble he had been experiencing from Norman Scott. (Alarmingly from Jeremy's point of view, Scott had gone to live with friends at South Molton in North Devon during the autumn of 1972; but he seems to have given relatively little trouble during the early months of 1973, being under medical supervision and the influence of sedative drugs.)

But though they had much to learn about each other, it was nevertheless a love match. He brought into her life a warmth and humour which had been lacking, and tremendously admired her qualities. He told friends that they were bound together by a shared sense of suffering, having both 'been through the fiery furnace' owing to the traumatic loss (under different circumstances) of partners upon whom they had depended. His natural exuberance complemented her natural reserve: yet both possessed tough, secretive inner natures. There were common elements in their backgrounds: they had both had gentle, talented fathers whom they had adored and rather fierce, possessive mothers, Jeremy's still very much alive. The prospect of Marion, whose own sons had just grown up and left home, becoming stepmother to Rupert, now approaching his fourth birthday, was appealing to them both. Each appears to have felt that the other would add an element of excitement and glamour to their life: he (who had once dreamed of marrying Princess Margaret) was undoubtedly fascinated by her royal connections, while she regarded him as a rising star destined for great things. At the outset of their marriage, they both put the miseries of the recent past behind them and made each other happy, while developing a relationship strong enough to withstand trouble ahead.

Once Marion had accepted Jeremy's proposal, they proceeded to break the news to those closest to them. Jeremy met Marion's three bohemian sons aged eighteen to twenty-two, who were surprised at the sight of a bowler hat in the hall at Orme Square but pleased that their mother had found someone who evidently made her happy: they all took to little Rupert, their future stepbrother. Jeremy meanwhile took an arch pleasure in informing his mother, his sisters, and various friends that he was 'practically marrying into the Royal Family', Ursula being thrilled at the prospect of acquiring stepgrandchildren who were in line to the throne. As in the case of Caroline, he was concerned to keep the engagement secret from the public for as long as possible; but on Saturday 24 February, while he was spending the weekend in North Devon, his new press adviser Stephen Bonarjee* rang him to say that the *People* had got hold of the story and would be running it next day on their front page. Jeremy broke the news that evening to a meeting of his constituency association, which gave him a standing ovation, and returned to London the following morning to give a press conference with Marion at Ashley Gardens. Bonarjee, who had hurriedly organised the event, found Jeremy 'in his most boyish, skittish mood, joking with the cameramen in his best manner. Marion seemed unaccustomed to such things but very sweet and natural, and their obvious delight in each other was touching.'[3]

After this, the marriage was organised with the greatest speed, taking place by special licence on 14 March. This time, Jeremy managed to pull off the coup he had failed to achieve in 1968: no one had any notice of the ceremony except for the few who had been invited to it and it was not reported in the press until the couple had departed on their honeymoon. (As before, it was planned to give a huge party towards the end of the parliamentary session.) They were married at Paddington Register Office, Jeremy wearing his father's morning dress and Marion a navy hat and coat, the witnesses being Ursula, Marion's eldest son David, Viscount Lascelles, and Jeremy's best man Robin Salinger. They proceeded to Westminster Abbey where they received Holy Communion from the Dean and a blessing from the Archbishop,

* Formerly head of BBC Radio current affairs.

also attended by Marion's two other sons and by Rupert, following which they gave a luncheon for forty of their closest family and friends in the Jerusalem Chamber. Of his parliamentary colleagues, Jeremy asked only two Liberal peers, Avebury and Byers; while on Marion's side, Britten came with Pears despite suffering from heart trouble and being about to undergo an operation.

Owing to rapid exciting developments on the political scene (to be described in the following chapter), Jeremy was unwilling to absent himself from London for long, but they enjoyed two short honeymoons, a few days in the South of France after the wedding and two weeks in the Bahamas and the United States (where Marion had never been before) during the Easter recess in April. On the latter trip they were guests of Jack Hayward, who told the press that he expected Jeremy to be Prime Minister one day. It was not all pleasure, for Hayward had mentioned to Jeremy that he was thinking of selling his business interests in the Bahamas,* and Jeremy had offered to try to find him a buyer through Peter Bessell and his American business contacts: were they to succeed, he and Bessell might earn huge sums in commission. In New York, Bessell told Jeremy that he believed he could interest the Mobil Oil Corporation in the purchase, provided certain guarantees were forthcoming from the United States Government; and Jeremy saw officials in Washington to discuss this, receiving no assurances but impressing Hayward by his contacts. As will be seen, these inconclusive negotiations were to have a dramatic sequel.

Another enterprise into which Bessell drew Jeremy during this visit, which casts interesting light on them both, was an attempt to establish that the Russian Imperial Family had not, as commonly

---

* There was uncertainty as to the future political complexion of the Bahamas, which was due to become independent later that year – though in the event, the rather corrupt Pindling Government remained friendly to private enterprise.

supposed, been murdered in Siberia in July 1918 but had somehow escaped, and that the British Government were withholding documents proving this to be the case. Bessell had heard this story from a writer named Guy Richards, who believed that an investigation of the true fate of the Romanovs would lead the investigators to a hoard of 'Russian gold'. Jeremy, who considered himself to have a family link with the Tsar on account of his grandfather having been decorated by Nicholas II just before the Revolution, was intrigued by this fantastic tale and seems to have accepted it at face value. At the start of the new session, he tabled a parliamentary question to the Foreign Secretary, Sir Alec Douglas-Home, claiming to have seen a copy of a letter from Lord Hardinge of Penshurst, the contemporary head of the Foreign Office, confirming the escape of the Tsar and his family. The Government denied all knowledge of the matter, and the 'Hardinge letter' was subsequently exposed as a ludicrous forgery.[4]

Between their two honeymoons, the Thorpes attended a wedding rather different from their own, when Marion's second son, the nineteen-year-old James Lascelles, married his American girlfriend at a hippy commune in Norfolk, Lord Harewood and his second wife also being present. The groom wore a sheepskin jerkin and leather jeans, the bride the lace dress worn by the Princess Royal at her wedding in 1921. The rock group of which James was a member sang songs composed in honour of the occasion.

On their return from America in May, Jeremy and Marion settled down to married life in England. They decided to sell his flat in Ashley Gardens and live together at her house in Orme Square, which she had come close to selling after her divorce but which now proved an ideal residence for a married statesman with a sense of the theatrical. Its spacious, rather sombre rooms, crammed with fine pictures and furniture, had something of the air of a royal residence: mementoes of Queen Mary jostled with Empire Jack's sword and other memorabilia. In these atmospheric surroundings, they could hold a reception for sixty or a dinner for thirty, or have half a dozen guests to stay. The square was a private one set back from the Bayswater Road; its solid buildings, attractively faced in sandstone, had rear entrances on to adjoining streets. It therefore afforded some privacy; but the house also had a large first-floor balcony from which Jeremy might address the multitude or acknowledge their cheers.* Orme Square would be the scene of some dramatic episodes over the next six years.

They were at first unable to occupy the cottage in Cobbaton, which Jeremy had quixotically lent the previous autumn to a family of Ugandan Asian refugees:† the newcomers had not been made very welcome in North Devon, where the local authority declined to re-house them, so that a stay of a few weeks extended to more than six months. Finally, Jeremy managed to find them accommodation elsewhere and was able to introduce his wife to his constituency. It took time for Marion to establish herself there, as comparisons were inevitably made between her reserve and the outgoing personality of Caroline. Having been in effect a minor member of the Royal Family, she also had to adjust to the rather different role of a politician's wife. However, she proved as always most adaptable; her qualities soon came to be appreciated; and by the time of the February 1974 General Election, less than a year after her marriage, she had won respect in the constituency and was an undoubted asset to Jeremy in his campaign. People were impressed by the fact that, having been used to servants, she seemed to have little trouble running the cottage on her own, and that she never seemed to mind that it remained a shrine to

---

* In the event, he only once used it for this purpose – after his acquittal in June 1979.

† At the Margate Assembly in September 1972, Jeremy had denounced the Ugandan dictator Idi Amin as 'a black Hitler' and urged Liberals to offer support to the influx of Asians fleeing from his persecution. He was somewhat taken aback when, shortly afterwards, his hospitality was invoked by the Patel family, but made the most of the headline-catching publicity.

Caroline's memory and that first-time visitors were whisked off on arrival to see her monument on Codden Hill.

In June 1973, they attended the Aldeburgh Festival, during which they stayed at Curlews and he was introduced to her local circle, presided over by the now ailing figure of Britten. This rather intellectual and exclusive (as well as fairly homosexual) world had certain initial reservations about Jeremy, feeling that whereas Marion's interest in music was intensely serious, his was that of a dilettante. But having witnessed her wretchedness during the breakdown of her former marriage, they recognised that he made her happy and indeed that her personality seemed to blossom after marriage to him. The locality also provided her with an introduction to campaigning for the Liberal Party.* The local Liberal candidate, the personable young Oxford-educated schoolmaster Denys Robinson, became a frequent visitor to Curlews; and she accompanied Jeremy on campaigning visits to nearby Ely, where a by-election was due to take place that July which the Liberals, represented by Jeremy's friend Clement Freud, had hopes of winning.

Marion willingly took on the role of being a mother to Rupert, who became attached to her. Viv, Caroline's old friend who since her death had lived with Jeremy and looked after Rupert, gracefully withdrew from the scene, declining the Thorpes' offer of the tenancy of the basement flat at Orme Square, which was taken instead by Jeremy's devoted secretary Judy Young.† Marion showed patience with Rupert, whose health problems were compounded by a sense of confusion arising from the fact that, during his early years, there was a profusion of mother figures in

---

* The constituency, the Eye Division of Suffolk, had been Liberal up to 1951, when the sitting MP, Lloyd George's former private secretary Edgar Granville, defected to Labour.

† Viv was hurt by a 'story' of the gossip columnist Nigel Dempster suggesting she had been sacked: she was in fact invited to stay on, but declined as she felt that 'Rupert could not have two mothers'. She remained a friend of the family.

his life. Having herself had a formidable and sometimes trying mother, Marion also proved adept at dealing with the phenomenon of Ursula as a mother-in-law.

The passing months seemed to confirm the success of the marriage. She became more cheerful and extrovert than her friends had ever known her. When they were apart even for a few days, she pined for him. When they appeared together that July on a radio phone-in – a medium at which he was a past master but with which she was unfamiliar – listeners were touched by his attentiveness towards her. She still had much to learn about him, some of which she would find disconcerting: but the element of intrigue in his nature was not entirely uncongenial to her. Life with him was full of laughter and never dull.

On Sunday 22 July, four months after their wedding, they commemorated it with a party at Covent Garden, Marion being President of the Friends of the Royal Opera House. It was attended by almost a thousand guests, including well-known figures from the worlds of politics and music as well as hippies from the commune of Marion's son James and his new wife.* A champagne reception in the crush bar was followed by a concert in the auditorium given by musicians who were friends of the couple. The programme included a Britten arrangement of British folk songs; Janet Baker singing Schubert and Handel; Beethoven's *Spring Sonata* performed by Yehudi and Hepzibah Menuhin; and a Mozart sonata for two pianos played by Clifford Curzon and Murray Perahia. The occasion was memorable for most of those present, though a few guests remained drinking in the bar after the start of the concert.

---

* Those who had been invited but did not come included the Oswald Mosleys, whose invitation had led to protests from senior Liberals, and Rostropovich, who was unable to obtain an exit visa. A guest whose presence caused surprise was the former Home Secretary, Reginald Maudling, then the subject of a fraud investigation.

Around this time, Susan Barnes, the American wife of the senior Labour politician (and former don at Jeremy's Oxford college) Tony Crosland, began work on a profile of Jeremy for the *Sunday Times Magazine*. In the course of her interviewing, she encountered disapproval of the Covent Garden party both from some radical Liberals, who thought it an inappropriately elitist occasion, and some Old Etonians, who considered it rather showy. When she put these criticisms to Jeremy, he exploded with rage. 'One has to bloody well lead one's own life ... It's my wedding. If one cannot have a reception such as one wants, then to hell with them. One has made enough sacrifices in one's personal life. They can find another leader.'[5]

17

REVIVAL
1973

DURING THE FIRST half of 1973, while Jeremy Thorpe was experiencing the personal security and public popularity arising from his marriage to Marion, the revival of the Liberal Party proceeded apace. On 1 March, his old Oxford Union rival Dick Taverne, who had resigned from the Labour Party the previous October and then recontested his Lincoln seat, was re-elected with a majority of more than 13,000. Although Taverne stood not as a Liberal but as a 'Democratic Labour' independent, he was supported by the Liberals, who put up no candidate against him; and like Jeremy (with whom he had often discussed the matter), he was in favour of a 'coalition of the centre' in which the Liberals would play a key part. Meanwhile, in the Labour strongholds of Chester-le-Street and Manchester Exchange, there was a huge swing towards the Liberals, who took votes from both the main parties and came a close second. While Jeremy was on his honeymoon, an article appeared under his name in the *Evening News* pointing out that, if one included Taverne, the Liberals had won more votes overall in the past six by-elections than either Labour or the Conservatives. 'People are beginning to realise we can win, and therefore we are doing so.' The other parties had surrendered to their 'wild men', and the electorate, who supported Liberal policies on industrial relations, racial harmony and the environment, were beginning to wonder why they had 'ever put up with such nonsense for so long'.

There was more good news in the council elections that May and June, the first to be held under the Conservatives' reform of the local government system. In Liverpool, the Liberals were swept to power under the leadership of the Party's President-elect Trevor Jones, an astonishing result in a city where five years earlier they had only possessed a single council seat. Liberal councillors were elected in places such as Bristol where they had had no presence since the war. They also captured Eastbourne and became the largest party in five other authorities and the second largest in twenty more. Altogether they won some 1,500 council seats, their greatest number for decades and vastly exceeding their expectations.

Then, on 26 July, four days after Jeremy and Marion had held their wedding party at Covent Garden, the Liberals achieved a feat unique in living memory by winning two by-elections on the same day, both in former Tory strongholds, Isle of Ely and Ripon. Ely (close to Aldeburgh, where Marion had her base) was captured by the celebrity chef and radio personality Clement Freud, a friend of Jeremy who had given much personal support to his campaign: largely the result of Freud's personal charisma, it was comparable to Cyril Smith's victory at Rochdale. Ripon, won by the Leeds bookseller David Austick, was the outcome of a 'community politics' campaign similar to that which had delivered Sutton to Graham Tope. Both victories represented a swing to the Liberals of more than 20 per cent. As always, Jeremy knew how to celebrate when things went well: next day, he held a champagne party at a Westminster pub before presiding with Marion at a reception for the new MPs at the National Liberal Club. He described the moment as 'a dramatic turning-point in British politics': both the main parties, he contended, were now 'on the run' from the Liberals.

The transformation of Liberal fortunes during the preceding twelve months had been remarkable, and for the first time, Jeremy began to be seriously regarded by many fellow politicians as a contender for public office. The day after Ely and Ripon, Tony Benn recorded a talk with him in his diary. Benn thought that, with the Tory majority dwindling, a coalition could soon come into being, in which Douglas-Home might return as premier and invite Jenkins, Wilson and Jeremy to join him. Jeremy did not think much of this speculation, replying that 'Home wouldn't be any good because he didn't know anything about economics'; but it is interesting that Benn – who two years earlier had dismissed Jeremy as a lightweight who was 'absolutely out of touch with modern trends and movements'[1] – now saw him as a potential player in government. He concluded: 'Jeremy was cock-a-hoop of course, and his bandwagon is rolling.'[2]

The Liberals were back in double figures with ten MPs. As so often in the past, they more resembled a group of independents than a parliamentary party, including as they did two mavericks (Freud and Smith), two old-fashioned radicals (Grimond and Pardoe), two new-fangled 'community politicians' (Austick and Tope), a right-wing traditionalist (Hooson) and two pragmatic managers (Johnston and Steel). At the beginning of August, Jeremy summoned them all to a two-day meeting at Kiddington Hall, the Oxfordshire seat of his old friends and benefactors Lawrence and Stina Robson: this was announced as 'a secret [sic] council of war' to 'discuss policy and strategy ... in the light of the continuing upsurge in the party's fortunes'. It was one of the few occasions during the Parliament when all the MPs met together, since Grimond, Hooson and Johnston were rarely seen at Westminster. As with so much that was organised by Jeremy, however, it turned out to be largely a public relations event: the MPs were presented with no proper agenda, and were surprised that Jeremy had invited their hostess (whom he would shortly nominate for a life peerage) to join their meetings. In the end, they spent most of their time deciding what statement to issue to the press.[3] The formula eventually agreed on was that the Liberals were seeking 'power and not the balance of power', but that if they held the balance, their participation would depend 'on the attitude of the other parties to the key Liberal policies of industrial democracy, Europe, devolution and help for the poor'. Later that month, Gallup put Liberal support at 28 per cent, the highest figure recorded in thirty-five years of polling: Jeremy declared that this heralded 'a massive Liberal bridgehead' at the coming General Election.

Under the circumstances, the Liberal Assembly gathered at Southport in September in an atmosphere of euphoria: it was a far cry from the Eastbourne Assembly three years earlier, which had been so depressing and poorly attended that many had believed it would be the last. In his opening speech, Jeremy trumpeted the electoral gains of the past year and set out an array of new, eye-catching Liberal policies: these included a weekly minimum wage of £24, higher pensions linked to average wages, a tax credit system and the creation of 'works councils' through which labour would participate in industry. These were radical proposals, but Jeremy took care to couch them in moderate language, and succeeded in getting the Young Liberals and other radical elements to keep their heads down during the Assembly. He wound up the proceedings with another rallying speech, lambasting the two main parties for their failures in office. 'Can we translate the goodwill, the enthusiasm and the support of recent months into solid parliamentary results? Can we at last make the breakthrough which has eluded us for two decades? ... We cannot ask for much more help from our opponents.'

The appearance of harmony was deceptive. Led by their hero Trevor Jones, the radicals had merely declared a truce in their war against Jeremy and the party traditionalists, and were biding their time until after the election. But Jeremy, his new wife by his side, was as popular as ever with the rank and file. And as ever, he spoke with the authority of a statesman in foreign affairs. He was listened to with respect when he spoke of the opportunities presented by the USSR–China conflict, and dismissed proposals for the 'denuclearisation' of Europe with the comment that 'without the nuclear deterrent, all Western Europe would have been overrun by now'. October 1973 saw the Yom Kippur War in the Middle East, a region Jeremy had visited the previous year and where he was knowledgeable about the issues and personalities. As in June 1967, he was sympathetic to the Israeli case, criticising the Government for operating an arms embargo which he claimed acted unfairly against the Israelis, who were denied spare parts for Centurion tanks while Britain continued to train Egyptian helicopter pilots. The war resulted in an Arab oil embargo against the West: this had the effect of exacerbating the economic and industrial difficulties of the Heath Government, particularly in view of an imminent clash with the National Union of Mineworkers which now threatened to leave Britain shorn of energy resources, and a serious conflict loomed between the Government and militant trade unionism which seemed likely to lead to an early election.

In this febrile atmosphere, the next test of Liberal advance occurred on 8 November, which saw four by-elections, in the English Conservative seats of Berwick-upon-Tweed and Hove and the Scottish Labour seats of Glasgow Govan and Edinburgh North. Jeremy concentrated his attention on the contest at Berwick, which had become vacant the previous May following the resignation of the Conservative defence minister Lord Lambton MP from both the Government and Parliament after the *News of the World* had taken photographs of him smoking marijuana with a call girl. At the time, Jeremy had tempted providence by declaring in a radio interview:

If you are in public life you are more vulnerable and must not put
yourself in a position where you can be subject to blackmail or
other pressures. Peccadilloes which might be acceptable for a private citizen can become a great danger to security with a person
in public life.[4]

He had also lost no time in sending to Berwick the Liberals' best
agent, John Spiller, who had five months to organise a campaign.
With the sprightly young academic Alan Beith as their candidate,
the Liberals were confident of victory; and they also had hopes
of winning Hove with the charismatic Des Wilson, founder of
the homelessness charity *Shelter* (with whom, however, Jeremy
did not get on). The Government continued to be unpopular,
having recently announced an extension of its incomes policy. In
the event, the results proved disappointing for the Liberals.
Beith, far from romping home at Berwick, won after several
recounts by a majority of fifty-seven. Wilson came no more than
a respectable second at Hove. With the Liberals well down in the
opinion polls from their summer peak of 28 per cent, there was
a sense that their revival had run out of steam. However, the
most sensational result of the night was the loss of Govan by
Labour to the Scottish Nationalists. Jeremy could still hope that,
with disillusionment rife among the electorate with both the
main parties, the coming election might yet present the Liberals
with their great opportunity.

In the autumn of 1973, as the Liberal revival seemed to falter,
Jeremy faced other problems. Norman Scott was again causing
trouble. A year earlier, he had gone to live in South Molton in the
heart of Jeremy's constituency, staying with his London friends
Jack and Stella Levy who had moved there. His attempt to start
a new life in North Devon followed much the same pattern as his
previous attempts in Ireland and Wales: after a brief period of
euphoria, during which he spoke of his now ancient affair with

Jeremy to anyone who would listen and came to be regarded locally as a colourful eccentric, he fell into a state of depression. A local GP, Dr Ronald Gleadle, prescribed strong sedatives: these resulted in Scott spending most of 1973 in a stupor but did not relieve his anguish, and eventually he slashed his wrists. At this, the Levys, like other past well-wishers, asked him to leave. Scott moved to an isolated cottage on the edge of Exmoor, where he scraped a living helping to look after the horses of neighbouring farmers, cursing Jeremy as always for the wretchedness of his lot.

It has been seen that, following the collapse three years earlier of his marriage and modelling career and the removal of Bessell's influence, Scott had done his utmost to publicise his allegations and thus damage Jeremy, but to little avail: few were willing to pay attention to the vindictive ramblings of a neurotic about the unprovable events of a decade earlier. In North Devon too, most of those to whom he told his tale regarded him as no more than an obsessed lunatic: at any rate, his efforts there had little effect on Jeremy's local popularity. However, throughout his career, Scott had shown an unusual ability to arouse the sympathetic interest in his case of priests, doctors and social workers, such as Father Sweetman in Dublin, Dr O'Connell at St George's Hospital and Mrs Parry-Jones in Talybont. He now managed to enlist as allies both Dr Gleadle, to whom he showed Bessell's 'retainer' letters, and an eccentric local Anglican vicar, the Reverend Frederick Pennington, who offered 'hypnotherapy' sessions to his parishioners in the course of which he tape-recorded Scott talking for hours on end about how Jeremy had ruined his life.

With a General Election looming, Pennington and Gleadle agreed that Scott's story bore on Jeremy's fitness for office and ought to be brought to the notice of others. In November 1973, Pennington, who believed it was impossible for Scott to have lied under hypnosis, mentioned the story to Jeremy's right-wing Conservative opponent Tim Keigwin, who had long been aware of rumours of the MP's homosexual past. Gleadle meanwhile passed the story on to a leading Liberal, the former Party President Desmond Banks, with whom he had once attended the same church in Harrow. Banks was in an embarrassing position, for he was an old friend of Jeremy from the 1950s when they had been involved together in the Radical Reform Group; Jeremy had also promised him a life peerage (which he duly received in 1974). He sought the advice of a friend, the former MP Lord Wade. Wade told Banks that Scott's allegations had already been investigated by Byers and found to be groundless, but suggested that Banks raise the matter with Jeremy himself. Jeremy made light of the affair, saying that he had been pursued for years by two nutcases, a man and a woman, and had gone to see Maudling when Home Secretary about the man: he showed Banks the letter he had solicited from Maudling in 1971 which gave the impression that the minister concurred with Jeremy's view. Banks was reassured and did not pursue the matter further.[5]

Although Jeremy had dealt deftly with the immediate threat, there can be no doubt that Scott's activities in North Devon caused him intense alarm. He had little to fear from his own supporters in the constituency, who willingly accepted his account of Scott as a troublemaking fantasist; but the prospect of his opponents making use of Scott assumed the proportions of a nightmare for him. He was also anxious that nothing should mar the success of his recent marriage and that Marion, who had suffered from her former husband's infidelities, should not be troubled by matters arising out of his past. Then as always, the wisest thing would have been to do nothing; but Jeremy was becoming ever more obsessed by what he perceived as the need to neutralise Scott.

In January 1974, soon after Jeremy's meeting with Banks, Scott's isolated existence on Exmoor was (according to his own account, which must be viewed in the light of the fact that he continued to be heavily sedated at this time) disturbed by a series of frightening incidents. The most alarming of these occurred when a helicopter landed near his cottage and two burly men emerged and hammered on the door, while the terrified Scott pretended not to be at home. As a result of this alleged episode, Scott telephoned Keigwin to say that he feared for his life and urgently wanted to see him. Keigwin, who already knew the outline of Scott's story from Pennington, visited Scott in the company of a local solicitor, John Palmer: Scott spoke to them for two hours and handed them a long handwritten statement about his association with Jeremy, beginning with the episode at Stonewalls on 8 November 1961. ('Though I realise now I had homosexual leanings, I had never had a complete relationship with another man until this seduction by Jeremy Thorpe.'6) Keigwin resolved to bring the matter to the attention of top figures in Party and Government. He sent Palmer to London to deliver Scott's statement to Conservative Central Office, where it was seen by the Party Chairman and cabinet minister Lord Carrington. Meanwhile, Keigwin spoke to the Attorney-General, Sir Peter Rawlinson, with whom he had served in the Irish Guards. Both these senior politicians, however, took the view that, at a time when the Government was trying to concentrate the public mind on serious issues, no use whatever should be made of Scott's allegations either by the Party in general or Keigwin in particular, a view with which the Prime Minister Edward Heath, when informed of the matter, fully concurred. Once again, Jeremy had little to fear: though he was understandably anxious when, on the eve of the General Election campaign, he learned of the encounter between Keigwin and Scott.

On 30 November 1973, while Jeremy was facing these personal problems, his public reputation, political career and economic circumstances experienced a serious reverse when London &

Counties Securities, Gerald Caplan's secondary banking firm of which he had been a non-executive director for the past two and a half years, collapsed amid allegations of fraud.

For more than a year, informed well-wishers had warned him of such an outcome and urged him to sever his links with Caplan, whose company was believed to be seriously under-capitalised and concealing this fact through dishonest accounting. Apart from private advice to this effect, he had also received public warnings from Patrick Hutber, the Oxford Union contemporary who was financial editor of the *Sunday Telegraph*. 'London & Counties is not the National Westminster,' wrote Hutber in August 1972, after Maudling had resigned following accusations (pushed home by Jeremy) of financial irregularity. 'It is not the Midland. It is not Warburgs. It is not Hill Samuel. If I were leader of the Liberal Party, conscious, as perhaps Mr Maudling should have been conscious, of the value of my name to a business, these are the calibre of names I should regard as giving me as much dignity as I lent them.' But Jeremy paid no heed and remained on the board. He seems to have been under the spell of Caplan, a persuasive rogue whose ability to carry along people who ought to have known better resembled that of Robert Maxwell.

Particularly surprising was Jeremy's failure to resign after he had survived one scandal arising out of his association with London & Counties. In January 1973, the *Daily Mail* claimed that 'the Jeremy Thorpe bank' had granted a second mortgage at a rate amounting to 280 per cent per annum, an allegation leading to questions in the House of Commons. Jeremy wanted to sue the newspaper for libel, and consulted Lord Goodman; but Goodman persuaded him that such action would be most unwise, and added his voice to the many who urged him to quit. With help from Goodman, Jeremy drew up a new code of practice for mortgage lenders and got most of them to agree to it, enabling him to emerge from the episode with some credit.[7] But he stated publicly that he would not be resigning his directorship, prompting another open letter from Hutber in the *Sunday Telegraph*:

> We were colleagues at Oxford and you did me more than one good turn. My effort to return the compliment failed, because candidly you did not seem to grasp the central point. It is that as leader of one of the three great political parties your name carries great prestige. If you do not exercise the utmost care and judgement in where you lend that name then you put yourself in a very vulnerable position ... In my opinion a company which thrives on second mortgages is either trading upon ignorance or trading upon desperation. This is no business for the leader of the Liberal Party.

It is something of a mystery why Jeremy did not resign at this time. The financial advantages he derived from his directorship – a salary of £5,000 per annum, shares which at their peak were worth perhaps twice that, plus a car and travelling expenses – hardly justified the risks to his career. And he remained personally close to Caplan: on Budget Day in March 1973, he embarrassed his staff by turning up at the House of Commons the worse for drink after a London & Counties boardroom lunch; and in August that year, he and Marion accepted an invitation to cruise in the Mediterranean on Caplan's yacht.

As 1973 progressed, the company got into increasing difficulties and Caplan resorted to ever more shady practices to prop it up. He illegally used the money of the bank's depositors to buy shares in his own company and maintain its stock market valuation. Criticism at the firm's AGM led the Department of Trade to set up an enquiry into its affairs. Then, in November 1973, the threat of a Monopolies Commission investigation forced Caplan to back out of a takeover bid for Inversk Paper in Scotland. The company's share price plunged from 138 to 39 pence before dealings were suspended. Up to the last, Hutber and others warned Jeremy of the imminent collapse and urged him to get out; but he was still opening bank branches in department stores that November. When the crash came, the *Sunday Telegraph* in a leader reminded readers of his disregard for Hutber's repeated warnings:

> It is all too easy to imagine the sanctimonious indignation, with merry quips, with which Mr Thorpe would have greeted the news of a Tory or Labour minister's involvement with the ailing London & Counties Securities. Another example, we would have been told, of the unacceptable face of capitalism or the hypocritical face of socialism. We will content ourselves more charitably with describing his own involvement with this unfortunate business as showing the all too human face of Liberalism ... Mr Thorpe, like other leading politicians in opposition, clearly wanted a job that was at once not too onerous and reasonably remunerative, and was not too choosy about where he found it ...

Once again, Jeremy managed to emerge from the disaster with some credit. He announced that he would remain on the board until he had managed to secure the deposits of the company's 12,500 banking customers, many of them small savers whom he had personally encouraged to entrust their savings to the bank. In the following days, he was active in negotiations which resulted in a consortium of the company's main investors, Eagle Star Insurance and United Draperies, and its principal rival, First National City Finance, putting up £35 million to save the depositors. The Department of Trade investigation ultimately reached the conclusion that Jeremy had been unaware of improper practices inside the company, though it criticised him for lending his name to a business without fully informing himself of its affairs. It was scathing, however, about Caplan (who had meanwhile fled abroad), referring to his 'inherent deviousness, a capacity amounting to genius not to give a straight answer to a straight question'.[8]

On 17 December, Jeremy announced that he had resigned from the board of London & Counties and all his other directorships to devote himself to politics in the run-up to the General Election. He had held six directorships in all, bringing in a combined income of some £8,000. However, within days of this self-denying gesture, which helped restore his public credibility and assuage criticism from party radicals following the London & Counties affair, he was involved with Peter Bessell in a plan to swindle Jack Hayward, the Liberals' greatest benefactor, of half a million dollars, though he afterwards insisted that he had been no more than an innocent dupe.

Bessell was now on the brink of ruin. He had run up massive debts; he had promised to repay his creditors by the end of the year; he had no money with which to do so; they would not wait. During the previous twelve months, he had hoped to bring off various important business projects which would have put him in funds; but none of these had been realised and it seemed unlikely that any of them would be in the deteriorating world economic climate. One of these was his plan, mentioned in the last chapter, to get the Mobil Oil Corporation to purchase Jack Hayward's Bahamas interests: on completion of this deal, he and Jeremy were due to share a commission amounting to more than $1 million. On 20 December, in Bessell's presence, Jeremy telephoned Hayward to say that the Mobil deal was on the brink of completion but that, in order to pay off an intermediary, Bessell needed $500,000 by way of advance commission. According to Jeremy, this is what he had just been told by Bessell, and believed (though having known him for so long, it seems incredible that he should have taken anything from Bessell at face value). Acccording to Bessell, Jeremy was perfectly aware of the true situation, and had indeed thought up this frankly fraudulent request in order to relieve the financial problems of both Bessell and himself (though one wonders how he thought he was going to explain matters to Hayward afterwards).

Hayward at first agreed to send Bessell the money, but then changed his mind. Feeling desperate, Bessell left for America, intending never to return: he had a girlfriend waiting for him in New York but did not bother to tell his wife in Cornwall that he was deserting her. On 29 December, after spending Christmas with Marion in Suffolk, Jeremy joined Bessell in Miami and they flew together to the Bahamas in a final attempt to persuade Hayward to pay over the $500,000. In the course of several meetings, Jeremy was 'very plausible',[9] but Hayward and his partners insisted that they would pay nothing until they had proof of the deal: among much else, Jeremy had assured them that it had the personal support of the Secretary of State, Henry Kissinger (to whom he had in fact briefly mentioned the matter, though receiving a wholly non-committal reaction). Following the failure of their efforts, Bessell (according to his later account) told Jeremy that he now proposed to evade his creditors by either vanishing in America or committing suicide there, but that he would first write to Hayward admitting the attempted fraud and taking full responsibility for it. (At the time, Hayward believed Jeremy had acted in good faith and been deceived by Bessell: he was later to revise his view.) Jeremy and Bessell parted with an embrace at Miami on 2 January 1974, neither imagining he would ever see the other again.

18

GLORY?

1974

JEREMY THORPE'S TRIP across the Atlantic in a failed attempt to help Bessell swindle Hayward was all the more extraordinary in that it occurred at a moment when he could hardly afford to be away; for he returned on 3 January 1974 to a Britain in crisis. Following the Arab oil embargo, and subsequent industrial action by the coalminers, supported by the railwaymen and power-station workers, the Government had been forced to introduce emergency measures in the New Year, including a three-day industrial week, a 50mph speed limit on the roads and a daily television shutdown at 10.30 PM. Jeremy's unexplained absence had aroused the fury of the Liberals' splenetic employment spokesman, Cyril Smith, who had written to him asking 'when the hell are we going to do something?', and without waiting for a reply, released the letter to the press. On his return, Jeremy airily dismissed these strictures, remarking that Smith had 'made rather an ass of himself' and vaguely explaining that he had 'been away having private and political talks in the Caribbean and America'.[1]

That January, as the Government struggled to find some

formula which would satisfy the miners while preserving their incomes policy, Jeremy played a clever game. His many statements inside and outside Parliament portrayed the Conservatives as intransigent and Labour as irresponsible, while representing the Liberals as the voice of moderation. On the one hand, he urged the miners to settle with the Government; on the other, he blamed Heath for the miseries inflicted on the nation. He sufficiently mastered the complexities of the industrial situation to talk about it with authority. To the general surprise (and against the advice of most of his colleagues), Heath did not go to the country that month, wishing first to be seen to exhaust all reasonable possibility of settlement; but at the beginning of February, the miners voted for an all-out strike. Jeremy held a much-publicised meeting with their leader, Joe Gormley, on 7 February, just before it was announced that Heath had called a General Election for the 28th. He subsequently claimed that he had found Gormley reasonable, that he believed a compromise had still been possible, and that the election was therefore unnecessary – though a host of ingenious solutions had been put forward during recent weeks and all rejected by the miners, who seemed more determined than the Government to force a showdown.

The Liberals had been expecting an early election and were well prepared. They were able to field 517 candidates in 635 constituencies, almost two hundred more than in 1970 and the greatest number in their history. The programme put forward at Southport – minimum wages, higher pensions, tax credits, works councils – became the basis of their manifesto. As in 1970, Jeremy retreated to his marginal constituency with his family and assistants, followed by an army of journalists; but whereas last time he had used North Devon as a base from which to tour the country, this time he resolved to stay there and nurse his fragile majority. His electorate had mushroomed from 50,000 to 70,000, owing to boundary changes and the absorption of much of the neighbouring (and now abolished) Torrington seat (including Bideford);* it was not yet clear how this would affect his prospects, and it meant that his local campaigning had to cover a far greater geographical area. In order to fight a national campaign without moving from his constituency, he arranged at considerable expense (which was eventually defrayed by Hayward) a closed-circuit television link between the Party's campaign headquarters at the National Liberal Club and the Liberal offices in Barnstaple where, sitting at an antique desk against a backdrop of leather-bound books, he gave at long distance a press conference every morning and interviews every evening.[2]

At the outset of the campaign, Liberal prospects looked bleak. Few opinion polls gave them more than 10 per cent, a far cry from their peak of 28 per cent of six months earlier. The Conservatives began with a comfortable lead, said to be especially strong in the West Country: bookmakers offered odds of only 6/4 on Jeremy retaining his seat. The one comfort for the Liberals was that an unusually large proportion of voters claimed still to be undecided. But their ratings improved steadily with the passing days. The closed-circuit link proved to be a masterstroke: for while Heath and Wilson came across as flinging mud at each other in the hurly-burly of London press conferences, Jeremy in distant Devon gave an impression of serene detachment from the conflict. The sight of him at his desk, looking and sounding statesmanlike, able to hear but not see his questioners, was reassuring for many voters, and wonderful theatre. He kept his message simple: the election was unnecessary; it had been caused by the confrontational attitudes of the other parties; the Liberals would bring the country together with their moderate policies. He gave suitably vague answers when asked what the

---

* Torrington had returned a Conservative MP since its brief tenure by Mark Bonham Carter in 1958–59.

Liberals would do in the event of their holding the balance. On the air, he guarded himself against appearing witty and light-weight; but in his constituency appearances he was in sparkling form, and won over the journalists covering his campaign on the ground. The BBC's documentary film-maker Michael Cockerell made an amusing film about him, shown on *Newsnight*: the days that he and his team had spent making it had been full of merriment.[3] Marion, whose devotion to her husband was evident and who had rapidly adapted her talents to suit the role of a political wife, proved a great asset to him.

A week before the election, Liberal ratings showed a sudden jump to around 20 per cent, double what they had been at the outset. Canvassing reports from the constituencies suggested that the increase largely consisted of women who had been impressed by Jeremy on television: in every region, large numbers of housewives on doorsteps proposed to change their former allegiances and 'vote for Jeremy'. On the final weekend, he gave what many considered his finest party political broadcast. With the air of a future Prime Minister, he declared:

> We still face a desperate crisis, and seldom in peacetime has there been such a need for national unity. At this election we Liberals are seeking to unite the centre, to isolate extremists whether on the Right or the Left ... In the next days, stand firm. Don't be bullied. Together we can make history and heal the self-inflicted wounds of Britain.

The next poll showed the Liberals back at their 1973 peak of 28 per cent. At this, Jeremy abandoned restraint and tempted providence. He told one reporter that 'the bandwagon is on its way', another that 'we are out for the jackpot'. He began speculating on the result: with 23 per cent of the vote, he told *The Times*, they would win forty seats; with 25 per cent, sixty-five; with 29 per cent, over one hundred. Evoking memories of 1906, he even spoke of a possible 'Liberal landslide'. Some commentators afterwards felt that this triumphalism had cost votes.

Amid all the excitement of the campaign, Jeremy never ceased to be haunted by Norman Scott, roaming around the constituency like an avenging angel. He had dealt with the Banks episode, but it had left him shaken. He had also had a stormy personal encounter with Scott's hypnotising vicar, Pennington.[4] There was no telling who else was getting to hear Scott's story, and Jeremy knew that Keigwin had got hold of it. He took precautions. His Devon solicitor Michael Barnes warned Keigwin not to mention Scott during the campaign, and went so far as to attend the Conservative candidate's meetings, brandishing a notebook and pencil. (This was in fact unnecessary, as Keigwin had already agreed, at the behest of leading members of his own party, not to embarrass Jeremy on personal grounds.) Meanwhile, Jeremy got David Holmes to ask Lord Goodman if there was any way of shutting Scott up during the campaign; but Goodman, then as always, advised Jeremy to put Scott out of his mind. (Holmes agreed; as he later said: 'Everybody in the constituency knew about [Scott] and it didn't make any difference because they thought he was a nut, which is in the end the tragedy of the whole thing, because Jeremy needn't have reacted.'[5])

During the weekend before the poll, Barnes was telephoned by Dr Gleadle (who had given Scott's story to Banks some weeks earlier) and asked whether he wanted to buy some letters embarrassing to the Liberal Party. Barnes reported the matter to Jeremy who begged him to sort it out with Holmes. On the Sunday night, Holmes went to see Gleadle who, 'making it sound like a social request', explained that he had a patient (he did not mention Scott by name) who needed some money to start a riding school and wanted £25,000 for some letters, which were not actually produced. Holmes consulted Jeremy, and they both agreed (as Holmes claimed to recall seven years later) 'that we had to have the [as yet unseen] letters because we dared not risk the publication Gleadle was threatening in the days immediately before the election.' On Monday night, Holmes returned to see Gleadle and offered him a cheque for £2,500 drawn on his own account, which the doctor accepted, handing over a file of some hundred letters. These turned out to be the originals of Bessell's 'retainer' letters, which Holmes burned that night in Jeremy's presence in Barnes' Aga – 'the most expensive bonfire ever', as he later described it.*

The transaction was foolish, because submission to blackmail gave credence to Scott's allegations, and Holmes had paid with a traceable cheque. It was unnecessary, because newspapers were being offered the story from various sources throughout the campaign,† and (except for one garbled reference in *Private Eye*) none of them would touch it. And it was futile, for Scott had kept copies of the letters, which he had already distributed in the past to people as diverse as the Liberal statesman Lord Byers and the South African agent Gordon Winter. But Jeremy seems to have reasoned that no avoidable risk could be allowed which threatened to compromise his election prospects:‡ when Holmes asked whether he should stop his cheque to Gleadle, Jeremy told him not to.

---

* This is the account Holmes gave the *News of the World* in 1981, which the author believes to be accurate. It differs from Holmes' earlier version (designed to protect Jeremy), and from Jeremy's own account, which is that Holmes saw Gleadle and bought the letters on his own initiative, without consulting Jeremy at all. In most published accounts, the purchase of the letters is said to have taken place on the eve of poll, i.e., the Wednesday; but in his *News of the World* interviews, Holmes says that it in fact occurred on the Monday night.

† For example, Gordon Winter returned from South Africa in a futile effort to interest the *Sunday Mirror* and *People* in publication. And Ronald Duncan, a playwright who lived in North Devon and had been approached by Scott, passed the story to *The Times*, which declined to use it. (*Rinkagate*, pp. 202–4.)

‡ It will be recalled that Bessell (according to his own later account) had been approached during the 1970 election campaign by a blackmailer claiming to have letters from Jeremy to Scott. Jeremy had begged Bessell (according to the latter) to do whatever might be necessary to avoid exposure: though, in the event, Bessell discovered the letters to be forgeries and scared the man off.

For he did not doubt that he was about to experience his greatest moment. The Conservative lead had almost vanished and the Liberals were riding high. A cartoon by Garland in the *Daily Telegraph* showed Jeremy as Cinderella, about to surprise the ugly sisters Heath and Wilson by appearing at the ball. At his eve-of-poll meeting in Barnstaple, he predicted 'a tremendous Liberal victory', and openly discussed the possibility of a hung Parliament and coalition, declaring that both Heath and Wilson would have to stand aside in such an eventuality and allow the Government 'to be led by a man who can unite the nation on the basis of a moderate policy'.

At the count the following night, he experienced his greatest personal triumph. The results (with 1970 figures in brackets) were:

Thorpe, John Jeremy (Liberal):	34,052	(18,893)
Keigwin, T. C. (Conservative):	22,980	(18,524)
Marston, T. K. (Labour):	6,140	(5,268)

Notwithstanding that his electorate had been diluted by the huge intake from formerly Conservative Torrington, Jeremy's majority had shot up from 369 to 11,072 and his share of the vote from 44 per cent to 54 per cent. With his wife and mother at his side, he thanked his supporters, saying that he had never dreamed of such a triumph, which represented 'a victory for moderation'. Keigwin, who had kept both his dislike of Jeremy and knowledge of Scott bottled up during the campaign, made an ungracious speech, claiming that the result had been distorted by the influence of television, and concluding: 'The truth will out and our time will come again.'

In the country, the result was extraordinary. The Liberals had polled over 6 million votes, more than in any previous election. Their percentage of the total was 19.3 per cent, compared to 7.5 per cent in 1970. But their one-fifth of the vote had delivered them barely one-fiftieth of the seats, fourteen in all. Except in a few places where candidates had strong personal followings, the resurgence was spread too thinly to deliver victory. All six MPs returned in 1970 were re-elected with greatly increased majorities; three of the five by-election victors of the late Parliament – Beith in Berwick, Freud in Ely and Smith in Rochdale – were returned; and Taverne was again re-elected with Liberal support in Lincoln. The two North of England MPs elected in 1966 and defeated in 1970 reappeared, Richard Wainwright in his old seat of Colne Valley, Michael Winstanley in the new seat of Hazel Grove. Two other seats which had recently been Liberal became so again – Cardigan, lost by Roderic Bowen in 1966 and now regained by the Welsh sheep farmer Geraint Howells, and Bessell's old seat of Bodmin, which (despite the trail of debts and scandals left behind by Bessell) was retaken by Paul Tyler after many recounts with a majority of nine. The only real surprise was the capture of the Isle of Wight, where Stephen Ross increased the Liberal share of the vote from 22.2 per cent to 50.2 per cent.

Heath's attempt to win a national vote of confidence had failed, the election producing the first hung Parliament since 1929. Though the Conservatives had won a fractionally higher percentage of the national vote than Labour, 37.9 per cent to 37.1 per cent, they gained four fewer seats, 297 to 301. The question immediately arose as to whether Heath would try to stay in office with Liberal support, though the prospect of doing so cannot have filled him with enthusiasm. Between him and Jeremy there had long existed the mutual mistrust of the dedicated plodder and the brilliant lightweight, the repressed introvert and the flamboyant extrovert. He was also aware, as he puts it in his memoirs, that 'there were matters in Thorpe's private life' which bore on his suitability for office.[6] Moreover, even with Liberal support, Heath would not have an overall majority in Parliament: he would also need Taverne, and the seven Ulster

Unionists (who had fought the election on a platform opposed to the Government's Northern Ireland policy), just to have a majority of one. Of those colleagues to whom he felt closest, the Energy Secretary Carrington and the Employment Secretary Whitelaw urged him to resign at once, on the grounds that the country saw the election in the crude terms of a football match, which he had simply lost.[7] (Margaret Thatcher, then Education Secretary, later claimed that this had also been her view.[8]) But Heath preferred the advice of the Lord Chancellor, Hailsham, a friend of Jeremy since the 1940s,* that he should not resign without first exploring the possibility of a coalition, seeing that 'an immense majority' had voted for the Conservative–Liberal consensus on Europe and the need to control prices and incomes. The Liberals, Hailsham suggested, should be offered a handful of government posts – 'one Cab. Min.: two Mins. of State: two Undersecs.' – to encourage them to share responsibility. 'If the Liberals turn us down,' he concluded, 'we should resign forthwith ... I think they *will* turn us down. If they do, I think they will be foolish, as they will have refused a chance of getting experience of Government and their best chance ever of electoral reform ...'[9]

The day after the election, Jeremy experienced mixed emotions of delight at the size of the Liberal vote, which he could justly claim to have been largely his personal achievement, and disappointment at the meagre complement of MPs. When asked what he thought Heath should now do, he replied that the Prime Minister would be 'entirely within his constitutional rights' to carry on and that resignation was 'entirely a matter for his own

---

* When Jeremy was at Oxford, and the then Quintin Hogg (before inheriting his viscountcy in 1950) was the local MP. They shared a love of showmanship and repartee. When Jeremy remarked that, if he ever lost his Commons seat, he believed he could claim a dormant barony and sit in the Lords, Hailsham replied: 'It's so expensive reviving dormant peerages nowadays that you would find it cheaper to buy a new one from the Prime Minister of the day.'

judgement'. He was celebrating his victory that evening with the traditional torchlight rally in his constituency when a policeman passed him a message to telephone the duty officer at 10 Downing Street as soon as possible. Jeremy showed no haste and waited until the end of the celebrations before doing so, and accepting Heath's invitation to talks the following day. Apart from his family and closest entourage, he told no one that he was going to London for this purpose, and made arrangements to slip away the following morning unnoticed by the press. He was later to be criticised for going to see Heath without first consulting his fellow MPs or indeed the Party as a whole. However, he took the view that, having been approached by the Prime Minister, he had a right and indeed a duty to hear what he had to say; and having decided to go, he could not easily consult anyone, given the urgency of the situation and the likelihood (which came to pass) that the Party would start tearing itself apart as soon as it became known that the meeting was taking place.*

On the morning of Saturday 2 March, Jeremy sneaked out of his cottage by the back door and walked across muddy fields to a lane where a car was waiting, driven by his young political assistant Tony Richards, who was to be his sole companion on the adventure. On the rail journey from Taunton to London, he spoke excitedly to Richards of the historic significance of the coming meeting, describing it as the first visit by a Liberal to

---

* In his memoirs Jeremy claimed that Heath 'suggested that we keep the fact that we were meeting private' (*In My Own Time*, p.114). However, the record kept by Heath's Private Secretary Armstrong (PREM/16/231) notes that 'the Prime Minister thought it desirable that an announcement about his meeting with Mr Thorpe should be issued as soon as possible. Mr Thorpe agreed . . . but asked that it should be delayed until after his train had left Taunton, so that he was not besieged by journalists on the train. I therefore sent the text to the Press Office for release at 12.45 PM. But by noon the press were already aware – apparently from Liberal Party sources – that Mr Thorpe was on his way to London to see the Prime Minister; and so, after consulting the PM, I authorised the release of the announcement.'

Downing Street for political negotiations since Lloyd George.*
Like an actor rehearsing his entrance, he polished his intended
opening line – to the effect that it was not clear who had won the
election but quite clear who had lost it. But he did not underes-
timate the problem: in the train, he opened a pile of telegrams
received from fellow Liberals since the election, most of which
urged against any dealings with Heath. By the time they reached
Paddington, the news had become public and they were greeted
by the press in force. Jeremy made a brief sortie to Orme Square,
where he changed into his most Edwardian clothes, and then
drove with Richards to Downing Street, where they arrived at
4 PM. The crowds there were mostly hostile to Heath but cheered
the Liberal Leader, shouting: 'Go on Jeremy, tell him to get out!'
To a hail of flashlights, they entered Number 10 by the front
door. Richards remained with Heath's Parliamentary Private
Secretary Timothy Kitson while Jeremy talked with Heath for an
hour and twenty minutes, the only witness to their meeting
being the Prime Minister's Principal Private Secretary Robert
(later Lord) Armstrong, an Eton contemporary of Jeremy.[10]

Both Heath and Jeremy described their meeting in memoirs
which were written some twenty-five years after the event, by
which time their recollections had become clouded. In his
autobiography, Heath, after remarking misleadingly that Jeremy
had 'turned up' at Downing Street that afternoon, wrote:

> ... [Thorpe] agreed that his party was much closer to the
> Conservatives than to Labour on the main issues of the day: like
> us, the Liberals favoured a prices and incomes policy, and they
> supported a constructive approach to Europe. I asked Thorpe to
> consider three possible arrangements if we remained in office.
> First, a loose arrangement within which the Liberals could pick

---

* This was a slight exaggeration: presumably Liberal Leaders had gone there in
1931 and 1940 to discuss their proposed participation in Government.

and choose which governmental measures they supported; secondly, full consultation on the contents of a government programme to be announced in a Queen's Speech, which the Liberals would then support; or thirdly, a coalition, in which Thorpe would be offered an unspecified Cabinet seat. I told him that the third arrangement would be my preferred option, to ensure stability. Thorpe expressed a strong preference for the post of Home Secretary, but I made no such offer to him. Before the meeting took place I had been warned by the Secretary to the Cabinet that there were matters in Thorpe's private life, as yet undisclosed to the public, which might make this a highly unsuitable position for him to hold. Thorpe also raised the subject of proportional representation. I replied that I would have to consult my colleagues before committing the party to electoral reform. He promised to hold consultations with his own senior colleagues.[11]

In fact, no specific Cabinet post seems to have been mentioned by either of them during the meeting (though Jeremy later claimed to have heard 'from a reliable source' that Heath had in mind for him 'a Foreign Office job with specific responsibility for Europe'). According to Jeremy's account, Heath began by stressing the fact that he had won the largest share of the popular vote, to which Jeremy replied that this presumably meant Heath was in favour of electoral reform (the expression 'proportional representation' was not used), which would in any case be the Liberal price for any deal. Heath admitted that the result strengthened the case for electoral reform, but warned that many in his party would strongly resist it.[12] However, according to the nine-page account of the meeting drawn up afterwards by Armstrong (and released in 2005 under the Thirty Year Rule), it was only at a late stage of the discussion that Jeremy raised the subject of electoral reform, which he 'recognised ... was of less immediate priority than the economic situation and dealing with inflation'. Armstrong's memorandum shows that Heath did most of the talking, Jeremy making it clear that he was there to listen but could express no views as Liberal Leader, still less enter into any commitments, until he had consulted colleagues. Jeremy's interventions were mostly to ask how far the Conservatives might be willing to modify their programme in order to accommodate the Liberals; he also wanted know the Conservatives' attitude towards their former Unionist allies (who had repudiated the government's 'Sunningdale Agreement' for a devolved power-sharing administration in Northern Ireland). Finally, they agreed on a press statement to be released by Downing Street: this merely confirmed that they had 'exchanged views about the current situation and the urgent need for an administration which can carry on the business of government', and would now consult with colleagues 'to see whether a basis exists for further discussions'.[13]

Soon after Jeremy's departure Heath reported on the talks to a group of senior colleagues.* He told them (as Armstrong recorded) that

> Mr Thorpe was evidently being held on a very tight rein, and unable to enter into any kind of commitment without consulting his colleagues. After about twenty minutes, when the Prime Minister had completed his opening analysis and invited Mr Thorpe to consider the possibility of an arrangement, Mr Thorpe had thanked him, made it clear that he could say nothing at that stage, had undertaken to consult his colleagues, and had made as if to go. The Prime Minister had felt that the interview should not be cut so short, and had therefore gone over some of the ground in more detail. Mr Thorpe had made another attempt to leave about 4.45 PM, and this too had been frustrated.[14]

---

* These were the Foreign Secretary, Home; the Lord Chancellor, Hailsham; the Chancellor of the Exchequer, Barber; the Northern Ireland Secretary, Pym; the Home Secretary, Carr; the Lord President, Prior; the Employment Secretary, Whitelaw; the Energy Secretary, Carrington; and the Chief Whip, Atkins.

This can be interpreted as indicating either Jeremy's scrupulousness, merely wishing to receive Heath's proposal without entering into further discussions, or his lightweightness – having discovered in general terms what deals were on offer, he did not want to go too deeply into discussions about policy.

Jeremy seems to have harboured more than a glimmer of hope, that Saturday, that he could 'pull off' a coalition. Throughout the day, he received encouraging messages from well-wishers on the Liberal right and Conservative left, as well as from such influential non-party figures as Rees-Mogg of *The Times*. Of the two main obstacles, neither can have appeared insuperable. The figures may not quite have added up: but the Conservatives and Liberals had between them won almost 60 per cent of the vote, and Labour would have brought down their coalition at its peril. (Nor would Labour have received much support from either the Ulster Unionists or the Scottish Nationalists, most of whom, as soundings indicated, were inclined towards keeping the Conservatives in office.) Grass-roots Liberals may have reacted with alarm to the prospect of a coalition: but many of them could have been won round by Jeremy, whose personal contribution to the huge Liberal vote was not in doubt, and who remained the darling of the faithful. All seemed to hang on how attractive Heath would make his offer to the Liberals. How much patronage would he allow Jeremy? (Jeremy certainly had high hopes on this front, telephoning several friends that evening to say he was bearing them in mind for 'a peerage and junior office'.)[15] And how far would he be willing to modify his programme to take account of Liberal wishes?

Meanwhile, Jeremy's thirteen fellow Liberal MPs, fresh from their election contests and all still in their constituencies, were amazed to hear on radio and TV that Jeremy had gone to London to see Heath, about which he had not informed or consulted any of them. They were still more amazed when it was announced, on the news that Jeremy had called a lunchtime meeting of

Liberal peers at Orme Square on Sunday, in advance of the full meeting of the Parliamentary Liberal Party which was to take place at Westminster on Monday morning. This was too much for most of the MPs: it seemed preposterous that the views of unelected peers should be sought before those of the fourteen newly elected members who, between them, spoke for 6 million Liberal voters. Having been made aware of these feelings, Jeremy speedily reorganised the Sunday meeting so as to include only the Liberal Leader in the Lords, Frank Byers, along with two senior MPs, Grimond and Steel.

Steel did not wait for Sunday. He had been 'confused and irritated' to hear on the radio, while touring his constituency to thank his supporters, that Jeremy had gone to Downing Street; he felt that, as Chief Whip and thus number two in the parliamentary hierarchy, he ought at least to have been informed; and he drove straight to London to see Jeremy, getting there late Saturday evening. He told Jeremy that 'the huge Liberal vote was largely a protest against [Heath's] incapacity to deal with the worsening industrial crisis' and that the Liberals could not risk 'propping up a defeated Prime Minister' unless they were offered 'a cast-iron commitment to change the electoral system'.[16] These expostulations had some effect, for by the time they were joined next day by Byers and Grimond, Jeremy's enthusiasm for the coalition project seems to have cooled. The four talked throughout Sunday afternoon. There was some discussion as to whether Jeremy should propose to Heath that he stand down as Prime Minister in favour of another Conservative, such as Whitelaw, with whom it would be easier for the Liberals to reach an accommodation. Byers supported Steel in his insistence that there could be no coalition in any case without electoral reform, while Grimond was in favour of Jeremy continuing coalition talks without preconditions, believing that the Liberals could ill-afford to pass their first chance in thirty years to participate in government. Rather to Grimond's surprise, Jeremy came down on the side of Steel and Byers. Grimond felt that he gave in too easily, and wondered how seriously he desired office: as he told his godson Magnus Linklater, 'he was ambitious to appear on the national stage but not to be a hard-working minister'. Finally they agreed on a compromise: that Jeremy should get in touch with Heath to find out how much he was willing to concede on electoral reform;* and that unless the response was satisfactory (which seemed unlikely), Jeremy should, at the meeting of the parliamentary party the following day, recommend not a coalition but rather the second of the three alternatives proposed by Heath on Saturday, whereby the Liberals might (as Jeremy later wrote to Heath) 'give consideration to offering support from the Opposition benches to a minority government on an agreed but limited programme'.[17]

At 5.40 PM Jeremy telephoned Heath, the conversation being tape-recorded by the Prime Minister's office. He came straight to the point, saying that, having consulted colleagues, he had encountered two problems in the way of continuing their discussions. 'The first is that there is a lack of enthusiasm for a proposition such as you suggested . . . in the light of your own position as PM, the feeling being that you called an election and failed to get the mandate that you sought. The second is that before there can be talk of an agreed package of economic proposals, [something must be done about] an electoral system [which produces] six million votes and fourteen MPs.' On the first matter, Jeremy did not consider the problem insuperable, 'I think I can handle my party on that issue', but on the second matter, 'I believe that I have to have something firm to put to them'. If Heath could come up with an acceptable set of proposals on electoral reform, to be implemented 'within six or nine months', the Liberals might agree to support him from the

---

* Steel in his memoirs says that Jeremy, at his insistence, went to see Heath on Saturday night for this purpose; but this is clearly an error.

Opposition benches with a view to entering a coalition once the proposals became law; but they felt that 'if they go into a coalition under the present system they are simply putting their heads under a chopper'. Could Heath consult his own colleagues regarding these matters so as to give Jeremy some indication of their views before he, Jeremy, met his parliamentary party the next morning? When Heath asked what sort of electoral reform proposals the Liberals had in mind, Jeremy suggested a formula once favoured by Winston Churchill – 'PR for the boroughs and the alternative vote for the rural areas'. 'But at the moment coalition is excluded?' asked Heath. Jeremy confirmed this was the case, adding, 'I personally hope we can work something out'.[18]

Following this conversation, Heath again consulted his senior colleagues, who 'made it clear that they were not interested in discussing any arrangement which involved a change in their own leadership'. Carrington said that 'the more he thought about it, the stronger was his view that nothing short of full Liberal participation in the government would constitute a satisfactory arrangement'. The others agreed: it might have been different had the Conservatives won more seats than Labour, but under the circumstances 'any arrangement short of full participation ... would not be a basis for an administration which could command sufficient support in parliament to enjoy the necessary degree of domestic and external confidence'. Most of those present still thought a Conservative–Liberal Government, stressful though it would be, preferable to a Labour Government, but all agreed that the Prime Minister should now tell Jeremy that any arrangement between the two parties would have to include 'full participation'. On electoral reform, the unanimous view was that 'the Cabinet could not go beyond a commitment to support the setting up of a Speaker's Conference to examine the matter and make recommendations which could then be the subject of a free vote in parliament'.[19]

Jeremy was then contacted and asked to call again at 10 Downing Street. This meeting, which began at 10.30 PM and lasted half an hour, received none of the publicity which the earlier one had attracted, Jeremy (who had been driven there by Steel) entering and leaving unobserved by a side entrance. (It was now raining, so there were no crowds.) Heath explained the views of his colleagues: that they were not willing to serve under another leader; that they had revised their view and now felt it had to be a coalition or nothing; and that on electoral reform they could offer no more than a Speaker's Conference followed by a free vote. Jeremy replied that he 'had to have in mind the need ... to keep his party together' and regretted that he saw 'no possibility of the Liberal Party agreeing to participate in government at this stage'. Regarding electoral reform, he understood that it was not currently possible to commit Parliament or even the Conservative Party to a particular policy, but 'if there were to be any prospect of an arrangement between the two parties, it would be necessary for the Prime Minister and his colleagues to give more indication that they had so far given that they recognised the injustice of the present system'. Heath asked what form of 'arrangement' the Liberals had in mind; Jeremy suggested that, if they could reach agreement on the contents of the Queen's Speech, the Liberals would undertake to support this until the next Queen's Speech. Jeremy added that, since his telephone conversation with Heath, he had been invited to see Harold Wilson the following morning, when he would hear what proposals the Labour leader might have to offer the Liberals: it was true that Wilson had declared he would do no deals with anyone, but that 'was before he realised that the government might wish to examine the possibility of a coalition with the Liberal Party'. Heath promised to put Jeremy's ideas to a meeting of the Cabinet due to take place the following morning at 10 AM, with a view to their reaching a decision which might be communicated by Jeremy to the meeting of the Parliamentary Liberal Party, due to begin at 11 AM.[20]

That Wilson, before Heath's resignation had become certain, asked to see Jeremy is a fact which was not generally known until Armstrong's record of the Heath–Thorpe meetings became public in 2005. What was Wilson's position that weekend? That he had won more seats than Heath had come to him as a considerable surprise; and he wisely decided that his best policy was to sit tight, accusing the Conservatives of 'clinging to power' while announcing that Labour would not enter into any pacts with other parties. Though the outcome of the election had been inconclusive, it seemed likely that Heath would have to resign after a few days, obliging the Queen to send for Wilson. How, then, did Wilson regard the Heath–Thorpe talks? We have two indications, both from senior aides who were constantly in touch with him during those days. His senior policy adviser Bernard Donoughue took a call from John Pardoe (they were friends and neighbours in Hampstead), suggesting that the talks (to which Pardoe himself was adamantly opposed) should be taken seriously as Jeremy was intent on 'getting his knees under the top table'.[21] And according to his press secretary Joe Haines, Wilson, on hearing that Jeremy was meeting Heath, said: 'If Thorpe joins the Cabinet and keeps the Tories in office, then we will tell the Norman Scott story.'* (It will be remembered that Wilson had become aware of that story after Labour ministers had been approached on Jeremy's behalf by Bessell during the 1960s – George Thomas at the Home Office, David Ennals at Social Security.) Wilson added that it would be ironical if Jeremy became Home Secretary and thus in charge of his own file; and that, even if Wilson himself (who, as we have seen, personally liked Jeremy) was unwilling to drag up Jeremy's murky past to prevent him supporting Heath, there were other senior Labour

---

* Wilson allegedly made these remarks at his Lord North Street house to a group of intimates that included Donoughue, the journalist Terry Lancaster, the ex-MP Albert Murray, and Haines himself.

politicians, notably the party's deputy leader Ted Short, who were in the know and would not hesitate to do so.[22] Haines is regarded by some as an unreliable witness, but credence is given to his account by the fact that one of Wilson's first acts on resuming the premiership the following week was to call for a summary of Scott's National Insurance card saga from government sources. (This was compiled by Jack Straw in his capacity as Barbara Castle's policy adviser at the Department of Health and Social Services; when it emerged in 2002 that Straw, by then Home Secretary, had drawn up this document, he protested that he had had no idea at the time that it was intended for possible use against Jeremy Thorpe.) Whether Wilson actually carried out his threat of blackmail, or merely kept it in reserve, will probably never be known. It is possible that, even before going to see Wilson, Jeremy had received a warning that any attempt by him to join Heath's Government would lead to certain disclosures; this might explain why, to Grimond's surprise, he had offered so little resistance to the Steel–Byers view that there could be no coalition without PR. Whether he received such a warning from Wilson when he saw him we do not know; all that is certain is that Wilson, true to his word, offered the Liberals no deals.

By Monday, the drama was effectively over, though this was not yet known to the public, which remained on tenterhooks as to whether Jeremy and Heath would strike a bargain. At 10 AM (while Jeremy was seeing Wilson), the Cabinet met at Downing Street. They endorsed the conclusions Heath had reached with senior colleagues (and then put to Jeremy) the night before, and discussed the draft of a letter to be sent to Jeremy embodying these conclusions. Discussion was prolonged by the fact that some ministers insisted that the letter, while offering a Speaker's Conference, be redrafted so as to avoid any suggestion that the government favoured electoral reform. Thus the letter was only delivered to Jeremy at the House of Commons when the meeting of the Parliamentary

Liberal Party was well underway. The mood of this gathering was stormy. Most of the MPs were furious at having been ignored over the weekend; in revenge for Jeremy's earlier attempt to summon the Liberal peers, they excluded the latter (who normally attended PLP meetings) except for Byers, who was only admitted on condition that he should not have a vote. Heath's letter was read out, confirming that all that was now on offer was a coalition, along with a Speaker's Conference 'to consider the desirability and possibility of a change in our election arrangements'. Grimond spoke in favour of a coalition; Cyril Smith said he might be in favour were it possible to obtain more on PR; but all the other MPs declared themselves firmly opposed to a coalition with Heath under existing circumstances. Jeremy sided with the majority and urged rejection of Heath's offer, while arguing that the Liberals had to be seen to be putting putting forward some constructive proposals of their own. After some discussion, they agreed that he should send a formal reply to Heath declining his invitation but adding that

> we believe that the only way in which the maximum degree of national co-operation can be achieved is for a government of national unity to be formed to include members of all Parties to carry out a limited programme on those matters of overriding priority ... [I]n the present economic emergency, I think that sufficient common ground and good will could be found between all Parties to sustain a national government ...[23]

This sounded patriotic; and it was possible to visualise a situation in which *elements* of all three parties – 'One Nation' Conservatives, 'Jenkinsites' and traditional Liberals – combined in a new centrist grouping. (Indeed, Jeremy had been discussing the prospects for such a combination with friends such as Taverne and Rees-Mogg for the past two years.) However, in the circumstances of the moment it was, as Hailsham wrote to

Heath, a 'ridiculous' proposal, given the ideological gulf between Conservative and Labour, and the fact that Wilson had already refused to enter into pacts. It also represented a fudge of the question the Liberals were being asked (and would continue to be asked) by many who had voted or considered voting for them: what, if any, were the circumstances in which they would be prepared to support a government in power?

At 4.30 that afternoon, Heath read Jeremy's letter to his last Cabinet, which agreed with him that that was an end to the matter. He then went to the Palace to submit his resignation, which in the opinion of some colleagues he ought to have done three days earlier. As leader of the largest party in the new House of Commons, Wilson was invited by the Queen to form an administration. He agreed to head a minority government, confirmed that Labour would rule without seeking any arrangements with other parties, and declared that, if his opponents defeated him on a confidence motion or made it impossible for him to govern, he would ask for a dissolution. Having refused a deal with the Conservatives which would have left them with a modest share of influence and little on electoral reform, the Liberals found Labour in office offering them no influence and nothing on electoral reform. 'The Liberals have put Labour in power', noted Hailsham. 'In doing so they have done, I believe, damage to themselves. It remains to be seen whether the country and the Conservative Party will suffer too.'[24] There was bitter disappointment among 'liberal' Conservatives and 'conservative' Liberals, many of whom would later attribute the rise of Mrs Thatcher to the failure of Jeremy and Heath to strike a deal.[25]

If Jeremy hoped that the fourteen Liberal MPs would be able to put the minority Labour Government under pressure, he was quickly disillusioned; for the Conservatives, fearing the electorate would not readily forgive them if they forced another General Election so soon after calling the last, decided to give Wilson an easy ride. This was demonstrated during the debate on the Queen's Speech, when the Conservatives suddenly withdrew an amendment which risked bringing down the Government, to the anger of the Liberals who had offered to support it. During May, after further Conservative failures to oppose Wilson, the Liberal MPs expressed their contempt by invading the Opposition front bench, from which the gargantuan Cyril Smith refused to budge – a gesture of protest which gave Jeremy and his colleagues a rare opportunity for a good laugh together. Secure in the knowledge that he was unlikely in the short term to suffer a major defeat, Wilson bought off the miners and went on to bribe the electorate with other populist measures, always intending to go to the country during the autumn before the cost of these had made itself felt.

Meanwhile, Jeremy's public prestige stood higher than ever, after he had appeared to sacrifice the prospect of office for the greater good of his party and country. Some disillusioned Conservatives who had voted Liberal may have been disappointed that he had not struck a deal with Heath, but this was not reflected in the opinion poll figures. The Liberals (though there were no by-elections to put this to the test) seemed to continue to enjoy much the same level of support as they had received at the general election, while Jeremy's approval rating as a party leader* was higher than that of either of the others – Gallup at the end of March put it at 73 per cent compared with 64 per cent for Wilson and 45 per cent for Heath. Both he and Marion spoke to friends as if it was only a matter of time before he achieved the office which had eluded him. The fact that the *Sunday Times Magazine* devoted the whole of its post-election issue to Sue Barnes' profile of him, a brilliant essay which touched on many of the complexities of his personality, was indicative of his stature as a national figure.

---

* In response to the question: 'Do you think Jeremy Thorpe is a good Leader of the Liberal Party?'

He continued to play the role of statesman on the international stage, now with the authority of one who had come within sight of power. In April he was the star of a conference of Liberal leaders in Ottawa, hosted by the Canadian premier Pierre Trudeau. When the Cyprus crisis erupted in July, followed by the fall of the Greek Colonels, he showed an impressive grasp of the issues involved, arguing that the Turkish invaders of Cyprus needed to be restrained and everything done to support the new Greek democracy. (It was around this time that he befriended the exiled King Constantine in London, whom he encouraged in his hopes of restoration.) When Nixon resigned in August over the Watergate affair, Jeremy paid tribute to the disgraced President, declaring that 'the event must not blind us to his great successes in foreign affairs'.

The spring and early summer of 1974 were, however, an uneasy time for Jeremy: he often seemed in a state of nervous exhaustion, as if drained by recent events. Whether as a cause or a consequence of this mood, he became more obsessed than ever by Norman Scott, whom he now saw as an obstacle prejudicing his future prospects of office. Despite assurances made on his behalf by Dr Gleadle that he would cause no more trouble, Scott continued remorselessly in North Devon with his campaign to discredit Jeremy. Flushed with the £2,500 paid by Holmes for the Bessell letters, he bought a car and began to frequent the centre of Barnstaple, where he became a well-known figure, standing drinks in pubs and spreading his story. Jeremy received a constant stream of letters from constituents who had met Scott and heard his tale, which (in the words of Holmes) 'were well meant but reinforced his feelings of permanent persecution'. It was little comfort to him that few seemed to take Scott seriously and that his antics had had no apparent effect on Jeremy's triumphant election result. Holmes later recalled that Jeremy rang him at least twice a week about Scott in the months following the election, often in despair, and eventually reverting to his old line that Scott had to be silenced once and for all.[26]

Jeremy was still on terms of friendship with Jack Hayward, whom he had persuaded that he had been an unwitting accomplice (if not a fellow victim) in Bessell's attempt to deceive the tycoon the previous December;* and Hayward had generously agreed to contribute £50,000 to the Liberal coffers at the general election. On 10 April 1974, Jeremy wrote to Hayward of the 'fantastic' Liberal election result, which was but a foretaste of things to come, and which owed much to Hayward's generosity, which had paid both for the Party's national publicity campaign and the closed circuit television link. He asked if Hayward might now pay the promised £50,000 in the form of two cheques – one for £40,000 to the Liberal General Election Fund, another for £10,000 to Nadir Dinshaw, a Parsee businessman resident in the Channel Islands whom Jeremy had befriended with Caroline in the late 1960s and appointed a godfather to Rupert. To both Hayward and Dinshaw, he confidentially explained that the £10,000 was needed to settle some 'irregular' election expenses which could not appear in the accounts. At the end of May, Hayward duly sent £10,000 to Dinshaw who, acting on Jeremy's instructions, sent a cheque for that sum to Holmes, who used it to pay off a bank overdraft. Holmes later claimed that he had in fact only 'kept' £2,500 of this money, by way of reimbursement for the cheque he had given Gleadle, using the remaining £7,500 to 'defray Jeremy's fringe election expenses'[27]. At the trial five years later of Jeremy and Holmes, the prosecution would insinuate that Holmes had in fact kept the whole of the money on the understanding that he would organise the murder of Scott – though it was to be many months before he took any steps in that direction.

Apart from his obsession with Scott, and the tensions of the political situation, there were other factors which contributed to

---

* As Jeremy wrote to Hayward the following November, 'frankly we were both taken for a ride. . . The whole thing has sickened me and could have undermined our friendship. It is a great blessing to me that it has not.'

Jeremy's state of strain that spring. On 16 May, his sister Camilla, aged forty-eight, was found dead at her house in Chester Square after taking an overdose of barbiturates. There was a dark history of self-destruction on the Norton-Griffiths side of the family, of which Empire Jack's suicide had been but the most spectacular manifestation; and Camilla (who suffered from epilepsy) was considered to have inherited her grandfather's wild temper and manic depressive tendencies to a strong degree. Jeremy had been close to her in childhood, especially when they had gone to America together in 1940; and she had regarded him with a mixture of hero-worshipping admiration and resentment that he was Ursula's spoiled and favoured child. Interviewed by Susan Barnes in 1973, she burst out: 'My life has been ruined by him, but I'm also proud of him. He was his mother's boy until he was forty: she ate him up.'[28] The marriage in 1955 of the basically lesbian Camilla and her much older millionaire admirer Enrique Ellinger had been unusual but happy, blessed by a son and a daughter: it was only after his death in 1969 that she had started to become seriously depressed. Her end was both a trauma and an embarrassment for Jeremy, who had to identify the body, and was followed within a fortnight by another sadness in the family – the death of his adored and adoring grandmother, Gwladys, Lady Norton-Griffiths, at the age of 101.

Since the election, Heath had been making speeches criticising the Liberals for having refused his coalition offer and implying that this still stood. The opinion polls also suggested that the electorate favoured some form of centrist coalition. On 24 June, both Jeremy and David Steel, the latter in a party political broadcast, the former in a television interview, announced that the Liberals wanted to see the Labour Government replaced by a coalition offering 'fair government based on partnership': they made clear their continued preference for a 'national' coalition but did not rule out the possibility that the Liberals might be willing to form an alliance with one or other of the main parties. This led to an outcry from the party radicals, who believed that Jeremy was about to 'sell out to Heath' as he had already tried to do in March. (Wilson continued to state that he would make no deals with anyone.) On 29 June, the Party Executive, always a thorn in the side of Jeremy's leadership, passed a resolution opposing an alliance with either of the other parties and criticising Jeremy and other Liberal MPs for ever having countenanced such a thing. Anxious to preserve party unity, Jeremy publically rejected Heath's latest offer and reaffirmed that the Liberals sought a national government, while saying nothing about other coalition possibilities. Steel, however, argued that the Liberals could hardly expect to form a government on their own and that, if they were politically serious, they would have to consider some kind of coalition arrangement sooner or later.

On 9 July, while the coalition argument was raging, the Party received an unexpected fillip when Christopher Mayhew, Labour MP for Woolwich East and a former navy minister, decided to join the Liberals. In his memoirs, Mayhew describes this as an impulsive step inspired by a combination of exasperation with Labour's leftward trend and personal liking for Jeremy: their fathers had been friends.[29] Jeremy reacted with delight: it was difficult to recall when a sitting MP, let alone a former minister, had last gone over to the Liberals. (It did not worry him that Mayhew was perceived as hostile to Israel of which Jeremy was always a conspicuous supporter, though some Jewish Liberals were unhappy about the new convert.) As always, he made the most of the moment, producing Mayhew at a press conference at which he described him as 'John the Baptist, the prophet and forerunner of great events': by a happy chance, an opinion poll that day gave the Liberals 22 per cent, their highest rating since the election. (That month, Jeremy's personal rating stood around 60 per cent compared with Wilson's in the 40s and Heath's in the 30s.) Although, to Mayhew's disappointment, none of his former colleagues on the Labour right followed him into the Liberal ranks,* his defection increased the pressure on Dick Taverne to abandon his independent status and join the Liberals: Taverne was personally favourable but explained that he would need time to prepare his supporters, mostly former Labour voters. Unfortunately the news leaked out prematurely and Taverne, faced with a constituency row, was forced to deny that he intended to apply for the Liberal whip.

With Wilson expected to go to the country in October, Jeremy now hit upon a campaigning idea which, for its novelty, its flamboyance, its lack of substance and the sheer bad luck that dogged it, would come to be regarded by many as symbolic of his leadership – a late summer tour of British holiday beaches by hovercraft. Though invented by the British scientist Cockerell in 1959, the hovercraft had only begun to be used commercially in the early 1970s and was still regarded by the public as a glamorous novelty. During the summer, Jeremy mentioned the idea in confidence to many people as a 'secret weapon' which Heath and Wilson would try to steal if they got hold of it, and planned the logistics of the operation down to the smallest detail. He announced the tour at a press conference at Bideford on 14 August, declaring in Churchillian tones that he would 'campaign on the beaches' and that it was fitting that the Liberals, 'so often the innovators of new thinking', should choose this novel mode of transport to take their message to the people. But what *was* the message? Typically, he had been so busy planning the spectacle that he had not even prepared a press handout for the journalists attending the conference, many of whom were disposed from the first to treat the whole enterprise as a joke.[30]

---

* Another Labour MP and ex-minister, John Stonehouse, contemplated joining the Liberals but did not finally do so – a fact which caused relief to Jeremy and his colleagues when, some months later, Stonehouse was involved in a bizarre attempt to escape charges of fraud by faking his own death.

The tour began on 28 August at Ilfracombe in Jeremy's constituency, the original passengers consisting of Jeremy, his wife Marion, his aides Wheeler and Richards, and his fellow West Country MPs Pardoe and Tyler, joined at the various ports of call by local Liberal candidates. For the first two days, all went splendidly. In superb weather, they hovered their way around the south-western peninsula, landing at Bude, Newquay, St Ives, Falmouth, Par, Looe, Plymouth, Kingsbridge and Torbay. The spectacle of their arrival was treated everywhere as a great local event, greeted by brass bands and witnessed by fascinated crowds of holidaymakers totalling almost one hundred thousand. After appearing to emerge Christ-like from the waves, Jeremy walked along the beaches in Edwardian seaside attire, glad-handing the crowds and addressing them through a megaphone. He may have begun the campaign with little thought of what to say, but his improvised speeches became ever more inspired: even Pardoe, who had originally disapproved of the whole plan as vacuous, was reminded of Nye Bevan and Robert Kennedy. At Plymouth, thousands thronged the harbour to hear his words. At Kingsbridge, where the party travelled up the River Dart in an old paddle steamer in glorious late afternoon sunshine, followed by a flotilla of sailing boats, he gave another memorable speech to a rapt crowd on the quayside.

Then, on the third day, the weather changed and disaster struck. The party had just disembarked at Sidmouth when a freak wave pounded the hovercraft, smashing the windows and disabling the engine: the captain and his wife were stranded aboard the impotent vessel, which had to be dragged onto the beach with ropes. Jeremy issued a statement to say that his faith in British technology remained unshaken: but the newspapers were unable to resist writing that his 'hot air crusade' had foundered as soon as the going got rough. Once the craft had been patched up, the party tried to resume the tour along the Isle of Wight and Sussex coasts, but were again frustrated by stormy weather and engine trouble, as a result of which they were unable to land on schedule and missed a series of advertised meetings. The final leg of the hovertour, on the north-west coast, also proved a disaster and had to be abandoned after a final breakdown, said to have been provoked by Cyril Smith clambering aboard at Southport with his enormous bulk.

Following this diversion, he had only a weekend to prepare for the Liberal Assembly at Brighton on 11 September. This was inevitably dominated by the question of how far the Liberals were prepared to enter into arrangements with other parties in the event of the forthcoming General Election producing another inconclusive result. (The election was correctly expected to take place on 10 October, though not announced until 18 September.) As always, the radicals were opposed to a coalition with anyone: Ruth Addison of the Young Liberals denounced Jeremy as 'a traitor to the Party' who put 'personal power before Liberal aims and ideals' in his quest for 'unsavoury political alliances'. In his opening speech, Jeremy begged to be allowed a free hand after the election. As a sop to his critics, he confirmed that the Liberal aim was to achieve their own majority, or failing that, a 'national' government; he also promised to consult the Party Council before engaging in negotiations; but he wanted to be able, after the election, to listen to 'any proposition from any party leader'. He was supported by Mayhew, and opposed by the radical standard-bearer Trevor Jones. When the matter came to a vote, he won by a resounding majority of six to one. But although his formula had succeeded in keeping the Party united, it mystified the electorate, who still had little idea of how the Liberals proposed to behave in the event of their holding the balance in another hung parliament.[31]

The following week, the election campaign began. The opinion polls showed a substantial Labour lead but put the Liberals at around 20 per cent – twice their starting level of February. The Party's hopes were high: they managed to contest every seat in

England and Wales with the exception of Lincoln, a considerable feat of organisation. As before, Jeremy based himself in Barnstaple; but after the five-figure majority he had received there in February, he felt free to tour around the country with his entourage and press followers: this he did in characteristic style in a fleet of helicopters, dubbed 'Jeremy's Flying Circus'. Although his appearances before large audiences were always effective, he somehow failed to make the national impact which, speaking from the aloofness of his leather-bound study, he had made in February. He showed hubris, predicting that the Liberals would gain 28 per cent of the vote and 150 seats. As the campaign progressed, the predicted Liberal share of the vote declined; but so did the Labour lead, making another hung parliament seem possible. The polls continued to show that Jeremy remained the nation's favourite party leader, while the press agreed that he fought the best campaign. As the election date approached, he tantalised the press with the news that he would soon be announcing another Labour convert to the Liberals, this time a peer. There was intense speculation as to the identity of the defector, generally thought to be Lord Chalfont, a former defence journalist and Foreign Office minister. Finally, Jeremy produced the 2nd Viscount St Davids, heir on his mother's side to a barony dating from 1299, an eccentric Old Etonian who had no obvious interest in politics, lived on a houseboat and devoted himself to organising aquatic activities for boys.

The 9th of October marked the fifteenth anniversary of Jeremy's original election as MP for North Devon, and he combined his eve-of-poll meeting with a celebration of this event, claiming to be the longest continuously serving member in the six-hundred-year history of the division. He was confident of winning an easy victory over his new Conservative opponent, the local businessman and county councillor Tony Speller (Keigwin having retired from politics in disgust after Heath had invited Jeremy to join the Cabinet). At his final press conference,

Jeremy warned that the country had to break the two-party system or 'sink back into the old ways of confrontation'.

The outcome represented a setback both for Jeremy in North Devon and the Liberals in the country. His local result (with February figures in brackets) was as follows:

Thorpe, John Jeremy (Liberal):	28,209	(34,052)
Speller, A. (Conservative):	21,488	(22,980)
Golant, Mrs A. J. (Labour):	8,356	(6,140)
Miller, H. F. (Nationalist):	568	

At 6,765, his majority still looked safe; but it had fallen by more than 4,000 and his personal vote by almost 6,000, many who had voted for him in February having for some reason (perhaps in some cases the reason he feared most) decided not to vote at all. In the country, the result was similarly disappointing. Despite contesting 102 more seats, the Liberals polled some 700,000 fewer votes, taking 18.3 per cent of the national total as compared with February's 19.3 per cent. Two seats won earlier in the year, Bodmin and Hazel Grove, reverted to the Conservatives. Taverne lost Lincoln. Mayhew failed to capture Bath. The only Liberal gain was Truro, where the dynamic Cornishman David Penhaligon defeated the sitting Conservative, Jeremy's Eton schoolfriend Piers Dixon. With thirteen MPs, the Liberals had the same strength in the House of Commons as five year earlier. However, the overall outcome of the election was a Labour majority of just three, making it likely that Wilson (or his successor) would try to seek support from among the thirteen Liberals, the fourteen Scottish and Welsh Nationalists and the twelve Northern Ireland MPs at some point during the coming parliament.

Only three years earlier, the prospect of winning over 18 per cent of the vote, and more than a dozen seats in a Parliament where the governing party might soon fall into a minority, would have seemed an impossible dream. And given the Liberals' disarray over the coalition question, it was a tribute to Jeremy that they had nevertheless secured their second highest ever total of 5,346,800 votes. Yet for Jeremy as for most Liberals, the sense of disappointment was overwhelming. As a Liberal historian has written, 'the promised land had again turned out to be a shifting mirage'.[32] 1974 had been the turning point when the Liberal Party had failed to turn: his great moment had come and gone. To Ted Wheeler, the old stalwart who ran the Liberal Party Organisation, he remarked that, unless they made 'some really spectacular progress soon', he felt his days were numbered as Leader.[33] The shadows were closing in; and as they did so, he brooded on his problem.

19

CONSPIRACY
1974–75

THOUGH BUT FORTY-FIVE years of age, and for long a well-established national figure, Jeremy Thorpe now found himself in a weaker position as Liberal Leader than at any time since the failed coup against him of June 1968. Many in the Party held him responsible for the disappointing Liberal performance at the October election, feeling that he had mishandled the situation in March 1974 and wasted the ensuing months. There was disapproval of his hovercraft and helicopter tours, ill-affordable extravagances which had made the Liberals look frivolous. His radical critics had held their fire so as not to prejudice the Party's electoral chances: now they felt free to resume hostilities against him. Nor did he have much support among his fellow MPs. His deputy, David Steel, had been demoralised by Jeremy's failure to give a lead on the coalition question, and asked to be relieved of his duties as Chief Whip as soon as a successor could be appointed.[1] Other MPs, notably Pardoe and Wainwright, had still not forgiven him for failing to consult them before going off to talk to Heath. At the first post-election meeting of the PLP, he caused irritation by presenting three earls he had persuaded to take the

Liberal whip in the House of Lords – Denbigh, Grey and Kimberley – before welcoming David Penhaligon, the Party's only new MP. During the first months of the new Parliament he aroused further annoyance – at a time when it was thought he should be concentrating on domestic politics and the problems of the Liberal Party – by going off to Rhodesia in a futile effort to persuade Ian Smith to end his 'rebellion', and attending such foreign junkets as the 'coronation' of the Shah of Iran.

Meanwhile, in the Conservative Party, there was much dissatisfaction with Heath, who was manifestly unpopular in the country and had now lost three elections out of four. Heath declined to step down, but a leadership election took place in February 1975 at which he was comfortably defeated by the strident (though still relatively unknown) Margaret Thatcher. Among the Liberals, there were many mutterings that they too could do with a new face: no machinery yet existed for replacing the leader but the creation of such machinery was certain to be high on the agenda at the September Assembly. Mrs Thatcher (whose victory, in the view of many of her Conservative opponents, might have been avoided had Jeremy struck a deal with Heath) quickly made it clear that she wanted no truck with either the Liberals or electoral reform, and had no intention of renewing her predecessor's coalition offer. She and Jeremy developed a sparring relationship.* (She once snapped at him: 'Why do you always wear that silly hat?' He replied: 'It's my trademark, like Chamberlain's umbrella or Churchill's cigar. And don't forget that, although we were called to the Bar on the same day and elected to Parliament on the same day, I beat you

---

* On 5 March 1975, Jeremy wrote to Jack Hayward: 'Margaret Thatcher is far more amenable than Heath. I could do business with her.' These words did not represent reality and Jeremy probably used them merely by way of attempting to persuade Hayward, to whom he was appealing for further funds, that his political prospects were improving.

to the Privy Council by three years and to party leadership by eight years.'[2])

Thatcher's arrival with her clear-cut policies gave a fillip to the Conservatives, who were set to benefit from the unpopularity of the Labour Government. (And this was not long in coming, for the year following the October election was one of unrelieved economic gloom, marked by rapidly rising inflation and unemployment.) This meant a decline in Liberal fortunes, as disillusioned Conservatives who had voted Liberal in 1974 returned to the fold. Jeremy's popularity suffered too, as he was perceived to have failed to take advantage of his opportunities in 1974. During most of 1974, Liberal support in the opinion polls had stood at around 20 per cent and Jeremy's personal rating well above 50 per cent; but in 1975, the Liberals generally polled only between 10 per cent and 15 per cent and Jeremy himself around 40 per cent, some points below both Wilson and Thatcher. This gave further ammunition to his critics, who argued that, as he had already been in the job for eight years, and his three predecessors had served for about a decade each, he ought to think of retiring before the next General Election.

Jeremy was also blamed, after the extravagances of 1974, for a chronic financial crisis in the Liberal Party, as a result of which its headquarters staff was cut from thirty-six to twenty-four. However, the situation was saved by the fact that two fundraising strategies on which Jeremy had embarked years earlier were at last bearing fruit. First, he had long been pressing for the public funding of the parliamentary activities of opposition parties; and in March 1975, this was finally agreed to by Wilson, the new arrangements being formulated by the Leader of the House, Ted Short. The annual funds earmarked for the Liberals were set at £33,250, making possible the engagement of new parliamentary staff to offset the shedding of headquarters staff. Secondly, ever since becoming Leader, Jeremy had been trying (despite protests from radicals) to win support from big business; and soon after the October election, he finally seemed to be achieving important results in this direction, thanks to an ingenious strategy. He had gone to see leading figures in the City, well-known Conservative backers, to point out that just 39 per cent of the vote had given an absolute majority to a Labour Government which was unfavourable to business, and that the private sector would do far better under a PR system which would guarantee a long period of centrist government. This argument impressed a number of tycoons, some of whom – including such big names as Sieff of Marks & Spencer, Stokes of British Leyland and Weinstock of GEC – contributed to the Liberal coffers and let it be known in Conservative circles that they now looked favourably on electoral reform.

As Jeremy struggled to maintain his position in the face of mounting criticism, his entourage was changing. David Steel was eventually replaced as Chief Whip by Cyril Smith, but Jeremy had stormy relations with the bombastic Smith and would not confirm his appointment until June 1975.[3] Richard Moore, the whiggish old friend who had served him as political secretary and speechwriter since the outset of his leadership, left to take up a job in the European Parliament, to be replaced by the youthful Tony Richards, who had been Jeremy's personal assistant during the 1974 elections and accompanied him to see Heath. His excellent press adviser Stephen Bonarjee also accepted a job elsewhere, believing that Jeremy was riding for a fall. The genial Ted Wheeler, another old Jeremy loyalist but regarded by some as ineffective, was gradually phased out as Head of the Liberal Party Organisation, though no successor was appointed until the autumn of 1976. A happier development was the election of the Yorkshireman Stephen Atack as Chairman of the Young Liberals in April 1975 in succession to Ruth Addison. Although Atack began office with a ritual denunciation of Jeremy, saying that he should 'get cracking or start packing', the two men soon became close friends. Like Jeremy, Atack was a charismatic showman with a talent for intrigue and a fondness for whisky; as one of the first openly gay politicians, he also had some understanding of the problems under which Jeremy laboured as a clandestine homosexual.

Despite Wilson's apparent willingness to exercise political blackmail against Jeremy in March 1974, and his becoming increasingly vague and reclusive during the two years of his second premiership, Jeremy resumed something of the cordial relationship which he had enjoyed with the Labour premier during the 1960s. He also took care as always to cultivate Wilson's political secretary Marcia Williams, now raised to the peerage as Baroness Falkender, who was rumoured to exercise complete dominance over the Prime Minister and to be responsible for many of his decisions. The benevolence of Wilson and Falkender towards him would become particularly apparent during the early months of 1976; but it manifested itself earlier in such matters as the decision on the public funding of opposition parties, and the allocation of life peerages. In the whole of his term, Heath had allowed Jeremy only two of the latter; but during 1974–75, Wilson let him have five.* In Parliament, however, Jeremy did not give the Labour Government an easy ride. He denounced the Social Contract, the informal agreement between the Government and TUC for voluntary pay restraint, as 'a charade', and Tony Benn's nationalisation of the shipyards as 'crazy'. He attacked the Government's proposal to grant the National Union of Journalists a 'closed shop' as a sinister development which would effectively give the Union a power of censorship over the press.

---

* These were awarded to two ex-MPs, George Mackie and Michael Winstanley; two former Party Presidents, Desmond Banks and Stina Robson; and a former Chairman of the Party Executive (and sometime President of the Oxford Union), Basil Wigoder QC. Three of the five – Mackie, Robson and Wigoder – were wealthy individuals who had contributed handsomely to party funds.

His greatest concern during the months following the October election, however, was with Europe. In opposition, Labour had opposed British entry into the EEC on the terms negotiated by the Conservatives; back in power, Wilson announced that his Government would 'renegotiate' these terms and put the results before the British public in a Referendum. Time and again, Jeremy lambasted Wilson for hypocrisy and dismissed the 'renegotiation' (which consisted of a few minor adjustments) as a farce. He also opposed the Referendum as contrary to Britain's political traditions and a waste of taxpayers' money. However, once the Referendum Bill had been passed, he announced that he would campaign heart and soul for a 'yes' vote and retire from politics unless this was achieved. As he declared in the House at the outset of the campaign:

> This country has been in retreat since the war – retreat from overseas possessions, overseas commitments and many of the responsibilities it accepted abroad. There are some who would wish to go further and turn this island into one with a siege economy. The time has come to end that retreat, to reverse it, to advance into Europe.[4]

The Referendum was fixed for 5 June 1975. Jeremy was one of the 'big three' campaigners on the 'yes' side, along with Heath and Jenkins. For two months, he threw himself into addressing meetings up and down the country, speaking eloquently without notes and usually sharing a platform with leading politicians from the other parties. At times, it almost seemed as if the 'government of national unity' for which he had called the previous year had come to pass. He was also able to forget the financial problems of the Liberal Party, for the 'yes' campaign was amply funded by contributions from industry, and private aeroplanes and lavish banquets were the order of the day. Two of his many appearances particularly impressed those who witnessed them.

He held a great rally in his constituency (which would turn out to be the last of his many jamborees there), addressed by Lord Hailsham, the trade union leader Vic Feather and the former Labour Foreign Secretary Lord George-Brown. And he took part in a televised debate at the Oxford Union, at which he and Heath spoke in favour of the EEC and two dissenting Cabinet ministers, Barbara Castle and Peter Shore, against it.* At one point he asked Mrs Castle whether, in the event of a 'yes' result, she would resign from the Government, to which she replied that 'my country would need me more than ever': at this, Jeremy assumed an ironical expression and traced a halo, whereupon the audience dissolved in laughter. It was a memorable moment for the watching millions.

At the end of the day, the Referendum produced a vote in favour of continued British membership of the EEC of more than two to one. Jeremy could claim that his personal campaigning had helped secure this unexpectedly good result for the 'yes' side: in the month preceding the vote, his own popularity rating in the opinion polls had risen from 39 per cent to 49 per cent. He did not know it, but it would be his last great moment as a politician on the national stage.

While fighting for his political survival, Jeremy continued to live in perpetual fear of Norman Scott. Friends in whom he confided, such as Clement Freud, urged him to try to forget that character; but he was constantly being reminded by events. In November 1974, builders doing conversion work at Peter Bessell's former office in Pall Mall discovered a briefcase concealed in a false ceiling containing (among other compromising

---

* Wilson had laid down a compromise whereby anti-EEC ministers were allowed to campaign for a 'no' vote in the country provided that, in Parliament, they refrained from opposing the Government's official recommendation that the 'renegotiated' terms be accepted.

material) a file of documents relating to the Scott affair, including the long, accusatory letter which Scott (then Josiffe) had sent Jeremy's mother in February 1965. The builders took this material to the *Sunday Mirror*. Both the editor of that newspaper, Bob Edwards, and the chairman of the company which owned it, Lord Jacobson, knew Jeremy personally and were already aware of the Scott story, which had been brought to them two years earlier by Gordon Winter. Now as then, they did not wish to make use of it; and they decided to return the documents to Jeremy (having first made copies for their legal manager's safe). Edwards visited the Liberal Leader at his Westminster office to hand over the file, Jeremy behaving as if the whole proceeding was the most natural thing in the world and offering Edwards a small whisky.[5] But while outwardly cool, inwardly he must have been appalled.

Meanwhile, Scott continued on the rampage in North Devon. His shrill denunciations of Jeremy in local pubs, and to such people of substance as he managed to meet, had reached such proportions that the head of Devon and Cornwall CID, DCS Proven Sharpe, felt obliged to report the matter to the security services in London, who were already well aware of it from other sources. In December 1974, Scott made a further attempt to stir things up when he instructed a local solicitor to try to 'recover' the Bessell letters which Dr Gleadle had sold on his behalf to Holmes ten months earlier. (Although Scott had benefited from this transaction to the tune of £2,500, he had now persuaded himself that his former GP had acted without his authority, and had also tried to poison him.) Scott's solicitor wrote to Jeremy's solicitor Michael Barnes, who replied that the letters in question had been destroyed – Jeremy once again being reminded that the threat posed by Scott was one which would not go away.[6]

By now, there had begun the chain of events which would lead to Jeremy's trial at the Old Bailey in 1979,[7] at which the principal allegation against him was that, at some point between the two elections of 1974, he had asked David Holmes to organise the murder of Scott, thus setting in motion a conspiracy. As has been seen, Jeremy had already talked of disposing of Scott to Bessell and Holmes (as confirmed by them both) as early as 1968–69, but Holmes and Bessell had concluded at the time that he was indulging in fantasy; they had humoured him, and he had eventually ceased to mention the matter. Since the early 1970s, when Bessell had moved to America and Scott to North Devon, Jeremy had relied on Holmes to 'handle' Scott. Unlike Bessell, Holmes never had any personal contact with Scott; and he seems to have been in two minds when it came to dealing with him. On the one hand, he agreed with Lord Goodman and others that the wisest course was to ignore Scott, and dismiss him as the 'nut' which most of those with whom he came into contact, in North Devon and elsewhere, believed him to be. On the other hand, he was strongly under Jeremy's influence, and felt he should at least be seen to be 'doing something' about Scott in order to satisfy Jeremy.* He was also under an obligation to Jeremy on account of the £10,000 from Hayward which Jeremy had arranged for him to receive in May 1974 and which he had used to pay off an overdraft. Interviewed in 1981, Holmes claimed that, from the summer of 1974 onwards,† Jeremy had indeed constantly urged him to have Scott murdered, but he insisted that he had never had any serious intention of killing Scott. The truth of the matter seems to be

---

* 'I always believed Jeremy should not react, and in the end we [sic] reacted not to Scott but to Jeremy because if you are going to have somebody totally panicked to the extent that he can't sleep, can't eat, can't work properly and because it's become an obsession to him in the way that Scott had become an obsession to Jeremy, then you have to try to do something.' (Holmes Transcripts.)

† For obvious reasons, Holmes places the moment at which the 'conspiracy' was launched after the Hayward payment, rather than (as would seem more likely) before it.

that Holmes did take steps which might have led to Scott's death, but that he did so in a decidedly dilatory and half-hearted (and ultimately bungling and ineffective) manner.

He seems to have done nothing until after the October 1974 election, when in the course of a visit to South Wales he met John Le Mesurier, a jovial carpet merchant with whom he had had business dealings for some years.* Holmes explained his problem to Le Mesurier, who responded sympathetically and suggested they might be able to hire someone to 'deal with' Scott through the intermediary of George Deakin, a prosperous Swansea gambling-machine manufacturer and nightclub owner in his thirties who lived (as Holmes later put it) 'on the fringes of a slightly rougher world': Holmes had already met him through Le Mesurier and given him some professional advice on overseas investment. Deakin was put in the picture by Holmes and Le Mesurier and agreed to 'see what he could do'. Neither Le Mesurier nor Deakin knew Jeremy Thorpe (or ever met him until the day in August 1978 when they were all arrested and charged); they knew nothing about Scott, or Jeremy's reasons for wishing to act against him, except what Holmes told them (which included some imaginative touches, such as that Scott had threatened to kidnap Rupert Thorpe, Holmes' godson); and in offering to help Holmes, they seem to have been motivated by nothing other than a desire to do a favour for a friend.

Holmes later claimed that, although asked by Jeremy to plan a murder, he had only ever envisaged giving Scott a fright, and that Le Mesurier and Deakin had offered to help him find someone to carry out 'a frightening job'. On the other hand, Le Mesurier, in

---

* According to private information from a source which the author believes to be reliable, Holmes also asked several muscular London rent boys with whom he was aquainted whether they would be willing to carry out a murder, but none of them wished to be involved in such a matter.

post-trial interviews, insisted that Holmes had made it clear that he was looking for a 'hit-man' to carry out a contract killing;* and the sum which (according to most of the parties involved) was mentioned, £10,000, would certainly suggest that something more than 'a frightening job' was contemplated. On the other hand, there may be an element of truth in Holmes' claim; for while idly planning the dastardly deed, he nevertheless seems to have hoped that it would still be possible to silence Scott by merely frightening him. During February 1975, Scott was robbed in Barnstaple of a briefcase containing copies of the Bessell letters by two men posing as foreign journalists; and a week later, he was beaten up as he emerged from a local pub. It later transpired that Holmes, assisted by Le Mesurier, was behind both these incidents (though he later denied that he himself had been one of the 'journalists').

However, if Holmes believed that Scott, having been deprived of his papers and given a fright, would cease to pester Jeremy, he had badly miscalculated; for the predictable effect of these incidents was that Scott became totally hysterical. At the North Devon Infirmary, where he was treated for his injuries, he denounced Jeremy to his fellow patients as well as to medical staff and social workers. He wrote to Gordon Winter in Johannesburg, requesting further copies of the Bessell letters and offering to write a book 'exposing' Jeremy. He made a special visit to London to tell his story to 'Up Against the Law', a radical legal advice group, which subsequently alluded to it in their newspaper. Finally, around Easter 1975, he drove up to the Thorpe cottage at Cobbaton, determined to confront Jeremy, whom (so far as is known) he had not seen for more than ten years. Rupert was playing in the garden, and the door was opened by Marion,

---

* Like Holmes, however, Le Mesurier claimed that, although he and Deakin were invited to take part in a murder plot, they never intended to be a party to murder, and were merely willing to 'put the frighteners' on Scott.

to whom he nervously introduced himself. She showed no surprise and merely remarked: 'I don't think he'll see you.'* Scott got back into his car and tried to drive off, but such was his state of panic that he found himself unable to reverse out of the drive and had to ask Marion to help him, which she did in grim silence. Since his marriage to Marion, Jeremy had been concerned to protect her from any unpleasantness arising out of his past; and this episode may have shocked him deeply, and caused him to renew his pressure on Holmes to take action against Scott.

By this time, Le Mesurier and Deakin had found someone who, they believed, would be able to 'take care' of Scott – Andrew 'Gino' Newton, a raffish airline pilot of twenty-eight who boasted to all and sundry that he was prepared to do anything for money. Neither Le Mesurier nor Deakin had previously met him, but Deakin knew of him by reputation, having heard about him from David Miller, a Cardiff printer. On 26 February 1975, at a drunken public dinner in Blackpool, Miller introduced Newton to Deakin, who asked him if he would like to undertake a job for which he would be well paid. Newton expressed interest and three days later spoke again to Deakin, who gave him Holmes' telephone number in Manchester and suggested he contact him directly. Newton rang Holmes to offer his services; and Holmes (as he later claimed) rang Jeremy to report that he believed he had at last found someone who might solve the problem of Scott.

There followed a coincidence which was to be crucial to the case against Jeremy. In October 1974, Jack Hayward had offered to make an unspecified contribution towards the Liberal election campaign; but he had subsequently had second thoughts when a £10,000 bank guarantee he had given Peter Bessell was called

---

* A year later, Jeremy told Dan Farson that, on reflection, he thought it would have been better if he had agreed to see Scott on this occasion. (Dan Farson, *Never a Normal Man* [London: HarperCollins, 1997].)

in. On 28 November, Jeremy wrote to him that he was 'horrified to hear of the extent to which that bastard Bessell landed you in the cart' and asking whether 'with incredible generosity' he might nevertheless contribute £17,000 to the Liberals, representing the sum still needed to pay off their election bills. This letter (which was full of flattery of Hayward and inside details of current politics) elicited no immediate response; and on 5 March 1975, he wrote again repeating his request for £17,000 and asking whether, as with Hayward's donation of May 1974, £10,000 of this might be sent to Nadir Dinshaw in the Channel Islands, 'since some expenditure could just conceivably be held by my opponents to be attributable to the North Devon campaign'. This second letter was written exactly a week after Deakin had met Newton and allegedly offered him £10,000 to take care of Scott, and just after Jeremy had allegedly heard from Holmes that someone had been found to do the job. At the same time, Jeremy telephoned Dinshaw to ask him if, as before, he would receive £10,000 from Hayward and transmit it to Holmes, this time in cash, to which Dinshaw reluctantly agreed (though he did not finally receive Hayward's cheque until November 1975, by which time he had already advanced most of the money to Holmes in the form of cash payments personally handed over on visits to England).

Whether because of the delay in getting hold of the money, or because Holmes was in no hurry to bring matters to fruition, or because Newton was only intermittently available in the intervals of his career as a pilot, there appear to have been no significant further developments in the affair for some months. Eventually, Holmes met Newton to clinch the deal and brief him, an encounter of which the two parties later produced different versions. According to Newton, they saw each other twice, at a London hotel and a Manchester railway station, Holmes confirming that Newton would be required to kill Scott, for which he would receive a fee of £10,000. According to Holmes, they only met once, at a pub near Bolton during the early summer of 1975, when he offered Newton £1,000 to 'frighten' Scott.* Holmes later described Newton as 'not exactly a typical tough but ... I felt sure he could deal with a hysterical type like Scott'. Holmes told him little about the motives underlying the operation, but gave him details of public houses in the Barnstaple area which Scott was known to frequent. After the meeting (as he later claimed), he telephoned Jeremy to report on how it had gone.

Yet further weeks passed without much occurring. Newton later made the astonishing claim that he had first gone looking for Scott in the Bedfordshire town of Dunstable rather than Barnstaple. Finally, in July or August, he discovered that Scott was living at Barnstaple's Market Inn, and telephoned him there, using an alias and claiming to represent an Italian fashion house which was eager to enlist Scott's modelling services. He invited Scott to discuss this matter at the Royal Garden Hotel in London (where, Newton later told the Old Bailey, he had planned to kill him with a poker concealed in a bunch of flowers, duly produced as an exhibit); but Scott was suspicious and did not keep the appointment. Soon afterwards, Newton rang again, using a different name and voice and this time asking Scott to a modelling session in Bristol; but again Scott failed to turn up. By the end of September, seven months had elapsed since Newton's recruitment to the plot and he had yet to catch sight of the intended victim. By this time, if one is to believe his evidence at the Old Bailey, he had also decided not to carry out the murder but merely to go through the motions.

Holmes later claimed that, in the course of numerous

---

* These divergent memories as to location are not as odd as they might at first seem. Holmes had three sets of contacts with Newton: in mid-1975, in connection with the 'contract'; between November 1975, when Newton was charged, and March 1976, when he was tried; and after his release from prison in April 1977. It is understandable that there may have been some confusion in their minds as to where they had met on particular occasions.

telephone conversations and personal meetings, he had kept Jeremy fully informed of such progress as there was. Jeremy, on the other hand, later maintained that he had been quite unaware of what Holmes had been up to, and that any 'incitement' had been unintentional and along the lines of King Henry II's remark about Thomas à Becket: 'Who will rid me of this turbulent priest?' (Though, as Auberon Waugh has written, 'Henry II did not send large sums of money to the four knights ... to reimburse them for any incidental expenses' in connection with Becket's murder.[8])

During the summer of 1975, Jeremy seems to have experienced some kind of breakdown, going to ground in North Devon and cancelling all his engagements for six weeks, Marion deputising for him. His mother told the press that this was due to the 'stress' of the Referendum campaign, but his now pathological anxiety about Scott, coupled (if one is to believe Holmes) with his impatience at Holmes' slow progress, may have played a part. He appeared, however, to have made a striking recovery by the time of the Liberal Assembly at Scarborough in September. This promised to be the most difficult of his leadership; but as usual, he rose to the challenge. His opening speech was a *tour de force* in which he lambasted the main parties and urged Liberals to dwell on the triumphs rather than the disappointments of the recent past. He announced a range of imaginative new policies, in particular calling for a tax to be levied on wage increases and used to create a fund for industrial development. Even the *Daily Telegraph*, not naturally sympathetic to the Liberals, described the speech as 'a magnificent parade of ideas' which 'other parties would do well to study' and 'should have convinced all but the most prejudiced that there is no comparable rival in sight for the party leadership'.[9] Calls for his resignation were easily put down; and pressure for a new system of electing the leader, including annual re-election, resulted only in the setting-up of a committee to examine this question, chaired by the academic Michael Steed.

Given the widespread criticism of his leadership earlier in the year, he had reasserted his hold over the Party in a remarkable manner. Even the normally hostile Radical Bulletin Group, which conducted a mock leadership election among its 177 members, found that Jeremy was their first-round favourite with fifty-two votes. The Liberals' opinion poll rating crept up to 16.5 per cent, their highest since the General Election, while Jeremy's personal rating returned to the 49 per cent he had achieved during the Referendum campaign. But soon after the Assembly,* those closest to him had the impression that he was relapsing into the state of anxiety which had gripped him over the summer. It was announced that, during the coming months, he would hold a series of rallies in different parts of the country: these, according to Tony Richards, were designed 'to revive his own spirits as much as the Party's'.

Jeremy's abstracted mood may have owed something to the knowledge that, at long last, Newton was going into the field. The latter planned to descend on Barnstaple during October, find some way of meeting Scott and winning his confidence, and then lure him to some remote spot where he could (depending on what view one takes as to his intentions) 'frighten' or kill him. At this period, Scott had found yet another patron to offer him help and sympathy – a Mrs Friendship, landlady of the Market Inn, where he lodged rent-free for some months. He was, however, in a more than usually nervous state, as he had been arrested by the police on 6 September, ostensibly for non-payment of a hotel bill: during two days spent in custody (for

---

* It had also been notable for the self-publicising activities of Young Liberal militant homosexuals, whose behaviour caused something of a scandal in respectable Scarborough. Jeremy avoided all contact with them, but they joked and sang ribald songs about his clandestine proclivities.

some reason in the female cells), he had been aggressively interrogated and warned that he might be in danger if he did not shut up about Jeremy Thorpe. On the afternoon of Sunday 12 October, Newton approached Scott as the latter was crossing Barnstaple's Pannier Market with a bundle of laundry and introduced himself as Peter Keene. He warned Scott that he was in great danger, as an assassin was coming from Canada to kill him, and that he would learn more if he allowed himself to be driven to a village ten miles away where someone was waiting to meet him. When Scott declined this mysterious invitation, Newton said: 'At least let me know why I'm being paid to protect you.' They subsequently spent several hours in the lounge of the nearby Imperial Hotel, where Scott showed Newton copies of the Bessell letters (a fresh set of which had been sent to him by Gordon Winter) and poured out his tale. Newton offered to warn Scott when 'the man from Canada' arrived; and Scott said he was going to stay with a friend in the village of Combe Martin near Ilfracombe and could be contacted there at the Pack of Cards public house.

Newton's next move was to provide himself with a gun, which he borrowed from an old schoolfriend in Chiswick who collected antique firearms. It was an odd weapon for the job – a 1910 model Mauser whose self-loading mechanism (as forensic examination subsequently confirmed) had a tendency to jam. On 23 October, he rang Scott at the Pack of Cards to say that 'the man from Canada' had arrived and ask if they might meet the following evening. Scott agreed, and at six o'clock on Friday the 24th of October, Newton drove up in a blue Ford Escort to their appointed meeting place outside a hotel in Combe Martin, observing with alarm that Scott was accompanied by an enormous Great Dane. Newton explained that he had some business in Porlock, twenty-five miles to the east on the Somerset coast, and suggested that Scott accompany him there so they could talk in the car. Scott agreed provided the dog, Rinka, came too. During the drive down the narrow coast road, they talked of the threat posed by the Canadian hit-man, Scott feeling at ease in Newton's company. At Porlock, Newton dropped Scott and Rinka at the Castle Hotel and said he would return for them at eight. Newton did not appear in the hotel bar at that time but was soon afterwards discovered by Scott waiting in the car outside, explaining that he had not come in as he did not wish to be seen with Scott. They drove off in the direction of Combe Martin until they came to a lay-by at the top of Porlock Hill, where Newton stopped.

It was a dramatic setting. To the south was the great barren expanse of Exmoor, to the north, the Bristol Channel with the lights of South Wales dimly visible in the distance. They were some way from any human habitation. It had started to rain. Newton said he was exhausted, and Scott offered to change places with him. He got out of the car and walked round to the driver's side, followed by Rinka, bounding along in a state of excitement. Newton emerged from the driver's seat, drew the Mauser, said 'this is it', and shot the dog through the head. As a stunned Scott knelt to examine the prostrated Great Dane, he felt the press of metal against his cranium and heard Newton say: 'It's your turn now.' But no second shot came. Newton seemed to be having difficulty with the gun, and swore vigorously. With the parting words 'I'll get you', he jumped back into the car and drove off, leaving Scott sobbing in the rain beside the canine corpse.

By chance, the incident took place just on the Somerset side of the Devon–Somerset border; and an hour later, a distraught Scott was trying to explain what had happened to the Avon and Somerset Police. (Had Newton continued another few hundred yards into North Devon, where Jeremy was regarded as a hero and Scott as a nuisance, the case would have become the exclusive responsibility of the Devon and Cornwall Police, who might well have handled it differently.) The local police at Bridgwater, aware of Scott's vendetta against Jeremy, immediately referred the case to their headquarters at Bristol. By one o'clock in the morning, the head of Avon and Somerset CID, DCS Michael Challes, was discussing it on the telephone with his Devon and Cornwall counterpart, DCS Proven Sharpe, who offered his co-operation, but suggested that Scott might have shot the dog himself to create publicity: they only had Scott's word that he had been lured on to the moor by a man he knew as Peter Keene. However, when Scott had first met that individual in the Pannier Market, their meeting had been observed by Scott's protective landlady Mrs Friendship, who had taken careful note of the registration number of the car 'Keene' was driving. On hearing of the shooting incident, Mrs Friendship took this information to the police, who were thus able, within a few days, to identify and track down Newton, whom they kept under observation in the hope that he would lead them to the gun. On 31 October, a week after the shooting, Newton, accompanied by a girlfriend and by David Miller, who had introduced him to the whole affair, left Heathrow on a flight bound for Karachi: on police instructions, his luggage and that of his companions had been thoroughly searched by airport security, but no gun was found.

Holmes had meanwhile been waiting anxiously to hear from Newton, who had not bothered to contact him in the immediate aftermath of the shooting. The first that either he or Jeremy heard of it was when the *West Somerset Free Press* published an item headed 'Mystery of the Dog in the Fog'. This stated archly that the police 'refused to confirm or deny . . . that the killer of the pet also tried to shoot the man, but that the gun jammed. Neither would they say whether the dog owner is a Mr Norman Scott.' This caused journalists who knew of Scott's story to contact Jeremy, who claimed to be as mystified as anyone and hardly to know Scott. ('I have been aware of this man Scott,' he told the *Sunday Express*. 'He once presented himself at the House. I did not see him. I made a report to the Home Secretary and this would be about three years ago.') It was not until a week after the shooting that Holmes had indirect news of Newton, who rang Deakin from

Heathrow to explain what had happened, adding that he was
going abroad on holiday while the dust settled. Holmes was
'appalled that he'd shot the dog and left a weeping, hysterical Scott
by the roadside':[10] he (and Jeremy) could only hope that the police
would fail to trace Newton and that the story would die down.

On Tuesday 18 November, Jeremy gave a dinner at Orme
Square for the Parliamentary Liberal Party on the eve of the State
Opening of Parliament, attended by his twelve fellow MPs and
seventeen Liberal peers. He told the press that he was reviving a
tradition of the 1920s, when an annual eve-of-session banquet
had been held at the palatial Curzon Street residence of the
Liberal Leader in the Lords, the Marquess of Crewe. The same
day, Newton returned from his overseas holiday and was detained
by the police at Heathrow and questioned by them there and at
Bridgwater. He concocted a bizarre story that he had been blackmailed by Scott, who had come into possession of some
compromising photographs, and that he had shot the dog, and
threatened to shoot Scott (without, however, having any intention
of actually doing so), in the hope of persuading him to desist
from his exactions, which amounted to £4 a month. He said nothing about Holmes or Jeremy, doubtless feeling that it would be to
his advantage to keep such matters to himself for the time being.
On 20 November, he was charged with possession of a firearm
with intent to endanger life, and released on bail after leading the
police to his mother's house in Chiswick where he had hidden the
Mauser in a garden shed. The police impounded the gun (the
jamming tendencies of which they were soon able to confirm)
along with some scrappy notes on pink paper referring to Jeremy
and other well-known figures which had been taken down by
Newton during his interview with Scott at the Imperial Hotel. On
his release, Newton rang Holmes with the alarming news that he
had been caught and charged by the police and was likely to be
committed for trial on account of the shooting incident.

On 21 November, the day after Newton had been charged at

Bridgwater, Jeremy was forty miles away in Salisbury, addressing the first of his morale-boosting rallies. He called for 'a constitutional rebirth', including fixed-term Parliaments, a reformed House of Lords, devolved assemblies for Scotland, Wales and the English regions, a written constitution with a Bill of Rights, and direct elections to the European Parliament. Normally, he gave an inspiring performance at such meetings, using his written text as the basis for a speech full of sparkling asides. ('You write the guts,' he would tell his speechwriter Tony Richards, 'and I'll add the fizz.') On this occasion, however, he looked and sounded grim and merely plodded through his speech, making little impact on his audience.[11]

For the remaining weeks of the year, he was closer to his usual form. Subsequent rallies went off better after he had accepted Marion's advice to dispense with written speeches altogether and speak 'off the cuff'. In Parliament, he attacked the Government's White Paper on devolution as inadequately 'federal'; he supported an amendment introduced by Lord Goodman in the House of Lords to prevent the NUJ exercising a stranglehold over the press; and he himself introduced an amendment in the House of Commons opposing the Dock Labour Scheme, reducing the Government's majority. He made a witty speech as guest of honour at a dinner to celebrate the one thousandth programme of *This Week*, and conducted (as he had done for some years) a carol service of schoolboys to raise money for Help the Aged.

But those around him continued to find him distracted – and well might he be. For the press were starting to take an interest in Scott's story, which Scott would at last have an opportunity of publicising when he gave evidence at Newton's trial. That might cost Jeremy his career. And in the course of that trial, it might be alleged that Jeremy had been the instigator of a conspiracy to do Scott harm. That might cost him his liberty.

20

RESIGNATION
JANUARY–MAY 1976

IF, AS IS sometimes said, Jeremy Thorpe suffered from a Houdini complex – a love of getting into complicated situations for the thrill of extricating himself from them – it is hard to think of a more challenging entanglement than that in which he found himself at the outset of 1976. For years he had lived in fear of the exposure of his relationship (whatever its nature) with Scott; and thanks to the incident on Porlock Hill, that relationship had suddenly become of intense interest to the press. Following the 'Dog in the Fog' article, he was having to give explanations to colleagues (including the Chief Whip Cyril Smith, and his fellow West Country MP John Pardoe) who had formerly been unaware of Scott's allegations.[1] There was a risk that the explanations he had already given to the three Liberals who had examined those allegations in 1971 – Byers, Hooson and Steel – would be shown to have been lacking in frankness. Meanwhile, Newton was due to be tried at Exeter in March. Until then, the whole matter was *sub judice*; but at the trial, Scott would have an opportunity of airing his allegations in public as a prosecution witness. Last but not least, elements in both the police and the press, knowing of

Jeremy's interest in silencing Scott, were suspicious that he might have had a hand in the events leading to the incident: were it ever to emerge that Holmes had hired Newton to harm Scott, further criminal proceedings could follow which might involve Jeremy.

Under the circumstances, he might have been expected to lie low; but, perversely, he began the year by drawing attention to himself with an extraordinary statement. In his New Year's message, he declared that he had reason to believe that the Soviet Union had bribed African leaders with £25 million paid into Swiss bank accounts to secure their recognition of the Marxist MPLA regime in Angola. This caused a sensation not just in Britain but in Africa, where Jeremy counted many of the national leaders as his friends. However, a week later, having been challenged to explain himself by the Foreign Secretary and others, he had to admit that he had no evidence to support his allegations (which seem to have been fed to him by UNITA, the MPLA's Angolan rivals).* It was not the first time he had caused a stir by

---

* Concerning this episode, the Liberals' recently appointed Parliamentary Press Officer Stuart Mole wrote in his diary on 8 January:

> Now here is a story worthy of Ian Fleming. Soviet gold – Swiss bank accounts – bribery and corruption in steaming Africa – South African agents – a crucial peace summit – the dramatic intervention of *Jeremy Thorpe* ... The accusation was dropped out as a vague aside in Thorpe's New Year message. It was obvious that it would create a considerable furore but Thorpe appeared to me to be unprepared with any details and unsure of how he was going to handle the issue. The result was that I was pestered by journalists all over the New Year holiday ... while Thorpe preferred to remain 'tight-lipped'. In the ensuing week, a series of exchanges with the FO left himself severely bruised and palpably one down ... If the matter is allowed to rest ... he will be a lucky man. This pompous quasi-Palmerstonian behaviour – Privy Counsellor discussions, meetings with the FCO, solemn 'no comment' statements to the press, telephone calls to Lusaka, secret messages to African Heads of State – all appears more than faintly ludicrous coming from the Liberal Party Leader.

When he wrote these words, Mole knew nothing of the personal problems hanging over Jeremy.

making sensational claims he could not substantiate: there had
been his suggestion at the time of Profumo that other ministers
would have to resign because of indiscretions in their private
lives, and the suggestion in 1973 that the British Government
were concealing information indicating that the Tsar and his
family had escaped from Russia.

He also attracted attention that month with a series of robust
comments on the domestic matter which, next to the economy,
was most in the news at the time – that of regional devolution,
a controversial cause which the Labour Government, with its
vanishing majority, was half-heartedly espousing in the hope of
securing parliamentary support from the Scottish and Welsh
Nationalists. In the House of Commons on 14 January, he
called for the United Kingdom to adopt a federal system, saying
that it was unlikely that such countries as Canada and Nigeria
would have developed as successfully as they had without fed-
eralism. Speaking at Stowmarket in Suffolk on 24 January, he
went so far as to say that, if the Scots and Welsh felt unable to
achieve what they regarded as their 'just rights' by peaceful
means, they might be tempted to follow the example of the
Irish and take them by force. 'The drama of Gladstone's first
attempts to introduce Home Rule for Ireland is being played
out again ... the parallels are frightening in their similarity.' On
28 January, he warned the Conservatives that their hostile attitude towards devolution could break up the United Kingdom
just as their attitude towards Home Rule had led to the end of
a United Ireland.

Throughout the month, however, he remained under intense
strain. This was evident at Stowmarket, the last of the regional
rallies which had begun in November. Local Liberals had worked
hard to ensure a turn-out of almost a thousand; but Jeremy's
speech, for all the sensation of its content, mystified his audience
by a delivery which (in the view of the local Liberal candidate,
Denys Robinson) was 'sepulchral'.[2] He also caused surprise by

making a fuss about the service at a dinner which had been organised by a local Liberal restaurateur.[3] By that time, however, there had been further developments in the Scott affair which had plunged him into a desperate mood.

Since Newton had been charged in November, Holmes had been keeping in touch with him with a view to limiting the damage. Whether Newton's brief had been to kill Scott or merely frighten him, it was clear that he had made a complete mess of his mission. It was equally clear, however, that, were he to reveal the true background to that mission, he would be putting Holmes (not to mention Jeremy) in a most awkward position. It has been seen that, at the time of his arrest, Newton had made up a story which did not implicate either Holmes or Jeremy – namely that he personally had been blackmailed by Scott and that this had been his motive for 'staging' the incident on Porlock Hill. From the point of view of both Holmes and Jeremy, it was vital that Newton stick to this story. In the course of several uncomfortable meetings between late November and early January, Holmes offered to pay Newton £5,000 after the trial so long as he continued to keep the names of himself and Jeremy out of his evidence. He also assured Newton that a plan was being hatched which would probably result either in his acquittal or his receiving no more than a suspended sentence.[4]

That plan, in which there can be little doubt of Jeremy's involvement, concerned a figure from the past, Peter Bessell. Jeremy had last seen him at Miami in January 1974, following the failure of their attempt to obtain money from Jack Hayward. Since then, Bessell had been in virtual hiding at Oceanside near San Diego in Southern California with his American girlfriend Diane Kelly, while he tried, with the aid of Diane's wealthy father and the Plymouth solicitor Lord Foot, to work out a settlement with his creditors. Jeremy had had little contact with him during those two years, in the course of which (as Bessell recalled in his memoirs) they spoke only twice on the telephone. Both Jeremy and Marion had, however, remained friendly with Bessell's abandoned wife Pauline, who had gone to live with them at Orme Square for several months in 1975. As so often in the past, Jeremy decided to appeal to Bessell for help in getting him out of trouble. In the spring of 1971, when Jeremy had been confronted by Hooson and Steel with evidence that Bessell had paid money to Scott, Bessell had allowed him to say that these payments had been made as a result of Scott's blackmailing Bessell. Now that Newton was telling a similar tale, Jeremy wanted Bessell to corroborate, so to speak, Newton's story that Scott was a blackmailer. The idea was that, were Scott's lawyers to be informed that Jeremy possessed evidence which could result in their client being charged with blackmail, it might induce Scott to remain silent about Jeremy during Newton's trial. By confirming Newton's picture of himself as a blackmail victim, it might also help secure Newton's acquittal or lenient sentence.

Holmes claimed (at his meeting with Bessell, and again in his 1981 interviews) that Jeremy had assured him that this course of action had been sanctioned by Lord Goodman; but it is difficult to believe that that wily solicitor would have encouraged Jeremy in so dangerous a plan. Apart from the inherent risks of trying to corroborate one lie with another, to bring Bessell, who had otherwise vanished from sight, back into the affair was to risk opening Pandora's box. For no one was better placed than Bessell to tell the world the truth of the Scott affair and the efforts made down the years to cover it up. And although Bessell was an old friend of Jeremy's, who had often helped him out of trouble in the past, it was rash to assume that he would still be happy to go out of his way to do so – particularly as, since their last meeting, Jeremy (as Bessell would soon discover) had been disparaging him both to his wife Pauline and to Jack Hayward (to whom he had written of 'that bastard Bessell'). However, almost as soon as the crisis arose, Jeremy seems to have thought of turning to

Bessell, who heard from his daughter in November 1975 that Jeremy was 'muttering' that he might soon visit him in California.[5]

In the end, however, Bessell received a visit from Holmes, who stopped at San Diego on 19–20 January in the course of an American holiday with his partner Gerald Hagan. Having met no one from England for two years, Bessell was delighted to see Holmes; but he was surprised to hear that Scott was still giving trouble. Holmes gave him two things from Jeremy – a letter and a present of a book. The letter, written in circumspect language lest it fall into the wrong hands, asked if Bessell, for reasons which would be explained to him by Holmes, might write a statement confirming that he had once been blackmailed by Scott. The book was *Life With Lloyd George* by A. J. Sylvester, the recently published diaries of the great statesman's private secretary. Jeremy had inscribed it:

> For Peter from Jeremy with affection
> From one Liberal to another Liberal about a third Liberal
> Vive les trois Mousquetaires!
> New Year 1976

Holmes drew Bessell's attention to Chapter 9, which dealt with Lloyd George's fears that his political career might be ruined if it became generally known that he was having a sexual affair with his secretary, Frances Stevenson, and his plans to try to ensure that the relationship did not become public.

There is some conflict of evidence between Holmes and Bessell as to what transpired between them.[6] Bessell later claimed that Holmes had at first told him that Newton was genuinely being blackmailed by Scott and that Jeremy's only fear was that Scott would use Newton's trial to repeat his allegations in public: given these facts, Bessell agreed to write a letter to Jeremy's solicitor Michael Barnes accusing Scott of blackmail, on the understanding that it would not be produced as evidence or otherwise made public but merely used by Barnes to try to deter Scott from embarrassing Jeremy. However, while being driven by Bessell to the airport, Holmes suddenly confessed that, under pressure from Jeremy, he had hired Newton to kill Scott: this alarmed Bessell, who considered retrieving his letter but had no opportunity to do so before Holmes and Hagan caught their plane. Holmes, on the other hand, later claimed that he had told Bessell frankly that he and Jeremy were in a tight spot as a result of a botched plot to 'frighten' Scott, and that Bessell, while regarding the hiring of Newton (not to mention the purchase of his own letters to Scott in February 1974) as foolish beyond belief, had been happy to help by writing the suggested letter (on the understanding – on this point at least the two accounts agree – that it should not be made public: Bessell was concerned to avoid scandal which might spoil his efforts to rehabilitate himself). At all events, Bessell did write a letter, incorporating a number of true facts about how he had tried to help Scott with his National Insurance problems, but falsely alleging that he had paid Scott small sums of money over a period in order to prevent him revealing 'that I was having a relationship with my private secretary'. It concluded: 'Although I have always had some sympathy for him since he is clearly mentally sick, I have no doubt that he is also vicious. He does not hesitate to turn on those who, like myself, genuinely tried to help him.'[7] As soon as the letter was in his hands, Holmes telephoned Orme Square and asked Marion to give Jeremy the message 'Mission Accomplished'.

When he left Bessell on 20 January, Holmes imagined that he and Jeremy had at least a month in hand to prepare for the moment when Scott threatened to go public with his allegations, at Newton's trial in March. However, he returned to England a few days later to discover that the period of grace had shrunk to less than a week, and that Jeremy was in a frantic state. For Scott was himself due to be tried for having made a fraudulent social security claim (amounting to £58.40) the previous June: this case was set down to be heard before Barnstaple magistrates on Thursday 29 January, and Scott made it known to journalists that, in the course of it, he would have something to say about Jeremy Thorpe. The dam was therefore about to burst. Jeremy learned of the imminent hearing on the eve of the Stowmarket rally, which explains his nervous mood at that appearance (which he almost cancelled).[8] It happened that, around this time, the report was due to be released of the Department of Trade enquiry into the collapse of London & Counties Securities in November 1973, and this too would have something to say about Jeremy, who had been a director of that company and associated with it in the public mind. In the event, the report was also published on 29 January, the day of Scott's court appearance. It has been said that it was extraordinarily unlucky for Jeremy that two such sensationally embarrassing statements about him should have been made on the same day (though it is conceivable that persons who were well disposed towards him may have helped contrive the coincidence in the mistaken belief that the London & Counties story would eclipse Scott's nebulous allegations).

The London & Counties investigation had been carried out by two inspectors appointed by the Department of Trade, D. C. Hobson, a chartered accountant, and A. P. (later Sir Andrew) Leggatt, a QC (later a distinguished judge) who, like Jeremy, had begun his legal career as a pupil of Rodger Winn at the Inner Temple in the 1950s. Having interviewed him, they noted his contention that he had on several occasions wished to resign but had been persuaded that, after the publicity the company had received thanks to him, it would not survive his departure. They did not remark on his personal closeness to Caplan (about whom they were scathing). They noted that, although Jeremy had encouraged depositors to entrust their savings to the bank, this was 'irrelevant' as none of them had ultimately lost their money. But they concluded, in language reminiscent of Patrick Hutber's warnings in the *Sunday Telegraph*, that

> this venture into secondary banking must remain a cautionary tale for any leading politician. For unless he is properly informed of the affairs of the company he joins he cannot make his own judgement on the propriety of its transactions; and he is liable to be reminded, as Mr Thorpe must have been, that his reputation is not only his most marketable, but also his most vulnerable commodity.

While the newspapers were digesting this, the other story came through from Barnstaple. After the prosecution had stated the case against him, to which he pleaded guilty, Scott, ignoring the efforts of the clerk to restrain him, burst out:

> It has been fifteen years. I really would like to get this matter cleared up. It has been so sick. I am being hounded all the time by people just because of my sexual relationship with Jeremy Thorpe. It gets worse and worse. I am sorry but I must say it. I am so tired and upset and that is why all this has happened.

Scott was ordered to refund the sum defrauded and was put on two years' probation. When he left the court, he eagerly gave interviews to the waiting reporters, mentioning not only details of his alleged affair with Jeremy but such matters as the 'retainers' he had received from Bessell and the pre-election sale of Bessell's letters in 1974.

That evening, Jeremy issued two brief statements through Lord Goodman. Regarding the London & Counties report, he admitted an 'error of judgement', adding: 'I placed total reliance and faith in quarters where it is now, alas, all too clear that confidence was wholly misplaced.' The other statement simply read: 'It is well over twelve years* since I last saw or spoke to Mr Scott. There is no truth in Mr Scott's allegations.' The following (Friday) morning, *The Times* and the *Telegraph* ran long articles about the inspectors' report, concentrating on the remarks concerning Jeremy (though these covered less than two pages out of more than two hundred), alongside short articles about Scott's outburst; the *Guardian*, *Express* and tabloids, on the other hand, gave huge coverage to the Scott story. Tony Benn wrote in his diary: 'The papers are full of Jeremy Thorpe who is in real trouble over this man Scott who has claimed a sexual relationship with him. It looks as if he's on the way out.'[9] The event which Jeremy had been dreading for more than a decade had finally come to pass, and he would not now know peace.

Apart from issuing his brief statements, Jeremy was unavailable for comment that eventful Thursday: he spent much of it with Goodman, and also consulted Lord Byers and the Liberal legal peer Lord Wigoder QC, before retreating to Orme Square where he refused to receive visitors or answer the telephone. The press therefore directed their enquiries to the Liberal Chief Whip, Cyril Smith. Since his election victory at Rochdale three years earlier, Smith's relations with Jeremy had been difficult and sometimes stormy. There did not seem to be room in the tiny parliamentary party for two such massive egos; and Smith, though a tough political operator and popular among the rank and file, was regarded by Jeremy and other traditionalist colleagues as a quarrelsome buffoon. Jeremy had delayed for months before announcing his appointment as Chief Whip in June 1975, and had been unamused when Smith subsequently attended the State Opening of Parliament wearing a T-shirt bearing the legend 'Electoral Reform Now!'. Smith (who was rumoured to have gay tendencies himself, though no one outside his constituency

---

* In fact, it was just over eleven years since their last known meeting in December 1964.

seems to have known at the time about his shocking predilection for children of both sexes) had heard a certain amount of informed gossip about Jeremy's proclivities from gay activists in the party;[10] and early in January, Jeremy told him about Scott, describing him as a 'hothead' who had been making false allegations of a sexual nature which he might repeat during the coming court case over his shot dog. Smith at first treated this as a joke, but agreed to a suggestion of Jeremy that he raise the matter with the Home Secretary, Roy Jenkins: Jenkins took note, but said he could not interfere in what was a police matter.[11]

Nevertheless, Smith was unprepared for the storm which burst on 29 January, having been given no warning of the Barnstaple episode. Judging by what he heard from the journalists who besieged him, it was clear that Jeremy had by no means told him the whole story: in particular, Scott was claiming that Bessell had paid him money to keep quiet. Smith stonewalled, describing Scott's allegations as 'ludicrous and irrelevant' and insisting that the entire parliamentary party stood solidly behind Jeremy; but he demanded explanations when he saw Jeremy the following day. Jeremy's reaction was to tell Smith 'in confidence' about the letter Bessell had written Barnes. Apparently satisfied, Smith went off to preside at a weekend conference of Liberal candidates and agents at Totnes in Devon, where he was again put under pressure by the press to comment on Scott's allegation (of which the newspapers were now full) that he had been paid by Bessell. Finally, Smith told them that he had knowledge of a letter by Bessell confirming that the latter had been blackmailed by Scott, a 'revelation' which was sensationally reported in the Sunday newspapers of 1 February.

The press (as well as several leading Liberals) were now frantically trying to locate Bessell, who was rumoured to be in Venezuela. On Sunday night, Bessell (who saw no British newspapers in California) received telephone calls from both his London solicitor Charles Negus-Fancey and David Holmes, from whom he learned about Scott's outburst at Barnstaple and its consequences – that the story of Bessell's payments to Scott had been published in the *Guardian* alongside reproductions of Bessell's covering notes, that the existence of Bessell's letter to Barnes had been revealed to the newspapers, and that he was being hunted by the press. Bessell was alarmed to think that his cover was about to be broken and that the untrue story of his having been blackmailed by Scott had (contrary to Holmes' assurances) become public. He asked Negus-Fancey to get Jeremy to telephone him as soon as possible. On Monday morning, before hearing from Jeremy, he was finally tracked down to Oceanside by the *Daily Mail*, and soon a host of journalists were ringing him up or on their way to see him, a development which Bessell found disturbing but also, after two years of being ignored by the world, rather flattering.[12]

When Jeremy did telephone, he sounded surprisingly relaxed. 'We've just seen you on TV,' he began. Bessell (according to his memoirs) expressed sympathy for Jeremy but said that he could not afford a scandal, suffering as he did from a heart condition and being in the process of restoring his business reputation. He wanted to know how the letter had leaked out: Jeremy said that he had been forced to mention it to Smith to prove that Scott had been blackmailing Bessell. Bessell said that he had now heard from the press and got the impression that no one believed the blackmail story (though it almost seemed to Bessell as if Jeremy himself had started to believe it). Accordingly, he proposed to instruct Negus-Fancey to prepare a statement to the effect that, although Bessell had paid Scott on his own account and not Jeremy's, he had done so merely out of charity. When Jeremy expressed alarm ('You can't do that – it'll ruin everything!'), Bessell agreed to Negus-Fancey's consulting Jeremy and taking his suggestions into account before issuing the statement. The final text, which filled the front pages on Tuesday 3 February, stated that, 'many years ago', Bessell had given Scott '£200–300 . . . solely

to help him establish himself at a time when he was destitute';
that he 'utterly rejected' the suggestion that they were made on
behalf of a third person; that he knew nothing of any alleged
payment to Scott of £2,500;* and (this being a touch suggested
by Jeremy) that he could say no more as 'I understand that it is
possible that I might be required to give evidence in these matters'.[13] When the *Daily Mirror* asked Smith, the source of the
earlier blackmail story, to comment on this statement, he produced the ripe remark: 'Someone is telling bloody lies.'

   With his reputation dented, and many questions remaining
to be answered, Jeremy now had to face the Liberal Party, both
in the country and in Parliament. One option open to him, now
Scott had gone public, was to 'come out' as a homosexual: but
although some Liberals (notably among the Party's growing
body of gay militants) urged him to choose this course, it was
not one he would ever have contemplated. He had for too long
inhabited a world of secret and guilty pleasures to be capable
of doing so; the climate did not yet exist to allow politicians to
survive such self-disclosures; and it would have embarrassed
his wife, shocked many traditional Liberals, and compromised
him for having denied his nature down the years to so many
people. However, despite his inability to make admissions
about his private life, he attracted enormous sympathy from
Liberals everywhere in the light of the attempt to 'smear' him
on account of it. At a Young Liberal rally in Ealing which he
attended on the Saturday after Scott's outburst, the Chairman,
Stephen Atack, declared: 'Our main concern was with his
involvement with London & Counties Bank. His frankness and
honesty in admitting his mistake has increased his personal
standing among Young Liberals considerably. As regards the
court case accusation, we totally accept Jeremy's statement and

---

* This story had broken on Monday morning, no mention at this stage being
  made of Holmes.

we don't regard it as anything that is politically relevant.'* This was greeted by loud cheering, as was the assurance to Jeremy by the former Chairman Peter Hain that 'we are with you in resisting the politics of smear and innuendo'.[14] (These were astonishing words coming from a man who had been his greatest antagonist six years earlier, but as will be seen, there was a special reason for them.) These feelings were reflected by Liberals all over the country: Jeremy received a huge postbag from party members affirming their enthusiastic support for and continued faith in him in the face of the accusations against him.[15]

It was in this atmosphere that the Parliamentary Liberal Party assembled at Westminster on 4 February for their weekly Wednesday meeting.[16] Inevitably, the main item on the agenda was the position of Jeremy following the extraordinary developments of the past week. Of his twelve fellow MPs, five of the most senior – Grimond, Hooson, Pardoe, Steel and Wainwright† – believed that he had brought the latest events upon himself; that the Party was being severely damaged by those events; that there was worse to come; and that he ought to step down as Leader. (Of the five, Grimond, Hooson and Wainwright had long doubted his fitness to lead the Party, while Pardoe and Steel, though close to him in the past, both hoped to

---

* Earlier during the meeting, Atack's predecessor Ruth Addison had asked Jeremy: 'Why do you not come out and say that Liberals believe in love, that peaceful sexual acts between adults are not illegal and nobody else's business?' Jeremy had replied: 'I think it is better that these matters should be allowed to run their natural course, to work their way through, as I think they will in a very short period of time. Then perhaps I may be rather more anxious to answer your question than now. There are so many matters involved that I prefer to leave it as it is.'

† Around this time, four of the five – excluding Wainwright – dined at Pardoe's house to discuss the affair, on which occasion Grimond produced his quip that 'I suspected [Jeremy's homosexuality] from the moment I met him, and when I met his mother, I had no further doubts'.

succeed him as Leader.) However, it was obvious that Jeremy was not going to step down of his own accord; and there was nothing for the moment that anyone could do to make him. On the one hand, the great majority of Liberals in the country were rallying loyally to his side. On the other hand, the mild strictures against him in the London & Counties report were hardly a resigning matter; and he could hardly be required to resign – at least by Liberals with their philosophy of tolerance – on account of alleged and unproven private indiscretions of fourteen years earlier. As in 1971, the man who assumed the role of Jeremy's prosecutor was Hooson; but he took care not to overplay his hand, merely seeking to establish the point that if it emerged that Jeremy had lied about his relationship with Scott – either to the 1971 'enquiry' (which most of those present had just learned about) or to the current meeting – then he ought to go.[17] Jeremy, however, always at his best when cornered, defended himself and repeated his denials in an impressive speech; and even those who were not persuaded by it were left breathless by his performance. He was therefore given a unanimous vote of confidence by what the newspapers described as the 'jury' of twelve MPs. He received especially staunch support from three colleagues, Clement Freud, Russell Johnston and Stephen Ross, all of whom would stand by him to the end, as well as from the ever-loyal Lord Byers, who chaired the meeting. Even Smith, who had been given ample cause to doubt Jeremy's frankness during recent days, declared his 'thousand per cent support' and said that he considered the matter closed. That not all shared this view was evident when, at the dinner following the meeting, Hooson raised his glass to Jeremy with the words: 'I drink to your health, Jeremy, though I fear for your future.'

Jeremy's self-confidence at this dramatic meeting may have owed something to the fact that, by this time, he had been assured of support in his battle for survival by the Prime Minister himself. According to Wilson's press secretary Joe Haines, the ubiquitous Marcia Falkender 'burst into [Wilson's] office [when the Barnstaple story broke] and said, "Harold, you must save Jeremy!"'[18] Cyril Smith tells the following story in his memoirs. On Tuesday 3 February – the day preceding the PLP meeting – he was discussing with Jeremy the latter's speech of welcome to the new Speaker, George Thomas, who was due to be installed that day, when the Prime Minister entered. After making some friendly remarks to the effect that he did not believe everything he read in the press, Wilson asked Jeremy to come to his room that afternoon during a break in the installation ceremony. At the appointed time, Jeremy absented himself from the Liberal bench for half an hour. When he returned, Smith asked him what had happened. 'We were talking on Privy Council terms,' replied Jeremy. Smith would have none of this, and demanded to know at least whether what Wilson had said was good or bad. Jeremy replied: 'It's good. It will be pushed on to South Africa.' 'What the hell does that mean?' asked Smith. Jeremy's reply failed to dispel the Chief Whip's bafflement: 'The Prime Minister believes there are South African influences at work.'[19]

Some mystery still surrounds Wilson's involvement. By this stage of his premiership, his health was failing, his mind was becoming clouded, and he was increasingly obsessed by the thought that sinister forces were working to destabilise his Government, including the South African secret service. These fears were not discouraged by Lady Falkender, who saw a South African hand in recent burglaries at Wilson's houses as well as an episode involving her own sister. As a leading British critic of apartheid, Jeremy was regarded by the South African regime as a dangerous adversary; and it was known that Scott had been encouraged to publicise his allegations by the South African journalist (and reputed BOSS agent) Gordon Winter. (This had now been revealed by the *Daily Mirror*, to which Winter had offered Scott's story three years earlier.) Wilson had of course long known about Jeremy's efforts to 'manage' Scott – indeed, he had (according to Haines) been prepared to use this information against Jeremy in March 1974; but either because in his addled state he had forgotten about this, or because he now wished to give Jeremy friendly support while at the same time taking a swipe at their common South African 'enemies', he was willing to promote the theory that the Scott story was in essence a South African 'smear'.

Moreover, Wilson was not alone in finding virtue in this theory. On 24 October 1975 – by an amazing coincidence, the same day as the incident on Porlock Hill – the South African-born former Young Liberal Chairman Peter Hain, a militant anti-apartheid campaigner who had led the opposition to the South African cricket tour of 1970, had been charged with attempting to carry out a robbery at a building society near his home in Putney. Such conduct was so absurdly uncharacteristic of Hain (who was subsequently acquitted of the charge) that it not unreasonably occurred to both him and others that he may have been the victim of a South African plot to discredit him. When, three months later, Jeremy became the subject of similarly bizarre allegations, it occurred to Hain (who knew nothing of Jeremy's homosexuality) that he too may have been a victim of such machinations. Hence his surprisingly friendly declaration to Jeremy at Ealing, that 'we are with you in resisting the politics of smear and innuendo'.* Soon afterwards, Hain was approached by a mysterious businessman who claimed to possess evidence (which he never produced) that BOSS had framed Hain by getting a lookalike to stage the attempted robbery, and was out to destroy other prominent Liberals including Jeremy. Hain took this information to Jeremy, who on 24 February had another meeting with Wilson to discuss this development, also attended by both Marcia and Marion, which (according to Haines) 'went on to 1 AM with much drinking'.[20]

---

* Jeremy had thanked him, adding: 'Without in any way involving myself in matters which could be *sub judice*, may I say the same for you?' According to Hain, this was the first word of support Jeremy had offered him in his troubles.

34. Speaking at the National Liberal Club, in the shadow of the 'Grand Old Man', January 1974.

35. At the Liberal Office in Barnstaple (with Rupert, aged four) during the February 1974 General Election campaign.

36. Heath to Wilson: 'What on earth does she mean – "See you at the ball"?' (Garland in the *Daily Telegraph*, February 1974.)

37. Within sight of power: on the train to London for coalition talks with Heath, 2 March 1974.

38. Leaving 10 Downing Street with his assistant Tony Richards.

39. A *Punch* cover after the 'Hovertour' of August 1974.

40. With Pierre Trudeau, Liberal Prime Minister of Canada, March 1975.

41. Jeremy and Marion looking preoccupied at the Liberal Assembly at Scarborough, September 1975 – a month before the shooting incident on Porlock Hill.

42. No longer Leader, but still wearing an anxious look – with his successor David Steel, and the Party Chairman Geoffrey Tordoff, at the time of the Lib–Lab Pact, 1977.

43. Campaigning in Barnstaple, April 1979.

44. Arriving at the Old Bailey, May 1979.

45. Acquittal, 22 June 1979.

46. At the Oxford Union, 1981.

47. At Harold Wilson's memorial service, 1995.

Following these talks, Wilson asked the security service MI5 to look for evidence of a South African plot against Jeremy. Meanwhile, in a parliamentary answer of 11 February, he criticised the press for their 'nauseating' treatment of 'a classic innuendo' against an MP and 'democracy as a whole'. Other public figures were also helpful to Jeremy. One of the many revelations of recent days was that, in February 1974, Jeremy's Conservative rival Tim Keigwin had sent a dossier on Scott to Conservative Central Office; but Mrs Thatcher declared that she had not read it and had no intention of doing so or of allowing it to be used to 'smear' Jeremy. The new Speaker, George Thomas, was also most friendly towards Jeremy* and discouraged some right-wing Conservative MPs who tried to ask parliamentary questions calculated to embarrass him. It has been suggested that the support he obtained from such quarters amounted to 'an establishment cover-up'; and although it might more charitably be said to arise from natural sympathy towards a popular fellow-politician who (as it then seemed) had experienced the misfortune of having a minor and ancient indiscretion raked up by the press, Jeremy himself encouraged the development of a conspiracy theory by remarking to all and sundry that he was certain of winning through as he had the three most powerful forces in Britain on his side – Harold Wilson, Lord Goodman and MI5.[21]

In his many statements and denials at this time, Jeremy

---

* It will be recalled that Thomas (himself a clandestine homosexual) had, as a junior Home Office minister, a minor involvement in the Scott affair in 1965 (see Chapter 10). In his memoirs, *George Thomas, Mr Speaker* (London: Century, 1985), he wrote that 'my feeling has always been that Jeremy Thorpe was destroyed by his parliamentary colleagues as much as by the press campaign against him'. He told the author in May 1993: 'It was as if a wounded man was lying on a battlefield bleeding to death and his so-called comrades fled for cover when they should have been pulling him out of the firing line.' He also remembered a conversation with Wilson at Chequers in which the Prime Minister spoke of his liking for Jeremy and desire to help him.

impressed his interlocutors with his air of total sincerity. When DCS Proven Sharpe of Devon and Cornwall CID called on him at Cobbaton on 8 February, he appeared relaxed and co-operative. Sharpe explained that, following the Porlock Hill incident, he had been asked by the DPP to conduct an enquiry into Scott's activities in Devon, which now had to take account of the allegations made by Scott since 29 January, notably that letters belonging to Scott had been sold on his behalf by Gleadle in February 1974 for £2,500. Without bothering to consult his lawyers, Jeremy offered to make a statement. He began by declaring that he was 'in the process of drafting a comprehensive statement relating to my knowledge of Mr Norman Josiffe, otherwise known as Scott, which, subject to the advice of my legal advisers, I would have no objection to supplying to those investigating this case'. (It was never in fact supplied.) He insisted that he had 'no knowledge whatsoever' of the payment of £2,500. He did, however, know that Gleadle had approached Lord Banks at the time, claiming to 'be in possession of documents which could be embarrassing to the Liberal Party'; and he recalled that he had himself been approached by the Rector of North Molton (Pennington), who had alluded to these documents and Scott's allegations and suggested 'that the Liberal Party might like to "set up" this young man financially ... I robustly rejected the suggestion that I or any of my colleagues should be involved in these "good works".' Indeed, why should he buy these documents when copies of them had been seen by the Liberal enquiry of 1971 and were in the hands of the newspapers? As for the incident of 24 October 1975, Jeremy had 'never met the accused, Mr Newton' and knew 'no more than I have read in the press'.[22]

Jeremy was now like a general fighting a battle on several fronts: no sooner had he contained an attack from one quarter than he had to dash to prevent the enemy breaking through in another part of the field. Having dealt with the PLP and the police, he returned to Bessell. Since being tracked down by the press on 2 February, Bessell had enjoyed himself (and made some money) giving interviews about himself and Jeremy, full of colourful and often conflicting details. On the whole, he had been protective of Jeremy (though he had now heard from his deserted wife Pauline, who had until recently lived with the Thorpes, that Jeremy had 'regaled her with endless accounts of [Bessell's] misdeeds' and 'told Marion so many different stories that even she doesn't know what to believe'[23]). Although Bessell had not yet given the game away in any important respect, his rediscovered passion for talking to the press was disturbing for Jeremy, as were several specific developments. He had been approached by Hooson and others, urging him to return to England to 'clear things up': Bessell replied that he had neither the health nor the funds for the trip but would always be happy to see old colleagues in California. At the same time, he wrote to Barnes saying he wished to 'withdraw' the 'blackmail' letter, which was at odds with various accounts he had given since.

On 19 February, alarm over this last move prompted Jeremy to write Bessell a letter which, illustrating as it does both the ingenuity with which he was attempting to manage the situation and his ability to present a fantasy account of events with total conviction, is worth quoting at length.

My dear Peter,

I tried telephoning but wisely you are off the hook. I think we are emerging from the Tunnel and I owe you an explanation and hope to be allowed to give a piece of advice.

Your letter was shown to *no one* (that is including Cyril Smith). However, his Loyalty was crucial and I did *paraphrase* the broad outlines of your letter. *Phase I* Cyril having panicked, *wrongly* referred to its contents ... This was disastrous & quite unauthorised by me. *Phase II* you were caught off the hop by the Press & denied almost *everything* in the letter. I don't blame you but it didn't enhance anyone's credibility. *Phase III* you put out your statement confirming the broad outline & *Phase IV* to my horror you *now* tell Barnes that you want to withdraw the letter . . . What I want you to consider is a) the letter is now with the police b) they are not likely to publish & nor is anyone else. No more publicity is likely. c) the only result of withdrawal is to suggest (i) that your letter was a fabrication – *which it wasn't* (ii) that there may be some other explanation for those payments *which frankly there isn't* (iii) that we are lying like troopers *which we are not.*

The police I gather don't know whether to believe the dog man (Newton) or Scott. Scott has some ridiculous theory that Marion, self and/or the Government hired Newton! Newton according to the D. Mirror crime reporter had been living with Scott homosexually, went straight & was then blackmailed by Scott. Who do they believe? There is nothing to compel you to come to Britain to give evidence against Scott, particularly if you are not prepared to allege blackmail. But if they think that Scott at least tried to pressurise you as he did then it appears consistent with Newton's experience.

In view of the denials & counter-denials it is not impossible that the Police may want to interview you. My advice is a) Your letter is correct b) You wanted to withdraw since the undertaking of confidentiality was breached c) Scott *is* a Lunatic d) whatever interpretation may be placed on the [retainer] letters you do not wish to prefer a charge of blackmail against Scott – partly because your health would not permit travelling to Britain, & partly because Scott has tried to wreck enough lives without having a go at yours.

All the above is vital if justice is to be done. The Press are still being bloody & trying to destroy me. Harold [Wilson] on the other hand is being quite superb.

The Police asked me what my view was & I said I thought it looked as if Scott had tried to pressurise you but you slapped him down. Am I right? Alas I think the press would have hounded

you in *any event* since 3 papers had copies of your letters & had
them for several years ...

The whole story has been a nightmare, but I am damned if that
bloody Lunatic is going to destroy the Party. So far I've had 700
letters in support ... Stand firm and we shall win through. You
need say nothing more. Your letter is enough. Bless you. Take
care of yourself & remember Ll[oyd] G[eorge]!*

Ever yours affectionately,

Jeremy

Your letter was superb to Emlyn

None of us have anything to hide

Bessell replied that he had to withdraw the letter, but was telling
Barnes that he was doing so purely because it had been hurriedly
written and contained some inaccuracies. He assured Jeremy that
he had no intention of talking to the police, but hoped that
Jeremy in return would protect what remained of his good name.
He ended on a warning note:

Alas, too often, innocent people are destroyed by their persecutors.
The fact of your innocence does not, of itself, guarantee your survival ... Nixon did not fall because some idiots broke into the
Watergate Hotel. He didn't (in my view) fall entirely because of the
cover-up. He fell because at the end he trusted no one, not even his
friends and he betrayed even those who were trying to help him.

Bessell was saying in effect that Jeremy could rely on his support
so long as Bessell could rely on his – a warning which, within a
month, Jeremy was to ignore to his peril. These were the last

---

* Probably a reference partly to the book Jeremy had sent Bessell via Holmes,
  which dealt with the great man's private-life problems, partly to Lloyd George's
  philosophy that one should never give up.

direct communications which passed between Jeremy and Bessell.

By the middle of February, Jeremy seemed (for the time being, for no one could tell what would happen at Newton's trial a month hence) to be in the clear. He had given plausible explanations to his fellow MPs and the police. He had won sympathy and support among the general public and the party at large. The general view, encouraged by the statements of Wilson and other public figures, was that he had behaved with dignity in the face of a campaign of denigration by the press. Even some of the press itself supported this view: the tabloid *Sun*, in an article entitled 'The Hounding of Jeremy Thorpe', wrote that 'rarely has a national figure had his public and private life ripped apart on such scanty evidence'.[24] Jeremy received loud applause on BBC Radio's *Any Questions* when he spoke of his recent ordeal and complained of the unfairness of the system whereby witnesses could make slanderous accusations in court without fear of consequences. Personal friends were impressed by the staunchness with which Marion stood by him (though she disapproved of Bessell and Holmes who, on the basis of what Jeremy had told her, she regarded as largely responsible for his troubles). By the end of the month, he seemed back on form as a working politician, presiding on the 26th at a dinner of European Liberals at Orme Square, at which they agreed a common platform for future elections to the European Parliament.

Jeremy's critics, however, looked to see how far the affair had affected the electoral fortunes of the Liberal Party. These had not been bright for some time, and events since 29 January had not been calculated to enhance them. Gallup on 19 February suggested that the Party's support had dropped by almost a third during the past month from 14 per cent to 10.5 per cent, Jeremy's personal rating less dramatically from 45 per cent to 41 per cent. Three by-elections were due in March – in the Labour stronghold of Coventry North-West, the Conservative stronghold of Wirral, and the Surrey commuter seat of Carshalton which in happier times the Liberals might have had hopes of capturing (it being adjacent to Sutton and Cheam where they had had their great win in December 1972). Jeremy campaigned in all these seats, making speeches in which he casually referred to his recent troubles. On Thursday 4 March, at Coventry North-West, the Liberals registered a slight fall in their vote of October 1974 (the first post-war election at which they had fought the seat), narrowly forfeiting their deposit. This was hardly a disgrace; but the press made much of Grimond's reply when asked whether he thought the result reflected a lack of public confidence in Jeremy: 'Well, it certainly begins to look like it.'

However, the by-election was now the least of Jeremy's troubles. For the *Daily Mirror* had just discovered that Holmes was the purchaser of the letters which had been sold by Gleadle for £2,500. (This was probably the result of a leak from police quarters: for during February, Holmes, realising that the fact was bound to emerge eventually, had confidentially seen the Deputy Director of Public Prosecutions, a fellow member of the Reform Club, to confess that he had bought the letters, being subsequently interviewed about the matter by the police.[25]) Jeremy astonished Cyril Smith by remarking to him: 'A press-man has told me that the £2,500 came from someone close to me. I'd love to know who it was.' On Friday, while campaigning in the Wirral, he was telephoned by Smith to be told that the *Mirror* was about to identify Holmes as the purchaser. 'Where does that leave me?' asked Jeremy. 'In a bloody mess,' replied Smith, who dispatched Alistair Michie, a recently appointed Liberal Party official, to meet Jeremy's train at Euston and help him elude the press. Michie told Jeremy that a statement had just been issued by Holmes admitting the purchase of the letters, but adding that he had carried out the transaction entirely on his own initiative and without Jeremy's knowledge. Jeremy professed to be astonished and shocked by this news. When they reached Orme Square, Jeremy invited Michie in and telephoned Holmes in his presence, beginning the call with the theatrically delivered words: 'David, how *could* you . . .'[26]

Next day, Saturday 6 March, the Holmes revelation was the lead story in most newspapers, eclipsing the news that the value of the pound had sunk below $2 for the first time. The *Mirror* sported the celebrated headline: 'I PAID NORMAN SCOTT £2,500, SAYS THE GODFATHER'.* Among the press and most of the colleagues who had given Jeremy the benefit of the doubt a month earlier, his credibility was shattered. As Steel writes in his memoirs, it was just believable that Holmes might have bought the letters without Jeremy's knowledge: it was inconceivable that he should have continued to keep Jeremy in the dark once the transaction had been disclosed by the press.[27] That Jeremy's astonished reaction to Holmes' statement was mere play-acting is suggested by the fact that it had been issued on Holmes' behalf by David Freeman, the Prime Minister's personal solicitor. (Indeed, Holmes subsequently claimed that Wilson himself had vetted the statement before publication.[28]) Holmes did not increase his plausibility by giving a number of artless interviews in which he kept contradicting himself.

Most of the Liberal MPs would now have agreed with Hooson, who declared in a weekend radio interview that Jeremy 'should recognise that the Thorpe era is coming to an end'. It seemed likely that, at the next PLP meeting, he would formally be called on to resign. However, that Sunday, Jeremy confounded his colleagues by announcing that he *would* resign as soon as the proposed new rules for the election of the Leader had been adopted, probably at the Liberal Assembly at Llandudno in September, and would stand for re-election. He made this announcement without consulting anyone except the Party President Margaret Wingfield, his loyal supporter. The new rules,

---

* Holmes was godfather to Jeremy's son; Mario Puzo's novel *The Godfather* had recently been made into two Oscar-winning films.

formulated by a committee set up at the previous Assembly, had not even been published, though were due to appear in the coming issue of *Liberal News*: in essence, they provided that the Leader should be chosen from among Liberal MPs by an electoral college consisting mostly of delegates from constituency associations, where support for Jeremy remained strong (though ironically, he himself had been resisting such a change for years).

This ingenious coup disarmed the colleagues who sought to oust him: they were taken unawares, and risked offending fellow Liberals if they either opposed the new rules or tried to force an election before they came into effect. Hooson and Pardoe unwittingly strengthened Jeremy's hand still further by declaring that they would stand against him, thus both implicitly accepting that he should be able to stay until the rules were adopted, and appearing as disloyal colleagues. As for Cyril Smith, so shocked was he by Jeremy's artful move, and the fact that, as Chief Whip, he had not been consulted about it, that he suffered some kind of seizure that Sunday night and was rushed to hospital in Rochdale. Jeremy promptly offered his job to Alan Beith, the last Liberal to have won a by-election, who accepted on condition that he should not have to concern himself with Jeremy's personal problems. As he lay half-delirious in his hospital bed that Monday, Smith provided further headlines for a bemused public by mumbling to reporters the following surreal phrases:

> I am frightened of what may yet come out. I have not been told everything known about the affair, even by members of my own Party. There are things going on I know nothing about. I am being made to carry the can for something that's nothing to do with me ... You simply wonder what is going to happen. You just don't know.

Quoting these remarks, the *Daily Telegraph* commented: 'Liberals at Westminster had to pinch themselves yesterday to believe that they were not involved in a Feydeau farce.' But the most bizarre development was about to come. On Tuesday 9 March, in reply to a planted question in the House of Commons, the Prime Minister declared: 'I have no doubt at all there is strong South African participation in recent activities relating to the Leader of the Liberal Party.' He qualified this remarkable statement by saying that he believed that this participation involved 'private agents' backed by 'massive resources of business money': he had seen 'no evidence that the South African Government or its agencies have any connection with these unsavoury activities'. When John Pardoe, sitting next to Jeremy, asked what action the Prime Minister proposed to take, Wilson merely replied that he hoped fellow-members would be 'revolted' that such things should be going on in a democratic country.

What lay behind this statement? Wilson had asked MI5 to 'investigate' the possibility of a South African plot to discredit Jeremy, but they had come up with very little. Unprecedentedly, he had discussed his proposed answer with none of his usual advisers, nor did he produce the slightest evidence for his state-ment. Tony Benn wrote in his diary:

> You can see why Harold said it. First of all, his interest in trying to boost the Liberals lies in the fact that their lost votes would go to the Tories. Secondly, from a PM's point of view, to be generous to a man who is down might do him some credit. Thirdly ... I wonder whether Harold himself is vulnerable and wants to estab-lish the principle that the South Africans are trying to destroy British political leaders.

Another diarist, Wilson's senior policy adviser Bernard Donoughue, one of the few people who knew that the Prime Minister himself meant to resign within a few days, had a blunter explanation: 'He does not want Thorpe to go now and steal the thunder from his own departure.' But although in the short term Wilson's words helped Jeremy survive politically, in the long run they did him harm. For the journalists who rushed to investigate Wilson's sensational claims soon discovered that, although the South Africans were doubtless delighted that Jeremy should encounter problems as a result of his private life, and may have played a role in helping publicise those problems, the truth was that Jeremy's original relationship with Scott, his subsequent hounding by Scott, and his eventual decision to do something about Scott were real matters which had nothing to do with South Africa.

Asked to comment, Jeremy remarked that he had been interested but not surprised by the Prime Minister's words. No doubt they gave him comfort as he faced two new tests – the by-elections at Carshalton and Wirral on Thursday, and the trial of Newton, due to begin in Exeter the following Tuesday. Accompanied by Marion, he put in several appearances at Carshalton, hoping to salvage his political reputation with a good result there for the Liberals. Although it was too much to hope for another Orpington, it was rather a tribute to Jeremy that their vote there held up; but at Wirral they slipped badly, losing their deposit for the first time since 1950. These results were really no worse than those which the Liberals had experienced in the mid-term of the last Labour Government, but they provided ammunition to the colleagues who wanted him to go.

By this time, Orme Square was under permanent siege by journalists and television camera crews, much to the annoyance of Marion, and Jeremy was being inundated with requests for interviews from newspaper editors. On Friday 12 March, the day after the by-elections, Jeremy, bearing in mind that Scott would be giving evidence in Exeter after the weekend, accepted the advice of Lord Goodman that he should receive the leading editor who appeared to be most sympathetic to him, Harold Evans of the *Sunday Times*. He replied to Evans' questions and handed him a statement which he invited his newspaper to publish. This began:

When Norman Scott made his outburst in court I issued a brief statement that I had not seen him for 12 years and that the allegations were baseless. I would have thought that that assurance would have sufficed, but I am advised that a further refutation in the most categorical and unqualified terms is necessary.

Mr Scott has made the following allegations against me:

(a) the existence of a homosexual relationship with me;

(b) that I stole his National Insurance card;

(c) that the Liberal Party, Lord Byers and others have made him from time to time subventions to keep him quiet;

(d) that, in the incident of the shot dog, my wife or I hired a gunman at a five-figure sum to kill the dog, or Scott, or both, towards the cost of which the Government contributed;

(e) that the identity of the gunman was variously, my helicopter pilot, or a Liberal worker in the Devon and Cornwall region.

(f) In addition, it is alleged that I was acquainted with or involved in a correspondence between Scott and Bessell and that I knew of, or was involved in, the purchase of the Bessell letters from Scott for a sum of £2,500.

All these allegations are totally false.

It was a clever statement: on the one hand, it made Scott sound ridiculous; on the other hand, it contained little, on the available evidence, which could be impugned. Allegations (a) and (f) were the ones which Scott had been making and Jeremy denying since 29 January. Allegation (b) was one which Scott had been making to all and sundry since 1962, and was indeed absurd. Allegation (c) corresponded to Scott's own distorted view of Bessell's 'retainers', which he had described to friends as 'hush money' from the Liberal Party. Allegation (d) represented the accusation which Scott was expected to make from the witness box at Exeter: the implication that the Government might have been involved was one which Newton himself had planted in Scott's mind. Only allegation (e) was in effect a distortion of Jeremy's, for Scott knew that Newton was neither of these things – though there were other hostile incidents of which he had spoken and which had allegedly involved a helicopter and West Country Liberals.

That Sunday, the newspaper published the statement (which had already been broadcast on television the night before[29]) on its front page under the title 'THE LIES OF NORMAN SCOTT', while its inside pages contained a long 'report' on the affair by its Insight team which was highly favourable to Jeremy. Whatever had occurred between Jeremy and Scott in the early 1960s, it suggested, had been 'essentially trivial', while Jeremy's word had 'proved reliable throughout a long career in public life'. Whenever Jeremy, in his interview with Evans, had given details which could be checked, these were found to be accurate. For example, Scott claimed to have received a present of Cartier cufflinks from Jeremy, who denied this and suggested the newspaper consult Cartier, who confirmed that they had no record of supplying such an item to Jeremy, nor was Scott able to produce them.* The piece was scathing not only about Scott, whom it depicted as a malicious liar, but also about Bessell, whom it portrayed as both a knave and a fool: it gave details of Bessell's past business affairs with a view to demonstrating his incompetence, dishonesty and propensity to fantasy. The article was invaluable to Jeremy, as it went some way towards discrediting in advance whatever Scott might say in Exeter or Bessell might say in future; but the denigration of Bessell, in which Jeremy had clearly collaborated, threatened to alienate the ex-MP, who had hinted in his last letter to Jeremy that his willingness to be used could not be taken for granted.

---

* The cufflinks in question may have been those of Jeremy's father sporting the Thorpe crest, which Jeremy told Bessell in 1965 that he regretted having given Scott (see above, p. 232).

On 29 January, it was arguably Jeremy's bad fortune that the London & Counties report should have appeared on the same day as Scott's outburst. On 16 March, it was certainly his good fortune that Newton's trial opened on the same day as two even more sensational news items which drove it off the front pages – Wilson's resignation and the announcement that Princess Margaret was divorcing Lord Snowdon. It has been suggested that this coincidence was not entirely fortuitous. Given that Wilson (as is now known) had long harboured the intention to resign that month, two years after resuming office, but presumably had no reason to choose any particular date, and that, spurred on by Falkender, he had already gone out of his way to help Jeremy, by attacking the press treatment of him and attributing his problems to South African 'influences' and even (we are told) casting a friendly eye over David Holmes' statement, it seems plausible that he may have timed his announcement to distract attention from the embarrassments of both the Royal Family and Jeremy. (The Princess, who was still something of a friend of Jeremy, would presumably have consulted the Prime Minister about the timing of her announcement: hers was only the second case of a person in the line of succession to the throne being party to a divorce, the first having been that of Marion and Harewood a decade earlier.*)

The Exeter proceedings contained elements of farce. The prosecuting counsel, Lewis Hawser QC, was an old friend of Jeremy, and is said to have had unusual consultations beforehand with both the Attorney-General and Lord Goodman.[30] He treated

---

* On 22 March 1977, Lady Falkender purportedly told Penrose and Courtiour that 'the date of Sir Harold's surprise resignation announcement had been inextricably linked to the announcement that the royal marriage ... was officially at an end' and 'that the Palace might probably [sic] have played an equally crucial role in the timing of Andrew Newton's trial'. (The Pencourt File, pp. 330–1.) But all of this was denied by Wilson when it was published in February 1978.

Scott more like a defendant than a prosecution witness, and tried to steer him off the subject of Jeremy while taking him through his main evidence, based on the statement he had given the police following the shooting incident. During cross-examination, Scott was asked by Newton's counsel: 'Has anyone ever told you that you are an incorrigible liar?' He replied: 'Yes, Mr Thorpe on Sunday.' From that moment, Scott was unable to keep off his usual theme (though the police stated that they had found nothing to link Jeremy with the case). As for Newton, he trotted out the story he had told the police in November, that he had been blackmailed by Scott over a nude photograph; but despite a jaunty manner, he made an unconvincing impression. The depths of absurdity were reached when a girlfriend of Newton gave evidence in his defence, claiming to have met Scott when he had made a 'blackmailing' visit to Newton. From the dock, Newton appeared to be prompting her replies. Finally she was asked to identify Scott in the courtroom: as she looked around desperately, Scott suddenly stood up. 'Well, that's the end of that experiment,' said the judge. Newton was sufficiently confident of acquittal to purchase an air ticket for use after the trial. However, forced to choose between two most peculiar stories and witnesses, the jury finally accepted Scott's contention that Newton, for whatever reason, would have killed him but for the jamming of the gun. Convicted of possession of a firearm with intent to endanger life, Newton faced a maximum sentence of twenty years' imprisonment, and was sent down for two.

The trial left Jeremy in an uncomfortable position. On the one hand, his name had again been dragged through the mud by Scott; on the other, there was uncertainty as to what Newton would now say or do. (If he kept silent and served his sentence, he could expect to collect the £5,000 promised by Holmes when he came out. But what then?) And yet, by the time Newton was sentenced on Friday 19 March, Jeremy had cause to congratulate himself. A week earlier, following the by-elections, he had been

under much pressure to resign. Wainwright had visited him at
Orme Square (where Jeremy, recovering from the strain of recent
events, received him in bed) and told him bluntly that he had no
alternative to resignation unless he could clear his name by suing
Scott for slander.[31] Steel, who had been flabbergasted to hear
from Nadir Dinshaw about his role in passing money from
Hayward to Holmes, told Jeremy that 'the lifeblood was ebbing
from the entire Party because of this interesting mess' and that
'in the interests of both the Party and himself he ought now to
resign'.[32] John Pardoe had a stand-up row with him at a dinner
given by Professor Ralf Dahrendorf of the LSE.[33] Cyril Smith continued to issue denunciations of him from his sickbed in
Rochdale. The latest Gallup poll suggested that his troubles were
doing the Party real harm: the Liberals were down to 9.5 per
cent, while his personal rating had dropped to 32 per cent, more
people now disapproving than approving of him as Liberal
Leader. And yet, the PLP, at its weekly meeting on Wednesday 17
March (the second day of the Newton trial), did not, as had been
predicted by the press, express its lack of confidence in him, but
confirmed its willingness to wait for a leadership election in the
autumn. In a leader entitled 'Mr Thorpe Rides Again', the *Daily
Telegraph* wrote of his 'seemingly miraculous resuscitation'.[34]

How is one to explain this failure of his colleagues, most of
whom had by now certainly lost confidence in him and were passionately keen to get rid of him, to wield the axe? There appear to
have been four reasons. First, the unexpectedly vigorous defence
of him by the *Sunday Times* had caused even his critics to wonder
whether there might yet be an innocent explanation for the matters of which he stood accused. Secondly, the commanding figure
of Byers again came to his rescue with strong support. Thirdly, the
Party Chairman Kenneth Vaus announced the result of a poll of
constituency associations, three-quarters of which supported the
continuance of Jeremy's leadership, often in adamant terms. (This
came as little surprise to the MPs, all of whom were receiving post-

bags to the same effect.) Fourthly, there was the surprise of Wilson's resignation: it would have looked odd if two of the historic parties had simultaneously engaged in leadership contests.

Among Jeremy's supporters, the general feeling was that, whether or not there was any truth in the Scott allegations, it was outrageous and ridiculous that he should suffer on account of alleged sexual indiscretions of fourteen years earlier, before he had become Party Leader and married. Some actually felt that his troubles elevated him to a heroic stature. Michael Foot compared him to Byron: 'They pretend to be against you for your morals, but really hate you for your politics.'[35] Even those who had negative feelings about him were often unable to resist a sneaking admiration for the courage and ingenuity with which he parried the blows. An interesting perspective is provided by the diary of Stuart Mole, aged twenty-six, who a few months earlier had been appointed Parliamentary Press Officer to the Liberal Party. He did not find Jeremy easy to work for; like most of the staff, he was demoralised by the Scott affair and believed Jeremy was being far from frank; but he paid tribute to the way he battled through. 'When Thorpe is up against it,' he wrote on 16 February, 'he knows how to fight.' Two weeks later, after the Holmes revelations, he wrote: 'It says much for the skill and nerve of Thorpe that he amazingly held off the challenge and survived.' On 22 March, after the PLP meeting, he wrote of Jeremy's 'Rasputin-like resistance to political extinction'.[36]

There now followed a strange interlude. For seven weeks, the name of Scott had hardly been off the front pages; but for the next seven, it was hardly mentioned by the press. Except in that he showed an icy reserve towards colleagues, Jeremy appeared to resume his normal political life, almost as if nothing had happened. Wilson's departure had left him as the longest-serving party leader, the last survivor of the trio which had personified British politics for almost a decade; and he graciously welcomed the new Prime Minister, James Callaghan, when he took office on 3 April following the Labour leadership election. In a widely reported speech, he declared that 'political parties must stop blaming institutions, individuals, circumstances for their own failures', and described Mrs Thatcher, the 'Iron Lady', as suffering from 'rust on the bodywork'.[37] He committed the Liberals to supporting budget measures which otherwise risked being defeated but which the Government considered vital to the maintenance of its 'social contract' with the unions: this was the first indication to Callaghan, whose majority seemed likely soon to vanish, that the Liberals might be prepared to come to an arrangement with his administration.[38] He spoke at a gathering of European Liberals at Stuttgart to found a common bloc in the European Parliament. He and Marion were guests at a ball given by the Queen at Windsor on 20 April to celebrate her fiftieth birthday.

All the while, however, nemesis was drawing near. Inspired by Wilson's remarks, journalists were still trying to get to the bottom of the Scott affair, and coming up with some surprising discoveries. Richard Rowntree, a leading Yorkshire Liberal from the famous Quaker confectionery dynasty and a friend of Richard Wainwright, was ringing up Bessell every few days urging him to come clean about the affair. Bessell was still reluctant to betray Jeremy, but his loyalty had been strained by the denigration of him in the *Sunday Times*, based on information much of which could only have come from Jeremy. Eventually, he began to reveal some of the truth to Rowntree, who had once helped him in business; and tapes of these conversations came to circulate among members of the PLP. Fortified with this knowledge, some parliamentarians began to plan a coup against Jeremy, to take place after the local elections on 6 May, the leading plotters being Smith and Wainwright among the Liberal MPs and Beaumont and Mackie (both of whom had been ennobled on Jeremy's recommendation) among the Liberal peers.

Jeremy still had the support of most Liberals in the country, along with that of Byers and other party figures, and he might have survived this latest attempt to oust him, but for another development. When Norman Josiffe (as he then was) had complained about Jeremy to the Chelsea police in December 1962, he had given them, along with his statement, two letters from Jeremy – one of February 1962, remarking that 'Bunnies can and *will* go to France', the other of September 1962, commiserating with Josiffe on the death of his dog. Through a ruse, Jeremy had managed, in June 1965, to retrieve most of the letters he had written Josiffe, but not these, which remained on the police file. Technically, they remained Scott's property; and on 30 April 1976, Scott announced that he had asked his solicitor to write to the Metropolitan Police Commissioner demanding their return. Goodman ascertained that the Commissioner intended to accede to Scott's request unless, within the next few days, he was presented with a reason not to. The letters (of which Goodman obtained copies) were not especially compromising in themselves; but they were potentially devastating for Jeremy as they showed that, contrary to what he had been telling everyone for months, his relations with Scott had been affectionate if not intimate. (The 'Bunnies' letter was signed 'yours affectionately' and contained the postscript 'I miss you'.)

He now tried a desperate ploy. For twenty years, he had known the journalist Dan Farson, a sometime colleague on *This Week*. Farson was never exactly a friend, but his parents, the American writer Negley Farson and his wife, who had lived at Appledore in North Devon in a house which their son had now inherited, had been friends of Jeremy. Farson was also a homosexual who inhabited the raffish, heavy-drinking Soho demi-monde.* In December

---

* In his subsequent memoirs, Farson claimed that Jeremy was aware of his homosexuality, though he himself never suspected Jeremy's until the Scott matter arose. Scott told Newton and others that Jeremy had associated with Farson in homosexual circles in the early 1960s, but this has been denied by both Farson and Jeremy and does not appear to be supported by any evidence.

1975, at the twentieth anniversary party of *This Week*, Jeremy had
taken him aside to say that he was being pursued by a 'nut' in
North Devon and asking if Farson might let him know if he ever
came across this person. Soon afterwards, Farson wrote to
Jeremy that he had run into Scott in Barnstaple who indeed
seemed determined to 'destroy' him. On Monday 3 May, after
sending Farson several curious messages in code, Jeremy drove
all the way from London to Appledore to ask him a delicate
favour. Would Farson sign a statement testifying that Scott had
'posed a threat' to Jeremy? If so, the police would refrain from
releasing Scott's letters which would be required as evidence in
the ensuing investigation. Farson was unenthusiastic; he insisted
that Scott's threat had merely been to destroy Jeremy's reputation,
not harm him physically; he was unimpressed by Jeremy's assurances (similar to those Holmes had given Bessell in January) that
Lord Goodman had given his blessing to the plan and that
Farson's name would not be made public. Jeremy seemed desperate, saying that 'the Queensberry Rules don't apply in this
case'; but Farson refused to commit himself, and Jeremy left
empty-handed.[39]

Meanwhile, Bessell was still wrestling with his conscience.
Even now, he was reluctant to reveal the truth in public, as
Wainwright and Rowntree were urging him to do; but at the
beginning of May, two events occurred which eliminated his
remaining inhibitions. The first was the news that Scott had
applied to the police for the return of the letters: Bessell reckoned
that, once this happened, Jeremy's final exposure would be
inevitable. Secondly, Holmes rang Bessell to warn him that, if he
did anything to damage Jeremy, the latter would ensure that he
was pressed to repay the £35,000 he owed Jack Hayward. Bessell
was provoked by this threat. On Monday 3 May, he contacted the
local correspondent of the *Daily Mail*, Douglas Thompson, and
offered to give him a sensational story on condition that
publication was held back until after the local elections on

Thursday the 6th: Bessell did not wish to be responsible for increasing the electoral misfortunes of his old party. Having received this assurance, he told Thompson how he had been visited by Holmes in January asking him to fabricate the blackmail story in order to cover up for Jeremy. The *Mail* originally planned to run this on 7 May, but learned that the *Daily Mirror* also planned to do a big feature that day, revealing the latest Liberal 'plot' against Jeremy and also making use of the documents which had been brought to them by workmen refurbishing Bessell's former office in November 1974. Not wishing to be scooped, the *Mail*'s editor, David English, broke Thompson's promise and ran Bessell's story on 6 May under the headline 'I TOLD LIES TO PROTECT THORPE'.[40] As Bessell had foreseen, this set the seal on the Liberals' disaster at the local elections, in which most of the seats they were trying to hold fell to the Conservatives: they lost control of their great prize of Liverpool, while at Eastbourne, their other gain of 1973, their seventeen seats were reduced to one.

The previous evening, clad in full evening dress on his way to the Royal Academy Dinner, Jeremy had gone to the Royal Automobile Club in Pall Mall to meet Harold Evans at the latter's request. Evans told him that the *Mail* was about to break the story of Holmes' visit to Bessell and asked what Jeremy knew about this. Jeremy was in such a confused state that he hardly seemed aware of what he was saying. He appeared to know all about the Bessell–Holmes meeting, and described Bessell as 'a Judas' for revealing it to the press. Yet he denied ('I would not lie to you') having asked Holmes to ask Bessell to write as he had done to Barnes. At one point he went off to telephone Holmes, with whom he had evidently been in touch for much of the day. 'It struck me as odd,' wrote Evans in his note of the meeting, 'that a man going about his party business should be in such incessant contact with one of the denied parties to a cover-up.' However, by the time he left the Royal Academy that night, Jeremy had pulled himself together and showed his usual fluency in addressing the press. 'It is quite possible,' he said, 'that Mr Holmes may have visited Mr Bessell – he often travels to America – but he certainly did not do so on my behalf or acting on my instructions.' He also claimed to be wholly unaware of Bessell's latest revelations, about which he had been informed in some detail by Evans a few hours earlier. On reading this statement, Evans noted: 'It creates a serious doubt in my mind about the honesty of Jeremy Thorpe.'[41]

Bessell's interview was not in itself fatal for Jeremy: as it represented the fifth version of events he had so far given, it was sceptically received. Moreover, Bessell himself backtracked to some extent that Thursday, saying that he did 'not want to give the total lie' to Jeremy's assertion that he had been ignorant of the purpose of Holmes' visit. However, it acted as the signal which triggered off a torrent of new headlines about the Scott affair, which had hardly been mentioned since the Newton trial seven weeks earlier. Facts which the press had dug up and sat on during that period – such as that Jeremy had paid the bill of Scott's divorce solicitor – were now sensationally produced. It also acted as a starting pistol for the 'plot'. On Friday, Beaumont and Mackie announced that, unless Jeremy resigned as Leader, they would resign the Liberal whip in the House of Lords, while Smith made similar threats as an MP. There was talk of a Liberal parliamentary delegation going to see Bessell in California to get the full facts.

The most pressing problem facing Jeremy, however, was the release of his letters to Scott. He reluctantly accepted the advice of Goodman that, as these were bound to become public within days, his safest course was to publish them himself in a context over which he had some control. Following the latest Bessell story, he had already agreed to give another interview to the *Sunday Times*; and on Friday 7 May, Evans was invited to a meeting at Goodman's office attended by a glum-looking Jeremy and his financial adviser Robin Salinger. On behalf of his client,

Goodman offered the letters (which were in Jeremy's copyright) to the newspaper provided they did not publish them in a blatantly hostile way. After their talk at the RAC two days earlier, Evans was now 'taking a more jaundiced view of Thorpe's story',[42] but he felt unable to refuse this scoop. He agreed to publish the letters along with Jeremy's comments – though he rejected a suggestion of Salinger that the publication should omit some phrases in the letters which 'could be misunderstood'.[43] Later that day, Jeremy was interviewed by a senior journalist of the paper, Bruce Page. Asked to explain why he was publishing the letters, he said:

> I am sick and tired of the mystery being whipped up around these two letters and I am therefore making them available. I have never made a secret that my family* and I befriended Mr Scott fifteen years ago when these two letters were written and we were trying to help him at a time when he was in a desperate and depressive state of mind. I have readily taken the step of publishing these two letters and would certainly do so with any other relevant letters shown to me for authentication.

Page was prepared to believe Jeremy when he continued to insist that he had not had sexual relations with Scott, but felt obliged to ask him whether he had ever been a homosexual. Jeremy said nothing. Page took this to be an admission, and his original article said as much; but Evans felt this would be unfair to Jeremy and, in the final copy, the matter was not mentioned.[44]

That Saturday, Jeremy and Marion left to spend the weekend at their house in Suffolk, to await publication of the *Sunday Times*. Meanwhile Richard Wainwright, interviewed that morning on BBC Radio Leeds, remarked: 'Very serious questions

---

* Presumably a reference to the fact that he had taken Josiffe to spend the night at his mother's house.

have not been answered. Why does Jeremy not sue for libel, which is the proper way in England of clearing one's name?' Given the preoccupation of the mass media with Jeremy's fate that weekend, these words were repeated on radio and television programmes all over the country and highlighted in the Sunday newspapers. Wainwright was later portrayed as Brutus in the political assassination of Jeremy, but he afterwards insisted that it was never his intention to wield the dagger. Although he had been telling Jeremy for months that he should either sue Scott or resign, he had not meant to say so in public and was annoyed to be asked about Jeremy by the interviewer, having been assured that this would not happen – though once asked, he felt he ought to speak his mind.[45]

Under the circumstances, the *Sunday Times* was as favourable to Jeremy as he could have expected. Apart from publishing the two letters along with his explanations, and the Page interview (edited at the last moment so as to exclude his supposed admission of homosexuality), it cited several supportive recent statements about him – including a speech by Harold Wilson at Halifax on Saturday referring to 'underground forces ... at work against the elected Leader of the Liberal Party'. However, the immediate effect of the 'Bunnies' letter was to make both Jeremy and the Liberals a laughing stock throughout the land.

Jeremy still had friends, even among his fellow MPs. Interviewed on the radio, Russell Johnston said that Jeremy was given to writing extravagant letters which meant less than they said, and that it was 'intolerable that someone who has given so much to public life should be hounded in this way on a tissue of allegations for which no proof has been produced at all'. Another friend was Clement Freud, whom the Thorpes visited that Sunday afternoon at his house near Ely. Freud gently advised Jeremy that the situation was now such that he ought to resign, and after some talk, Jeremy unhappily accepted this advice. So far as is known, Freud never revealed to anyone the details of their discussion. It is possible that he took the same view as Lord Byers, who also now believed Jeremy should resign, not so much because he had been discredited – Byers thought him more sinned against than sinning – but because he was 'at the end of his tether and faced a nervous breakdown if he did not give up ... The press made life hell.'[46] Another likely consideration was that, with the prospect of senior figures quitting the Party, it was probable that Jeremy would have been forced out within a matter of days in undignified circumstances had he not now gone voluntarily.

Jeremy then rang David Steel, standing in for the Chief Whip, Alan Beith, who was abroad, and asked for a meeting with him the following morning. At noon on Monday 10 May 1976, having taken elaborate measures to avoid the press, they met at Freud's London house 'in a tired and dejected atmosphere'.[47] Jeremy tendered his resignation to the man destined to succeed him in the form of a letter (designed for general publication) which contained an understandable element of bitterness, but which, in a characteristic touch, concluded with the same salutation as the 'Bunnies' letter.

My dear David,

In the absence of Alan Beith, I am writing to you in your capacity as acting Chief Whip. You will recall that the Parliamentary Liberal Party having passed a unanimous vote of confidence in the leadership subsequently agreed that the Party would hold a Leadership election in the autumn. This was a course which I myself had suggested to the President. Until such time it was clearly agreed that we act as a united party.

Since then two things have happened: first, sections of the press have turned a series of accusations into a sustained witch hunt and there is no indication that this will not continue; second, a parliamentary colleague has taken to the air publicly to challenge my credibility.

Although other parliamentary colleagues have come to my support, and agree that nothing has changed since our decision to hold an autumn election, I am convinced that a fixed determination to destroy the Leader could itself result in the destruction of the Party.

I have always felt that the fortunes of the Party are far more important than any individual and accordingly I want to advise you that I am herewith resigning the leadership.

You will appreciate the sadness with which I do this, but I feel I owe the decision to my family, my constituents, and the many loyal Liberals who deserve better of us than the continued spectacle of a Party wrangling with itself with more concern for personality than policy.

You will know that from the very beginning I have strenuously denied the so-called Scott allegations and I categorically repeat those denials today. But I am convinced that the campaign of denigration which has already endured for over three months, should be drawn by me as an individual and not directed at the Liberals collectively through their Leader. No man can effectively lead a Party if the greater part of his time has to be devoted to answering allegations as they arise and countering continuing plots and intrigues.

To Liberals all over the country, whose loyalty and understanding has been quite superb and a source of great strength to my wife and myself, I ask that they use this period to redouble their efforts to build up the Party and to re-create the unity upon which alone we can build on our substantial and dedicated Liberal support.

Perhaps you would make this decision known to my colleagues and be responsible for making it known to my fellow Liberals in the country.

Yours affectionately,

Jeremy

21

INTERLUDE
1976–77

JEREMY THORPE WAS down but not yet out. After nine years and four months, he had ceased to be Liberal Leader; but he remained an MP and a Privy Counsellor, and had only just turned forty-seven. He was still held in much affection and respect by the public, the Liberal Party, 'establishment' circles and the mass media. The view was widespread that he owed his fall to a mixture of bad luck and shabby treatment. Harold Wilson declared that he had been a victim of 'evil' and treated 'contemptibly' by colleagues.[1] The Young Liberal Chairman Stephen Atack deplored the 'most illiberal' manner in which he had been 'hounded out of office' and predicted that 10 May 1976 would 'go down in history as a black day for Liberalism'. Although Jeremy himself largely blamed the press for his misfortunes, the newspapers were generous to him in his downfall: in the leader columns, editors paid tribute to his original gifts and distinction as a public figure, wished him well in the interesting career which doubtless still lay ahead of him, and wondered whether the Liberals would find anyone of equal calibre to succeed him.

Following Jeremy's resignation, Jo Grimond agreed to become Caretaker Leader while arrangements were made to approve the new election procedure and elect a successor as quickly as possible. On 12 June, a Special Assembly at Manchester approved the new rules, a complex formula under which candidates had to be nominated by at least three fellow MPs and constituency associations were allotted votes according to how their parliamentary candidates had fared at the last General Election. After Grimond had made his speech, Jeremy and Marion appeared and were cheered all the way to their seats, while Cyril Smith stormed off the platform in protest. As expected, David Steel and John Pardoe announced their candidatures, the difference between them being more of style (Steel's ice and Pardoe's fire) than of policy: Russell Johnston, one of the few MPs to have supported Jeremy to the end, also wished to stand, but could not find enough colleagues to nominate him, while Jeremy's old adversary Emlyn Hooson, having announced his intention of standing while Jeremy was still Leader, withdrew from the contest. On 7 July, after a month-long campaign marked by extraordinary unpleasantness, Steel was declared elected by some 12,500 votes to Pardoe's 7,000.

Though it represented release from strains which had become almost intolerable to him, Jeremy's resignation was naturally accompanied by some trauma. It was a wrench for him to leave the parliamentary office which he had occupied by virtue of his status (though as Steel wanted modern furniture, he managed to hang on to the fine Pugin desk used by Lloyd George and take it with him to the new office which he shared with the House of Commons Chaplain).[2] But he soon seemed to shake off his depression and recover much of his old sparkle. As always, he could count on unlimited comfort and support from his wife and mother (though it was a time of sadness for Marion, marked by the final illness of her beloved Benjamin Britten who died in December 1976). He remained popular in his constituency and attracted much sympathy there on account of his recent troubles: in the months following his resignation, he and Marion lived mostly at their Devon cottage, where they cultivated their garden and had friends to stay.

Steel offered Jeremy the post which he himself had held for the past year, that of the Party's chief foreign affairs spokesman, which Jeremy accepted with good grace. His portfolio included responsibility for European matters, and on his first day in the job, he made a plea in the House of Commons for Direct Elections to the European Parliament under a PR system,* a subject on which he also spoke at the Liberal Assembly at Llandudno in September, where his enthusiastic reception confirmed his continuing popularity with the rank and file. He was also hopeful that recent developments in Southern Africa would lead to a settlement in Rhodesia based on 'majority rule', hopes he discussed with the new Foreign Secretary, Tony Crosland. During the summer, he took on two further jobs: the Chairmanship of the United Nations Association, the national organisation dedicated to promoting the ideals of the UN, and the Presidency of the Liberal Centenary Committee, set up to commemorate the founding in Birmingham in May 1877 of the National Liberal Federation, Britain's first mass party organisation. He resumed his broadcasting career, presenting a special edition of *This Week* to mark the twenty-first anniversary of the launch of British commercial television. He also took up the causes of various individuals: early in 1977, he became a prominent supporter of the dashing young émigré Soviet dissident Vladimir Bukovsky, and tried to protect some Buddhist monks

---

* The first elections to the European Parliament were due to take place in June 1979, but each EEC member state had the right to choose which electoral system to adopt, as well as an option not to hold elections at all but continue the existing system of co-opting national parliamentarians. Given the lukewarmness of many of its backbenchers towards the EEC, the Labour Government was disinclined to introduce legislation providing for direct elections.

from being deported to Nepal, where he claimed they would suffer persecution (though he was unable to produce any evidence to substantiate this claim, causing Stuart Mole to comment wearily that it looked like 'the Angolan gold all over again'[3]).

By the spring of 1977, memories of the Scott affair were fading, and Jeremy looked set to establish himself as an elder statesmen in his late forties; but he suffered a setback when, on 24 March, a man calling himself George de Chabris, who had been appointed Secretary of the National Liberal Club the previous July on Jeremy's recommendation, absconded with club funds. Chabris (whose real name was Marks) was a flamboyant and apparently wealthy Canadian businessman whom Jeremy had originally got to know when he had offered his services as a fundraiser. He was given wide control over the ailing NLC and its finances on the understanding that he would use some of his own fortune to revive it, but instead he stripped the Club of such assets as its cellar and library and used the proceeds to finance a lavish lifestyle for himself and his family. He struck up close relations with the Party Treasurer, Jeremy's protégé Philip Watkins, who vouched for his financial standing. It eventually emerged that Chabris' wealth was non-existent and he was being sued for large sums on account of his former business activities. While it is uncertain how far Jeremy was aware of Chabris' true background, their association was all too reminiscent of his earlier involvement with such dubious (and equally flamboyant) operators as Bessell and Caplan; he emerged from the affair looking foolish, having once declared in an after-dinner speech that 'throughout history there have been whole families who have devoted themselves to Liberalism – the Gladstones, the Lloyd Georges, the Asquiths and now the De Chabris'. *Private Eye*, for whom Jeremy and the Liberals had become favourite targets, helped expose Chabris and derived much amusement from the affair – especially when it emerged that a manager appointed by Chabris, a former police officer, had organised homosexual entertainments involving the club's (sometimes unwilling) young male staff for the benefit of various members and himself.[4]

Chabris timed his vanishing act with care, for Liberals had other things to think of on 24 March 1977 than the fate of the NLC. In recent months, the Government had lost its majority through defections and by-election losses and only survived thanks to the support of nationalists and independents. When the Conservatives tabled a no-confidence motion for Wednesday 23 March, the Scottish and Welsh Nationalists announced they would vote against the Government, which faced certain defeat if the Liberals followed suit. In a series of hectic meetings between Monday night and Wednesday morning, Callaghan and Steel hammered out a deal whereby the Liberals agreed to 'work with the Government in the pursuit of economic recovery', support-ing it until the end of the current parliamentary session in return for a consultative role. Steel, aware that Jeremy had been lam-basted three years earlier (not least by Steel himself) for talking to Heath without first consulting his colleagues, took care to confer at every stage of the hurried negotiations with his fellow MPs, as well as with Byers in the Lords and the Party Chairman Geoffrey Tordoff who was in touch with the grass roots. The agreement – the so-called Lib–Lab Pact – remained secret until after the debate on Wednesday, in which Mrs Thatcher, imagin-ing that her hour had come, made a fool of herself and the Government survived by 322 votes to 298. When the Joint Statement of Callaghan and Steel was published the following morning, it transpired that the Government, in addition to setting up a Joint Consultative Committee with the Liberals, had agreed in advance to some watered-down Liberal demands: to prepare legislation providing for Direct Elections to the European Parliament and new Scottish and Welsh Assemblies, which might contain clauses on proportional representation subject to free votes; to provide time for a bill on housing the homeless; and to drop some nationalisation proposals.

All the Liberal MPs supported the agreement apart from Grimond and Penhaligon, who acquiesced in the interests of unity. When the Conservatives bitterly accused the Liberals of being Labour's catspaw, as they had struck a deal with Callaghan having failed to strike one with Heath, Jeremy was quick to point out that he and his colleagues *had* in fact offered to maintain Heath in office on 'an agreed programme in the national interest' – though they had felt unable to accept the formal coalition upon which Heath had finally insisted. It was natural, however, that he should experience a sense of regret that he no longer led the Liberals at this long-awaited hour. It must also have been galling for him that, whereas he had been put under pressure in 1974 (not least by Steel) to accept no agreement with Heath which failed to offer firm guarantees on proportional representation, the undertakings now obtained from Callaghan on this issue were pitiful – a mere offer to consider including PR clauses in legislation concerning European, Scottish and Welsh elections, such clauses to be subject to free votes. The difference was that, whereas in March 1974 the Liberals had just won their greatest popular vote and felt bitter that this had translated into a mere handful of seats, the polls in March 1977 showed the worst Liberal ratings for years, lower even than during Jeremy's troubles a year earlier: the alternative to the pact was therefore a General Election at which the Liberal MPs risked being wiped out.*

During the early months of the pact, Jeremy played a leading role in consultations with the Government on the key issue of Direct Elections to the European Parliament. This had led to such heated discussions during the original Steel–Callaghan negotiations that they had almost broken down on the point, but it had finally been agreed in the Joint Statement that the

---

* At a by-election that summer in Birmingham Ladywood, the Liberals, who had actually won the seat at a by-election eight years earlier, experienced the humiliation of being beaten into fourth place by the National Front.

Government would introduce legislation for Direct Elections, to be subject to a free vote, and in so doing would 'take account' of the Liberals' preference for PR. During May, however, the Liberals were dismayed to discover that the bill being considered by the Cabinet invited Parliament, if it accepted the principle of Direct Elections, to choose between alternative options of a PR or first-past-the-post system. The Government insisted it could not go further in view of the dislike felt by many on its own side for both 'Europe' and PR. In a series of meetings with the Leader of the House Michael Foot and Home Secretary Merlyn Rees, Jeremy expressed understanding for the Government's position but warned that the disappointment of Liberals in the country would be such that it would be impossible to get the pact renewed for the coming session. He therefore proposed that, in publishing its bill, the Government should at least express a 'recommendation' in favour of the PR option.[5] The Cabinet accepted this solution and an immediate crisis was thus averted – though the 'recommendation' failed to prevent many Labour backbenchers and even some Cabinet ministers from combining with the Conservatives to defeat the PR option when the clause was finally debated in December.

As Liberal Foreign and Commonwealth Spokesman, he also had consulations under the pact with the glamorous new Foreign Secretary David Owen, who had been appointed at the age of thirty-eight after Crosland's sudden death in February. These were relaxed occasions, described by Owen in his memoirs as 'an obligation but also a pleasure': as fellow Devon MPs since Owen's election for a Plymouth seat in 1966, they had always got on well and co-operated on such West Country issues as the rescue of Lundy. From his long knowledge of the subject, Jeremy gave Owen both useful advice and parliamentary support on policy concerning Rhodesia, along with a friendly warning 'that the Tory right were just waiting to put a motion of censure down on [Owen] personally'. They also discussed the future of the pact, Owen recognising that 'when one could stop [Jeremy] acting the showman he was an astute politician'.[6]

May 1977 witnessed the celebrations organised by Jeremy as President of the Liberal Centenary Committee (in which role he was assisted by the former Head of the LPO Ted Wheeler, who had also been unwillingly driven from office the previous year). These were characteristically lavish and theatrical, culminating in a huge banquet at Birmingham attended by Liberals from all over the world, pride of place being given to descendants of the Liberal Prime Ministers Gladstone, Rosebery, Campbell-Bannerman, Asquith and Lloyd George. They also included a concert by the Birmingham Symphony Orchestra, featuring Yehudi Menuhin, and a 'Centenary Service' at Westminster Abbey, conducted by the former Archbishop Michael Ramsey who had been a Liberal undergraduate. These festivities, coinciding with celebrations for the Queen's Silver Jubilee, brought kudos to Jeremy and welcome distraction to the Party at a time of troubled self-examination over the Lib–Lab Pact – though such was their extravagance that what had originally been conceived as a fundraising exercise ended up as a costly loss-making operation. It was to be the last time for some years that he would hit the headlines for reasons unassociated with scandal.

A year after his resignation, Jeremy remained a popular figure and was widely expected to make some sort of comeback in the near future. But he knew that his troubles were not over, for at least three developments threatened to revive public interest in the Scott story and implicate him in the incident on Porlock Hill. First, there was the uncertainty as to what Newton, sent to prison for up to two years in March 1976, would say or do once released. In return for his silence, Holmes had promised him £5,000 as soon as he came out – but Newton, who was always on the lookout for ways of enriching himself and whose career as an airline pilot lay in ruins, was likely to regard this merely as a first instalment of 'hush money' and, unless satisfied, was likely to sell his story to the press. In Jeremy's world of fears and fantasies, Newton (although Jeremy had never actually met him) seems in effect to have replaced Scott as the possessor of a compromising secret who somehow had to be kept quiet.

Secondly, there was Bessell, his former confidant and 'fixer' whom he had tried to use in 1976 to discredit Scott but who had ended up confirming to the press that Scott's allegations were essentially true. Following Jeremy's resignation, Bessell contemplated writing a memoir of the Scott affair for publication: he consulted a firm of New York literary agents, and by the autumn of 1976 had produced a substantial typescript.[7] (He later claimed that his motive had been 'to help root out corruption in public life': it was just two years since America had been rocked by Watergate, and even at this stage, before anything had been heard of the alleged murder plot, Bessell planned to represent the affair as a 'cover-up' in which British ministers had helped Jeremy evade the consequences of past wrongdoing.) The prospect of Bessell publishing a book in America (revealed by *Private Eye* that October) cannot have failed to alarm Jeremy: not only had he 'managed' Scott between 1965 and 1971, but Jeremy had spoken to him of murder, and Holmes had told him that Newton had been hired to kill Scott. Since March 1976, Jeremy had had no direct contact with Bessell, whom he had described to Harold Evans as 'a Judas'; but he tried to put pressure on him to abandon his project through two men to whom Bessell still owed large sums of money, Tim Beaumont and Jack Hayward (to both of whom Jeremy appealed with some success at this time, claiming that he was being persecuted by Bessell, they obviously having no idea of Jeremy's true reasons for wishing to muzzle Bessell).

The third worrying development for Jeremy was that, following Wilson's sensational and unsubstantiated claim in the House of Commons in March 1976 that sinister South African elements were responsible for Jeremy's troubles, various journalists had set out to investigate this story – investigations which inevitably concluded that the issue was a red herring and that South Africans had had no role in the affair other than to encourage Scott to publicise allegations which had a substantial basis in fact. It must have been a relief for Jeremy when, in June 1977, an imminent book on the subject, by the freelance journalists Geoffrey Allen and William Raynor, was withdrawn by its publishers, Penguin Books.* Jeremy had no success, however, in attempting to discourage another firm of publishers, Secker & Warburg, which had commissioned a book from two former BBC reporters, Barrie Penrose and Roger Courtiour: indeed, the investigation undertaken by this pair (jointly dubbed 'Pencourt' by *Private Eye*, after the Watergate journalists Woodward and Bernstein who had become known as 'Woodstein') was remarkable not least for the reason that it had been initiated by Wilson himself.

It has been seen that, during the final months of his premiership, Wilson, who was getting rather senile and paranoid, had become persuaded (with some prompting from Lady Falkender) that South African agents were responsible both for various difficulties he had experienced as premier and Jeremy's troubles. On 12 May 1976, two months after his own resignation and just two days after Jeremy's, he invited Penrose and Courtiour, who had earlier approached his office about a news story (which proved spurious) concerning an alleged South African agent, to his house in Westminster. To the amazement of the journalists, neither of whom he knew personally, Wilson received them warmly and offered to help them 'investigate the forces that are threatening democratic societies like Britain'. He then talked

---

* Although some believed that the decision not to publish was at least partly due to pressure from Jeremy, it was in fact entirely due to the judgement of the responsible editor, Michael Dover, that there was insufficient evidence to support the theories put forward in the book.

discursively for ninety minutes about these alleged 'forces', which included not just South African agents but also right-wing elements in the British security services. Reiterating his willingness to help them get to the bottom of these nebulous matters, he added, with a (probably tongue-in-cheek) touch of John Buchan:

> I see myself as the big fat spider in the corner of the room. Sometimes I speak when I'm asleep. You should listen. Occasionally when we meet I might tell you to go to the Charing Cross Road and kick a blind man standing on the corner. That blind man may tell you something, lead you somewhere.

For the moment, however, the only concrete issue which Wilson suggested 'Pencourt' investigate was the alleged disappearance of Norman Scott's social security file. (Many months later, they learned from Lady Falkender that both she and Wilson believed that this had been stolen by an as yet unidentified 'South African mole in the Cabinet Office' who had used it to 'smear' Jeremy and had also worked to undermine Wilson as Prime Minister.[8])

'Pencourt' reported this meeting to incredulous superiors at the BBC, and a few days later returned to see Wilson with the Director-General, Sir Charles Curran, to whom the ex-premier said much the same things. Curran found the whole thing bizarre but agreed to give 'Pencourt' facilities to investigate Wilson's allegations. At the start of their quest, 'Pencourt' looked into suggestions of South African involvement in the Scott affair – but discovered that most of those who claimed to have knowledge of such involvement were frauds. They also examined the question of Scott's social security file – but learned that, although it had been considered politically sensitive by the Wilson Government, it had not in fact 'disappeared' but been weeded in the course of normal procedure.* They soon found that their only line of enquiry to yield results was into Scott's allegations themselves, and to this they began to devote their energies, believing that eventually some genuine link would present itself with the sinister 'forces' mentioned by Wilson. They met Scott, spoke on the telephone to Bessell, made a research visit to North Devon and approached Jeremy's fellow MPs. They had soon learned more about the affair than any of the journalists who had tried to investigate it during the recent crisis leading to Jeremy's resignation: Scott, for example, gave them a copy of the statement he had made at Chelsea police station in 1962, which he had just recovered along with his letters, and they obtained information from such figures as Scott's solicitor and psychiatrist in Devon and Jeremy's disenchanted colleagues Emlyn Hooson and Cyril Smith.

The direction of their research soon began to alarm their superiors. It was one thing to investigate claims about destabilising forces made by the former Prime Minister; it was quite another to seek to expose the efforts of a recently humbled but still popular politician to avoid the disclosure of ancient sexual indiscretions. In August 1976, some ten weeks into their investigation, Penrose and Courtiour were presented with new contracts by the BBC which would have deprived them of control over the eventual use of their material. Believing that they were about to uncover intrigues of untold implications, and that the 'establishment' was out to 'muzzle' them, they decided to leave the BBC and write instead a book for Secker, whose managing director, Tom Rosenthal, shared their fascination with conspiracy theories. Wilson continued to help them, and they had further talks with him and Lady Falkender, learning such alleged facts as that Wilson had timed his resignation to distract attention from Princess Margaret's divorce. During the

---

* The contents of the file had however been summarised in the report on Scott which had been drawn up for Wilson by Jack Straw: see p. 397.

following months, they failed to establish any connection between the Scott affair and a wider conspiracy – but they managed to pull off two sensational coups in their research into the affair itself. They visited Bessell in California and extracted his entire story from him, which (as with all their interviews) they secretly tape-recorded. And they succeeded in visiting Newton in Preston Prison and tricking him into admitting that he was in the pay of Holmes – the first time any of those investigating the Porlock Hill incident had established such a connection.

Jeremy observed the progress of 'Pencourt' (which was regularly reported in *Private Eye*) with increasing alarm. He refused their requests for interviews; and when they approached him outside his Devon cottage early in 1977, he reacted with some violence, threatening them with an action for criminal libel.* On 4 May 1977, Jeremy and Lord Goodman saw Wilson at his Westminster office and asked him to cease helping the journalists, who they suggested might be in South African pay.[9] As a result, 'Pencourt' had no further direct contact with Wilson and Falkender; but at a meeting with Tom Rosenthal later that month, Wilson agreed not to obstruct their book. Wilson admitted that he had tried to help Jeremy as a friend, but accepted the publisher's view that the former Liberal Leader had been involved in inappropriate doings which were bound to come out, and that Wilson could do nothing further to protect him without compromising himself.[10]

Meanwhile Newton, having served just over half his sentence, had been released from prison in April 1977. Within days of his release, he received the £5,000 promised by Holmes (which presumably came out of the Hayward money which Dinshaw had transmitted to Holmes in cash) from John Le Mesurier at a

---

* Much to Jeremy's satisfaction, his Eton contemporary Sir James Goldsmith was currently conducting a rare private prosecution for this antiquated offence against *Private Eye* and its distributors, finally settled out of court in May 1977.

cloak-and-dagger meeting in South Wales. (Interviewed in 1981, Le Mesurier claimed that, to maintain Newton's silence, he had subsequently paid him a further £12,000 on behalf of Holmes, though this was never admitted by either Holmes or Newton.*) Holmes also offered to help Newton find work, and suggested he apply for service with either the South African or Rhodesian Air Force. This was a curious suggestion, given that both those governments must have been aware of the rumour that Newton had been hired to kill Scott, and were hardly likely to help Jeremy, one of their most vocal critics, by employing Newton: it seems that the motive behind it was to be able to discredit Newton as a South African agent should he ever try to tell his story in future. Newton for his part was quite attracted by the idea of starting a new life in Southern Africa, but before he went there planned to double-cross Holmes and sell his story to a British newspaper for the fortune he imagined it to be worth.

By the summer of 1977, therefore, Jeremy knew that a fresh outbreak of scandal could not be long delayed: it was merely a question of when it would occur, which of the various threatening parties would set it off, and whether he would survive it. Now that Newton was at large, Jeremy could only hope that Holmes would succeed in keeping him quiet. Bessell had postponed his plan to publish his memoir of the Scott affair, while he

---

* '[Newton] said he needed another £12,000 to qualify as a jet pilot and he would then get out of our hair immediately. I was sceptical and remember telling David that with Newton we had acquired an albatross round our necks far more dangerous than Scott ... In any event, David stumped up the money ... [which] came ... out of funds directed to him by Thorpe.' (Interview of John Le Mesurier by Barrie Penrose, 1981, quoted in *Rinkagate*, pp. 287–8.) In his interviews given to the *News of the World* around the same time, Holmes merely said that Newton 'asked for £18,000 [*sic*] to train as a pilot and would not believe me when I said such money was not available. It was rather a relief when Newton spilled the beans and the blackmail threat disappeared.' (Holmes Transcripts.)

coped with a debt recovery action brought (with Jeremy's encouragement) by Tim Beaumont: but Jeremy knew that he still had much to fear from Bessell, who – as disclosed by *Private Eye* – had been actively helping 'Pencourt'. As for 'Pencourt', Jeremy, now that Penguin had abandoned publication of a book delving into his past, tried to persuade Secker & Warburg to do the same; but this only confirmed the doughty Rosenthal in his view that Jeremy had much to hide, and that the discoveries of 'Pencourt' would cause a sensation (though the two journalists had still discovered nothing to link the Scott affair with Wilson's tale of 'forces' undermining democracy, and had little idea how to contrive a book combining the two subjects).

Yet as the autumn of 1977 began, Jeremy did not seem particularly downcast. On 27 September, at the Liberal Assembly at Brighton, he received a standing ovation after a rousing speech in favour of a resolution (which was overwhelmingly carried) that the Liberals should fight the coming Direct Elections to the European Parliament in coalition with continental members of the Federation of Liberal and Democratic Parties.* A week later, he hailed the Government's decision to construct a link road joining Barnstaple to the Exeter–Taunton motorway at Tiverton, an amenity for which he had been pressing for years in order to relieve his constituency's isolation. Throughout the first half of October, he was involved in talks with both party colleagues and government ministers about the future of the Lib–Lab Pact; and on 18 October, he took part in a meeting of the Liberal Shadow Administration (as the Party's parliamentary spokesmen now grandly termed themselves) to discuss the measures the Liberals would require to be included in the coming Queen's Speech if the pact were to continue.

---

* Radical Liberals had objected to this on the grounds that the Federation included the quite right-wing party of the French President Giscard d'Estaing. But as Jeremy put it, 'we can never be as pure as we would wish ...'

It was on the day after this meeting that the dreaded exposure occurred. In the end, Bessell and 'Pencourt' were scooped, while Newton was duped. Shortly before flying out to Rhodesia at Holmes' expense, Newton offered his story to the *Evening News* for £75,000, with an extra £25,000 to be paid in the event of his confessions returning him to prison. When the newspaper asked for evidence, Newton allowed them to hear a tape-recording he had made of a telephone conversation with Holmes. For this privilege, they paid him £3,000; but having done so, they decided that they had their story and had no further need of Newton. Their edition of Wednesday 19 October 1977 carried the banner headline: 'I WAS HIRED TO KILL SCOTT'.

22

PROSECUTION
1977–79

THOUGH HE HAD long lived in fear that the Newton story would break, its timing appears to have come as a complete surprise to Jeremy Thorpe, who was in Devon that day. Less than a week earlier, Newton, encouraged by Holmes (who paid his fare), had flown off to Southern Africa with the supposed intention of making a new life there, reassuring news which Holmes had doubtless reported to Jeremy. Jeremy first learned of the bombshell from David Steel, who rang to warn him shortly before the *Evening News* hit the stands.[1] He thus had time to prepare a brief statement for the press: 'I know nothing about an alleged plot, but welcome any inquiries the police may make.' The following day, he and Marion returned to London, the popular press remarking that they looked 'grim' on arrival at Paddington and drove off to Orme Square without a word to the waiting journalists. The *Daily Mail* suggested that it was 'the worst day of Jeremy Thorpe's life', but those who met him during the following days were surprised at how calm and normal he seemed in the face of the crisis.

The *Evening News* article of 19 October 1977 caused a national sensation and its content was reproduced by the entire mass media. It proclaimed that Newton had been paid £5,000 to murder Norman Scott,* and described the paymaster as 'a leading Liberal'. (It was some days before the press, fearful of libel, began to name Holmes, who was in fact scarcely known in Liberal circles except as a personal friend of Jeremy.) After reminding readers of Scott's allegations, and their part in bringing about Jeremy's downfall seventeen months earlier, it went on to reveal that DCS Michael Challes of Avon and Somerset Police, who had originally investigated the shooting incident which had led to Newton's trial, had been asked to undertake a new investigation by the Director of Public Prosecutions, Sir Tony Hetherington. This development arose from the fact that Stuart Kuttner, the *Evening News* journalist dealing with Newton, had gone to see Hetherington to report Newton's story and enquire whether, in the event of further criminal proceedings, Newton was likely to be given immunity from prosecution in return for acting as a crown witness. The close relations between the press and the police and prosecuting authorities were to be a striking feature of the case.

While Jeremy showed his usual sang-froid in time of crisis, Steel and other senior party figures were appalled. The claim that Newton had been hired by 'a leading Liberal', followed by statements of Bessell that the idea of murdering Scott had first been raised at 'Liberal meetings',† gave the impression that the whole Party was implicated in the alleged plot, an impression no denials would easily dispel. Moreover, the scandal broke at an embarrassing moment for the Liberals, just as the party

---

* This story differed somewhat from that which Newton later told in court, which was that he had been offered £10,000 to kill Scott and subsequently paid half that sum after failing to do so.

† A reference to the private discussions of Jeremy, Bessell and Holmes at Jeremy's office in the late 1960s.

leadership was engaged in delicate negotiations with the Government for the renewal of the Lib–Lab Pact. Since an early General Election now threatened to wipe out the Liberal MPs, they had little alternative but to renew on the best terms they could get. Jeremy's crisis may thus be said to have affected the political history of Britain by helping prolong the life of the minority Labour Government: for the pact continued to operate officially until the spring of 1978 and unofficially for six months after that, despite giving very little to the Liberals and causing increasing disenchantment among them.

It was obviously vital to the Liberals that the matter should be cleared up quickly, and the key to this seemed to lie with Jeremy himself. When he saw Steel on the afternoon of the 20th, he declared his intention to 'tell all' at a press conference – though as Steel ruefully noted in his diary: 'He won't tell me what "all" is until he has cleared it with his lawyers.' Steel then issued a press release saying that Jeremy would shortly be making 'a full considered statement', adding that the 'leading Liberal' said to have hired Newton was in fact nothing of the kind. He also saw the Home Secretary, Merlyn Rees, to request that the police inquiries 'be speeded up and efficiently conducted at the highest level'.[2]

The press and police were now frantically searching for Newton, who seemed to have vanished. He had in fact flown to Johannesburg in mid-October, proceeding from there to Salisbury, where Holmes had apparently advised him that the local defence commander, General Peter Walls, would give him a job. In the Rhodesian capital, however, Newton, whose name had just become notorious throughout the English-speaking world, was detained on arrival, held for two days and then deported. On his return to Heathrow on 26 October, he voluntarily gave himself up to the police and was taken to Bristol to be interviewed by Challes. The story he now told was very different from the one he had spun two years earlier, and essentially confirmed the *Evening News* story that he had been hired by Holmes to kill Scott. He told the police where they could find some £3,000 in cash, the remains of the £5,000 he had received from Le Mesurier in April. He also let them copy the tapes he had made of his telephone conversations with Holmes, though these did not prove much except that Holmes was a frightened man who had been associated with Newton in some clandestine enterprise and was anxious to appease him.

For almost two weeks, the story dominated the news, every day bringing fresh revelations and allegations. Bessell, flattered to be the object of attention again, gave a series of press interviews, tracing the history of the 'murder plot' back to the night in December 1968 when Jeremy had allegedly first broached it to him. 'Pencourt', bitter at having been scooped, made the best of things by publishing their main findings about the Scott affair in the *Observer*. Newton, as soon as he was released from police custody on 28 October, began hawking further details of his story around Fleet Street, along with his tapes. Newspapers began investigating what they called 'the South Wales connection', getting most of their information from Miller, the man who had introduced Newton to Deakin, who even managed to sell a blurred and virtually indecipherable photograph which he claimed showed Le Mesurier about to hand over the money to Newton on a foggy moor in mid-Glamorgan.

The story the world was waiting for, however, was that of Jeremy himself, who finally held his press conference on Thursday 27 October, a week after it had been announced. It was a curious occasion, attended by eighty-two invited journalists: they were summoned to Westminster only to be redirected to the National Liberal Club, a ploy enabling Jeremy to evade photographers. Flanked by his wife, Lord Goodman's partner John Montgomerie, and Clement Freud MP, he read out a long statement. He began by warning that 'anyone expecting sensational revelations is likely to be disappointed', as 'not a scrap of evidence has been produced to implicate me in any alleged plot to murder Norman Scott'. Of Scott, he said: 'He is neither the only nor the first person I have tried to help, but a close, even affectionate relationship developed from this sympathy. However, no sexual activity of any kind took place.' He admitted having asked Bessell to 'help out with the Scott problem', but denied ever having been party to a 'cover-up'. He insisted as before that Holmes' purchase of letters from Scott had been made without his knowledge: 'Had I known of these negotiations, I would have stopped them at once.' Regarding Wilson's statement about South African involvement, he 'had no reason to disbelieve this, coming from so authoritative a source. I did not myself promote this belief, and it is fair to say that Sir Harold himself has now expressed his doubts.' Regarding Bessell's latest allegations, 'it is my considered opinion that if he had credible evidence to offer, he should have gone to the police rather than the press'. He concluded: 'It would be insane to pretend that the re-emergence of this story has not placed an almost intolerable strain on my wife, my family, and me. Only their steadfast loyalty and the support of many friends ... has strengthened my resolve to meet this challenge. Consequently I have no intention of resigning [the North Devon seat], nor have I received a single request to do so from my constituency association.'

As Jeremy sat down, he put his arm around his wife. Questions were then invited. After a few uncontroversial ones, the BBC reporter Keith Graves rose to his feet and said: 'The whole of this hinges on your private life. It is necessary to ask you if you have ever had a homosexual relationship.' At this, Marion angrily interjected: 'Go on, stand up and say that again!' Graves duly obliged. This time Montgomerie replied, saying he could not allow his client to answer the question. Graves replied: 'I thought this press conference had been called to clear the air, and that is the major allegation.' Jeremy then replied: 'That is not the major allegation. The major allegation is that there was a

Liberal hired to murder a man [*sic*].' Graves replied: 'Because he was having a homosexual relationship with you.' Jeremy replied: 'It may be that our priorities are different. It has been alleged that a man was hired to murder somebody. That is a very serious allegation ...' Although he answered further questions before thanking his audience and leaving by the back stairs, it was this exchange which dominated the coverage in the following day's newspapers.

Had the exercise been worthwhile? It had certainly been wonderful theatre, *The Times* complimenting him on having 'carried off magnificently his act of appearing relaxed and scornful of the whole business'. In the short term, it aroused sympathy for him, as both the opinion and correspondence columns of the newspapers testified. However, it served to fan the flames of publicity; it did nothing to help him in the police inquiries which were commencing; and it compromised him in various respects. There were inconsistencies between it and the previous statement he had published in the *Sunday Times* on 14 March 1976 under the title 'The Lies of Norman Scott'. There, he had insisted that it was 'totally false' to suggest that he had been 'acquainted with ... a correspondence between Scott and Bessell', whereas he now admitted to having asked Bessell to 'help out with the Scott problem'. There was nothing in the former version to suggest the 'close, even affectionate relationship' to which he now confessed. And evidence was not lacking that Jeremy, contrary to what he now claimed, had promoted the theory that a South African hand lay behind his troubles. He also tempted providence by suggesting that Bessell 'should have gone to the police rather than the press': before the year was out, Bessell, stung by these words, would be talking to the police most eagerly. On the whole, friends and advisers believed the press conference to have been a mistake; and it was the last time he spoke in public about his involvement with Norman Scott.

*

Challes had meanwhile started his new investigation. Being under pressure from the Home Secretary to proceed with it as quickly as possible, he took the unusual step of approaching Penrose and Courtiour for their assistance. This 'Pencourt' willingly gave, feeling that their work would not have been in vain if it led to serious criminal charges being brought against Jeremy Thorpe, and that their involvement in the case might contribute to the success of their coming book. They put their eighteen months of research at Challes' disposal and helped him fix up meetings with various witnesses. When Challes interviewed Bessell in California in December 1977, 'Pencourt' were not only present but allowed to tape-record the proceedings, of which they gave an account later that month in the *Observer*.[3] In February 1978, their book was published as *The Pencourt File*, but aroused relatively little attention. This was partly because much of its content had already been in the press for months, partly because its text had been neutered by lawyers, partly because it largely consisted of what one reviewer described as 'a wholesale scattering of half-formulated assertions of interference and cover-up'. It was, however, read with interest by Jeremy's lawyers; for as Sir David Napley later wrote: 'While we did not appreciate that *The Pencourt File* would disclose the whole of the prosecution's case, we rightly assumed that it would cover much of it ... If it provided a blueprint for the police, it equally provided a guide to us as to what we had to meet which is seldom available in other cases ...'[4]

Nevertheless, the publication of the long-dreaded book was a bad moment for Jeremy, going into detail as it did about a murky slice of his past along with his efforts down the years to cover it up. It coincided with another painful episode, the acrimonious ending of his friendship with David Holmes. Jeremy took the view that Holmes (whom he henceforth dubbed 'Whole-Mess') had made a complete mess of things by choosing the incompetent and untrustworthy Newton in the first place and then mishandling him at every stage. He felt that, in the event of the police managing to prove that Holmes had hired Newton for criminal purposes, Holmes should take full responsibility and claim to have acted without Jeremy's knowledge, as he had already done when identified as the purchaser of Bessell's letters to Scott. Holmes, however, having acted reluctantly and at Jeremy's insistence, felt it was outrageous that, if it came to the worst, he should have to shoulder the entire blame. As Jeremy had been advised by his lawyers to avoid further direct contact with Holmes, their exchanges mostly took place through the intermediary of another Oxford friend of Jeremy, Michael Ogle;* but there seems to have been at least one stormy meeting between them. On 19 March, an ITN journalist rang Challes to report that one of his colleagues had recently been visited by Holmes, who had just seen Jeremy and was 'shaking with rage'. Holmes had told him: 'If you want to know where the money for Newton came from, it was from Jack Hayward in the Bahamas. He passed it to a man called Nadir Dinshaw in Jersey who . . . brought it to London in several lots of cash . . .'⁵ By asking the journalist (a neighbour of Holmes' mother) to pass this infor-mation on to Challes without revealing its source, Holmes presumably sought to tip off the police about the one piece of provable evidence linking Jeremy to the plot. But he got more than he had bargained for: within a month, the story had appeared in *Private Eye*, and the involvement of Hayward and Dinshaw was being discussed throughout the press.

Four months earlier, Jeremy had lunched with Dinshaw and asked him whether, should the police question him about the £20,000 he had received from Hayward during 1974–75, he might say that this had been part of a business deal with

---

* Ogle was very supportive of Jeremy at this time, offering sanctuary to him and Marion on his isolated estate on Dartmoor when they came under pressure from the press.

Hayward, and not mention either Jeremy or Holmes. Dinshaw was shocked, and said he would have to tell the truth if asked about the money: he had acted purely on Jeremy's instructions and had never even met Hayward. On 13 April, following Holmes' compromising disclosures, Jeremy approached Dinshaw again. He made light of the possibility that criminal charges might be brought against him, but said there were people out to destroy him and that his political career might be finished unless Dinshaw helped him by telling the police no more than he was asked and in particular saying nothing about the second £10,000. Dinshaw repeated that he would have to tell the truth and urged Jeremy to do the same. At this, Jeremy remarked: 'It will be curtains for me, and you will be asked to move on.' Dinshaw interpreted this as meaning that Jeremy would commit suicide, while Dinshaw would be deported to his native Pakistan: he was saddened that a man he had regarded as a friend should threaten him in so crude a manner. Without waiting to be approached by the police, he got in touch with them and told them the whole story, including his latest exchanges with Jeremy.[6]

This was not Jeremy's only attempt to interfere with the course of justice. Next to Dinshaw's revealing to the police that he had been asked to receive money and pass it to Holmes, what he most feared was Bessell's coming to England to give evidence: Challes (this time unaccompanied by 'Pencourt') had made a second visit to America in March 1978 to secure Bessell's agreement to be an eventual witness in court. Hitherto, Bessell had been constrained from returning by Beaumont's lawsuit; but this was settled that month, leaving Hayward, to whom he owed £35,000, as his last remaining substantial creditor. On 4 April, Jeremy saw Hayward in London and asked if he might dissuade Bessell (whom he referred to as 'the rat') from coming to England by threatening him with a writ of bankruptcy should he do so. Hayward refused, saying he did not do business that way. Soon afterwards, Hayward was staggered to hear from the police (and read in *Private Eye*) about Dinshaw's payments to Holmes, and wrote to Jeremy demanding to know what had happened to the £20,000 he had sent Dinshaw, a question to which he never received a reply. 'I am rapidly getting the impression,' he wrote on 20 April, 'that my friends have not told me the truth and that I am being set up as a fall guy and a sucker of the first degree.'[7]

So artless were Jeremy's attempts to manipulate Hayward and Dinshaw that April, so lacking not just in moral sense but awareness that his behaviour was unlikely to achieve anything except to alienate two good friends and provide potentially damning evidence against him, that one may wonder how far his mental stability had been affected by his troubles. Certainly the nine months of the police investigation, with all its terrors and uncertainties, was a time of strain, during which he drank heavily and was frequently depressed. With a wild look in his eye, he would sometimes mutter to friends: 'It won't go away. They're going to get me . . .'[8] Attending a gaudy at his Oxford college, he broke down and lamented that he had ruined his life: his fellow Trinity men stayed up half the night with him, trying to talk him out of this mood.[9] A fellow MP who had known him since the Oxford Union met him in a BBC studio and thought he looked so desperate that he might kill himself; he insisted on accompanying him back to Westminster, where Jeremy astonished him by saying: 'I know what you're thinking, but I had a sister, a grandfather and a great-uncle who committed suicide, and that's enough.' Even at such grim moments, his sense of humour never quite deserted him: before the fellow MP left, the telephone rang and Jeremy, answering it, assumed the voice of a cockney charwoman to tell the caller that Mr Thorpe's current whereabouts were unknown.[10]

Indeed, the surprising thing about this period is not that he often seemed in a state of half-crazed despair, but that for much of the time he appeared to carry out his normal duties with his customary style. During January 1978, he made a spirited but doomed effort to rescue the PR clause in the European Assembly Elections Bill; he presided, as Chairman of the United Nations Association, at a two-day Conference on Peace and Disarmament, featuring the veteran pacifists Lords Noel-Baker and Brockway; and he attended a Special Assembly at Blackpool at which the Party reluctantly confirmed its support for the Lib–Lab Pact. The following month, he made a succession of parliamentary speeches about Ian Smith's attempt to implement an internal power-sharing settlement in Rhodesia, supporting the cautious position adopted by David Owen as Foreign Secretary; he presented a television programme on the history of Parliament; and he was an active co-founder of a British Campaign for Human Rights in the Soviet Union. He also wrote charming letters that winter to a Cambridge postgraduate student* who was contemplating writing a biography of one of Jeremy's heroes, the pre-war Liberal historian Philip Guedalla (1889–1944), another President of the Oxford Union famed for his wit and style.

In May 1978, Lord Goodman learned through his official contacts that it was probable that Jeremy would shortly be charged with conspiracy to murder. As Goodman's firm did not handle major criminal cases, he arranged for Jeremy to be represented henceforth by Sir David Napley, a recent President of the Law Society. Napley had a reputation as a brilliant defence solicitor and was completely dedicated to his practice and clients, though he was also a man of considerable vanity. The Thorpe case was clearly destined to be the most sensational of his career and for the next twelve months he devoted much of his time to it, while his partner Christopher Murray, a pleasant young man who happened to come from Barnstaple, remained in permanent contact with Jeremy and worked on nothing else. Napley's first task was to prepare Jeremy for his police interview, scheduled for 3 June.

---

* The author, then aged twenty-four.

Challes had already seen Holmes and Le Mesurier two months earlier, both of whom had refused to answer questions;* and Napley advised Jeremy that he should hand over a prepared statement and then also decline to answer any questions that might be put to him. There was a perfect justification for this policy, as the details of Challes' investigation were constantly being leaked to the press and anything said by Jeremy was likely to find its way into *Private Eye*: in the event, Jeremy replied to Challes' first question with 'no comment' and subsequent questions with 'ditto', giving rise to a *Private Eye* story entitled 'The Ditto Man'.

In his new statement, Jeremy went into some detail about his relationship with Scott, whom he had considered 'desperately in need of help and support' but who had repaid his 'kindness and compassion' with 'malevolence and resentment'. Jeremy had 'formed the opinion at an early stage' that Scott 'was a homosexual and was becoming too dependent on me'; and although Scott's allegations of a homosexual affair were 'without the slightest foundation', Jeremy had feared they might involve 'baring my soul in public which could have . . . serious . . . repercussions for myself and the Liberal Party'. (This was the closest he came to admitting his own homosexuality.) Regarding the conspiracy, he maintained that 'any desire to kill or cause physical harm to any person is wholly alien to my nature', and that it would in any case have been pointless to try to 'silence' Scott as his allegations were already well known in North Devon and had had no obvious effect on Jeremy's vote there in 1974. He denied that he had been responsible for either the £2,500 paid to Scott or the £5,000 paid to Newton. It was true that Hayward had given him two

---

* Deakin, on the other hand, had given a statement to the police as early as November 1977, admitting that he had been involved in a 'conspiracy to frighten' Norman Scott but claiming that his involvement had been confined to putting Newton in touch with Holmes.

gifts of £10,000, but these had been made 'not to the Party but to me personally ... to be used by me in any way I thought appropriate in relation to campaigning expenses'. (This assertion was to be denied by Hayward, and indeed contradicted by letters from Jeremy which Hayward was later able to produce.) As it had proved 'unnecessary to have recourse to these funds' after the 1974 elections, Jeremy had arranged for them 'to be deposited with accountants and to be held as an iron reserve against any shortage of funds at any subsequent election. At no time, however, have I ever authorised the use of these funds for any payment ... to either Scott or Newton.' He concluded that, 'having regard to the unusual way in which these current allegations have emerged', he felt it 'neither incumbent upon me nor desirable to add anything further'.

On 4 July, Challes delivered his report on the case to the Director of Public Prosecutions, who (as is customary in cases involving unusual problems) consulted his superior, the Attorney-General. The latter office was then held by Sam Silkin, a conscientious man who contrived to keep his role as public prosecutor separate from his political capacity as legal adviser to the Government. He was in a difficult position: on the one hand, so much had already come out about the case (including claims that senior ministers had 'protected' Jeremy in the past) that the authorities would be accused of a cover-up in the event of a decision not to prosecute; on the other hand, the case was a shaky one in that it was largely based on the uncorroborated evidence of witnesses whose characters could easily be discredited. Silkin deferred his decision and asked the police to make further enquiries; but at the end of July, relying on the advice of the DPP, he decided to allow the prosecution to proceed.

The next act took place at the magistrates' court in the Somerset coastal resort of Minehead, whose jurisdiction covered Porlock Hill: it was there, on 2 August 1978, that Challes obtained warrants for the arrest of Jeremy Thorpe, David

Holmes, John Le Mesurier and George Deakin. Two days later, on the morning of Friday the 4th, the four men presented themselves at different times at Minehead police station, where they were formally arrested and charged with conspiring 'together and with others' to murder Norman Scott; in addition, Jeremy was charged with having incited Holmes to murder Scott in 1969. That afternoon, they appeared together before the magistrates and were remanded until 12 September on bail of £5,000 each: it was here that Jeremy first set eyes on Le Mesurier and Deakin, though they exchanged no words. Jeremy was accompanied by Napley and Lord Avebury, the latter standing surety for his bail. None of the accused made any reported comment, except that Jeremy, when Challes read out each of the charges against him, replied: 'I am totally innocent of this charge and will vigorously challenge it.'

For Jeremy, the worst uncertainties were over. The police investigation had been completed; the charges had been brought; the world knew that he was soon likely to be the principal defendant in a sensational trial. During the preceding months, he had often been depressed, almost desperate; but during the ensuing weeks, his dominant mood seems to have been one of manic euphoria (fuelled, as the earlier depression had been, by alcohol). As always when facing a challenge, he rose to it, stimulated by the fact that the eyes of the world were on him. His lawyers were amazed by the enthusiasm with which he discussed his case, like a child absorbed in a new game. Friends found him confident to the point of jauntiness and in his most exhibitionist form: sometimes he would entertain them with imaginary scenes from his coming trial, to which he almost seemed to be looking forward as a social occasion.[11] Indeed, well-wishers urged him to moderate his high spirits on the grounds that it was unwise to draw attention to himself at such a time. Napley, on the other hand, encouraged him to carry on as usual and so advertise the fact that he felt no guilt. Thus barely a week after being charged, Jeremy applied to the police for the return of his passport to attend a conference in Geneva, where he stayed with the British Ambassador to the United Nations, Sir James Murray, an old friend with whom he engaged in much banter, some of which got reported in the press.

Some months earlier, Jeremy had promised David Steel that, in the event of his being charged, he would resign his seat and refrain from attending the coming Liberal Assembly at Southport.[12] By August 1978, these matters were of some moment, as Callaghan, following the demise of the Lib–Lab Pact, was expected to call an autumn election within weeks. However, after a weekend of emotional meetings in his constituency, at which local Liberals affirmed their support for him and belief in his innocence, Jeremy announced that he would not resign but accept their invitation to recontest the seat at the coming election. He made this decision against the advice of his devoted agent Lilian Prowse, who believed he would be humiliated at the polls, but with the blessing of Napley, who thought that to do otherwise might be interpreted by the public as a sign of guilt.[13] Most of his parliamentary colleagues were horrified by his decision, fearing that the publicity he was bound to receive would wreck the Liberals' national campaign. Steel promptly relieved him of the Party's foreign affairs portfolio. Jeremy was supported, however, by his fellow West Country MP (and former adversary) John Pardoe, who applauded his courage in standing again despite the likelihood that it would damage Pardoe's own electoral prospects. Meanwhile, as the election was expected to take place on 5 October, he obtained a postponement of the next hearing in his case from 12 September to 9 October (it being later postponed again until 20 November).

All were now waiting to see whether Jeremy would turn up at Southport. Steel made a public appeal to him to stay away, while Cyril Smith and others threatened to leave if he came. Then, on the eve of the Assembly, Callaghan made the surprise announcement that he did not propose to call an election that autumn after all. This news was most unwelcome to the Liberals, who had no strategy to deal with the aftermath of the Lib–Lab Pact, and feared they might now have to fight an election after rather than before Jeremy's trial with its disastrous publicity. It meant, however, that Jeremy could attend the Assembly without causing pre-election embarrassment, and he decided to put in a token appearance on Thursday 14 September. Even this caused a sensation which overshadowed the proceedings. His arrival was characteristically theatrical: in an interval between debates, he flung open the doors and marched down the aisle to a mixture of thunderous applause and embarrassed silence, while the press surged forward in a stampede. When he reached the platform, Steel (as one observer put it) shook him by the hand looking as if he would rather have gripped him by the throat. It happened that the Assembly Chairman, Roger Pincham, was about to read out a police announcement: this produced a humorous look from Jeremy, at which the hall dissolved in laughter. He stayed just twenty-five minutes before slipping out by a back entrance.* Some Liberals complained that, thanks to his appearance, the press had ignored their debates; but these were generally considered the most tedious for years, whereas thanks to Jeremy, the Assembly received more media attention (if not perhaps of a wholly helpful kind) than any since his 'Bomb Rhodesia' speech at Brighton in 1966.[14]

Following what had been a stressful summer, Jeremy enjoyed

---

* Jeremy later spoke briefly at two meetings, a rally of the Liberal Candidates Association (of which he remained Vice-Chairman) and a foreign affairs press conference (to which he himself had sent out the invitations while still party spokesman). At both events, he gave the impression of being nervous and the worse for drink. But he was in high spirits when he and Marion entertained friends that night in their hotel suite, hanging a 'do not disturb' sign round the neck of Kenneth Rose.

a three-week holiday in Morocco with Marion before applying himself to the preparatory work on his case. The QC whom Napley had retained to represent him was George Carman: he and Jeremy had already collaborated thirty years earlier at Oxford, when Jeremy had helped Carman (a Balliol man) get started at the Union in return for assistance with his college law essays.* At this time, Carman had a thriving practice on the Northern Circuit but was not yet well known in London, where his most celebrated case had been the successful defence of the manager of Battersea Funfair in 1973 on a manslaughter charge after five children had been killed on the 'Big Dipper': Napley, representing another client in that case, had been struck by his skill as a cross-examiner and persuasiveness in addressing the jury. Carman was delighted to have been briefed in 'the case of the century', confident (as he put it to his son) that he would 'get Jeremy off' and in so doing put himself on the path to becoming the most famous counsel in England. This thought had also occurred to Jeremy and Napley, and Carman was offered (and accepted) the derisory fee of £15,000 for what would turn out to be a year of dedicated and difficult work.[15]

Carman (according to his son and biographer) 'had great admiration for [Jeremy's] achievement in public life' and 'was impressed by his resilience and good humour'. (He may also have admired Jeremy's talent as a risk-taker; for Carman himself, as emerged after his death in 2001, was a drunkard, a wife beater and an addicted gambler; despite his three marriages and repu-tation as a ladies' man, he also led a secret homosexual life.) However, Carman soon discovered that Jeremy, though a model client in some respects, was a trying one in others. On the one hand, he was evasive even with his lawyers, and it was not easy to get him to produce a comprehensive and plausible version of

---

* Carman was in fact Napley's second choice; his first, John Matthew QC, had already been retained for Holmes.

the facts. On the other hand, imagining that his former legal career enabled him to grasp all the legal and forensic issues involved, Jeremy sought to direct the planning of his own defence; and Carman had to keep reminding him that, while he would naturally take note of any instructions, he as senior counsel was ultimately in charge of the case.[16] This combination of lack of frankness and excessive interference would result in a moment of fiasco during the trial which might easily have been disastrous for Jeremy.*

The next legal stage was the committal proceedings, the preliminary hearing before magistrates which precedes every crown court trial in order to establish whether there is 'a case to answer'. On Napley's advice, Jeremy opted for a procedure (since abolished) known as 'Section 7 Committal' which obliged the prosecution to set out its full case,† which the defence could then test by cross-examining witnesses: such proceedings could not be reported in the press unless a defendant requested otherwise. It was generally assumed that, at this dress rehearsal for his trial, Jeremy would be represented by Carman – until Napley announced that he would appear for his client himself. This astounded the entire legal profession, as it was almost unheard of for a solicitor to appear in a case of such magnitude and complexity where distinguished counsel had been retained. (Of the other defendants, Homes and Deakin were represented by their QCs, John Matthew and Gareth Williams; and Carman had to struggle to contain the deep frustration and apprehension which he not unnaturally felt at being passed over in this unprecedented way.) Napley was to be bitterly attacked for this decision. It was said that he was motivated by vanity, being unable to resist the limelight in this, the greatest case of his career, and that his

---

* See below, pp. 532–3.

† As the other three defendants also opted for a 'Section 7' hearing, it would have happened anyway whether Jeremy had wanted it or not.

handling of the proceedings proved to be inept in various respects. In his memoirs, published in 1982, Napley defended himself against these charges, advancing a number of practical reasons as to why he had considered himself more suitable than Carman to appear before the magistrates,* and suggesting that, if he had an ulterior motive, it was to strike a blow for his profession by dispelling the myth that only a barrister possessed the skill to appear under such circumstances.[17] Whatever the merits of the controversy, the fact remains that Jeremy, who was taking the closest personal interest in all decisions affecting his case, did not object to being represented by Napley. On the other hand, he did object to Napley's recommendation that they apply for a lifting of reporting restrictions – he saw no reason to expose himself unnecessarily at this stage – and accordingly no such application was made on his behalf.

The proceedings opened at Minehead on 20 November and lasted more than three weeks. Although reporting restrictions were expected to remain in force, and only some thirty places had been allocated to the press in the small courtroom, an army of journalists descended on the out-of-season resort. Napley and his wife moved in with Jeremy and Marion at Cobbaton, which was also besieged by reporters and cameramen. Every day, Jeremy and Napley drove to Minehead, passing the spot where Newton had shot Rinka, receiving waves and shouts of encouragement along the way from constituents who recognised Jeremy's white Rover. They were usually accompanied by Ursula and Marion, who sat in the front row of the public seats to demonstrate their support for Jeremy. The proceedings began with a surprise when Gareth Williams QC, on behalf of Deakin, asked for reporting restrictions to be lifted. As Napley wrote: 'The remainder of us gasped, since this was the first we had

---

* Such as that the prosecution witnesses, having got used to Napley's methods, would be unprepared for Carman's.

heard of this decision, and as the law then stood any one accused could unilaterally lift the ban on reporting.* Apart from the momentary shock, this did not unduly distress me . . .'[18] If Jeremy himself was distressed by the thought that, contrary to his wishes, the case would be splashed all over the press, he did not show it: throughout the proceedings, he registered scarcely a flicker of emotion as he sat on a bench at some distance from his co-defendants, looking for all the world as if he was listening to a debate in the House of Commons, and engaging in easy banter with journalists between hearings.

Peter Taylor QC, future Lord Chief Justice, opened the case for the Crown with a series of bald statements. 'In 1959, Jeremy Thorpe became an MP. In the early 1960s, he had a homosexual relationship with Norman Scott . . . Scott was a danger to his reputation and his career, a danger of which Mr Thorpe was constantly reminded . . .' In rapid detail, he went on to describe Jeremy's alleged 'rape' of Scott at Stonewalls on 8 November 1961, subsequent episodes in the relationship, Scott's letter to Jeremy's mother and Jeremy's appeal to Bessell. He came to the alleged talk between Jeremy and Bessell in December 1968, in which the former spoke of disposing of Scott with the words: 'It's no worse than shooting a sick dog.' (This provided the main headline for the following day's newspapers.) He spoke of Holmes' purchasing Bessell's letters to Scott for £2,500; Holmes' approaching Le Mesurier to find someone to kill Scott; Deakin's putting Newton in touch with Holmes; Holmes' offering Newton £10,000; and Jeremy's asking Hayward to send £10,000 to Dinshaw. He described the shooting on Porlock Hill, resulting in

---

* As a result of this episode, the law was changed the following year so that restrictions could only be lifted at the instance of all co-defendants, the relevant amendment being proposed by Lord Wigoder QC, the Liberal lawyer who had been ennobled on the nomination of Jeremy in 1974 and taken a close interest in his case.

Newton's trial, prison sentence and eventual 'pay-off' by Le Mesurier. He described Jeremy's efforts to get Bessell to lie in January 1976, and his attempt to use Hayward in April 1978 to prevent Bessell coming to England. Despite this attempt, Taylor declared dramatically in conclusion of his opening address, Bessell had come and would now give evidence.

Having something of the air of a retired film star, with his glamorous, sunburned looks and sonorous voice, Bessell was taken carefully by Taylor through his evidence. In a lengthy cross-examination, Napley tried to establish three things: that Bessell was a proven liar whose word was not to be trusted; that he had concocted his story in cahoots with 'Pencourt'; and that his evidence was largely motivated by financial considerations. Bessell proved a match for Napley and occasionally got the better of him. Napley got him to admit that he had told many lies and had 'a credibility problem'; but he overworked the point until Bessell sharply reminded him that 'I am here under oath and everything I have said here is under oath'. Napley quoted a snippet of a letter from Bessell to Lady Falkender, stating that 'I worked fairly closely with Barrie and Roger in the preparation of *The Pencourt File* ...', whereupon Bessell pointed out that the letter continued, '. . . but not as closely as I would have liked ... If they had confided more to me, I would have steered them away from some unfortunate errors of fact and judgement.' Despite such lapses, Napley succeeded in exposing weaknesses in Bessell's evidence and obtaining some important admissions from him, notably that he had signed a contract with the *Sunday Telegraph* for the eventual publication of articles based on his story. (It later transpired that, under the terms of this contract, Bessell was due to be paid £50,000 upon Jeremy's conviction but only £25,000 in the event of an acquittal – a spectacular gift to the defence.)

The next witnesses were Hayward and Dinshaw, who told the story of the money, and how they had been respectively asked by Jeremy, the previous April, to put pressure on Bessell not to return to England, and lie to the police. Wisely, Napley did not seek to challenge their evidence, merely to get them to confirm that they had admired Jeremy prior to the alleged episodes and that he had always denied to them that he was guilty of the matters of which he stood accused. They were followed by Newton, who made as poor a witness as he had done at his own trial, with his cocky, wisecracking manner and the ever-shifting details of his story. Jeremy had never before set eyes on him, but he was dealt with effectively by Deakin's counsel, the future Labour Attorney-General Gareth Williams, who got him to admit that he was a liar and fantasist by nature who was out to 'milk the case for all it was worth'.

Next came Norman Scott: the press had long been aware of his story, but were now able to publish anything he cared to mention without fear of libel, and he gave them good copy. They looked to see how Jeremy was reacting, but he remained as impassive as ever. In cross-examination, Napley soon established (as he had done with Bessell, and Williams with Newton) that Scott had regularly lied in the past, and stood to make money out of his story. He also sought to establish that Scott was emotionally unbalanced, assisted by Scott himself who was easily provoked into a series of petulant outbursts. Then came a surprise. On the second day of cross-examination, Scott suddenly claimed that he could prove he had enjoyed an intimacy with Jeremy Thorpe by the fact that he knew of certain physical peculiarities. During lunch, which they had together in the private room of a hotel, Napley asked Jeremy if he possessed any distinguishing marks which might lend credence to Scott's story, whereupon Jeremy removed his shirt and invited his solicitor to examine him. When the hearing resumed, Napley asked Scott to write down the peculiarities he had in mind. Scott wrote – 'warts or nodules under the arms'. Having seen no sign of these during his inspection, Napley asked Scott to read his note aloud. The court dissolved in laughter, and Scott did not pursue the matter.

The last witness was Challes, who read out the statements given by Jeremy to the police in February 1976 and June 1978. Napley's cross-examination concentrated on the propriety of the detective having sought assistance from 'Pencourt', and the fact that much of his investigation had been leaked to the press. Finally, the four lawyers made submissions to the court that there was 'no case to answer' against their clients – though counsel for Holmes and Le Mesurier hinted that they might have admitted to a lesser charge. Napley argued that, while all three of the main prosecution witnesses had confessed to being 'inveterate liars', the only one who really mattered from Jeremy's point of view was Bessell, of whose evidence he said: 'Mendacity was oozing out of every pore in his body.' However, on 13 December 1978, after sitting for sixteen days, the magistrates decided that the prosecution had established a *prima facie* case against all four defendants, and committed them for trial. Indeed, their decision was virtually inevitable after the publicity the case had attracted, which had brought their little town a moment of world fame.[19]

As an exercise to test the case against him, the committal proceedings had been useful for Jeremy; but as a public relations exercise, they had been a disaster. Even if the actual charges against him remained unproven, all the world had now heard, in lurid detail, of his past association with a louche individual, his long efforts to cover up that relationship with the aid of a parliamentary colleague, his diversion of political funds to improper purposes, his recent attempts to get two unwilling friends to connive in the suppression of evidence. Many who had been his admirers found their faith in him shaken; and some who had been his staunch supporters – such as Jo Grimond's wife Laura, and the former Archbishop Michael Ramsey – felt betrayed. The list of those who continued to stand by him remained impressive; but Jeremy did not assist his cause by his unwillingness to confide much in any of them. Even his wife and mother, whose solidarity with him was total, only ever heard part of the story; and an old friend who offered support as one who shared his covert inclinations was surprised to be told by Jeremy that he had never experienced homosexual feelings for Scott or anyone else. In the face of the latest blows, he continued to affect indifference and nonchalance; but behind the mask, he suffered increasingly from strain. He continued to drink heavily, and sometimes exhibited slurred speech and unsteady gait even when he had not touched alcohol – possibly the early symptoms of Parkinson's disease, its onset hastened by stress.

On 10 January 1979, the case was set down to be heard at the Old Bailey on 30 April.* This gave Jeremy a breathing space, much of which he spent with his lawyers, studying the transcripts of the Minehead hearings and planning tactics for the trial. It was now fairly clear what approach Carman should take in cross-examining the prosecution witnesses: the great question was what case, if any, Jeremy should offer in his defence. Soon after being charged, he had been advised by Lord Wigoder QC 'to let the three main prosecution witnesses hang themselves and not to give evidence himself on the grounds that no case against him had been proved';[20] and this advice continued to be put to him, in the months leading to the trial, by Napley and Carman. Circumstances might arise – if Holmes, for example, testified in court (as he was subsequently to do in the press) that Jeremy had incited him to kill Scott – which would force Jeremy to go into the witness box; but in the absence of such circumstances, his lawyers – doubtless fearing that, like Oscar Wilde, he would compromise himself by being too clever – were strongly of the view that he should say nothing. Jeremy was far from happy at

---

* Normally, a trial takes place at the Crown Court local to the scene of the alleged crime (in this case, Exeter, where Newton had been tried), but at the behest of a defendant (in this case, Holmes), it may be heard instead at the Central Criminal Court in London.

the thought of being confined to a walk-on part in the most spectacular public appearance of his career – as one friend put it, 'he felt cheated of the performance of his life' – but in the end he reluctantly deferred to the advice of his lawyers (though not, it was said, before Carman had threatened to quit).

Another decision for Jeremy, which must have caused him some agony, was whether (through Carman) to admit during the trial that he had been a homosexual at the time he met Scott. The prosecution were proposing to call witnesses to testify to this fact from personal experience,* as well as to produce love letters,† and the only way Jeremy's lawyers could stop this happening was to do a deal with their opposite numbers whereby such evidence would be rendered unnecessary by a suitable admission on Jeremy's part. The problem with an admission was that it would cast doubt on Jeremy's contention, from which he had never wavered in his statements, that he had never had a sexual affair with Scott. The deft manner in which Carman got round this problem will be seen in due course.

Jeremy was also preoccupied with money matters. The previous summer, Hayward had walked into Liberal Party Headquarters and demanded to know what had happened to the £150,000 he had given Jeremy in 1970 and the £49,000 in 1974–75. (This did not include the £20,000 he had sent Dinshaw at Jeremy's request, which was being separately investigated by the police.) At the Southport Assembly, a committee was set up to enquire into these and other funds which had never appeared in the party accounts, chaired by the Party President, Michael Steed. When Jeremy was approached by Steed and his colleagues in the New Year, he was unco-operative, receiving them with bare civility

---

* Such as William Shannon, the boy who had written a 'blackmailing' letter (now in the hands of the prosecution) to Jeremy in 1967 and been handled at the time by Bessell (see Chapter 12).
† Including the 'Brewin' letters (see Chapter 10).

and refusing them access to the special bank accounts into which he had paid Hayward's cheques at the time. David Steel, however, had access to the account records as an original co-signatory, and reported to the committee that, so far as he could see, the Hayward money had been properly used by Jeremy for election and other political purposes. Steed found it revealing of Jeremy's obsession with secrecy that he had refused to 'come clean' even when, as it seemed, he had nothing to hide.[21] Another worry was how to pay the costs of his defence.* A Jeremy Thorpe Defence Fund was set up by Lord Lloyd of Kilgerran, the rich patent lawyer who had defrayed the expenses of his private office as Leader and been rewarded with a peerage: contributors ranged from Sir James Goldsmith (£5,000) to a porter at the Reform Club. As we have seen, Carman contented himself with a nominal fee; and Napley, recognising the publicity which the case was giving his practice, also gave his professional services for relatively little; but the expenses alone incurred by Napley's firm over twelve months were enormous, and Jeremy also had to find £20,000 with which to 'repay' to Hayward the money for which he was unable to account (though Hayward refused to accept any repayment before the trial). To help him meet his expenses, his mother sold the upper floor of her house in Limpsfield to its sitting tenants, while Marion sold various artefacts she had received under her divorce settlement with Lord Harewood.

Meanwhile, he did his best to give the appearance of 'business as usual'. He continued to attend the House of Commons (though he rarely spoke), and to perform his constituency duties (though his local party, shaken by the Minehead revelations,

---

* On 3 August 1978, the day before he was charged, Jeremy had brazenly advertised this problem by asking the Attorney-General in the House of Commons to specify the capital sum which precluded an applicant from legal aid. (The answer was £1,600.)

were no longer quite so unanimous in their support). When his stepson, Lord Lascelles, decided to marry the partner by whom he had had two children, Jeremy not only attended the wedding with Marion but got in touch with the Privy Council Office to obtain the consent which the groom, being in line to the throne, required under the Royal Marriages Act. When the Conservatives tabled a motion of no confidence, to be debated on 27 March, Jeremy attended the meeting of the Parliamentary Liberal Party to decide what they should do: to the general surprise, he spoke impressively in support of the majority view that they should vote with the Conservatives to bring down the Government.* The Government duly fell, and Callaghan called a General Election for 3 May, scheduled to be the fourth day of Jeremy's trial. His local party again invited him to stand as their candidate, though with noticeably less enthusiasm than the previous August; and he again accepted their invitation, against the advice of Lilian Prowse, who knew he was bound to lose, but with encouragement from Napley, who seems to have taken the view that the jury would be impressed if he won and sympathetic if he lost. Under the circumstances, he was able to obtain an adjournment of the trial for eight days.

The Party distanced itself from his campaign to the point where he was virtually fighting as an independent. He received no support from Liberal Headquarters, nor most parliamentary colleagues. Only John Pardoe came down to speak for him, along with two of the ten life peers who owed their elevation to him, Stina Robson and John Foot. They, like the press, noticed that he had lost much of his sparkle, and that his efforts at jovial

---

*Some of those present argued that it would be a mistake to bring the Government down at that moment, as the General Election would then take place on the same day as the local elections, resulting in the Liberals faring poorly in the latter. Jeremy, however, suggested that the Liberals would actually do better in the local elections on account of the higher turnout, and was proved correct. (Information from Michael Steed.)

electioneering seemed forced. The strain of the past eighteen months was beginning to tell; and he was probably already suffering (as may be discerned from his election photograph, with its set features and blank stare) from the preliminaries of Parkinson's disease. Still, with the support of his wife and mother and a loyal band of helpers, he campaigned throughout the constituency, even if voters were often too embarrassed to turn out to hear him; and he made some good speeches, if delivered with less than his usual panache. Of Margaret Thatcher, he said: 'She is the headmistress personified. Given a working majority, she would be the most autocratic Prime Minister since the war and would stamp the Government with her abrasive brand of Toryism.' He argued that he had 'put North Devon on the map' and secured many advantages for its people, who would need him to fight for their interests in the face of her threatened cutbacks. In public, he expressed confidence of victory, albeit with a less than confident air; to close friends in private, he confessed that he did not expect to win.

However much he spoke of politics, the campaign was inevitably dominated by the issue of his trial, due to begin just five days after the election. Voters were apt either to express admiration for his courage and wish him luck, or shun or vilify him on account of the charges that hung over him. He was obliged to preface every speech with the words: 'You are aware that the political fight is taking place in circumstances which are without parallel. Matters are to be resolved elsewhere which it would be improper to discuss in this campaign. Suffice it to say that I have vigorously asserted my innocence and am determined to establish it.' He remarked to one friend that it was 'hard to run two shows at the same time'. (It was a telling remark: to Jeremy, both the election and trial were 'shows', dramas in the theatre of life.) The unusual circumstances of the contest attracted half a dozen fringe candidates – 'the liquorice allsorts', as Jeremy called them – including Auberon Waugh, who as a columnist in *Private*

Eye had been consistently hostile to Jeremy and who had been commissioned to write a book about the trial. In a reference to Rinka, Waugh stood as the 'dog-lovers' candidate, and in a facetious election address published in the pre-election issue of the *Spectator*, he wrote:

> Before Mr Thorpe has had time to establish his innocence of these extremely serious charges, he has been greeted with claps, cheers and yells of acclamation by his admirers in the Liberal Party, both at the National Conference at Southport and here in the constituency. I am sorry but I find this disgusting ... Rinka is NOT forgotten. Rinka lives. Woof, woof ...

Jeremy's lawyers applied for an injunction to prevent the further dissemination of these words on the grounds that they were prejudicial to his trial: this was refused by the Divisional Court but granted by the Court of Appeal, where the Master of the Rolls, Jeremy's old friend Lord Denning, declared that he had no doubt that Waugh's motives in standing for Parliament were improper. Jeremy showed a different attitude towards another of the fringe candidates, Henrietta Rous, who lived with her mother, a granddaughter of Asquith, on the beautiful Clovelly estate near Bideford. She was standing for the Wessex Regional Party, an eccentric grouping led by Viscount Weymouth which preached free love and naturism. Jeremy, who had known her since her childhood, helped her complete her nomination papers and write her election address, at the possible cost of a handful of votes to himself. [22]

On 29 April, five days before the poll and ten days before his trial was due to begin, Jeremy celebrated his fiftieth birthday. It had been an extraordinary career: President of the Oxford Union at twenty-one; Member of Parliament at thirty; Leader of the Liberal Party at thirty-seven; effectively offered the deputy premiership of Britain at forty-four; now facing the prospect of losing his parliamentary seat within a week and going to prison within two months.

The declaration, watched by the nation on television, was an emotionally charged event. The result (with October 1974 figures in brackets) was as follows:

Speller, Anthony (Conservative):	31,811	(21,488)
Thorpe, John Jeremy (Liberal):	23,338	(28,209)
Saltern. A. J. (Labour):	7,108	(8,365)
Whittaker, A .M. (Ecology):	729	
Price, J. P. (National Front):	237	
Hansford-Miller, F. H.		
(English Nationalist):	142	(568)
Waugh, Auberon (Dog Lovers):	79	
Rous, Miss H. (Wessex Regionalist):	50	
Boaks, Lieutenant-Commander W. G.		
(Democratic Monarchist Public		
Safety White Regionalist):	20	

Under the circumstances, Jeremy had not done too badly: his vote had fallen by less than 5,000, despite the large national swing to the Conservatives; and although the Conservative vote had risen by just over 10,000, this was partly attributable to an influx, since 1974, of mostly Tory-voting immigrants from the Home Counties. Elsewhere in the country, two other Liberals lost the seats they were defending, his neighbour John Pardoe (who may have suffered by association with him) and his old adversary Emlyn Hooson: the remaining eleven Liberal MPs* hung on with reduced majorities. The total Liberal vote, at about 4.3 million or 13.8 per cent, was almost double what it had been

---

* The thirteen Liberal MPs had been swelled to fourteen by David Alton's surprise win, only days before the calling of the General Election, at a by-election in the Liverpool seat of Edgehill.

in 1970,* before the revival under Jeremy's leadership: but the Party did distinctly worse on average in the West Country than the rest of England, a phenomenon attributed to 'the Thorpe effect'. The overall result of the election was a Conservative parliamentary majority of forty-three, Mrs Thatcher becoming Prime Minister.

Although he could scarcely have hoped for a much better personal result, Jeremy appeared to be stunned. Throughout the campaign, the press had camped outside his house; on the morning after his defeat, he invited them in. As he sipped whisky, and his wife by his side smoked cigarettes, he uttered some affecting words. He had no regrets, and would 'rather have stood and lost than not have stood at all'. But his defeat had been 'shattering'.

> I never expected to get hammered. You never do ... I gave this constituency a voice in Westminster. I made it mean something. I knew it better than anything. I knew which houses would be flooded after an hour's rain. I even knew the people who had got new bathrooms. I knew it ... People said I looked tired, didn't they Marion? They said I'd lost my energy, my drive. Well, I don't think so. I was going twelve hours a day, I actually felt good. No, it must have been the Tories going home ... So, the headmistress has done it, eh? I'm horrified. She makes Ted Heath look like a moderate ... You know, the circumstances in which I fought the election were astonishing, even historic. Quite fantastic. I don't think people really understood ...[23]

---

* The Liberals contested 577 seats in 1979 as compared to 332 in 1970, in itself an indication of how the Party had revived during the decade.

23

TRIAL
MAY–JUNE 1979

THE TRIAL OF Jeremy Thorpe – and his alleged fellow conspirators Holmes, Le Mesurier and Deakin – opened before Mr Justice Cantley in Court Number One at the Old Bailey on Tuesday 8 May 1979, five days after the General Election. Having all pleaded not guilty to the charges against them, the defendants took their places in the dock. Jeremy sat at the end nearest the press, wearing a velvet-collared overcoat and supporting his back with three red cushions: he looked pale and grave, and rarely showed much animation. Next to him sat Le Mesurier, fidgeting constantly; then Deakin, looking anxious; finally Holmes, following the case with an air of nonchalance. The four men scarcely acknowledged each other during the seven weeks of the trial. Every day, Marion accompanied Jeremy to court and sat in the public gallery, often being joined by Ursula and her brother Peter (the latter – who also performed a secret liaison role between Jeremy and Holmes – appearing to enjoy the proceedings immensely). The press benches included two celebrated authors, Auberon Waugh and Sybille Bedford, both of whom had been commissioned to write books about the trial.

Waugh's book, *The Last Word*,* was to be a compelling read, though he took a satirical approach and made no secret of his personal dislike of Jeremy. Mrs Bedford, on the other hand, saw herself as an admirer and defender of Jeremy, but so disillusioned was she by what she heard about him during the case that her book was never written.[1]

The judge, Sir Joseph Cantley, was sixty-eight and had been sitting on the High Court bench for fourteen years. Like Jeremy's father (and Jeremy's counsel, George Carman QC), he had begun his career and made his reputation on the Northern Circuit. He was regarded as a competent judge, conventional in outlook, and something of a wag: he was given to expressing blimpish opinions from the bench and lightening the proceedings with witty or sarcastic remarks. While unfailingly courteous to the jury, he could be quite sharp with counsel and witnesses, and rattle his sabre at the press: his first reported words in the case were that any journalist thinking of interviewing a juror 'had better bring a toothbrush'. He was rather a snob: he described Deakin as 'the sort of man whose taste might run to a cocktail bar in his living room', and seemed highly conscious of the fact that he was trying 'a Privy Counsellor ... and national figure with a very distinguished public record'. He was a gift to a writer of Waugh's comic talents; and had they met under other circumstances, Jeremy would no doubt have done a superb impersonation of him.

The impatience with which he treated the main crown witnesses (Bessell, Scott and Newton) and their evidence was to give rise to the view that he had been biased in favour of the defence. Judges are human, and Cantley (as he told his friends) did not relish the thought of sending a distinguished Privy Counsellor to prison. But he was also undoubtedly guided by the thought that

---

* After a remark of the judge: 'Remember, I have the last word.'

the case, though supported by some persuasive circumstantial evidence, was weak in legal terms. Of the three main witnesses, one was an accomplice, two had been given unusually wide immunity, all gave evidence which was only incidentally corroborated, and all stood to gain financially from guilty verdicts (Bessell literally so, having signed a contract with the *Sunday Telegraph* promising him a double fee in the event of Jeremy's conviction). Indeed, the trial began with a day and a half of defence submissions that the evidence of all three witnesses should be ruled inadmissible on account of these factors. While Cantley dismissed these submissions, he had been given notice that, unless he drew attention to these factors himself, they might form the basis of an appeal – and no judge likes having his judgments reversed on appeal.

What had been heralded by the press as 'the trial of the century' proved to be something of an anti-climax. Taking place during the first weeks in office of the new Conservative Government, it occupied a secondary place in the news. Sensational as it was, the prosecution case had already been exposed to the world at Minehead, and produced few further surprises. The cross-examination of prosecution witnesses by defence counsel (though now starring Carman rather then Napley) also proceeded along very similar lines. While some interesting admissions would be made on their behalf, neither Jeremy nor Holmes were to give evidence, or have witnesses called in their defence. (It was not of course clear at the start of the trial – either to the press or indeed the defendants themselves – that this would happen, but the likelihood was always strong.) It might be said that the only great imponderable at the beginning of the trial was what verdict would be returned by the jury at the end.

Peter Taylor opened for the Crown with a summary of his case in simple and compelling language.

Twenty years ago, in 1959, Mr Jeremy Thorpe was elected Member of Parliament for North Devon. During the early 1960s, he had a homosexual relationship with Norman Scott. From then on, Scott was a continuing danger to his reputation and career. It was a danger of which Mr Thorpe was constantly reminded by Scott pestering him and talking of their relationship with others.

In 1967, Mr Thorpe was elected Leader of the Liberal Party. But the higher he climbed on the political ladder, the greater was the threat to his ambition from Scott. His anxiety became an obsession, and his thoughts desperate.

Early in 1969, at his room in the House of Commons, he incited his close friend David Holmes to kill Norman Scott. Peter Bessell, a fellow Liberal MP, was present. Holmes and Bessell tried, over a period of time, to dissuade Mr Thorpe from this plan, and to humour him. Other, less dramatic measures, were tried – seeking to get Scott to America, trying to get him a job, paying him money, purchasing damaging letters from him. But Scott remained a constant and serious threat.

Shortly before the first of the two General Elections of 1974, Scott went to live in Mr Thorpe's constituency. He had been talking openly about his relationship with Jeremy Thorpe, and he was seeking to publish a book about it.

The accused David Holmes eventually became convinced that, as Mr Thorpe had repeatedly urged, the only way to stop this threat both to Mr Thorpe and to the Liberal Party was effectively to kill Scott.

Mr Holmes had connections in South Wales. He knew the accused John Le Mesurier, a carpet dealer. Through him he met the accused George Deakin, a dealer in fruit machines, and a plot was hatched to find someone who would kill Scott for reward.

Mr Deakin recruited Andrew Newton, an airline pilot, as the hired assassin. Mr Deakin met him and briefed him. Mr Holmes also met Newton and briefed him further.

The reward was to be £10,000. Attempts were made – but

failed – to lure Mr Scott to his death, but eventually in October 1975 Mr Newton met him in Devon, gained his confidence and drove him out on to the moors.

There Newton produced a gun. Scott had brought a dog with him. Newton shot the dog but failed to shoot Scott.

Mr Newton was arrested, charged, and convicted in March 1976. He had been charged with possessing a firearm with intent to endanger life, but at his trial the true history of the shooting did not emerge.

He was sent to prison and on his release in 1977 he was paid £5,000, half the contract price. The cash was handed over to him by Le Mesurier at a remote spot in South Wales.

The money to pay for this contract was procured by Jeremy Thorpe. He had persuaded Mr Jack Hayward, a wealthy benefactor, to make a substantial contribution to Liberal election funds. Mr Thorpe then personally arranged for the money to be delivered by a devious route through the Channel Islands to Holmes, so that payment could be made to Newton.

In a nutshell, this is what the case is about.

Following this summary, Taylor laid out his case in detail, taking two days to cover ground which had taken him a single morning at Minehead. His narrative fell into three main chapters: the relationship of Jeremy with Scott from 1961 to 1964 (mostly based on the evidence of Scott); the efforts of Bessell to 'manage' Scott on Jeremy's behalf from 1965 to 1971 (mostly based on the evidence of Bessell); and the doings of Holmes and his South Wales friends in 1974–75 (mostly based on the evidence of Newton and Miller) coupled with Jeremy's action in arranging for Holmes to receive £20,000 during those two years (mostly based on the evidence of Hayward and Dinshaw).

Taylor's first witness was Bessell, who seemed less self-confident at the Old Bailey than at Minehead: his health had since deteriorated, he was (according to his memoirs[2]) moved to pity by the sight of Jeremy in the dock, and he was conscious of hostility on the part of the judge, who rebuked him sharply (after witnesses had been warned not to give interviews) for casually remarking to a journalist that he was 'still drinking as many cups of tea as at Minehead'. Bessell cut a plausible figure as he was taken through his story by Taylor; but the air of gloom and hesitancy which hung around him was quickly exploited by the defence in cross-examination. John Mathew, counsel for Holmes, got him to admit that he had a strong financial interest in the outcome of the trial (which he could hardly deny in view of his contract with the *Sunday Telegraph*), that he suffered from a 'credibility problem', and that it had been 'very wrong and irresponsible' of him never to have told anyone that Jeremy had murder on his mind. Carman, using classic techniques, then went on to reduce the unfortunate ex-MP to a state of breast-beating penitence, in which he was willing to confess to being 'a thoroughly amoral person', 'a hypocrite', even 'all things to all men'. The judge joined in the baiting; when Carman accused Bessell of telling 'whoppers', and then asked if it might be a suitable moment to adjourn, Cantley remarked: 'Oh, I think we've got time for one whopper if you like.'

One matter raised by Carman in his cross-examination was Bessell's uncorroborated claim that, just before the 1970 General Election, Jeremy had asked him to deal with a blackmailer named Hetherington, if necessary by murdering him. This caused surprise as, although Bessell had mentioned the episode in his written statements, Taylor had chosen not to raise it in his examination-in-chief. Carman now used it as a basis for mocking Bessell. 'You have now told us there were two people Mr Thorpe wanted murdered. Is that all? Or will you have some others to tell us about tomorrow morning?' The judge joined in: '*Did* you kill Hetherington, Mr Bessell?' Bessell explained that he had scared off Hetherington on the Sunday before the election, and telephoned Jeremy in North Devon on the Monday morning to say he had dealt with the problem. However, Carman produced a press cutting to show that Jeremy had in fact spent that Sunday night in Cornwall, where Bessell himself shared a platform with him on the Monday. 'It takes a long time to nail down your lies,' declared Carman triumphantly. 'At last we have nailed one.' In fact, the discrepancy could be explained by Bessell just having made a mistake as to dates; but Jeremy, whose remarkable memory had enabled his counsel to score this point, was delighted: for once, he seemed to brighten up in the dock, and it was to be one of the few moments of the trial which he enjoyed recollecting in later years.[3]

Carman continued his cross-examination remorselessly for three days. Eventually Bessell was so worn out that he seemed to agree with practically everything put to him. His attempt to defraud Hayward in 1973 was 'a disgraceful, damnable, totally inexcusable episode'. On that and other occasions he had been 'guilty of deviousness, of quite disgraceful behaviour'. Finally, Carman put his last question: 'May I suggest to you that you have reached the stage of being incapable of belief by anyone else?' For a moment, it almost seemed as if Bessell was going to accept this too, when the judge intervened: 'You can't expect him to agree to that.' Bessell collected himself to reply: 'If I believed I were no longer capable of being believed, I would not be here at the Old Bailey, I would be at Oceanside, California.'

Scott followed Bessell in the witness box. He too was less impressive than at Minehead: the surroundings of the Old Bailey, the sight of Jeremy in the dock and the unfriendly attitude of the judge all seemed to intimidate him. During the two days it took him to tell his story, there were times when he was close to tears, others when he had to be asked to speak up. Carman's cross-examination, the ground for which had been well prepared by Napley at Minehead, was masterly. He began by enquiring gently after Scott's health, and within minutes had got him to admit that he had a long history of psychiatric illness, that he suffered from delusions, and that one of those delusions, which he had aired to various people in 1960–61, was that he had had a love affair with Jeremy Thorpe at a time when they had in fact only met once for a few minutes. Within half an hour, Scott was admitting to having told innumerable lies and 'done many wicked things in the past'. Having got what he wanted, Carman adopted a harsher tone, predictably provoking a hysterical outburst from Scott. This produced a taunt from the judge: 'If only you had spoken up like that when you began your evidence, we could have heard everything you said.' So upset was Scott at this that he threatened to refuse to give further evidence, even if it meant going to prison for contempt, and had to be cajoled into continuing. Then came a surprise:

CARMAN: You knew [*sic*] Thorpe to be a man of homosexual tendencies in 1961?

SCOTT: Yes, sir.

CARMAN: He was the most famous and distinguished person you had met at that time?

SCOTT: Yes, sir. I think so.

CARMAN: You were flattered that for a short time he introduced you into a different social world. I suggest you were annoyed because he did not want to have sexual relations with you.

SCOTT: Of course that is ridiculous because he did.

Towards the end of the afternoon and his cross-examination, Carman had casually slipped in an admission that Jeremy had possessed 'homosexual tendencies' at the time he met Scott – though he continued to insist that Jeremy had never had sexual relations with Scott. It had been necessary to make some admission of this sort to prevent the prosecution calling further witnesses to Jeremy's past sex life, and Carman had done so skilfully, inferring that Scott was a predator who had accurately assessed Jeremy's 'weakness' at their first meeting and set out to exploit him.

Next came Newton, his jauntiness in grotesque contrast to Scott's plaintiveness. Whereas the evidence of Bessell and Scott had been essentially identical to that given at Minehead, the scatterbrained Newton often diverged from his previous story and produced some colourful new details. He claimed to have told Deakin at Blackpool: 'I understand you want someone bumped off. If you've got nobody, I'm your man.' Newton stuck to his story that he had at first agreed (indeed, volunteered) to commit murder, but that by the time of the shooting incident he had changed his mind and decided merely to frighten Scott.* At the end of his evidence, the court heard some tape-recordings of his telephone conversations with Holmes and Le Mesurier soon after his release from prison. These were cryptic, but one exchange was capable of being interpreted as supporting the case against Holmes. Newton said: 'There is a charge, you know, of conspiracy to bloody murder.' Holmes replied: 'I'm remembering that very carefully.' Newton said: 'So let's keep it quiet, OK?' Holmes replied: 'Just fine, and you may rely on that.'

Mathew's cross-examination of Newton began with another surprise, for Mathew did not deny that Holmes had conspired to frighten Scott and had hired Newton for this purpose. His aim was to show that Newton was lying about the purpose of the conspiracy, partly because it was in his nature to fantasise and exaggerate, but mainly because he stood to make more money out of selling his story to the press if it involved a murder plot. Mathew's manner was sneering, Newton's was cocksure, and their exchanges soon began to resemble a music hall double-act. The judge added to the entertainment by remarking, when Newton mentioned his early plan to kill Scott with a poker concealed in a bunch of flowers: 'But you were going to meet a man.

---

* Newton had originally produced this story for the press in 1977 and had stood by it, though the immunity he had subsequently been granted meant he would have risked nothing by admitting that he had tried to kill Scott.

Why was it necessary to have flowers?' Under fire from Mathew, Newton cheerfully admitted that he had told 'a pack of lies' at Exeter (in order to save his skin, as the defendants were now doing) and was out to 'milk the case for all it was worth' (having lost his normal livelihood thanks to the affair): but he stood resolutely by his story that he had been hired to kill.

Newton's evidence was hostile to Deakin – he insisted Deakin had approached him to carry out nothing less than a murder – but favourable to Le Mesurier: he said he had never even heard of the carpet dealer before the pay-off of April 1977, and had no reason to suppose that he had been involved in the earlier stages of the conspiracy. However, the next witness, Newton's former friend David Miller – the Cardiff printer who had introduced Newton to Deakin and subsequently sold information to the press – gave evidence which was favourable to Deakin, who he claimed had only ever spoken of 'a frightening job', but hostile to Le Mesurier, whom he described as 'far more than just a contact man'. Even more compromising to Le Mesurier was the following witness, the ex-soldier Colin Lambert, who testified that Le Mesurier (his employer at the time) had told him that 'we should have hired someone like you, because the chap who went to do the shooting was an idiot'.

Next came Hayward and Dinshaw, later described by the judge as 'nice respectable witnesses'. They were vital to the case against Jeremy, as their evidence (which was not challenged by the defence) showed that Jeremy had arranged for Holmes to receive £10,000 in cash at the time of hiring Newton,* and that, while the police investigation against him was in progress, he had tried

---

* It transpired during the case that Jeremy had already given at least three conflicting explanations as to why he had channelled the £10,000 to Holmes: to Hayward and Dinshaw, that it was needed to settle 'irregular' election expenses; to Michael Ogle, that it was to repay money Holmes had lent him in the past; and to the police in June 1978, that it was 'to be held as an iron reserve against a shortage of funds at any subsequent election'.

to get both of them to pervert the course of justice. As usual, Carman showed skill in getting the witnesses to say what he wanted them to say. He began by telling Hayward that he wished 'to make it perfectly clear on behalf of Mr Thorpe that there is no suggestion that you have been guilty of any kind of financial or commercial impropriety'. Although Hayward's evidence implied that Jeremy was guilty of such impropriety, Hayward seemed relieved to hear this and asked Carman to thank Jeremy. He went on to say how highly he had always regarded Jeremy's political gifts, and hammered another nail into Bessell's coffin by confirming that he had lent large sums to the latter which had not so far been repaid. Like Hayward, Dinshaw agreed with Carman that he had always found Jeremy to be a generous man and a dedicated politician: politics were as vital to him as the air he breathed, and it was doubtless his fears for his career which had caused him to act as he had.

The last prosecution witnesses were the two police officers who had taken statements from Jeremy in 1976 and 1978 and investigated his possible role in the events leading to the shooting incident – DCS Sharpe of Devon and Cornwall CID and DCS Challes of Avon and Somerset CID. After Sharpe had read the 1976 statement, Carman asked him what he knew of a request made by Jeremy in 1971 to the Metropolitan Police Commissioner and the Home Secretary to investigate Scott's allegations. Sharpe replied that he knew nothing of this but would look into the matter. The fact was that Jeremy had never made any such request, but had written to Maudling at the time asking if he might confirm two relatively minor facts concerning Scott: Maudling had sent an ambiguous reply that he had consulted the Commissioner and 'neither of us see any reason to disagree'.* Jeremy had shown this reply to so many people down the years,

---

* See pp. 336–7

inaccurately claiming that it referred to Scott's story having been investigated by the police and found baseless, that he had come to believe in the fantasy himself, even to the extent of instructing his lawyers to raise the matter during the trial. A few days after doing so, Carman was forced to make a humiliating admission that 'no request, whether oral or in writing, was made by Mr Thorpe for an investigation . . . as to the truth of Norman Scott's allegations . . .' This provided some comfort to the prosecution on what turned out to be the last day of its case, the presentation of which had lasted almost a month.

The next day – Thursday 7 June – was to see the opening of the defence; and in the event, it did not get beyond that day. Mathew, Cowley and Carman rose only to declare that they wished to call no evidence on behalf of Holmes, Le Mesurier and Thorpe. Although there had long been speculation that Jeremy and his co-defendants might decide not to give evidence and face cross-examination, these stark announcements took most listeners by surprise. (However, according to Napley's memoirs, the decision not to call Jeremy was only made 'at the last possible moment': for Jeremy would have gone into the witness box had Holmes done so, and it only became certain that Holmes would not do so on the day itself.[4]) The only one of the four defendants to give evidence was Deakin, whose story (which had not varied since he had first given it to the police in November 1977) was that he had been asked by Holmes and Le Mesurier to find someone to 'frighten a blackmailer' and had subsequently put Holmes in touch with Newton, which was the end of his involvement in the affair. Cross-examined by Taylor, he denied that anyone had ever spoken to him of murder, or that – contrary to the evidence of Newton and Miller – he had been either involved in briefing Newton before the shooting incident or in touch with him after it.

That concluded the evidence. The jury intimated that there were still things they wished to know; but the judge told them that 'the curtains are down and you must decide the case on what you have heard'. There followed the closing addresses for the prosecution and defence. Taylor began with the dramatic statement that the story of Jeremy Thorpe was 'a tragedy of truly Greek or Shakespearean proportions – the slow but inevitable destruction of a man by the stamp of one defect'. But he urged the jury to put pity out of their minds: the charge was grave, even if the conspiracy had failed. He defended the crown witnesses against the mud which had been flung at them. Some of them may have lied in the past; but there was no reason why they should not now be telling the truth, and the fact that they were making money out of the case did not of itself invalidate their evidence. He listed more than sixty facts which had not been disputed by the defence, and which alone constituted damning evidence against the defendants.* He made much of Jeremy's false claim that he had asked the police to investigate Scott, which gave 'insight into the way Thorpe worked ... trying to fix the record'. Jeremy had 'lied, lied and lied again' with his conflicting explanations as to why he had arranged for the £20,000 to be paid to Holmes. His efforts to get Hayward and Dinshaw to pervert the course of justice showed his 'preparedness to go to any lengths to avoid being exposed' – including, the jury might think, 'the lengths of taking a life'.

On behalf of Holmes, Mathew reiterated that if his client had been involved in a conspiracy, it had only been one to frighten

---

* The most important of these were 'that Thorpe in 1961 was a bachelor with homosexual tendencies; that he gave Scott money, wrote him affectionate letters; that Holmes had paid £2,500 to recover letters from Scott; that Thorpe had arranged for £20,000 to be paid to Holmes; that Holmes and Le Mesurier asked Deakin to find someone; that Newton took Scott and shot his dog without harming Scott; that Holmes met Newton and discussed his defence; that Le Mesurier arranged through Miller to meet Newton and pay him £5,000; that Thorpe tried to persuade Mr Dinshaw to give different accounts of the money; and that he tried to persuade Mr Hayward to put pressure on Mr Bessell not to come to England.' (Auberon Waugh, *The Last Word*, p. 188.)

Scott. The accusation that it had been to murder rested 'on the evidence of two people [Bessell and Newton] who are self-confessed liars and perjurers and who have accepted that their behaviour ... has been deceitful, devious and dishonest'. The £20,000, he suggested, could be explained by the possibility that Holmes had arranged to settle Jeremy's 'illicit election expenses'. He pleaded for 'a fair and fast ending to the agonies which, albeit brought on by himself, have been suffered by Mr Holmes in recent times'.

On behalf of Deakin, Gareth Williams QC said that the decision to prosecute Thorpe (of whom he spoke with scorn) had been an act of courage, which upheld the principle that 'even the mighty in this land are in the end subject to the same ventilation as the obscure'. And obscure was what George Deakin was – 'just someone of no consequence who could be used and not told the whole story, someone of no account, a tool'. Deakin had nothing to hide: he alone of the defendants had co-operated with the police, given evidence in court and submitted to cross-examination. The notion that he might have been involved in a murder plot rested entirely on the worthless evidence of Newton, whom Williams described as 'a sort of moral amputee ... not just a man from whom you would hesitate to buy a second-hand car, you would not even sell him one'.

Dennis Cowley QC, who had hardly uttered a word during the trial, then spoke. His client Le Mesurier had introduced Holmes and Deakin; and in 1977, he had paid £5,000 to Newton. 'There is not one iota of evidence to connect him with anything in between.' Le Mesurier was a man of impeccable character who had served for six years in the RAF. 'Is he the sort of man that you think is going to be engaged in a scheme to kill somebody he does not know and has never met and has nothing to do with?'

Carman began his address in defence of Jeremy with an appeal to the jury's emotions. 'Privately, he is a man whose life has had more than its fair share of grief and agony. Nature so fashioned him that, at the time he had the misfortune ever to meet Norman Scott, he was a man with homosexual tendencies . . . Because of the prominence he has achieved in the public life of this country . . . his frailties . . . have been remorselessly exposed to the public gaze.' Taylor had told them not to be swayed by pity in reaching their verdict, but they should nevertheless not lose sight of 'compassion and humanity in assessing the man'. He mentioned the 'untimely death' of Caroline, and paid tribute to Marion, 'whose constant presence in this court speaks eloquently for itself', before declaring that Jeremy was 'human like us all' and had paid dearly for any transgressions with the ruin of his political career.

Turning to the substance of the case, Carman launched a vitriolic attack on 'Pencourt', suggesting that they had 'fabricated' evidence and 'launched' the prosecution with a view to gain. There was in fact no reliable evidence on which Jeremy could be convicted: that of Bessell, Scott and Newton was so tainted as to be worthless, while that of Hayward and Dinshaw was insufficiently incriminating. Regarding Jeremy's admitted past 'homosexual tendencies', Carman pleaded for 'tolerance, sympathy and compassion' towards 'people who have propensities which we personally may not understand'. But he pointed out that Jeremy was not on trial for his sexual proclivities, and that if he had had a motive for silencing Scott, it existed whether they had actually had a sexual affair or not. As for the £20,000, 'I'm not going to solve for you the mystery of the money . . . The Crown has to prove that it is referrable to guilt. That is one possibility, but there are many others the prosecution has not explored.' Nothing could be read into Jeremy's refusal to give evidence. 'We are not here to entertain the public or provide journalists with further copy. We are here . . . to determine whether these charges have been made out.' He concluded:

You have the right as citizens to vote in elections ... Mr Thorpe
has spent twenty years in British politics and obtained thousands
and thousands of votes in his favour. Now the most precious
twelve votes of all come from you. [At this point, Carman paused
theatrically to indicate each juror in turn.] I say to you, on behalf
of Jeremy Thorpe – this prosecution has not been made out.

In the course of his speech, Carman had suggested that, if
there had indeed been a murder plot, it must have been initiated
by Holmes without Jeremy's knowledge. This came as a cruel
blow to Holmes, as there had been an understanding between
the defendants that they would do nothing to incriminate each
other.[5] Both Holmes and Le Mesurier had been advised by their
lawyers that they stood a better chance of acquittal if they gave
evidence, which in Holmes' case would almost certainly have
cooked Jeremy's goose: but Jeremy, communicating with his co-
defendants through intermediaries and notes scribbled in the
dock, had persuaded them that they should all stand together.[6]
Indignant at what he regarded as a betrayal of Holmes, Le
Mesurier later quoted against Jeremy his most famous words:
'Greater love hath no man than this, that he lay down his friends
for his life.'

On Monday 18 June, Cantley began his summing-up. It has
been suggested (notably by Auberon Waugh in his book, and in
a brilliant parody by Peter Cook for *The Secret Policeman's Ball*)
that this was ludicrously biased in favour of the defence in
general and Jeremy in particular. The judge certainly did not
restrain himself in expressing his views on the shortcomings of
the main prosecution witnesses and their evidence, but this was
at least partly due to the consideration that a failure to draw
attention to those shortcomings might leave the door open to a
successful appeal against conviction. He began: 'This is a very
serious charge and a rather bizarre and surprising case. It is right
for you to pause and consider whether it is likely that such

persons would do the things they are said to have done. But if ...
you are ultimately convinced by the evidence that they did, then,
however sadly, you will have to convict.'

He said the jury could take account of the defendants'
'unblemished reputation' in reaching their verdict. On the other
hand, they should not read too much into allegations of sexual
misconduct which were only indirectly relevant, and nothing at
all into the fact that three of the defendants had chosen not to
give evidence. The judge then discussed at some length the law
relating to conspiracy and its bearing on the case. It did not
matter if some of the alleged conspirators were unacquainted
with each other, provided they were all links in a chain. But one
could not join a conspiracy after the event: if, as suggested by
Cowley, Le Mesurier had only become involved after the shooting, then he had not been a member of the original conspiracy.
Two of the defendants had admitted to the existence of a conspiracy to frighten, but none of them was charged with that: the
jury could only convict on the conspiracy charge if persuaded of
the existence of a conspiracy to murder.

The judge then reviewed the evidence, beginning with that of
Bessell, whom he described as 'a very intelligent, very articulate
man. He must have impressed the electors of Cornwall very
much. He told us he was a lay preacher at the same time as
being sexually promiscuous. And therefore a humbug.' His
evidence had to be treated with care as most of it was uncorroborated, his account of Jeremy's alleged incitement of
Holmes in 1969 (which was all that charge rested on) entirely
so. The judge was dismissive of Carman's suggestion that Bessell
had concocted his evidence with the help of 'Pencourt' – the
dates suggested that it had 'crystallised' before the journalists
had come on the scene – but attached much weight to the fact
that Bessell had a financial interest in the outcome of the case,
and regarded the *Sunday Telegraph* contract as 'deplorable'.
'These are matters which question Mr Bessell's credibility,' he

concluded, 'but the fact that a man tells a lie does not mean that he is telling lies all the time.'

The judge did not conceal his contempt for Scott, 'a hysterical, warped personality, accomplished sponger and very skilful at exciting and exploiting sympathy'. Affectionate letters had been produced to suggest a homosexual affair, but 'we must not assume that mere affection implies buggery ...' And did it really matter whether an affair had taken place or not? The motive existed in either case, for Scott's was 'the kind of story people are so ready to believe these days, even if it wasn't true'. He spoke of Scott's 'amazing lies' and his predatory and dishonest behaviour, concluding: 'He is a crook ... He is a fraud. He is a sponger. He is a whiner. He is a parasite. But of course, he could still be telling the truth ...'

The judge described Newton as 'a highly incompetent performer for all his self-advertisement', and seemed positively annoyed with the ex-pilot for his bungling of the plot. He had armed himself with a defective weapon, driven about in an easily traceable car. 'What a chump the man is! To frighten or to murder – that is no way to go about it.'* His evidence at Exeter showed he was 'capable of inventing an entirely false story', and he had admitted that he was out to 'milk the case' as hard as he could. 'One has to look at his evidence with great care, not only because he is an accomplice ... but also because he has the clearest possible motive for making a sensational story.'

The judge made a point in favour of the prosecution by casting doubt on the suggestion – on which the defence of Holmes and Deakin rested – that the plot had been one to frighten. 'You have seen Scott for yourselves. He is a neurotic, spineless creature, addicted to hysteria and self-advertisement, rushing to others for help whenever he felt it would do any good. Would he

---

* Or as Peter Cook put it in his parody: 'He [Newton] is a piece of slimy refuse, unable to accomplish even the simplest murder plot without cocking it up ...'

be expected to keep quiet if thoroughly frightened?' On the other hand, 'it could be argued that, if the intention was to murder, then even a conceited bungler like Newton might have been stimulated to take a little more care to avoid detection'. Whatever kind of conspiracy it may have been, nothing seemed to have been properly thought out.

The judge then dealt with the cases against each of the defendants in turn. Holmes had admitted to being involved in a conspiracy to frighten: the contention that the conspiracy was to murder was supported by the evidence (for what it was worth) of Bessell and Newton, arguably corroborated by the taped conversation between Newton and Holmes. The case against Deakin (which Taylor had admitted was weaker than that against the other three) rested entirely on the word of Newton, contradicted by that of Miller. Le Mesurier's claim that he had played no part until the pay-off of April 1977 would, if accepted, clear him of the charge, but was contradicted by the evidence of Miller, as well as that of Lambert, who had allegedly been told by Le Mesurier that 'we [sic] should have hired somebody like you ...'

Finally, the judge turned to the case against Jeremy, which he described as 'almost entirely circumstantial'. Regarding the incitement charge, there was only the dubious word of Bessell. Regarding the conspiracy charge, a motive certainly existed: at a crucial moment of Jeremy's career, 'this wretched Scott is still in his constituency with his file and his grievance and his story and his visits to public houses and so on ... It would be in his interest if ... one way or another Scott was silenced ...' But the existence of motive did not constitute proof. Nor did the fact of Jeremy's obtaining money from Hayward under false pretences 'amount to proof that he was a member of a conspiracy to murder someone else'. The judge failed to make much of the unchallenged facts that Jeremy had arranged for Holmes to receive £10,000 in cash at the period when the latter was hiring

Newton, and had attempted to get Hayward and Dinshaw to interfere with evidence. He seemed, however, unimpressed by Carman's suggestion that Holmes might have been acting on his own, wondering what motive Holmes might have had for so doing.

The judge had now been summing up for two days and could have closed his speech that afternoon. But he chose to adjourn until next morning, when he merely spoke for a few minutes, reminding the jury of the burden of proof and the main questions they had to ask themselves in reaching their verdict. There was speculation that he did so to spare the defendants a night in prison, as (in accordance with normal procedure) their bail was withdrawn as soon as the jury retired. They were handcuffed together and driven in a police van to Brixton: as they entered the prison yard, a supportive cheer went up from the overlooking cells. Along with the others, Jeremy suffered the usual indignities of being stripped and searched, but he managed to avoid being consigned to a communal cell by pleading a stomach upset and asking to be taken to the prison hospital. In the morning, they were all brought back to the Old Bailey to await the jury's verdict. During the long wait, a sense of companionship developed between the defendants, who had been at pains to keep their distance from one another during the trial. They joked and played cards together, enjoying a game taught to them by Deakin in which the players were required to accuse each other of lying. When Carman came in, Jeremy greeted him jovially with the words: 'Hello, George, you look as if you've had a rough night.' He also invited his fellow defendants to lunch at Orme Square after their acquittal* (an invitation which was not subsequently confirmed). As the jury did not reappear that day,

---

* Throughout the period of the trial, Jeremy had been extending invitations for the future to friends he met socially, dismissing the case as a minor difficulty the outcome of which could hardly be in doubt.

the defendants were taken back to Brixton for a second night,
Jeremy again going to the prison hospital after pleading illness –
which did not stop him enjoying a good lunch the next day of
smoked salmon and cold fillet of beef, provided for the defendants by Jeremy's loyal friend Clement Freud MP.

Several of the jurors were later interviewed about their delib-
erations, and one of their accounts was published in the *New
Statesman*, giving rise to controversy and a tightening of the law.
By coincidence, the forewoman, the South London schoolteacher
Celia Kettle-Williams, was a member of the Liberal Party and an
admirer of Jeremy: she and others were influenced by the reflection (planted by Carman) that Jeremy and Marion had suffered
enough. Other factors which weighed with them were the dubious characters of the main witnesses and the fact that Bessell
stood to gain financially from Jeremy's conviction. They joked
about 'queers', but reminded themselves that they were not
trying Jeremy for homosexuality and that it was not strictly relevant whether or not he had actually had an affair with Scott.
They liked the judge and saw nothing wrong with his summing-
up. By the end of their first day in the jury room, eleven of them
had agreed to acquit all the defendants, Jeremy of both charges:
the remaining day and a half were spent in an ultimately successful effort to get the remaining juror on board. Having been
out for fifty-two hours, they returned their unanimous verdict at
half-past two on the afternoon of Friday 22 June. Jeremy, who
had sat impassively throughout the proceedings, and awaited the
verdict with much the same coolness as he would have awaited
the outcome of an election, suddenly became the showman once
again: he broke into a broad smile, tossed the three red cushions
on which he had been reclining over the dock, then lent over it
himself and kissed his wife.

24

AFTERMATH
1979–2014

JEREMY THORPE PROCEEDED to celebrate his acquittal as if it were an election victory. 'Darling, we won!' he exclaimed to his wife; while he congratulated Carman with the words, 'Well rowed, Balliol!'* Outside the courthouse, surrounded by a police cordon and wearing his brown trilby at a jaunty angle, he flung his arms into the air in his traditional victory gesture and read a statement to the waiting press. 'I have always maintained I was innocent of the charges brought against me. The verdict of the jury ... I regard as ... a complete vindication. Apart from the devoted and unswerving support of my wife and family ... I want to express my deep appreciation of the countless messages of encouragement and support received from all over the world ...' Back at Orme Square, he appeared on the balcony with his wife and

---

* Carman had to content himself with these peremptory thanks. It was not until October that Jeremy (prompted by Napley) wrote to express his appreciation of his efforts; and an earlier promise to present him with Empire Jack's Sword of St Vladimir 'if you get me off' was quietly forgotten. (Dominic Carman, *No Ordinary Man*, p. 101.)

mother, posing for photographers and waving to the crowd. He was in high spirits at the victory party he held there that evening, attended by his lawyers, family and friends.

He was still in triumphal mood when he and Marion returned to North Devon the following weekend. Leading local Liberals had published a message congratulating him and declaring that they wanted to re-nominate him as their prospective candidate. They organised a celebratory coffee evening: two hundred attended, to hear Jeremy announce that he looked forward to being their MP once again. More controversial was the decision of the Reverend John Hornby, a flamboyant local vicar who was chairman of his village Liberal association, to hold a service of thanksgiving for the acquittal at his eleventh-century church on the edge of Exmoor, based on a text from St Luke: 'With God nothing shall be impossible.' Friends pleaded in vain with Jeremy not to lend himself to this incongruous event. 'I felt no doubt,' wrote Napley in his memoirs, 'that it was the most crass folly, and would do more harm than all the misfortunes which had already befallen him.'[1] It aroused much scornful publicity: the Gay Liberation Front threatened to send a coach party to the service (though in the event, the small congregation was outnumbered by journalists), while the Archdeacon of Barnstaple issued a statement 'vigorously disassociating' himself from it and denouncing it as 'unfitting, unseemly and unsavoury'.

On the first day of his closing address to the jury, George Carman, seeking to enlist their sympathy for his client, had declared that 'a political life and political future are now irreversibly denied to him'. This evidently did not please Jeremy; for when Carman resumed his address the following morning, he qualified his statement by saying that 'there may still be a place somewhere in the public life and service of this country for a man of his talents'. In the aftermath of his acquittal, Jeremy told friends that he hoped to win back his seat at the next election and resume his political career. He declared his intention of attending the forthcoming Liberal Assembly at Margate and Liberal International Congress at Ottawa. Slowly the truth dawned: that as a result of the evidence produced at the trial, much of it uncontested, he had been discredited in the eyes of the world; that he was widely considered lucky to have 'got off'; that the embarrassment he had caused the Liberals had effectively wiped out the loyalty and admiration he had won among them over the years; and that, with the exception of the North Devon Liberals, and a few loyalists elsewhere, no one in the Party, even among those who continued to regard themselves as his friends, wanted him back, at least for the time being.

The extent to which he had been compromised by the trial was brought home when, soon after its conclusion, Jack Hayward issued a statement complaining that he had never received any explanation from Jeremy as to what had happened to the political donations totalling £20,000 which he had sent Nadir Dinshaw at Jeremy's request (and which the prosecution had contended had been used to finance the alleged murder plot), and demanding that the Liberal Party investigate the matter. Some Liberals felt that Jeremy should be expelled from the Party and even prosecuted again for his failure to account for this money: but David Steel urged against this course, which would only have prolonged the Liberals' agony; and Hayward, still having received no explanation, finally agreed to let the matter rest after Jeremy had repaid him the £20,000. In the circumstances, few in the Party disagreed with Steel's public statement that the ex-Leader's political career was over and it was to be hoped that he would find some other outlet for his talents. His closest friends in the Party, Clement Freud and Lord Avebury, who had stood by him throughout his troubles, persuaded him that any attempt to make a comeback would be rebuffed, that it was in his interests to lie low to allow wounds to heal. Reluctantly, he agreed to stay away from Margate and Ottawa, and announced that he would not after all put his name forward for the North Devon candidature, though he would keep his house in the constituency and always remain keenly interested in and supportive of the local Liberal cause. A whip-round to thank him for his twenty years of representation raised just over a thousand pounds, which he used to build an ornamental bridge over the duck pond in his garden at Cobbaton.

Following the euphoria of his acquittal, and the weeks during which he dreamed of returning to politics, there began a long dark period in Jeremy's life. Despite the outcome of the trial, he had to face up to the fact that he was effectively in disgrace. Whether out of disapproval or embarrassment, he was shunned by many who had been his friends. It was suggested to him that he might care to resign his Privy Counsellorship; but although for some years that status produced few official invitations, he clung to it as one of the few honours remaining to him from his great days. He had to endure the steady appearance of a series of books and articles about the trial and its background, including the reminiscences of Bessell and Holmes, further nails in the coffin of his reputation. (He considered suing some of the authors, but was bluntly advised by Lord Goodman that it would be madness to do so.) There was also a series of belated and messy trials arising out of the collapse of London & Counties in 1973, in which (though he was not directly implicated) his name was raised. Then, before the end of 1979, he was diagnosed as having Parkinson's disease, from which (as he later wrote) he had probably already been suffering for at least two years: he first became aware of it when he experienced difficulty in doing up his shirt buttons.[2] Anxious to find some sphere of work, however, he did not publicly admit to being afflicted with this incapacitating but slowly developing illness for some years, as a result of which many had the impression that he had fallen into a state of depression or taken to drink or drugs. When, in December 1979, he made his first public appearance since the trial, speaking alongside Dame Peggy Ashcroft, Sir John Gielgud and others at an event to commemorate United Nations Human Rights Day, a newspaper wrote of his 'immobile features' and 'unblinking eyes' and concluded that 'his bitterness seemed to weigh like a coat of lead'.[3]

It was in fact in a positive mood that he began the search for a new career. The next few years were to be frustrating, however, for no one seemed disposed to offer work to this discredited figure from the past in visibly declining health. He first thought of television, where he had made a dazzling impact in the 1950s and 1960s. But ITN turned him down; and although ATV showed some interest in giving him a chat show, to the extent of making a pilot programme in which he interviewed Peter Ustinov, this came to nothing when it emerged that many of the celebrities he proposed to invite were likely to refuse. With his long knowledge of Central Africa, he thought of playing a role in the transition, during 1980, of Rhodesia to Zimbabwe. But the British Governor, Lord Soames, wanted little to do with him, and he was out of favour with the African leader Robert Mugabe, having been close in the past to Mugabe's rivals Muzorewa and Nkomo. In 1981, he applied for two advertised posts, as Administrator of the Aldeburgh Festival, and Race Relations Adviser to the Greater London Council; in both cases his application received some consideration thanks to his record and contacts, but was ultimately rejected.

Then, in February 1982, it was announced that he had been appointed to a job for which he seemed eminently suited: that of Director of the British Section of Amnesty International, at a salary of £15,000 a year. Jeremy had been one of the founders of Amnesty in 1961; he had shown a close interest in its activities down the years and taken many initiatives on its behalf; and his general record as a champion of human rights was second to none. Yet his appointment provoked protests from among the organisation's staff and 19,000 members, as well as from members of its governing council who had failed to attend the meetings at which Jeremy had been interviewed and selected. Did he have the necessary administrative ability, it was asked, and the essential probity? Had one forgotten the London & Counties affair, the whole Scott business, the lies told down the years, the money obtained from Hayward under false pretences, the failure to bring a libel action against David Holmes who, a year earlier, had published articles confirming that Jeremy had incited him to murder? Two council members resigned; complaints were received from some 200 of the membership; and a letter in *The Times*, its prominent signatories headed by David Astor, former owner and editor of the *Observer*, declared that they were 'disturbed' by the appointment of Jeremy, who had shown himself to be 'a man of unsound judgement'. For a month the controversy raged, until Jeremy himself ended it by standing down. For him, it seemed, there was to be no amnesty.

This was a moment when he knew real despair. At the age of fifty-two, he could no longer see much future for himself. What made the episode particularly hard to bear was that it occurred at a time when the Liberals, in alliance with the new Social Democratic Party of Roy Jenkins, were experiencing a spectacular revival, with huge poll ratings and stupendous by-election results. It looked like a re-run of 1962 and 1972–73, when a fractious Labour Opposition had failed to provide an attractive alternative to an unpopular Conservative Government. The difference was that, with more than two dozen moderate Labour MPs breaking away to join the SDP, the 'realignment of the centre' for which Jeremy, Dick Taverne and others had called a decade earlier at last seemed to be taking place. At this thrilling hour, it was galling for Jeremy to find himself without a role. But the revival fizzled out like its predecessors: by the middle of 1982, Mrs Thatcher had been restored to popularity by the Falklands War. At the General Election of June 1983, the Social Democrats were reduced from thirty to six seats while the

Liberals won seventeen – admittedly their greatest number since the war, but a far cry from the absolute majority which had been predicted for them and their allies fifteen months earlier. In North Devon, which Jeremy refrained from visiting during the campaign, his successor as Liberal candidate, the college lecturer Roger Blackmore, polled some 4,000 votes fewer than Jeremy had done in 1979.

Although life for Jeremy was difficult in the 1980s and sometimes traumatic, it was not without consolations. Marion remained devoted to him, as did his secretary Judy Young. His mother also continued to be robustly supportive until she suffered a stroke in 1989; she died in 1992. He showed close interest in the progress of Rupert, who after overcoming various health and learning difficulties was happily established at Frensham Heights School, where he won a prize for photography and decided to make a career in that field. Many friends remained faithful at home and abroad, including such world figures as Yehudi Menuhin and President Kaunda. He continued to travel extensively. He was kept busy by his Chairmanship of the United Nations Association, his involvement with various charities, and a succession of eccentric and generally not very successful business ventures, such as a project to build housing in Africa using bricks made from elephant grass. His financial problems were relieved thanks to the munificence of an elderly bachelor admirer based in Luxembourg. He was still capable of displaying much of his old charm: his young cousin Christina Morgan, daughter of his Eton schoolfriend Richard Morgan and Sir Peter Norton-Griffiths' daughter Anne, who was invited to live at Orme Square while studying at a London art college in 1980, found him a delightful companion, avuncular in his attentions towards her and full of amusing gossip. When, in the autumn of 1981, Christina and her sisters were married in an unusual triple wedding at the family home, the Château d'Oursières in Normandy, Jeremy, who had often stayed there as a boy, made a speech in French which contributed to the jollity of the occasion.[4]

All the while, his illness was visibly progressing; but it was not until 1985 that he let it be officially known that he was suffering from Parkinson's disease. This led to a change of feeling in his favour, for even those who were not among his usual supporters had to admire the courage with which he faced his illness, and the devotion with which Marion cared for him. He showed no trace of self-pity and a strong will to carry on, seeking every form of available treatment. When, in 1989, a potential but hazardous cure for the disease was announced, based on implanting part of a foetus into the brain of the sufferer, he began a long campaign to receive it on the NHS, which he finally did in the autumn of 1991. It did not seem to do him much good, but he never gave up the battle. When I met him in 1993, he was finding it difficult to walk without falling over: within a year, he had trained himself to do so. Whatever his condition, he was determined to lead as normal and active a life as was possible under the circumstances. He travelled all over the world; he never missed a party or a memorial service; until he lost the ability to eat normally, he attended dinners at the Oxford Union, Trinity College, the National Liberal Club and the Other Club. As well as keeping up with old friends, he made some new ones, such as the exiled King Michael of Romania: Jeremy offered him advice on how he might regain his throne, and was instrumental in getting him invited, as the last surviving head of state of the wartime alliance, to the VE-Day anniversary celebrations in 1995. Younger friends included a talented and personable sculptor.

As the trial receded, he experienced something of a revival. In March 1987, he was elected President of the North Devon Liberals; and he took as active a part in local campaigning as his condition allowed, still being held in much affection by his former constituents. At the General Election of June 1987, his friend Aza Pinney halved the Conservative majority from around

8,000 to 4,000. Then, at the next election in April 1992 – the Liberals having meanwhile merged with the Social Democrats – Nick Harvey won the seat for the Liberal Democrats with a majority of 794. This was a great moment for Jeremy: Harvey, who possessed something of his own charismatic quality, was thirty, exactly the age Jeremy had been at the time of his own first election (also by a three-figure majority) in 1959. The two men became close:* Harvey was grateful for the experienced advice of Jeremy, who in turn revelled in the opportunity to get first-hand gossip from Westminster. At the General Election of May 1997, at which the Conservatives were swept from power by a Labour landslide, Harvey increased his majority to 6,181 and the Lib Dems broke through by winning forty-six seats, most of them on the 'winnable' list targeted by Jeremy in the early 1960s. Jeremy gave a reception at Orme Square for the now large contingent of West Country MPs: a decade earlier, they would have been embarrassed to be asked; now they saw him as the Grand Old Man of Liberalism. He made a charming speech, noting that they now held Land's End and John O'Groats and merely had to do some filling-in. For the first time since his trial, he turned up at the Party Conference (as the annual Assembly now called itself), where he was treated coolly by the leadership but given an ecstatic welcome by the rank and file, his presence also attracting intense interest from the press.

Since 1979, he had never ceased to dream that he might return to Westminster himself one day, not as an MP but as a peer. He resurrected the fantasy that he was the rightful claimant to a medieval peerage and went so far as to consult the relevant officials, being advised that, even were he able to prove a title, it was no longer legally possible to claim peerages which had been dormant or abeyant for centuries.[5] Approaching everyone he knew

---

* Although Harvey, unlike Jeremy and unusually for a Liberal Democrat, was an opponent of closer European union.

who might be able to exercise influence, he then tried to get himself nominated for a life peerage. When it was pointed out that his condition would not even permit him to make an audible speech, he riposted that special peerages (in addition to the normal allocation to opposition parties) had sometimes been created in the past for distinguished personages in failing health, such as Lady Violet Bonham Carter in 1964. John Major let it be known that he would consider allowing such a creation for Jeremy were it to be recommended by the LD Leader Paddy Ashdown – but his old Party had not yet forgiven him to that extent.

Increasingly he lived in the past, reminiscing to friends in his study at Orme Square, its walls covered with photographs of his meetings with the famous and of the great moments of his career. Historians and broadcasters were usually welcome to consult him about political events in which he had been involved and personalities he had known. (One visiting historian was reminded of Lord Randolph Churchill: like that brilliant but erratic statesman, Jeremy evidently believed that he had been destined for the greatest things, but that his career had somehow become derailed.) In April 1993, I had the first of some twenty memorable meetings with him and Marion, both of whom always treated me with courtesy and patience, though their feelings on learning that a biography was being undertaken had been understandably mixed. During these meetings I heard many interesting facts and anecdotes, and saw frequent flashes of his old, magnetic, roguish self. It was perhaps too much to hope that I might eventually win his confidence to the point where he would be willing to talk about the less conventional aspects of his past: whenever I tried to touch on his private life, his trial, or any other subject which showed him in a less than straightforward light, the shutters came down.

The autumn of 1996 saw the publication of a book entitled *Rinkagate*, by Simon Freeman and Barrie Penrose. It contained a first-hand account of how *The Pencourt File* came to be written; otherwise it was mostly an account of Jeremy's life and trial as seen by Norman Scott. Its appearance was followed by a television documentary in the revisionist *Secret Lives* series. This unflattering publicity did not seem to depress Jeremy, who rather revelled in the upsurge of interest in his past, and was inspired by it to put together his own book of anecdotal reminiscences. This he did with the help of Judy Young, who lived in the basement flat at Orme Square and had spent thirty years in his devoted service. When published in the spring of 1999 by the new firm of Politico's, under the rather witty title *In My Own Time*,* it turned out to be a miscellany of titbits, mostly family lore and tales of his encounters with the great. It also included a few weighty documents, such as his recent submission to the Jenkins Commission on Electoral Reform, and some passages recalling key episodes in his career, those which might have been expected to be of greatest interest, on his coalition talks with Heath and his trial, containing few revelations. It incorporated tributes solicited from such well-known figures as Sir Cyril Smith and Lord Briggs, who wrote that it would enable the public to acquaint themselves with the humorous stories Jeremy's friends had so often heard in the past. The reviews, while noting that the book contained little of substance and bore witness to the decline of his faculties, were mostly sympathetic to Jeremy personally, recalling what a splendid performer he had been in his prime and saying how sadly his style was missed in an age of conformity.

As always, Jeremy could not resist throwing a party whenever there was something to celebrate; and he held a huge reception at the National Liberal Club to mark the book's publication on the eve of his seventieth birthday. The crowd which filled the Lloyd George Room reflected much of his past, including as it did Ted Heath and Roy Jenkins, his former fellow MPs Clement Freud and Alan Beith, his faithful aides

---

* The reply he had given down the years to those who asked him when he would write his memoirs.

Richard Moore and Tom Dale, his old adversaries Lords Beaumont and Mackie, his favourite journalist Kenneth Rose, his childhood friend (from the Lloyd George circle) Baroness Trumpington, the gay politician and former Young Liberal chairman Steven Atack, and George Carman QC. Rupert, now working in America, came over for the occasion, and his step-sons were loyally present. Jeremy was having one of his bad days: he was visibly in pain and unable to stand, suffered from a severe tremor and found it difficult to speak. Yet he showed no embarrassment, and seemed thoroughly aware of the occasion; with an effort of will, he made a speech, those parts of which one could hear being lively and amusing. Ensconced in the centre of the room, frail but alert, the handsome figure of Marion standing protectively by his side, he drew his guests towards him with a certain magnetism.

Astonishingly, Jeremy proceeded to outlive most of those attending this party, struggling on for another fifteen and a half years. His Parkinson's specialist did not know of any sufferer who had survived the disease longer than he. Marion continued to care for him until she suffered a stroke in 2007, and became wheelchair-bound. Among the more dramatic episodes in their lives was a trip to Los Angeles in September 2001 to attend the marriage of Rupert,* aged thirty-two, to a woman some years older than himself; their return journey coincided with '9/11' and their plane was grounded, marooning them for some days. Despite extreme frailty, Jeremy's name continued to pop up in the news from time to time. In 2003 he complained to the Broadcasting Standards Authority that he had been unfairly

---

*A year earlier, Rupert had acquired some notoriety by taking unauthorised photographs at the wedding of Michael Douglas and Catherine Zita Jones, sparking off a series of highly publicised law actions as a result of which *Hello!* magazine, which bought the pictures, was obliged to pay damages amounting to more than a million pounds.

treated in a TV documentary about himself and Norman Scott (the complaint was dismissed). During the 2005 General Election he himself appeared on television, an emaciated ghost from the past, lambasting the two main parties for having supported the Iraq War.

Longevity forgives all, and as memories of his trial faded Jeremy began to be claimed as a national treasure not just by his own party but the political establishment as a whole. In 2009 he celebrated his eightieth birthday with a party for 150 at the National Liberal Club, at which tributes were paid to him by his political successors David Steel, Paddy Ashdown, Menzies Campbell and Nick Clegg. A few weeks later, another celebration took place when a bust which had been executed in the early days of his leadership was unveiled in the Grimond Room of the House of Commons by the new Speaker John Bercow, who declared himself a lifelong fan. To the general amazement, Jeremy in his whispered reply announced that he intended to campaign at the forthcoming General Election. But the unveiling turned out to be his last public outing: when the election took place a year later, followed by Conservative–Liberal coalition talks more successful than those in which Jeremy had engaged in 1974, the press tried in vain to canvass his views.

Marion died on 6 March 2014, aged eighty-seven. Jeremy followed on 4 December the same year, aged eighty-five.

His funeral took place on 16 December at St Margaret's, Westminster, where his parents had been married ninety-two years earlier. All his successors as party leader attended; eulogies were read by Sir Nicholas Harvey (as he had become after serving in the coalition government) and Stephen Atack, the great friend of his later years. His coffin was draped with a Union Jack, topped with one of his trilbies. The order of service was emblazoned with the crest of the medieval Barons de Thorpe.

BIOGRAPHICAL NOTES

AUSTICK, David (1920–97): MP (L) Ripon, 1973–74; Leeds city councillor and bookseller.

AVEBURY, 4th Baron, see *LUBBOCK, Eric*.

BANKS, Desmond Anderson Harvie (1918–97): Member, with JT, of Liberal Party Radical Reform Group, 1950s; Chairman of Party Executive, 1961–63 and 1969–70; Party President, 1968–69; cr. life peer, 1974.

BANNERMAN, John MacDonald (1901–69): Legendary rugby player; Chairman, Scottish Liberal Party, 1956–65; cr. life peer as Baron Bannerman of Kildonan, 1967.

BEAUMONT, the Rev. Timothy Wentworth (1928–2008): Eton and Oxford contemporary of JT; benefactor of Liberal Party; Joint Treasurer, 1962–63; Head of LPO, 1965–66; Party Chairman, 1967–68; President, 1969–70; cr. life peer as Baron Beaumont of Whitley, 1967.

BEERBOHM, Sir Max (1872–1956): Humorist; famous in early life as a theatre critic and author of *Zuleika Dobson*, in later life (spent mostly at Rapallo in Italy) for his essays and irreverent caricatures of the famous; friend of JT's great-uncle Ralph Wood, and a great influence on JT.

BEITH, Alan James (b. 1943): MP (L & LD) Berwick-upon-Tweed from 1973; Liberal Chief Whip, 1976–83; Deputy Leader of Liberal Party, 1985–88, and of Liberal Democrats, 1992–2003; knighted, 2008.

BENN, Anthony Neil Wedgwood (1925–2014): President of Oxford Union, 1947; MP (Lab) Bristol SE, 1950–60 and 1963–83; fought, with support of JT, to disclaim Viscountcy of Stansgate, 1960–63; Postmaster-General, 1964–66; Minister of Technology, 1966–70; Industry Secretary, 1974–75; Energy Secretary, 1975–79; MP (Lab) Chesterfield, 1984–2001.

BESSELL, Peter Joseph (1921–85): MP (L) Bodmin, 1964–70; confidant of JT who 'helped out with the Scott problem'; prosecution witness at trial.

BONHAM CARTER, Mark Raymond (1922–94): Son of Lady Violet Bonham Carter; MP (L) Torrington, 1958–59; Chairman of Race Relations Board, 1966–70; cr. life peer as Baron Bonham-Carter, 1986; publisher.

BONHAM CARTER, Lady Violet (1887–1969): Daughter of the Prime Minister H. H. Asquith, to whom she devoted herself until his death in 1928, thereafter becoming a leading supporter of Winston Churchill; Party President, 1945–47; cr. life peer as Baroness Asquith of Yarnbury, 1964.

BOURKE, Christopher (1926–2013): Close Oxford friend of JT, succeeding him as President of OULS; a Metropolitan Stipendiary Magistrate, 1974–96.

BOWEN, (Evan) Roderic (1913–2001): MP (L) Cardigan, 1945–66; QC, 1952.

BRADLEY, Lavinia (b. 1923): Elder of JT's two sisters; married Colonel Eric Bradley of USAF.

BYERS, (Charles) Frank (1915–86): Leader of Liberal Party in House of Lords, 1967–86; President of OULC, 1937; MP (L) North Dorset, 1945–50; Party Chairman, 1950–52 and 1965–67; cr. life peer, 1964.

CHITNIS, Pratap Chidamber (1936–2013): Professional Officer of Liberal Party from 1960; Head of LPO, 1966–69; Director of Rowntree Trust, 1974–88; cr. life peer, 1977.

CHRISTIE-MILLER, Colonel Sir Geoffry (1881–1969): JT's rich uncle, married to his father's elder sister; owner of Christie & Co., hat manufacturers.

DALE, Tom (b. 1931): Personal assistant to JT, 1967–76; International Officer of Liberal Party, 1977–85; Chairman of Essex County Council, 1994–95.

DAVIDSON, James Duncan Gordon (b. 1927): MP (L) West Aberdeenshire, 1966–70; Chief Executive of Royal Highland and Agricultural Society of Scotland from 1970.

DAVIES, Clement (1884–1962): Leader of Liberal Party, 1945–56; MP (L) Montgomeryshire, 1929–62; said to have saved Party from extinction by declining Churchill's offer of a Cabinet seat, 1951.

DEAKIN, George (b. 1940): Swansea nightclub owner and fruit-machine vendor, allegedly implicated in plot to kill Norman Scott; co-defendant of Le Mesurier, David Holmes and JT.

DINSHAW, Nadir (1925–2002): Old Harrovian accountant of Parsee origin, resident in Jersey; befriended in 1969 by JT, who later asked him to transmit money secretly from Jack Hayward to David Holmes; prosecution witness at trial.

DOUGLAS-HOME, Sir Alec (1903–94): Prime Minister, 1963–64, and Leader of Conservative Party, 1963–65; succeeded father as 14th Earl of Home, 1951; Secretary of State for Commonwealth Relations, 1955–60; Foreign Secretary, 1960–63, 1970–74; disclaimed peerage, 1963; MP (C) Kinross & West Perthshire, 1963–74; cr. life peer as Baron Home of the Hirsel, 1974.

ELLINGER, Camilla (1925–74): Younger of JT's two sisters; married Enrique Ellinger, German-born South American mining tycoon (d. 1969); committed suicide.

FOOT, Sir Dingle (1905–1978): Early political mentor of JT; President of OULC and Oxford Union; MP (L) Dundee, 1931–45; Parliamentary Secretary to Ministry of Economic Warfare, 1940–45; QC, 1954; joined Labour Party, 1956; MP (Lab) Ipswich, 1957–70; Solicitor-General, 1964–67; brother of John (Lord Foot), Hugh (Lord Caradon) and Michael (Leader of Labour Party, 1980–83).

FOOT, John Mackintosh (1909–99): Plymouth solicitor and former Liberal parliamentary candidate who gave JT his first brief at the Bar in 1954, being rewarded with an unwanted life peerage in 1967.

FREUD, Clement Raphael (1924–2009): MP (L) Isle of Ely, 1973–83; celebrity chef and radio personality; knighted, 1987.

GILBERT, Dr John William (1927–2013): Oxford Union friend of JT; MP (Lab) Dudley, 1970–97; served in Labour Government, 1974–79; cr. life peer, 1997; Minister for Defence Procurement in Blair Government.

GLADWYN, Gladwyn Jebb, 1st Baron (1900–96): Deputy Liberal Leader in House of Lords, 1967–88; spokesman on foreign affairs and defence, 1965–88; career diplomatist; UK Permanent Representative to United Nations, 1950–54; Ambassador to France, 1954–60; ennobled, 1960.

GRIMOND, Jo (1913–93): Leader of Liberal Party, 1956–67 and

May–July 1976; MP (L) Orkney & Shetland, 1950–83; married Laura, daughter of Lady Violet Bonham Carter; cr. life peer, 1983.

HAIN, Peter (b. 1950): South African-born Chairman of Young Liberals, 1970–72; MP (Lab) Neath, from 1991; minister in Labour governments, 1997–2010.

HAYWARD, Jack Arnold (b. 1923): businessman and philanthropist resident in the Bahamas; benefactor of JT and Liberal Party, 1969–75; prosecution witness at trial; knighted, 1986.

HEATH, Edward Richard George (1916–2005): Prime Minister, 1970–74, and Leader of Conservative Party, 1965–75; MP (C) Bexley, 1950–2001; Minister of Labour, 1959–60; Lord Privy Seal (responsible for negotiations with EEC), 1960–63; President of Board of Trade, 1963–64; KG, 1992; Father of House of Commons from 1992.

HOLME, Richard Gordon (1936–2008): Vice-Chairman of Liberal Party Executive and Director of Campaigns, 1966–67; Party President, 1980–81; cr. life peer, 1990.

HOLMES, David (1930–90): Oxford contemporary of JT; subsequently worked as schoolmaster, textile manufacturer, management consultant and merchant banker; based in Manchester during 1960s and '70s and raised funds there for Liberal Party; appointed Party Deputy Treasurer by JT as Treasurer, 1965; best man at JT's wedding to Caroline Allpass, 1968, and godfather to their son Rupert, 1969; alleged to have hired Andrew Newton to kill Norman Scott, 1975; co-defendant at JT's trial.

HOLT, Arthur (1914–95): MP (L) Bolton West, 1951–64; Liberal Chief Whip, 1962–63; hosiery manufacturer.

HOOSON, Emlyn (1925–2012): MP (L) Montgomeryshire, 1962–79; QC, 1960; JT's rival for Liberal Leadership, 1967; Leader of Wales and Chester Circuit, 1971–74; Chairman of Welsh Liberal Party, 1966–79; cr. life peer, 1979.

HOWELLS, Geraint (1925–2004): MP (L) Cardigan, 1974–92; cr. life peer as Baron Geraint, 1992; Welsh sheep farmer.

JOHNSTON, (David) Russell (1932–2008): MP (L) Inverness, 1964–97; Chairman of Scottish Liberal Party, 1970–87; knighted, 1985; cr. life peer as Baron Russell-Johnston, 1997.

JONES, Trevor (b. 1927): Leader of Liverpool City Council, 1971–73; 'community politician'; Party President, 1972–73; knighted, 1981.

JOSIFFE, Norman, see SCOTT, Norman.

LAWLER, Wallace (1912–72): Leader of Liberals on Birmingham City Council, 1962–72; MP (L) Ladywood, 1969–70; 'community politician'.

LE FOE, Dominic (born William Cooper-Smith) (1932–2010): actor-manager and administrator; managed a brilliant series of Liberal by-election campaigns in late 1950s, and JT's campaigns in North Devon in 1959 and 1964; ran Winnable Seats, 1961–65, with JT and Ted Wheeler; joined Conservative Party, 1965; later managing director of Players Theatre.

LE MESURIER, John (b. 1932): Swansea carpet dealer and friend of David Holmes, allegedly implicated in plot to kill Norman Scott; co-defendant of Holmes and JT.

LLOYD, (Rhys) Gerran (1907–91): Welsh inventor, patent lawyer and director of companies, who subsidised JT's private office as Liberal Leader; cr. life peer as Baron Lloyd of Kilgerran, 1969; Party President, 1973–74.

LLOYD GEORGE, David, 1st Earl (1863–1945): Liberal statesman; Prime Minister, 1916–22; JT's greatest hero and role model.

LLOYD GEORGE, Gwilym (1894–1967): Son of David Lloyd George and friend of JT's father; MP Pembrokeshire, 1922–23 and 1929–50, Newcastle North, 1951–57 (describing himself from 1945 as 'Liberal and Conservative' and from 1951 as 'Conservative and Liberal'); Minister of Food, 1941–42 and 1951–54; Minister of Fuel and Power, 1942–45; Home Secretary, 1954–57; cr. Viscount Tenby, 1957.

LLOYD GEORGE, Megan (1902–66): Daughter and worshipper of David Lloyd George; friend of JT's mother and mentor of JT; MP (L) Anglesey, 1929–51; joined Labour Party, 1956; MP (Lab) Carmarthen, 1957–66.

LUBBOCK, Eric Reginald (b. 1928): Liberal MP for Orpington 1962–70, following victory in the famous by-election; Liberal Chief Whip, 1963–70; JT's rival for Liberal Leadership, 1967; succeeded cousin as 4th Baron Avebury, 1971; stood surety for JT's bail, 1978–79.

MACKAY, Simon (b. 1934): Son of 2nd Earl of Inchcape; Managing Director, Inchcape & Co., 1967–71; Treasurer of Scottish Liberal Party, 1971–72; cr. life peer as Baron Tanlaw, 1971; later sat as cross-bencher.

MACKENZIE, Alisdair (1910–71): MP (L) Ross & Cromarty, 1964–70; Gaelic-speaking Scottish farmer.

MACKIE, George Yull (b. 1919): MP (L) Caithness & Sutherland, 1964–66; Chairman of Scottish Liberal Party, 1965–70; cr. life peer as Baron Mackie of Benshie, 1974.

MACMILLAN, (Maurice) Harold (1894–1986): Prime Minister and Leader of Conservative Party, 1957–63; MP (C) Stockton-on-Tees, 1924–29 and 1931–45, Bromley, 1945–64; Minister of Housing,

1951–54; Defence Secretary, 1954–55; Foreign Secretary, 1955; Chancellor of Exchequer, 1955–56; Chancellor of Oxford University, 1960–86; cr. Earl of Stockton, 1984.

MAYHEW, Christopher (1915–97): MP (Lab) Woolwich East, 1950–74; Minister of Defence (RN), 1964–66; joined Liberal Party, July 1974.

MILLER, David (b. 1946): Cardiff printer who introduced George Deakin to Andrew Newton; prosecution witness at trial.

MOORE, Richard (b. 1931): political secretary and speechwriter to JT, 1967–75; President, Cambridge University Liberal Club and Cambridge Union; leader-writer, News Chronicle, 1955–60; Secretary-General of Liberal International, 1960–64; Secretary to Liberal Peers, 1965–67; later Secretary to Liberal (EDU) group in European Parliament.

NEWTON, Andrew (b. 1946): Airline pilot, allegedly hired by David Holmes to kill Norman Scott; prosecution witness at trial.

NORTON-GRIFFITHS, Gwladys, Lady (née Wood) (1873–1974): JT's tough and intelligent maternal grandmother, who lived to be 101.

NORTON-GRIFFITHS, Sir John ('Empire Jack') (1872–1930): JT's maternal grandfather; engineering contractor and imperial federalist; MP (C) Wednesbury, 1910–18, Wandsworth, 1918–24; knighted, 1917; cr. baronet, 1922; committed suicide.

NORTON-GRIFFITHS, Sir Peter, 2nd Bt (1904–83): JT's uncle; married American heiress Kay Schrafft.

OGLE, Michael (1930–2000): JT's best friend at Trinity College, Oxford; pursued successful business career.

PARDOE, John Wentworth (b. 1928): MP (L) North Cornwall, 1966–79; Party Treasurer, 1968–69.

PENHALIGON, David (1944–86): MP (L) Truro (defeating JT's school-friend Piers Dixon), 1974–86; killed in car crash.

PROWSE, Lilian (b. 1920): JT's excellent constituency agent in North Devon, 1956–79; awarded OBE.

REES-MOGG, William (1928–2012): Oxford Union rival of JT, later involved with him in discussions about 'coalition of the centre'; Editor of The Times, 1967–81; cr. life peer, 1988.

RICHARDS, Tony (b. 1947): Director of Research at LPO, 1971–75; JT's 'minder' during February 1974 election, subsequently accompanying him to see Edward Heath; political secretary and speechwriter to JT (succeeding Richard Moore), 1975–76.

ROBSON, Stina (1919–99): Formidable Swedish wife of Liberal bene-factor Sir Lawrence Robson (1904–88; Party President, 1953–54);

Party President, 1970–71; cr. life peer as Baroness Robson of Kiddington, 1974.

ROSS, Stephen Sherlock (1926–93): MP (L) Isle of Wight, 1974–87; cr. life peer, 1987.

SCOTT, Norman (b. 1940): Horseman with whom JT had 'a close, even affectionate relationship' in 1961–62; changed name from Norman Josiffe, 1967; prosecution witness at trial.

SEEAR, (Beatrice) Nancy (1913–97): Teacher at London School of Economics, 1946–78; cr. life peer, 1971; Leader of Liberal Party in House of Lords, 1986–88.

SMITH, Cyril (1928–2010): MP (L) Rochdale, 1972–92; Liberal Chief Whip, 1975–76; knighted, 1988.

SMITH, Leonard (1907–93): Professional Officer of Liberal Party; Party Treasurer, 1967–68; knighted, 1982.

STEEL, David (b. 1938): Leader of Liberal Party, 1976–88; MP (L) Roxburgh, Selkirk & Peebles, 1965–83, Tweedale, Ettrick & Lauderdale, 1983–97; Liberal Chief Whip, 1970–75; knighted, 1990; cr. life peer as Baron Steel of Aikwood, 1997; Presiding Officer of Scottish Parliament, 1999–2003.

STEELE, Mike (b. 1936): Australian-born Parliamentary Press Officer of Liberal Party, 1966–72.

TANLAW, Lord, see *MACKAY, Simon.*

TAVERNE, Dick (b. 1928): Dutch-born Oxford Union rival of JT, later involved with him in discussions about 'coalition of the centre'; MP (Lab) Lincoln, 1962–72; served in Labour Government, 1966–70; resigned Labour whip 1972 and recontested seat, holding it until October 1974 with Liberal support as independent social democrat, 1973–74; later joined Liberal Democrats; cr. life peer, 1996.

THORPE, Caroline (née Allpass) (1938–70): JT's first wife, whom he married in 1968; died in car crash.

THORPE, John Henry ('Thorpey') (1887–1943): JT's father; MP (C) Rusholme, 1919–23; KC, 1935.

THORPE, the Venerable John Henry (1855–1932): JT's paternal grandfather, son of a Dublin police officer; Anglican clergyman and leading Evangelical preacher; appointed Archdeacon of Macclesfield, 1922.

THORPE, Marion (née Stein) (1926–2014): JT's Austrian-born second wife, whom he married in 1973 (she having previously been married to 7th Earl of Harewood, from whom she obtained a divorce, 1967).

THORPE, Rupert (b. 1969): JT's son by his first wife; ed. Frensham Heights; made career as photographer; emigrated to California, where JT attended his wedding in September 2001.

THORPE, Ursula (née Norton-Griffiths) (1903–92): JT's mother; a Surrey county councillor (first Conservative, then Independent), 1949–61.

TOPE, Graham Norman (b. 1943): MP (L) Sutton & Cheam, 1972–74; Leader of Sutton Council from 1986; cr. life peer, 1994.

TYLER, Paul Archer (b. 1941): MP (L) Bodmin, February–October 1974, and (LD) North Cornwall, 1992–2005; cr. life peer, 2005.

UPTON, Hon. Henry Eric Patrick Mountjoy Spalding (b. 1917): Son and heir of 5th Viscount Templetown; early homosexual friend of JT; disappeared mysteriously at sea, 1957.

WADE, Donald William (1904–88): MP (L) Huddersfield West, 1950–64; Liberal Chief Whip, 1956–62; cr. life peer, 1964; solicitor.

WAINWRIGHT, Richard (1918–2003): MP (L) Colne Valley, 1966–70 and 1974–87; Party Chairman, 1970–72; accountant.

WATKINS, Philip (1930–95): Oxford contemporary of JT, succeeding him as President of OULC; Party Treasurer, 1972–76; accountant.

WHEELER, Edward (b. 1924): Professional Officer of Liberal Party from 1950; Chief Agent, 1960–70; ran Winnable Seats (from 1961) with JT and Dominic le Foe; Head of LPO, 1970–76.

WIGODER, Basil Thomas (1921–2004): President of Oxford Union, 1946; Chairman of Liberal Party Executive, 1963–65; QC, 1966; cr. life peer, 1974; Liberal Chief Whip, House of Lords, 1977–84.

WILSON, Harold (1916–94): Prime Minister, 1964–70 and 1974–76; Leader of Labour Party, 1963–76; MP (Lab) Ormskirk, 1945–50, Huyton, 1950–83; Treasurer, OULC, 1936; President of Board of Trade, 1947–51; cr. life peer as Baron Wilson of Rievaulx, 1983.

WINSTANLEY, Michael (1918–93): MP (L) Cheadle, 1966–70, Hazel Grove, February–October 1974; cr. life peer, 1975; doctor and television personality.

YOUNG, Judy (b. 1939): Personal secretary engaged by JT as Liberal Party Treasurer in 1965, who served him for rest of his life.

NOTES

1: ANCESTRY

1. Information from Baroness Robson and Mary Hodgkinson. In 1952, Jeremy expressed his hope of being confirmed in the title in time to attend the Coronation in his peer's robes!
2. Little is known for certain about these brothers; but one of them may have been Francis Thorpe, who during the 1640s subscribed £10 to a fund to raise a parliamentary army to defeat the Catholic rebels in Ireland and redistribute land there: in the roll of the so-called 'Adventurers for Land in Ireland' he appears as No. 1,132 and is described as 'servant to Major-General Skippon'. (See Prendergast, *The Cromwellian Settlement of Ireland*, 1870 edition, p. 440.) One Gervase Thorpe was Dean of Waterford in 1640, but this may have been a different family. According to O'Hart's *Irish Pedigrees* (3rd edition, 1892, Vol. I, p. 372), Thorpe is also a native Irish name, being a corruption of the Gaelic 'O'Torpa' – 'the bulky one'.
3. Notebooks of Archdeacon Thorpe in possession of the late Dr Colin Knowles; information from Colonel J. A. Christie-Miller; attestation and service record of William Thorpe in archives of the DMP, Garda Museum, Dublin.
4. See, for example, James Joyce's short story 'Grace' in *Dubliners* (London: Penguin Books, 1999; first published 1914).
5. Parliamentary Papers 1873, Vol. XXII.
6. Probate archives, Irish Record Office.
7. He attended the recently founded Erasmus Smith School (later known as the Dublin High School) from February 1871 to December 1872. (Information from Archivist of Dublin High School.)
8. I am grateful to Professor R. B. McDowell for obtaining this information from the Trinity College archives.

9. A volume of his sermons was published after his death under the title *No More Sundays and Other Reflections* (Stockport, 1932).

10. Information from the Lord (Julian) Aylmer; Sir Fenton Aylmer, *The Aylmers of Ireland* (London: Mitchell, Hughes & Clarke, 1931). Jeremy was born just in time to be included in this impressive work of genealogy, on p. 345.

11. Information from Colonel J. A. Christie-Miller.

12. Stephen Jones, *The Foundation of St George's Church, Stockport* (Stockport, 1993).

13. See his contribution to *Anglican Essays* (1921), and his pamphlet *Prayers to the Blessed Virgin Mary* (1925). Those who worshipped her, he wrote, were committing 'a blasphemous sin ... We may only hope that their ignorance and want of reflection will in some way mitigate their guilt on the Day of Judgement ... Her name has been steeped in rhapsody, poetical extravagance and amorous imagination even to the shocking assertion of her beauty causing God the Father to burn with love for her.'

14. Susan Barnes, *Behind the Image* (London: Jonathan Cape, 1974), p. 267.

15. Archives of Trinity College, Oxford; Gerald B. Hurst, *With Manchesters in the East* (Manchester, 1918); *Handbook of the Order of the British Empire* (1921).

16. *Hansard*, 2 March 1923.

17. Ibid., 11 April 1921.

18. Ibid., 18 April 1923.

19. Information from Christopher Hurst and others.

20. Typescript memoirs of Gwladys, Dowager Lady Norton-Griffiths, 1950s, in possession of Lavinia Bradley.

21. Ibid.

22. Robert Keith Middlemas, *The Master Builders* (London: Hutchinson, 1963), p. 258. This brilliant monograph, which requires some reading between the lines, remains the best published source on the life of Norton-Griffiths.

23. For example, he gave a series of lavish parties at the time of the Coronation in 1911 to introduce dignitaries from the Dominions to British politicians; and he founded the new town of Wednesbury in Canada as a destination for unemployed emigrants from his constituency.

24. See his parliamentary questions of 20 March 1911, 16 May 1912, 26 March 1913, 8 April 1914 and 4 April 1921.

25. Quoted in Stephen Roskill, *Hankey: Man of Secrets* (London: Collins, 1970), p. 423.

26. A year later, Empire Jack suggested that Lloyd George send him back to Russia with £1 million in cash to reverse the Bolshevik Revolution and restore the Tsar to the throne, a proposal to which the Prime Minister did not bother to reply. (Lloyd George Papers, F94/1/74, F201/3/6.)

27. Letter of 1929 in Baldwin Papers, Cambridge University Library, quoted by Richard Davenport-Hines in his entry on Norton-Griffiths in *The Dictionary of Business Biography* (London: Butterworths, 1985), Vol. IV.

28. Mervyn Jones, *A Radical Life: The Biography of Megan Lloyd George, 1902–66* (London: Hutchinson, 1991), p. 38.

29. Thorpey attended this meeting but was unable to stay for the vote; he did, however, scribble on his voting card that he believed 'the Coalition should cease and the Conservative Party fight as a separate unity'. (Davidson Papers, House of Lords Record Office.) Empire Jack was absent in Brazil; presumably he was happy at the fall of the coalition which he had always opposed, though of which his friend Worthington-Evans was a prominent member.

2: CHILDHOOD

1. For many of the details in this chapter, and much else, I am indebted to Jeremy's sister, Lavinia Bradley.

2. See 'Dostoevsky and Parricide' in Vol. XXI of James Strachey (ed.), *The Standard Edition of the Complete Psychological Works of Sigmund Freud*. I am grateful to Leo Abse for drawing my attention to this source.

3. For a description of this establishment, situated at 90, Queen's Gate, see Sir Anthony Wagner, *A Herald's World* (London: Wagner, 1988), pp. 1–5.

4. Photo feature in the *Daily Express*, 8 October 1935. The judge was Sir Alfred Tobin.

5. Barnes, *Behind the Image*, p. 268.

6. Information from Robin Carey Evans, Sir Eustace Gibbs, Robin Macnaghten, Patrick Marlowe, Sir William Shakespeare, Mike Shaw, Viscount Tenby and Baroness Trumpington.

7. Information from Patrick Marlowe and his sister 'Pixie' Balfour-Paul.

8. Information from Jeremy's cousin, Dr Timothy Wood.

9. Joseph Macleod, *The Sisters d'Aranyi* (London: Allen & Unwin, 1969).

10. Information from Ruth Araujo.

11. Letter from Robin Carey Evans to the author, 17 February 1994; information from Lord Tenby (the drowning episode occurred in 1937, when Jeremy was eight).

12. Colin Cross (ed.), *Life With Lloyd George: The Diary of A. J. Sylvester, 1931–45* (London: Macmillan, 1975), p. 130.

13. Information from Mrs Heather Prescott.

14. Information from 'Scottie' Cheshire, Sir Eustace Gibbs and Sir William Shakespeare; George Pike, *The Cothill Story* (Abingdon: Cothill House, 1991), p. 95.

15. Interview of Jeremy and Marion Thorpe on *Friday Call*, 6 July 1973: National Sound Archives LP 35489 f.4.

16. Sir Geoffrey Shakespeare, *Let Candles Be Brought In* (London: Macdonald, 1949).

17. Alistair Horne, *A Bundle from Britain* (London: Macmillan, 1993), pp. 113–16.

18. Information from Captain Michael Prest.

19. Information concerning Jeremy's early months in America from Ann Morgan, George Moser, Michael Prest and Bill Schultz.

20. Jeremy Thorpe, *In My Own Time* (London: Politico's, 1999), p. 8.

21. John Bigelow to the author, 14 July 1994; information from Robert Fisher, a classmate of Jeremy and later master at the school.

3: ETON

1. I am grateful to the following contemporaries for their information about Jeremy at Eton: Anthony Allfrey, the Rt Rev. Simon Barrington-Ward, Anthony Blond, Peter Blond, Colonel Simon Bradish-Ellames, Nigel Cockburn, Piers Dixon, Sir Eustace Gibbs, Julian Gibbs, Christopher Hurst, Lord Lloyd of Berwick, Robin Macnaghten, Lord Marlesford, Patrick Marlowe, Lord Montagu of Beaulieu, Richard Morgan, Michael Mosley, Robert Ponsonby, Lord Snowdon, Tom Stacey, Robin Warrender, Stephen Willink and Philip Ziegler. I am grateful also to Paul Quarrie and Neil Flanagan at the Eton College Library, and to Colin Merton, who took me there.

2. Ian Anstruther, *Oscar Browning: A Biography* (London: John Murray, 1983).

3. Wilfred Blunt, *Slow on the Feather: Further Autobiography, 1938–59* (Salisbury: Michael Russell, 1986).
4. Nora Byron, *Eton: A Dame's Chronicle* (London: William Kimber, 1965), pp. 48–9.
5. Information from Colonel J. A. Christie-Miller.
6. Jeremy Thorpe interviewed for *The Incomparable Max*, broadcast 27 August 1972: National Sound Archives T34698.
7. Lord Marlesford to the author, 24 September 1993.
8. Information from Simon Barrington-Ward, Sir Francis Dashwood, Christopher Hurst and Richard Morgan.
9. Information from Tom Houston and others.
10. The Reverend Douglas Macdonald to the author, 25 October 1994.
11. For information about Henry Upton and his involvement with Jeremy, I am grateful to Major Anthony Maycock and to Stephen Carroll, the current custodian of Henry's surviving papers.

4: OXFORD

1. For information on Jeremy at Trinity, I am grateful to the College Archivist and the following college members: David Cairns, 'Scottie' Cheshire, Robin Fletcher, Lord Kingsdown, Michael Maclagan, Christopher Martin, Sir Patrick Moberly, John Morrell, Sir Angus Ogilvy, Michael Ogle, Robert Ponsonby, John Shakespeare, George Watson and Stephen Willink.
2. See James Rattue, *Kissing Your Sister: A History of the Oxford University Liberal Club and Its Successors, 1913–1993* (1993). For information on Jeremy's role in the Club and Liberal politics generally during this period, I am grateful to the following: Judge John Baker, Lord Banks, Lord Blaker, Professor George Bull, Patric Dickinson, Ann Dummett (née Chesney), Lord Foot, Tom Houston, Keith Kyle, Dominic le Foe, Baroness Robson, Godfrey Smith, Michael Turner-Bridger, Philip Watkins and George Watson.
3. *Oxford Guardian*, 12 January 1950.
4. Information from Lord Beaumont, Michael Ogle, Earl Russell, Philip Watkins and George Watson. Jeremy wrote to the Editor of *The Times* on 4 May 1950 asking if any members of the old club could help the revival by contributing documents or information.
5. I am most grateful to the following, who have given me their reminiscences of Jeremy at the Union: Richard Allen, Tony Benn, Lord Blaker, Stanley Booth-Clibborn, Stanley Brodie, George

Carman, Patric Dickinson, Sir Peter Emery, Gerald Kaufman, Oleg Kerensky, Uwe Kitzinger, Keith Kyle, Bryan Magee, Lord Rees-Mogg, Michael Ryle, Howard Shuman, Godfrey Smith and Lord Taverne.

6. *Isis*, 9 February 1949.
7. Ibid., 15 June 1949.
8. Ibid., 9 November 1949.
9. Ibid., 1 February 1950; *Oxford Guardian*, 10 February 1950.
10. Several contemporaries have given versions of this story, notably Tom Houston, whom Jeremy asked to hide the clothes in his rooms – Houston refused, but Stanley Myers, a Balliol music student, obliged.
11. Committee Minutes of the Oxford Union Society, report of proceedings on 6 October 1950 (consulted by kind permission of the Senior Treasurer).
12. Interview with Philip Watkins.
13. *Isis*, 22 November 1950.
14. Ibid., 29 November 1950.
15. Ibid., 24 January 1951.
16. For these anecdotes I am indebted to Jeremy's Eton friend Patrick Marlowe, who heard them at the time from his father, a Bencher of the Inner Temple and Conservative MP.
17. For this information, and much else in the final pages of this chapter, I am indebted to Christopher Bourke.

5: CAREER

1. Information from Lord Banks.
2. Information from Baroness Robson.
3. The minutes of the Party Executive show that Jeremy attended only twice between 1954 and his becoming Party Leader in 1967. This was in 1956, when he reported on behalf of a committee on monopolies. The Party Council minutes only survive from 1958: between then and 1968, Jeremy attended five times, once in 1958, once after each of his General Election wins of 1959 and 1964, and twice after his appointment as Party Treasurer in the autumn of 1965. (LPO Archives at the London School of Economics.)
4. Information from Lord Banks.
5. For information on Jeremy's career at the Bar, I am indebted to the following: Lady (Elizabeth) Anson, Judge John Baker, Christopher Bourke, Stanley Brodie QC, Julian Byng, Judge Thomas Dewar,

NOTES 571

Judge George Dobry QC, Sir John Drinkwater QC, Thomas Field-
Fisher QC, Lord Foot, John Hall QC, Patricia Hastings, Sir Denis
Henry, Sir Patrick Mayhew QC, Judge Arthur Mildon QC, Florrie
O'Donoghue, Sir Hugh Park, Hubert Picarda QC, Judge George
Shindler QC, Sir Swinton Thomas, Richard Threlfall QC, Sir Henry
de Waal QC, Judge Victor Watts and Lord Woolf.

6. Thorpe, *In My Own Time*, p. 39.
7. This account is based mostly on information from Brian Taylor and press cuttings supplied by him.
8. Information from James Moxon.
9. Thorpe, op. cit., p. 45.
10. Magnus Linklater's interview with Jo Grimond, February 1979.
11. Information from Richard Lamb and John Baker.
12. Jo Grimond, *Memoirs* (London: Heinemann, 1979), p. 197.
13. Information from Ludovic Kennedy.
14. Information from Christopher Booker.
15. Susan Barnes' notes of interview with Laura Grimond, 1973.
16. Information from Lord Bonham-Carter, Dominic le Foe, Jeremy Thorpe and Ted Wheeler.
17. Nicholas Parsons, *Straight Man: My Life in Comedy* (London: Weidenfeld & Nicolson, 1994), p. 231.
18. Information from Antony Fletcher.
19. Jeremy Thorpe to Piers Dixon, October 1959.
20. Tom Pocock to the author, May 1994.
21. Information from Keith Kyle.

6: TENDENCIES

1. Information from Emlyn Hooson.
2. For information about Henry Upton and his part in Jeremy's life, I am grateful to the late Major Anthony Maycock and various other persons identified in the text.
3. Peter Bessell, *Cover-Up: The Jeremy Thorpe Affair* (Wilmington: Simons Books, 1980), pp. 21–2; information from Paul Bessell.
4. Document in possession of Stephen Carroll.
5. Magnus Linklater papers.
6. Francis Wheen, *Tom Driberg: His Life and Indiscretions* (London: Chatto & Windus, 1990), pp. 190–1.
7. Letter in possession of Stephen Carroll.
8. Susan Barnes' notes of interviews with Jeremy Thorpe in 1973.

9. Barrie Penrose and Roger Courtiour, *The Pencourt File* (London: Secker & Warburg, 1978), p. 75.
10. Bessell, op. cit., p. 39.

7: PARLIAMENT

1. *Spectator*, 16 October 1959.
2. Tony Benn, *Office Without Power: Diaries, 1968–72* (London: Hutchinson, 1988), entry for 20 May 1971.
3. *Spectator*, 16 October 1959.
4. *Daily Telegraph*, 11 November 1959.
5. *Hansard*, 10 November 1959.
6. This was the view of Michael Ryle, who had known Jeremy at the Union and went on to become a Clerk to the House of Commons.
7. *Guardian*, 25 June 1960.
8. *Punch*, 13 June 1961.
9. *Daily Telegraph*, 15 March 1961.
10. *Daily Herald*, 21 February 1962.
11. Minutes of Standing Committee in the LPO Archives at the London School of Economics; information from Lord Bonham Carter.
12. For detailed information about both Winnable Seats and the by-elections of this period, I am grateful to Dominic le Foe and Ted Wheeler.
13. Information from John Marshall and Richard Lamb.
14. Fourth Edition, 1992.
15. Information from Derek Ingram, Richard Kershaw, Eric Silver, Jeremy Thorpe and others.
16. *Daily Telegraph*, 5 June 1961.
17. *Hansard*, 19 October 1961.
18. Speech to the OULC, October 1962.
19. For information on Jeremy's work as a constituency MP, I am grateful to many Devonians who spoke to me, in particular Lilian Prowse and Percy Browne.
20. *Hansard*, 7 February 1964.
21. Gerald Kaufman, 'Jeremy Thorpe's Devon' in the *New Statesman*, 27 August 1965.
22. Information from Jeremy Thorpe and Kenneth Rose.
23. Notes on Jeremy Thorpe's relations with John Mansel in Magnus Linklater's papers; Bessell, *Cover-Up*, pp. 18–19.
24. Information from Grenville Jones and George Knapp.

25. *Hansard*, 2 December 1960; correspondence in *The Times*, 8, 14 and 16 December 1960; information from Tom Baistow and Richard Moore.
26. Tony Benn Archives.
27. Jeremy Thorpe to Tony Benn, 2 May 1961: Tony Benn Archives.
28. Ibid., 26 November 1960.
29. Jeremy Thorpe to Michael Zander (Benn's legal adviser), 4 August 1961: Tony Benn Archives.
30. *Hansard*, 27 June 1963.
31. *Hansard*, 16 December 1963; *New Statesman*, December 1963. I am grateful to Dominic le Foe and Richard Lamb for information about this affair, interesting details of which are also provided in Simon Freeman and Barrie Penrose, *Rinkagate: The Rise and Fall of Jeremy Thorpe* (London: Bloomsbury, 1996), pp. 68–72.

8: NORMAN

1. The following account of Norman Scott's early life and association with Jeremy is largely based on the evidence produced at Jeremy's trial and the well-researched details given in *Jeremy Thorpe: A Secret Life*, by Lewis Chester, Magnus Linklater and David May (London: André Deutsch, 1979). I am also grateful to Magnus Linklater for allowing me to see the extensive collection of documentary material in his possession concerning Scott's life and the various police inquiries into his relationship with Jeremy; to Christopher Murray of Kingsley Napley & Co., and Dominic Carman, for showing me further material on Scott, much of it the result of the enquiries of private detectives; and to others for private information.
2. Chester, Linklater and May, op. cit., p. 34.
3. David Steel, *Against Goliath* (London: Weidenfeld & Nicolson, 1989), p.109.
4. Quoted in Freeman and Penrose, op. cit., p. 66: the authors give no indication of how they came by this alleged letter, which they mistakenly assume must date from 1963.

9: MANOEUVRING

1. Diary of Lord Beaumont, 3 September 1964.
2. Tom Pocock to the author, May 1994.
3. Information from Grenville Jones and Richard Lamb.

4. Information from Dominic le Foe.
5. Steel, *Against Goliath,* pp. 40, 109.
6. Information from Michael Cartwright-Sharp, Private Secretary to the Law Officers in 1965.
7. Ian Waller in the *Sunday Telegraph*, August 1965.
8. Magnus Linklater's interview with Len Smith, 1979.
9. Minutes of Liberal Party Council on 30 October 1965. (LPO Archives, LSE.)
10. Diary of Kenneth Rose, 1 March 1966; diary of Tony Benn, 13 February 1968; information from Jeremy Thorpe.
11. Jeremy Thorpe to John Marshall, 7 April 1966.

10: EDGE

1. The first part of this chapter is largely based on the evidence produced at Jeremy's trial, and information contained in Penrose and Courtiour, *The Pencourt File*; Chester, Linklater and May, *Jeremy Thorpe: A Secret Life*; and the memoirs of Bessell.
2. Information from Paul Bessell.
3. Bessell's account in *Cover-Up*, pp. 57ff; Soskice's account in Penrose and Courtiour, op. cit., pp. 110–11.
4. This story was revealed to the authors of *Jeremy Thorpe: A Secret Life* (who felt unable to use it in their book) by an MI5 contact, and confirmed to them in most of its essentials by Tim Beaumont, Pratap Chitnis and Jo Grimond.
5. Information from Richard Wainwright; correspondence of John Wilkins in possession of Stephen Carroll.

11: SUCCESSION

1. Information from Richard Wainwright.
2. Information from Roderic Bowen, Lord Bonham Carter, Lord Hooson and Lord Mackie of Benshie.
3. Diary of Lord Beaumont.
4. Ibid., 13 December 1966. Even Lady Violet only learned the news from the *Evening Standard*: see Mark Pottle (ed.), *Daring to Hope: The Diaries and Letters of Violet Bonham Carter, 1946–69* (London: Weidenfeld & Nicolson, 2000), p. 312.
5. Diary of Lord Beaumont, 22 December 1966.
6. Ibid., 21, 22, 29 December 1966.

7. Ibid., 14 January 1967.
8. Ibid., 16 January 1967.
9. Ibid., 18 January 1967.
10. Magnus Linklater's interviews with Beaumont and Chitnis.
11. For information about the Liberal Leadership election, I am grateful to Lord Avebury, James Davidson, Lord Hooson, Lord Mackie of Benshie, Michael Meadowcroft, John Pardoe, David Steel, Jeremy Thorpe, Lord Tordoff and Richard Wainwright. The diaries of Lord Beaumont, the memoirs of Peter Bessell and Magnus Linklater's interviews were invaluable written sources.
12. Bessell, *Cover-Up*, pp. 107–8.
13. Information from David Steel.
14. Note in diary of Lord Beaumont added on 6 November 1981, following a conversation with Donald Wade.
15. This account comes from Bessell, op. cit., pp. 117–18, and is corroborated by Wainwright.
16. Jeremy Thorpe to Piers Dixon, February 1967: 'And how I miss my beloved Megan!'
17. Bessell, op. cit., pp. 118–20.

12: LEADERSHIP

1. Miles Jebb (ed.), *The Diaries of Cynthia Gladwyn* (London: Constable, 1995), p. 321.
2. *Sunday Times*, 22 January 1967.
3. *Guardian*, 19 January 1967.
4. *Daily Telegraph*, 19 January 1967.
5. *Sunday Times*, 22 January 1967.
6. Ibid.
7. *Sunday Express*, 22 January 1967.
8. *Hansard*, 19 January 1967.
9. I am grateful to many people for general information about the early part of Jeremy's Leadership, especially Lord Avebury, Lord Beaumont, Alan Beith, Tom Dale, Bernard Greaves, Lord Holme, Richard Moore, John Pardoe, Adrian Slade, David Steel, Mike Steele, Celia Thomas, Richard Wainwright, Ted Wheeler and Margaret Wingfield. Much further interesting information came from the interview notes which Susan Barnes and Magnus Linklater kindly made available to me.
10. Diary of Lord Beaumont, June 1968.

11. Information from Bernard Greaves.
12. *Hansard*, 9 November 1967.
13. Ibid., 22 February 1968.
14. Ibid., 21 November 1967.
15. Diary of Lord Beaumont, 4 December 1967.
16. Bessell, *Cover-Up*, p. 119.
17. Ibid., Chapter 11.
18. Freeman and Penrose, *Rinkagate*, pp. 123ff.
19. Bessell, op. cit., pp. 127–8.
20. Ibid., pp. 128–32.

13: CAROLINE

1. This account is mostly based on the original transcripts of David Holmes' interviews with the *News of the World*, extracts from which were published in that newspaper in 1981.
2. Bessell, *Cover-Up*, p. 139.
3. Information from Mike Steele.
4. Diary of Lord Beaumont, 7 June 1968.
5. Ibid., 25 March 1968.
6. Bessell, op. cit., pp. 132–42.
7. Holmes Transcripts.
8. Information from Michael De-la-Noy.
9. Diary of Lord Beaumont.
10. *Daily Mail*, 20 June 1968.
11. Barnes, *Behind the Image*, p. 279.

14: MISFORTUNE

1. Holmes Transcripts: 'It was in fact one of the happiest relationships I had ever seen. Perhaps if one's slightly cynical it didn't last long enough for the gilt to wear off.'
2. Information from Tom Dale.
3. Ian Waller in the *Sunday Telegraph*, 21 September 1969.
4. Bessell, *Cover-Up*, Chapter 13.
5. Ibid.; Holmes Transcripts.
6. Penrose and Courtiour, *The Pencourt File*.
7. Diary of Lord Beaumont, 14 May 1970.
8. The stormy correspondence between Jeremy and Medlicott is discussed and quoted in some detail in Chester, Linklater and May,

Jeremy Thorpe: A Secret Life, Chapter 7.

9. Information on the 1970 election campaign from Lord Banks, Chris Mullin, Michael Ogle, Lilian Prowse, Mike Steele and Ted Wheeler.
10. Bessell, op. cit., Chapter 15.
11. Information from Humphry Berkeley.
12. *Hansard*, 29 June 1970.
13. Steel, *Against Goliath*, p. 68.

15: Abyss

1. Information from Lord Tenby.
2. Information from John Pardoe.
3. *Sunday for Sunday* on BBC Radio 4, 2 May 1971: National Sound Archives, AC/MTO 42694.
4. *With Great Pleasure*, 15 March 1971: National Sound Archives, KM/TO 33717.
5. Quoted in Chris Cook, *A Short History of the Liberal Party, 1900–1976* (London: Macmillan, 1976), p. 151.
6. Information from Antony Grey and Michael Launder.
7. Information from Francis Wheen and Christopher Hitchens.
8. An account of the dealings between Scott and Ross based on their correspondence is given in Chester, Linklater and May, *Jeremy Thorpe: A Secret Life*, Chapter 8.
9. The correspondence between Mrs Parry Jones and Hooson is quoted in Chester, Linklater and May, op. cit., Chapter 9.
10. There are abundant sources for the Scott episode of May–June 1971. The account which follows is largely based on Chester, Linklater and May, op. cit., Chapter 9; Steel, *Against Goliath*, Chapter 5; Bessell, *Cover-Up*, Chapter 17; and the author's interviews of Steel and Hooson.
11. Magnus Linklater's interview of Byers, 8 February 1979.
12. Lord Hooson to the author, September 1993.
13. Magnus Linklater's interview of John Pardoe.
14. Information from Lords Rees-Mogg and Taverne.
15. *Hansard*, 5 June 1972.
16. Cyril Smith, *Big Cyril* (London: W. H. Allen, 1977), pp. 118–21.

16: MARION

1. I am most grateful to Marion Thorpe for talking to me about her background and early life.
2. Lord Harewood, *The Tongs and the Bones* (London: Weidenfeld & Nicolson, 1981), p. 216.
3. Information from Stephen Bonarjee.
4. Chester, Linklater and May, *Jeremy Thorpe: A Secret Life*, pp. 175–7; *Daily Telegraph*, 15 May 1973.
5. Barnes, *Behind the Image*, pp. 290–1.

17: REVIVAL

1. Diary of Tony Benn, 20 May 1971.
2. Ibid., 27 July 1973.
3. Information from Lord Tope.
4. Interview with William Hardcastle on *The World at One*, 24 May 1973: National Sound Archives, LP 35347/b/3.
5. Information from Lord Banks.
6. Copy of undated handwritten statement by Norman Scott made available to the author by Colonel Robin Keigwin. (Penrose and Courtiour in *The Pencourt File* and Chester, Linklater and May in *Jeremy Thorpe: A Secret Life* uncovered extensive details about the activities of Scott in 1973 and the roles of Pennington and Gleadle. Robin Keigwin provided the author with further information.)
7. Information from Stephen Bonarjee.
8. Report by Department of Trade Inspectors into London & Counties Securities Group Ltd, 1976.
9. Hayward's partner Edward St George to Simon Freeman, quoted in Freeman and Penrose, *Rinkagate*, pp. 190–1. (The Bahamas episode is unravelled in some detail in Chapter 11 of *Jeremy Thorpe: A Secret Life*; some further details, based on the authors' interviews with Hayward and St George, being contained in *Rinkagate*.)

18: GLORY?

1. A self-glorifying account by Smith of his row with Jeremy, and their subsequent interventions in the industrial crisis, appears in his memoirs *Big Cyril* (1976).
2. For the February 1974 campaign: Lord Banks, Stephen Bonarjee,

Michael Cockerell, Robin Keigwin, Lord Mackie, John Pardoe, Tony Richards, Earl Russell, John Spiller, Mike Steed, Celia Thomas and Paul Tyler.

3. Information from Michael Cockerell.

4. *The Pencourt File*, p. 184.

5. Holmes, Transcript 3.

6. Edward Heath, *The Course of My Life* (London: Collins, 1998), p. 518.

7. Lord Carrington, *Reflect on Things Past* (London: Collins, 1988), p. 266; see also William Whitelaw, *The Whitelaw Memoirs* (London: Aurum, 1989).

8. Margaret Thatcher, *The Path to Power* (London: HarperCollins, 1995), pp. 238–9.

9. Quoted in Geoffrey Lewis, *Lord Hailsham* (London: Jonathan Cape, 1997), p. 324.

10. Information from Tony Richards.

11. Heath, op. cit., p. 518.

12. Jeremy Thorpe, *In My Own Time*, pp.114–5, and conversations with the author.

13. 'Note for the Record', PREM/15/2069/7.

14. 'Events Leading to the Resignation of Mr Heath's Administration on 4 March 1974', PREM/16/231.

15. Information from Richard Lamb and Robin Salinger.

16. Steel, *Against Goliath*, pp. 78–80.

17. Steel, op. cit., p. 80; Magnus Linklater's interview with Grimond; information from Tony Richards; letter by Jeremy Thorpe in *The Times*, 27 July 1977.

18. PREM 15/2069/13.

19. PREM/16/231.

20. PREM 15/2069/15.

21. Bernard Donoughue, *Downing Street Diary: With Wilson in No. 10* (London: Jonathan Cape, 2005), entries for 1 March, 3 March, 4 March 1974.

22. Joe Haines, *Glimmers of Twilight*, (London, Politico's, 2003), p. 81; *Punch*, 28 September 1996, pp. 9–10.

23. Exchange of open letters between Edward Heath and Jeremy Thorpe on 4 March 1974.

24. Lewis, op. cit., p. 325.

25. This view was expressed to the author by two former MPs on the 'liberal' wing of the Conservative Party, Sir Charles Fletcher-Cooke and Sir Robert Rhodes James.

26. Holmes, Transcript 3.
27. Ibid.
28. Susan Crosland's papers.
29. Christopher Mayhew, *Time to Explain* (London: Hutchinson, 1977), pp. 201–3.
30. For the hovertour: David Hall, John Pardoe, Tony Richards, John Spiller, Paul Tyler; Memoirs of Christopher Mayhew and Cyril Smith.
31. Steel, op. cit., pp. 83–4.
32. Chris Cook, *A Short History of the Liberal Party*, Chapter 13.
33. Information from Ted Wheeler.

19: CONSPIRACY

1. Steel, *Against Goliath*, pp. 84–5.
2. Information from Robin Salinger. The exchange took place at the house of Duncan Sandys in Vincent Square.
3. Smith, *Big Cyril*, pp. 177–80.
4. *Hansard*, 7 April 1975.
5. Information from Robert Edwards.
6. Chester, Linklater and May, *Jeremy Thorpe: A Secret Life*, pp. 206–11.
7. Apart from the mass of evidence produced at Jeremy's trial, the main sources on the conspiracy are the media interviews given at various times by Holmes, Le Mesurier, Miller, Newton and Scott.
8. Auberon Waugh, *The Last Word: An Eyewitness Account of the Trial of Jeremy Thorpe* (London: Michael Joseph, 1980), p. 210.
9. *Daily Telegraph*, 18 September 1975.
10. Holmes Transcripts.
11. Information from Tony Richards and Margaret Wingfield.

20: RESIGNATION

1. Information from John Pardoe; Cyril Smith, *Big Cyril*, pp. 184–6; Christopher Mayhew, *Time to Explain*, p. 207.
2. Information from Denys Robinson.
3. Information from Stuart Mole.
4. Holmes Transcripts; see also Chester, Linklater and May, *Jeremy Thorpe: A Secret Life*.
5. Bessell, *Cover-Up*, pp. 271–2.
6. Bessell's fullest account is given in *Cover-Up*, Chapter 21; Holmes Transcripts.

7. The full letter is given by Bessell in the endnotes to *Cover-Up*, pp. 546–7.
8. Information from Denys Robinson.
9. Diary of Tony Benn, 2 February 1976.
10. Information from Bernard Greaves.
11. Smith, op. cit., Chapter 11.
12. Bessell, op. cit., pp. 289–95.
13. Ibid., pp. 295–300.
14. *Sunday Telegraph*, 1 February 1976.
15. Information from Celia Thomas.
16. The meeting, of which garbled versions appeared in the press at the time, is described in the memoirs of Cyril Smith and David Steel. Further details about it have been provided by Alan Beith, Lord Hooson, John Pardoe, David Steel, Richard Wainwright, and the then Party President, Margaret Wingfield, who also attended.
17. Smith, op. cit., pp. 196–8, quotes a memorandum which was circulated by Hooson to those attending the meeting, advancing this case.
18. Magnus Linklater's interview of Haines, 1979.
19. Smith, op. cit., pp. 193–5.
20. Peter Hain, *A Putney Plot?* (Nottingham: Spokesman, 1987) and interview with author; Magnus Linklater's interview of Haines.
21. Among the many known recipients of this remark were Cyril Smith (op. cit., pp. 205–6) and Peter Hain (Penrose and Courtiour, *The Pencourt File*, p. 22).
22. Evidence of DCS Sharpe at Jeremy Thorpe's trial.
23. Bessell, op. cit., pp. 302, 371.
24. *Sun*, 7 February 1976.
25. Holmes Transcripts: Holmes believed that 'the press were unleashed' on him 'by the police'.
26. Magnus Linklater's interview of Michie, 1979; Smith, op. cit., pp. 199–200.
27. Steel, *Against Goliath*, p. 98.
28. Holmes Transcripts.
29. Diary of Tony Benn, 13 March 1976.
30. Holmes Transcripts.
31. Information from Richard Wainwright.
32. Steel, op. cit., pp. 99–101.
33. Information from John Pardoe.
34. *Daily Telegraph*, 18 March 1976.

35. Information from Michael Foot.
36. Diary of Stuart Mole in his possession.
37. *The Times*, 20 March 1976.
38. *Daily Telegraph*, 8 April, 10 April, 12 April 1976.
39. Farson summarised this episode in a witness statement which was never used by the prosecution at Jeremy Thorpe's trial. He wrote about it in detail in Chapter 18 of his memoirs, *Never a Normal Man*, published shortly before his death in 1997 (London: HarperCollins). A fictionalised account is given in his novel *The Dog Who Knew Too Much* (London: Jay Landesman, 1979).
40. Bessell, op. cit.; diary of Stuart Mole.
41. Chester, Linklater and May (quoting Evans' memorandum), pp. 265–7.
42. Ibid., p. 267.
43. Ibid., pp. 267–8.
44. Ibid., p. 268; *Sunday Times*, 9 May 1976.
45. Information from Richard Wainwright.
46. Magnus Linklater's interview of Lord Byers, 1979.
47. Steel, op. cit., p. 102.

21: INTERLUDE

1. Televised interview of 22 October 1976, reported in the following day's newspapers.
2. 'Peterborough' in the *Daily Telegraph*, 22 September 1976.
3. Diary of Stuart Mole, 11 January 1977.
4. A more detailed account of Chabris' involvement with the NLC, based on the subsequent police investigation, is contained in Chester, Linklater and May, *Jeremy Thorpe: A Secret Life*, pp. 277–80. Some material on the affair is also to be found in David Steel's papers at LSE, file 6/3.
5. Some of these meetings are described in detail in David Steel, *A House Divided: The Lib–Lab Pact and the Future of British Politics* (London: Weidenfeld & Nicolson, 1980), pp. 53–8.
6. David Owen, *Time to Declare* (London: Michael Joseph, 1991), pp. 298–9.
7. Bessell, *Cover-Up*, Chapter 26.
8. Penrose and Courtiour, *The Pencourt File*, pp. 176, 325.
9. Ibid., p. 396.
10. Freeman and Penrose, *Rinkagate*, pp. 277–8.

22: Prosecution

1. Steel, *A House Divided*, p. 87.
2. Ibid., pp. 88–9.
3. Freeman and Penrose, *Rinkagate*, pp. 296–305.
4. Sir David Napley, *Not Without Prejudice* (London: Harrap, 1982), p. 395.
5. This story is described in detail in Bessell, pp. 398–9. In his source note, Bessell says that his account is 'taken almost verbatim from a document supplied to me privately by an undoubted source'. The ITN journalist who rang Challes is identified as Sam Hall.
6. Dinshaw gave detailed evidence of these matters (none of which was challenged by Jeremy's counsel) at Minehead and the Old Bailey (4 June 1979). He had earlier reported his discussions with Jeremy to a friend, Canon Trevor Beeson, who carefully noted them in his diary. See Trevor Beeson, *Window on Westminster* (London: SCM Press, 1998), pp. 61–6.
7. Evidence given at the Old Bailey (again unchallenged by Carman) on 4 June 1979.
8. Information from Michael Ryle and Lord Russell-Johnston.
9. Information from the Reverend Christopher Martin.
10. Information from Bryan Magee.
11. Information from Kenneth Rose.
12. Steel, *Against Goliath*, p. 105.
13. Information from Lilian Prowse; Napley, op. cit., pp. 405–6, 416–17.
14. For information on Jeremy's visit to Southport: Alan Beith, Viv Bingham, Ann Dawson, Sir Hugh Jones, Michael Meadowcroft, Roger Pincham, Kenneth Rose, Michael Steed, David Steel, Lord Tordoff and Richard Wainwright.
15. Dominic Carman, *No Ordinary Man: A Life of George Carman* (Hodder & Stoughton, 2002), pp. 76–9.
16. Napley, op. cit., pp. 402–15.
17. Ibid., pp. 407–8.
18. Peter Chippendale and David Leigh, *The Thorpe Committal* (London: Arrow, 1979); Chester, Linklater and May, *Jeremy Thorpe: A Secret Life*, pp. 294–99; Napley, op. cit., pp. 407ff.
19. Diary of Kenneth Rose, 15 September 1978, quoting Lord Wigoder.
20. Information from Michael Steed; Steel, op. cit., pp. 107–8.
21. Napley, op. cit., pp. 417–18; Waugh, *The Last Word*, pp. 29–32.

22. For information on the 1979 election: Percy Browne, Lord Foot, John Morrell, John Pardoe, Lilian Prowse, Tony Richards, Denys Robinson, Baroness Robson, Henrietta Rous and Michael Ryle.
23. *Daily Mail*, 5 May 1979.

23: TRIAL

1. The case was extensively reported in the press at the time. Auberon Waugh's *The Last Word* is devoted to it, and detailed and interesting accounts are contained in Bessell, *Cover-Up* (Chapters 22–23), Chester, Linklater and May, *Jeremy Thorpe: A Secret Life* (Chapters 20–22) and Freeman and Penrose, *Rinkagate* (Chapter 20). Holmes gave his account in the *News of the World*, June–July 1981, and Le Mesurier in a number of press and television interviews. In the ten pages he devotes to the trial in *In My Own Time* (pp. 197–206), Jeremy Thorpe merely repeats some of the defence arguments used to discredit the evidence of Bessell and Scott, which 'were ... not given their full significance by the media', and explains that he decided not to give evidence as 'to have done so would have prolonged the trial unnecessarily for at least another ten to fourteen days'. I am grateful to both Auberon Waugh and Sybille Bedford for letting me see their notes of the trial, to Magnus Linklater for access to his extensive collection of material from the prosecution files, to Dominic Carman for showing me the notebooks in which his father planned the defence, and to several others involved in the case for private information.
2. Bessell, op. cit., Chapter 32.
3. Thorpe, op. cit., pp. 199–200.
4. Napley, *Not Without Prejudice*, p. 425.
5. Holmes in *News of the World*, 28 June 1981.
6. Freeman and Penrose, op. cit., p. 358.

24: AFTERMATH

1. Napley, *Not Without Prejudice*, p. 248.
2. Thorpe, *In My Own Time*, pp. 206–10.
3. *Evening News*, 11 December 1979.
4. Information from Christina White.
5. Information from Patric Dickinson, Piers Dixon, Michael Ryle and James Vallance-White.

INDEX